Other books sponsored by the Society include:

Career Development in Organizations
Douglas T. Hall and Associates

Productivity in Organizations
John P. Campbell, Richard J. Campbell, and Associates

Training and Development in Organizations
Irwin L. Goldstein and Associates

Organizational Climate and Culture
Benjamin Schneider, Editor

Work, Families, and Organizations
Sheldon Zedeck, Editor

Personnel Selection in Organizations
Neal Schmitt, Walter C. Borman, and Associates

Team Effectiveness and Decision Making in Organizations
Richard A. Guzzo, Eduardo Salas, and Associates

The Changing Nature of Work

The Changing Nature of Work

Ann Howard, Editor

Foreword by Sheldon Zedeck

Jossey-Bass Publishers • San Francisco

Substantial discounts on bulk quantities of Jossey-Bass books are available to corporations, professional associations, and other organizations. For details and discount information, contact the special sales department at Jossey-Bass Inc., Publishers.
(415) 433-1740; Fax (800) 605-2665.

For sales outside the United States, please contact your local Paramount Publishing International Office.

 Manufactured in the United States of America on Lyons Falls Pathfinder Tradebook. This paper is acid-free and 100 percent totally chlorine-free.

Library of Congress Cataloging-in-Publication Data

The Changing nature of work/Ann Howard, editor.—1st ed. p. cm.—(The Jossey-Bass management series) (The Jossey-Bass social and behavioral science series)
   Includes bibliographical references and index.
   ISBN 0-7879-0102-4 (alk. paper)
   1. Work—Forecasting. 2. Work—Psychological aspects. 3. Industrial sociology.
4. Industrial relations. I. Howard, Ann, date. II. Series. III. Series: The Jossey-Bass social and behavioral science series.
HD4904.C453   1995
306.3'6—dc20   95-14580

FIRST EDITION
HB Printing   10 9 8 7 6 5 4 3 2 1

A joint publication in
The Jossey-Bass Management Series
and
The Jossey-Bass
Social and Behavioral Science Series

Frontiers of Industrial and Organizational Psychology

Contents

Foreword

The Society for Industrial and Organizational Psychology established the *Frontiers of Industrial and Organizational Psychology* series in 1982, in part, to advance the scientific status of the field. The series was specifically designed to include volumes that would deal with a single topic considered to be of major contemporary significance in the field. The volume editor, a leading contributor to the topic, would take responsibility for the development of the volume with a particular goal of presenting cutting-edge theory, research, and practice in chapters contributed by individuals doing pioneer work on the topic. Each volume is to be aimed at members of the Society for Industrial and Organizational Psychology—for researchers, practitioners, and students. Volumes are to be published on a timely basis rather than on a fixed schedule, though at a projected rate of one volume per year.

The first editor of the series was Raymond Katzell, who was followed by Irwin Goldstein. I began my term as series editor in May 1993. The practice of choosing volume topics and editors that I am following is the one successfully established by my predecessors. Specifically, the choice of topics and volume editors is determined by the *Frontiers* series editorial board; there is considerable exchange between the board and the volume editor in the planning stages of each volume. Once the volume is under contract, the series editor works with the volume editor to coordinate and oversee the activities between the board, the publisher, the volume editor, and the volume authors.

Under the excellent leadership and guidance of the premiere editor, Raymond Katzell, three major volumes were developed and published: *Career Development in Organizations*, edited by Douglas T. Hall (1986); *Productivity in Organizations*, edited by John P. Campbell and Richard J. Campbell (1988); and *Training and Development in Organizations*, edited by Irwin L. Goldstein (1989). Under the equally excellent stewardship of Irwin Goldstein, three additional volumes were produced: *Organizational Climate and Culture,* edited by Benjamin Schneider (1990); *Work, Families, and Organizations,* edited by Sheldon Zedeck (1992); *Personnel Selection in Organizations,* edited by Neal Schmitt and Walter Borman (1993); and *Team Effectiveness and Decision Making in Organizations,* edited by Richard A. Guzzo and Eduardo Salas (1995). The success of the series is evidenced by the high number of sales (over 25,000 copies have been sold), by the excellent reviews written about the volumes, and by the frequent citation of volumes and chapters in papers by scholars.

The choice of this volume, *The Changing Nature of Work,* represents a departure from the previous volumes. It is not rooted in a single topic, but rather draws from many disciplines and concentrations and causes us to broaden our view as well as to rethink the nature of work as we move into the next century. We are constantly being reminded by many commentators on the economic, social, and political scene that the nature of work and the workforce is changing. The challenge for industrial and organizational psychologists is to anticipate what lies ahead and to determine ways in which we can contribute to the knowledge base of the psychology of work behavior. This volume examines how work is changing, how organizations are changing, and the implications of such changes for psychological research and theory. The volume editor, Ann Howard, has done an excellent job in identifying the topics, selecting a diverse group of authors, and working with them to provide a focused volume that is sure to direct our research for many years to come. The Society owes Howard and her chapter authors a considerable debt of gratitude for undertaking such an ambitious and perhaps atypical volume. Integration of chapters on technological, demographic, and social changes, making projections about these domains, and then relating them to changes in work and workers is a difficult task, but one that is necessary if we are to be prepared to study the new age. We anticipate that this volume will serve as an important stimulus for researchers seeking to move forward and study the work and worker of tomorrow.

The production of a volume such as this one requires the cooperation and efforts of many individuals. The volume editor, the volume chapter authors, and the series editorial board all played an obvious major role. They deserve our sincere appreciation and thanks for devoting their time and efforts to a task that is undertaken for the sole purpose of contributing to our field without any remuneration whatsoever. Also to be thanked is Bill Hicks, senior editor of the Management Series, and his colleagues at Jossey-Bass, who worked with us in the planning stages and took the manuscript through production. Finally, I want to acknowledge and thank Ray Katzell and Irv Goldstein for the standards they set and the accomplishments they achieved. I hope that the series under my editorship meets those standards and achieves equal success.

May 1995

SHELDON ZEDECK
University of California, Berkeley
Frontiers Series Editor

Preface

The body of knowledge underlying the psychology of work behavior is rooted in jobs and organizations of the past. Yet work is currently undergoing such a fundamental transformation that this knowledge base must necessarily be questioned, tested, revised, expanded, or replaced. Workers, too, are changing, and a haunting question is the extent to which these simultaneous changes in work and workers represent a mismatch beyond the power of behavioral science to reconcile.

This book examines post-industrial transformations in work, workers, and the experience of working and the psychological implications of these changes. Because post-industrial workplaces will be so fundamentally different from those in past eras, almost no subject in the repertoire of industrial and organizational (I/O) psychology is unaffected, and the book initially threatened to become a text encompassing the entire field. The content of the book is less ambitious than that, but it is still necessarily broad: in terms of standard I/O topics, it ranges from organizational structure and job design to personnel selection, training, organizational attachment, careers, teamwork, leadership, and performance appraisal. It is not, however, a handbook. We focus pointedly on change—less on what we know than what we need to know. Nor is it a manual advising organizations on how to prepare for a new era of global competition, although we delve deeply into the human ramifications of competitive strategies and how these may help or hinder the organization's cause. Clearly, organizational responses to the challenges of post-industrial capitalism will determine in great measure the structure of work and the conditions people will face at work. We thus have much to say about the human challenges, rewards, and hazards implied by organizations' strategic choices.

The breadth of subject matter is magnified by pursuit of another objective—that is, to explore the causal texture of work change: what is driving it, what is constraining it, and where it is headed. To that end, this volume reaches both within and beyond the expertise of I/O psychologists to professionals in other fields—electrical engineering, sociology, political economy, and labor economics—for insights on how technological advances and the social-political-economic milieu are determining the fate of everyone who works. Despite the expansiveness of subject matter and of perspective, strong themes emerge and interconnect the stories told here. We urge readers to move patiently through the book from front to back in order to appreciate fully how the themes weave together into a post-industrial fabric.

Intended Audience

As with all the books in the *Frontiers* series, I/O psychologists are a prime audience, whether professors, students, or practitioners. In the academic arena, the breadth of the book gives it a distinct advantage for integrative or broadband courses where major goals include placing the field in a larger context or generating enthusiasm for the research and practice opportunities stemming from the changing nature of work. This could be a textbook of choice for seminars on "current directions" in I/O psychology, integrative symposia for advanced graduate students, or introductory core courses that will entice students into the field or introduce others to the excitement offered in the rapidly shifting world of work. It should serve a similar purpose in business schools, especially within the domain of organizational behavior.

Other audiences should benefit as well. The breadth of perspective offered in the book will allow scholars in various fields to build bridges to I/O psychology and to examine their own place within the post-industrial milieu. Various subspecialties of psychology and business are obvious candidates, as are economics and sociology. Psychological and human resource practitioners and managers of various functions should also benefit from a deeper understanding of how the world of work is changing and the possibilities and pitfalls for the human beings who will inevitably struggle to manage work change.

In the broadest sense there are lessons in this book for everyone expecting to work in the twenty-first century. Change is here now, and much more is coming. The authors of this volume anticipate the future and foresee how people can and must transform themselves to meet the challenges of post-industrial life.

Overview of the Contents

Two types of contributions characterize the book. Six authors, assorted into pairs, provide a broad perspective on the forces driving and influencing the changing nature of work (Chapters Two, Three, and Six). The remaining authors focus less on what is driving change and more on how work and workers are changing or should change. Their charge was to project into the future; identify needs for new and different research, theory, and practice; and offer fresh ideas to help advance the psychology of work behavior.

Part One establishes the connections between the workplace and its social-political-economic milieu. In the first chapter I offer a framework for work change that captures the various perspectives of the volume. Technological and demographic/social developments are the primary instigators of change in work and workers, respectively, but their passage into the workplace is inevitably bumped and tossed by the broader environment, including the actions of governments and work organizations. A brief historical tour highlights how all these factors have codetermined work life in the past and anticipates how they are likely to in the future. Chapter Two provides a deeper analysis of two aspects of the political context of employment. Kirsten Wever, using a cross-cultural analysis, illuminates some of the subtleties involved in the interaction of political institutions and beliefs, industrial relations, and the nature of work. Jim Ledvinka homes in on the direct impact of the American government on human resource management, underlining fundamental and perhaps irreconcilable differences between the philosophies and objectives of psychology and the law.

Part Two concerns work—what is pushing its transformation and how that is manifested in both manufacturing and office environments. Chapter Three, as background, addresses technology and organization. Jan Van der Spiegel leads us through the micro-electronics revolution and points toward more humanlike computing in the future. Don Davis shows how computer-based interconnections, knowledge growth, and global competition have broken down the boundaries within and around work organizations, stretching human capacities. In Chapter Four, Toby Wall and Paul Jackson single out three technology-driven initiatives in the manufacturing environment—just-in-time inventory control, total quality management, and advanced manufacturing technology—and argue for rethinking the psychological factors in job design. Mike Coovert, in Chapter Five, visualizes the future office and shows how technological advances will affect human resources research and practice.

Workers come to center stage in Part Three, particularly how the U.S. labor force, so different from that of the past, measures up against the requirements of the new workplace. Chapter Six describes key demographic and social changes and explores the difficulties of bringing worker skills to the level necessary for an increasingly complex work environment. Paul Osterman discusses the school-to-work transition and the potentials and limitations of public policy in remedying skill deficiencies of youth. Tony Carnevale identifies needs for greater employee training and discusses approaches to motivate more skill building within organizations. The next three chapters address the merging of workers and the workplace. Frank Landy, Laura Shankster-Cawley, and Stacey Moran highlight in Chapter Seven the evolution in personnel selection and placement methods as work requirements expand and shift. In Chapter Eight, Denise Rousseau and Kimberly Wade-Benzoni explore how people will relate to organizations in the future as psychological contracts undergo major revisions and organizational commitment takes on new meanings. Tim Hall and Phil Mirvis, in Chapter Nine, reconceptualize careers for the twenty-first century as significantly more flexible and changeable.

Part Four explores the process of working. Sue Mohrman and Susan Cohen concentrate in Chapter Ten on how people will relate to and depend on each other in the new lateral organization. In Chapter Eleven, Bob House brings together emerging concepts of leadership and management most needed in the future with a theoretical integration of different streams of leadership research and thought. New ways of working, organizing, and managing challenge traditional approaches to performance appraisal, discussed by Jerry Hedge and Wally Borman in Chapter Twelve.

In Part Five we reflect on the meaning of working and living in post-industrial society. Jerry Hage, in Chapter Thirteen, draws parallels from work life to the family and community and challenges people to grow and develop in ways that will counter the many evidences of role failure in society. Finally, in Chapter Fourteen, I draw together the themes articulated in the various chapters to help us rethink the psychology of work.

Acknowledgments

One privilege of editing a book in the *Frontiers* series derives from the guidance and support of interested and inspiring colleagues. A talented editorial board—Wally Borman, Irv Goldstein, Dan Ilgen, Allen Kraut, Ben Schneider, and Shelly Zedeck—carefully considered my proposal for this volume and offered many valuable suggestions about topics and possible authors. Irv Goldstein was the editor of the series at the time, and I would have found launching the book considerably more difficult without his encouragement and ideas. I also thank Paul Goodman, who despite being unable to accept my request to write a chapter, gave me thoughtful and useful feedback on the prospectus and made the important suggestion of going outside the field of I/O psychology for contributors. Shelly Zedeck was the series editor by the time the chapters began to arrive, and I am thankful for his prompt attention and insightful comments about each first draft. Bill Hicks and his colleagues at Jossey-Bass lent their support and encouragement at each step of the process, despite the fact that the volume departed from a more comfortable niche aligned with specific academic subspecialties.

Those of us within I/O psychology have a special interest in contributing to a volume in our field, and I am grateful to the authors who donated their time to this effort. But we all owe special thanks to those outside our profession who were willing to participate, fully cognizant that the book would lie outside the mainstream of their professional literatures and that their royalties would go to the Society for Industrial and Organizational Psychology. This spirit of interdisciplinary cooperation heralds a new future for our field and others that I hope will expand and multiply in the interconnected post-industrial world we face together.

Tenafly, New Jersey   ANN HOWARD
May 1995

The Authors

ANN HOWARD is president of the Leadership Research Institute, a nonprofit organization dedicated to research on the selection and development of leaders and managers, and senior consultant for Development Dimensions International, a leading human resource development and consulting firm with nearly seventy offices and affiliates around the world. She received her B.A. degree (1960) from Goucher College, her M.S. degree (1967) from San Francisco State University, and her Ph.D. degree (1976) from the University of Maryland, all in psychology. She holds an honorary doctor of science degree from Goucher College.

Her books include *Managerial Lives in Transition: Advancing Age and Changing Times* (1988, with D. W. Bray), which won the George R. Terry Award of Excellence from the Academy of Management in 1989, and *Diagnosis for Organizational Change: Methods and Models* (1994, with others). For twelve years (1975–1987) she directed two longitudinal studies of the lives and careers of managers at AT&T. Dr. Howard is a past president (1988–89) and fellow of the Society for Industrial and Organizational Psychology and has served as its secretary-treasurer, editor of the *Industrial-Organizational Psychologist,* and chair or member of several other committees. She received the society's Distinguished Service Contributions Award in 1994.

Walter C. Borman is professor of psychology at the University of South Florida and president of Personnel Decisions Research Institute in Minneapolis, Minnesota. He received his B.A. degree (1964) from Miami University in Ohio in psychology and his Ph.D. degree (1972) from the University of California, Berkeley, in industrial psychology. Dr. Borman is currently on the editorial boards of *Journal of Applied Psychology* and *Personnel Psychology.* He served as president of the Society for Industrial and Organizational Psychology (1994–95) and is co-author of a previous volume in the *Frontiers* series, *Personnel Selection in Organizations* (1993, with N. Schmitt and Associates).

Anthony P. Carnevale is vice president and director of human resource studies for the Committee for Economic Development in Washington, D.C. He was formerly vice president and chief economist with the American Society for Training and Development. He received his B.A. degree (1968) from Colby College in government, history, and economics and his Ph.D. degree (1971) from the Maxwell School of Citizenship and Public Affairs at Syracuse University in public finance economics. In August 1993 the president of the United States appointed him to chair the National Commission on Employment Policy, and in February 1994 the secretary of commerce appointed him to the board of overseers for the Malcolm Baldridge National Quality Award. Dr. Carnevale is the author of numerous articles and books on employment and training issues.

Susan G. Cohen is research scientist at the Center for Effective Organizations at the University of Southern California. She received her B.A. degree (1972) in psychology from the State University of New York, her M.A. degree (1977) from Whitworth College in applied behavioral science, and her M.Phil. (1984) and Ph.D. (1988) degrees from Yale University in organizational behavior. She is an author of *Designing Team-Based Organizations* (1995, with S. A. Mohrman and A. M. Mohrman, Jr.) and is currently working on *Teams and New Technology: Developing Information Systems for Collaborative Work* (with D. Mankin and T. K. Bikson).

Michael D. Coovert is associate professor of psychology at the University of South Florida, where he is also the founding director of the Institute for Human Performance, Decision Making, and Cybernetics. He received his B.A. degree (1979) from Chaminade University of Honolulu in computer science and psychology, his M.S. degree (1981) from Illinois State University in psychology, and his Ph.D. degree (1985) from The Ohio State University in industrial and organizational psychology with a minor in computer science.

Dr. Coovert's research interests include human-computer interaction, the impact of technologies on organizations, quantitative methods, and statistical models of human performance.

Donald D. Davis is associate professor of psychology at Old Dominion University, where he served as director of the doctoral program in industrial and organizational psychology from 1986 to 1993. He is a member of the editorial board of the *Journal of High Technology Management Research.* He received his B.A. degree (1973) in psychology, sociology, and philosophy and his M.A. degree (1977) in psychology from Central Michigan University. His Ph.D. degree (1982) in psychology is from Michigan State University, where he also served as assistant director of the Center for Evaluation and Assessment. He has previously published *Managing Technological Innovation* (1986) and articles in a variety of professional journals and books. Dr. Davis has consulted with more than eighty-five public- and private-sector organizations throughout the United States and abroad.

Jerald Hage is professor of sociology and director of the Center for Innovation at the University of Maryland at College Park. He received his B.A. degree (1955) from the University of Wisconsin and his Ph.D. degree (1963) in sociology from Columbia University. He completed post-doctoral studies in the sociology of mental health at the University of Wisconsin in 1964. His primary interests are theory-building and research on organizations and society. His fourteen books include *Post-Industrial Lives* (1992, with C. H. Powers) and *Organizations Working Together* (1993, with C. Alter). His book *State Intervention in Medical Care* (1990, with others) received an award in 1991 from the International Political Science Association for best book in comparative public policy.

Douglas T. (Tim) Hall is professor of organizational behavior and director of the Executive Development Roundtable in the School of Management at Boston University. He received his B.S. degree (1962) with high honors from the School of Engineering at Yale University, and his S.M. (1964) and Ph.D. (1966) degrees from the Sloan School of Management at the Massachusetts Institute of Technology. He has held faculty or research positions at Northwestern,

Columbia, Yale, York, and Michigan State Universities and the U.S. Military Academy at West Point. He is the author of *Careers in Organizations* (1976) and co-author of six other books, including the first book in the *Frontiers* series, *Career Development in Organizations* (1986). He is co-editor of *The Handbook of Career Theory* (1989). His research interests include work/life balance, career planning and development, executive succession, and managing diversity.

Jerry W. Hedge is senior research scientist and chief operating officer at Personnel Decisions Research Institute. He has worked in both the public and private sectors planning, implementing, and evaluating research in the areas of job/task analysis, criterion development and performance measurement, personnel selection and classification, training program evaluation, and attitude assessment. He received his B.A. degree (1976) from Texas Lutheran College in psychology, and his Ph.D. degree (1982) from Old Dominion University in industrial/organizational psychology.

Robert J. House holds the Joseph Frank Bernstein Chair of Organizational Studies at the Wharton School of Management, University of Pennsylvania. He received his Ph.D. degree (1960) in management from The Ohio State University. Dr. House is a co-founder of *The Leadership Quarterly* and the Organizational Behavior Division of the Academy of Management. He has published over one hundred articles and academic papers and several books. He is the recipient of the Irwin Career Award for Distinguished Scholarly Contributions to Management, administered by the Academy of Management (1991), and several best paper awards. He is currently the principal investigator of the Global Leadership and Organizational Behavior Research Program (GLOBE), which is a collaborative effort with co-investigators from sixty-six countries.

Paul R. Jackson is senior lecturer in the department of psychology at the University of Sheffield, England, and a member of the Institute of Work Psychology. His main research interests are advanced manufacturing systems, unemployment, and research methodology. He received his B.Sc. (1972) and Ph.D. (1981) degrees in psy-

chology from the University of Sheffield and his M.Sc. degree
(1983) in applied statistics from the Council for National Academic Awards.

Frank J. Landy is professor of psychology and president of Landy,
Jacobs and Associates, a human resources consulting firm. He
received his B.A. degree (1964) from Villanova University and his
M.A. (1967) and Ph.D. (1969) degrees from Bowling Green State
University, all in psychology. He has published and practiced extensively on issues related to personnel selection, test validation, and
performance evaluation. His books include *The Psychology of Work
Behavior* (1989), *The Science of Human Behavior* (1987), and *The Measurement of Work Performance* (1983, with J. Farr). He is senior author
of the Selection and Placement chapter of the 1994 *Annual Review
of Psychology.*

James Ledvinka is professor of management and psychology in the
Terry College of Business at the University of Georgia. He received
his B.A. degree (1962) from Michigan State University and his
M.A. (1964) in psychology and Ph.D. (1969) in social psychology
from the University of Michigan. He co-authored *Federal Regulation
of Personnel and Human Resource Management* (1991, 2nd ed., with V.
G. Scarpello) and *Human Resource Management* (1995, 2nd ed., with
V. G. Scarpello and T. J. Bergmann). His professional and research
interests include the legal environment of human resource management, human resource planning, sexuality and organization,
utility analysis, and post-modern organization theory.

Philip H. Mirvis is a private researcher and consultant concerned
with large-scale organizational change and the character of the
workforce and workplace. He received his B.A. degree (1973) in
administrative science from Yale University and his Ph.D. degree
(1981) in organizational psychology from the University of Michigan. He has authored or edited six books, including *Failures in
Organization Development and Change* (1977, with D. Berg), *Managing the Merger* (1992), *The Cynical Americans* (1989, with D. L. Kanter), and most recently, *Building the Competitive Workforce* (1993). Dr.
Mirvis has been a professor in the School of Management, Boston

University, and held research positions at the Center for Applied Social Science, Boston University, and Institute for Social Research, University of Michigan.

Susan Albers Mohrman is senior research scientist at the Center for Effective Organizations at the University of Southern California. She received her A.B. degree (1967) in psychology from Stanford University, her M.Ed. degree (1970) from the University of Cincinnati, and her Ph.D. degree in organizational behavior from Northwestern University (1979). Her books include *Self-Designing Organizations: Learning How to Create High Performance* (1989, with T. G. Cummings) and *Designing Team-Based Organizations* (1995, with S. G. Cohen and A. M. Mohrman, Jr.).

Stacey Kohler Moran is an industrial and organizational psychologist with the St. Paul Fire and Marine Insurance Company. She served as the research coordinator for St. Paul's nationwide study, *American Workers Under Pressure,* and has continued research and consulting in all areas of workforce excellence, including human factors risk management, occupational stress, and employee burnout. She received her B.A. degree (1986) from the University of Wisconsin, Madison, and her M.S. (1988) and Ph.D. (1991) degrees from Pennsylvania State University, all in psychology. Dr. Moran is a member of SIOP and APA, and she serves as an elected member on the American Association of Nurse Anesthetists' Council for Public Interest in Anesthesia.

Paul Osterman is professor of human resources and management at the Sloan School of Management, Massachusetts Institute of Technology. He received his B.A. degree (1968) from Oberlin College and his Ph.D. in economics (1976) from M.I.T. He is the author of four books (*Getting Started: The Youth Labor Market,* 1980; *Internal Labor Markets,* 1984; *Employment Futures: Reorganization, Dislocation, and Public Policy,* 1988; and *The Mutual Gains Enterprise,* 1995) as well as articles on topics such as employment policy, internal labor markets, human resources within firms, poverty, and social policy. Dr. Osterman has served as deputy administrator of the Job Training Partnership Act in Massachusetts and has consulted widely with federal and state governments and foundations.

Denise M. Rousseau is professor of organizational behavior at the H. John Heinz III School of Public Policy and Management, Carnegie-Mellon University, with a joint appointment at the Graduate School of Industrial Administration. Previously on the faculty at Michigan and Northwestern Universities, she received her A.B. in psychology and anthropology, and M.A. and Ph.D. (1977) degrees in industrial/organizational psychology from the University of California, Berkeley. Her main research interests include the study of organizational culture and performance and the psychological contract in employment. Dr. Rousseau's books include *Developing an Interdisciplinary Science of Organizations* (1978, with K. H. Roberts and C. L. Hulin), the *Trends in Organizational Behavior* series (beginning in 1994), and *Promises in Action: Contracts in Organizations* (1995).

Laura Shankster-Cawley is a graduate student at Pennsylvania State University. She received her B.A. degree (1989) from the University of Wisconsin, Madison, in psychology and her M.S. degree (1992) from Pennsylvania State University in industrial and organizational psychology. Her research interests include job analysis, employee selection, and employee involvement. Her dissertation investigates applicants' reactions to selection tests and the impact on test performance. She is also co-author of the Selection and Placement chapter of the *Annual Review of Psychology* (1994).

Jan Van der Spiegel is associate professor of electrical engineering at the University of Pennsylvania, where he holds the Bicentennial Class of 1940 Chair and is the director of the Center for Sensor Technologies. He received an engineering degree in electro-mechanical engineering (1974) and Ph.D. degree (1979) in electrical engineering from the Catholic University of Leuven, Belgium. Dr. Van der Spiegel's research interests are in artificial neural networks; computational optical sensors; and low-noise, low-power, and high-speed analog integrated circuits. He received the Presidential Young Investigator Award (1984) and the R. Warren (1987) and C. & M. Lindback (1990) awards for distinguished teaching. He is the editor for North and South America of *Sensors and Actuators* and is on the editorial board of the *International Journal of High Speed Electronics*.

Kimberly A. Wade-Benzoni is currently a doctoral student in organizational behavior at Kellogg Graduate School of Management at Northwestern University. She received a B.S. degree (1989) in electrical engineering from Cornell University and worked for GTE Corporation for three years. Her research interests include psychological contracts in relationships, ethics and intergenerational justice, and the role of biases in environmental degradation. Her current research projects include the role of psychological contracts in research collaborations, the effects of relationships on market efficiency and individual effectiveness, positive illusions and environmentally relevant behaviors, the role of egocentric interpretations of fairness in asymmetric resource dilemmas, and the psychological effect of arbitrary standards.

Toby D. Wall is professor of psychology at the University of Sheffield, England, where he is director of the Institute of Work Psychology. His main research interests have been in industrial and organizational psychology, and recently have been focused on the implications of advanced manufacturing technology for shopfloor work organization, work performance, and strain. He received his B.A. (1968) and Ph.D. (1971) degrees in psychology from the University of Nottingham, England.

Kirsten S. Wever is a political economist, currently Hans-Böckler-Stiftung Fellow and director of the German-American Project of the International Industrial Relations Association (IIRA). She received her B.A. (1980) and M.A. (1981) degrees in international politics from the University of California, Berkeley, and her Ph.D. (1986) degree from the political science department and the Sloan School of Management, Massachusetts Institute of Technology. She is author of *Negotiating Competitiveness: Employment Relations and Organizational Innovation in Germany and the United States* (in press). Dr. Wever has published articles on German and American employment relations and labor politics in journals in a variety of disciplines, including *Industrial and Labor Relations Review*, the *Journal of Public Policy, Industrial Relations,* and *Harvard Business Review.*

The Changing Nature of Work

Part One

Connections

Chapter One

A Framework for Work Change

Ann Howard

When was the work of the head severed from the work of the hand? The current fashion is to scapegoat Frederick Taylor and his ideas of scientific management that flourished at the turn of the twentieth century, but it would be more accurate to say that he helped put into place notions about work that go back at least as far as the classical age. Aristotle did not see knowledge within productive activity, for he believed that manual workers act without knowing what they do. Head and hand were reconciled across the ages: St. Benedict cultivated the dignity and sanctity of labor in early monasteries; Leonardo da Vinci demonstrated that doing was the ultimate way of knowing; Francis Bacon grasped that knowledge is power and called for the application of science to technology (Katz, 1990). Somehow we forgot these lessons in the mass production factories that broke down work into simple, monotonous tasks. But the new age of work—the post-industrial, post-modern, information-rich, knowledge age—is rediscovering these truths and applying them with vengeance.

Work does not exist in a vacuum. It is deeply embedded in a political-economic-societal context that nudges and constrains the translation of technology into work activities and people's participation in them. In the classical age an intellectual elite speculated about the good, the true, and the beautiful and considered the technical arts the proper business of slaves. When Diderot and his colleagues traversed the French countryside on the eve of the

French Revolution pursuing knowledge of the industrial trades for their Encyclopedia, they were kept under police surveillance, for elevation of the trades dangerously implied the elevation of those who practiced them (Katz, 1990). As physicist and Nobel prize winner Arno Penzias observed, "Technology is nonpersonal. It is society that decides how to use it" (Tobagi, 1991, p. 193).

In the modern age the forces acting on the transformation of work are many and complex. Figure 1.1 provides a framework for conceptualizing the catalysts and restraints. The two light sources on either side of the figure are the primary drivers of workplace transitions. Technological changes stimulate the demand side of work—what needs to be done and in what form. Demographic/social changes, the supply side, influence the kinds of workers available to assume work roles and the nature of their interface with the institutions of work. Governments and work organizations respond to technological and demographic/social changes in ways that serve their own agendas. They appear in Figure 1.1 as lenses or filters between the roots of change (the light sources) and the actuality of work (in the spotlight). This is not to suggest that forces toward change operate in a linear fashion, for the lenses and light patterns reflect back and permeate one another. Moreover, all forces are shaped by a political-economic-societal context of institutions, ideologies, and ideas about acceptable behavior.

Figure 1.1. Forces on Work Change.

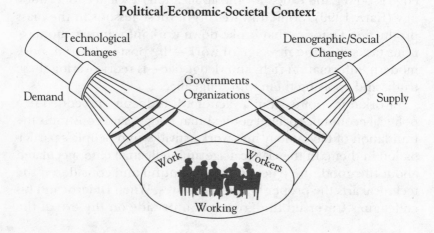

In several chapters of this volume we explore the pattern of interactive influences on work, which is too often ignored by industrial-organizational (I/O) psychologists and other organizational scholars (Nord, Brief, Atieh, & Doherty, 1990). But the primary focus of the book is on the spotlight in Figure 1.1; that is, the nature of future work and its psychological implications. The three words around the perimeter of the spotlight correspond to the volume's central sections.

- *Work.* In light of a technology-driven economic environment, how is work being transformed in psychologically significant ways? What is happening to its content and context? What will work be like in the factory and the office? What are the implications for job design and work roles?

- *Workers.* As demographic and social patterns shift, how will workers fit the new demands of work? What does this imply for how workers are selected and placed in organizations? What kinds of arrangements and contracts will workers negotiate with organizations, and what will be the nature of individuals' careers?

- *Working.* As labor force members confront both novel work and new co-workers, how does this affect their experience of working? How will people relate to each other in work organizations, and what will leadership involve? How will organizations understand and appraise worker performance?

The next two sections of this chapter illustrate the framework in Figure 1.1 with examples from two key periods in American history—the establishment of industrialization around the turn of the twentieth century, and the flowering of bureaucracy following World War II. The final section introduces the post-industrial era and shows how the chapters in this volume meld together to depict a future work world that departs in major ways from those of the past.

Industrialization

- *The Farm.* A man "works hard with his muscles from about five in the morning until half-past eight in the evening . . . it takes the earnings of about five days to buy a pair of top boots and overalls" (Ginzberg & Berman, 1963, p. 80).

- *The Factory.* "The job consisted of putting great bundles and coils of wire from a platform into freight cars . . . the chief superintendent . . . decided that with Toné around the other two workers had nothing to do . . . so he ordered them off the job and left Toné alone to do the work of three men" (Ginzberg & Berman, 1963, p. 41).

- *The Office.* "I got the position, beginning with a salary of $15 a week, which was to be increased to $20 provided I could fill the position. . . . My work consisted for the most part of taking dictation from the editor of the periodical published weekly by the house—letters to contributors, editorials, and special articles" (Ginzberg & Berman, 1963, p. 100).

Political-Economic-Societal Context

The latter years of the nineteenth century brought industrialization, urbanization, and immigration. For American industrial organizations it was a time of gathering capital and accumulating resources, of enhancing production facilities and forming a distribution network (Chandler, 1962). The basic infrastructure of railroads, telegraph, and telephone was in place, enabling firms to distribute goods and services on a national scale (Chandler, 1977). Industry generated unprecedented demands for labor. Although the early textile mills had to rely on young women expendable from family farms as workers, by the late 1870s mechanized farm tools and large-scale production invaded agriculture and pushed men into the paid labor force.

The industrial revolution may, in fact, be less significant for introducing machinery and work processes than for creating a social upheaval as people left their homesteads and workshops to sell their labor power on the open market (Baldry, 1988). Families had been self-sufficient on their farms with minimal needs to exchange goods and services. They comprised their own production teams, scheduled their work by the season and the sun, completed a series of whole tasks, and thrived in accordance with their own efforts and accomplishments.

The workers lured into factories were uncomfortable with industrial discipline (Jacoby, 1985). Wage working jarred ideals of democracy; it made people dependent and brought visions of slavery. It also raised issues of conflict and incentives, unlikely problems on the farm or in the workshop. The resolution of these dilemmas lay in the promise of upward mobility through individual achievement sanctioned by a secularized version of the Protestant work ethic (Rodgers, 1978).

Laissez-faire capitalism dominated the political economy in the late nineteenth century, and government interfered little with business. As industrialists consolidated production and monopolized markets, the government passed antitrust legislation, but it had little teeth until President Teddy Roosevelt invoked the Sherman Act in 1901. His administration ushered in the Progressive Era, intent on social and economic reforms. Job situations were often risky, and workers had no protections for injuries (Nelson, 1975). Legislators in Maryland passed the first workmen's compensation law in 1902, but other legislative efforts moved slowly. Fortunately, industrialists discovered that clean and safe workplaces were to their advantage; proper lighting and fresh air encouraged workers to take care of expensive equipment (Ginzberg & Berman, 1963). Legislators also regulated the physical environment of the factory with sanitation laws. Manufacturers in those times typically gave little thought to conditions such as the location of toilets or the provision of meals (Nelson, 1975).

The other major category of laws passed before World War I restricted the labor of women and children. Enforcement of these laws was lax, however; government inspectors frequently colluded with employers and overlooked obvious infringements. But to some extent economic considerations again drove internal reforms. For example, manufacturers gradually realized that it was not profitable to employ young children and replaced them with machinery (Nelson, 1975).

The industrial system greatly enhanced the wealth of the national economy. Between 1860 and 1920 population increased by a little more than three times while the volume of manufactured goods increased twelve to fourteen times (Rodgers, 1978). Although workers were not highly paid, most earned enough to support their families and even to put some money aside to buy homes or start businesses (Ginzberg & Berman, 1963). Men worked on average sixty hours per week in 1890 (Robertson, 1973), and laboring from sunup to sundown six days per week was common. The family's economic status was affected not only by the husband's wages but by those of children or other relatives and by the indirect contributions of the wife. Most women engaged in long and arduous days of unpaid labor, raising large families, doing laundry in washtubs, raising vegetables, and tending cows, chickens, pigs, and goats. Whether grown or purchased, food came in a natural state, and women had to preserve, pickle, can, and bake. Although men customarily bought their clothes, women made their own and their children's (Braverman, 1974; Ginzberg & Berman, 1963).

Many workers turned to labor unions to negotiate for better wages and working conditions, despite public fears about labor violence in the last two decades of the nineteenth century (Wren, 1987). Nearly two million workers had joined labor unions by 1903, primarily in the transportation and building trades but also in mining, heavy manufacturing, food, liquor, and tobacco. Samuel Gompers threw out a wide net to bring craftsmen and skilled workers into the American Federation of Labor (AFL). But employers vehemently resisted union organizing, using such tactics as economic pressure, blacklisting, labor spies, private armies, and bribery. Between 600,000 and 700,000 workers engaged in work stoppages during the first five years of the twentieth century, and the turbulence and turmoil continued (Ginzberg & Berman, 1963).

Work

At the turn of the century, 42 percent of the labor force was still in the agricultural sector of the economy. The rest were almost equally divided between the goods-production (28 percent) and service-production (30 percent) sectors, the latter including such things as government, transportation, wholesale and retail trade, and finance (U.S. Bureau of the Census, 1975).

Manufacturing depended on crude iron and steel machinery, but the appearance of electric power spurred technological innovation. By installing motors in each tool or machine, manufacturers could eliminate the expense of steam engines, shafts, and belts (Nelson, 1980). The newer factories were larger, well lighted by electricity, and usually clean. But many small plants were sweatshops. Iron and steel mills were hot, dirty, and physically exhausting, and workers in machinery factories had to cope with dust, heat, and smoke (Nelson, 1975). Much work required physical strength, posing a disadvantage to women, older men, and people in poor health. In fact, one major objective of unions was to assist those unable to continue working because of injury or illness (Ginzberg & Berman, 1963).

The manufacturing process involved the gradual development of interchangeable parts, division and specialization of labor, and continuous process assembly. These methods of work were taken up in the quest for efficiency, and they paid off handsomely. After Henry Ford adopted the moving assembly line in 1914, the time required to put together a Model T declined to 10 percent of what was formerly needed (Braverman, 1974).

Charles Babbage had explicated in 1832 the efficiency of the division of labor touted by Adam Smith in 1776. Babbage explained how breaking work into parts and using lower-skilled workers on the simpler parts of the process led to tremendous wage savings. He cited other advantages, including the reduction of learning time, reduction of waste during learning, elimination of time shifting from one task to another, attainment of high skills on each task, encouragement of labor-reducing innovations, and allowing more careful matching of people and task (Duncan, 1989).

Specialization and automation meant that most factory jobs consisted of small tasks that unskilled workers could readily perform. A shoemaker's 1879 testimony to the U.S. Congress illustrates well the consequence. "By the subdivision of labor a man now is no longer a tradesman. He is part of a tradesman. In my own trade of shoemaking, twenty years ago the work was done almost entirely by hand, and the man had to learn how to make a shoe. Now, with the use of machines of almost superhuman ingenuity, a man is no longer a shoemaker, but only the sixty-fourth part of a shoemaker, because there are sixty-four subdivisions in making shoes; and a man may work forty years at our trade, and at the end of forty years he will know no more about making a whole shoe than when he commenced business" (Yellowitz, 1969, p. 88).

Clerical work was rooted in early management practices, and at the turn of the century three-fourths of clerks were men who engaged in bookkeeping and the like (Braverman, 1974). Women began to take clerical positions during the last two decades of the nineteenth century, following the introduction of the typewriter. Simple office machines extracted some of the more laborious manual tasks from the clerk's job, such as copying, preparing and checking data, preparing correspondence, and billing (Zuboff, 1988). But similar to factory work, automation stimulated the specialization of clerical work to improve its efficiency.

Workers

Streams of immigrants, mostly from southern and eastern Europe, passed through Ellis Island to find work in America, primarily in factories. During each decade before and after the turn of the century, immigrants accounted for 37 percent of population growth (Simon, 1989). In 1907 they numbered 1.3 million. Most brought no capital and few possessions beyond the clothes on their backs. They desperately needed to find work immediately, but their numbers pushed down the level of wages for unskilled laborers. With long hours in the factories, they had little time to enhance their education and training to qualify for better work (Ginzberg & Berman, 1963). To make ends meet, immigrants often had to send their children to work: breaker boys sorted coal in the mines, and young girls worked as doffers, tending bobbins in the textile mills.

In 1900, manual laborers were nearly as large an occupational group (35.8 percent) as farm workers (37.5 percent). Managers represented less than 6 percent of the workforce, other white collar workers a little over 11 percent, and direct service workers 9 percent. Women constituted only 18 percent of the total workforce (U.S. Bureau of the Census, 1975); most of them were unmarried and filled in the bottom of the wage scale (Ginzberg & Berman, 1963).

Applied psychology was just getting established during this period, and scientific selection and training methods were scarce. Entrepreneurs selected their successors through family ties or by their own impressions. Andrew Carnegie put Charles Schwab on the fast track to the presidency of his steel company after the young Schwab made a favorable first impression by learning to sing and play Carnegie's favorite tunes on the piano (Sloat, 1979).

Foremen generally hired friends and relatives or selected unskilled workers from the masses who waited anxiously outside the factory gates. In a Philadelphia factory, a foreman tossed apples into a throng and gave a job to any man who caught one (Jacoby, 1985). Selection was often guided by racial and ethnic stereotypes. A correspondence course in 1919 advised that Italians and Swedes were effective railroad builders; Norwegians, Greeks, Russians, and German Poles were good for all-round rough work; and Jews, French, and Irish didn't take well to monotonous, repetitive tasks but were suited to work requiring action, artistry, and enthusiasm (Hale, 1982).

Hugo Munsterberg, often considered the father of industrial psychology, introduced scientific methods of selection in 1909, but his efforts were not always successful. For example, in 1911 he was asked by the New York director of the Hamburg-American shipping line to develop a test to eliminate incompetent ship captains. Munsterberg's test, oriented toward rapid decision making, required candidates to sort a set of cards according to whether A, E, O, or U predominated in a random list of vowels. An independent attempt to replicate his experiment showed not only that good decision makers often scored low, but that the highest scorer was a woman—considered a crushing blow to the test (Hale, 1980). Similarly, Walter Dill Scott's tests to select textile workers at Joseph and Feiss proved to correlate with performance only .002 after five years (Hale, 1982). Fortunately, some testing efforts did succeed. Munsterberg's tests for telephone operators—measures of attention, memory, intelligence, exactitude, and rapidity, including a paper simulation of plugging in a jack—demonstrated creditable validity when stacked up against rankings of job performance (Hilgard, 1987).

Competing with psychologists' tests were various forms of pseudo-psychological selection methods, such as character analysis or physiognomy. One popular treatise recommended that managers be mental types; a large head and triangular face supposedly indicated that the brain and nervous system were highly developed, and that such an individual would be unhappy doing physical labor (Blackford, 1916).

Formal education meant little in hiring staff; in 1900 only 6.3 percent of the population over age seventeen had graduated from high school (U.S. Bureau of the Census, 1975). Even management was generally considered an art that was not subject to formal study, and managers were expected to learn on the job (Gilbreth, 1914). Early business schools, established during this period, covered practical subjects such as accounting and commerce; they were nonintellectual, sometimes anti-intellectual (Hofstadter, 1962). About one-half of top executives in 1900 attended college, but they did so primarily for social reasons, not to learn the techniques of business (Newcomer, 1955). Employers valued skilled workers for their technical and mechanical ability and their experience, regardless of education (Nelson, 1975). Unskilled workers were often illiterate.

Workers did not adapt easily to factory discipline. They were often truants, malingerers, and quitters (Hale, 1980). There was little commitment on the part of either organizations or employees to each other. Rousseau and Wade-Benzoni (Chapter Eight) describe such relationships as transactional contracts, or short-term arrangements that result in little learning, weak identification, and easy exit. At the Ford plant in Highland Park, Michigan, turnover was 370 percent in 1913; the company hired 52,000 men that year to fill 13,000 jobs. Henry Ford took strong action. Of the men who left, foremen had discharged at least 8,000, so Ford stripped the foremen's authority, including the right to set wage rates, which they did idiosyncratically. He established job classifications and raised hiring rates from $2.30 to $5.00 per day. He also set up a sociological department to investigate workers' home and family life to be certain they adhered to middle-class values and were worthy of the higher pay. His methods succeeded in reducing both turnover and absenteeism (Nelson, 1975).

More important, Ford demonstrated that it was good business to pay attention to the human element—a strong boost for the emerging discipline of industrial psychology (Baritz, 1960). Fledgling, reform-minded personnel managers were able to use analysis of the costs of turnover to change their image from dreamers to hard-headed realists (Jacoby, 1985); this was, perhaps, the first utility analysis.

Working

Risk-taking, dynamic entrepreneurs like Ford dominated business at the turn of the century. Four-fifths of the chief executive officers

(CEOs) were the first to head up their companies (Newcomer, 1955). Middle management was relatively undeveloped (Chandler, 1977), and authority over the workers was concentrated at the bottom of the managerial hierarchy. In addition to hiring and setting wages, foremen made their own work rules and imposed discipline, and they did so with unfettered license. First-line management methods were known as the drive system. Foremen used profanity, threats, abuse, and scare tactics to encourage more work. Because immigrant laborers were abundant, foremen fired them recklessly and hired others as replacements (Jacoby, 1985; Nelson, 1975).

The workers protected themselves by slacking off when they weren't being watched. The inefficiency of this system motivated engineers at the 1886 convention of the American Society of Mechanical Engineers to begin the systematic study of management (Duncan, 1989). In attendance was Frederick W. Taylor, who had observed the deliberate restriction of labor, which he called soldiering. He differentiated natural soldiering, or the instinctive tendency to take it easy, from systematic soldiering, a second thought caused by relations with other men (Braverman, 1974). Thus he understood that group norms could restrict productivity, although he failed to recognize that group norms could also work the other way (Weisbord, 1987).

The engineers proposed various forms of the piece rate to provide incentives for better work. They argued that this gave the worker the spirit of being in business for himself, an "entrepreneur in overalls" (Rodgers, 1978). But manufacturers usually maintained ultimate control of wage rates, and as soon as workers began to earn a little more, they would cut the rates, thus undermining incentives (Nelson, 1975). Taylor believed that the fault lay not in the piece rate itself but in the crude guesswork by which the rates were set. He thought he could overcome soldiering by tying a system of stable incentive rates to a scientific analysis of the work process. He advocated a differential piece rate system that punished those who did not come up to standards and rewarded those who met or exceeded them.

Taylor went on to develop what became known as scientific management in the United States or rationalization in Germany. Through time study he analyzed each element of work to find the "one best way" of performing a job and to establish a fair day's work and pay. Taylor aimed to raise output and bring order to the chaotic workplace, but he also believed that his methods would improve labor-management relations and increase wages. He reasoned that management and labor fundamentally had the same interests and that both would benefit from scientific management. Taylor also extended his methods to management with the notion of functional foremen. Instead of one foreman he called for eight specialists with functional authority over a task—a speed boss, repair boss, inspector, and so on (Nelson, 1980; Taylor, 1911).

Various aspects of scientific management proved valid and useful over time, including standardization, time and motion study, goal setting with work measurement and feedback, the motivational value of money, management's responsibility for training, and shorter hours and rest pauses (Locke, 1982). But Taylor's methods resulted in even more precise jobs and narrower responsibilities (Rodgers, 1978). He also seized more control from workers by insisting that they perform work in the precise manner that he specified (Braverman, 1974).

A psychologist in the scientific management fold called attention to some psychological factors that the engineer Taylor did not consider. Lillian Gilbreth, who worked with her husband Frank on motion study, argued that standardization does away with discrimination, offers workers a "square deal," and removes their fear of losing their jobs. She thought that managers needed psychological knowledge in order to give and receive information, which she considered a large part of their job (Gilbreth, 1914).

Munsterberg approved Taylor's principle of having independent experts apply science to work. But he faulted him for relying on bribery and coercion to get workers to accede to the new rates, for assuming that workers were motivated by conscious reason and not irrational personality factors, and for ignoring human and individual variation by focusing mechanically on the task (Hale, 1980). Yet Taylor's notion of a "first-class man"—ambitious, willing to work hard, and suited to his work—indicated that he was aware of the need to match people's abilities to the requirements of the job (Wren, 1987). Applied psychology's major approach to reconciling individual differences with the "one best way" of scientific management became personnel selection (Kraus, 1986). Munsterberg believed that workers should be placed in positions that fit their mental types. He argued that even jobs that seemed the most boring and monotonous might be fascinating to the right people, although he did not consider whether there were enough people of this type to fill all the boring jobs (Hale, 1980).

Whereas psychologists thought the answer to monotony was appropriate matching of people to work, labor reformers thought the answer was to give workers something else to think about (Rodgers, 1978). In the spirit of Progressivism, reformers brought "welfare work" or "industrial betterment" into the factories to improve workers' lives (Nelson, 1975; Rodgers, 1978). Welfare secretaries instituted recreational, educational, and health care activities, such as pleasant surroundings, dramatic performances, libraries, lunchrooms, and company picnics. Many practices were paternalistic and intruded into workers' personal lives (Gilson, 1940); the home visits conducted by Ford's sociological department are an example. Workers often found these practices demeaning. Women in a Maine textile mill, for example, called their welfare secretary "Sanitary Jane" and refused to submit to hygienic examinations (Jacoby, 1985).

Proponents of scientific management criticized welfare work because of its remote reward system. Lillian Gilbreth (1914) argued that a worker feels that decent, comfortable surroundings are his right and not a reward or incentive to added activity. Companies later curtailed welfare work, but it had laid the foundations for personnel departments, and the welfare secretaries gradually extended their activities to such things as recruitment and training (Eilbert, 1959; Jacoby, 1985).

Reformers changed their allegiance from welfare work to industrial democracy during World War I. Woodrow Wilson wrote to Congress in 1919 that industrial democracy would give all workers the right to "participate in some organic way in every decision that affects their welfare or the part they are to play in industry" (Rodgers, 1978, pp. 58–59). In practice, businessmen pursued industrial democracy through company unions or works councils, although these practices were not widespread compared to scientific management or welfare work. Company unions pulled together representatives of management, foremen, and workers to evaluate suggestions, and foremen were encouraged to get employees to think for themselves (Nelson, 1975). But the AFL soon concluded that the committees were toothless and easily intimidated. Moreover, the concerns that the workmen brought to the councils—wages and hours, grievances, working conditions, discipline—suggested that they were more interested in steady, well-paid employment than control of the enterprise (Rodgers, 1978).

Bureaucracy

• *The Farm.* "In my county of Floyd, with 53,000 population, there is not a half-dozen farms where one could make a living on farming alone" (Ginzberg & Berman, 1963, p. 298).

• *The Factory.* "My job is to weld the cowl to the metal underbody. . . . Exactly twenty-five spots. The line runs according to schedule. Takes me one minute and fifty-two seconds for each job. . . . When everything's laid out for you and the parts are all alike, there's not much you feel you accomplish. The big thing is that steady push of the conveyor—a gigantic machine which I can't control. . . . My job is all engineered out. The jigs and fixtures are all designed and set out according to specifications. There are a lot of little things you could tell them, but they never ask you" (Ginzberg & Berman, 1963, pp. 283–284).

• *The Office.* "I work on lapsing and reinstating policies. I am called a clerk. . . . I don't like the monotony of the work I do. Every week your work is set up for you and you do the same thing at the same time every week. . . . In my job I make decisions that are so small you really can hardly consider them decisions. . . . My job is considered unimportant around here, though; there are so many people doing the same thing and they don't require special qualifications for it. . . . They could do without me and anybody else could take my place" (Ginzberg & Berman, 1963, pp. 324–325).

Political-Economic-Societal Context

Americans lost faith in capitalism in the 1930s when the Depression left so many unemployed—25 percent in 1933 (U.S. Bureau of the Census, 1975). The government sought a course correction, and President Franklin Roosevelt's New Deal had a significant impact on business practices. For example, the Fair Labor Standards Act of 1938 guaranteed a minimum wage and outlawed child labor. The Wagner Act of 1935 gave employees the right to unionize and bargain collectively and also outlawed the company unions. Keynesian economics gave government a role in fiscal and monetary policy to stimulate recovery from the Depression, and the Employment Act of 1946 gave explicit recognition of the responsibility of the government to maintain high employment (Committee on Science, 1992).

American science and technology policies grew during the cold war years after World War II. The government focused on defense-related research and development and subsidized university-based basic research. It gave minimal support to industrial technology adoption, but the defense research led to spinoffs in the commercial sector (Committee on Science, 1992). The infrastructure took more steps forward: jets broke the sound barrier in 1947, computers entered the marketplace by the 1950s, and the first telephone cable snaked across the Atlantic in 1956.

The United States experienced the longest sustained economic expansion in its history between 1940 and 1960 (Ginzberg & Berman, 1963). Japan and Europe, recovering from the war, posed little competition. John Kenneth Galbraith argued in *The Affluent Society* (1958) that the problems of economic production were solved. Bidding for the newly affluent American market, manufacturers enticed customers with splashy goods—Fords and Chevrolets sprouted colored paint and tail fins. Profits and efficiency declined as major corporate goals, and self-help became government help (Wren, 1987).

Unions continued to gain members during World War II, and by 1950 they had enlisted one-fourth of the U.S. workforce. But violent postwar strikes proved disruptive, and Congress passed the Taft-Hartley Act of 1947 to curtail unions' powers. The legislation outlawed the closed shop and branded some labor practices of employees as unfair. Most workers joined unions to push up their wages and benefits and savored organized labor's bargaining power. Very few thought unions should serve to make labor and management more cooperative (Viteles, 1953).

But by this time evidence mounted that economic rewards were not the only values pursued at work. The Depression and resulting social legislation demarcated a cultural attitude shift away from ambitious individualism and toward a social ethic that sought protection and security among other people (Wren, 1987). The human relations movement that was fed by the Hawthorne studies in the 1930s culminated in conformity in the 1950s. Social critics decried over-attention to the social group. In *The Lonely Crowd* Riesman (1950) noted the shift from the "inner-directed" to the "other-directed" man, from the market's invisible hand to the glad hand. Psychologist David McClelland (1961) found a notable shift between 1925 and 1950 in individual motives, with need for achievement receding and need for affiliation rising.

People sought security under the protection of the big organization, wrote Whyte in *The Organization Man* (1956). He accused companies of using personality tests to select "yes" men on traits of tranquility, content, and stability. Getting along was valued above getting ahead (Wren, 1987). We had gone from Andrew Carnegie to Dale Carnegie, striving to win friends and influence people.

Work

Large organizations and mass production dominated the bureaucratic era. Goods-production industries occupied a greater proportion than ever (35 percent) of the workforce in 1950. Service-production (employing 51 percent) expanded even more, while the agriculture sector reduced its human needs to only 13 percent of the workforce (U.S. Bureau of the Census, 1975). Organizations diversified their products, created divisional structures, and expected their managers to direct operations on a larger scale than ever before (Chandler, 1962).

Although the engineers of the industrialization era had excelled at dividing work into simple elements for systematic study, they were not so good at melding the parts into a smoothly functioning whole (Duncan, 1989). As organizations grew they created more and more jobs for specialists, staff, and multiple layers of management to coordinate the enterprise. As Weisbord (1987) put it, "You can't simply break jobs down indefinitely without spending pots of money to put everything back together" (p. 62).

These were the rigid line and box organizations that Mohrman and Cohen describe in Chapter Ten. The vertical specialization of labor had resulted in steep hierarchies; for example, Bell System telephone companies had seven levels of management, from the foreman to the president, and the AT&T holding company had several levels above that. The horizontal specialization of labor involved well-defined functions or tasks with strict lines of demarcation between departments. Bureaucratic managers had less power to exercise their personal will than did their predecessors; in line with the social ethic, they had to go through the proper channels and work through committees (Baritz, 1960).

The work week declined to forty or even thirty-seven hours, and piece work was replaced by day work. Employers generally financed an array of fringe benefits for employees, including holidays, vacations, health insurance, and pensions. Work life was routine but comfortable.

Office work was rationalized as factory assembly lines had been. Although mechanization of factory jobs had relieved physical labor, automation in the office brought fatigue, backaches, and other physical complaints (Zuboff, 1988). Mainframe computer technology transformed clerks into keypunch operators and isolated them into work stations. Said an insurance company vice president, "All they lack is a chain." A worker commented, "This job is no different from a factory job except I don't get paid as much" (Braverman, 1974, p. 336). The bookkeeper's job succumbed to automation, although executives clung to private secretaries as status symbols, despite the inefficiency of the practice (Braverman, 1974).

Workers

Restrictive laws in the 1920s nearly halted immigration. The labor force settled down, and most workers were an integral part of American society (Ginzberg & Berman, 1963; Jacoby, 1985). Low-cost mortgages for veterans and the automobile stimulated a massive exodus to the suburbs, and the social ethic encouraged a war-weary population toward family values (Howard & Bray, 1988). One result was the great baby boom that would constitute the next generation of workers.

By 1950, most organizations were run by professional managers, who made up nearly 9 percent of workers, with other white collar workers accounting for another 28 percent. Manual laborers represented 41.1 percent of the labor force, farm workers 11.8 percent, and direct service workers 10.5 percent. Men constituted almost three-fourths of the paid workforce, while women tended households and raised families. But women who had plunged into the labor force to support the war effort were not always willing to retire to the hearth; by 1960 three-fifths of the female labor force was married (U.S. Bureau of the Census, 1975).

Only 10 percent of top executives were entrepreneurs at mid-century, and four-fifths had been promoted from within their own organizations. CEOs now resembled gray eminences rather than the flamboyant figures who had seized the initiative at the turn of the century. The bureaucratic CEO approved decisions flowing upward from subordinates, persuaded others to cooperate, and participated in group actions (Newcomer, 1955). The GI Bill supported many ex-servicemen through college, and a bachelor's degree became a prerequisite to middle and higher management (Newcomer, 1955). I/O psychologists began to migrate to business school faculties in the 1960s, assuring that future managers would be exposed to psychological theory and research.

To select personnel to staff the burgeoning bureaucracies, companies used interviews, biodata, and a wide variety of intelligence and personality tests (Scott, Clothier, & Spriegel, 1949). Employers in 1947 could choose among 783 different kinds of tests (Baritz, 1960). Unfortunately, many tests were not subjected to rigorous job-related validation research. Leadership researchers still concentrated on leader traits, as they had in the 1920s and 1930s, but the Ohio State studies, which commenced in the 1940s, began to turn attention toward behaviors. Douglas Bray, hired by AT&T in 1956 to study the development of telephone company managers, created the first management assessment center, which emphasized behavior rather than traits and used simulations of managerial work to identify them.

Workers were highly committed to their organizations in the bureaucratic era. Rousseau and Wade-Benzoni describe psychological contracts during this period as primarily relational (see Chapter Eight). They engendered long-term expectations, emotional commitment, and strong identification with the organization. As Hall and Mirvis note in Chapter Nine, careers were secure

and stable, shaped by the organization, and directed toward movement up the hierarchy. But factory workers and clerks had short
advancement ladders.

Not everyone thought this secure internal labor market was a
positive transformation. Companies lost labor market flexibility
and economic efficiency. Workers gained security but lost freedom.
The unions had succeeded so well in advancing labor's interests
that workers could no longer afford to leave their benefit-rich jobs.
As Clark Kerr put it, fraternity was triumphing over liberty. But the
system promoted greater equality among a large middle class, with
blue-collar workers sharing in the rewards of their labor nearly as
much as the white-collar class (Jacoby, 1985).

Working

Labor productivity declined after World War II, a phenomenon
noticed by 46 percent of executives surveyed in 1946. Part of the
cause was boredom; a 1947 *Fortune* study showed that 20 percent
of factory workers found their work dull or monotonous most or
all of the time. Clearly those concerned with the human side of
work needed to attend to satisfactions and not just efficiencies—
the will to work, not just the capacity to work (Viteles, 1953). This
discontent came to a head in the early 1970s, publicized by a strike
of factory workers in the General Motors plant in Lordstown, Ohio.
Clerical and other office workers also complained of authoritarian
practices and repetitive work, adding "white-collar woes" to the
"blue-collar blues." A consultant admitted in 1972 that job designers may have created "too many dumb jobs for the number of dumb
people to fill them" (Braverman, 1974, p. 35).

Taylor, Gilbreth, and others in the scientific management tradition had focused on defining and measuring the task. The human
relations writers, including Mayo and Roethlisberger of the Hawthorne studies, recognized that tasks were accomplished in a social
setting and that feelings of belonging and significance must be
massaged to ensure harmony and cooperation. Both of these
approaches focused on extrinsic rewards for work. Several other concepts took hold in the bureaucracy era that formed what Nord and
associates (1990) called the neoconventional view of organizational

behaviorists. This approach homed in on the content of work and its relationship to intrinsic motivation. One outcome of this shift was that industrial psychology formed a partnership with organizational psychology, augmenting its concern with fitting people to work with that of fitting work (job, work group, and organization) to people (Katzell & Austin, 1992).

The neoconventional writers paid attention to higher-order needs as conceptualized by Maslow (1954); beyond security and social needs, Maslow postulated that humans needed to fulfill self-esteem and self-actualization needs. White (1959), too, wrote of a competence motive, a theme that Argyris (1957) and other organization theorists applied to the workplace. Herzberg, Mausner, and Snyderman (1959) called attention to the importance of intrinsic work content factors to motivate work performance and stimulated work on job enrichment. As Nord and associates (1990) point out, this view of motivation differed significantly from the Protestant work ethic, which had a religious basis, assumed that all work was good, and stressed only extrinsic rewards. The neoconventional view is that individual psychological development stems only from specific types of work.

Other theorists paid attention to the amount of control workers have over their work. The notion of participative management grew from work on group dynamics by Kurt Lewin and his colleagues. During World War II experiments to influence Iowa housewives to cut their consumption of rationed foods, Lewin and Margaret Mead discovered that groups that reached consensus during discussion were more likely to change than those who were given expert advice on the matter (Weisbord, 1987). Another significant outcome from the war was Bion's work on leaderless groups, which inspired Eric Trist to begin his research with sociotechnical systems and self-managed teams among coal miners. McGregor's (1960) conceptualization of Theory X and Theory Y, and Likert's (1961) System 4 also added principles that underlie psychological thought about participation and treatment of workers. All these pioneering efforts contributed underpinnings to the high-involvement work practices of the information age. The practices they spawned in the bureaucratic era, however, were criticized as illusory and trivial in their impact on work (Braverman, 1974).

The Post-Industrial Information Age

•   *The Farm.* Observing that the cow was sick, he turned to the personal computer on his tractor and logged onto the network for an interactive diagnosis (Tapscott & Caston, 1993).

•   *The Factory.* "Gone the heroic workman, a WPA mural in living flesh, ruddy in the glow of the blast furnace; now she's likely to be a middle-aged mom, sitting in front of a screen, who attends night school to study statistical process control" (Stewart, 1993).

•   *The Office.* She passed her handheld computer over the map and stopped at Bedminster, site of the field office she needed to visit. "Rain, heavy at times" flashed on the computer screen. "Traffic tie-up on interstate 287; take route 206" (see Coovert, Chapter Five).

In the post-industrial information age, the balance of work has tipped from hand to head, from brawn to brain. Workers don't just run machines and push paper; they control information. And information is displacing capital as the essential resource for industrial success.

The fundamental transformation from hand to head, capital to information, and goods to service and knowledge attracts labels such as discontinuity, paradigm shift, even revolution. What are the economic, political, and societal implications of post-industrial, information age work? What are the psychological implications when work, workers, and working undergo fundamental transformations? The authors of this volume confront these issues in the remaining chapters. Table 1.1 outlines how the thrust of each chapter contrasts with the major themes of the early industrial and bureaucratic eras.

Political Economy

Transportation and electronic communications have condensed time and space. Competition in this compressed market is fast paced and global, either directly or indirectly (see Davis, Chapter Three). Customers demand flawless goods and services customized to their needs, delivered any time, any place (Davis, 1987). The

Table 1.1. Historical Development of Work Themes.

	Chapter	Industrialization	Bureaucracy	Post-Industrialism
Political economy	2	Laissez-faire capitalism Antitrust legislation Employment-at-will Rise of unions Regulation of work conditions	Powerful unions Regulation of labor relations Trade policies for mass products Defense-related R&D Keynesian economic policies	Fast-paced, global competition Concern with job creation Union decline Cooperative union model? Regulation of HR—More?
Work:				
Technology	3	Crude machinery Emerging electric power National infrastructure	Large mass-production machinery Primitive mainframe computing	Personal computing; multimedia Networked computing Mobile, global communications Computing based on biological systems
Organization structure	3	Autocracy Flat, few management levels	Bureaucracy Line and box Hierarchical	Boundaryless Adhocratic Lateral

Manufacturing jobs	4	Dirty, dangerous Narrow tasks Mass production Scientifically determined tasks	Monotonous, mindless	JIT, TQM, AMT Knowledge based Interdependent Worker control
Office jobs	5	Clerks mostly male Typewriter; simple machinery Beginnings of specialization	Automation of business process Pink ghettos of routine paperwork	Computer-supported cooperative work Ubiquitous computing Augmented reality
Workers:				
Demography; Labor force	6	European immigrants Child labor 80 percent male Most working women single	White male dominated Women's role directed home Low immigration	Aging workforce Strong participation of women Educated; high expectations Hispanic, Asian immigrants Illegal and refugee immigrants Disabled?

Table 1.1. (cont.) Historical Development of Work Themes.

	Chapter	Industrialization	Bureaucracy	Post-Industrialism
Education/Skills	6	Many unskilled, illiterate Technical skills more important than formal education	Mass-production pedagogy	Half go beyond high school Poor quality elementary, secondary schooling Importance of corporate training
Personnel selection	7	Ad hoc by foreman Primitive testing	Empirical, atheoretical Wide use of unvalidated tests Beginnings of assessment centers	Expanded cognitive knowledge Personality, values, motivation Team selection Affirmative action
Organization attachment	8	Transactional contracts Low commitment High turnover	Relational contracts Lifetime stability Internal labor market	Variable contracts Short-term and long-term Insiders and outsiders
Careers	9	Unskilled largely unprotected Unions seek seniority for skilled Homemaking for women	Vertical movement for men Shaped by organization Seniority in one firm important Low mobility for women, minorities	Lateral movement Protean, shaped by person Multiple careers in lifetime Lifetime learning Self-development

Working:

Co-workers; Hierarchy 10	Foremen in control Soldiering	Rigid hierarchical relations Boss mediates between workers Low employee involvement Competition between employees	Collective webs Diverse, lateral interconnections High employee involvement Cooperative; interdependent
Leadership/Management 11	Drive system Entrepreneurial owners Few middle managers	Rise of middle management Instrumental leadership Human relations overlay	Neocharismatic Revised instrumental for ambiguous tasks Empowerment
Performance appraisal 12	Ad hoc by foreman	Top down Evaluation of individuals Supervisory ratings	Multiple sources; 360° feedback Typical + maximal Team performance Functional + contextual
Social context 13	Agricultural family Company towns Factory work separated from other social life Individual ethic	Distinct realms of work, family, leisure Rigid gender role scripts Stable families; paternalistic Social ethic	Interpenetration of work, family, leisure Complex role-sets Fluid roles

United States is challenged in high technologies by Japan, Europe, and the Pacific Rim countries, and on mass-produced goods by third world countries that can offer labor at lesser wages. With work easily outsourced beyond national borders, governments search for ways to enhance the quantity and quality of jobs for their own constituents.

Today's nation-states intervene in a variety of processes that ultimately impact the nature of work. Among other things these include monetary and fiscal policies, financial support for research and development, trade policies that protect domestic industries or open markets to nationally produced goods and services, and construction and maintenance of a supportive infrastructure. But the nature of the post-industrial political economy renders many of these approaches less effective than they might have been in the past.

The success of the Japanese industrial model of collaborative groups of companies *(keiretsu)* and government favoritism for some industries suggests that American antitrust concerns, which so consumed the government at the turn of the twentieth century, may be misguided in today's economy. Nevertheless, American businessmen fiercely attack proposals for an industrial policy whereby the government picks and subsidizes "winners" in the commercial market, not least because political pressures in a constituent-oriented democracy tend to favor losers and not winners (Committee on Science, 1992).

Although the U.S. government continues to support basic research, in recent years defense spinoffs have become fewer and less important. Military and civilian technology development have diverged, and the pace of technological innovation in civilian firms has outstripped that of the defense industry (Kash & Rycroft, 1993). The government fortuitously created the information network known as the Internet, but private industry stands poised to take the next steps, including the fiber-optic superhighway (the Infobahn).

Most analysts agree that industrialized countries will succeed best by encouraging high-technology industries, where knowledge is a prime source of competitive advantage. It is not the size of these industries that draws attention but their implications for other segments of the economy. According to economist Paul Krugman (1992), when many firms congregate in a geographical area (for example, Silicon Valley or Boston's route 128), they encourage workers to develop relevant skills or encourage other people who have the appropriate skills to migrate there. As these firms communicate they introduce technological spillovers, which cause both these industries and others that apply their technologies to grow and develop. Thus high technology has many perceived economic benefits, including more productive and higher-paying jobs. To date, Japanese success in high-technology trade has been bought at the expense of American and European producers. But as Krugman's analysis suggests, the national ownership of production may be less important than where it is located (Tyson, 1992). The critical knowledge may be tacit, resting in the minds and skills of the firm's employees. As long as those employees stay within a national economy, that economy gains.

Trade policy commands attention as jobs and living standards come to rely increasingly on international exchange, but this, too, may be less useful in high-technology industries. Compared to, say, steel and automobiles, high-technology industries have added risk, short product life cycles, limited appropriability, and competitive advantages for those who enter a market first. These characteristics put a premium on speed, and the typical slow resolution of trade disputes limits governments' ability to be helpful (Yoffie, 1992).

Economists claim that the key to creating jobs and greater wealth is higher productivity. But productivity increases initially lead to fewer jobs. For example, a Nucor minimill, using computer-controlled manufacturing processes, can make a ton of steel with less than one-twelfth the labor needed by a large integrated mill a decade ago (Magnet, 1993). The move to bar codes contributed to the loss of 400,000 jobs in retailing between 1990 and 1993 (Rattner, 1993). Companies have also been substituting capital for labor in the office; investment in information technology has soared over the past few years, automating and replacing clerical jobs, including secretarial positions (Mandel, Zellner, & Hof, 1993).

If technology increases the productivity of labor and demand doesn't increase, then employment must fall. But economic doctrine holds that productivity increases lead to price reductions that open new markets and create more jobs. Thus job displacement, which forces people to learn new skills, must be distinguished from job replacement, which shrinks the overall job market. For example, the rise in health care costs, which has made workers more expensive, generated over 240,000 jobs in the health care industry in 1992 (Mandel et al., 1993). If productivity enhancement is the key, then "the primary threat to jobs is not too fast a pace of technological change, but a pace that is too slow in comparison with the competition" (Adler, 1992).

Government policies inadvertently affect the quantity of jobs when they establish conditions that affect the cost of employment. When governments add to the cost, they make private firms reluctant to hire new workers and thus constrict the supply of jobs. Economists and business writers contrast the United States with Europe to underscore this point. Between 1973 and 1991 the U.S. economy created more than thirty-five million new jobs while the European community generated only eight million, despite having one-third more people. The unemployment rate in Europe in the last quarter of 1994 (about 12 percent) was approximately double that of the United States (Friedman, 1994). Economists explain that European governments offer relatively comfortable social safety nets that encourage people to stay on welfare rather than to take low-paying jobs, as many do in the United States. Some writers also hold labor laws, environmental regulations, and union demands responsible for encouraging western European firms to move manufacturing to cheaper locations, including the southern United States (Rapoport, 1993). On the other hand, the more flexible U.S. system creates greater heterogeneity in wage levels, leading policymakers to balance the demand for job quantity with job quality and general living conditions.

Meanwhile, as Chapter Two elaborates, new ways of working clearly clash with old rules guiding labor relations in the United States from the early industrial and bureaucratic eras, such as prohibition of works councils or company unions. Kirsten Wever demonstrates how government policies and society's political and economic institutions mold work and employment relations, illustrating her points with current developments in the United States, eastern Germany, and Poland. She questions whether the competitive pressures of the environment will be powerful enough to enable the political choices required to change current institutions.

The American government wrapped personnel practices in a blanket of regulation in the 1960s and 1970s, the most prominent

being the Equal Pay Act (1963), Title VII of the Civil Rights Act
(1964), the Age Discrimination in Employment Act (1967), the
Occupational Safety and Health Act (1970), and the Employee
Retirement Income Security Act (1974). Jim Ledvinka cites three
recent developments—the 1991 Civil Rights Act, the Americans
with Disabilities Act of 1990 (ADA), and legal initiatives relative to
privacy—to illustrate that the same regulatory dynamics have been
at work for the past century. He analyzes the divergent models of
employment held by psychology and the law and underscores the
inevitability of conflict when the law adjudicates challenges to psychological interventions.

Work

Despite its name, the post-industrial economy hasn't done away
with industry any more than the industrial revolution did away with
agriculture. Agriculture, industry, and services all make significant
contributions to the economy, but each sector's need for human
beings to accomplish its mission differs widely. In the post-industrial economy most workers provide services, few make products,
and very few plow fields. By 1990 almost three-fourths of the U.S.
labor force was in the service-producing sector, and analysts expect
the proportion to continue to expand. Fewer than 3 percent were
in the agricultural sector.

Yet no sector of the economy is immune to the influence of
high technology. Industrialized countries are now immersed in
electronics, bio-technologies, advanced materials, and other high
technologies. Workers are being replaced or augmented by a new
kind of machine—robots, made possible through advances in electronics. Microcomputers are ubiquitous and networked; notebook
computers and mobile telecommunications can be taken on the
road; and satellites, microwaves, and fiber-optic cable can potentially connect us all, instantaneously.

This new technology is not an incremental advance over that of
the past; as Chapter Three reveals, it represents a discontinuous revolutionary breakthrough. Information technology is unique in its
ability to produce information. At the same time devices translate
information into action, they also register data about the automated
activities and thus generate new streams of information. The new

technology can be used merely to automate, or it can be mined for its information generating function. The latter approach sets into motion a series of dynamics that can reconfigure the nature of work and social relationships (Zuboff, 1988). Whether technology enriches or starves job content was the central issue in the deskilling debate that arose in the 1970s and continues today. Chapter Three examines ways in which post-industrial work may inevitably involve more upskilling than deskilling as more jobs become saturated with knowledge and information.

The driver of this new technology is the microchip. In Chapter Three Jan Van der Spiegel traces the development of this technology and explains how it is pushing work in new directions. Advances in microprocessing power, semiconductor memory, and telecommunications technologies have catapulted us into the information age, but he contends that intelligent machines of the future will be based on biological systems and have humanlike capabilities. Don Davis depicts how the information technologies described by Van der Spiegel are being used by organizations to promote flexibility. He notes that knowledge is not just a source of power, as Bacon understood in the sixteenth century; knowledge is an inexhaustible source that must be continuously regenerated for organizations to learn and adapt. By removing internal and external boundaries, organizations gain the flexibility to respond to the demands of global competition. Davis relates organizational forms to strategies such as just-in-time inventory control (JIT) and total quality management (TQM). Foreshadowing themes pursued later in the volume, he calls for research and theory in I/O psychology to address consequent human resource requirements, such as teamwork and organization attachments.

Picking up on some of the organizational strategies described by Davis, Toby Wall and Paul Jackson draw implications in Chapter Four from three initiatives that are making dramatic changes in manufacturing—JIT, TQM, and advanced manufacturing technology (AMT). They contend that by focusing too exclusively on issues of motivation, psychologists have failed to recognize the power of learning and knowledge in job design. They argue that deficiencies in job design research are not just in quantity but also in kind and cite specific job content variables, organizational contingencies, and psychological mechanisms that should be included. Their chapter offers a fresh perspective and new dimensions that reinforce critiques of the narrowness of the neoconventional view of work (Nord et al., 1990).

Michael Coovert examines in Chapter Five the influences of information technology and global competition on clerical, professional, and other nonmanagement office jobs. He revisits the issue of deskilling and attends to worker control in automation, health concerns, and human-technology interfaces. Coovert paints a picture of future office work that includes computer-supported cooperative work, augmented reality, and ubiquitous computing, all of which have implications for human resource practices, especially employee training. Consistent with the biological approach of Van der Spiegel, Coovert argues for naturalness—future office technology will be most useful where workers can use or augment existing knowledge, skills, and attributes. He also makes the case for developing and testing richer models of the interaction of workers, technology, and the organization, again challenging the narrowness of current psychological theory.

Workers

White-collar jobs employed more workers than any other category (45.9 percent) in 1990, and the proportion of managers was at 12.3 percent. Farmers represented only 2.3 percent of the labor force, and manual labor 26.2 percent (U.S. Bureau of the Census, 1992). The growth in white-collar and managerial workers has meant that researchers increasingly develop a psychology of such workers, which may color their theoretical perspectives (Nord et al., 1990).

The American workforce differs sharply from that of the past—less young, less male, and less white. Chapter Six considers changing demographic characteristics and what this may mean for the distribution of work. The middle-aging of the baby boom, advent of the baby bust, and general population aging have diminished the relative availability of younger workers. Labor-saving machinery in the home, processed foods, ready-made clothing, and small families freed women from the arduous unpaid labor they had endured at the beginning of the twentieth century. The rush of women into the labor force in the 1960s and 1970s changed its gender composition remarkably to more than 45 percent female in 1990 (U.S. Bureau of the Census, 1992).

As at the start of this century, American gates are open to new waves of immigrants, but this time few are from Europe. Residents on American coastal and southwestern borders feel the effects most, as immigrants swarm through the airports of Los Angeles, New York, and Miami and across the Rio Grande. Most new arrivals are Hispanics and Asians, but the cultural composition of the total group of immigrants ranges widely. Children from 188 countries entered New York City's schools in 1993; they speak more than fifty languages and dialects in Intermediate School 237 in Flushing (Jones, 1994). Contrary to the overt stereotyping and prejudice at the turn of the last century, diversity today meets awakened social sensitivities in an atmosphere of political correctness and more open attitudes, despite complaints about free speech and extremes of the changing lexicon. Nevertheless, immigration arouses public concerns about the impact on jobs and social services.

Immigrants range widely in the skill levels they bring, from highly trained scientists and engineers to unskilled laborers with only a few grades of education. But native-born Americans also show huge disparities in educational levels. The average level of education has increased (nearly one-fourth are college graduates) and with education have come higher expectations and more liberal values. Workers are no longer content, for example, with routine work and taking orders; increasingly they want a say in what they do and want their work to offer a means of self-fulfillment (Howard & Bray, 1988). Given that more than one-fourth of college graduates major in business and another 4 percent or 5 percent in psychology, it is not clear to what extent these values were socially constructed by the writings of psychological and management theorists.

Despite the higher average levels of education, nearly 22 percent of Americans were high school dropouts in 1991 (National Center for Education Statistics, 1993), and the average student in a public elementary or secondary school, according to many studies, was receiving an inadequate education. The bureaucracy era had dumb jobs and smart people; the post-industrial era threatens to have smart jobs and dumb people.

Paul Osterman (Chapter Six) considers the employment difficulties facing American youth because of the increasing emphasis on competitiveness and worker skills. From his analysis of longitudinal data on the transition from school to work, he concludes that a significant portion of young people have not settled down by age thirty and that the casual American system does not work well, especially for those who fail to finish high school. He finds many reasons why the dual model of apprenticeship training of western Germany, often suggested as an alternative, may not be a viable solution for the United States. Osterman explores a more fundamental question: Will increased worker skills lead to better jobs? His answer is not encouraging.

Workforce skills and knowledge are subject to continual obsolescence and displacement. This is part of the nature of capitalism, described by economist Schumpeter as "creative destruction"—creative by developing novel products, processes, and firms; destructive by abandoning outmoded technologies and products, devaluing costly investments and hard-won skills, and bankrupting firms that fall behind (Attewell, 1992). Normally such skill transitions are absorbed as older generations retire or move on, but the pace at which high technologies are racing through the global economy suggests that skill displacement may happen much more abruptly.

Another factor affecting needed skills is the greater efficiency achieved by multiskilling. Because jobs change quickly, training a worker for one narrow task, as recommended by Taylor, is inefficient. It is more practical to take advantage of human flexibility by having workers master several jobs and work where and when needed (Locke, 1982).

Tony Carnevale (also Chapter Six) analyzes worker education and skills within the context of an expanded set of competitive standards and consumer demands in the new economy. He notes that traditional pedagogy produces workers for outmoded mass-production workplaces, not for high-performance work systems. Yet he argues that education, technology, and even high-performance work organizations will not assure success without more training by American employers. He discusses the kinds of training workers need beyond formal schooling and describes alternative public policy initiatives to stimulate such worker training.

Demographic characteristics are just boxcars that carry psychological qualities, according to Frank Landy, Laura Shankster-Cawley, and Stacey Kohler Moran (Chapter Seven), and it is the latter that psychologists must try to unmask for personnel selection in the future. Much more needs to be learned, they claim, about the complexity of cognitive abilities and the role of tacit or job knowledge. Psychologists will also need to explore the "O" or other personality and motivational characteristics in addition to the classic KSAs (knowledge, skills, and abilities), especially to reduce the adverse impact of exclusively cognitive tests and to consider qualities important to teamwork. In fact, a key departure for personnel selection in the future will be analyzing jobs and personal characteristics that relate to working in teams. The authors' projections for the course of personnel selection are often driven by responsiveness to the force of federal regulation, as discussed by Ledvinka in Chapter Two, particularly the ADA, the Civil Rights Act of 1991, and the Age Discrimination in Employment Act. Despite the problems the ADA poses for practice, these writers remain sanguine about its influence on research and theory-building within I/O psychology.

Personnel selection will continue to be important as organizational adaptations create demands for workers with different configurations of skills and other characteristics. At the same time, organizations are recruiting or downsizing employees, partly because one type of employee is being substituted for another and partly as a reflection of restructuring to become more nimble. With information readily transmitted, layers of supervision become superfluous and the cubbyholes of traditional bureaucracies become traps for fast-paced competition.

The spate of downsizing in large organizations, releasing droves of employees from both the blue-collar and white-collar ranks, has had a powerful impact on employee-employer relationships. Despite hundreds of thousands of layoffs in the 1990s and significant economic recovery from a recession, in the first quarter of 1994 companies announced staff reductions of 192,572, or 3,100 per day (Byrne, 1994). According to a Sirota and Alper Associates survey, in 1980–1982 some 79 percent of management and 75 percent of nonmanagement employees reported their job security as "good" or "very good"; by 1992–1994, the proportion had dropped to 55 percent in management and 51 percent in nonmanagement (O'Reilly, 1994).

Besides reducing hierarchical layers and corporate staff, organizations are pursuing flexibility by using more contingent workers. The types of employment relations between organizations and workers will be much more variable in the future, according to Denise Rousseau and Kimberly Wade-Benzoni in Chapter Eight. In an adhocratic era of boundaryless organizations, employment relationships may be short term or long term and involve insiders or outsiders, raising issues such as the effects of core and peripheral workers on each other. Rousseau and Wade-Benzoni examine issues in psychological contract violation, often the case with downsizing. They explore new schemata for employment relations, speculating that organizations and workers will take less for granted in the future.

Contingent arrangements raise troublesome issues concerning workers' rewards, protections, and careers. Contract workers may lack proper supervision and training, particularly because employers who provide such oversight risk legal liabilities as "co-employers." The absence of supervision and training in turn can lead to more accidents. Contingent workers have no protections from employers or from U.S. labor law. Moreover, when they do get some training, it is likely to be for specific job-related skills rather than broader abilities, such as interpersonal skills that would develop them for other jobs or careers (Geber, 1993).

Yet not even core employees can count on long-term careers within one organization. As expressed by an advertising agency executive, it is "the end of work as marriage" (Calabresi, Van Tassel, Riley, & Szczesny, 1993, p. 37). As organizations adapt to a turbulent environment, the traditional career will die and be an unlikely candidate for resurrection, predict Tim Hall and Phil Mirvis in Chapter Nine. But they believe that careers can be protean, evolving and adapting to new environmental conditions, shaped by the individual and not the organization. They also visualize several careers per person and the need for lifelong learning and continual self-development. This will not necessarily come easily, and they raise troublesome questions such as whether self-development has life-enriching dimensions beyond interesting and challenging work. Thus they strike one more blow at narrow psychological conceptualizations and neoconventional assumptions.

Working

As hierarchies shrink, organizations empower their employees by moving decision-making responsibility to those close to internal and external customers. This high-involvement or high-performance workplace views workers as true partners in achieving its objectives (Howard & Wellins, 1994). To support its empowered workers, organizations must share information, knowledge, power to act, and rewards throughout the workforce (Lawler, 1992). High involvement can trace its roots to the company unions that basked briefly in the sunlight of industrial democracy after World War I; the work on group dynamics of Lewin and its extension to the tenets of participative management propounded by Likert, McGregor, and others; sociotechnical systems and self-managed teams explored by Trist, Emery, and other colleagues at Tavistock; and the importance of work content explicated by Herzberg and colleagues.

Yet high involvement is more than any of these, for it calls for a level of top-to-bottom involvement and realignment of roles that doesn't survive without massive rethinking and restructuring. Perhaps the most explicit ancestor was the ultra progressive Mary Parker Follett, who consulted with managers in the 1920s and early 1930s. Her ideas of "power with" rather than "power over," of integrative unity, the law of the situation, and authority vested with knowledge and experience (Follett, 1949) come closest to the holistic rethinking needed for high involvement to work. Full implementation of her ideas would have been difficult in the political-economic-societal context and organizational conditions of the industrial and bureaucratic eras. But the competitive push of the post-industrial age in combination with information technology that enables decision making at frontline levels has made high-involvement work settings possible. This does not, however, make high involvement easy to implement nor guarantee its acceptance (Howard & Wellins, 1994).

Where machinery takes over the task of making products, factory workers are elevated to the role of ensuring efficient system functioning, which includes sharing information with other workers. Such a worker has a much higher level of interdependence and considerably less individual autonomy. This new work situation is therefore not a revival of craft production (Kern & Schumann, 1992) but a new form of working. Sue Mohrman and Susan Cohen depict in Chapter Ten how the lateral, boundaryless organizations (described by Davis in Chapter Three) lead to different interaction patterns and integrating mechanisms. They describe people as emerging from the traditional organizational chart's boxes and lines to a new interconnectedness in high-involvement teams and other collective webs. These new co-worker attachments carry serious psychological implications, including what may be an uncomfortable dependency on co-workers. Managers must also assume difficult and unfamiliar roles, and Mohrman and Cohen depict how they will relate to both their direct reports and each other. The authors uncover large gaps in psychological knowledge about collectives of individuals who work together.

Bob House expands on the new roles of managers and leaders in Chapter Eleven. Mary Parker Follett, who was critical of the trait emphasis of psychologists in her era, specified in the 1920s that leaders must see the whole, find the unifying threads, and have a vision of the future. She stated that the higher the leader's position in the organization, the more important this becomes (Follett, 1949), a position House affirms for leaders at the top of modern organizations or major subunits. He proposes that leaders at various levels must engage in additional aspects of the neocharismatic paradigm (for example, self-sacrifice, selective motive arousal, high expectations of and confidence in followers). The stress and uncertainty of the future will also call for special managerial roles and elements of earlier leadership theory, such as clarifying paths and goals for ambiguous tasks. He demonstrates various ways that empowerment of followers can be accomplished and offers two integrative meta-propositions for the essence of leadership.

House speculates that a substantial proportion of organizational members will be without direct supervision in the future. If this is the case, how will the organization know how well these workers, including telecommuters, are performing their work? Jerry Hedge and Wally Borman examine such performance evaluation issues in Chapter Twelve. They evaluate the usefulness of appraisal sources beyond the supervisor, such as those included in 360-degree feedback methods—peers, self, subordinates, and customers. How to evaluate team performance is another difficult problem they address. Information technology lends itself to electronic performance monitoring, but they observe that this method carries mixed blessings. Building on the need for new personality measures cited by Landy, Shankster-Cawley and Moran in Chapter Seven, Hedge and Borman tie such "will do" measures to typical performance and relate "can do" measures to maximal performance. They see another duality emerging in performance appraisal: technical proficiency and contextual performance. Although performance appraisal will be more complex in the future, the authors note that it will connect employees to shifting organizational terrain and help them to identify what is expected and how they need to adapt.

Reflections on Post-Industrial Society and the Psychology of Work

Adjustments to post-industrial society will not be easy. In Chapter Thirteen Jerry Hage argues that the many institutional and role failures, including high levels of violent crime, divorce, out-of-wedlock births, and poverty-stricken one-parent families, suggest discontinuities in social life. He argues that to adjust to the constant changes in society, people must learn to perceive reality in more complex ways that can be defined as post-modern. Work, family, and leisure are becoming interpenetrated, and people must learn to negotiate within large, complex role-sets. He postulates that to make the transition to post-industrial society, people will need complex and creative minds, adaptive and flexible selves, and the capacity to understand symbolic communications.

The rich chapters that follow—on post-industrial work, workers, and working and their political-economic-societal context—explore many pathways, but they also connect in thematic avenues of thought. I bring together these various themes in Chapter Fourteen to help us rethink the psychology of an exhilarating but intimidating future world of work.

References
Adler, P. S. (1992). Introduction. In P. S. Adler (Ed.), *Technology and the future of work*. New York: Oxford University Press.

Argyris, C. (1957). *Personality and organization*. New York: Harper.

Attewell, P. (1992). Skill and occupational changes in U.S. manufacturing. In P. S. Adler (Ed.), *Technology and the future of work*. New York: Oxford University Press.

Baldry, C. (1988). *Computers, jobs, and skills: The industrial relations of technological change*. New York: Plenum.

Baritz, L. (1960). *The servants of power: A history of the use of social science in American industry*. Middletown, CT: Wesleyan University Press.

Blackford, K.H.H. (1916). *The job, the man, the boss*. New York: Doubleday.

Braverman, H. (1974). *Labor and monopoly capital*. New York: Monthly Review Press.

Byrne, J. A. (1994, May 9). The pain of downsizing. *Business Week*, pp. 60–69.

Calabresi, M., Van Tassel, J., Riley, M., & Szczesny, J. R. (1993, November 22). Jobs in an age of insecurity. *Time*, pp. 32–39.

Chandler, A. D., Jr. (1962). *Strategy and structure: Chapters in the history of the industrial enterprise*. Cambridge, MA: MIT Press.

Chandler, A. D., Jr. (1977). *The visible hand: The managerial revolution in American business*. Cambridge, MA: Harvard University Press.

Committee on Science, Engineering, and Public Policy; Panel on the Government Role in Civilian Technology. (1992). *The government role in civilian technology: Building a new alliance*. Washington, DC: National Academy Press.

Davis, S. M. (1987). *Future perfect*. Reading, MA: Addison-Wesley.

Duncan, W. J. (1989). *Great ideas in management: Lessons from the founders and foundations of managerial practice*. San Francisco: Jossey-Bass.

Eilbert, H. (1959, Autumn). The development of personnel management in the United States. *Business History Review, 33*, 345–364.

Follett, M. P. (1949). *Freedom and co-ordination: Lectures in business organisation*. London: Management Publications Trust, Ltd.

Friedman, T. L. (1994, March 14). World's big economies turn to the jobs issue. *New York Times*, pp. D1, D6.

Galbraith, J. K. (1958). *The affluent society*. Boston: Houghton Mifflin.

Geber, B. (1993, December). The flexible work force. *Training*, pp. 23–30.

Gilbreth, L. M. (1914). *The psychology of management: The function of the mind in determining, teaching, and installing methods of least waste*. New York: Macmillan.

Gilson, M. B. (1940). *What's past is prologue: Reflections on my industrial experience*. New York: Harper.

Ginzberg, E., & Berman, H. (1963). *The American worker in the twentieth century: A history through autobiographies*. New York: Free Press.

Hale, M., Jr. (1980). *Human science and social order: Hugo Munsterberg and the origins of applied psychology*. Philadelphia: Temple University Press.

Hale, M., Jr. (1982). History of employment testing. In A. K. Wigdor & W.

R. Garner (Eds.), *Ability testing: Uses, consequences, and controversies, Part I.* Washington, DC: National Academy Press.

Herzberg, F., Mausner, B., & Snyderman, B. B. (1959). *The motivation to work.* New York: Wiley.

Hilgard, E. R. (1987). *Psychology in America: A historical survey.* San Diego: Harcourt Brace.

Hofstadter, R. (1962). *Anti-intellectualism in American life.* New York: Random House.

Howard, A., & Bray, D. W. (1988). *Managerial lives in transition: Advancing age and changing times.* New York: Guilford Press.

Howard, A., & Wellins, R. S. (1994). *High-involvement leadership: Changing roles for changing times.* Pittsburgh: Development Dimensions International.

Jacoby, S. M. (1985). *Employing bureaucracy: Managers, unions, and the transformation of work in American industry, 1900–1945.* New York: Columbia University Press.

Jones, C. (1994, June 12). Melting pot still bubbles at I.S. 237. *New York Times,* pp. 41, 48.

Kash, D. E., & Rycroft, R. W. (1993, November–December). Nurturing winners with federal R&D. *Technology Review,* pp. 58–64.

Katz, B. M. (1990). *Technology and culture: A historical romance.* Stanford, CA: Stanford Alumni Association.

Katzell, R. A., & Austin, J. T. (1992). From then to now: The development of industrial-organizational psychology in the United States. *Journal of Applied Psychology, 77*(6), 803–835.

Kern, H., & Schumann, M. (1992). New concepts of production and the emergence of the systems controller. In P. S. Adler (Ed.), *Technology and the future of work.* New York: Oxford University Press.

Kraus, M. P. (1986). *Personnel research, history and policy issues: Walter Van Dyke Bingham and the Bureau of Personnel Research.* New York: Garland.

Krugman, P. R. (1992). Technology and international competition: A historical perspective. In M. C. Harris & G. E. Moore (Eds.), *Linking trade and technology policies* (pp. 13–28). Washington, DC: National Academy Press.

Lawler, E. E., III. (1992). *The ultimate advantage: Creating the high-involvement organization.* San Francisco: Jossey-Bass.

Likert, R. (1961). *New patterns of management.* New York: McGraw-Hill.

Locke, E. A. (1982). The ideas of Frederick W. Taylor: An evaluation. *Academy of Management Review, 7,* 14–24.

McClelland, D. C. (1961). *The achieving society.* New York: Van Nostrand Reinhold.

McGregor, D. (1960). *The human side of enterprise.* New York: McGraw-Hill.

Magnet, M. (1993, March 8). Why job growth is stalled. *Fortune,* pp. 51–57.

Mandel, M. J., Zellner, W., & Hof, R. (1993, February 22). Jobs, jobs, jobs. *Business Week*, pp. 68–74.

Maslow, A. H. (1954). *Motivation and personality*. New York: Harper.

National Center for Education Statistics. (1993). *Projections of education statistics to 2004*. Washington, DC: U. S. Superintendent of Documents.

Nelson, D. (1975). *Managers and workers: Origins of the new factory system in the U.S., 1880–1920*. Madison: University of Wisconsin Press.

Nelson, D. (1980). *Frederick W. Taylor and the rise of scientific management*. Madison: University of Wisconsin Press.

Newcomer, M. (1955). *The big business executive: The factors that made him, 1900–1950*. New York: Columbia University Press.

Nord, W. R., Brief, A. P., Atieh, J. M., & Doherty, E. M. (1990). Studying meanings of work: The case of work values. In A. P. Brief & W. R. Nord (Eds.), *Meanings of occupational work: A collection of essays*. Lexington, MA: Lexington Books.

O'Reilly, B. (1994, June 13). The new deal: What companies and employees owe one another. *Fortune*, pp. 44–52.

Rapoport, C. (1993, October 4). Europe tackles its job crisis. *Fortune*, pp. 133–134.

Rattner, S. (1993, September 19). If productivity's rising, why are jobs paying less? *New York Times Magazine*, pp. 54, 96–97.

Riesman, D. (1950). *The lonely crowd*. New Haven, CT: Yale University Press.

Robertson, R. M. (1973). *History of the American economy* (3rd ed.). New York: Harcourt Brace.

Rodgers, D. (1978). *The work ethic in industrial America: 1850–1920*. Chicago: University of Chicago Press.

Scott, W. D., Clothier, R. C., & Spriegel, W. P. (1949). *Personnel management* (4th ed.). Chicago: Shaw.

Simon, J. L. (1989). *The economic consequences of immigration*. Cambridge, MA: Blackwell.

Sloat, W. (1979). *1929: America before the crash*. New York: Macmillan.

Stewart, T. A. (1993, December 13). Welcome to the revolution. *Fortune*, pp. 66–78.

Tapscott, D., & Caston, A. (1993). *Paradigm shift: The new promise of information technology*. New York: McGraw-Hill.

Taylor, F. W. (1911). *The principles of scientific management*. New York: Harper.

Tobagi, F. A. (1991). Telecommunications: The nervous system of a modern society. In J. D. Meindl (Ed.), *Brief lessons in high technology: A primer of seven fields that are changing our lives*. Stanford, CA: Stanford Alumni Association.

Tyson, L. D. (1992). Managing trade conflict in high-technology industries. In M. C. Harris & G. E. Moore (Eds.), *Linking trade and technology policies*. Washington, DC: National Academy Press.

U.S. Bureau of the Census. (1975). *Historical statistics of the United States: Colonial times to 1970.* Washington, DC: U.S. Department of Commerce.

U.S. Bureau of the Census. (1992). *Statistical abstract of the United States.* Washington, DC: U.S. Department of Commerce.

Viteles, M. S. (1953). *Motivation and morale in industry.* New York: W. W. Norton.

Weisbord, M. R. (1987). *Productive workplaces: Organizing and managing for dignity, meaning, and community.* San Francisco: Jossey-Bass.

White, R. W. (1959). Motivation reconsidered: The concept of competence. *Psychological Review, 66,* 297–333.

Whyte, W. H., Jr. (1956). *The organization man.* New York: Simon & Schuster.

Wren, D. (1987). *The evolution of management thought.* New York: Wiley.

Yellowitz, I. (1969). *The position of the worker in American society, 1865–1896.* Englewood Cliffs, NJ: Prentice Hall.

Yoffie, D. B. (1992). Technology challenges to trade policy. In M. C. Harris & G. E. Moore (Eds.), *Linking trade and technology policies* (pp. 103–115). Washington, DC: National Academy Press.

Zuboff, S. (1988). *In the age of the smart machine: The future of work and power.* New York: Basic Books.

Chapter Two

The Political Context of Employment

How governments set the rules for relationships between employers and employees is a critical component of the political context of work. But this is not a topic that warms the hearts of industrial-organizational psychologists. Labor relations are often detached from other human resource functions in the workplace, and psychologists have traditionally served management rather than organized labor (Baritz, 1960). Industrial psychologists have been more closely concerned with direct government regulation of human resource activities, particularly personnel selection, but as Ledvinka points out later in this chapter, their attitudes toward this regulation are souring. Neither of these political contexts can be ignored, for both affect the nature of work and psychological interventions in the workplace.

Industrial Relations

Labor Day 1994 was observed in New York City without the traditional parade. Labor unions were unable to muster enough support to march down the city's streets. The parade died from lack of interest, and some anticipate that unions, at least in the private sector of the United States, will suffer a similar fate.

Union membership has declined sharply. From a high of 35.5 percent of the workforce soon after World War II, unions claimed fewer than 16 percent of the workforce by 1994, a smaller proportion than before passage of the 1935 Wagner Act (National Labor Relations Act), which granted labor's right to organize. Within the private sector, only 11 percent of the labor force were union members in 1994, and that proportion is predicted to drop to 5 percent or lower by the year 2000 (Bernstein, 1994).

The declining power of organized labor has had a noticeable social impact. Unions have been quite successful in one of their major objectives—raising wages. In the mid-1980s, union workers were said to earn an average of one-third more than their nonunion counterparts (AFL-CIO, 1985). But declining union membership has been held partly responsible for the decline in blue-collar wages in the 1980s. Weakening unions have also been cited as a key reason for simultaneous declines of employees with company pension plans and employer health plans, and for a 125-fold increase in unlawful discharge suits (Bernstein, 1994).

One reason advanced for labor's decline is that management has deprived unions of their right to organize or strike (Seligman, 1994). The diminution of labor's influence is often traced to President Reagan's breaking the air traffic controllers' union in 1981, when a strike cost workers their jobs. Others point to the success of unions in organizing in the public sector as evidence that management opposition in the private sector is the chief culprit in unions' decline. Private firms can often outsource or relocate to avoid unions, while public sector employees don't face such a threat to job security.

On the other side are those who argue that structural factors have led to unions' decline. These include the shifting of employment to sectors that have been difficult to organize, such as services and small, entrepreneurial firms; and the difficulty of paying negotiated higher wages in light of deregulation and international competition (Seligman, 1994). In this sense unions were victims of their own success. Higher wages, credited with thrusting blue-collar workers into the middle class after World War II, made union-intensive industries vulnerable to foreign competition, resulting in company losses and unemployment (Greenhouse, 1992).

Unions are viewed more as social partners than enemies in Europe (Bernstein, 1994). But recent reports suggest that Europe is lagging behind in productivity because of strong unions and protective governments that have resulted in high wages and employment costs. For example, a McKinsey survey of nine large manufacturing industries found that Germany was the productivity leader in none; Japan led in five and the United States in four (Stevenson, 1994a).

A gnawing debate is whether unions have outlived their usefulness. U.S. managers would generally agree, but supporters argue that helping workers bargain collectively rather than individually is a legitimate social role and that unions give workers the clout to help pass safety and pension laws (Bernstein, 1994). Many suspect that without a strong labor voice, management will give priority to factors other than worker interests. Worsening job conditions could, in fact, result in renewed union strength (Osterman, 1988).

Even stalwart labor supporters find it difficult in today's competitive business environment to defend the traditional, adversarial model of labor-management relations, which has devolved all too often into situations high in conflict and low in trust. This model was codified in New Deal legislation that separated the domains of management and labor—management had control over the organization of work, while unions were constrained to focus on wage levels and industrial jurisprudence. Although collective bargaining and job control strategies stabilized labor-management relations, they also fostered "growth of a thick underbrush of rules, customs and agreements governing the organization of many workplaces" (Thomas & Kochan, 1992, p. 216).

Industrial relations show the greatest promise of reform in organizations that adopt models of high involvement, which rely on a highly skilled workforce, teams, and rejection of the traditional dichotomy between thinking and doing. This is most likely to occur where organizational strategy emphasizes competing with quality, speed, and technological superiority in niche markets as opposed to competing with lower costs and high volume in mass, standardized markets. The latter is a linear extension of past practice, now prey to international production, outsourcing, and anti-union campaigns (Thomas & Kochan, 1992).

The AFL-CIO recently issued a report urging a model of work organization with a flatter management structure and greater worker responsibilities centered in teams. They proposed a new labor-management partnership, but they were careful to define unions' role as representing workers in strategic decision making with management (including decisions about implementation of

new technologies) and collective bargaining to compensate workers for their enhanced contribution to organizational productivity
(AFL-CIO, 1994). Whether unions are necessary to promote and
sustain high-involvement work models is at the heart of the debate
about unions' future. There is ample evidence of organizations
embracing such models for their own self-interest, and they may
be able to implement them more effectively without the union
bureaucracy. Even in Germany, unions' centralized and nonpar-
ticipatory organizational forms have been seen as impediments to
their taking on a needed new role as political brokers of a more
democratic workplace (Kern & Schumann, 1992). Meanwhile
American labor leaders' energies are still taken up in fights for survival and legitimacy—issues long ago resolved by European countries and Japan (Kochan & Osterman, 1991).

Government Regulation of Human Resource Activities

"Society cannot function by rat race alone" (Dornbusch, 1994,
p. 14). Without financial and social stability, work organizations
cannot survive, and the state functions to assure that these pre-
requisites are met.

In the United States, efforts toward social stability and the solution of social problems in the last twenty-five years have led the federal government to impose increasingly elaborate rules that govern
the workplace. Regulation has permeated five primary areas: equal
employment opportunity, employee safety and health, employee
pay and benefits, employee privacy, and job security (Ledvinka &
Scarpello, 1992). Although the government has been regulating
business for many years, most of the older laws pertained to specific industries (vertical regulation), while the newer laws affect
managerial functions across industries (horizontal regulation)
(Weidenbaum, 1977).

The newer regulatory agencies were created to solve social
rather than industry problems and serve constituencies other than
industry. In fact, organizations are often targets of the regulation,
for it is poor management practices (by some organizations, not
necessarily by most) that create the problems that the regulation
is supposed to solve (Ledvinka & Scarpello, 1992).

The growing number of complex regulations has widened business exposure to lawsuits and enhanced the need for knowledge and understanding of regulatory issues by managers and human resource professionals. As international competition intensifies, there are other drawbacks as well. European social welfare policies, financed by high taxes and mandates on business, have contributed to high rates of unemployment. Because regulations restrict layoffs, mandate paid leaves, and impose taxes for other costly benefits, employers have tended toward not replacing employees or using temporary workers. In Spain, where firing a worker on the payroll is almost impossible, about one-third of employees are temporary (Becker, 1993), and unemployment exceeds 24 percent (Stevenson, 1994b).

Implications

The intention of both labor organizations and regulatory bodies is protection of individuals, an intention entirely aligned with a profession like psychology, whose purpose is to promote human welfare. Historically, concern for worker interests has been the province of collective bargaining and human resource professionals (Jacoby, 1985). Whereas government regulations and labor organizations impose themselves to protect individuals from the misuse of power by work organizations, I/O psychologists are more inclined to seek common interests and mutual advantages—thus their continued search to maximize both productivity and job satisfaction.

The changing nature of work and work organizations suggests that there may finally be synergy between the interests of employers and employees. High-involvement organizations shift power away from management and toward frontline associates to capitalize on the knowledge and skills of such workers and their creativity in cutting inefficiencies and waste. Associates gain autonomy, respect, and opportunities for personal mastery by committing themselves to the organization's goals. Organizations and workers have never needed each other more.

As this new way of working spreads, the protections afforded by political institutions designed for another era seem increasingly inappropriate. As both Wever and Ledvinka point out, protections for labor against company-dominated unions in the 1935 Wagner Act now militate against the kind of joint problem solving on which high-involvement organizations depend. Recent rulings by the National Labor Relations Board found that workplace committees at Electromation and Du Pont were illegal, setting the stage for labor-law reform. But as Wever explains, a recommendation by the Commission on the Future of Worker-Management Relations, headed by former Labor Secretary John Dunlop, to liberalize the section prohibiting employer-dominated labor organizations, desired by management, in exchange for enhancing organizing rights, desired by unions, has generated little support from either side ("This is one," 1995).

Ledvinka illustrates how adversarial premises underlying government regulations are restricting other psychological interventions, particularly those that emphasize individual differences. It is tempting to draw a parallel between the government's thrust and the criticisms of industrial policy mentioned in Chapter One; that is, political pressures in constituent-oriented democracies tend to favor those who, for whatever reason, are losing out in the competition for jobs. Psychological approaches to future work may be curtailed, then, unless the political context can be reformulated into less confrontational models of employer-employee relationships. Both Wever and Ledvinka teach us how difficult that challenge is.

References

AFL-CIO. (1985). *The changing situation of workers and their unions* (2nd report, Committee on the Evolution of Work). Washington, DC: Author.

AFL-CIO. (1994). *The American workplace: A labor perspective* (3rd report, Committee on the Evolution of Work). Washington, DC: Author.

Baritz, L. (1960). *The servants of power: A history of the use of social science in American industry.* Middletown, CT: Wesleyan University Press.

Becker, G. S. (1993, October 4). Down and out all over Europe: A lesson for America. *Business Week,* p. 18.

Bernstein, A. (1994, May 23). Why America needs unions but not the kind it has now. *Business Week,* pp. 70–82.

Dornbusch, R. (1994, June 27). Sure, fight inequality, but set the markets free. *Business Week,* p. 14.

Greenhouse, S. (1992, April 19). The union movement loses another big one. *New York Times,* sec. 4, p. 1.

Jacoby, S. M. (1985). *Employing bureaucracy: Managers, unions, and the transformation of work in American industry, 1900–1945.* New York: Columbia University Press.

Kern, H., & Schumann, M. (1992). New concepts of production and the emergence of the systems controller. In P. S. Adler (Ed.), *Technology and the future of work.* New York: Oxford University Press.

Kochan, T., & Osterman, P. (1991). *Human resources development and utilization: Is there too little in the U.S.?* Paper prepared for the Council on Competitiveness, Massachusetts Institute of Technology, Cambridge, MA.

Ledvinka, J., & Scarpello, V. G. (1992). *Federal regulation of personnel and human resource management* (2nd ed.). Belmont, CA: Wadsworth.

Osterman, P. (1988). *Employment futures: Reorganization, dislocation, and public policy.* New York: Oxford University Press.

Seligman, D. (1994, July 11). Why labor keeps losing. *Fortune,* p. 178.

Stevenson, R. W. (1994a, July 17). Europe Inc. has a novel idea: Cut costs. *New York Times,* sec. 3, pp. 1, 6.

Stevenson, R. W. (1994b, September 27). Spanish economy picking up, but many people still suffer. *New York Times,* p. A6.

This is one government report that was born already an orphan (1995, January 13). *Inside Labor Relations,* pp. 1–5.

Thomas, R. J., & Kochan, T. A. (1992). Technology, industrial relations, and the problem of organizational transformation. In P. S. Adler (Ed.), *Technology and the future of work.* New York: Oxford University Press.

Weidenbaum, M. L. (1977). *Business, government, and the public.* Englewood Cliffs, NJ: Prentice Hall.

Political Economic Institutions, Labor Relations, and Work

Kirsten S. Wever

This chapter section is about how government policies and society's political and economic institutions influence work and employment relations outcomes. Such policies and institutions, which allocate resources and decision-making power, reflect preexisting conditions and structures but are also mediated in important ways by historical contingencies and often case-specific political configurations embodying particular ways of thinking. Diverse constellations of institutions and ideas can lead to very different sorts of jobs, skills, and labor-management relations. For the purposes of breadth, this discussion focuses on different national contexts; in particular, key current developments in employment relations in the United States, eastern Germany, and Poland. Recent research points out, however, that differences can be just as impressive at subnational levels (Locke, 1992).

The quality and quantity of work are both strongly influenced by the political economic institutions within which employment relations take place. An obvious example is that of the former Soviet bloc before 1990. Most eastern European jobs served the bureaucracy that was supposed to carry out the economic plans of often huge public enterprises, states (or republics), and the central government/party. Administrators often dominated producers; workers' creativity was channeled toward the achievement of (often extremely difficult to achieve) goals determined far from the point of production. Workers could not simply make the most of the resources available to them; they had to harness whatever was available for fairly narrow purposes for which these resources were often ill suited. Heavy bureaucracy and administration ensured that everyone had a job, but the nature of work was sharply constrained by the way in which the enterprise was embedded in the political economy. As the institutions of the former Soviet bloc countries are changing, so is the nature of work (as discussed later with reference to the Polish case).

Political economic institutions play an enormous role in influencing how the economy and enterprises are structured and how work is conceived and carried out, but how people think about work and its role in society and the economy plays an equally powerful role. Different theories about how a capitalist political economy should be articulated, which are often deeply rooted in structures and strategies, influence both the goals that are deemed worthy of attainment and the methods that are seen as appropriate in attaining them. The assumptions underlying these different perspectives inevitably promote some options and players while disadvantaging, or entirely obscuring, others.

For example, Germany's historic preoccupation with inflation, linked to the experience of particularly devastating hyperinflation in the 1920s, has led German governments to pursue policies that favor low inflation over low unemployment. This, for instance, is one of the reasons why the central Bundesbank has tended to keep interest rates higher than would seem to be in the interests of both business and labor (to say nothing of other domestic interests, or neighboring countries in the European Community). Thus for much of the 1970s and 1980s Germany suffered from higher levels of unemployment than many of the other advanced industrial countries.

The role of ideas and ideologies is often complicated and subtle. Consider the contrast between the Anglo-Saxon "free market" ideology and more "social market" northwestern European approaches. In the United States, for instance, regulation of any kind is typically avoided as long as possible. The ideal capitalist system is seen as one in which individual firms compete against each other on the basis of whatever cost advantages they can gain, and interference with managerial prerogative (of any kind, whether by unions or by government) is viewed with hostility. But once accepted, regulation in the United States is quite minute and detailed, entailing extensive red tape and curtailing the actors' activities substantially. For instance, the Wagner Act, governing union-management relations in this country, lays out in extremely specific detail precisely the conditions under which workers can organize a union, how they can and cannot bargain with management, the exact subject matter the parties are required to negotiate about, the particular governance structure of joint labor-management forums, and so on. Most other industrial relations systems are much more loosely structured.

The American mistrust of government regulation has its roots in the way in which the U.S. economy developed in relative isolation from the state (as opposed to the development patterns of Japan, France, or Germany, for instance), and the general view of government intervention as aiding disadvantaged groups in society to the detriment of capital. One example, of course, is the Wagner Act itself, created to protect labor from the excesses of capital that were thought to underlie the Great Depression (see Vogel, 1978).

The German case exhibits a more subtle "social market" understanding of the role of government institutions. The German political economic framework creates numerous incentives for the parties to negotiate among and between themselves—to bargain jointly over the nature and effects of organizational, industrial, and institutional change. Relations among unions and employers (and the government) center on consensus, cooperation, and compromise. In this view of capitalism, extensive cross-employer cooperation is seen as enabling companies to compete on bases other than labor costs, thus allowing for relatively harmonious industrial relations, but also entailing significant institutional coordination, co-determination, and some government intervention. The central principle underlying the institutional arrangements governing business-labor relations in Germany is that of "framework regulation": flexible negotiation among the parties about socioeconomic change is actively supported within stable outer boundaries. The security of the context—quite different from the rough-and-tumble environment of the "free market"—allows all the actors in the political economy to expend their resources on bargaining for advantage within the system rather than trying to destroy other actors or to bypass the system altogether as frequently happens in the United States and the United Kingdom (Wever & Allen, 1993; Katzenstein, 1987).

What do these broad institutional and ideological factors have to do with the nature of work and jobs? The answer to this question lies in the connections between, on the one hand, the broader business strategy a company pursues and the representational strategy of a union (or works council), and on the other, the way that labor-management relations are structured at the point of production. Imagine, for example, a country in which employers are all-powerful, the government depends entirely on business for its continued political survival, and unions and other forms of worker representation are outlawed. At the same time, competition among different local businesses is intense. This is a poor country relying heavily on foreign capital, and companies frequently are driven out of business by local competitors offering lower and lower costs in order to attract capital.

In this country employers have every incentive to compete for capital and market share on the basis of low labor costs. The government offers no national training system, there is no organized interest that might successfully push for higher labor standards (for example, skills, wages), and the business sector has insufficient time or capital to enhance the quality of its human resources on its own. Note that this is a matter of structural incentives rather than moral imperatives; under these circumstances it makes no sense for employers to act differently. Thus employers in this country pursue a competitive strategy based on low-wage, low-skilled labor, and industry will most likely be concentrated on mass-produced, relatively cheap, and relatively low-quality goods and services. This scenario in some ways reflects employment relations conditions in many of the least developed countries in the world.

This example is extreme for the purposes of illustration. The discussion that follows looks at a variety of more subtle ways in which employment relations, and broader political economic institutions, influence work, skills, and jobs in the United States, eastern Germany, and Poland.

Institutions, Industrial Change, and Work

In all three cases considered here, environmental changes and pressures are challenging government, business, and organized labor to restructure the institutions of employment relations—for instance, worker representation mechanisms, co-determination rights, and training measures. In all three, deeply historically rooted institutions are failing to meet the needs of many of the main actors involved. In each, preexisting institutions to some extent shape current debates and events in employment relations, but the role of ideas and ideologies is considerable as well. Finally, in each case it is the competitive pressures of the environment—domestic and international economic pressures—that underlie the impetus for changes in what jobs are done, how, by whom, under what circumstances, and the organizational and institutional conditions that influence these factors.

United States

The major public debate about employment relations in the United States has to do with the so-called competitiveness problem of the U.S. economy and associated shortcomings in the training and education levels of the U.S. workforce. American industry has become increasingly concerned about its economic strength, in part because of the loss of both domestic and international markets to foreign competitors, not least the Japanese. The solution is seen in the popular and business press as having to do with "flexibility"—the ability to deploy resources, including human resources, in flexible ways that allow companies to respond quickly to changes in technologies, production requirements, and markets. Tangibly, for instance, many companies have shifted from assembly line operations to teamwork. In the former case each worker possesses the skill(s) to accomplish her or his particular task in a series of specific jobs all along the line. In the latter, all workers may be trained to do many or even all necessary tasks, so that they can fill in for each other, moving around to do whatever task needs to be done at a given moment rather than being tied exclusively to one specific task. The shift toward more flexible deployment of workers can entail a general increase in skills (and wages), and in the level of cooperation among workers and between workers and managers. In general, workers' discretion on the job comes to play an increasingly important role. Managers, formerly charged with supervising the line, might now be required to facilitate team problem solving. The nature of work and the labor-management relationship is transformed.

Current labor law (the Wagner Act of 1935, as amended), which grants unions fairly rigid control over certain aspects of how labor is deployed (such as seniority rights and strict job demarcations), is widely viewed as interfering with the ability of American firms to compete effectively. Labor has not articulated a convincing argument to the contrary. This clash is reflected in the bitter disputes and battles that have characterized labor-management relations in the United States over the past fifteen years, as well as isolated (though often impressive) examples of joint labor-management efforts to redefine the nature of their relationship and the nature of work at the point of production (Kochan, Katz, & McKersie, 1986). In some places the shift to more cooperative forms of work has been dramatic (see Rubinstein, Bennett, & Kochan, 1993). In others it has been resisted and/or tried and rejected by all involved.

Many in the employer community would prefer to avoid unions altogether and believe that an entirely unorganized (or, as the British say, disorganized) labor movement would benefit the economy, and therefore society, as a whole (see Wever, 1995). This view reflects the prevailing neoclassical assumptions underlying mainstream thinking about how employment relations function in advanced capitalist societies. Many employers assume that without any unions they can more effectively and flexibly deploy their human resources. Evidence to the contrary, however, is mounting (see Applebaum & Batt, 1993; Soskice, 1991).

The unions, on the other hand, have been actively seeking changes in labor law over the past fifteen years, hoping to shore up their rights under the current institutional framework to organize workers and engage in collective bargaining with employers more easily and quickly (see AFL-CIO, 1983). They have been considerably less forceful in articulating a new role for themselves in promoting more cooperative and participative worker-management relations. Although both sides see the current situation as gravely flawed, neither has articulated how the institutions of employment relations could be fundamentally reshaped to work more effectively in the interests of all concerned. One important reason for the business community's failure to do this is again institutional: unlike their counterparts in many other advanced industrial countries, employers in the United States are highly unorganized and come together mainly for issue-specific political lobbying purposes. On the labor side, the resistance to change has a lot to do with the unions' traditional source of power: the ability to control the structure of jobs ("job control unionism")—that is, who does which tasks at what times. They have little or no experience with a model of worker representation that is more flexible on this dimension while entailing more influence on others (for instance, decisions about what new technologies to adopt or what training workers should receive to implement new forms of work organization).

New ideas have been introduced into the competitiveness debate by the current government, whose labor department has established a commission to look into the future of labor-management relations. The commission's mandate includes consideration of the ways in which worker representation (not necessarily by unions) might play a positive economic role. The commission's deliberations led to a report in early 1995 that suggests some minimal changes in the nature of the laws and institutions governing employment relations in this country that will be required to make it easier for labor and management to cooperate in reorganizing work and production. But it is noteworthy that the impetus behind these changes comes (with a few exceptions) not from the parties operating within the structure of the old institutions, but from a disparate group of varied interests including a small segment of the employer community and a few still unrepresentative union leaders, the academic and research community, and some of the new voices in the current Democratic administration in Washington. The commission's report was received coolly by both the labor and business communities, signaling that the ideology underlying the old structures still dominates in both communities. Both sides appear to continue to see the role of government in these matters in a rather binary fashion: regulation (for example, the Wagner Act) or no regulation (for example, employers' efforts to avoid unions altogether). For the time being, this understanding of how political economic institutions shape employment relations and the nature of work sharply limits the possibilities for structural changes in the United States.

Although single voices within both the labor and business communities have tried to articulate the connection between the nature of employment relations and the nature of work, neither "side" has developed a cohesive and consensual platform for addressing the problem tangibly. Everyone agrees that a highly skilled, well-paid, participative workforce, cooperating with management in the development of new ways of organizing work and production (that is, the shift to teamwork) would be a good thing. However, many employers still value low labor costs too highly, and many unions still prefer a job control orientation too strongly, to take concrete steps toward changing the structures of employment relations.

Eastern Germany

The problem in the eastern part of the newly united Germany is a very different one. Here, the economy as a whole has been in serious crisis since the social and economic institutions of the former East Germany were more or less entirely destroyed within a matter of weeks in 1990. In the former West Germany, employment relations reflected a highly stable negotiated pattern of accommodation and adjustment. Large industrial unions negotiated with employer associations (representing individual employers in a broadly defined industry and a large bargaining region) over the distribution of the benefits of steady increases in productivity, linked to a highly successful export-oriented model of growth during most of the postwar period. A number of interventionist labor market policies, along with a highly developed national vocational training system, helped to buffer relatively high levels of unemployment. In short, the (west) "German model" was based on a high-skill, high-wage, high-quality approach to production in which unions, works councils (which represent worker interests at the enterprise level, while unions operate primarily at the industry and regional level), employers, and managers generally cooperated in the perpetuation of this national competitiveness strategy.

The economic crisis in the eastern part of the country poses a formidable set of challenges to the western model. Real unemployment in the eastern part of the country lies between 30 percent and 40 percent and could get worse as uncompetitive companies continue to shed labor. In the mid-1990s, productivity levels in the east were still 25 percent to 50 percent of those in the west. Industrial production accounts for a mere 6 percent of total eastern gross domestic product (GDP). About 90 percent of the markets for goods produced by the large combines of the former East Germany were wiped out in 1990, in part by currency union with the west (in July 1990) and in part by the breakdown of the other eastern European economies. Private investment in the eastern part of the country remains far below predicted levels. In eastern Germany, labor-management relations have to do not with sharing productivity gains but with minimizing the dislocation involved in the crisis and finding politically and economically acceptable ways of distributing the costs of an economy that continues to be in real trouble (see Wever, 1995, chap. 6). While the overall level of training in the German Democratic Republic (the former East Germany) was high, in general the skills needed by Western investors apply to technologies not widely in use in the GDR.

The government, employers, and unions have responded in a wide variety of ways to these manifold problems. Some employers, fearing that they are unable to pay wages as high as those of their regional competitors, have opted to remain outside the employer associations, hoping to avoid having to deal with the unions altogether. Other employers are actively working toward increasing employer membership in the associations in order to enhance their overall bargaining power with the unions. Some unions have acquiesced to employer demands for lower and more flexible wages and working hours (for instance, the chemical workers' union; see Silvia, 1993) while others have demanded rapid parity with western wages (for example, the metal workers' union). Federal government measures have focused on expanding labor market policies developed in the west, such as retraining programs and short-term work. Some of the unions and local and regional governments have developed new innovations to deal with high levels of unemployment as well as other social problems—such as the disastrous state of the natural environment—by creating full-fledged semiprivate sector enterprises operating in the areas of environmental or regional development consulting, for example (Knuth, 1993; Kern, 1993). In other words, the restructuring of employment relations in the eastern part of Germany reflects a variety of different strategies regarding worker skills and the organization of work. As a result, the nature of work remains extremely heterogeneous, ranging from a low labor cost approach to the most advanced, high-technology-oriented, skill-based models.

While it is impossible to extract definitive trends from the array of developments currently under way in eastern Germany, it is clear that business, labor, and government are not terribly constrained by the institutional forms of the western part of the country, which have been transferred wholesale into the east. Labor and local and regional governments in particular have been able to develop innovative ways of accommodating the pressing and unfamiliar needs of the eastern economy along the pattern of negotiated industrial adjustment that has prevailed in the west (Wever, 1995, chap. 7). The terms of labor management have changed; the subjects of bargaining between the parties are in flux (and broader than in the western part of the country); the nature of work and of future employment relations are very much open questions. While elements in the business community and the government (particularly the Treuhand, the institution responsible for privatizing the eastern economy) favor a relatively laissez-faire approach, the institutions of the former West Germany do not appear to inhibit needed change. The ideology of the negotiation-oriented social market economy appears to be allowing the parties ample room to experiment with and begin to institutionalize new ideas and new ways of doing things. Thus the interrelation between preexisting structures and emerging ideas has been relatively fluid and has resulted in an array of different types of social and economic innovation in eastern Germany. In this respect, the German case contrasts sharply with that of the United States.

Poland

The case of Poland, as described by Weinstein (1993), is quite different. Here, as in eastern Germany, most of the institutions of the old socialist order have been swept away and replaced with new ones, more oriented to the free market. As in eastern Germany, privatization and the establishment of new markets are the chief orders of the day, but the path for achieving these is different from the one followed in the new (formerly East) German states. A number of institutions of employment relations were established in Poland during the transitional period of the Solidarity union's rise to power, and ultimately to political power; now, many of these are apparently being dismantled largely as a result of the power of a free (as opposed to a more German-style social) market ideology.

In the past three years, the workers' councils that Solidarity had established at the workplace level have in most enterprises been replaced—with the acquiescence of the union—by supervisory boards that have considerably less influence over how work is carried out. In some instances, local unions, uncertain of their roles, have actually disbanded themselves. That is, Solidarity has more or less agreed to minimize organized labor's voice in the structuring of work. At the same time, the union has supported a broad economic austerity plan based on significant wage restraint and resulting in sharply increased wage dispersion (disadvantaging the least skilled). Finally, the union appears relatively uninterested in active involvement in the privatization process or the governance of privatized and commercialized firms. The union's power has steadily eroded both at the national and at the local and regional levels, while managerial autonomy and initiative have increased commensurately. Workers' sense of job insecurity appears to be on the rise. Wage determination is increasingly a matter of managerial discretion, based on often subjective assessments of performance (Weinstein, 1993). The implications of these developments for the nature of work in Poland are potentially far reaching. By diminishing its influence on employment relations and worker-management relations at the point of production, the labor movement removes one important incentive for Polish companies to pursue high skill/wage/quality strategies.

This surprising retreat on the part of the country's main trade union—the mainstay of the organized labor movement—reflects a clear shift from the period before 1989. Weinstein (1993) argues that this departure is closely linked to the power of a more or less American version of free market ideology. This ideology has contributed to the indecisiveness and uncertainty of the union and its strategy, the rapid ascendancy and public acceptance of independent entrepreneurs, and the creation of new human resource practices in firms that arguably affect the nature of work negatively from the standpoint of the workers and their representatives. (Something of a puzzle is why the German model of the social market economy did not emerge at least as a competitor of the strict neoclassical approach.)

For historical reasons, it is not surprising that preexisting political economic institutions and structures carry relatively little weight in Poland. Unlike eastern Germany, Poland has no ready-made alternative institutional landscape to import and implement wholesale throughout the economy. The institutions that have been undermined, such as the workers' councils, do not represent long-standing structures deeply rooted in the socioeconomic fabric of Poland. Solidarity's rise occurred during the 1980s, and only in the late part of that decade was the union finally able to establish these councils. Nonetheless, the labor movement has virtually renounced its interest, stated earlier, in helping to shape the way work and employment relations are structured and carried out. This retreat is astonishing by any measure, particularly as Solidarity's declining influence did not result from a structurally unfavorable power position of the union in society and the economy at a broader level.

Conclusion

In each of the three cases considered here, changing economic conditions, environmental pressures, and political circumstances challenge the existing structures and institutions that influence how work is carried out and managed. This interrelationship is closely linked to how workers are trained and how work and production are organized, which in turn are strongly influenced by the institutions of employment relations and the broader political economy. In each, these changes both reflect and have led to significant changes in the way people are thinking about the problems of employment relations and the nature of jobs. Preexisting structures are shaping and being shaped by new ideas, and objective interests are not always the most important factors in determining strategies and policies.

It is too early to say with certainty what the outcome of any of these ongoing dramas is likely to be. For the purposes of this chapter section, however, processes are more important than outcomes. The role of political economic institutions is dynamic, and is influenced in important and often unpredictable ways by how the people involved think about them and their own proper places and functions within them. Institutions constrain the extent to which the actors can change the nature of work and employment relations, but institutions can be—and in at least two of these three cases actively are being—changed as well. Such change, however, will depend on the extent to which old structures are open to new ideas. When these structures are torn to the ground and rebuilt completely new, there is bound to be a particular openness to new ideas.

Some observers have argued that the current historical juncture offers a turning point or "industrial divide" throughout the advanced industrial world—a point at which new ideas can be particularly influential in reshaping political economic institutions, processes of production, and constellations of labor-management relations (Piore & Sabel, 1984; Kern & Schumann, 1985). In Sweden, Italy, France, Japan, the former east bloc, and other countries, political economic institutions and employment relations have indeed been undergoing profound changes over the past five to fifteen years. Although the changes in these countries are highly varied, in each there are tendencies toward emphasizing the role of negotiations between labor and management at the point of production over those at higher levels, such as the industry or region. These developments are still very much in the making, and outcomes remain unclear at this point. Provisionally, in Sweden and Italy local labor-management cooperation and participation appear to be taking root and leading to the development of new organizational and institutional forms of employment relations. Developments in France and Japan so far appear to be more company-specific, and to involve less significant roles for collective worker representatives.

The social and economic effectiveness of political economic institutions is inevitably time-bound. But how amenable to change those institutions are, both within the frameworks they establish and of those frameworks themselves, may be in substantial measure a function of political choice. Thus the American employers' and unions' apparent unwillingness to create a coherent and mutually beneficial institutional framework within which new ideas about work and labor-management relations can be developed and implemented may well render any significant institutional changes unlikely, and ensure the continuation of an employment relations system that is satisfactory to very few of those affected by it. The Polish labor movement's uncertainty about how to use its own (and other available) ideas about labor participation in work- and production-related decisions may consign Poland to an employment relations future based on a relatively uncoordinated rather than a more skill- and labor participation-oriented model. The implications for who does what kind of work under what circumstances are significant.

References

AFL-CIO. (1983). *The future of workers and their unions* (Report of the Committee on the Evolution of Work). Washington, DC: Author.

Applebaum, E., & Batt, R. (1993). *The new American workplace: Transforming work systems in U.S. firms.* Ithaca, NY: Industrial and Labor Relations Press.

Katzenstein, P. (1987). *Politics and policy in the Federal Republic: The semi-sovereign state.* Philadelphia: Temple University Press.

Kern, H. (1993). *Gewerkschaftliche industriepolitik: Beiträge der gewerkschaften in ost und west zur erneuerung des deutschen produktmodells.* [Unions' industrial policies: Contributions of the eastern and western unions to the renewal of the German production model.] Working Paper, Soziologisches Forschungsinstitut, Goettingen.

Kern, H., & Schumann, M. (1985). *The end of the division of labor.* Frankfurt: Campus Verlag.

Knuth, M. (1993, March). *Employment and training companies: Bridging unemployment in the East German crash.* Paper presented at the Conference of the Society for the Advancement of Socioeconomics, New York.

Kochan, T., Katz, H., & McKersie, R. (1986). *The transformation of American industrial relations.* New York: Basic Books.

Locke, R. (1992). The decline of the national union in Italy: Lessons for comparative industrial relations theory. *Industrial and Labor Relations Review, 45*(2), 229–249.

Piore, M., & Sabel, C. (1984). *The second industrial divide.* New York: Basic Books.

Rubinstein, S., Bennett, M., & Kochan, T. (1993). The Saturn partnership: Co-management and the reinvention of the local union. In B. Kaufman & M. Kleiner (Eds.), *Employee representation: Alternatives and future directions.* Madison, WI: Industrial Relations Research Association.

Silvia, S. (1993, July). *Holding the shop together: Old and new challenges to the German system of industrial relations in the mid-1980s.* Berlin Working Papers and Reports on Social Science Research, No. 83, Free University, Berlin.

Soskice, D. (1991). *The institutional infrastructure for national competitiveness: A comparative analysis of the UK and Germany.* Paper presented at the International Economic Association Conference, Venice, Italy.

Vogel, D. (1978). Why businessmen distrust their state: The political consciousness of American corporate executives. *British Journal of Political Science, 8,* 45–78.

Weinstein, M. (1993). *The emergence of human resource systems in post-socialist Poland: The role of economics, institutions, and ideas in the creation of new institutional arrangements.* Dissertation proposal, Sloan School of Management, Massachusetts Institute of Technology, Cambridge.

Wever, K. S. (1995). *Negotiating competitiveness: Employment relations and organizational innovation in Germany and the United States.* Cambridge, MA: Harvard Business School Press.

Wever, K. S., & Allen, C. S. (1993). The financial system and corporate governance in Germany: Institutions and the diffusion of innovation. *Journal of Public Policy, 12*(3), 183–202.

Government Regulation
of Human Resources

James Ledvinka

Over the past twenty years, the reaction of industrial and organizational psychology to government regulation of employment has changed. The field generally welcomed the *Griggs* v. *Duke Power* (1971) opinion and other early expressions of government support for professional standards in employee selection. Encouraged by government's involvement, psychologists explored issues such as situational validity, validity generalization, fairness, and gender differences more vigorously than they probably would have otherwise. But more recently, judging by articles in professional newsletters, the field apparently regards regulation as a threat. Three regulatory developments seem especially ominous: the 1991 Civil Rights Act, the Americans with Disabilities Act (ADA) of 1990, and a series of legal initiatives that challenge the use of psychological tests because of alleged invasion of privacy. Those three are controversial because they appear to conflict in fundamental ways with the model that has traditionally guided the profession's involvement in the employment process.

The conflict, however, is not new; psychology and the law have long held different models of employment. This chapter section compares psychology's model of employment with the model used by the law. Viewed from the perspective of the law's model, the

Note: I am grateful to Robert D. Gatewood and Robert J. Vandenberg for their comments on an earlier draft of this material.

three recent developments are not radical departures from the past but understandable extensions of regulatory dynamics that have been at work for the past century.

Contrasting Models of Employment: Psychology and the Law

To understand the differences between the two models, it is helpful to realize that today's regulated employment relationship is the product of a century-long evolution from a largely unregulated labor market. In the nineteenth century, the law viewed the employee-employer relationship in the same way that psychology continues to view it: as a consensual relationship, a market transaction freely undertaken by employer and employee. In legal terminology, this free-market principle is called *employment at will:* the employment relationship may be terminated by either party "for good cause, for no cause, or even for cause morally wrong" (*Payne* v. *Western and A. R.R. Co.*, 1884). It follows logically that either party is free to leave the relationship if that party finds unacceptable the conditions that the other party imposes on the relationship. Under the employment-at-will model, then, the employment relationship is self-regulating in the sense that any conditions governing the relationship are ones freely negotiated by the parties to the relationship rather than ones imposed by an external authority.

Government regulation arose as a set of exceptions to free-market principles such as employment at will. This development was a gradual process, beginning around the turn of the century, as legislatures attempted to solve various social problems and respond to political forces by limiting the employer's legally permissible sphere of action with respect to employees. Those legislative enactments are discussed later. More recently, the judiciary in many localities has added its own exceptions. Some courts have construed the employment relationship as a contractual one, governed by the limitations that the common law imposes on the freedom of contracting parties. Other jurisdictions consider certain employer acts, such as dismissal without reasonable cause, to be torts—unjustifiable inflictions of harm prohibited by common law. The combined result of the legislative and judicial exceptions to employment at will is a legal environment in which employers must contend with a growing set of limitations on their freedom in negotiating the terms and conditions of the employment relationship.

For most of that legal history, psychology continued its professional activities uninhibited by the law. Not until Title VII of the 1964 Civil Rights Act was government regulation of employment extended into areas where psychology as a profession was involved. By that time, however, psychology had cultivated a perspective on employment shaped by decades of professional practice in a largely unregulated, employment-at-will environment. With the *Griggs* opinion in 1971, the profession suddenly found itself immersed in a new institution: the law. Before then, a few psychologists had helped shape the federal government's employee selection guidelines, but for the most part, the law was an unfamiliar domain to psychologists.

Because the *Griggs* opinion expressed support for professional psychology's standards, it was easy to assume that the law and psychology held similar views of the employment relationship. The Supreme Court's clear endorsement of job relatedness seemed to be a call for employers to come to their senses and recognize that test validity was good for them. Only after the passage of some time did the conflict between the law and psychology become apparent. The law's fundamental model of the employment relationship had changed while the profession's had remained more or less the same.

Psychology's Model of Employment

From the outset, psychology's model has assumed that the psychologist intervenes in an employer-employee relationship that is *consensual* in nature: it endures because both parties consent to it. Because the relationship is consensual rather than coerced, the psychologist serves values that are *intrinsic* to the relationship, not ones imposed from without. As a behavioral scientist, the psychologist serves those values by helping to bring about a *behavioral* outcome of interest to one or both of the parties.

In that effort, the psychologist typically follows Edward Tolman and Kurt Lewin by regarding work behavior as caused by worker *traits* and work *situations*. Accordingly, the psychologist might recommend that management alter traits, situations, or both—whatever intervention best serves to bring about the outcome of interest, as judged by scientific standards rather than legal or political ones. In exercising scientific judgment about such interventions, the psychologist usually seeks *correlational* evidence regarding employees as an *aggregate:* What traits and what situations are associated with the outcome of interest for employees on average? The most common example is the use of predictor-criterion correlations measured for an aggregate of employees as evidence to support the use of selection tests.

The foregoing is industrial and organizational psychology's normative model of employment as a professional domain—its model of what employment ought to be and how psychologists ought to fit in. The model allows the profession of psychology its own free market in which it can most efficiently and profitably provide its service of applying the science of psychology to the world of work. Any departure from that model runs the risk of compromising the psychologist's science and the psychologist's professional freedom. But compromise is precisely what the law has imposed, compromise in the form of external limitations based on an unfamiliar model of employment that emerges not from professional practice but from the political system's resolution of conflict.

The Law's Model of Employment

The law's model of employment varies from jurisdiction to jurisdiction. Thus the model described here is not universal; instead, it is a prototypical one that applies to the more "liberal" judges and legislatures. Other judges and legislatures adhere to a legal model that is somewhat closer to psychology's model. Nonetheless, the model here captures the essence of what psychologists and managers complain about when they lament the loss of the free relationship they enjoyed under employment at will.

The loss of freedom has occurred because government regulation implicitly introduces a third party to the employment relationship, namely society. Society's interest demands that certain obligations not be bargained away in that relationship, and the law supports that interest. Even if employer and employee agree on a discriminatory pay plan or an unsafe work environment, the law does not permit the agreement to take effect. The employee's rights to nondiscriminatory pay and safe work are non-negotiable; regulation sees to that by giving any individual employee the power to enforce those rights through the legal process. The entry of society as a third party vastly transforms the relationship from that which prevailed under the traditional doctrine of employment at will.

Understandably, then, the law's model of employment differs in all respects from psychology's model of employment described earlier. First, the law gives employees a measure of power to insist that employers respect their rights. In this aspect, the law's model anticipates an employer-employee relationship that is *adversarial* rather than consensual in nature, one in which a psychologist serving one of the parties becomes an adversary to the other party. The legal system thus views the psychologist not as a disinterested scientist but as a source of evidence favorable to one party rather than the other. Further, by introducing society as an implicit third party to the employment relationship, the law introduces values that are *extrinsic* to that relationship, ones that emerge not from the interests of employer, employee, or psychologist but from the body politic. Those extrinsic values include equality and the resolution of political conflict.

As a consequence, employer and employee are obliged to pursue other outcomes besides behavioral ones such as performance. In particular, the law forces them to pursue *equitable* outcomes of interest to the larger society. Thus the law responds to the values embodied in the American Dream by requiring employers to treat employees fairly by providing equal opportunity. But equal opportunity is largely a *situational* intervention; it alters employment not by changing the mix of employee traits but by enhancing opportunities for groups that have traditionally been deprived of those opportunities. Even employee training, an intervention that attempts to alter traits, is often justified for the credentialing it provides rather than the traits it instills, which does seem to reflect an assumption that the problem lies with the situation rather than the person.

The law goes beyond encouraging situational interventions; it also discourages trait-based interventions. Because trait-based interventions such as employment tests have unequal consequences for different groups, the legal system imposes a heavy burden of justification for their use, as the following discussion points out. That burden includes evidence not merely that the intervention correlates with an outcome of interest to the client, but that the intervention has a *causal* connection to that outcome. Implicitly, courts sometimes seem to seek evidence that desired outcomes such as performance improvement will occur only when management uses the intervention. Consequently, the psychologist's aggregate evidence that a requirement is job related can sometimes be defeated by a few *individual* cases to the contrary (as in the *Griggs* opinion, discussed below).

When Models Meet: Legal Challenges to the Work of Psychologists

Table 2.1 summarizes the differences between the two models. Those differences create conflict when the two models meet. When psychologists take part in a deposition or a trial, they lose control of their work and become subjected to demands that arise not from science but from the adversarial relationship between employer and employee. Attorneys for each side carefully control what psychologists may disclose about their work. Disclosures that would hurt either side's case seldom emerge, regardless of their scientific import, unless they are called for by the other side.

It might be tempting, then, to claim that psychologists seek truth while lawyers represent their clients regardless of the truth. Yet both professions, in their ethical standards, claim a commitment to truth. Perhaps the two models employ different methods for uncovering the truth. Psychology uncovers truth not through a Baconian search for facts but through paradigmatic observation guided by the hypothesis in question, which may be appropriate for the task of building a science, even if research outside the paradigm never gets published. The law uncovers truth not through disinterested inquiry into the facts of the case but through adversarial discovery, which may be appropriate for the task of settling conflicts between parties to a case, even if one party succeeds in suppressing evidence. In both professions, truth means something other than brute fact, something other than the absence of empirical error. And for both professions the search for truth relies on a playing out of interests in an empirical arena according to a set of rules that represent the best the profession can come up with as a way of being right most of the time.

**Table 2.1. Contrasting Models of Employment:
Psychology and the Law.**

	Psychology	The Law
Relationship	*Consensual* Employer and employee cooperate to pursue shared goals in the employment relationship; the psychologist enters to further the client's interests by applying scientific principles, with the implicit or explicit consent of the other party.	*Adversarial* Employee and employer are usually adversaries in a lawsuit or complaint; the psychologist is an adversary of whichever party is not the psychologist's client. The psychologist is not so much a scientist as a producer of evidence.
Values	*Intrinsic* The values that determine whether an outcome is desirable are ones indigenous to the parties involved in the psychologist's work (for example, employers) rather than ones held by external agents. Examples: productivity, satisfaction	*Extrinsic* Thc values that determine whether an outcome is desirable are those held by external agents (for example, legislators) rather than values that are indigenous to the parties involved in the psychologist's work. Examples: equality, resolution of political conflict
Outcomes	*Behavioral* The psychologist attempts to improve work performance, job satisfaction, and the like.	*Equitable* The law attempts to ensure that the parties to the employment relationship treat each other fairly.
Intervention Target	*Traits and situations* The psychologist considers behavior to be a function of both; based on	*Situations only* The law discourages the distribution of rewards based on a person's traits

**Table 2.1. (cont.) Contrasting Models of Employment:
Psychology and the Law.**

	Psychology	The Law
Intervention Target (cont.)	*Traits and situations* (cont.) scientific evidence, the psychologist could recommend an intervention that involves altering either.	*Situations only* (cont.) by prohibiting discrimination; thus it encourages interventions that alter the situation.
Evidence	*Correlation* The psychologist seeks evidence that desired outcomes occur *more often* when management takes the action in question than when management does not take the action in question.	*Causation* The law seeks evidence that the desired outcomes occur *only* when management takes the action in question, *never* when management does not take the action in question.
Level of Analysis	*Aggregate* The psychologist looks for the outcome to occur for *most* people when management takes the action in question.	*Individual* The law looks for the outcome to occur for *each* person when management takes the action in question.

Those similarities notwithstanding, the legal system does impose unfamiliar values that ultimately conflict with psychology's traditional values. The clearest example is the conflict between the value that the law places on economic *equality* and the value that psychology has traditionally placed on economic *productivity*. By imposing economic equality as a criterion, the law forces psychologists to examine unfamiliar outcomes such as the racial impact of a selection procedure. And it is rare to find a case in which a court has upheld a selection procedure that has unequal racial impact. Instead, the law appears to regard equal impact as a de facto prerequisite for fairness: if courts find disparate impact, they tend to regard the employer's evidence of job relatedness as insufficient to redeem the practice in the eyes of the law. Because the psychologist's selection devices usually assess traits that are unequally distributed among ethnic groups, selection usually exacerbates the economic inequalities that employment discrimination law was intended to alleviate—thus the conflict.

Economic inequality is the reason that the legal system imposes the burden of causal justification on trait-based interventions such as selection tests. The courts pay attention not only to the strength of the evidence supporting such interventions but also to whether the evidence indicates a causal connection between the intervention and an outcome of legitimate employer interest. That explains why the term *business necessity* figures so prominently in legal discourse, for necessity is a type of causal relationship. It also explains why the courts sometimes use clinical evidence to refute arguments based on actuarial evidence, as the Supreme Court did in the *Griggs* case when it pointed out that some employees performed satisfactorily even though they had not met the employer's testing and education requirements. The Court's observation was tantamount to demanding both that the requirements correlate with satisfactory performance and that they satisfy the logical criteria for necessity. Other courts have subsequently applied a more relaxed standard, but the *Griggs* standard remains an available yardstick by which a court can measure the work of industrial and organizational psychology.

How the Recent Changes in Regulation Fit the Law's Model of Employment

To some extent, then, the law's model and psychology's model are not just different but conflicting, which makes it easy for psychologists to regard the law as an alien intruder. The law's model, however, is of long standing; recent legal changes are more an extension of an old model than the beginning of a new one. They are understandable, if not predictable, in that they reflect a precedent of government involvement that goes back at least a century. By examining each feature of the model in turn, we can see how the three recent developments (the 1991 Civil Rights Act, the Americans with Disabilities Act, and the anti-testing initiatives) fit the law's longstanding model.

Adversarial Relationship Between Employer and Employee

The law focuses on the adversarial aspect of employee-employer relationships because it is the purpose of legal institutions to manage conflict. The judiciary exists to settle disagreements between adversaries, while legislatures exist to pass statutes that resolve conflict in society as a whole. It is somewhat natural, then, that the law approaches employment as something other than a consensual relationship.

The value that U.S. culture places on individualism has throughout history reinforced the law's adversarial perspective on employment. In the nineteenth century, legal institutions were reluctant to impose collective norms on relationships that were freely negotiated between individuals. Legislatures in particular were reluctant to pass the kinds of laws that would settle disputes between employers and employees by mandating specific rights and responsibilities. If workers wanted a right, they had to fight for it in court, a situation that brought the employer-employee relationship to the attention of the law as a relationship between adversaries. Courts in turn refrained from mandating anything more than the minimal norms of decency provided by the limited standards of common law that prevailed at the time. In the case of work injuries, for example, no statute forced employers to compensate injured employees. Instead, workers had to sue under common law, which required them to prove that fault lay with the employer. And the standards for acceptable proof of fault were imposing.

It was not until the cumulative consequences of individual conflicts were severe enough to cause problems for society as a whole that legislators began to intervene by regulating the adversarial relationship between employee and employer. For example, not until work injuries became a matter of public indignation did state legislatures pass workers' compensation laws. Workers' compensation laws attempted to ensure financial reparation for injured workers by removing work injury cases from the adversarial atmosphere of the courts and settling them administratively. In the process, they conferred specific statutory rights on employees and imposed specific statutory responsibilities on employers.

With the advent of those workers' compensation laws, the legal system began the process of abandoning the *laissez-faire* principles that had theretofore guided its approach to employment. But it did so in a fashion that enhanced the law's adversarial approach to the employment relationship. Rather than allow for the possibility that employers and employees could come to agree on injury prevention as a common goal, workers' compensation takes restitution as its purpose and makes employers pay to remedy the losses that workers suffer with work injuries. In that respect, the law makes employer-employee relations into a zero-sum game.

A similar dynamic underlies most of the laws governing labor-management relations. Initially, the individualistic orientation of nineteenth-century U.S. law created an environment that was indifferent to labor-management cooperation and hostile to collective action by employees. That legal environment encouraged two developments that created problems for society at large. First, it allowed individual conflicts between companies and striking workers to escalate into acts of armed violence such as the Haymarket Massacre. Second, it left employees in a position of economic powerlessness that culminated in widespread destitution during the Great Depression.

Congressional efforts to solve those problems ultimately resulted in the passage of the Wagner Act in 1935. The Wagner Act gave employees "the right to . . . engage in . . . concerted activities for . . . mutual aid or protection." "Concerted activities" means activities taken in concert with other employees, including the activity of organizing themselves into a union. To ensure that right, the act defined certain antiunion actions to be unfair labor practices. Most important, it prohibited employers from discriminating against any employee who engaged in concerted activities. In effect, then, the Wagner Act was Congress's first employment discrimination law. Like later antidiscrimination laws, it gave employees the legal power to enforce their rights to nondiscrimination by employers.

But the Wagner Act went beyond merely outlawing discrimination—it outlawed virtually any employer involvement in employees' "concerted activities." Thus the U.S. legal system's individualistic orientation once again expressed itself in the form of a statute based on the assumption that the relationship between employers and employees is an adversarial one. The separation of labor and management that has resulted from laws such as the Wagner Act has made labor relations less cooperative in the United States than in just about any other nation.

More recent statutes such as the 1964 Civil Rights Act make it even clearer that the history of employment law is a history of government attempts to solve social problems by granting legal power to employees in their market transactions with employers. Government alters the free market by declaring that employees are legally entitled to certain treatment by the employer, treatment that they had previously been obliged to seek through free-market bargaining. Other laws do the same. The Occupational Safety and Health Act gives employees the right to safe work, the Fair Labor Standards Act gives them the right to overtime pay, unemployment compensation law gives them the right to unemployment insurance, and the Employee Retirement Income Security Act gives them a variety of rights involving employee benefits.

The three recent legal developments fit that historical pattern. The frank intent of the 1991 Civil Rights Act is to increase the power of employees in their employment discrimination battles with employers. Specifically, the 1991 act:

1. Makes it easier for complainants to prevail in "mixed motive" cases, where a discriminatory motive exists but where the decision would have been the same even in the absence of the discriminatory motive.
2. Raises the limit on monetary damages in cases of discriminatory intent.
3. Makes it easier for complainants to win disparate impact cases by requiring employers to "demonstrate that the challenged practice is job related for the position in question and consistent with business necessity."
4. Gives complainants more time to file discrimination lawsuits.
5. Allows complainants to seek jury trials.
6. Makes it difficult for outsiders to challenge court settlements of discrimination lawsuits.
7. Makes it illegal for employers to eliminate adverse impact by raising test scores for members of low-scoring groups or by using different cutoff scores for different groups.

The Americans with Disabilities Act also grants legal power to employees in their market transactions with employers. It does so by identifying a new group—disabled employees—as entitled to legal protection against discrimination. Specifically, ADA makes it illegal for employers to discriminate against a "qualified individual with a disability" because of that person's disability. "Disability" means "a physical or mental impairment that substantially limits one or more . . . major life activities," or a record of such impairment, or being regarded as having such an impairment. Among other things, ADA:

1. Defines "qualified" as being able to "perform the essential functions of the employment position that such individual holds or desires."
2. Requires employers to make "reasonable accommodation" to the known disabilities of any qualified employee or applicant, provided that the accommodation does not impose an "undue hardship" on the employer. "Reasonable accommodation" includes all of the following:
   a. Making the job accessible to persons with disabilities
   b. Restructuring the job to eliminate tasks that a disabled person cannot perform
   c. "Appropriate adjustment or modification" of examinations
   d. Modification of work schedules
   e. Transfer to a job that the disabled person can perform
3. Prohibits employers from using employee selection practices that screen out, or tend to screen out, individuals with disabilities, unless the practice is "job related for the position in question and is consistent with business necessity."
4. Prohibits the use of preemployment medical examinations and inquiries.

Finally, the recent anti-testing initiatives are designed to give employees added privacy rights by granting them the legal power to restrict the questions that employers can ask them. An entire test would be illegal if it included a single offending question. Thus various state legislatures have been considering the elimination of tests that ask about a job applicant's religious, political, or sexual activities or beliefs. State courts have also been active. For example, in California, the state court of appeals in *Soroka* v. *Dayton Hudson Corporation* (1991) prohibited an employer from administering tests such as the Minnesota Multiphasic Personality Inventory

(MMPI) and the California Psychological Inventory (CPI) that include questions about those things unless the employer could demonstrate a "compelling interest" in the information. Finally, the U.S. Office of Technology Assessment has issued a report critical of integrity tests, and that report may lead to increased efforts to limit their use.

In continuing the tradition of granting legal power to employees in their dealings with employers, the three recent developments also continue to constrain the practice of psychology. The "business necessity" provisions of the 1991 Civil Rights Act and the ADA ratify the courts' demand for convincing validity evidence in defense of methods that have disparate impact. Other provisions of the ADA control preemployment tests and job design. And the recent antitesting initiatives limit the use of construct validity in employment testing. A construct-valid employment test measures a construct that correlates with some legitimate interest of the employer. For example, the construct of "psychopathic deviancy" might correlate with illegal employee behavior. A construct-valid test of psychopathic deviance would behave as a test of psychopathic deviancy ought to behave. Perhaps it would accurately separate individuals with a history of lying, stealing, and other asocial acts from individuals without such a history. Such a test would probably attempt to sample a broad range of behavioral domains, including sexuality. Given that, a prohibition of questions about sexual matters would probably reduce the test's construct validity, because sexuality is at the heart of how society defines deviancy, and an individual who violates society's standards in the area of sexuality might be more likely to violate society's standards in other areas as well. The *Soroka* court, however, held that the questions on sexuality did not serve the employer's legitimate interests, thus rendering the test unacceptable regardless of whether the test did serve those interests when taken as a whole. Nothing about the case suggests that the holding would have been different for most other employers.

In sum, all three recent legal developments discussed here are part of the ongoing tradition through which a pluralistic society deals with the demands of various groups by awarding them legal power in their dealings with other groups. The reality that those developments limit the freedom of professional psychologists simply reflects professional psychology's relative lack of political influence. There is nothing particularly mysterious or sinister about that; it is straightforward politics, the same politics that has been at work in one form or another in government regulation of employment for a century.

Extrinsic Values

The shifts of power brought about by changes in the law reflect the value that society places on the resolution of social conflict. Such resolution is an extrinsic value in that employees and employers would not ordinarily negotiate for it in a free exchange relationship. Social conflict is what economists call an externality, an outcome that is felt outside the market transaction between employer and employee. Society as a whole experiences the effects of conflict due to strikes, unsafe work conditions, and discrimination. Those effects take the form of violence, added demands for medical care, and increased welfare dependency. The law is society's mechanism for asserting the collective interest in controlling such externalities.

The shift in the relative power of the adversaries also serves a second extrinsic value: the value of equality. Here, equality means equal distribution of wealth among race, ethnic, and gender groups. Those two extrinsic values, conflict resolution and equality of wealth, are connected by an assumption that has guided Congress repeatedly throughout this century: social conflict can be abated by equalizing the distribution of wealth. Many laws reflect that assumption. For example, Congress passed the Wagner Act not only to end labor unrest but also to relieve the poverty that supposedly created such unrest. Other laws reflect the additional assumption that equality of wealth can be brought about by ending discrimination. For example, Congress passed the 1964 Civil Rights Act on the assumption that outlawing employment discrimination would not only quiet the social unrest of the 1960s but also reduce the economic inequality that was thought to have contributed to that unrest. Clearly, the 1964 Civil Rights Act has not brought about equality of wealth. The 1991 Civil Rights Act may in part be a response to the ineffectiveness of the 1964 Act in promoting the extrinsic value of equality.

Conflict resolution rather than equality is the extrinsic value that explains the provision of the 1991 act outlawing test score adjustments. That provision was added to the bill in response to a controversy over the U.S. Department of Labor's policy for scoring its General Aptitude Test Battery (GATB). To eliminate the adverse impact of the GATB on minorities, the Department of Labor added points to the scores of minority test-takers. The score adjustments helped to equalize the racial and ethnic impact of the GATB, but they also penalized individuals who belonged to groups that did well on the test, and that created controversy. When public indignation over score adjustments reached Congress, the provision outlawing them was added to the bill, thus avoiding a continuation of the controversy.

Equitable Outcomes

The public rejected score adjustments because they violated the fundamental American principle that the distribution of opportunities should be based on a person's achievements, not on ascribed characteristics such as race and gender. Distribution based on achievement is a "fair" distribution, one that appeals to the prevailing conception of what is equitable. But psychology is a neutral science, and science is agnostic to prevailing notions of fairness and equity. If left unrestrained, psychology will produce models that freely mix achieved and ascribed characteristics according to whatever best predicts the outcomes of interest. In this day and age, racial impact is an outcome of interest, so psychology will naturally produce models that incorporate race into test scoring, as the GATB score-adjustment policy did. By prohibiting such scoring methods, the 1991 Civil Rights Act imposes the prevailing conception of equity as a restraint on the practice of psychology as a neutral science, even at the cost of exacerbating economic inequalities.

This legal restraint on reverse discrimination in test scoring may seem difficult to reconcile with the hundreds of court cases upholding "affirmative action," a euphemism for other approaches that equalize impact, often less formally than do test score adjustments. But the euphemistic approach to labels is revealing. It suggests that the fundamental distinction making affirmative action more acceptable than test score adjustment is that affirmative action is less blatant—thus less likely to create conflict.

Moreover, the subjectivity of affirmative action is consistent with equity, as it allows management to incorporate subjective equity considerations into employment decisions. For example, if a preference system creates an undue hardship for a particular employee or group of employees, affirmative action could incorporate a modification. Test score adjustment, by contrast, is a mechanical approach that incorporates nothing besides subgroup norms—preferential treatment without a human face. It may be the mathematically optimal way to maximize productivity and equalize impact, but the courts seem to believe that equity is a matter to be ensured not by an objective mathematical standard but by the subjectivity of fair human judgment with fair intentions. The leading court case, *Steelworkers* v. *Weber* (1979), warns that a preferential treatment system must not "unnecessarily trammel" the rights of the majority, and that it should be "intended" to break down old patterns of discrimination. That standard is subjective, in that someone must exercise judgment regarding whether any "trammeling" of majority rights is unnecessary, and also in that management must have a certain intent, namely, the intent to eradicate previous patterns of discrimination.

Situational Interventions

Thus the primary purpose of employment discrimination law is to prohibit employers from basing employment decisions on certain characteristics of the person—the prohibited classifications. Psychology, by contrast, attempts to identify those characteristics of the person that are functionally related to the outcomes of interest. There is a natural antipathy here: the psychologist's purpose is to determine how to discriminate among persons in the way that maximizes those outcomes, whereas regulation limits the forms of discrimination that the psychologist can use.

This variance of purpose may help to explain why regulation discourages some of psychology's more notable contributions to human resource management. Most regulatory challenges involve interventions that attempt to alter outcomes by changing the person, such as selection, recruiting, and performance appraisal. Far fewer regulatory disputes involve interventions that change the situation, such as job design, incentive systems, organization development, employee involvement, and governance. Because they do not inherently discriminate among persons, such situational interventions raise fewer legal issues.

The three recent developments further limit the psychologist's use of person characteristics in favor of situational characteristics. The test score adjustment provision in the 1991 Civil Rights Act explicitly prohibits the use of ethnicity and gender in test scoring, even when the results benefit groups that are traditionally the victims of discrimination. By contrast, affirmative action allows employers to grant preferential treatment when "the situation" calls for it. The Americans with Disabilities Act adds disability to the list of prohibited person characteristics. It calls upon employers to alter the situation by making "reasonable accommodation" to disabilities. Finally, the recent anti-testing initiatives prohibit employers from collecting information on two types of person characteristics: political beliefs and sexuality. In sum, these three developments confer a competitive advantage on situational interventions in employment.

Causal Evidence

In their references to "business necessity," the 1991 Civil Rights Act and the Americans with Disabilities Act evince a concern with causation that is missing from the wording of the 1964 Civil Rights Act. Further, the ADA defines a "qualified" individual with a disability to mean someone able to perform the "essential" functions of the job, a term that indicates necessity. But what does it mean to be "consistent with business necessity"? It probably means showing the same kind of evidence that the courts have been requiring ever since the *Griggs* case told us that "the touchstone is business necessity." Specifically, it means that the employer's defense of an employment practice will fail the business necessity test whenever there exists an alternative practice that would serve the employer's interests equally well with lesser disparity of impact.

Here again, recent legislation does not seem to change things much. On the scales of justice, necessity evidence will continue to weigh on the employer's side, while the lack of necessity evidence will continue to weigh on the complainant's side (which I suppose to mean that necessity evidence is not a necessity).

Individual Level of Analysis

The individual orientation that the law takes to employment practices is evident in both the Americans with Disabilities Act and the recent anti-testing initiatives. The ADA states that the employer must make reasonable accommodations to the "known physical and mental limitations of a qualified *individual* who is an applicant or an employee" (emphasis added). If a disability makes an individual unable to perform a job, the fact that most incumbents can perform the job without accommodation is not a defense. Likewise, if a disability makes an individual unable to pass a test, the fact that the test is valid for most candidates is not a defense. Employers must adapt to individuals by implementing job redesign and alternate methods of test administration, or else demonstrate that any such accommodation would impose an "undue hardship." Test validities are actuarial evidence, and the ADA requires that such evidence be suspended in the case of disabled individuals. For a disabled individual, the ADA requires that the employer substitute clinical judgment regarding the possibility of accommodation to the individual's disability. In that sense, the law mandates that clinical judgment replace actuarial judgment when a disabled individual challenges a job requirement.

The recent anti-testing initiatives pose a different sort of challenge to actuarial judgment. Personality testing in employment rests on an elaborate actuarial argument. In the example above concerning an employer who gives a test of psychopathic deviancy, the justification for using any question, including questions about sex, rests on an empirical correlation between the answer to that question and a diagnosis of psychopathic deviancy, plus an empirical correlation between psychopathic deviancy and dysfunctional employee behavior. Though quite acceptable from the perspective of construct validity, such an approach is likely to result in test items that appear far-fetched. Any applicant might argue that his or her own answers to those questions have no bearing on his or her own fitness for employment. By accepting that clinical argument, the recent anti-testing cases have concluded that those answers are none of the employer's business, regardless of their place in a sound actuarial judgment of the candidate's fitness for employment.

Beyond recent developments, the very existence of court cases gives the law an individual focus. In most court cases an *individual* complains about something an employer did. That frames the matter in individual terms, so that the employer must often defend by arguing that its action is reasonable for the particular individual filing the complaint. But because actuarial judgment is *not* always reasonable when judged against the circumstances of certain individual cases, it is inevitable that such an argument will sometimes fail.

Conclusion

The three recent legal developments discussed here impose substantial limits on psychologists' freedom to practice their craft. This discussion suggests that the same sort of thing has been going on for some time in the world of government regulation. Other recent developments besides the three discussed here seem to fit the same pattern. If space had permitted, this section would have discussed developments such as the new "reasonable woman" standard in sexual harassment case law, the emergence of wrongful termination legislation at the state level, and the recent legal challenges to employee involvement programs under the National Labor Relations Act. Like the three discussed here, those other developments are puzzling if we assume that the law views employment in the same way that industrial and organizational psychology does. They are more understandable if we recognize that the law operates from a model of employment that is somewhat different from that of psychology. Comprehending the law's model probably does not give us any special ability to forecast future regulatory developments, but it does help us avoid imagining that such developments are a temporary phenomenon. On the contrary, they have been going on for the past century. Barring a revolution, we can expect them to go on well into the next.

References

Griggs v. *Duke Power,* 401 U.S. 424 (1971).
Payne v. *Western & A. R.R. Co.,* 81 Tenn. 507 (1884).
Soroka v. *Dayton-Hudson Corp.,* 1 Cal. Rptr. 2d 77 (Calif. Ct. App., 1991).
United Steelworkers of America v. *Weber,* 443 U.S. 273 (1979).

Work

Chapter Three

Technology and the Organization of Work

For most of human history, technology did not seem powerful enough to have a pervasive influence on society (Katz, 1990). The industrial revolution and the severe social dislocations it wrought challenged that view, of course. "But the world has never seen anything like the computer" (Verity, 1994, p. 14). This new technology is the most powerful tool ever invented for recording and communicating symbolic information, and its ability to disseminate human knowledge will change forever the ways we work and live.

Information Technology

What makes the computer so unique? Like the hammer or the car, it is a tool developed by and for humans. But instead of being an extension of the human extremities (the arm or the legs), it is an extension of the brain, primarily because it is instructable (Cheriton, 1991). It can extend or displace a variety of intellectual skills; diagnose problems within a predetermined range; operate with exceptionally high reliability; perform in a variety of contexts, including those hostile to humans; and respond faster than human reaction times (Baldry, 1988). And it can be applied to many, many uses; it is malleable. As Jan Van der Spiegel points out in the next segment of this chapter, it continues to advance according to what some call the holy trinity of computing—faster, smaller, and cheaper (Deutschman & Tetzeli, 1994). A consequence is the astounding spread of microelectronic power throughout the economy—from cars to watches and children's toys. Today a greeting card that plays "Happy Birthday" when you open it has more computing power than existed in the world before 1950 (Huey, 1994).

For the last four years, U.S. industry has spent more on computers and communications equipment than on all other capital equipment combined, creating a new economy based on the silicon microprocessor (Huey, 1994). Van der Spiegel traces the development of the microchip and related technologies. He also prophesies the next model of computing, one that simulates the biological system. Humanlike capabilities underlie the most dramatic projections of tools that will revolutionize the workplace. As Michael Coovert emphasizes in Chapter Five, computers have the greatest utility when they allow people to work naturally.

Van der Spiegel's historical tour demonstrates that computing is now entering a second era, evolving from a tool of computation to one of communication (Deutschman & Tetzeli, 1994; Huey, 1994; Tapscott & Caston, 1993). During the first few decades of computers (1950s through 1970s), managers used models based on the semiconductor to automate business processes and reduce clerical costs. They confined computing to specialized, inwardly focused departments in hierarchical bureaucracies. When engineers developed the microprocessor and essentially put the computer on a chip, they enabled the movement of intelligence out into the enterprise. The old master/slave computing, of mainframes or minicomputers summoned by dumb terminals, is now being replaced not just by personal computing but by client/server or network computing, whereby operators are in control of processing but able to share information and system resources (Tapscott & Caston, 1993). Although most desktop machines today are still focused on personal productivity, collaborative work (discussed by Coovert in Chapter Five) is expected to be the primary use of state-of-the-art machines within two years (Deutschman & Tetzeli, 1994). Van der Spiegel describes how multimedia and mobility enhance their functionality, again promoting the natural qualities of computing.

Electronic communications interconnect people not only within organizations but across and around, culminating in the worldwide web represented today by the Internet. Though primitive compared to the wide bandwidth model of the upcoming fiberoptic information highway (Infobahn), the Internet joins more than 32,000 computer networks and 20 million users around the world. At its current rate of growth, the Internet could connect 40 million people within two years (Deutschman & Tetzeli, 1994) and everyone on the planet by 2001 (Tetzeli, 1994). That's communication. But it is not necessarily an interchange of quality or usable information; according to management consultant Tom Peters, global communications could become "garbage at the speed of light" (Tetzeli, 1994, p. 61). Later in this chapter Don Davis discusses the challenge to organizations of siphoning out from the glut of information what is useful for competitive advantage.

Organizations and Job Context

The more important message that Davis imparts is how information technology, along with the growth of knowledge and global competition (which derive at least in part from that technology), has broken down the barriers within and around work centers and created boundaryless organizations. The symbolic representation or "virtualization" of business is eliminating slack at every level—removing intermediaries, speeding transactions, and distributing power (Verity, 1994). As Davis points out, globalization, information technology, dismantling of hierarchy, and knowledge growth and dissemination feed on one another and magnify their impact.

When organizations remove external and internal boundaries, they create fundamental change in the context of work. When they remove layers of hierarchy they also redistribute power toward front-line workers, as embodied in self-managed teams and total quality management practices. Organizations have traditionally used hierarchies for their coordination advantages, and vertically integrated businesses conducted transactions between divisions. But computers have so reduced coordination costs that many companies have decided to buy what they once produced in-house; in other words, they rely on the market rather than the hierarchy for competitive advantage. One consequence is that more than three of ten large U.S. firms outsource over half their manufacturing (Stewart, 1993) with consequent loss of internal jobs.

Davis lays the foundation for changes in job context in the lateral, networked organization. Various authors elaborate on this theme later in the book, especially Sue Morhman and Susan Cohen in Chapter Ten.

Job Content

"Jobs are not the issue. Slaves had jobs. The issue is what kind of jobs." With these words (Seligman, 1992), Senator Tom Harkin dramatized governmental concerns that even though the United States continues to excel in creating jobs, they will not necessarily be jobs that will raise the standard of living and support the American economy. The quality of jobs derives from both the context in which they operate and their content. Both Coovert (Chapter Five) and Toby Wall and Paul Jackson in Chapter Four address technology-driven changes in job content and their psychological implications. They delve into the issue of control, which resonates with the historical but recurring debate about deskilling.

Deskilling

The deskilling debate flared in the 1970s. Marxist writer Harry Braverman (1974) contended that management deliberately fragmented jobs into smaller and smaller subtasks, separating the thinking parts from the doing parts, in order to increase its control over the process of production. The deskilling proponents derided the notion that technology itself determined how work would be applied and placed the blame on the capitalist class. Critics of this point of view argued that the causal chain may be considerably more roundabout than a management desire for control (Baldry, 1988) and firms often embark on innovation with little thought to the consequences (Attewell, 1992). Moreover, the deskilling hypothesis ignores the possibility of resistance by workers or unions (Baldry, 1988), and overlooks the reality that craft labor is not necessarily the main target; it is easier to automate out of existence work that is already narrow and repetitious (Attewell, 1992).

Contextualism began to replace the deskilling view in the late 1970s and early 1980s. The contextualists claimed that the technology-work relationship was dependent on the situation (Adler, 1992)—identical technologies can be implemented in a variety of ways, some of which deskill and some of which enhance skills (Attewell, 1992). Management has a choice in how technology will be implemented (Zuboff, 1988). The contextualist view is still dominant today, supported by research like that Coovert describes in Chapter Five.

Still another view has emerged during the last several years, one that emphasizes a distinct upgrading trend. While not disputing the importance of context, the upgrading proponents claim that competition is forcing firms to seek out more productive combinations of machine and human capacities that more often than not lead to raising skill requirements. They do not imply that all technology carries with it a predetermined work content or work organization. Nevertheless, the upskilling view is, in effect, a softer form of technological determinism (Adler, 1992).

Some examples demonstrate how upskilling is gaining impetus. Skill may be thought of as reflecting the ability to respond to the unexpected and unpredictable. For example, both a football player and a brain surgeon are skillful because they must respond to an ever-changing situation, whereas a chocolate-bar packer is merely dexterous. Skill also includes the ability to control the work process in some way, because if workers can't control the process, they can't decide how to tackle the job, what sequence of operations would be most effective, what pace is best to get the job done, and so forth. Jobs must be controlled from somewhere, and deskilling may occur when control passes from the machine operator to the designer or programmer (Baldry, 1988).

Manufacturers of computer-controlled machine tools originally tried to lure purchasers with this idea of passing control from operator to programmer and replacing skilled labor with cheaper unskilled labor. But this promise proved to be a mirage. Companies needed the knowledge and initiative of skilled machinists to make best use of the machines, and the technology shifted to enable the operator to engage in programming, proofing, and editing. Flexible manufacturing should encourage such practices because shorter production runs require more programming and setup work, which in turn require more worker skills. Moreover, increased worker interdependence in the modern plant and the high cost of its equipment put a high premium on avoiding errors and reducing uncertainty, which require greater responsibility and initiative on the part of shopfloor workers (Attewell, 1992).

Trends in the office environment offer similar examples. Interactive computing allows a clerk to link, update, and transfer calculations from multiple data bases in a fraction of a second. It is therefore more efficient to have one clerk perform functions previously handled by several workers, each specializing in order entry, check inventory, customer credit, and the like. This requires more knowledge on the part of the clerk and also more responsibility and care, for errors in integrated data bases will have far-reaching consequences (Attewell, 1992).

Job Projections

Estimating the effects of technology on skills is not a simple matter. Analysts must consider skill shifts due to changes within individual jobs over time, changing relative sizes of occupations within an industry, and different growth rates of various industries that employ different kinds of workers (Attewell, 1992). Hiring patterns in the American economy suggest that the process of obsolescence and replacement is substituting higher-skilled jobs for lower-skilled ones. Most of the 5.5 million jobs added in the last two-and-one-half years were in occupations with above-average pay. More than two-thirds of the new jobs created in the last several years have been managerial and professional, especially in health care, education, business services, banking, retailing, and telecommunications—notably in the service sector (Nasar, 1994). At the same time, manufacturing jobs have generally declined, replaced by outsourcing, robotics, or other efficiencies.

Labor Department projections for jobs in the future also support more growth in higher-skill jobs than lower-skill jobs (Johnston & Packer, 1987). One of every four new jobs created between 1992 and 2005 is expected to be for technical workers, with paralegals and medical technicians setting the pace. Technicians are likely to become a new worker elite, representing one-fifth of total employment (Richman, 1994).

Work in the Office and the Factory

Van der Spiegel makes clear that rapidly advancing information technology with its inherent malleability offers unimaginable and perhaps unlimited applications. Few workers will be unaffected— by one estimate no more than 10 percent of the workforce by 2010 (Hines, 1994). Recognizing that information technologies are often introduced and used haphazardly today, Hines further predicts that they will be integrated into systems fifteen years from now. Coovert dramatically illustrates this in Chapter Five as he describes ubiquitous computing in future office work and its implications for human resources practice, especially training.

Contemplating work in the factory, Wall and Jackson suggest in Chapter Four that I/O psychology may be pursuing unproductive job design themes. Job satisfaction research has been criticized for taking one of two approaches: (1) proffering a model of what human beings ideally desire, in the tradition of Maslow and Herzberg, and assessing jobs against this model, or (2) assessing workers' attitudes toward their work and suggesting ways to modify jobs to modify the attitudes. Both approaches measure the degree to which workers have adjusted to their jobs; they fail to analyze the nature of jobs themselves and the assumptions and priorities built into their design (Baldry, 1988). Wall and Jackson break with this tradition by questioning I/O psychology's approach to job design. The conditions of the industrial age may have trained psychologists too intently on motivational issues and blinded them to other implications of individuals' control over their work. The post-industrial information age may finally bring these neglected factors into focus.

References

Adler, P. S. (1992). Introduction. In P. S. Adler (Ed.), *Technology and the future of work*. New York: Oxford University Press.

Attewell, P. (1992). Skill and occupational changes in U.S. manufacturing. In P. S. Adler (Ed.), *Technology and the future of work*. New York: Oxford University Press.

Baldry, C. (1988). *Computers, jobs, and skills: The industrial relations of technological change*. New York: Plenum.

Braverman, H. (1974). *Labor and monopoly capital*. New York: Monthly Review Press.

Cheriton, D. R. (1991). Software: A new form of literature. In J. D. Meindl (Ed.), *Brief lessons in high technology*. Stanford, CA: Stanford Alumni Association.

Deutschman, A., & Tetzeli, R. (1994, July 11). Your desktop in the year 1996. *Fortune*, pp. 86–98.

Hines, A. (1994, January–February). Jobs and infotech: Work in the information society. *The Futurist*, pp. 9–13.

Huey, J. (1994, June 27). Waking up to the new economy. *Fortune*, pp. 36–46.

Johnston, W. B., & Packer, A. E. (1987). *Workforce 2000: Work and workers for the twenty-first century*. Indianapolis: Hudson Institute.

Katz, Barry M. (1990). *Technology and culture: A historical romance.* Stanford, CA: Stanford Alumni Association.

Nasar, S. (1994, October 17). Statistics reveal bulk of new jobs pay over average. *New York Times,* pp. A1, D4.

Richman, L. S. (1994, August 22). The new worker elite. *Fortune,* pp. 56–66.

Seligman, D. (1992, December 14). Two dumb laws: A no-progress report. *Fortune,* p. 180.

Stewart, T. A. (1993, December 13). Welcome to the revolution. *Fortune,* pp. 66–78.

Tapscott, D., & Caston, A. (1993). *Paradigm shift: The new promise of information technology.* New York: McGraw-Hill.

Tetzeli, R. (1994, July 11). Surviving information overload. *Fortune,* pp. 60–65.

Verity, J. W. (1994). The information revolution: How digital technology is changing the way we work and live. Introduction. *Business Week,* pp. 10–18.

Zuboff, S. (1988). *In the age of the smart machine: The future of work and power.* New York: Basic Books.

New Information Technologies and Changes in Work

Jan Van der Spiegel

The second half of this century has witnessed the birth of the information age. Computers and communication systems are reaching new levels of sophistication at increasingly reduced prices that seem to drop every quarter. They are being used in all areas of society, ranging from education, the workplace, health care systems, and consumer products, to manufacturing.

A few decades ago this picture was very different. Computers were accessible to only a privileged few, mainly engineers or scientists working on complex problems at universities or analysts supporting administrative services in large corporations. The advent of the microprocessor and the personal computer, together with powerful and user-friendly software packages, has given a large fraction of the population access to new information technologies.

Despite these advances, the information revolution is still in its infancy and will continue to change our society profoundly well into the next century. There will be a virtually unlimited ability to sense, manipulate, store, display, and communicate large amounts of information almost instantaneously. This will cause a paradigm shift from *computational speed* to *information processing* (Chatterjee, 1991). As we move into the next century, the role of computers is changing from calculators to information delivery systems. Moreover, the emergence of portable systems such as cellular phones, faxes, notebook computers, personal digital assistants, and pen-based computers provides multimedia capabilities to the user independent of space or time.

Several years ago John Sculley of Apple Computers described a system called the Knowledge Navigator (Sculley, 1987). It would bring individuals in contact with a wealth of information at the push of a button: libraries, museums, data bases, archives, even movies. A large, high-definition screen would present the information in full color showing text, pictures, and computer animation together with high-fidelity stereo sound. The user could expect easy access to the wealth of information, in the form that he or she needs most.

This system requires computers with more humanlike characteristics and user-friendly interfaces. The input and output of these intelligent machines will be not just a keyboard, mouse, or video display and printer, but will encompass a range of sensors and actuators that act as the computer's eyes, ears, nose, and fingers. Also, the interface should be sufficiently responsive that if one speaks in Japanese to the computer, the reply would be in Japanese. The evolution of information technologies will help us to realize such a system.

The Microchip: The Underlying Driving Force

People have always been fascinated by building machines. Fueled by the need to be more efficient and by a vision of machines that could take over human tasks, modern civilization has made tremendous strides. One such demand came in the late nineteenth century from the U.S. Census Bureau, which predicted that it would take up to ten years to manipulate and correlate the U.S. census data of 1890. This led to the invention of Hollerith's tabulating machine, which was able to complete the census tabulation in about six weeks. Hollerith founded the Tabulating Company, which later became the International Business Machines Corporation (IBM) (Van Zant, 1990).

During the early 1900s, computers were made of electrical and mechanical switches. It was not until 1946 that the first large-scale all-electronic computer, called ENIAC, was developed at the Moore School of Electrical Engineering at the University of Pennsylvania. Although the ENIAC was a breakthrough at that time, when compared to current-day calculators and computers, its performance and technology looks very primitive. For example, the ENIAC could handle 750 instructions; today, a handheld pocket calculator (HP-48SX) can perform over 2,100 functions. Moreover, the ENIAC came with a heavy price tag. In 1946 it cost about $480,000, occupied a room of 1,899 square feet, weighed thirty tons, had 5,000 manual switches and 18,000 vacuum tubes, consumed 174 kilowatts, and required highly skilled operators.

The principal driving force behind the microelectronics revolution has been the explosive growth in integrated circuit capability. The advances made in semiconductor technology, coupled with the ingenious designs of circuits and sophisticated computer-aided design tools, enabled the semiconductor industry to put millions of transistors on an area the size of a fingernail, thus creating incredibly powerful and fast systems at low cost. A few years ago we witnessed the first chip that contained one million elements; before the end of this century we anticipate a gigachip, which will house over one billion elements. According to some optimistic predictions there is a chance that a one-trillion-transistor chip may be a reality by the year 2020! (Meindl, 1993). These chips will give rise to more powerful and intelligent information processing systems at ever-decreasing prices, as discussed later on.

Figure 3.1 shows how the integrated circuit has allowed the building of powerful computers. Computational capabilities are expressed in million instructions per second (MIPS). In terms of MIPS, the microprocessor-based computer has increased in computational power at a considerably faster rate than have mainframe computers. As a result, the distinction between mainframes, workstations, and personal computers is beginning to blur.

While computers have become more powerful, their price has dwindled, as illustrated in Figure 3.2. Over the last fifteen years the price/performance ratio of microprocessors has come down by two orders of magnitude. If this trend continues, we can expect to have a personal computer with supercomputing power on our desks by the end of the century. Such powerful systems will give rise to improved ways to communicate, as will be explored later in this chapter section.

In parallel with microprocessors, semiconductor memories have undergone a similarly impressive growth (Prince, 1991). In fact, during the 1970s semiconductor memories were the fastest growing segment of the semiconductor industry. As manufacturing techniques improved during the 1980s, the price of memories fell from about 50 millicents per bit in 1989 to 0.1 millicent per bit

**Figure 3.1. Evolution of Computing Power
Expressed in Million Instructions per Second (MIPS).**

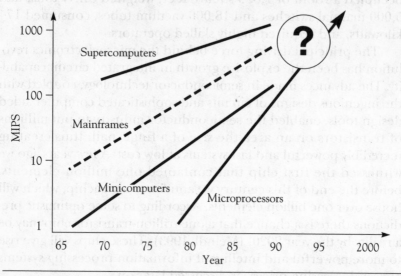

Source: L. Roffelsen, IEEE International Conference on Computer Design, Rye, New York, 1990; and DataQuest, Inc., San Jose, California.

in the early 1990s. This has made memories affordable for a large range of applications. Many of the technological advances to be described in subsequent sections depend heavily on storing and retrieving huge amounts of information quickly and inexpensively.

A recent trend in integrated circuits has been the development of low-power chips, especially for microprocessors, memories, and the application-specific circuits for communications. This important technological development is boosting the mobile computer market. The major computer manufacturers have developed many types of low-voltage, low-power products for use in nomadic computing and wireless local area networks (LAN), which are expected to boom in the next few years.

Telecommunications Technologies

The integrated circuit (IC), which houses billions of tiny electronic components, together with very fast fiber communication net-

**Figure 3.2. Evolution of Price Paid in Dollars per Million
Instructions per Second (MIPS) for Mainframe, Mini,
and Micro Computers.**

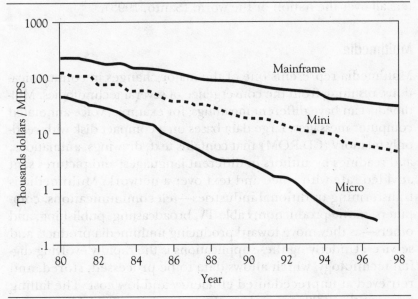

Source: Gartner Group.

works, will usher us well into the information age. While communication is as old as mankind, the ways of communicating have become increasingly more sophisticated and efficient. Telecommunication networks are often considered the nervous system of the commercial world (Tobagi, 1991; Brian, 1990), allowing messages to be sent at unprecedented speed around the globe, twenty-four hours a day. Until now, different networks were built to optimize the information they transmit: voice communication, cable TV, and data communication. Increased bandwidth (that is, transmission capacity), coupled with the demand for more information, has led to the development of networks that can simultaneously transmit multimedia information: voice, video, and data.

Presently, several companies are developing high-speed access roads to connect the customer to a fiber-optic, high bandwidth data highway. These access roads will be sufficiently intelligent to re-route the data automatically in a few tens of milliseconds in case of damaged cables or equipment. Thus the customer will be able to establish reliable, high-speed connections between the workplace, the home, the shopping center, or other information centers all over the nation or the world (Santo, 1993).

Multimedia

Multimedia represents one of the major changes in communications, resulting from the convergence of several technologies. Multimedia can have different meanings; for example, voice-annotated computer messages; large data bases on a compact disk with read-only memory (CD-ROM) that contains text, drawings, animations, and readings by authors in different languages; and pictures sent at video rate with voice and text over a network. Multimedia is transforming traditional industries—telecommunications, computers, movie production, cable TV, broadcasting, publishing, and others—as they move toward producing multimedia products and services. Underlying these applications is the rapidly evolving digital technology, which allows data to be processed, stored, and retrieved at unprecedented efficiency and low cost. The falling prices in the 1990s are making the technology affordable not only for business but for the consumer as well.

Multimedia requires state-of-the-art hardware. For instance, storing ten minutes of digitized video in a compressed format of 30:1 needs 550 megabytes (Mb) of space. Larger and less costly mass storage together with aggressive compression algorithms are needed to make multimedia attractive. Also, the transmission of such large amounts of data puts high demands on the network. Transmitting video signals requires data rates on the order of 100 Mb/s. Compression techniques and other signal processing techniques can reduce the data rate significantly, but the requirements on the system remain high. An Ethernet or token ring local area network that operates typically at 10–20 Mb/s has problems handling such large amounts of data. The limiting factor is not so much the fiber-optic communication channels, which can transmit at rates of 10^{14} Hz or higher, but rather the switching elements. These are the processors that switch or store and forward incoming packets of data to the right destination. Microelectronic switching elements are currently running at 150 million bits per second, and architectures capable of handling data rates up to several billion bits (gigabits) per second are being developed. More advanced systems, consisting of photonic switches, have the potential of being much faster but are still in their infancy.

Mobile Communications

Another emerging application is mobile communications and cellular telephone technology. An area such as a city is divided into different cells that have a number of frequency channels with short-range capabilities that broadcast to the base station in the cell. The station connects via a land network to a special switching network that routes the call to the proper destination. This technology gives people access, using modems, to electronic mail (e-mail), facsimile (fax), and other information resources anywhere they travel.

The ultimate vision for personal communications is a wireless, go-anywhere system (Kobb, 1993). An individual can be reached anywhere using a single phone number, making multiple numbers for home, the office, fax, and so forth redundant. Several experiments, being conducted in cities all over the world, are making this vision a reality. Moreover, national and international standards are being developed while new high-capacity voice and data networks are being given new allocations of the radio spectrum.

This has led to what is known as *personal communications services* (PCS). PCS is an emerging technology and generic term for mobile and portable *radio* communications service to individuals and businesses that are integrated into a variety of networks. A family of services will be available as part of the PCS including personal communications networks (PCN), which make use of a pocket telephone that will work anywhere. Also included in PCS is a cordless pay phone service that operates within a limited range of base stations in public places. Another service is wireless local area networks (LAN) for computers and portable personal information handling systems. As these telecommunications services become more widely available at affordable prices, working at home or on the road will become commonplace. The mobile office will become a new way of doing business.

As with the microelectronics revolution, telecommunications technology is progressing at such a high rate that by the twenty-first century, technology will provide horizons and opportunities that are currently still beyond our imagination. The merging of computer and communications has just started and will provide tremendous capabilities for a wide range of communications services.

New Approaches to Building Truly Intelligent Machines

From the previous discussions it should be clear that technology to sense, process, and communicate large amounts of information is progressing at an unprecedented pace. A wide range of tools, from supercomputers to powerful workstations, backed by high-speed data, voice, and video communication networks, are at our disposal. Where technology has fallen short, however, is in dealing with real-life problems, such as vision. Recognizing a face in a crowd is an almost impossible task for a computer, even the most powerful supercomputers. Vision, speech, natural language processing, and even translations are the kind of tasks that we, as humans, find effortless but which conventional computers do poorly. It is fascinating to see how elegantly biology has succeeded in solving these complex sensory processing tasks. It is even more impressive when one realizes that the brain has a volume of only about one deciliter, consumes about eight watts of power, and consists of slow processing elements (neurons). This raises the important question, what is so special about the way the biological system operates?

Without going into detail on the anatomy of the nervous system, we can recognize several major operational differences between the biological system and conventional computers. The nervous system is highly parallel and consists of many nonlinear processing elements (neurons) massively interconnected by synapses. Information is stored in a distributed fashion in the interconnections between the neurons. The network processes information in a fully parallel, dynamic fashion and evolves to a stable state within a few neural time constants. The synaptic time constant serves as short-term memory and enables the brain to represent time as an independent variable that permits the network to do spatiotemporal processing. This corresponds to solving a large set of coupled nonlinear differential equations—a task that is very computationally intensive for conventional serial digital computers.

This approach to data processing is very different from the one found in current von Neumann–based digital computers, which have a central processor (CPU), a main memory, and peripheral input/output devices, as shown in Figure 3.3. The CPU processes the data, engaging in calculations, decision making, and controlling the overall computer operation. The memory, which is separated from the processor through a communication bus, stores the information. This architecture has proven to be extremely powerful for solving well-defined problems such as complicated mathematical calculations, sorting large data bases, or manipulating spreadsheets. But it has fallen short in dealing with real-world problems, mainly because of the serial nature of the processor and the limited bandwidth between the processor and the memory.

The unique architecture of the nervous system is only one characteristic that gives biology its ability to process sensory information so effectively. The nature of the sensors and the sensory data preprocessing and representation at the cerebral cortex are equally important. Again, the visual system best illustrates the complexity of the task. From progress made in understanding the biological vision system, we know that many early vision tasks occur in parallel at the sensor sites without input from the brain. In other words, the retina is more than just an array of photodetectors. The sheet of neural tissue located at the back of the eye carries out some form of image analysis. Certain features of the raw visual input are accentuated while others are downplayed (Masland, 1986). This is accomplished by five layers of nerve cells in which information flows both vertically and horizontally. The intricate coupling of photocells with the processing layers is essential for the

Figure 3.3. Schematic of the Architecture of a Digital Computer.

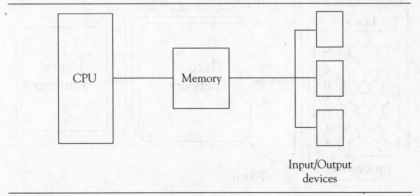

Input/Output
devices

formation of visual images and the reason the biological system is so efficient, notwithstanding the slow response of the individual nerve cells (Mahowald & Mead, 1991).

If we ever want to build intelligent machines with capabilities similar to those of humans, we will have to develop new architectures that are modeled to a certain extent after the biological system. Figure 3.4 shows schematically an example of such an approach (Van der Spiegel, 1994). Intelligent front-end sensors link to a neural network and further connect to a digital processor. The data are transformed at the sensor site in order to eliminate redundant information and to extract features from the visual or acoustical image patterns. This is usually done in parallel and real time before the data are fed into the next stage for further processing.

The processor, which generally will be a neural network-based computer, integrates sensory data from different sensing modalities and performs higher-level, more global processing. Neural networks process information in a parallel fashion, which makes them effective at dealing with large amounts of information. They are also capable of dealing with noisy, incomplete, and ill-defined problems, typical for real-world situations. In addition, they have the capability to learn or adapt and to make optimized guesses. During the past ten years, impressive progress has been made with neural networks at both the theoretical level and the implementation level. Several neural systems are currently being developed at major research laboratories (Hirai, 1992; Van der Spiegel et al., 1992).

Figure 3.4. Schematic Diagram of an Intelligent Machine.

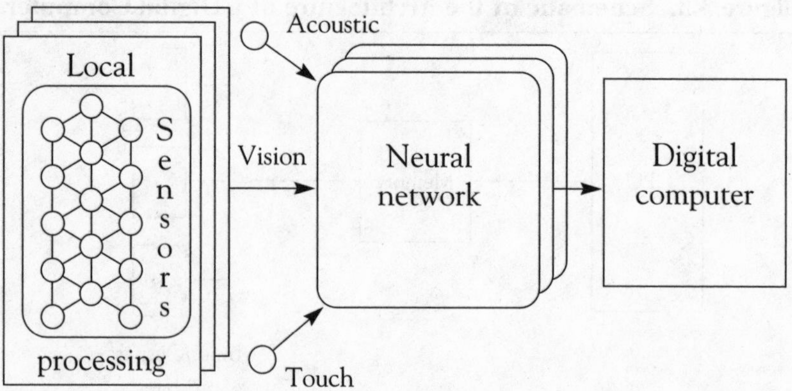

A digital computer follows the neural network processor because it offers flexibility in programming and the ability to implement algorithmic abstract computations. The current trend in computers is massive parallelism. The architecture of massive parallel processors (MPPs) is based on the interconnection of thousands of microprocessor-based nodes rather than a few but more powerful and expensive processors. By the end of this decade it is expected that MPPs with processing power of ter-aFLOPS (10^{12} floating point operations per second) will be available (Zorpette, 1992).

Thus intelligent machines of the future will combine smart sensors, neural network-based systems, and parallel digital processors. These machines are expected to have capabilities to interact with humans in real-world situations in an intelligent way.

Information Technologies and the Workplace

The new information technologies will drive new work environments and work habits. Computers with ever-increasing processing power are currently available at modest prices and are becoming more affordable for even the smallest companies. Computers and communications are merging and increasingly incorporating graphical and sound media. These combinations create unprecedented opportunities for almost instantaneous access to powerful data bases from all over the world, as well as improved and more efficient communications between workers and customers. Advances in operating systems, software packages, and interface standards make the complexity of the system transparent to the user and ensure ease of use. In the not-too-distant future we will see the emergence of machines with learning capabilities that can understand natural language instructions and make intelligent decisions.

Microsoft, the software company, and major office equipment manufacturers are making intense efforts to link office equipment together to enable cooperative operation over local and wide area networks. According to industry specialists, microprocessor-driven equipment, such as personal computers, phones, faxes, copiers, and handheld personal assistants, will all talk to each other. In addition, application-specific programming interfaces will ensure easy access to a host of outside services, such as phone, e-mail, and fax broadcast services. Collaborations between computer companies, software houses, and the telecommunications industries are shaping up and will give users wireless messaging capabilities for both data and voice. These developments will provide every worker with essentially a full-fledged desktop in the office or on the road. Distance working is expected to gain importance where workers may be located all over the world, giving rise to the global office. In addition, personal mobile communication systems are being installed worldwide and will provide workers with full access to office resources no matter where they are located (Kobb, 1993).

The information technologies will undoubtedly have an impact on office space and facility usage. Pilot studies around the concept of a *waking week* in contrast to the *working week* are being considered, where productivity is decoupled from space and time (Melvin, 1992). This concept will require interchangeability of office workers as well as redistribution and optimization of space. Related to this will be the emergence of home offices. It may be more efficient to work at home for several days where one can work uninterrupted using a personal desktop that provides the worker with access to the same resources that are available in the office (Kinsman, 1991).

Training and education will involve educational communications with multimedia and life interactions. Companies will have the capability to introduce distant learning, with a remote instructor for a workforce distributed worldwide. For example, organizations might train staff in a U.S. office using a Japanese instructor with simultaneous translation while showing real-life pictures of the manufacturing facilities in an offshore plant. Video conferencing, a somewhat sleeping market up to now, is expected to take off quickly. Digital video technologies will make face-to-face communication possible, even between people miles apart, increasing communication and work efficiency. In addition, participants will be able to exchange information, such as pictures or movies explaining the product being discussed (Tobagi, 1991; Meall, 1992).

A more sophisticated technology is *virtual reality* (VR), which describes a family of techniques and instruments that can create computer-generated sensations that closely resemble real-life experiences (Clark, 1993). Users put on head-mounted displays, which provide images and 360° sound; body gloves; and tactile-feedback devices. When users turn their heads, the displays are programmed to change, as if the wearers were really present in the surroundings that they observe. Users can also affect their environment and manipulate objects in the virtual space through joysticks and control gloves. As a result, those wearing the equipment have the sensation of being at the center of the display, whether in a distant country, on a mountain, or inside the organ of a patient to be operated on. Originally developed for flight simulators, VR can have more far-reaching consequences for areas such as medicine, education and training, design, sales, entertainment, and aiding the disabled. A variation of the VR technologies is tele-existence, which allows the operator to manipulate objects at a remote location (Tachi, 1991). Research is being conducted in using the operator's brain waves to communicate with the equipment. One of the obvious applications of tele-existence is the performance of tasks in dangerous and hazardous environments from the safety of the office.

These technologies will have a profound impact on the work environment and work practices. A group of people will be able to share the same experience and the same environment, even though they are miles apart. All the users' senses may be involved. The participants will hardly be able to distinguish between the virtual and actual reality. This technology will create opportunities for salespeople, product designers, maintenance people, and others to reach out to a national and even worldwide clientele and to become more efficient at addressing customers' needs.

One of the negative side effects of the information technologies in the office is "technostress," described as a computer-generated form of physical and emotional burnout. Technostress is often caused by workers' inability to adapt to the new technologies. Seminars that teach workers how to use the equipment at a level on which they feel comfortable, and that explain the implications of the human-machine interface on emotional well-being, are important in helping workers to cope with technostress and to reduce its effects (Baldwin, 1990).

Conclusion

Digital technologies and the underlying integrated circuits have progressed at a remarkable rate. The microprocessor, semiconductor memories, and communication chips form the technological foundation for these rapidly emerging information technologies. Sophisticated software packages, operating systems, interface standards, and telecommunications advances make these technologies user-friendly and available to a large section of the population. Computer architectures modeled on the biological system offer the promise of building intelligent machines with capabilities approaching those of humans.

Information technology will have a profound impact on how we live, communicate, and work, even on the psychological well-being of the individual workers. The technology will give us new tools, and it will influence our thinking processes. It will provide opportunities for increased teamwork and collaboration that promise to make the workplace more integrated and efficient.

The goal of the new technologies has been and must continue to be the improvement of quality of life and quality of work. Whether for work, education, environment, energy usage, personal security, communication, or health care, these technologies provide new opportunities to solve many needs of our society (Sheth & Janowiak, 1991). Predicting the future is always difficult, but it is fair to say that the horizons of the new information technologies are to a large extent still unexplored.

References

Baldwin, B. (1990, October). Managing the stress in technology. *CPA Journal, 60,* 94–96.

Brian, H. (1990, January). Future trends in telecommunications. *Information Age, 12,* 15–18.

Chatterjee, P. (1991). ULSI: Market opportunities and manufacturing challenges. *Digest IEEE International Electron Device Meeting,* 11–17.

Clark, R. S. (1993, August). Virtual reality: A world of applications. *OE Reports, 1,* 7.

Hirai, Y. (1992). VLSI neural networks. *IMC 1992 Proceedings,* 12–19, Yokohama, Japan.

Kinsman, F. (1991, November). Home sweet office. *Accountancy, 108,* 118.

Kobb, B. Z. (1993, June). Personal wireless. *IEEE Spectrum, 30,* 20–25.

Mahowald, M. A., & Mead, C. (1991, May). The silicon retina. *Scientific American,* pp. 76–82.

Masland, R. H. (1986, December). The functional architecture of the retina. *Scientific American,* pp. 102–110.

Meall, L. (1992, April). The shape of things to come. *Accountancy, 109,* 70–71.

Meindl, J. (1993). Evolution of solid-state circuits: 1958–1992–20??. *1993*

Commemorative Supplement of the Digest of the IEEE International Solid-State Circuits Conference, 36, 23–26. Castine, ME: Wuorinan.

Melvin, J. (1992, November). Office for the 1990s. *Facilities, 10,* 16–19.

Prince, B. (1991). *Semiconductor memories.* New York: Wiley.

Santo, B. (1993). Three pave data-highway access roads. *EE Times.*

Sculley, J. (1987). *Odyssey, Pepsi to Apple: A journey of adventure, ideas, and the future.* New York: Harper.

Sheth, J., & Janowiak, R. M. (Eds.). (1991). *2021 AD: Visions of the future. The ComForum summary and research report.* Chicago: National Engineering Consortium.

Tachi, S. (1991). Sensors and sensing systems in advanced robotics. *Digest of the 1991 International Conference on Sensors and Actuators,* pp. 601–606.

Tobagi, F. (1991). Telecommunications: The nervous system of a modern society. In J. Meindl (Ed.), *Brief lessons in high technology.* Stanford, CA: Stanford Alumni Association.

Van der Spiegel, J. (1994). Computational sensors—The basis of truly intelligent machines. In H. Yamasaki (Ed.), *Intelligent sensors.* Amsterdam: Elsevier Sequoia.

Van der Spiegel, J., Mueller, P., Blackman, D., Change, P., Donham, C., Etienne-Cummings, R., & Kinget, P. (1992). An analog neural network with modular architecture for real-time dynamic computations. *IEEE Journal of Solid-State Circuits, 27,* 82–92.

Van Zant, P. (1990). *Microchip fabrication* (2nd ed.). New York: McGraw-Hill.

Zorpette, G. (1992, September). The power of parallelism. *IEEE Spectrum,* pp. 28–33.

Form, Function, and Strategy in Boundaryless Organizations

Donald D. Davis

> *My center is giving way, my right is pushed back,*
> *situation excellent, I am attacking.*
> MARSHAL FERDINAND FOCH
> (SECOND BATTLE OF THE MARNE, 1918)

Organizations operate today within a worldwide web of nations that are joined together by virtually instantaneous communication. National boundaries fade into insignificance. Knowledge accumulates exponentially, while the rate of change itself moves at breakneck velocity. Organizations must strive to take advantage of opportunities provided by this complex new environment while at the same time they must avoid threats that may come from anywhere in the world. Unfortunately, this new environment may be too complex to predict and respond to in a planned, incremental way, the manner of change most preferred by organizations. Instead, organizations must prepare for change by instilling in their members the flexibility to sense and respond rapidly to global windows of opportunity.

I discuss in this chapter section the manner in which organizations may respond to opportunities and threats, paying particu-

Note: I am grateful to Ann Howard for her many helpful suggestions. Thanks also to David Pendlebury, of the Institute for Scientific Information, for his assistance regarding bibliometric methods.

lar attention to changes in organization form and structure. I also discuss some of the implications of social and technical change for research and theory in industrial and organizational psychology. I try to provide a sweeping context for the material to follow in this volume. As a consequence, my treatment of these ideas is broad and general rather than deep and detailed.

Currents of Change

Three currents of change impinge on modern organizations: (1) information technology, (2) growth in knowledge, and (3) globalization. Although other trends such as demographic change affect organizational functioning as well, I emphasize these three trends because they are likely to influence organizations in a long-lasting and pervasive manner. Moreover, these currents of change are potent because they are synergistic and therefore more difficult to predict and forestall.

Information Technology

Information technology refers to the use of computers to store, analyze, retrieve, and disseminate information. Information systems include computerized technology and the knowledge necessary to achieve advantage from its use. Information technology has revolutionized the organization and performance of work in manufacturing and service industries.

Information systems must be considered in any organization strategy, although this link is not often recognized and exploited by managers (Kantrow, 1980). Moreover, when technology strategy is explicitly formulated, it must be integrated with other strategies in manufacturing or service delivery, human resources, and marketing (Davis, 1986a). Furthermore, technology strategy must consider the organizational and human adaptation necessary to ensure that the technology achieves its productive promise (Davis, 1986b; Majchrzak, 1988).

The mere possession and use of information technology is not enough to ensure success. It is the system in which the technology is embedded and the manner in which the technology is deployed that provide advantage. New forms of organization and new methods of managing must accompany new information technology if it is to achieve its potential. For example, the failure to achieve large gains in organizational performance at General Motors (GM) despite billions of dollars of investment in advanced manufacturing technology during the 1980s resulted from management's inability or unwillingness to sufficiently change the form of organization and the methods of managing. GM automated but did not "informate" (Zuboff, 1984); human effort was replaced with robots and other forms of automation, but the sources of information that were newly available to the organization, and the new forms of social relationships that were required to take advantage of this information, were not adequately exploited.

Just as the use of steam power led to changes in the organization of factory work during the industrial revolution, information technology will lead to equally dramatic change in the form or "architecture" of future organizations (see Nadler, Gerstein, & Shaw, 1992). Organizational scientists are only now beginning to revise theories of organization to consider the influence of information technology in the creation of new organizational forms (for example, Huber, 1990; Pennings & Buitendam, 1987).

Managers who fail to recognize the need to redesign their organizations cannot fully take advantage of information technology. More important, managers who fail to recognize the close link between information technology and organizational design are likely to be caught off guard by changes in the organization that occur without deliberation and forethought, or by problems inevitably arising from the conflict between the constraints of the old organizational form and the new patterns of behavior required by the new technology. That is, with information technology there is an *organizational design imperative*.

The changes in organizational form made possible by information technology provide numerous strategic opportunities. One important advantage of information technology derives from its obliteration of boundaries within the organization and between the organization and elements in its external environment, as discussed later. Information technology may even create an economic environment in which temporary partnerships between organizations, or "virtual organizations," will gain ascendancy through their greater flexibility and responsiveness to rapidly changing markets and ability to provide customization of products and services

(Davidow & Malone, 1992). This new population of organizational forms may demonstrate evolutionary superiority similar to that previously manifested by bureaucratic forms of organization during the nineteenth century.

Knowledge

As Francis Bacon noted, knowledge itself is power. More important for organizations, knowledge is an *inexhaustible* source of power. The growth of knowledge resembles the long-sought grail of a perpetual motion machine; knowledge can perpetually create new knowledge. Just as with humans, the ability of an organization to acquire or create knowledge is an important requirement for survival. The ability to transform knowledge into action and to learn from the consequences of action provides further competitive advantage. The capacity to learn from experience in this circular manner—knowledge to action to reflection to knowledge to action to reflection—is diminished by the fact that the consequences of organizational actions stretch over many years and do not obviously result from previous decisions (Senge, 1990). Moreover, as with technology, some organizational designs are better able to develop and exploit knowledge as a resource and, as a consequence, increase their chances for survival (Hage, Collins, Hull, & Teachman, 1993).

Under the right circumstances, as organizations gain experience it becomes easier for them to acquire further knowledge (Argote, Beckman, & Epple, 1990; Epple, Argote, & Devadas, 1991). Achievement of this advantage is made difficult, however, because organizations strive to install systems that replicate past responses through programmed decision making (March & Simon, 1958; Weick, 1991). The desire to produce similar responses when confronted by novel stimuli underlies all organization design efforts. Consequently, organizations have great difficulty when trying to adapt previously successful organizational designs to new environmental demands. Past success restrains future choices. Highly successful organizations, therefore, find it more difficult to change themselves.

Knowledge may be located inside or outside of the organization. Employee involvement programs represent a common attempt to tap knowledge located inside the organization. Asking those who do the work to improve production processes and to provide suggestions for quality improvement, in contrast to consulting only those who merely oversee the doing of the work, represents an understanding of the power of this fundamental source of knowledge. But merely learning new ways of doing things provides only momentary advantage. Instead, organizations must *learn to learn* so that their store of knowledge constantly increases over time, much as compound interest makes investments grow. Organizations that learn how to learn gain more advantage than those that merely correct problems (Argyris & Schön, 1978; Senge, 1990).

Knowledge located outside the organization must be discovered, acquired, and assimilated. Organizational learning is made increasingly difficult by the need to keep abreast of a burgeoning store of knowledge, especially for firms in high-technology industries. This is only partially due to the increasing number of scientific and technical journals published each year; according to Bradford's Law of Scattering, only a few journals (about 10 percent of the total number published in any given field) account for the majority of citations and therefore require monitoring (Bradford, 1950; Garfield, 1980). More difficult is monitoring the bewildering variety of new sources of scientific information made available by information technology. In the past, scholars communicated their ideas and findings in letters, archival journals, and occasionally face to face. Today opinions and findings are shared daily on the Internet and by fax. Scientific entrepreneurs sell proprietary information to those who will pay for their newsletters. Scholars travel with ease to conferences and meetings throughout the world. The difficulty in the future will be to establish an intelligence network sufficiently complex and varied to match the variety of sources of scientific information.

While scholars have long sought to achieve intellectual advantage by seeking knowledge wherever it may be found, managers have also begun to seek knowledge widely to gain advantage. The popularity of management books such as *In Search of Excellence* (Peters & Waterman, 1982), *The Change Masters* (Kanter, 1983), and previously obscure books first published centuries ago in Asia, such as *The Art of War* (Sun-tzu, 1988) from the sixth century B.C. and *A Book of Five Rings* (Musashi, 1974) from the sixteenth century, testify to the eagerness with which managers seek knowledge located outside their organizations. Scholars such as Rosabeth Kanter, Edward Lawler, and Warren Bennis, among others, have achieved popular recognition far beyond the walls of academe.

New management knowledge and practices such as total quality management, statistical process control, employee involvement, quality circles, and downsizing and flattening of organizational hierarchies have diffused quickly and broadly throughout the world during the past twenty years. Although some of these practices surely represent temporary fads, many are likely to endure. In fact, "high-performance" organizations appear to derive competitive advantage by implementing a combination of these practices (Lawler, Mohrman, & Ledford, 1992). Such innovative practices can increase the overall level of organizational competency, but this effect is difficult to achieve. For example, surveys have revealed that firms attempting to implement a multitude of quality improvement practices such as statistical process control frequently fail to achieve positive results because their organizations are overwhelmed by the changes required of them; these new practices seldom become part of daily operations (Fuchsberg, 1992); that is, organization learning does not occur.

Globalization

Organizations can no longer confine their competitive focus to their own national boundaries. Corporations increasingly seek competitive advantage by searching for markets and sources of labor, capital, raw materials, and ideas throughout the world. Because of the global distribution of organizational functions, even determining the national identity of many firms is becoming more difficult (Reich, 1991). Like the other two trends previously discussed, the trend toward globalization is growing.

U.S. firms are increasingly investing abroad, although only 1 percent of U.S. industry is responsible for 80 percent of exports (President's Commission on Industrial Competitiveness, 1985, vol. 2). During the period 1988 to 1990, U.S. investment abroad grew from $335.89 billion to $421.49 billion, an increase of more than 25 percent (Bureau of Economic Affairs, 1991). Whereas most of this investment was in Europe, particularly the twelve

Economic Community countries, the greatest percentage increase of investment was in Latin America and other countries located in the Western hemisphere. This trend is likely to accelerate because of the fast population growth rate in Latin America and its expanding markets, and passage of the North American Free Trade Agreement (NAFTA), which eliminates trade barriers and opens markets between Canada, Mexico, and the United States.

Foreign firms also seek opportunities in the United States. For example, during the period from 1988 to 1990, foreign direct investment in the United States went from $314.75 billion to nearly $403.74 billion, an increase of about 28 percent (Bureau of Economic Affairs, 1991). Firms from Europe, particularly the United Kingdom and the Netherlands, accounted for the greatest dollar value of investment. Firms from Japan increased their investments at the greatest rate (63.3 percent) over the three-year period. This investment is often made by entering into partnerships with American firms, such as the joint venture between General Motors and Toyota (NUMMI). This trend means that it is increasingly likely that Americans will work for foreign firms doing business in the United States.

Countries in Asia dominate U.S. foreign trade. By 1986, transpacific commerce exceeded trade with European nations (President's Commission on Industrial Comp etitiveness, 1985, vol. 1). U.S. foreign trade with Pacific Rim nations continues to surpass trade with countries in Europe (Bureau of Economic Affairs, 1993). This movement of the U.S. commercial center of gravity from the Atlantic to the Pacific will provide unique opportunities and threats (Kotkin & Kishimoto, 1988). These changes will be difficult to negotiate because few Americans share an Asian heritage or understanding of Asian cultures.

International standards exert another, indirect influence on the behavior of American firms. ISO 9000, a series of standards created by the International Standards Organization of Geneva, was formulated to standardize the quality of products and services sold to members of the European Community (EC) after 1992. These guidelines require companies to document the performance of every organizational function that pertains to quality. Examples include specifications for products and services, verification of all production steps, specification of methods used to select suppliers, instructions for providing after-sale service and support, and records of employee training. Although originally designed for EC firms, ISO 9000 has become a de facto world standard for judging quality. The Big Three auto producers; makers of steel, semiconductors, and chemicals; and federal agencies such as the Department of Defense are adopting ISO standards (Levine, 1992). Suppliers to these organizations are consequently required to meet these standards as well.

ISO standards demonstrate how global events can shape the choices of American firms, regardless of whether they conduct business abroad. While not all agree with the wisdom of adopting ISO standards—for example, they fail to consider customer needs or desires in determining product or service specifications—achievement of these standards provides powerful evidence of a firm's commitment to quality, evidence not likely to be ignored by its marketing and sales departments when pursuing advantage against competitors.

While each of these trends—information technology, growth of knowledge, and globalization—pushes organizations to change the manner in which they organize work, it is their interaction that exerts the greatest influence. Computers and other forms of information technology such as e-mail networks and fax machines make global expansion easier, just as steam technology and the telegraph gave rise a century ago to the first railroad companies and the modern form of the American corporation (Chandler, 1977). Global alliances also facilitate the diffusion of new knowledge such as human resource management practices across national and cultural borders (Badaracco, 1991). Global electronic networks amplify these flows of information.

Information technology expands immensely the availability of and access to knowledge. Computerized data bases such as Dow-Jones News Retrieval, Lexis, Nexis, and IQuest, and electronic networks such as CompuServe and Internet, provide virtually instantaneous global access to vast amounts of information concerning management and organizations throughout the world. The ability to access and process such data bases already provides competitive advantage by, for example, facilitating environmental scanning (McCann & Gomez-Mejia, 1992).

The interaction of information technology, growth in knowledge, and globalization provides a worldwide information system in which all organizations are embedded. The interaction of these trends accelerates the rate of change of this information system beyond that of any one of them operating alone and greatly increases their complexity. The complexity goes far beyond the simple interactions described by earlier organization theorists (for example, Emery & Trist, 1965). The result is that organizations will have to rely less on forecasting (which presumes linear, incremental change) and more on developing an organizational form that can quickly respond to unpredictable events (see Leifer, 1989; Prigogene & Stengers, 1984). These new forms of organization will be characterized by flexibility, amorphous boundaries, and the ability to learn. Managers will need to respond eurhythmically by moving their organizations in harmony with these changes (Davis, 1988).

Strategy and Organization Form

Strategy represents the organization's anticipation of and response to an uncertain future, although most managerial attempts to formulate strategy reflect current problems more than future events (Hamel & Prahalad, 1989). Common organizational strategies emphasize (1) quality and customer satisfaction, (2) speed and timeliness, (3) customization and flexibility, (4) cost-cutting, productivity, and efficiency, and (5) innovation (Kanter, 1983; Lawler, 1992; Miles & Snow, 1978; Porter, 1985). Some of these strategies may complement each other while some may work against each other. For example, increasing the timeliness of service delivery with overnight mail services such as Federal Express often results in increased customer satisfaction (Blackburn, 1991; Jones, 1993). On the other hand, emphasis on cost-cutting, particularly in research and development departments or universities, may reduce innovation (Kanter, 1983; Miles & Snow, 1978).

Organizations develop strategies to exploit opportunities and avoid threats in their environments. To achieve performance gains, the organization must adopt a form that complements its strategy (Frederickson, 1986; Hrebiniak, Joyce, & Snow, 1989). For example, the anticipated economic benefits of downsizing often fail to materialize because organizations do not also emphasize organization redesign as part of their cost-cutting strategy (Cascio, 1994).

Managers can achieve strategic goals through many potential organizational forms. Some believe that organizational form results directly from external forces such as technology (for example, Woodward, 1965). This "technological determinism" constrains the behavior of individuals and organizations (Markus & Robey, 1988). Organizational form may also emerge from the complex interactions of people and organizational processes (Markus & Robey, 1988). In the case of information technology, for instance, managers learn through their experience with the technology that it may be able to achieve unanticipated desired outcomes; they then redesign the organization to take advantage of these benefits (Huber, 1990). A hybrid perspective, "interactive determinism," presumes that some aspects of the organization may change directly as a consequence of external influences such as technology or global events, whereas others emerge from social interactions and cannot be predicted from knowledge of external factors alone (Majchrzak & Davis, 1990).

The focus in this section is on changes in organizational form that eliminate boundaries between processes and subsystems within the organization (internal) and between the organization and elements in its environment (external). Boundary elimination is today a common organizational response to the environmental influences of information technology, knowledge, and globalization and one that I believe will permit organizations to prepare successfully for change. Elimination of boundaries increases the requisite variety of the organization, thus strengthening its ability to adjust to the complexity of turbulent environments (see Ashby, 1956).

Internal Boundaries

Many boundaries exist within organizations. These include the boundaries between (1) groups, (2) departments, (3) levels of authority, (4) cultures, (5) permanent and temporary status, and (6) time periods (see Table 3.1). This list is more illustrative than exhaustive, but these internal boundaries are likely to be affected by the environmental trends and strategic emphases previously discussed.

Pursuit of increases in quality, speed, flexibility, and innovation frequently lead to the elimination of boundaries between groups, departments, and levels of authority. For example, traditional forms of work design emphasizing individual responsibility may be changed to those emphasizing teams. Organizations frequently

Table 3.1. Organizational Boundaries, Organizational Form, and Strategic Emphases.

Boundary Eliminated	Organizational Form Feature	Strategic Emphases
Between groups	Parallel processing Groupware Cross-functional teams Liaison roles	Quality/Customer satisfaction Speed/Time Customization/Flexibility Innovation
Between departments	Cross-functional teams Employees as customers Internal integration Electronic networks Liaison roles	Quality/Customer satisfaction Speed/Time Customization/Flexibility Innovation
Between levels of authority	Employee involvement Electronic networks Downsizing Flattening hierarchies	Quality/Customer satisfaction Speed/Time Customization/Flexibility Cost-cutting Innovation
Between cultures	Cultural diversity	Quality/Customer satisfaction Innovation
Between permanent and temporary employees	Virtual staffing Temporary/Contract workers	Customization/Flexibility Cost-cutting
Between time periods	Flexible work schedules Continuous work	Speed/Time Customization/Flexibility Quality/Customer satisfaction

Internal

External		
Between competitors and collaborators	Mergers and acquisitions Joint ventures Spin-offs	Speed/Time Customization/Flexibility Cost-cutting Innovation
Between suppliers	JIT Outsourcing	Quality/Customer satisfaction Speed/Time Cost-cutting
Between customers	TQM Beta-testing	Quality/Customer satisfaction Customization/Flexibility Innovation
Between work and home	Virtual staff Telecommuting	Customization/Flexibility Speed/Time Cost-cutting

adopt mechanisms to improve employee involvement, provide group-based forms of compensation, and improve total quality through methods such as statistical process control (Lawler et al., 1992). Eliminating layers of employees and flattening hierarchies through downsizing provide another course of action to eliminate internal boundaries. Downsizing is often chosen to reduce costs or confront global competition (Kozlowski, Chao, Smith, & Hedlund, 1993).

Information technology aids the conjoining of groups, departments, and different levels of authority. This technology may be used to support decision making or communication (Kraemer & Pinsonneault, 1990). By using conferencing software, advanced multimedia electronic mail, and groupware, for example, individuals and groups may work on shared information around the clock, around the corner, or around the world (Dennis, George, Jessup, Nunamaker, & Vogel, 1988; Johansen, 1988; Olson & Atkins, 1990). This form of computer-mediated communication allows work to be processed in parallel in addition to serially, thus increasing innovation and reducing processing time. Moreover, when using these methods in product or service design and development, employees may detect errors and correct them at an earlier stage in the development process, thus increasing quality and reducing cost.

The boundary between subcultures is slowly falling in firms throughout the United States. Although early efforts to increase rates of hiring and promotion of women and minorities were undoubtedly spurred by federal legislation, many current endeavors to broaden the participation of such groups are inspired by perceived competitive advantage (Jackson & Associates, 1992). This expanded inclusion increases the potential pool of talent available to the organization, thus strengthening its human resource system. Increased innovation and quality may result. The need to eliminate cultural boundaries will grow more acute in the future with demographic shifts in the U.S. labor market.

During the past decade there has been a trend toward increasing use of what I call *virtual staff*, employees who come together temporarily to work on projects. Virtual staff includes (1) temporary and contract workers who work in lieu of full-time workers, (2) full-time employees of the organization who may work on site on temporary teams, (3) full-time employees from multiple organizations who cooperate on joint projects, (4) office temporaries, and (5) special project teams. The peacekeeping force that was sent to Somalia from the United States and other nations under the aegis of the United Nations represents a large-scale use of virtual staff. Impermanence and reduced reliance on traditional work groups and lines of authority are what define the virtual nature of staffing. Use of virtual staff allows an organization to reduce fixed costs yet marshal more resources than it has on its own.

The trend toward relying on part-time workers is growing in the United States (Carey & Hazelbaker, 1986) and in most other industrialized nations (Thurman & Trah, 1990). In recognition of this social change in the nature of work, some nations such as France, Germany, and Spain have provided statutory protection of part-time workers (Thurman & Trah, 1990). This preference for temporary employees reflects organizations' attempts to reduce the costs associated with maintaining permanent staff and to increase staffing and scheduling flexibility, although age and gender considerations may also play a part in this decision (Thurman & Trah, 1990; Verespej, 1989; Zeytinoglu, 1992). This trend toward part-time employment is also a reaction to organization downsizing, particularly in response to the elimination of support staff. Virtual staff require special attention because they have a unique relationship with their work and the organization in which they are employed (Feldman, 1990).

Psychologists have only recently devoted their attention to time as a variable in organizational processes, despite the fact that time exerts a ubiquitous influence on organizational behavior (McGrath & Kelly, 1990). Elimination of temporal boundaries, particularly the traditional workday, can better align schedules with employee and customer needs. It can even lead to around-the-clock work scheduling. Information technology frequently helps to eliminate these temporal boundaries. Examples include automatic teller machines that permit twenty-four-hour banking services, help forums on computer networks such as CompuServe and Internet that make possible twenty-four-hour customer service, and electronic trading around the clock in stock and monetary markets throughout the world. In each case, elimination of temporal boundaries provides competitive advantage but requires significant organization change (Jones, 1993).

External Boundaries

Information technology, growth in knowledge, and global competition principally affect two external boundaries: (1) the boundary between the organization and other organizations in its environment and (2) the boundary between the organization and individuals who may be part of the organization only occasionally, another form of virtual staff. Organizational scholars have paid the greatest attention to the boundary between organizations. This boundary is discussed first.

Organizations may focus on the boundary between collaborators or competitors. In some cases the boundary between two or more organizations may be breached; in other cases, new boundaries may be created where none existed previously. Mergers and acquisitions dissolve the boundary between two organizations. Joint ventures and spin-offs create new boundaries.

Mergers and acquisitions result in dissolution of the boundary between organizations through one organization's absorption of another. Mergers and acquisitions often result from the organization's attempts to expand and diversify into new markets, acquire new technology, eliminate competitors, or grow larger to avert being taken over by competitors (Glueck & Jauch, 1984).

Joint ventures provide a common mechanism for extending the boundary of an organization. In joint ventures one firm enters into a temporary partnership with one or more other firms in order to achieve mutually desired goals. Such actions provide strategic flexibility and facilitate transfer of technological and administrative innovations such as human resource management practices (Badaracco, 1991; Harrigan, 1985; von Glinow & Teagarden, 1988).

In spin-offs, one organization divests itself of one of its units, or personnel leave to form an independent unit. Spin-offs produce new organizational boundaries. In fact, the new organizations may enter into alliances on their own and compete or collaborate with their parent organizations. Spin-offs may be motivated by (1) efforts to reduce costs, (2) desire to focus more narrowly on markets, (3) government intervention, as in the break-up of AT&T, or (4) unwillingness to fully develop new ideas resulting from technological innovation. Financial success of spin-offs is not assured. A six-year longitudinal study of fifty-one voluntary spin-offs by nonfinancial firms found that financial performance was as likely to decline as to improve after divestiture (Woo, Willard, & Daellenbach, 1992).

Developing close links with suppliers provides another example of the manner in which the border between organizations can blur. Just-in-time delivery (JIT) represents a common means for closely integrating organizations and their suppliers. JIT emphasizes the delivery of raw materials and other inputs to feed the organization's transformation process on an as-needed basis. It is used widely in manufacturing to reduce costs associated with storage of materials and to improve quality (Ettlie & Reza, 1992; Harmon & Peterson, 1990). The organization and its suppliers may be linked by shared computer systems. The organization can download to suppliers designs for parts and other product-related information to speed up manufacturing and delivery and increase the quality of inputs. In some cases suppliers may even be involved in the product design process (Ettlie, 1988). The organization and its suppliers become fused together by their shared electronic information systems.

Outsourcing may also make indistinct the boundaries between organizations and their suppliers. Outsourcing is the subcontracting of the organization's functions; frequently this occurs in manufacturing although it is also found in service firms such as banks (Huber, 1993) and in staff functions such as human resources (Flatley, 1992). In some cases, the organization may outsource most of its functions and focus instead on its core competency (Huber, 1993). Outsourcing may be pursued to increase flexibility and customization or to cut labor costs.

Organizations may eliminate the boundary between themselves and individuals in their environment who can help them. This leads to temporary relationships that are instrumental in nature. These temporary relationships often occur between the organization and its customers. Customers become virtual staff of the organization. They expend effort on behalf of the organization without becoming formal members of it. For example, customers of fast-food restaurants clean their own tables after eating even though they are not employed by the restaurant. Customers may also spend considerable time providing suggestions for improvement when they are asked to do so.

Practices associated with total quality management (TQM) cause firms to seek advantage by involving customers in quality improvement efforts. TQM practices typically start with identifying the needs of customers (for example, Juran, 1988). These needs are then incorporated into product or service design. Suggestions to improve quality receive special attention. Customers, particularly those who present strong demands that will become more pervasive throughout the marketplace in the future ("lead users"), can also provide ideas for new products and services, thus increasing the firm's capacity to be innovative and flexible (von Hippel, 1986).

Beta-testing provides another mechanism for user input, thus blurring the boundary between the organization and customers who work as virtual staff. It is a procedure in which lead users receive an early version of a product under development. Beta-testers identify flaws and provide suggestions for improving subsequent versions of the product. Firms such as Microsoft may use several thousand beta-testers from around the world to test a software product during early stages of development. Although mostly confined to the computer industry, beta-testing can be used to advantage by most manufacturing and service organizations.

Computer forums and bulletin board services (BBSs)—electronic meeting places where people from throughout the world can share information—provide another connection between the organization and its customers. Customers link their personal computers or workstations via modem to the organization's information system. BBSs are commonly located on for-profit networks such as CompuServe, GEnie, America Online, and Prodigy, or on nonprofit networks such as Internet, although Internet cannot be used by private firms for marketing or sales purposes. The organization may also maintain its own BBS. For example, SPSS, the statistics software company, maintains a BBS that provides around-the-clock technical support to its customers.

The chief advantage of computer forums and BBSs is that they allow thousands of people separated widely by geography and time to communicate immediately. These electronic meeting places pull customers and other interested parties into the organization to serve as virtual staff in efforts to increase quality and customer service, customization and flexibility, and innovation.

The boundary between the organization and its full-time personnel is also becoming blurred. Traditionally, personnel have worked within the physical confines of the organization. Today information technology allows employees to work as telecommuters, another form of virtual staff. Telecommuters may work many miles from their employer, often at home. Some may work from around the globe. For example, new software code may be written by programmers located in several countries and then pieced together in yet another country. In some ways, this form of virtual staff represents a return to older forms of craft technology, where home and workplace were often one and the same rather than separate.

The number of telecommuters in the United States grew by more than 100 percent from 1988 to 1992, from three million to more than six million, representing about 5 percent of the U.S. workforce (Caudron, 1992). The number of telecommuters is expected to reach nine million by 1995 (Churbuck & Young, 1992). Estimates of productivity increases for telecommuters have ranged from 15 percent to 100 percent, with the average projected at 25 percent to 30 percent (Fisher, Schoenfeldt, & Shaw, 1990, p. 743). These increases in productivity typically result from the greater ability to focus on the task and reduction of interruptions among those who work at home. Telecommuters also report lowered stress, greater efficiency, and increased flexibility in balancing personal and work demands (Caudron, 1992; National Research Council, 1985).

Implications for Industrial and Organizational Psychology

Current changes in organizations provide numerous opportunities for research and practice for industrial and organizational psychologists. Space allows only a cursory discussion of three of them: (1) human resource requirements of these new organizational forms, (2) importance of personal mastery, and (3) need to focus on organizational competencies.

Human Resource Requirements

Elimination of the boundaries within and between organizations presents new challenges for managing human resources. The need for greater teamwork runs counter to the emphasis on individual accountability and career mobility historically maintained in U.S. organizations. When teamwork is coupled with increased employee involvement, organizations strain to adjust to the new demands of this collectivist and egalitarian orientation. Managers at all levels may resist these changes because their power and status are threatened. In many cases, despite receiving training, they are unable to develop new styles of leadership that emphasize coaching over direction. Lower-level employees may resist these changes because they often are unwilling or unable to accept new forms of responsibility. Many employees do not have the quantitative or cognitive ability to succeed in such endeavors as using statistical approaches to quality improvement. A history of worker-manager animosity, particularly in unionized firms, often leaves a residue of suspicion that is difficult to overcome. All of these change efforts are made virtually impossible when they are directed by managers who themselves do not function well as a team, do not link the elimination of boundaries to achievement of strategic goals, do not consider the need to change the organization's culture, or are not willing to act as the vanguard of the organizational change effort.

Elimination of the boundaries between organizations and customers and suppliers also requires new behaviors. Interpersonal relationships increase in importance as boundaries are lowered. Negotiation and compromise are essential. Leadership must be exercised through persuasion and example. Managers have to alternate leading and following. Although the organization may be tempted to dictate terms in relationships with customers or suppliers, this push will undermine the sense of partnership that the non-organization members must feel to perform extra-role behaviors such as providing suggestions for improvement.

Elimination of the boundary between permanent and temporary staff and between work and home presents new challenges for human resource management. Virtual staff work only temporarily on projects. Because of the short duration of assignments, accurate job analysis is essential. Selection and classification become more important than training.

Employees working at a distance also require special attention. They must be managed through emphasis on achievement of goals rather than monitoring of work processes, the traditional form of supervisory control. Employees may feel isolated and may reduce their attachment to their work group or the organization. For workers at home, self-discipline must replace the social cues that maintain effort in the work setting. It becomes easy to work too little or too much. Families of employees working at home may resent the intrusion of work into what they view as personal and private time, creating new sources of friction between work demands and family life. Successful telecommuting may require selection and training of families in addition to the employees involved, as is necessary when preparing employees for overseas assignments (Black, Gregersen, & Mendenhall, 1992).

Personal Mastery

The elimination of boundaries requires all organizational members to stretch beyond their specific work role. This need is most obvious in quality improvement practices and efforts to increase organizational citizenship behaviors. The competitive advantage of these practices results from the degree to which all organizational members pursue personal mastery. Organizations learn only when individuals learn; pursuit of personal mastery encourages individuals to learn (Senge, 1990).

Personal mastery is the result of the continuous process of self-refinement. It is a discipline of constant refinement, not the achievement of perfection itself. This difference in focus distinguishes personal mastery from mere obsessiveness or compulsiveness. Personal mastery is the primary emphasis in many Asian martial arts such as aikido, kendo, and tai chi ch'uan, as well as other arts such as the Japanese tea ceremony. At a superficial level, physical techniques are mastered through countless repetition so that they may be used correctly and effortlessly. At a deeper level, artists refine themselves.

In the case of martial arts, this refinement occurs through practiced patterns of physical movements, simulated combat exercises, and most important, self-reflection throughout the entire process. Martial artists observe their own reaction to events around them and strive to reach a point at which each action becomes *mindful* rather than merely a reaction driven by momentary agitation or other fleeting influences. This mindfulness is similar in some respects to the notion of double-loop learning, in which the organization steps back to observe its response to external events and strives to act reflectively rather than merely react (Argyris & Schön, 1978). After a time, mindfulness itself dissolves.

Personal mastery may be a specific aspect of conscientiousness, one of the "Big Five" personality characteristics that emphasize duty, hard work, self-discipline, perseverance, and achievement (Digman, 1990). Conscientiousness validly predicts many important organizational outcomes (Barrick & Mount, 1991). Unlike most personality traits, which by definition are stable and resist change, personal mastery may be learned and taught. Personal mastery has been taught successfully throughout Asia for many centuries. In fact, the Japanese cultural value for personal mastery may contribute to the success of quality improvement efforts in Japanese firms.

Personal mastery also shares some qualities with the optimal experience known as *flow*, a state of concentration that leads to complete absorption in some activity so that no attention is left over to devote to other thoughts or concerns (Csikszentmihalyi & Csikszentmihalyi, 1988). This feeling of flow is so gratifying that people are willing to engage in activities that lead to it for prolonged periods of time without the expectation of receiving anything in return. Flow results from becoming one with the action, as exemplified by art, dance, and music. The experience of flow may come from the pursuit and exercise of personal mastery. Whether personal mastery is a specific aspect of conscientiousness, a cause of experienced flow, or something different is empirically verifiable and deserves research attention.

Organizational Competencies

Organizational scientists have long known that individual performance is a function of knowledge, skills, and abilities (KSAs). These individual differences are often measured and used as the basis for selection, placement, and training in organizations. It is also true that organizations develop differences in their competencies; organizations have unique KSAs. Organizational competencies include the sum of knowledge possessed collectively by all employees in the organization. Collections of organizational competencies ("compools") may be seen as the genotype of the organization that can be used to distinguish populations of organizations (McKelvey, 1982).

Organizational competencies are transmitted over time through socialization and training and allow the organization to continue to exist over succeeding generations of employees. These competencies, particularly core competencies used to coordinate diverse production skills and integrate multiple technologies, have a strategic advantage: unlike physical assets that deteriorate over time, they grow with use (Prahalad & Hamel, 1990). Moreover, unlike specific practices such as JIT or quality circles, organizational competencies are difficult for other firms to imitate and thus provide greater long-term advantage. The elimination of organizational boundaries renders more important competencies such as team process, use of electronic communication and decision-making systems, and the ability to manage virtual staff. If the requisite feedback loops are in place, the organization can learn from its experience and strengthen its competencies in these areas.

Methods of job analysis are available to discover the KSAs required to perform individual jobs successfully. Needed are methods to determine organizational KSAs. Organizational KSAs may be simply the aggregation of individual KSAs. On the other hand, they may be different in meaning. This difference may be similar to the distinction between organizational climate and organizational culture (James, James, & Ashe, 1990; Reichers & Schneider, 1990).

Methods for assessing organizational competencies would be very useful for selecting potential organizations for collaborative relationships such as mergers and acquisitions, temporary partnerships, joint ventures, or outsourcing. Attributes currently used to make such decisions, such as cost or financial values, are important to know but are narrow and insufficient. Organizational competencies such as use of gain-sharing and other innovative reward systems, quality improvement adeptness, and so forth, could provide greater insight for selecting partners for long-term relationships.

Conclusion

Information technology, knowledge growth, and globalization are leading organizations to remove their internal and external boundaries. Advantage can be gained from these changes only when they are appropriately pursued as part of a deliberate strategy. These organizational changes provide new opportunities for industrial and organizational psychologists. Identification of human resource requirements, measurement and fostering of personal mastery, and measurement and management of organizational competencies represent new areas for research and practice.

References

Argote, L., Beckman, S. L., & Epple, D. (1990). The persistence and transfer of learning in industrial settings. *Management Science, 36*(2), 140–154.

Argyris, C., & Schön, D. (1978). *Organizational learning: A theory of action perspective.* Reading, MA: Addison-Wesley.

Ashby, W. R. (1956). *Introduction to cybernetics.* New York: Wiley.

Badaracco, J. L. (1991). *The knowledge link: How firms compete through strategic alliances.* Cambridge, MA: Harvard Business School Press.

Barrick, M. R., & Mount, M. K. (1991). The big five personality dimensions and job performance: A meta-analysis. *Personnel Psychology, 44*(1), 1–26.

Black, J. S., Gregersen, H. B., & Mendenhall, M. E. (1992). *Global assignments: Successfully expatriating and repatriating international managers.* San Francisco: Jossey-Bass.

Blackburn, J. D. (Ed.). (1991). *Time-based competition: The next battleground in American manufacturing.* Homewood, IL: Business One Irwin.

Bradford, S. C. (1950). *Documentation.* Washington, DC: Public Affairs Press.

Bureau of Economic Affairs. (1991, August). *Survey of current business.* Washington, DC: Bureau of Economic Affairs, U. S. Department of Commerce.

Bureau of Economic Affairs. (1993, June). *Survey of current business.* Washington, DC: Bureau of Economic Affairs, U. S. Department of Commerce.

Carey, M. L., & Hazelbaker, K. L. (1986). Employment growth in the temporary help industry. *Monthly Labor Review, 109*(4), 37–44.

Cascio, W. (1994). Downsizing: What do we know? What have we learned? *Academy of Management Executive, 7*(1), 95–104.

Caudron, S. (1992, November). Working at home pays off. *Personnel Journal,* 40–49.

Chandler, A. D., Jr. (1977). *The visible hand: The managerial revolution in American business.* Cambridge, MA: Harvard University Press.

Churbuck, D. C., & Young, D. S. (1992, November 23). The virtual workplace. *Forbes,* pp. 184–190.

Csikszentmihalyi, M., & Csikszentmihalyi, I. S. (Eds.). (1988). *Optimal experience: Psychological studies of flow in consciousness.* New York: Cambridge University Press.

Davidow, W. H., & Malone, M. S. (1992). *The virtual corporation: Structuring and revitalizing the corporation for the 21st century.* New York: Harper.

Davis, D. D. (1986a). Integrating technological, manufacturing, marketing, and human resource strategies. In D. D. Davis (Ed.), *Managing technological innovation: Organizational strategies for implementing advanced manufacturing technologies.* San Francisco: Jossey-Bass.

Davis, D. D. (Ed.). (1986b). *Managing technological innovation: Organizational strategies for implementing advanced manufacturing technologies.* San Francisco: Jossey-Bass.

Davis, D. D. (1988). An integrative strategy for innovation and change in high-technology firms. In L. Gomez-Mejia & M. Lawless (Eds.), *Managing the high-technology firm.* Boulder: University of Colorado.

Dennis, A. R., George, J. F., Jessup, L. M., Nunamaker, J. F., & Vogel, D. R. (1988, December). Information technology to support electronic meetings. *MIS Quarterly,* pp. 591–618.

Digman, J. M. (1990). Personality structure: Emergence of the five-factor model. In M. Rosenzweig & L. Porter (Eds.), *Annual review of psychology.* Palo Alto, CA: Annual Reviews.

Emery, F. E., & Trist, E. L. (1965). The causal texture of organizational environments. *Human Relations, 18,* 21–32.

Epple, D., Argote, L., & Devadas, R. (1991). Organizational learning curves: A method for investigating intra-plant transfer of knowledge acquired through learning by doing. *Organizational Science, 2*(1), 58–70.

Ettlie, J. E. (1988). *Taking charge of manufacturing: How companies are combining technological and organizational innovations to compete successfully.* San Francisco: Jossey-Bass.

Ettlie, J. E., & Reza, E. M. (1992). Organizational integration and process innovation. *Academy of Management Journal, 35*(4), 795–827.

Feldman, D. C. (1990). Reconceptualizing the nature of and consequences of part-time work. *Academy of Management Review, 15*(1), 103–112.

Fisher, C. D., Schoenfeldt, L. F., & Shaw, J. B. (1990). *Human resource management.* Boston: Houghton Mifflin.

Flatley, K. (1992, November). Outsourcing 401(k) administration yields benefits. *Personnel Journal,* pp. 99–102.

Frederickson, J. W. (1986). The strategic decision process and organizational structure. *Academy of Management Review, 11*(2), 280–297.

Fuchsberg, G. (1992, May 14). Quality programs show shoddy results. *Wall Street Journal,* pp. B1, B9.

Garfield, E. (1980, May 12). Bradford's law and related statistical patterns. *Current Contents,* pp. 5–12.

Glueck, W. F., & Jauch, L. R. (1984). *Business policy and strategic management* (4th ed.). New York: McGraw-Hill.

Hage, J., Collins, P. D., Hull, F., & Teachman, J. (1993). The impact of knowledge on the survival of American manufacturing plants. *Social Forces, 72,* 223–246.

Hamel, G., & Prahalad, C. K. (1989, May–June). Strategic intent. *Harvard Business Review,* 63–76.

Harmon, R. L., & Peterson, L. D. (1990). *Reinventing the factory: Productivity breakthroughs in manufacturing today.* New York: Free Press.

Harrigan, K. R. (1985). *Strategies for joint ventures.* Lexington, MA: Lexington Books.

Hrebiniak, L. G., Joyce, W. F., & Snow, C. C. (1989). Strategy, structure, and performance: Past and future research. In C. C. Snow (Ed.), *Strategy, organization design, and human resource management.* Greenwich, CT: JAI Press.

Huber, G. P. (1990). A theory of the effects of advanced information technologies on organization design, intelligence, and decision making. *Academy of Management Review, 15*(1), 47–71.

Huber, R. L. (1993, January–February). How Continental Bank outsourced its "crown jewels." *Harvard Business Review,* pp. 121–129.

Jackson, S., & Associates. (1992). *Diversity in the work place: Human resource initiatives.* New York: Guilford Press.

James, L. R., James, L. A., & Ashe, D. K. (1990). The meaning of organizations: The role of cognition and values. In B. Schneider (Ed.), *Organizational climate and culture.* San Francisco: Jossey-Bass.

Johansen, R. (1988). *Groupware: Computer support for business teams.* New York: Free Press.

Jones, J. W. (1993). *High-speed management: Time-based strategies for managers and organizations.* San Francisco: Jossey-Bass.

Juran, J. M. (1988). *Juran on planning for quality.* New York: Free Press.

Kanter, R. M. (1983). *The change masters: Innovation for productivity in the American corporation.* New York: Simon & Schuster.

Kantrow, A. M. (1980, July–August). The strategy-technology connection. *Harvard Business Review,* pp. 6–21.

Kotkin, J., & Kishimoto, Y. (1988). *The third century: America's resurgence in the Asian era.* New York: Crown.

Kozlowski, S.W.J., Chao, G. T., Smith, E. M., & Hedlund, J. (1993). Organizational downsizing: Strategies, interventions, and research implications. In C. Cooper & I. Robertson (Eds.), *International review of industrial and organizational psychology* (Vol. 8). London: Wiley.

Kraemer, K. L., & Pinsonneault, A. (1990). Technology and groups: Assessment of the empirical research. In J. Galegher & R. E. Kraut (Eds.), *Intellectual teamwork: Social and technological foundations of cooperative work.* Hillsdale, NJ: Erlbaum.

Lawler, E. E., III. (1992). *The ultimate advantage: Creating high-involvement organizations.* San Francisco: Jossey-Bass.

Lawler, E. E., III, Mohrman, S. A., & Ledford, G. E. (1992). *Employee involvement and total quality management.* San Francisco: Jossey-Bass.

Leifer, R. (1989). Understanding organizational transformation using a dissipative structure model. *Human Relations, 42*(10), 899–916.

Levine, J. B. (1992, October 19). Want EC business? You have two choices. *Business Week,* pp. 58–59.

McCann, J. E., & Gomez-Mejia, L. (1992). Going "on-line" in the environmental scanning process. *IEEE Transactions on Engineering Management, 39*(4), 394–399.

McGrath, J. E., & Kelly, J. R. (1990). *Some concepts for a social psychological theory of time.* Unpublished manuscript, University of Illinois, Department of Psychology, Champaign.

McKelvey, B. (1982). *Organizational systematics: Taxonomy, evolution, classification.* Berkeley: University of California Press.

Majchrzak, A. (1988). *The human side of factory automation: Managerial and human resource strategies for making automation succeed.* San Francisco: Jossey-Bass.

Majchrzak, A., & Davis, D. D. (1990). The human side of flexible factory automation: Research and management practice. In S. Oskamp & S. Spacapan (Eds.), *People's reactions to technology in factories, offices and aerospace.* Newbury Park, CA: Sage.

March, J. G., & Simon, H. A. (1958). *Organizations.* New York: Wiley.

Markus, M. L., & Robey, D. (1988). Information technology and organizational change: Causal structure in theory and research. *Management Science, 34,* 583–598.

Miles, R. E., & Snow, C. C. (1978). *Organizational strategy, structure, and process.* New York: McGraw-Hill.

Musashi, M. (1974). *A book of five rings.* Woodstock, NY: Overlook Press.

Nadler, D. A., Gerstein, M. S., & Shaw, R. B. (Eds.). (1992). *Organizational architecture: Designs for changing organizations.* San Francisco: Jossey-Bass.

National Research Council (1985). *Office workstations in the home.* Washington, DC: National Academy Press.

Olson, G. M., & Atkins, D. E. (1990). Supporting collaboration with advanced multimedia electronic mail: The NSF EXPRES Project. In J. Galegher & R. E. Kraut (Eds.), *Intellectual teamwork: Social and technological foundations of cooperative work.* Hillsdale, NJ: Erlbaum.

Pennings, J. M., & Buitendam, A. (Eds.). (1987). *New technology as organizational innovation: The development and diffusion of microelectronics.* Cambridge, MA: Ballinger.

Peters, T. J., & Waterman, R. H. (1982). *In search of excellence: Lessons from America's best-run companies.* New York: Harper.

Porter, M. E. (1985). *Competitive advantage: Creating and sustaining superior performance.* New York: Free Press.

Prahalad, C. K., & Hamel, G. (1990, May–June). The core competence of the corporation. *Harvard Business Review,* pp. 79–91.

President's Commission on Industrial Competitiveness. (1985). *Global competition: The new reality* (Vols. 1 & 2). Washington, DC: U.S. Government Printing Office.

Prigogene, I., & Stengers, I. (1984). *Order out of chaos.* New York: Bantam Books.

Reich, R. (1991). *The work of nations.* New York: Knopf.

Reichers, A., & Schneider, B. (1990). Climate and culture: An evolution of constructs. In B. Schneider (Ed.), *Organizational climate and culture.* San Francisco: Jossey-Bass.

Senge, P. M. (1990). *The fifth discipline: The art and practice of the learning organization.* New York: Doubleday/Currency.

Sun-tzu. (1988). *The art of war.* Boston, MA: Shambala.

Thurman, J. E., & Trah, G. (1990). Part-time work in international perspective. *International Labour Review, 129*(1), 23–40.

Verespej, M.A. (1989). Part-time workers: No temporary phenomenon. *Industry Week, 238*(7), 13–18.

von Glinow, M. A., & Teagarden, M. B. (1988). The transfer of human resource management technology in Sino-U.S. cooperative ventures: Problems and solutions. *Human Resource Management, 27*(2), 201–229.

von Hippel, E. (1986). Lead users: A source of novel product concepts. *Management Science, 32*(7), 791–805.

Weick, K. (1991). The nontraditional quality of organizational learning. *Organization Science, 2*(1), 116–124.

Woo, C. Y., Willard, G. E., & Daellenbach, U. S. (1992). Spin-off performance: A case of overstated expectations? *Strategic Management Journal, 13*(6), 433–447.

Woodward, J. (1965). *Industrial organization: Theory and practice.* London: Oxford University Press.

Zeytinoglu, I. U. (1992). Reasons for hiring part-time workers. *Industrial Relations, 31*(3), 489–499.

Zuboff, S. (1984). *In the age of the smart machine: The future of work and power.* New York: Basic Books.

Chapter Four

New Manufacturing Initiatives and Shopfloor Job Design

Toby D. Wall, Paul R. Jackson

Our primary thesis in this chapter is that the changing nature of manufacturing exposes the limitations of established psychological approaches to shopfloor job design. The resultant deficiencies in empirical research are, in our view, not just a matter of quantity but of kind. In particular, job design research has considered a restricted set of job content variables, ignored important contingencies, and given insufficient attention to the psychological mechanisms linking job design to outcomes.

The development of our thesis begins with a description of the forces for change in manufacturing and of the key practical initiatives that have arisen in response to these pressures, namely, just-in-time inventory control, total quality management, and advanced manufacturing technology. The implications of these initiatives point to specific job content variables, organizational contingencies, and psychological mechanisms that should be included in job design research. After exploring these aspects individually, we relate them to each other and to cognate areas of inquiry with the aim of stimulating the development of more integrated theory and method.

The Changing Manufacturing Environment

There has been considerable change within manufacturing over the last decade. At one level this can be characterized as a reaffirmation of traditional market values in response to economic pressures. In the face of world recession it has become widely accepted that to succeed, perhaps even to survive, companies have to further enhance their competitiveness. This is today's theme, as reflected not only in the management and I/O psychology literature, but also in the language of practitioners, which is now replete with such phrases as "achieving a competitive edge" and "regaining the competitive advantage."

Of more particular interest is how this drive for greater competitiveness is being translated into practice. During the 1980s a number of factors coalesced to shape the response. Against a background of shrinking world markets for manufactured goods, it became increasingly apparent that some countries were trading much more successfully than others. By 1986, for example, (West) Germany had displaced the United States as the world's leading exporting nation (Hayes, Wheelwright, & Clark, 1988). Similarly, by 1987 Japan's share of the world gross domestic product (GDP) had risen to more than 10 percent (Okumura, 1989). Meanwhile, manufacturing in the United States and the rest of Europe was in decline.

At first, explanations for this differential performance were based on macroeconomic arguments. The finger was pointed at a range of contributory factors within the less successful economies, such as high interest rates, overvalued currencies, inflated wage rates, unfavorable international trading agreements, and lack of coherent domestic industrial policy. However, as Japanese and German companies began to manufacture successfully abroad and evidence grew that their products were still superior to those of the home competitors, this view lost ground. Explanations were sought instead in terms of differences in manufacturing approach (Hayes et al., 1988).

With the spotlight on manufacturing itself, the issue became one of identifying what led some companies to be more successful than others. Opinion converged on two interrelated factors. First, with regard to strategy, the successful companies were seen as those that competed not only on cost, but also on quality and responsiveness to market demand (Lawler, 1992). The latter involves offering a wider diversity of products, customizing products, rapid accommodation to new product designs, and meeting tight delivery deadlines. The second factor concerns the production methods and technologies used to support that strategy. Partly inspired by the techniques employed by the visibly successful Japanese industries, and reinforced by such influential books as Peters and Waterman's (1982) *In Search of Excellence* and Schonberger's (1986) *World Class Manufacturing,* just-in-time inventory control (JIT) and total quality management (TQM) were identified as the key practices. Closely associated with these was the adoption of advanced manufacturing technology (AMT).

Superficially, each of these manufacturing initiatives can be seen as linked to alternative competitive objectives. Thus JIT focuses on cost control, TQM on quality, and AMT on responsiveness. In reality, the relationships between these initiatives and the objectives are much more complex. For example, while AMT exploits the flexibility of computer control to enhance responsiveness through greater diversity and customization of products, it also helps to control costs (through reduced setup, changeover, and lead times) and increase quality. Similarly, diversity of products will tend to increase inventory requirements and consequently make the disciplines of JIT more salient. JIT in turn benefits from predictable workflow, whereas TQM plays its part by keeping disruptions due to quality problems to a minimum. Because of these and many other interdependencies, JIT, TQM, and AMT have been identified as the core components of a "new paradigm" of "integrated manufacturing" (Dean & Snell, 1991).

The significance of JIT, TQM, or AMT as determinants of manufacturing competitiveness remains to be systematically demonstrated. Nevertheless, those faced with the reality of the market cannot afford the luxury of awaiting proof. Thus in one form or another, these initiatives are increasingly being adopted, often in combination. A survey of UK manufacturing companies, for example, showed that by 1991 nearly 70 percent were employing JIT techniques, with the vast majority of the remainder planning to do so (Oliver & Wilkinson, 1992). Most companies had implemented the method since 1988. Similarly, use of TQM was reported by almost two-thirds of the companies surveyed, and typically had been introduced within the previous three years. Despite the recession, investment in AMT reveals an equivalent picture. By the mid-1980s almost two-thirds of all machine-tool sales in advanced industrialized countries were of computer-controlled models (Edquist & Jacobsson, 1988). The manufacturing landscape is changing dramatically.

The emergence of JIT, TQM, and AMT has naturally stimulated discussion of their implications for organizational practice, especially as this relates to shopfloor job design. There is both concern about the impact of these manufacturing initiatives on shopfloor work, and interest in the forms of job design that determine their effectiveness. Less consensus exists, however, about the nature of these relationships. Some argue that JIT and AMT in particular will increase job simplification and will operate successfully with rigidly defined, low-skill, and low-discretion jobs (for example, Braverman, 1974; Klein, 1991). For others, the development of the new manufacturing initiatives "heralds the end of Fordism and Taylorism" (Wood, 1990, p. 169) and provides the context for a move toward more enriched, autonomous, and responsible forms of job design (Jessop, Bonnet, Bromley, & Ling, 1988; Lawler, 1992). Wood (1989) portrays this view evocatively when he states: "We are witnessing the new specialized firm that can quickly respond to sudden changes in costs, market opportunities, and/or new technologies through adopting flexible multipurpose equipment and creating a flexible re-integrated and cooperative workforce free of the shackles of rigid job specification, narrow job-centered orientations, and excessive regulation and control" (p. 11). According to this view, JIT, TQM, and AMT require an approach to job design long, but unsuccessfully, recommended by applied psychologists concerned with enhancing the quality of working life (Buchanan & McCalman, 1989). Thus social and economic goals have converged.

Such contradictory views survive only in the absence of adequate evidence to decide between them. That is the present state of affairs. As Dean and Snell (1991, p. 777) observe, "Empirical research assessing the relationship between new manufacturing practices and job design has been limited" (see also Wall & Davids, 1992). Thus advancing our knowledge of this important relationship might be seen as simply a matter of time, of waiting until research catches up with practice.

Our position, however, is that the limitation of empirical research is not simply a matter of quantity but is also one of kind.

So far, the relationship between the new manufacturing initiatives and shopfloor work has been addressed largely within the parameters of conventional approaches to job design. These approaches evolved mainly in response to traditional manufacturing methods and, like the context from which they derive, are narrowly conceived. The new manufacturing context reinforces the need for a broader perspective on job design. While it is too early to specify this in full, three priorities are evident. The first concerns content. The traditional focus on the discretionary dimension of jobs should remain a core issue, but the nature of JIT, TQM, and AMT makes additional job variables salient. The second priority is to pay explicit attention to organizational context. The existing controversy over the impact of the new manufacturing practices on shopfloor work, coupled with evidence that traditional approaches to job design have variable effects on performance, suggest there are important contingencies to take into account. Finally, and perhaps most fundamentally, research has to take a much closer look at the psychological mechanisms that relate job variables to outcomes. Current approaches primarily are based on motivational assumptions. The nature of TQM, JIT, and AMT suggests that attention should also be paid to knowledge-based and learning processes. This is a perspective that has been neglected within job design research, as it has within industrial and organizational psychology more generally (Lord & Maher, 1991; Weiss, 1990).

The New Manufacturing Initiatives

Our focus in this section is on the implications of JIT, TQM, and AMT for the content, contingencies, and mechanisms encompassed by research on shopfloor job design. To set the scene we first describe those initiatives in more detail.

Just-in-Time Inventory Control

JIT is essentially a system for improving productivity by reducing the costs that result from high levels of stocks of raw materials and components, work-in-progress (WIP), and stores of finished goods. Traditionally, manufacturing has relied on high levels of such inventory to meet fluctuating demands, constituting a "push" system in which operations are triggered by the availability of materials and labor rather than by specific customer requirements (Monden, 1983; Schonberger, 1986). Materials are stored to cater to a wide variety of possible orders from customers, buffer stocks of WIP are kept to absorb imbalances between different stages of production, and finished goods are stored for distribution on demand.

The objective of JIT is to remove as much of this inventory as possible by manufacturing only to order, in a "pull" system in which each stage of production is carried out just in time to enable the next to be completed. Materials and components are purchased for immediate use and only for particular customer requirements. Without a stock of finished products for immediate supply, a company requires short lead times in order to be responsive to customer demand. This in turn necessitates little WIP because products have to pass rapidly from one stage of the manufacturing process to the next until finished. Finally, by completing the product for a given delivery date, the company will experience minimum delay before payment is received against the investment in materials and labor. On the factory floor, this typically involves the manufacture of much smaller batches, which demands reduced setup and changeover times (Hutchins, 1988).

In practice, JIT takes many forms and is implemented to varying degrees (for example, Voss and Robinson, 1987, found that companies had selected only the easy-to-implement elements of JIT). Perhaps the most common application, especially among smaller companies that can exert less control over their suppliers, is focused on the reduction of WIP. It is not uncommon to hear of reductions in lead times from several weeks to only a few days, and of WIP reduced by some 80 percent (for example, Schonberger, 1987).

Total Quality Management

As Dean and Snell (1991) have pointed out, TQM is the most elusive of the new manufacturing initiatives because it is a management philosophy rather than a particular set of practices. Nevertheless, its central concept is relatively simple: to ensure that high quality is built in throughout all stages of manufacturing from product design to delivery. Traditionally, much of quality control in manufacturing has been carried out only at the end of the production process by a separate group of employees, and defects detected then are rectified in a rework department. Those advocating TQM have pointed out that this separation of production from inspection institutionalizes the expectation of quality problems, and involves rework that would be unnecessary if production were "right first time" (for example, Crosby, 1979; Deming, 1986; Juran & Gryna, 1988; Schonberger, 1986).

Thus the emphasis in TQM is on preventing quality problems. A wide variety of methods and techniques are deployed toward this goal, including improvements in product design (Gryna, 1988a), design for manufacturability (Bessant & Lamming, 1989), upgraded technology, responsibility for quality at the point of production, statistical process control (for example, Harrington, 1987), and the development of a production culture based on continuous improvement in both products and processes (*Kaizen*) (for example, Imai, 1986). The aim is to make quality assurance an integral part of manufacturing itself rather than a subsequent stage. In practice, there is considerable variation in the focus of TQM initiatives, especially the extent to which nonconformances are designed or engineered out as opposed to actively managed.

Advanced Manufacturing Technology

AMT refers to computer-based manufacturing machinery and processes. Our emphasis is on direct applications, which include stand-alone computer-controlled equipment such as computer numerically controlled (CNC) machine tools, CNC assembly machines, and robotic installations. Where several such pieces of equipment are integrated under shared computer control through various materials-handling and transfer devices, they form a flexible manufacturing system (FMS).

The significance of computer control is not simply that it guides the machinery through a sequence of operations required for a given manufacturing process, but more important, that it allows the sequence to be easily and rapidly changed through modifications in software. For these reasons, AMT has been described as "soft automation," in contrast to the conventional dedicated "hard automation" based on built-in mechanical devices such as cams and timers (Sharit, Chang, & Salvendy, 1987). Thus AMT offers the normal advantages of automation in the form of reduced labor costs, consistent product quality, and enhanced output, but at the same time can be used for a much wider range of products. The capacity of many applications to improve quality, cope with different products, and minimize setup and changeover times (Majchrzak, 1988) complements both TQM and JIT.

Other aspects of AMT encompass computer-aided design, engineering, process planning, and production scheduling. More detailed descriptions of the various forms and characteristics of AMT are provided elsewhere (Gunn, 1987; Majchrzak, 1988; Wall & Kemp, 1987).

The New Initiatives and Job Content

In the literature to date, the relationship between the new manufacturing initiatives and shopfloor work has been addressed largely from the point of view of established approaches to job design. Two of these have been particularly influential. One is the job characteristics approach, as epitomized by the Job Characteristics Model (JCM) (Hackman & Oldham, 1976; 1980). The other is the more general sociotechnical systems perspective (STS) (for example, Cherns, 1976; Trist, Higgins, Murray, & Pollack, 1963), and especially its development in terms of "autonomous work groups" or "self-managing teams" (for example, Gulowsen, 1972; Susman, 1976).

There are clear differences between these approaches. The JCM, for example, is focused on individual job design and encompasses individual difference variables, whereas the STS approach emphasizes group work design and organizational factors. Nevertheless, with regard to job content, they have much in common. This is because both approaches developed against a background of job simplification, where the trend in manufacturing was toward limiting both the range of tasks within jobs and the discretion of individuals over how to carry out those tasks. Consequently, their primary focus is on the impact of such constraints on employee attitudes and behavior. Thus the JCM identifies skill variety, task identity, task significance, autonomy, and feedback as the "core job dimensions" that affect employee satisfaction, motivation, absence, turnover, and performance. Among the independent variables, autonomy is regarded as particularly important. The same emphasis is evident within the STS approach, where the design of autonomous work groups is based on the principle of creating "meaningful tasks" that allow employees to exercise control in the execution of their work. Indeed, the similarity between the approaches has led several authors to argue that they should be integrated (Cummings, 1978; Denison, 1982; Hackman, 1977; Rousseau, 1977).

The traditional approaches, therefore, place the spotlight clearly on the question of autonomy or job control. The application of this focus to the new manufacturing initiatives has been of considerable benefit in providing direction and in enabling work in the new context to build on an established body of knowledge. Thus as mentioned earlier, one of the key questions raised with regard to JIT and TQM is the extent to which they enhance or restrict the opportunity for shopfloor employees to exercise discretion over their work (Turnbull, 1988; Ramsey, 1991). Correspondingly, the debate on AMT has been dominated by concern over its potential to deskill jobs (Adler & Borys, 1989; Braverman, 1974) and how the effectiveness of computer-based technology relates to the degree of operator control (Wall, Corbett, Martin, Clegg, & Jackson, 1990; Wood, 1990). Indeed, it is for such reasons that there has been a revival of interest in job design (Buchanan & McCalman, 1989; Lawler, 1992).

Nevertheless, there is also a negative aspect to this perspective—that it perpetuates the weaknesses as well as the strengths of those earlier approaches. One such deficiency is especially important: traditional approaches encompass only a very limited number of potentially important job properties. This was noted in a critique of the job characteristics literature by Roberts and Glick (1981), who concluded that "investigations have become narrower over time. A restricted set of task characteristics . . . has been focused on" (p. 210). Six years later, Wall and Martin (1987) found it necessary to reinforce the point. Discussing several relevant job features not covered by research, they observed: "It is not that they have been investigated and found wanting as salient job properties, but that they have been largely ignored" (p. 75).

Recent studies of the job design implications of JIT, TQM, and AMT give added weight to that criticism by suggesting that attention needs to be paid to several job features not encompassed by existing approaches. Three in particular stand out, namely cognitive demand, production responsibility, and work interdependence. We shall advance the argument for the inclusion of each of these within a broader approach to job design that is more relevant to the modern manufacturing environment.

Cognitive Demand

One of the most common observations about the new manufacturing initiatives is that they alter the balance between the physical and cognitive demands of jobs. With cognitive demands, an important distinction lies between attentional demand (involving the essentially passive monitoring aspects of the work) and problem-solving demand (entailing more active diagnostic, error recovery, and fault prevention requirements). In these respects, however, the implications of the new initiatives for shopfloor jobs are far from uniform. In the case of JIT, where the objective is to keep production flowing with a minimum of disruption without the protection afforded by buffer stocks, shopfloor employees are often under pressure to maintain a systematic, and often augmented, rate of production. This has resulted in increased attentional demand but minimal problem-solving demand (for example, Booth, 1987). Turnbull (1988), for example, describes JIT as "recreating the rhythm of the assembly line" (p. 13), as does Klein (1989). In contrast, other instances have been recorded where the main impact of JIT is to augment problem-solving demand. Cases have been reported of employees being given added responsibility for dealing with any problems that threaten to interfere with the flow of production (Tailby & Turnbull, 1987; Young, 1987). This is the theme of Schonberger's (1986) analysis, that JIT "calls for assemblers to learn multiple job *skills,* data collection *duties,* and diagnostic and problem-solving *talents*" (p. 38, italics in original).

Similar implications follow from TQM practices. Where the approach to quality improvement is focused on improved materials supply, product design, and technology, the impact on employees can be to increase pressure on them to maintain standard methods of working (Sewell & Wilkinson, 1992). In cases where the emphasis is on integrating quality inspection and fault rectification within the job itself, TQM increases the attentional and problem-solving demands in the work (Gryna, 1988b).

Advanced manufacturing technology has similarly divergent consequences for shopfloor work. Van Cott (1985), for instance, argued that AMT "has rearranged man's [sic] role from an active element to one of passive monitoring" (p. 1140); and Perrow (1983) asserted that "machine monitoring is a growing activity in automated and high technology systems" (p. 535). Yet others have observed that advanced technologies "create for humans new tasks in which manual labor is replaced by thoughtful labor" (Shulman & Olex, 1985, p. 98).

Production Responsibility

The second key aspect of job content is that of production responsibility. A common characteristic of the new manufacturing initiatives is that they increase the visibility and significance of individuals' contribution to production. The nature of JIT is such that any disruption to the workflow often has obvious and serious effects because, in the absence of the protection afforded by local buffer stocks, it has an immediate and frequently far-reaching impact (Jackson & Martin, 1993). To the extent that such problems can arise directly from employee error, or indirectly from the failure to observe system faults, the consequence is that individuals are made more aware of their contribution to and accountability for production costs. In the extreme case, inappropriate actions can result in no work for "downstream" workers carrying out the next stage of production, and ultimately failure to meet delivery deadlines.

TQM can have very similar implications. Its emphasis on quality, and the pursuit of such principles as right first time (Oakland, 1989), highlights the role of individuals in the production process. In some applications there is even a requirement for employees or work groups to halt the production process when a quality problem arises, and not to resume work until it has been resolved. The philosophy and practice of TQM is thus one that can place the shopfloor employees' contribution to quality squarely in the public domain and accentuate the responsibility they feel for achieving the requisite standards (Delbridge & Turnbull, 1992).

With regard to AMT also, it is clear that operators often have considerably more responsibility for both valuable machinery and output than in most other forms of manufacturing (Zicklin, 1987).

The technology itself is typically expensive and can in many cases suffer damage as a result of operator error or failure to notice a malfunction. At the same time, AMT typically has the capacity to provide a much greater volume of output in a shorter time than has conventional technology. As a result, any downtime the operator causes or could have prevented carries much greater costs, which are visibly attributable to individual employees (Rasmussen, 1986; Sharit, Chang, & Salvendy, 1987; Sinclair, 1986).

As in the case of cognitive demand, the new manufacturing practices do not necessarily entail high cost responsibility. That depends on a variety of factors: the degree of slack and likelihood of disruption in a JIT system; the tolerances allowed and the probability of encountering quality problems in the case of TQM; and the intrinsic properties of the particular application (for example, reliability, potential for "crashing," and value of the product) with regard to AMT.

Work Interdependence

The final job content area we wish to emphasize is that of *work interdependence.* We use this term to refer to the degree to which employees collaborate with and are dependent on others in the execution of their work. It is the job-level equivalent of such organizationally defined constructs as sequential interdependence (Thompson, 1967), workflow integration (Pugh, 1973), coupling (Corbett, 1987), and functional integration (Lawrence & Lorsch, 1969).

A feature of the new manufacturing practices is that they can lead to much greater work interdependence. By eliminating or reducing the buffers of work-in-progress between production stages, JIT can make employees much more reliant on others' work in order to complete their own tasks. Similarly, TQM practices emphasize the importance of meeting the requirements of both internal and external customers, thus increasing employee awareness of their interdependence. The problem-solving aspect of TQM also links shopfloor employees more intimately with support staff, as does the use of AMT, where close collaboration between operators, programmers, and engineers is often fundamental for effective system performance.

Of course, the extent to which the new practices increase work interdependence is related to many other factors. For example, if

JIT is implemented in the context of individually operated "cells" (Mortimer, 1985), which provide for all or most of the required manufacturing operations to be completed within one group of machines, the effect on work interdependence may not be very great. In contrast, where products have to go through a sequence of separate operations (or cells), the impact of JIT on work interdependence will be much more pronounced.

It is interesting to observe that, in one form or another, work interdependence has regularly surfaced within the earlier job design literature. For example, it was a focus of attention within the original sociotechnical systems research (for example, Trist & Bamforth, 1951; Trist et al., 1963), and was among the key job properties identified within Turner and Lawrence's (1965) seminal work from which the current job characteristic perspective developed. More recently Kiggundu (1981) has argued for the integration of "task interdependence" into the Job Characteristics Model; and Corbett (1987) demonstrated that work interdependence, in the form of "coupling," was related to job attitudes (see also Corbett, Martin, Wall, & Clegg, 1989). The new manufacturing context under consideration in this chapter gives added impetus for research to encompass this aspect of shopfloor work, whose importance has been periodically documented but which so far has been inadequately investigated.

Overview

In summary, the nature of the new manufacturing initiatives makes more salient the levels of cognitive demand, production responsibility, and interdependence involved in shopfloor work. It is evident that JIT, TQM, and AMT can all accentuate these job features, and that the extent to which they do so differs across applications. However, we have not highlighted these particular variables simply for descriptive reasons. Equally important is that they are of known psychological significance, even though they have been neglected by traditional approaches to shopfloor job design. For example, they are prominent within the job stress literature where they are identified as determinants of job-related strain and mental health at work, either as individual job features, in combination with each other, or in combination with job control. High levels of attentional demand have been found to increase strain both directly (for example, Cox, 1985; Smith, 1981) and when associated with high levels of responsibility (for example, Cobb & Rose, 1963; Martin & Wall, 1989) or low levels of job control (for example, Karasek & Theorell, 1990). Thus inclusion of these variables within the approach to job design enhances the links with job stress research, as well as the prospect of integrating two areas of inquiry that have developed in relative isolation from one another to the probable detriment of both (Jackson, 1989). Similarly, the focus on job control, problem-solving demand, and work interdependence increases the potential to link theory and research on job design to developments in organizational theory and cognitive psychology, as will become clearer as the chapter develops.

The New Initiatives and Job Design Contingencies

A general issue throughout the literature on the new manufacturing initiatives, and indeed within job design research as a whole, is the existence of contradictory views and inconsistent effects. On closer examination, these seem to reflect the failure to adapt the new initiatives to the existing contingencies of the workplace.

The Case for a Contingency Perspective

As highlighted in the previous section, the impact of the new initiatives on job content is clearly variable. JIT, TQM, and AMT have all been reported to be associated with both increases and decreases in job control, and to affect cognitive demand, cost responsibility, and interdependence to varying degrees. This is reflected in a recent study reported by Dean and Snell (1991). They examined the relationship between the degree of implementation of JIT, TQM, and AMT and job characteristics in a sample of 123 companies and found no consistent association. They concluded that there are "serious doubts about the popular assumption that changes in manufacturing practices lead to widespread changes in job design" (p. 795).

The same picture emerges from more general evidence on the relationship of job design to job attitudes and performance. Kelly (1992), for example, reviewed outcomes from thirty-one of the more methodologically rigorous case studies and field experiments on job redesign and found divergent effects. Improvements in job satisfaction were recorded in seventeen cases, but not in thirteen others; and whereas performance gains were reported in twelve cases, in thirteen there were none. In this study as in others (for example, Iaffaldino & Muchinsky, 1985), there was no clear or strong relationship between job satisfaction and performance. Together such findings are something of an embarrassment to current job design theory because job satisfaction and performance are deemed to have common determinants.

The implication of these findings is that the effect of the new manufacturing initiatives on job design, and the consequent impact of job design on attitudes and performance, varies according to circumstances. This possibility is not accommodated within mainstream approaches to job design. As Roberts and Glick (1981) concluded, "Most research [has] failed to examine the relationship of task characteristics and job responses to their organizational contexts" (p. 210). Clearly, consideration of that relationship is a priority for research, and the primary need is to identify relevant contextual contingencies. One contingency with the potential to explain much of the apparent inconsistency within job design research is production uncertainty.

Production Uncertainty as a Key Contingency

To date, the notion of uncertainty has been most strongly developed within organizational theory. Interest in uncertainty has its roots in the work of Burns and Stalker (1961), who observed that the type of organizational structure that worked best in relatively stable, simple, and predictable settings was different from that needed in more complex and uncertain environments. On the basis of a study of twenty industrial firms, they argued that mechanistic structures (involving formal relationships, centralized decision making, and routinized tasks) were appropriate under predictable conditions but that more organic structures (with more flexible, decentralized, and informal practices) were required under uncertain conditions. Subsequent work has elaborated on this proposition, identifying several different sources and kinds of uncertainty that affect organizations, such as those due to market demands, the technology, or the inherent nature of the production task (for example, Brass, 1985; Galbraith, 1977; Lawrence & Lorsch, 1969; Mintzberg, 1979; Perrow, 1967; Thompson, 1967). However, the core proposition remains the same: as the degree of uncertainty increases, so does the need for more devolved decision making. Indeed, this remains one of the most pervasive and resilient perspectives within the organizational literature.

Given that shopfloor job design is an integral part of the wider organizational structure, this core proposition is clearly relevant at this more particular level of analysis. Basically, it follows that under relatively stable production conditions, narrowly defined low-discretion jobs will tend to arise and be compatible with good performance; but where there is greater uncertainty about how to complete the task, more autonomous or enriched forms of work design will be required for effective performance. This is implicit in much of the sociotechnical systems analysis of the significance of environmental instability (for example, Emery & Trist, 1965) and has been proposed as a more general development of job design theory (Clegg, 1984; Slocum & Sims, 1980). Nevertheless, the role of uncertainty as a contingency factor has not been assimilated into mainstream approaches to job design and has been neglected in empirical research.

The same picture emerges in relation to the new manufacturing practices, particularly with regard to AMT. Several authors have proposed that AMT increases technological uncertainty and thus requires job designs that enhance shopfloor job control. Susman and Chase (1986), for example, argued that sociotechnical systems principles imply an "upgrading strategy" so that operators can "deal with all key variances, either by writing software, or by taking real time action to correct them" (p. 266). Similarly, Cummings and Blumberg (1987) concluded that because AMT is "likely to result in higher levels of technical uncertainty," its effectiveness depends on operators' being "given the necessary skills, information and freedom to respond to unforeseen circumstances arising from the production system and its task environment" (p. 48). Equivalent arguments have been proposed by others, including Buchanan (1989), Majchrzak (1988), and Walton and Susman (1987).

The more general form of the argument relating to AMT, however, is that such technology varies with regard to uncertainty, and the appropriate form of job design will differ correspondingly. This possibility was investigated in a change study by Wall and others (1990), who examined the impact of increased job control for operators on the performance of CNC insertion machines. They found that the job change brought substantial improvements in output for machines characterized by greater operational uncertainty (high-variance systems) but had no effect on more predictable machines (low-variance systems).

The argument can be extended to JIT and TQM. Where production is predictable and stable, the disciplines of both these initiatives will encourage organizations to anticipate and standardize work methods in low-discretion jobs. Control of inventory, for instance, will be attempted primarily through more careful planning of materials supply and of WIP. Conversely, where demand, supply, and production processes are intrinsically more uncertain, greater reliance will be placed on flexibility to meet unanticipated problems, and the emphasis will be on jobs with higher discretion. Similarly, predictable production requirements enable organizations to invest in quality through building standards into the supply of materials, product design, and reliable technology, making discretionary job behavior relatively inconsequential. However, greater uncertainty requires that more reliance be placed on shopfloor discretion in order to attain quality goals because production problems cannot be eliminated at the source. Hence, one would expect the approach to shopfloor job design to vary systematically as a function of the uncertainty of a given production process, and the performance achieved to depend on the extent to which the appropriate job design approach is adopted.

The above arguments could in principle account for many of the inconsistencies noted in the research literature to date, although it is unclear to what extent they do so. This is because most research reports contain little information on the level of uncertainty examined in a specific study, and very few attempts have been made to test empirically the effects of different levels of uncertainty within the same study. We believe the potential of this line of inquiry is considerable and should be developed. That in turn requires closer attention to the construct of uncertainty itself, which at present is poorly and variably defined within the literature. A focus on job design as the level of analysis may be an advantage in this respect, because it makes less critical existing distinctions within the literature between sources of uncertainty, such as those emanating from the market, the materials, or the technology. From a job-level perspective, the important consideration is the extent to which meeting output, cost reduction (inventory), and quality goals entails dealing with operational problems. On any particular AMT system, for example, these problems may arise from a variety of sources but be equivalent in requiring action on the system itself in order to be properly controlled. Hence, the notion of production uncertainty, defined as a job-level construct, is likely to be a valuable approach. Operationalization at this level of analysis opens the way for proper empirical inquiry into the impact of uncertainty on the choice and effects of job design.

So far we have focused on production uncertainty as a potentially important contingency for understanding the relationship between the new manufacturing initiatives and job design, and for the development of job design research more generally. The more fundamental point, however, is that context needs to be considered in this domain as it does within I/O psychology as a whole (Johns, 1993). The new manufacturing initiatives serve to remind us of this weakness within current job design research.

The New Initiatives and Job Design Mechanisms

Perhaps the most challenging notion raised by work on the new manufacturing initiatives concerns the nature of the mechanisms relating job design to effective work behavior. Traditional approaches to job design are based on motivational assumptions, and job enrichment is deemed to enhance performance by encouraging greater work effort. That assumption is often less than adequately articulated, and in many ways represents the "soft underbelly" of job design theory. Nevertheless, it is at the core of established approaches (Campion & McClelland, 1993; Locke & Henne, 1986; Wall & Martin, 1987). In contrast, many of those now recommending more responsible and autonomous jobs to support JIT, TQM, and AMT are taking a different perspective. They base their arguments on the role of job design in facilitating a more rapid and better quality response to the demands of production, where greater job control enables employees to "work smarter," not harder.

Arguments for a Knowledge-Based Mechanism

The idea that the success of the new manufacturing initiatives depends on harnessing and developing shopfloor expertise has gained increasing acceptance in the general literature. This is illustrated by Schonberger's (1986) analysis of "world class manufacturing" in which he recommends: "Do not put in equipment simply to displace labor. Equipment cannot think or solve problems; humans can. Our past failures to use shopfloor people as problem-solvers have shaped the view that labor is a problem. The World Competitive Manufacturing view is that equipment is a problem, and labor is an opportunity" (p. 75). Similarly, Wood (1990) noted that "the question of increasingly automated systems is often portrayed as being fraught with problems, and it is thought workers' experience and tacit knowledges may be a better way of overcoming these than any textbook formula or engineer's conceptions" (p. 170). John Towers, managing director of Rover (UK), reflects the same philosophy when he describes the advances made by his company since joining forces with Honda (Japan) as due to the fact that "everyone now has two jobs. First to build the car, second to find ways of doing the job better" (Caulkin, 1993, p. 24).

Underlying these views is the more particular assumption that the way to capitalize on and develop shopfloor expertise is through job redesign. This is exemplified by Susman and Chase's (1986) insightful sociotechnical analysis of the integrated factory. These authors reasoned that "aside from any motivational benefits they might derive from having enriched jobs . . . employees are in a better position to see the relationships between specific actions and their consequences" (p. 268) and to take action accordingly. Lawler (1992) argued along similar lines: "Quality may also be improved because employees have a broader perspective on the work process and as a result can catch errors and make corrections that might have gone undetected in more traditional work design in which employees lacked the knowledge to recognize them. And because they have the autonomy to make ongoing improvements, employees can also fine-tune and make adjustments in the work process as they become increasingly knowledgeable about how their work can best be done" (p. 85).

Interestingly, essentially the same assumptions are evident within the quite separate German tradition of work psychology based on Action Theory (for example, Hacker, 1985, 1986, 1987). Applied to job design, this general cognitive approach identifies job control as the key issue. Frese and Zapf (1993) described its implications as follows: "Action Theory's arguments are not based on the grounds that control is a prerequisite for democracy at work. Nor is the basis a humanistic type of psychology. It is also not a motivational theory as the one by Hackman and Oldham (1980). Rather it is the idea that people who have control can do better because they can choose adequate strategies to deal with the situation. They can plan ahead better, they are more flexible in case something goes wrong. Skills can only be acquired where there is control at work" (p. 77).

Similar ideas were evident in early job design theory. For example, Herzberg's (1966) notion of psychological growth, which he saw as enhanced by enriched work, was defined as "knowing more, seeing more relationships in what we know, being creative, being effective in ambiguous situations" (p. 70). It can also be argued that this theme is implicit in the current approaches to job design. The Job Characteristics Model, for example, includes feedback as a core job dimension, and knowledge of results as the intermediate "critical psychological state" linking it to performance and other outcomes. Although this linkage is cast within a motivational framework, it could alternatively be interpreted as reflecting an essential condition for the development of job knowledge and expertise.

Many further examples can be found in which informed opinion points to the importance of knowledge-based processes as the means through which shopfloor job design affects performance at work in general, and within JIT, TQM, and AMT systems more particularly (for example, Cummings & Blumberg, 1987; Majchrzak, 1988; Walton & Susman, 1987). In fact, two closely related but distinct arguments can be discerned (Wall, Jackson, & Davids, 1992). The "quick-response explanation," implicit in much of the sociotechnical systems literature, emphasizes the logistical advantages of greater job control. If the employees have the knowledge and the authority to deal with production problems that arise, then necessary remedial action will be much more prompt than if they have to call on support from others who are more remote. In a sense, this is an explanation based on ensuring the delivery of relevant knowledge immediately and at the point where it is required. The human role is primarily a reactive one. The "anticipatory explanation," in contrast, assumes a more proactive learning-based process. Job control is seen promoting employees' understanding of the dynamic properties of the work system, and hence their ability to anticipate, avoid, and prevent production difficulties. The importance of such behavior is illustrated in Hohn's (1988) analysis of machinists' jobs in a German textile factory: "It's not so important to be able to reconnect the broken thread, what matters is to see what's likely to happen and what you need to do to prevent it snapping" (p. 98). The assumption is that job control provides a learning environment that improves employees' predictive knowledge and empowers them to take advantage of that gain.

Evidence for Cognitive Mechanisms

Although there has been increasing emphasis on knowledge-based mechanisms in discussions of job design for the new manufacturing initiatives, the issue has attracted less empirical scrutiny. Nevertheless, some suggestive investigations have been reported. Most of these are case studies that provide rather indefinite support. An example is Buchanan and McCalman's (1989) account of innovative work practices developed by the Digital Electronics Corporation in the United States and Great Britain (see also Buchanan, 1989). With the objective of increasing both flexibility in response to change and the quality of the end products, management introduced "high performance teams." These were based on "a considerable increase in worker control through autonomous work groups" (Buchanan, 1989, p. 264). The reported success of the approach was attributed to "massive personal growth and skills development" on the part of shopfloor employees, especially in relation to factors such as "analysis and synthesis skills in problem diagnosis" and "process design and planning skills" (Buchanan, 1989, p. 268).

Complementary findings are described by Parker (1993; see also Parker, Jackson, & Wall, 1993), who compared the role orientations of employees in semiautonomous work teams within an integrated manufacturing environment with those of shopfloor counterparts working under more traditional job design conditions. The former group were found to place more importance on using and acquiring job knowledge, and on understanding how to tackle problems to best meet overall production goals. In short, they displayed much broader and strategic orientations toward their work.

Two recent field experiments with job design for operators of AMT systems provided more concrete and specific evidence on the role of job knowledge in linking job design to performance. Jackson and Wall (1991) further analyzed the data from the study by Wall and others (1990) described earlier, which showed a strong effect of increased operator control on the downtime, and hence output, of CNC insertion machines. They recognized that alternative indices of downtime could be used to test for different explanatory mechanisms. A reduction in time per incident would indicate that gains derived from more immediate response to system faults (the quick-response explanation); whereas a decrease in the number of incidents would indicate that benefits arose through operators learning to prevent faults (the anticipatory explanation). The results, based on time-series analysis, showed strong support for the latter explanation, with the prevention of downtime improving over time. A problem with this study, however, is that the interpretation of the data relating to the quick-response explanation is not straightforward. It is possible that the faults that were prevented were ones of shorter duration, thus masking a real effect on downtime per incident. This problem was overcome in an investigation by Wall, Jackson, and Davids (1992) of a complex robotics line. They tracked particular types of faults causing downtime over an extended period before and after an increase in operator control. The results were unambiguous: there was both an immediate and lasting reduction in downtime per fault, and a progressive reduction in the incidence of faults.

Thus there is empirical evidence from these two studies to support both the quick-response and anticipatory explanations of the effects of job control on performance. The more general implication is that there are two underlying processes: an initial application of existing knowledge, where the mandate to rectify faults necessarily brings benefits through enabling a quicker response, and a subsequent development of predictive knowledge through learning, which allows fault prevention.

Perspective

At present, the case for a knowledge-based approach to job design is markedly unbalanced. The argument that job control enhances performance through promoting the application and acquisition of job knowledge is both appealing and widely proposed. Moreover, this view has a long history within the job design literature and has been given fresh impetus by recent discussions of how best to implement new manufacturing initiatives. On the other hand, there is little empirical evaluation of that assumption. The results of the few relevant studies we have been able to find are encouraging but do not add up to a substantial body of evidence. Additionally, they address the issue somewhat obliquely by inferring job knowledge from its manifestations either through role orientations or in performance. A more direct approach would be to measure knowledge itself in order to examine (a) whether increasing employees' job control enhances the extent and nature of their job knowledge, and (b) whether increased job knowledge accounts for performance gains. As far as we are aware, no such studies have been reported.

Our view is that such a direct approach is now required. In part, this is because the assumption that knowledge-based processes underlie job design is so widespread that it should be put properly to the test. More important, however, is the wider potential this perspective holds for promoting theory and practice.

Conclusion

In this chapter we have argued that the new manufacturing initiatives have made more explicit the limitations of established approaches to shopfloor job design. Our position is that those approaches focus on too restricted a set of job variables, ignore important contingencies, and pay insufficient attention to cognitive processes linking job design to outcomes. Correspondingly, within each of these domains we have identified particular lines of development that we consider to hold most promise for strengthening research and practice. Thus we have recommended that investigators add the job properties of cognitive demand, production responsibility, and work interdependence to the established emphasis on autonomy or control; include production uncertainty as a key contingency variable; and encompass knowledge- or learning-based mechanisms in addition to motivational ones. With regard to the latter, the key issue is that job knowledge is not restricted to the role of a contingency or moderator as is often proposed (for example, Hackman & Oldham, 1980), but is also considered as a first-level outcome or mediating variable.

So far, we have considered each area of recommendation as if it were independent of the others and of equal importance. In fact, our view is that the issues of job content, contingency, and mechanism are closely interrelated, with the latter being the linchpin. Indeed, we consider the relationship between job control and job knowledge to be the single most important issue for future research and practice, because of its capacity to account for existing findings on job design and its potential both to integrate job design research with cognate areas and to identify new lines of inquiry. We elaborate on each of these points in turn.

The Relationship of Mechanism with Content and Contingency

The assumption that the mechanism of job design involves the use and development of job knowledge is consistent with research to date. From this perspective, it is apparent that many of the job characteristics of traditional interest within job design are essentially those necessary for learning. As we have already argued, autonomy represents a key factor for facilitating learning; active involvement in the control of a system is usually necessary to fully understand how it operates (compare Frese & Zapf, 1993). However, the other job characteristics typically identified are also salient. Feedback, for example, is essential if individuals are to learn from experience. Task identity is similarly relevant because it represents a grouping of interrelated tasks whose relationship one to the other will be obscured if they are split into separate jobs.

Together task identity and job control increase task variety, and task significance defines the conditions under which it is worthwhile to advance understanding. The argument can be extended to the additional job variables we have proposed for inclusion in job design research. Problem-solving demand, for instance, clearly represents the conditions necessary for the development of knowledge because there is little requirement for greater understanding where such demand is low.

The choice of production uncertainty as a contingency variable can similarly be interpreted as a logical consequence of a knowledge-based mechanism. Uncertainty can be defined as a lack of knowledge about cause and effect, or action and outcome, within a system (Jackson, 1989). Where such uncertainty is high, knowledge is incomplete, problem-solving demand is high, and thus there is much scope for learning. Under these conditions, designing jobs to promote learning will be both possible and most likely to contribute to effectiveness. Conversely, where there is little uncertainty, the knowledge requirements of a job are low, there is little problem-solving demand, and there is less scope for learning. In other words, production uncertainty is important as a contingency because it defines the conditions under which knowledge development and application can occur and affect performance.

Thus, approaching job design as an opportunity structure for the development and application of job knowledge provides a rationale for the choice of job content and contingency factors that characterize job design research. The key features of the traditional approach to job design and that proposed here are summarized in Table 4.1.

The Knowledge-Based Mechanism and the Link to Cognate Areas

Looking more widely, the assumption of a knowledge-based mechanism offers the prospect of greater integration with cognate areas. Nowhere is this more evident than in relation to job stress.

Many of the variables central to job design have parallels to those within job stress research. For example, early work focused on the direct effects of (low) control, uncertainty, and problem-solving and responsibility demands on strain (for example, Jackson, 1989; Kahn, Wolfe, Quinn, Snoek, & Rosenthal, 1964; Rizzo,

**Table 4.1. The Main Features of Traditional Approaches
to Job Design and Proposed Additions.**

	Traditional job design	Proposed addition
Job content	Autonomy/control, with skill variety, task identity, task significance, and feedback	Cognitive demand, cost responsibility, and interdependence
Contingency	Individual differences— growth need strength	Organizational factors— production uncertainty
Mechanism	Motivation	Knowledge application and development

House, & Lirtzman, 1970; Warr, 1987). Especially relevant to our present concerns, however, is the more recent line of inquiry, which suggests that strain occurs only under conditions that combine high demands with low control, resulting in increased anxiety, somatic complaints, and other symptoms. By contrast, conditions in which high demands are associated with greater control do not have these effects on employee well-being. Originally proposed by Karasek (1979), the framework developed from these observations is now known as the *demand-control model* (Karasek & Theorell, 1990).

Empirical support for the demand-control model is as yet less than conclusive, perhaps because research is beset by definitional and methodological difficulties (Kasl, 1989). The aspect we wish to focus on, however, is the underlying rationale, which has ensured continuing interest in the model. This rationale involves essentially the same mechanism that we have suggested for job design. Karasek and Theorell (1990) proposed an "active learning hypothesis" (p. 91) that "learning occurs in situations that require psychological energy expenditure (demands and challenges) and the exercise of decision-making capability" (that is, job control) (p. 92). Learning in turn is expected to affect strain through several avenues. The potential of the demands to cause strain is mitigated by learning, which prepares the individual to predict the occurrence of these demands better and to choose ways of avoiding or actively coping with them. At the same time, greater competence in dealing with presenting problems makes those demands less acute; the acquisition of job knowledge increases competence and feelings of mastery, which make the individual more resistant to those aversive demands that remain.

Thus, job design and job stress research are potentially linked not only because they share the same independent variables but, in a more fundamental way, by the assumption of a common mechanism focused on the relationship of control to the application and acquisition of job knowledge. More generally, this ties both areas to developments in other domains concerned with the psychological significance of personal control, self-efficacy, self-regulation, and personality development (Bandura, 1977; Greenberger, Strasser, Cummings, & Dunham, 1989; Sutton & Kahn, 1986; Tetrick & LaRocco, 1987; Walton & Wood, 1992; Wood & Bandura, 1989).

Ironically, given our emphasis on a learning perspective as an alternative to a motivational one, the same theme has emerged in relation to motivation itself. Both Peters and O'Connor (1980) and Blumberg and Pringle (1982) have argued that more attention needs to be paid to the notion of opportunity in addition to the customary focus on ability (capacity) and motivation (willingness) in accounting for performance at work. Among the opportunity factors they consider to be important is job design, which they see as affecting not only the willingness but also the ability of individuals to work effectively.

There is thus support from a wide variety of sources for the value of examining the role of job knowledge as a mechanism linking job content to outcomes. Nevertheless, the role of job knowledge remains a subject of discussion rather than of empirical investigation within these other literatures, just as it does in job design research. It is time for that nettle to be grasped.

Implications for Research

A focus on the role of job knowledge within job design has major implications for research, and an initial issue of great importance concerns the nature and measurement of job knowledge itself. This chapter follows the rest of the literature insofar as our discussion has remained at a very general level, and there is little clear specification of the types and levels of knowledge that should be examined. There are many leads, however, within cognitive psychology and related areas that can be exploited (for example, Anderson, 1987; Dorner, 1990; Moray, 1990; Rasmussen, 1987; Rogers, Rutherford, & Bibby, 1992). Many different emphases are evident, ranging from a focus on factual, context-specific knowledge through procedural knowledge to more complex suggestions of strategies or mental models. The question of how best to characterize and measure job knowledge is a difficult and challenging one which will need to be seriously addressed.

A complicating factor is the probability that some aspects of job knowledge are implicit. That is, individuals develop and use knowledge they are unable to verbalize and of which they may even be unaware. Labor-process perspectives on the nature of job skill have touched on this possibility (for example, Cavestro, 1989; Kusterer, 1978; Leplat, 1990). Laboratory studies on human control of complex systems have similarly brought this issue to the surface (for example, Berry & Broadbent, 1986; Broadbent, Fitzgerald, & Broadbent, 1986). They show that individuals can learn to induce the rules of system behavior at a level that enables them to predict and improve system performance, even though they are not necessarily able to make explicit the knowledge that they have gained. An interesting corollary that mirrors the argument we have put forward with respect to job design is that the development of such "implicit knowledge" appears to depend on active involvement in system control (Berry, 1991; Chmiel & Wall, 1995). To the extent that implicit knowledge underlies job behavior, measurement will require detailed observation of that behavior. Self-report verbal methods will not be adequate on their own.

The above considerations in turn have implications for the type of research methods that are required. To the extent that job knowledge is context related and implicit, large-scale cross-sectional investigations will be of limited value. Instead, emphasis needs to be placed on more detailed longitudinal investigations in specific situations or problem domains if researchers are to capture the dynamics of individuals' transactions with their work. As learning is the development of knowledge over time, it must be studied with research methods able to map such knowledge over time (compare the analysis of requirements for job stress research in Latack and Havlovic, 1992).

Final Comment

We believe that a key to understanding the psychological and behavioral impact of job design lies in focusing on how job control affects the development and use of job knowledge. We also acknowledge the many challenges researchers face in pursuing such a study. Addressing these challenges will require much greater integration of ideas and methods between job design, organizational, and cognitive research than has been evident to this point. Despite these difficulties, it appears to be a path well worth following. The emphasis on job knowledge clearly reflects the core job design issue emerging from experience of the new manufacturing initiatives. Ultimately, it seems likely that the problems of definition, measurement, and method that will arise will be more tractable than those associated with a continued emphasis solely on motivational processes.

References

Adler, P. S., & Borys, B. (1989). Automation and skill: Three generations of research on the NC case. *Policies and Society, 17*, 377–402.

Anderson, J. R. (1987). Skill acquisition: Compilation of weak-method problem solutions. *Psychological Review, 94*, 192–210.

Bandura, A. (1977). Self efficacy: Towards a unifying theory of behavioral change. *Psychological Bulletin, 84*, 191–215.

Berry, D. (1991). The role of action in implicit learning. *Quarterly Journal of Experimental Psychology, 36*, 209–231.

Berry, D., & Broadbent, D. E. (1986). Interactive tasks and the implicit-explicit distinction. *British Journal of Psychology, 79*, 86–94.

Bessant, J., & Lamming, R. (1989). Design for efficient manufacture. In R. Wild (Ed.), *International handbook of production and operations management.* London: Cassell.

Blumberg, M., & Pringle, C. (1982). The missing opportunity in organizational research: Some implications for a theory of work performance. *Academy of Management Review, 7*, 360–369.

Booth, J. (1987). JIT at Beavers: A case study. *Proceedings of the 4th European Conference on Automated Manufacturing,* 87–108.

Brass, D. J. (1985). Technology and the structuring of jobs: Employee satisfaction, performance and influence. *Organizational Behavior and Human Decision Processes, 35*, 216–240.

Braverman, H. (1974). *Labor and monopoly capital.* New York: Basic Books.

Broadbent, D. E., Fitzgerald, P., & Broadbent, M. (1986). Implicit and explicit knowledge in the control of complex systems. *British Journal of Psychology, 77*, 33–50.

Buchanan, D. A. (1989). High performance: New boundaries of acceptability in worker control. In S. L. Sauter, J. J. Hurrell, & C. L. Cooper (Eds.), *Job control and worker health*. Chichester, England: Wiley.

Buchanan, D. A., & McCalman, J. (1989). *High performance work systems: The Digital experience*. London: Routledge.

Burns, T., & Stalker, G. M. (1961). *The management of innovation*. London: Tavistock.

Campion, M. A., & McClelland, C. L. (1993). Follow-up and extension of the interdisciplinary costs and benefits of enlarged jobs. *Journal of Applied Psychology, 78,* 339–351.

Caulkin, S. (1993, May 8). British firms resurrected by courtesy of Japan. *The Guardian,* p. 24.

Cavestro, W. (1989). Automation, new technology and work content. In S. Wood (Ed.), *The transformation of work?* London: Unwin Hyman.

Cherns, A. (1976). The principles of socio-technical systems design. *Human Relations, 29,* 783–792.

Chmiel, N., & Wall, T. D. (1995). Fault prevention, job design and the adaptive control of advanced manufacturing technology. *Applied Psychology, 43,* 455–473.

Clegg, C. W. (1984). The derivation of job designs. *Journal of Occupational Behaviour, 5,* 131–146.

Cobb, S., & Rose, R. (1963). Hypertension, peptic ulcer and diabetes in air traffic controllers. *Journal of the American Medical Association, 224,* 489–492.

Corbett, J. M. (1987). A psychological study of advanced manufacturing technology: The concept of coupling. *Behavior and Information Technology, 6,* 441–453.

Corbett, J. M., Martin, R., Wall, T. D., & Clegg, C. W. (1989). Technological coupling as a predictor of intrinsic job satisfaction: A replication study. *Journal of Organizational Behavior, 10,* 91–95.

Cox, T. (1985). Repetitive work: Occupational stress and health. In C. L. Cooper & M. J. Smith (Eds.), *Job stress and blue collar work*. Chichester, England: Wiley.

Crosby, P. B. (1979). *Quality is free*. New York: McGraw-Hill.

Cummings, T. (1978). Self-regulating work groups: A socio-technical synthesis. *Academy of Management Review, 3,* 625–634.

Cummings, T., & Blumberg, M. (1987). Advanced manufacturing technology and work design. In T. D. Wall, C. W. Clegg, & N. J. Kemp (Eds.), *The human side of advanced manufacturing technology*. Chichester, England: Wiley.

Dean, J. W., & Snell, S. A. (1991). Integrated manufacturing and job design: Moderating effects of organizational inertia. *Academy of Management Journal, 34,* 776–804.

Delbridge, R., & Turnbull, P. (1992). Human resource maximisation: The management of labor under just-in-time manufacturing systems. In P. Blyton & P. Turnbull (Eds.), *Reassessing human resource management.* London: Sage.

Deming, W. E. (1986). *Out of the crisis.* Cambridge, MA: MIT Center for Advanced Engineering Study.

Denison, D. R. (1982). Sociotechnical design and self-managing work groups: The impact of control. *Journal of Occupational Behaviour, 3,* 297–314.

Dorner, D. (1990). On the difficulties people have in dealing with complexity. In J. Rasmussen, K. D. Duncan, & J. Leplat (Eds.), *New technology and human error.* Chichester, England: Wiley.

Edquist, C., & Jacobsson, S. (1988). *Flexible automation: The global diffusion of new technology in the engineering industry.* Cambridge, MA: Blackwell.

Emery, F. E., & Trist, E. L. (1965). The causal texture of organisation environments. *Human Relations, 18,* 21–32.

Frese, M., & Zapf, D. (1993). Action as the core of work psychology: A German approach. In M. D. Dunnette, L. M. Hough, & H. C. Triandis (Eds.), *Handbook of industrial and organizational psychology* (2nd ed., Vol. 4). Palo Alto, CA: Consulting Psychologists Press.

Galbraith, J. (1977). *Organization design.* Reading, MA: Addison-Wesley.

Greenberger, D. B., Strasser, S., Cummings, L. L., & Dunham, R. B. (1989). The impact of personal control on performance and satisfaction. *Organizational Behavior and Human Decision Processes, 43,* 29–51.

Gryna, F. M. (1988a). Product development. In J. M. Juran & F. M. Gryna (Eds.), *Juran's quality control handbook* (4th ed.). New York: McGraw-Hill.

Gryna, F. M. (1988b). Production. In J. M. Juran & F. M. Gryna (Eds.), *Juran's quality control handbook* (4th ed.). New York: McGraw-Hill.

Gulowsen, J. (1972). A measure of work group autonomy. In L. E. Davis & J. C. Taylor (Eds.), *Design of jobs.* Harmondsworth, England: Penguin.

Gunn, T. G. (1987). *Manufacturing for competitive advantage: Becoming a world-class manufacturer.* Cambridge, MA: Ballinger.

Hacker, W. (1985). Activity: A fruitful concept in industrial psychology. In M. Frese & J. Sabini (Eds.), *Goal directed behavior: The concept of action in psychology.* Hillsdale, NJ: Erlbaum.

Hacker, W. (1986). Complete v. incomplete working tasks: A concept and its verification. In G. Debus & H. W. Schroiff (Eds.), *The psychology of work and organization.* Amsterdam: Elsevier North-Holland.

Hacker, W. (1987). Computerization versus computer-aided mental work. In M. Frese, E. Ulich, & W. Dzida (Eds.), *Psychological issues of human-computer interaction in the work place.* Amsterdam: Elsevier North-Holland.

Hackman, J. R. (1977). Work redesign. In J. R. Hackman, & J. L. Suttle (Eds.), *Improving life at work.* Santa Monica, CA: Goodyear.

Hackman, J. R., & Oldham, G. R. (1976). Motivation through the design of work: Test of a theory. *Organizational Behavior and Human Performance, 15,* 250–279.

Hackman, J. R., & Oldham, G. R. (1980). *Work redesign.* Reading, MA: Addison-Wesley.

Harrington, H. J. (1987). *The improvement process: How America's leading companies improve quality.* New York: McGraw-Hill.

Hayes, R. H., Wheelwright, S. C., & Clark, K. B. (1988). *Dynamic manufacturing: Creating the learning organization.* New York: Macmillan.

Herzberg, F. (1966). *Work and the nature of man.* New York: Harper.

Hohn, W. (1988). What is qualification? Lifestyle and personality as selection criteria. In P. Windholf & S. Wood (Eds.), *Recruitment and selection in the labor market.* Aldershot, England: Avebury.

Hutchins, D. (1988). *Just in time.* Aldershot, England: Gower Technical Press.

Iaffaldino, M. T., & Muchinsky, P. M. (1985). Job satisfaction and job performance: A meta-analysis. *Psychological Bulletin, 97,* 251–273.

Imai, M. (1986). *Kaizen: The key to Japan's competitive success.* New York: McGraw-Hill.

Jackson, P. R., & Martin, R. (1993). *The impact of just-in-time on job content, employee attitudes and well-being: A longitudinal study* (Memo 1340). Sheffield, England: University of Sheffield, MRC/ESRC Social and Applied Psychology Unit.

Jackson, P. R., & Wall, T. D. (1991). How does operator control enhance performance of advanced manufacturing technology? *Ergonomics, 34,* 1301–1311.

Jackson, S. E. (1989). Does job control control job stress? In S. L. Sauter, J. J. Hurrell, Jr., & C. L. Cooper (Eds.), *Job control and worker health.* Chichester, England: Wiley.

Jessop, B., Bonnet, K., Bromley, S., & Ling, T. (1988). Popular capitalism, flexible automation and left strategy. *New Left Review, 165,* 104–124.

Johns, G. (1993). Constraints on the adoption of psychology-based personnel practices: Lessons from organizational innovation. *Personnel Psychology, 46*(3), 569–592.

Juran, J. M., & Gryna, F. M. (Eds.). (1988). *Juran's quality control handbook* (4th ed.). New York: McGraw-Hill.

Kahn, R. L., Wolfe, D., Quinn, R., Snoek, J., & Rosenthal, R. (1964). *Organizational stress: Studies in role conflict and ambiguity.* New York: Wiley.

Karasek, R. (1979). Job demands, job decision latitude and mental strain. *Administrative Science Quarterly, 24,* 285–308.

Karasek, R., & Theorell, T. (1990). *Healthy work: Stress, productivity and the reconstruction of working life.* New York: Basic Books.

Kasl, S. V. (1989). An epidemiological perspective on the role of control in health. In S. L. Sauter, J. J. Hurrell, Jr., & C. L. Cooper (Eds.), *Job control and worker health*. Chichester, England: Wiley.

Kelly, J. (1992). Does job re-design theory explain job re-design outcomes? *Human Relations, 45,* 753–774.

Kiggundu, M. N. (1981). Task interdependence and the theory of job design. *Academy of Management Review, 6,* 499–508.

Klein, J. A. (1989, March–April). The human costs of manufacturing reform. *Harvard Business Review,* pp. 60–66.

Klein, J. A. (1991). A reexamination of autonomy in light of new manufacturing practices. *Human Relations, 44,* 21–38.

Kusterer, K. (1978). *Know-how on the job: The important working knowledge of the unskilled workers*. Boulder, CO: Westview Press.

Latack, J.C., & Havlovic, S. J. (1992). Coping with job stress: A conceptual evaluation framework for coping measures. *Journal of Organizational Behavior, 13,* 479–505.

Lawler, E. E., III. (1992). *The ultimate advantage: Creating the high involvement organization*. San Francisco: Jossey-Bass.

Lawrence, P., & Lorsch, J. (1969). *Organization and environment*. Homewood, IL: Irwin.

Leplat, J. (1990). Skills and tacit skills. *Applied Psychology: An International Review, 39,* 143–154.

Locke, E., & Henne, D. (1986). Work motivation theories. In C. L. Cooper & I. T. Robertson (Eds.), *International review of industrial and organizational psychology* (Vol. 1). Chichester, England: Wiley.

Lord, R. G., & Maher, K. J. (1991). Cognitive theory in industrial and organizational psychology. In M. D. Dunnette & L. M. Hough (Eds.), *Handbook of industrial and organizational psychology,* (2nd ed., Vol. 2). Palo Alto, CA: Consulting Psychologists Press.

Majchrzak, A. (1988). *The human side of factory automation*. San Francisco: Jossey-Bass.

Martin, R., & Wall, T. D. (1989). Attentional demand and cost responsibility as stressors in shopfloor jobs. *Academy of Management Journal, 32,* 69–84.

Mintzberg, H. (1979). *The structuring of organizations*. Englewood Cliffs, NJ: Prentice Hall.

Monden, Y. (1983). *Toyota production system*. Atlanta: Industrial Engineering and Management Press.

Moray, N. (1990). A lattice theory approach to the structure of mental models. *Philosophical Transactions of the Royal Society, 327,* 577–583.

Mortimer, J. (1985). *Integrated manufacture*. Berlin: IFS/Springer-Verlag.

Oakland, J. S. (1989). *Total quality management*. Oxford: Heinemann.

Okumura, A. (1989). The globalization of Japanese companies. In K.

Shibagaki, M.Trevor, & T. Abo (Eds.), *Japanese and European management: Their international adaptability*. Tokyo: Tokyo University Press.

Oliver, N., & Wilkinson, B. (1992). *The Japanization of British industry: New developments in the 1990s*. Oxford: Blackwell.

Parker, S. K. (1993). *An alternative performance-based approach to job design research*. Unpublished doctoral dissertation, University of Sheffield, England.

Parker, S. K., Jackson, P. R., & Wall, T. D. (1993, July). Autonomous group working within integrated manufacturing: A longitudinal investigation of employee role orientations. *Proceedings of HCI Conference*.

Perrow, C. (1967). A framework for the comparative analysis of organizations. *American Sociological Review, 32*, 194–208.

Perrow, C. (1983). The organizational context of human factors engineering. *Administrative Science Quarterly, 28*, 521–541.

Peters, L., & O'Connor, E. (1980). Situational constraints and work outcomes: The influences of an often overlooked construct. *Academy of Management Review, 5*, 391–397.

Peters, T. J., & Waterman, R. H. (1982). *In search of excellence: Lessons from America's best-run companies*. New York: Harper.

Pugh, D. S. (1973, Spring). The measurement of organizational structures: Does context determine form? *Organizational Dynamics*, pp. 19–34.

Ramsey, H. (1991). Reinventing the wheel? A review of the development and performance of employee involvement. *Human Resource Management Journal, 1*, 1–22.

Rasmussen, J. (1986). *Information processing and human-machine interaction: An approach to cognitive engineering*. New York: Elsevier North-Holland.

Rasmussen, J. (1987). Cognitive control and human error mechanisms. In J. Rasmussen, K. Duncan, & J. Leplat (Eds.), *New technology and human error*. Chichester, England: Wiley.

Rizzo, J., House, R., & Lirtzman, S. (1970). Role conflict and ambiguity in complex organizations. *Administrative Science Quarterly, 15*, 150–163.

Roberts, K. H., & Glick, W. (1981). The job characteristics approach to job design: A critical review. *Journal of Applied Psychology, 66*, 193–217.

Rogers, Y., Rutherford, A., & Bibby, J. (1992). *Models in the mind: Theory, perspective and application*. London: Academic Press.

Rousseau, D. M. (1977). Technological differences in job characteristics, employee satisfaction and motivation: A synthesis of job design research and socio-technical systems theory. *Organizational Behavior and Human Performance, 19*, 18–42.

Schonberger, R. J. (1986). *World class manufacturing: The lessons of simplicity applied*. New York: Free Press.

Schonberger, R. J. (1987). *World class manufacturing casebook*. New York: Free Press.

Sewell, G., & Wilkinson, B. (1992). Empowerment or emasculation? Shopfloor surveillance in a total quality organisation. In P. Blyton & P. Turnbull (Eds.), *Reassessing human resource management*. London: Sage.

Sharit, J., Chang, T. C., & Salvendy, G. (1987). Technical and human aspects of computer-aided manufacturing. In G. Salvendy (Ed.), *Handbook of human factors*. New York: Wiley.

Shulman, H., & Olex, M. (1985). Designing the user-friendly robot: A case history. *Human Factors, 27*, 91–98.

Sinclair, M. (1986). Ergonomic aspects of the automated factory. *Ergonomics, 29*, 1507–1523.

Slocum, J. W., & Sims, H. P. (1980). A typology for integrating technology, organization and job design. *Human Relations, 33*, 193–212.

Smith, M. J. (1981). Occupational stress: An overview of psychosocial factors. In G. Salvendy & M. J. Smith (Eds.), *Machine pacing and occupational stress*. London: Taylor & Francis.

Susman, G. (1976). *Autonomy at work*. New York: Praeger.

Susman, G., & Chase, R. (1986). A sociotechnical systems analysis of the integrated factory. *Journal of Applied Behavioral Science, 22*, 257–270.

Sutton, R. I., & Kahn, R. L. (1986). Prediction, understanding and control as antidotes to organizational stress. In J. Lorsch (Ed.), *Handbook of organizational behavior*. Englewood Cliffs, NJ: Prentice Hall.

Tailby, S., & Turnbull, P. J. (1987, January). Learning to manage just-in-time. *Personnel Management*, pp. 16–19.

Tetrick, L. E., & LaRocco, J. M. (1987). Understanding, prediction and control as moderators of the relationships between perceived stress, satisfaction and psychological well-being. *Journal of Applied Psychology, 72*, 538–543.

Thompson, J. (1967). *Organisations in action*. New York: McGraw-Hill.

Trist, E. L., & Bamforth, K. W. (1951). Some social and psychological consequences of the long-wall method of coal getting. *Human Relations, 4*, 3–38.

Trist, E. L., Higgins, G., Murray, H., & Pollack, A. (1963). *Organizational choice*. London: Tavistock.

Turnbull, P. J. (1988). The limits to 'Japanisation'—just-in-time, labor relations and the UK automotive industry. *New Technology, Employment and Society, 3*, 7–20.

Turner, A. N., & Lawrence, P. R. (1965). *Individual jobs and the worker*. Cambridge, MA: Harvard University Press.

Van Cott, H. P. (1985). High technology and human needs. *Ergonomics, 28*, 1135–1142.

Voss, C. A., & Robinson, S. J. (1987). Application of just-in-time manufacturing techniques in the United Kingdom. *International Journal of Operations and Production Management, 7*, 46–52.

Wall, T. D., Corbett, J. M., Martin, R., Clegg, C. W., & Jackson, P. R. (1990). Advanced manufacturing technology, work design and performance: A change study. *Journal of Applied Psychology*, *75*, 691–697.

Wall, T. D., & Davids, K. (1992). Shopfloor work organisation and advanced manufacturing technology. In C. L. Cooper & I. T. Robertson (Eds.), *International review of industrial and organizational psychology* (Vol. 7). Chichester, England: Wiley.

Wall, T. D., Jackson, P. R., & Davids, K. (1992). Operator work design and robotics system performance: A serendipitous field study. *Journal of Applied Psychology*, *77*, 353–362.

Wall, T. D., & Kemp, N. J. (1987). The nature and implications of advanced manufacturing technology. In T. D. Wall, C. W. Clegg, & N. J. Kemp (Eds.), *The human side of advanced manufacturing technology*. Chichester, England: Wiley.

Wall, T. D., & Martin, R. (1987). Job and work design. In C. L. Cooper & I. T. Robertson (Eds.), *International review of industrial and organizational psychology* (Vol. 2). Chichester, England: Wiley.

Walton, E. J., & Wood, R. E. (1992). Self-regulation in organizational psychology. *Applied Psychology: An International Review*, *41*, 154–159.

Walton, R. E., & Susman, G. T. (1987, March–April). People policies for the new machines. *Harvard Business Review*, pp. 98–106.

Warr, P. B. (1987). *Work, unemployment and mental health*. Oxford: Oxford University Press.

Weiss, H. M. (1990). Learning theory and industrial and organizational psychology. In M. D. Dunnette & L. M. Hough (Eds.), *Handbook of industrial and organizational psychology* (2nd ed., Vol. 1). Palo Alto, CA: Consulting Psychologists Press.

Wood, R. E., & Bandura, A. (1989). Impact of conceptions of ability on self-regulatory mechanisms and complex decision-making. *Journal of Personality and Social Psychology*, *56*, 407–415.

Wood, S. (1989). The transformation of work? In S. Wood (Ed.), *The transformation of work?* London: Unwin Hyman.

Wood, S. (1990). Tacit skills, the Japanese management model and new technology. *Applied Psychology: An International Review*, *39*, 169–190.

Young, S. (1987). Achieving a material advantage: A JIT case study at ICL Letchworth. *Proceedings of the 4th European conference of automated manufacturing*, 51–59.

Zicklin, G. (1987). Numerical control machining and the issue of deskilling: An empirical view. *Work and Occupations*, *14*, 452–466.

Chapter Five

Technological Changes in Office Jobs

What We Know and What We Can Expect

Michael D. Coovert

Professional and clerical jobs are being changed, sometimes dramatically, by the introduction of new technologies in the workplace. Moreover, this change in the nature of work is proceeding at an ever-increasing rate. The technologies that are having the greatest impact on changing office jobs include software advances for personal computers and workstations, networking systems for intra- and interorganizational connectivity, practical knowledge-based systems emerging from artificial intelligence and artificial neural nets, videodisc and virtual reality systems, computer-supported cooperative work systems (groupware), and augmented realities.

This chapter describes changes in the nature of office work by addressing three major topics: (1) what we know about technology's impact on office work, (2) the emerging areas of computer-supported cooperative work and augmented realities, and (3) implications for human resources management. Two major themes emerge from the work described in the chapter. Technology in the office of the future will be most useful where it allows individual workers to utilize existing knowledge, skills, and abilities or augments those attributes. But in order to contribute fully to management of the changing nature of office work, psychologists will need to develop and test richer models of the nomological relations between workers, technology, and the organization.

Computational Infrastructure

Transformation of the very infrastructure of organizations is producing a fundamental change in jobs. Organizations are moving away from traditional communication and interaction channels, and are developing computational infrastructures to enhance coordination and increase competitiveness. A computational infrastructure links all individuals and jobs in the organization through computer networks and data bases. This connection allows immediate access to computing resources from a person's desk and facilitates the seamless coordination of individuals in work groups.

A second major change at the job level relates to the allocation of work activities. Information technologies have the potential to change all aspects of the typical work flow: how inputs come to the job, what happens after the worker receives the "raw material," and who receives the worker's outputs. Technologies therefore can force a complete reengineering of an office job, and a shift in the knowledge, skills, and abilities of office workers.

Expanded Definitions of Office and Office Worker

During the 1970s and 1980s the popular press paid a fair amount of attention to telecommuting—that is, individuals performing work for an organization from their home. Although telecommuting has steadily increased, for the majority of the workforce the home is not the office of the future. This may change, of course, if the much-touted information highway becomes a reality.

In addition to telecommuting, there are other modifications to the traditional definition of office and office worker. Work in certain industries is becoming increasingly mobile and electronic, often as a response to increased organizational competition. For example, corporations such as Ryder System, UPS, and M.S. Carriers are dramatically changing the job scope and responsibilities for individuals who formerly only drove a truck. These drivers are now being asked to take on tasks once thought well beyond their capabilities, and to take on those tasks not from a traditional office, but from an eighteen-wheeler loaded with a computer, fax machine, and satellite dish (Grossman, 1993). Jobs have been enlarged in scope, and the truck drivers are also trained to be salespersons and problem solvers. A truck driver for Ryder who delivers, and now sets up, Xerox copiers must be as well versed with Xerox document feeders as with the fuel and hydraulic lift system on the truck (Grossman, 1993). This increase in job responsibilities would not be possible without advanced technologies allowing for real-time connections with the company.

Another example of the change in the traditional definition of office and office worker is the delivery and pickup system employed by U.S. Express Inc. After truck drivers make a delivery, they notify the company by entering a command into a laptop computer that transmits an encoded message from the satellite dish affixed to the truck cab. The company, relying on the Global Positioning System, fixes the exact location of the truck and matches it against a list of pickup requests in order to route the driver to the closest destination.

Many manufacturing jobs are also being modified to resemble professional and clerical jobs. Just because a job is physically located in a factory setting does not mean it should be automatically classified as manufacturing, as opposed to an office or technical job.

What We Know

With these transformations of office work as a background, we can examine what we know about changes in professional and clerical jobs. We begin by considering a series of general issues and then explore user interfaces.

Impact of Technology on Office Work

A common theme of the several topics covered in this section is the individual's perception of control. The more technology allows an individual to retain control over the job, the more likely the worker will be to accept the technology, and the greater will be its success in aiding worker performance.

Deskilling

The earliest debate about the impact of technologies on work focused on widespread simplification of jobs and deskilling of the workforce. Those currently advocating the deskilling argument purport that today's jobs will suffer the same fate as those during the industrial revolution: jobs will become boring, mindless, and fatiguing. In addition, proponents argue that technology will negatively influence all jobs, including not just traditional blue-collar occupations (Vallas & Yarrow, 1987), but managerial, professional, and technical work as well (Perrolle, 1986).

A few recent studies have investigated the deskilling issue. For example, Gattiker and Howg (1990) examined the attitudes of both computer users and nonusers regarding the impact of technology. Although the groups differed regarding communication, job complexity, and feedback, upon closer investigation the differences were a function of other variables (salary, age, and educational levels) within each group. Yaverbaum and Culpan (1990), who studied changes over time in individual motivation and satisfaction scores on the Job Diagnostic Survey, found differences related to job type and educational level. Individuals in mundane jobs viewed the technology as more enriching than did individuals in more challenging positions.

So the deskilling debate continues. Proponents argue that deskilling can and will occur, whereas research suggests that although it might occur (in jobs that are *already* viewed as enriched), there is also an extensive set of background variables that moderate the relationship between technology and perceptions of deskilling.

Vallas and Yarrow (1987) maintained that the outcome of technological change (enriching versus deskilling) should be viewed as a process that can be controlled through the management of the change. Management should pay special attention to their relations with workers as well as to existing relationships among workers, to ensure the technology is implemented in a positive fashion.

Control and Work

Deskilling could be defined as the loss of control over the job, or aspects of the job, by the worker. Research suggests that individuals who retain some degree of control (for example, over what gets done, in what order) report higher degrees of satisfaction and less mental stress and strain. McInerney (1989) proposed that five control issues need to be addressed in examining the effects of technological change: (1) an individual's control over others, (2) an individual's control by others, (3) an individual's control over work, (4) planning and the uses of information, and (5) access to information and people within the organization. Although not reviewed here, literature from a variety of sources supports these five control factors.

The notion of discretion and control may, however, be moderated by individual differences. For example, Coovert (1980) demonstrated that locus of control can be used to predict naive users' attitudes toward computers. Internals are more likely to view the computer as a tool to be used in the accomplishment of their work, whereas externals view it as another controlling force in their lives. More recently, Nelson and Kletke (1990) confirmed this finding and argued for locus of control and attitude as moderators during technological innovation.

Gender is another possible moderator of the technology-control relationship. Hackett, Mirvis, and Sales (1991) found that, in general, women were more pessimistic than men toward the effect of an innovation on their working conditions (for example, job security, rewards). These gender differences persisted when education, seniority, age, and other relevant characteristics of the jobs were controlled.

Finally, culture may have an impact. Gattiker and Nelligan (1988), in a study of U.S. and Canadian workers, found intercultural differences relative to the type of computer used, gender, and level in the organization's hierarchy. Issues of concern to U.S. female workers about computer-mediated work did not necessarily apply to their Canadian counterparts.

So the deskilling effect is likely tied to perceptions of control on the job, and the relationship is moderated by various individual difference variables. When a job is being modified by technology, psychologists and managers of job change should focus on maintaining an individual's sense of control over the work. Unfortunately, this is not a simple task, given that we need to be concerned about five different types of control and about individual differences in acceptance of technology.

Health Issues

Health-related issues have concerned workers since the early days of computer systems. The initial concern was over emissions from video display terminals (VDTs). There is a huge body of literature on this topic, but the general finding is that there is no danger from emissions with correctly shielded equipment. Symptoms such as blurry eyes and backaches, initially blamed on VDT usage, were found to be associated with other components in the work environment. An ergonomically designed work environment (including chair, lighting, vision corrected for distance from the monitor) can alleviate real pressures and strains on the human body as well as somatic complaints.

More recently health concerns have focused on repetitive strain injury and carpal tunnel syndrome, which often occur in jobs that require only a limited range of motion. Long-term users of keyboards are especially vulnerable and need to take appropriate precautions to prevent injuries. Effective preventives include frequent breaks from the repetitive motion, a wrist rest, specially designed wrist supports, and exercises.

Some researchers are broadening the scope of variables studied in order to glean a more complete picture of the possible effect of these technologies on the health of individuals. For example, Kahn and Cooper (1991) found that the health of individuals who used the computer throughout the day for trading currency, bonds, and so forth was related to poor mental health, job dissatisfaction, and alcohol intake. Multivariate analyses revealed that a technology factor was not related to poor mental health, job dissatisfaction, or alcohol intake, but it was related to free-floating anxiety. Stress attributed to the computer, however, was negligible.

A second study examined the antecedents and consequences of emotional exhaustion among airline reservation workers (Saxton, Phillips, & Blakeney, 1991). Using covariance structure modeling, these authors demonstrated that in an environment of tight managerial control and little decision-making latitude, variables such as age, job tenure, job satisfaction, and job-related tensions were related to reports of exhaustion. Exhaustion was in turn significantly related to absenteeism, intentions to leave, and actual job change. This finding is important because it marks the first time that the nature of the relationship between these variables and their impact on the health of workers has been confirmed.

Finally, Linstrom (1991) found that nonspecific somatic complaints by workers in the banking and insurance industries were related to problems associated with the fragmentation of work brought on by computerization. Women reported more subjective symptoms than men. These findings should, however, be tempered by the fact that women in the sample outnumbered men by three to one.

The impact of technologies on the health of professional and clerical workers will continue to be of interest. Health workers must strive to develop effective measures to ward off the effects of such physiological injuries as repetitive strain injury and carpal tunnel syndrome. Also, further work is needed to identify those characteristics of the technology, the job, and the environment that lead to somatic symptoms. Research covering additional variables, including possible moderators and mediators, will enrich our understanding of the impact of these technologies on the physiology and psyches of professional and clerical workers.

Toward Models of Technological Impact

Most research so far has focused on relatively simple relationships between technology and its impact on work and jobs. These simple independent and dependent variable designs are useful for gaining an understanding of the relationship between various pairs of variables. However, if we are to gauge the true impact of technology on work and jobs, we need to develop and test models that contain a rich set of the variables of interest and the relationships among them. These variables can be of various types, both exogenous and endogenous, and serve not only as moderators but perhaps also as mediators of the relationship between other variables. In addition, it is likely that variables in a technology-job outcome model will relate to each other in several ways: by having a direct influence, merely covarying, or operating independently.

Advances in covariance structure modeling allow us to develop and test such complex models. The models may contain latent variables representing work, individual, or organizational constructs with measured variables serving as indicators of those constructs. Relationships between variables can be directional (causal) and nondirectional (correlational or nonexistent). It is only through the construction of models of this type that we will ever be able to determine the nomological relationships between technology, work, and the individual and organizational variables important to changes in office jobs.

In one such modeling study Schneider (1989) investigated the relationship between job satisfaction and how a job is modified by a technology. *Role ambiguity* and *job scope* (defined by the scales of the revised *Job Diagnostic Survey,* Idaszak & Drasgow, 1987) were included as mediational constructs. Technology has the potential to impact three areas: the inputs to the job, how the worker transforms the inputs, and what the worker does with the outputs. These sources of change were each represented as exogenous latent variables in the model. On the basis of the literature, Schneider hypothesized that the three correlated types of uncertainty brought on by technology would each directly influence job scope and role ambiguity and only indirectly influence the correlated satisfaction latent variables, *satisfaction with work* and *general job satisfaction.* Job scope and role ambiguity were each expected to influence the two satisfaction latent variables directly. Figure 5.1 depicts this conceptual model.

Schneider (1989) sampled individuals in thirty-one different clerical and professional jobs in a large organization. The primary hypothesis, that the technology-satisfaction relationship was mediated by the intervening variables, was supported. Further research of this type is needed to establish additional directional influences of variables involved when technological change affects office workers.

The nature of changes in office work brought about by technology is complex. Only when we construct and test specific theoretical models of the nature and impact of these changes will we be able to fully understand and monitor the change process. The next section considers an area critical for the successful application of technology in the office, that is, the connection between the technology and the human made possible by computer interfaces.

Human-Technology Interfaces

The interface between the human and the computer is perhaps the most critical aspect in the usage of the system. There are at least a couple of reasons for this. First, the interface is the most visible aspect of the computer system, and to many users it *is* the computer, not just a linkage or connection to it. Second, for an individual to use the computer as a tool, the computer must have

Figure 5.1. A Conceptual Model of the Relationship Between Technological Uncertainty and Job Satisfaction.

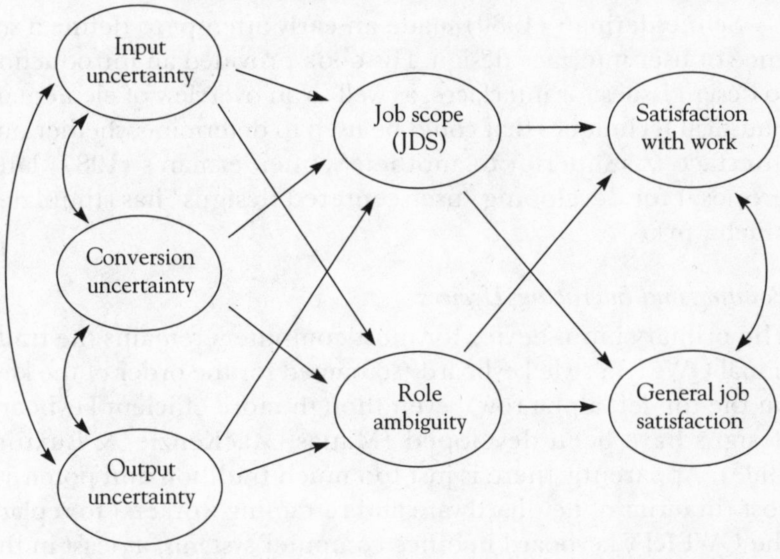

Source: Adapted from Schneider, 1989.

an effective interface. Just what makes an interface effective, however, is not always clear. But to the extent that it allows an individual to work with ease, utilizing existing skills and knowledge to accomplish the task at hand, the interface will be effective.

The early user interfaces were developed around anecdotal information, or designs that seemed to "make sense" to the software developers. But those interfaces reflected little other than the bias of the early scientists and engineers. It was a *broadening* of areas in organizations where the computer could have an impact that forced software developers to pay attention to the needs of the user.

The first major advance in user interface design was the Xerox Star, constructed in the early 1970s. The Star was targeted at a heterogeneous class of users—office workers with varying degrees of skills—and therefore the design team decided to simulate objects common in every office. They placed electronic forms of file cabinets, folders, waste baskets, and so forth onto an electronic desktop. The desktop metaphor served as the model for the Apple machines, which so successfully exploited the approach in their line of computers, as well as the modern graphical user interface (GUI) systems.

Schneiderman (1980) made an early attempt to define a science of user interface design. His book provided an introduction to design issues for interfaces, as well as an overview of elementary statistical techniques that could be used to determine whether one interface was superior to another. Schneiderman's (1987) later proposal for developing "user centered designs" has stimulated much work.

Pointing and Interacting Devices

The primary input device for most computers remains the traditional QWERTY-style keyboard (so named for the order of the keys on the top-left alpha row), even though more efficient keyboard designs have been developed (Matias, MacKenzie, & Buxton, 1993). Apparently there is just too much tradition and potential cost (in terms of new hardware and retraining workers) to replace the QWERTY keyboard in office computer systems, at least in the foreseeable future.

Other preferred input devices include the pen, mouse, touch screen, and stylus (Goldberg & Richardson, 1993). Voice input systems are becoming more popular in the office as the technology improves to make it feasible. Martin (1989) provided empirical evidence that speech input is in fact faster than typed and that it increases a user's productivity by providing an additional response channel. Although attractive for routine memos and correspondence, it is unlikely, due to privacy and security issues, that speech will be used for sensitive information (such as financial documents or performance appraisal forms).

The pointing and interacting devices that will be the most useful to professional and clerical workers are those that allow an individual to work in a natural fashion, exploiting existing knowledge and skills and augmenting those skills as required.

User Stereotypes

One approach to building an effective interface is to match it to the user's mental model of the task (Coovert, 1990). For example, an accounting package interface should look like a spreadsheet, albeit an electronic one, and users should be able to perform the same tasks in a manner similar to how they would perform them without the computer. LaLomia and Coovert (1992) presented some empirical support for varying numerical or graphical displays depending on the type of problem to be solved. For example, the interface should present information numerically for an identification problem, but graphically for a forecasting problem.

For a person with no knowledge of a substantive area, the interface should exploit knowledge structures that the individual should, or most probably does, have. Another way of saying this is that the interface can have embedded within it (Rivers, 1989) stereotypes of users, so that when an ambiguous command is issued, the system can refer to its active stereotype and respond in an appropriate manner.

To accomplish this type of interaction, we need to greatly expand the notion of a stereotype and to build representations of users that model various background variables (such as amount of work experience in this area), preferred interface (voice commands versus a pointing device), and preferred mode of learning new information (for example, working through an animated tutorial versus reading the new information). Ultimately this expansion could lead to very rich and elaborate stereotypes. Perhaps one way to deal with the complexity of the problem would be to develop and employ dual stereotypes: one with a broad class of expected behaviors (novice, intermediate, expert), and a second to represent each user of the system.

Extending the notion of a user stereotype, Pan and Tenenbaum (1991) argued for using intelligent agents to integrate people and computer systems. Intelligent agents model the reasoning, action, and communication skills involved in performing human job functions (see Riecken, 1994, for an overview). A cognitive task analysis is performed on an individual's tasks and activities, and intelligent agents are assigned to execute them. Humans then communicate with intelligent assistants, which in turn interact with other intelligent assistants and humans in a shared knowledge base.

One final comment about stereotypes: Keep in mind that models of users are an additional level of abstraction away from other issues related to the interface. The user stereotype is built below the level of the interface and interacts with the user through it. But from the perspective of most users, the behavior of the system controlled by the stereotype is part of the interface.

Interfaces for the Disabled

Interfaces for the disabled have the potential to greatly improve the lives of many individuals. Auditory interfaces (Edwards, 1989) allow access to blind individuals, and special input devices allow human-to-human interaction (through the computer) for individuals unable to speak (Alm, Elder, & Newell, 1993). An interface appropriate for individuals who know sign language has been developed, and other interfaces, such as those that track eye movement, enable paraplegics to use computers (see Glinert & York, 1992, for current developments).

Although the primary benefit of these systems is to facilitate the disabled in leading meaningful and productive lives, there are also two benefits for work organizations. First, by helping the disabled to work, these interfaces expand the pool of workers available to organizations. Second, they facilitate organizational compliance with the Americans with Disabilities Act (1990). In this regard, personnel psychologists and managers could no doubt learn much from educational and cognitive psychologists and other professionals to help them develop and administer tests producing scores that truly reflect the aptitude, skill, or ability of interest without being influenced by a disability.

International Interfaces

As organizations become more multinational and compete in a global market, it is important to consider how *international* (Russo & Boor, 1993) interfaces are. A fluent interface for international markets must go beyond translation of text and numerical symbols to communication of the concepts and intent of the user.

In a promising pursuit, Welsh and Toleman (1992) argued that the best way to develop a multilingual system is to work at the level of the concept rather than the physical interface. This places the focus of constructing the interface on concepts as the psychological building blocks. This approach may simplify the process, although much work needs to be done to determine which psychological concepts in one culture map onto concepts in other cultures and languages (assuming the concept exists in the alternate cultures).

What We Can Expect

The focus of the chapter now turns to how technological changes will affect professional and clerical jobs in the future. These changes reflect developments in systems that allow individuals to work together and advances that will greatly increase the number of computers in an office but help them recede into the background.

Computer-Supported Cooperative Work

During the early 1980s, a new field emerged that sought to have the computer truly *support and augment* the way individuals work. Going well beyond interface issues, *computer-supported cooperative work* (CSCW; a related term is *groupware*) is concerned with making the computer a tool that fits in and is totally a part of the process of getting work done in an organization. Consider a group of office workers, perhaps engineers, who must meet together on a regular basis to work on a project. Group members bring individual pieces of the project they have been working on, and after some discussion, the group integrates these pieces. CSCW augments and supports each part of this process. Individuals are supported by their individual systems, and one or more large computer displays, much like white boards, allow the separate individuals to work together in a shared space.

CSCW grew out of the need to have computers support workers in the way they traditionally work; that is, they work *with* each other, so the computer must facilitate these interactions and augment individual and group performance. Topics of interest to CSCW researchers include all the mainstream areas of those who study groups and teams as well as areas related to technological development. Early topical areas for CSCW included domain-specific coordination support (for example, project management support), support for meetings (for example, computer-based real-time conferencing systems), and organizational interfaces. An overview of CSCW appears in a variety of sources (see, for example, Baecker, 1992).

Colab is an early CSCW meeting room, designed to be used by small to medium-size work teams (Stefik et al., 1988). Separate workstations are linked together over a network that supports a distributed data base. The workstations are also connected to a large touch-sensitive screen and a stand-up keyboard. Individuals can share their work, and it can be displayed along with the work of others on the large screen display. The facilitator can operate in a traditional fashion without being restricted to a flip chart or white board. All the power of the computer is available for supporting the shared work.

CSCW may dramatically change the way people work together by effectively supporting larger groups of individuals. This development should reduce meeting and project time and enhance group member satisfaction (Valacich, Dennis, & Nunamaker, 1991). Valacich and colleagues have developed an Electronic Meeting System that is installed at over thirty corporate and university sites around the world. The system has the capability of linking together any or all of those sites simultaneously for interactive collaboration.

Another example of a device that facilitates collaborative interactions is the Electronic Paper (Brocklehurst, 1991), a flat panel display on which users write with a special scribing device. The computer interprets handwritten symbols, drawings, and characters and displays the results on the screen. Users with very little training are able to edit text, create tables, and insert diagrams.

Some researchers have studied individual behavior within CSCW groups to determine whether it differs from the behavior of workers in traditional groups. Heath and Luff (1992) found that the audiovisual technology used in many CSCW systems can introduce asymmetrical patterns into interpersonal communications. For example, although two individuals may ordinarily interact in an equitable fashion—each contributing equally to a discussion— the CSCW system could lead to one person's deferring to another because of discomfort with the technology. Thus the technology minimizes the input of one individual and thereby introduces an asymmetry into the typical interaction process. The effect seems similar to reports that television cameras in a courtroom can change the behavior of witnesses. Clearly, more work needs to be done to determine the impact of audiovisual technologies on the formal and informal aspects of collaborative work.

Other research has explored group decision making. In two different experiments, Gallupe et al. (1992) examined groups of various sizes (two, four, six, or twelve persons) under conditions where they brainstormed either verbally or electronically. In each experiment, more unique and high-quality ideas were generated in the larger group. Furthermore, individuals reported being more satisfied with the process when they brainstormed electronically. Kiesler and Sproull (1992) conducted seven experiments comparing face-to-face and electronic decision making in groups. They reported that computer-mediated discussions led to more delays, more explicit and outspoken advocacy, more extreme and risky decisions, greater equality of participation among group members, and "flaming" (rude language).

Broome and Chen (1992) argued that, for any of the CSCW systems to be successful in their support of groups, they must enable the individuals to move beyond the status quo and develop a greater focus on shared meaning. So until the technologies move beyond assisting individual decision making and problem solving, and toward a situation where the group becomes more than the sum of the parts, CSCW systems will not realize their potential impact on office jobs.

Augmented Reality

Most readers are probably familiar with virtual reality, where a reality is *created* for an individual who wears a set of goggles and perhaps a data glove. With virtual reality, a new (computer-generated) reality replaces the actual physical environment in which an individual resides. With augmented reality, on the other hand, computers augment or enhance but do not replace the physical environment.

One interesting application of augmented reality is the Digital Drawing board developed by Mackay, Velay, Carter, Ma, and Pagani (1993). They argued that offices will never get rid of paper (as in the "paperless office"), so the issue becomes one of augmenting people's ability to work with both paper and computers. They developed their system for graphical designers with the intention of letting them work as they normally do with paper and layout boards. Handwritten images can be replicated, rendered in 3D, rotated, and projected by the Digital Drawing board, allowing designers to have the advantages of both the traditional designer table and a three-dimensional computer-aided design (CAD) system.

Perhaps the most common device office workers will use in the future will resemble the Xerox DigitalDesk. Developers of the

DigitalDesk (Wellner, 1993) pointed out that people typically interact with documents in two different worlds: a paper world for "paper pushing" and an electronic world for "pixel pushing." Unfortunately, interaction in either of these two worlds loses the benefits of operating in the other. For example, people interacting in an electronic world lose the advantage of applying natural skills that have been developed over a lifetime, such as the use of their fingers, arms, three-dimensional vision, ears, and kinesthetic memory.

On the DigitalDesk, which really is a desk, papers obtain electronic properties and electronic objects gain physical properties; thus the advantages of both the physical and electronic worlds are retained in the augmented world. The system has three important characteristics: (1) electronic images are projected down onto the desk and onto papers residing on the desk, (2) the system responds to interactions with pens and the user's bare fingers, and (3) the system can read paper documents placed on the desk. DigitalDesk achieves these capabilities through a system of video cameras pointed down on the desk and an image processing system connected to a knowledge base that can sense what the user is doing. For example, to use the DigitalDesk as a calculator, an individual can point to each of several numbers on a piece of paper and the system will place them into an electronic calculator for further manipulations.

An application suitable for CSCW is the Double DigitalDesk, which allows two users in separate locations to "share" their own physical desks while each sees, edits, and writes on the other's paper documents (Wellner, 1993). Each DigitalDesk grabs images from its own physical desk and projects them onto the remote desk so that each user sees what is on both desks. As an example, Milt places a piece of paper onto his desk; an image of that paper is also projected onto Ann's desk, and vice versa. Each person can draw with a real pen on both paper and electronic documents, and the other user will see those marks appear on his or her documents. Furthermore, each user's hand is projected along with hand motion so the workers can also point to places on documents.

Feiner, MacIntyre, and Seligmann (1993) developed a system called KARMA, or Knowledge-based Augmented Reality for Maintenance Assistance; it generates virtual worlds that serve as an *over-*

lay and complement to the user's view of the real world. The system is called knowledge based because it includes a rule-based expert system that takes into account information about the user, the task the user is currently performing, and changes in the real world when selecting the image to project and how to project it. A test bed system for KARMA has been developed for the repair of laser printers. A technician wears a very small, see-through, head-mounted unit that has the capability of displaying the augmented view generated by the computer system. The system also has a motion sensor that is used for determining where the individual is looking. This cues the KARMA system as to what information the individual needs to see. As the worker looks through a beam splitter, his or her view of the world is combined with the display's image.

The KARMA system can be used to explain simple laser printer maintenance to end users. When looking at the laser printer, the user would see an image of the location and identity of the paper tray; the system would then show in virtual space the action of pulling out the paper tray and the resulting change in the tray's state, correctly oriented relative to the real laser printer (see Figure 5.2).

This type of system would be especially useful for jobs where individuals are trained in the use of tools, or have a general familiarity with the device needing repair, but are not experts in repair. The knowledge-based system could project enough information to guide individuals in any type of repair or maintenance work. Other applications of this type of technology in the office are clearly possible.

Augmented reality systems will play an ever-increasing role in the work of office personnel. These systems will be constructed around models of user abilities, accenting their knowledge and skills. In this fashion they will build on the strengths of individual workers and augment their ability to perform tasks of ever-increasing difficulty.

Ubiquitous Computing

Weiser (1991, 1993) and his group have proposed one of the most provocative accounts of what office work will be in the future, a work environment of *ubiquitous computing*. Computers will be literally everywhere; Weiser predicts there will be hundreds in every

**Figure 5.2. Augmented Reality to Show Action of Pulling
Out a Paper Tray on a Laser Printer and the Resulting
Change in the Tray's State.**

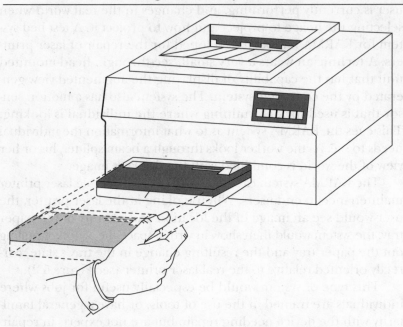

Source: Adapted from Feiner, MacIntyre, and Seligmann, 1993.

office! Not only will they be everywhere, but they will be "invisible."
The invisibility will come about for two reasons. First, many computers will be embedded in devices, the ceiling, and the walls, controlling the environment as well as office machines such as the
photocopier and answering machine. Second, computers will be
so commonplace that they will become psychologically invisible.
That is, the computer will move away from being the focal point—
something people have to deal with in order to accomplish a task—
and will be taken for granted. In the era of ubiquitous computing,
the computers will disappear and people will be free to focus on
their work goals. This invisibility of ubiquitous computing contrasts
sharply with multimedia systems, which are designed to grab attention, and with virtual reality systems, which create a universe
instead of augmenting or enhancing the actual reality.

According to Weiser (1991, 1993), three different types of ubiquitous computing systems will exist in the office of the future: tiny Post-it–sized computers called Tabs, notepad-sized computers called Pads, and wall-sized interactive surfaces called Liveboards. Tabs will be the most prevalent, serving primarily as an information doorway. A Tab has a pressure-sensitive screen on top of a display and three buttons. Tabs can be dedicated to each project the individual is working on; for example, a salesperson might have a Tab for each account. Tabs will function as an extension of a computer screen whereby the information in a window can be shrunk down into the Tab. Tabs are transportable, easily moved from office to office (or Liveboard to Liveboard) in one's pocket. Gathering up information on a project is accomplished by gathering up the Tabs associated with the project. The programs and other files of interest can be called up on any computer.

One current application of a Tab is an Active Badge system, which can broadcast an individual's identification for automatic door opening in restricted areas (Hopper, Harter, & Blackie, 1993). Other uses (implemented at Xerox PARC) include automatic call forwarding as individuals move about a building, customizing computer displays for each individual, quickly locating individuals for a meeting, and monitoring the general activity of a building.

Moving up in physical size from the tiny Tabs are the larger Pads. Pads are a family of notebook-sized computers (not laptops or PCs) that are meant to be used much as a piece of paper might be used. Pads will be lying around in a person's office and are intended to be picked up and easily used for any purpose. Some primitive examples of Pad systems are the recently introduced personal digital assistants and the handheld computers used by traders on the floor of the American Stock Exchange (Raghavan, 1993).

Much larger than Tabs and Pads are Liveboards, which will serve many of the purposes of the white boards found in today's offices. They are wall-sized interaction devices having an area about four hundred times the size of a Tab. Two current Liveboards, TIVOLI and SLATE, support the cooperative interaction of several individuals working on them at the same time. These systems allow individuals to work on the same page or even different pages of a project or report. Liveboards accept input from a variety of sources, including pens, scanners, and gestures.

Just how many computers will exist in the office of the future? Weiser (1991) suggested just looking around a typical office in order to get a feel for the answer. At the inch scale, for example, there are small pieces of paper and wall notes with information, titles on book spines, labels on controls of office equipment, thermostats, and clocks. Considering this, he predicted that the typical office will have one hundred or more Tabs, ten or twenty Pads, and one or two Liveboards. These devices will all be connected through a ubiquitous network of infrared, radio, and wire, allowing anyone in the room to work seamlessly with any of the devices. The computers in one office will also be connected with all the other computers throughout the organization. The result is a complete and total computational infrastructure in the organization.

Fitzmaurice (1993) described work on developing a ubiquitous computing environment with the Chameleon system. Consistent with the description provided by Weiser (1991), computers are embedded into the physical surroundings so that electronic information is accessible in the environment that holds meaning for people (thus leading to a blurring of the boundary between the electronic and physical environments). For example, workers planning to visit a branch office could obtain information on weather, traffic, and points of interest merely by passing a handheld computer over a map and stopping where they wished to receive information.

Another technology that represents a step toward making computers invisible is CHARADE (Baudel & Beaudouin-Lafon, 1993), which responds to commands issued with freehand gestures. For example, an individual using a projector to make a presentation in front of a group could gesture to CHARADE to go to the next page or to highlight an area. Baudel and Beaudouin-Lafon cited three advantages of using hand gestures: (1) they are a natural form of communication, (2) hand gestures are terse and powerful—a single gesture can communicate quite a bit of information, and (3) they allow direct interaction with the device—the presenter's hand is the input device. CHARADE can interpret and execute sixteen gesture commands (based on American Sign Language) issued in an active area of a large display device like a Liveboard.

In addition to supporting presentations, CHARADE has been used to orient construction cranes and conduct an orchestra of synthesizers, all through gestural control. People could also use it in noisy office environments to communicate with one another and with the computing system without interference from the noise. Freehand input would allow collaborative remote control when many workers share large displays, as in manufacturing plants, security services, and the stock exchange (Baudel & Beaudouin-Lafon, 1993).

While we may not see the widespread application of the exact systems described here in office work of the future, we will see systems with the same fundamental capabilities—facilitating group work and augmenting the knowledge and skills of office workers.

Human Resource Issues for Future Office Workers

As the nature of work in office jobs continues to change, human resource managers will face ever-increasing challenges. On the one hand, their job may become easier, as knowledge-based systems and intelligent agents replace some of the mundane tasks performed in the office and also augment workers' ability to perform difficult tasks. On the other hand, they may find it more difficult to match organizational members to the technologically intensive work environment. There will be greater demands on various subsystems of human resources management, including personnel selection, job design, and especially employee training. Issues related to each of these topics are presented in the following sections.

Personnel Selection

Perhaps the most important challenge to personnel selection will be finding the best predictors of job performance. The future organizational environment for professional and clerical jobs will continue to be increasingly technologically intensive, with new hardware and software systems constantly introduced to increase the effectiveness of office workers. The continual changes in office tools will increase input, conversion, and output uncertainty, resulting in a greater demand for workers who are smart, adaptive, and flexible.

Workers will have to be intelligent enough to handle the new technologies and to understand their capabilities at the appropriate operational level. But given further developments with intelligent agents and user interfaces incorporating stereotypes that "understand" the user's actions, computer systems will augment workers' intelligence, making it less necessary for individuals to know everything about the job. This is especially true for certain types of aptitude such as mechanical ability, as further advances in augmented reality can facilitate performance. For example, workers will no longer need to be able to mentally visualize the process of opening a laser printer door or mentally rotating an object in three-dimensional space because knowledge-based systems will show them what needs to be done.

Personality tests will likely take on more importance in selection. One reason is that workers will have to become increasingly flexible in adapting to the new technologies. In addition, psychologists may discover additional individual difference variables and personality constructs that moderate reactions to technology or that mediate other predictor-criterion relationships.

Advances in office technology will also increase the availability of work sample tests and situational exercises. It is a straightforward process to take operational technologies "off-line" and use them as work sample tests for selection purposes. Or, if decreases in hardware costs continue, high-fidelity simulators can be dedicated to work sample testing and situational exercises.

As technological advances increase the capability to augment and enhance worker performance, identifying stable predictor-criterion relationships may become more difficult. Consider, for example, an individual who is using one or more intelligent assistants but still performs poorly: Who is to blame—the worker or the assistants? On the other hand, new technologies will lend themselves to the development and use of work sample and job performance tests, leading to a potential increase in understanding of predictor-criterion relationships. Of course, this calls for redoubling our efforts to identify moderating and mediating variables, place them in nomological space with job criterion variables, and test the resulting models.

Job Design and Organizational Issues

Job design and organizational development are two different ways organizations might want to address the changing nature of office work. For job design, further effort is needed to identify relevant task attributes (such as control, autonomy, and skill variety), and critical psychological states related to implementation of successful technological systems in the office. Schneider's (1989) work, described earlier, is a step in this direction. It will be important to identify relevant job design variables at the individual and group level for workers in CSCW systems.

At the organizational level, managing change created by widespread automation is a major challenge. Some of the issues include gaining management commitment to the change, vendor and union relationships, employee resistance, education and training, job redesign, and organizational restructuring, among others (Kramer, Chibnall, & Pedersen, 1992). Management's influence in ensuring the successful introduction of the technology cannot be overstated. The management of the change (Majchrzak & Cotton, 1988) and the concomitant changes in the workplace and its culture (Collins & King, 1988; Milkman & Pullman, 1991) are as important as the technology itself. Implementing the changes within a sociotechnical systems framework has led to long-term success in a white-collar service setting (Taylor, 1986); overlooking inappropriate and conflicting sociotechnical structures (human and organizational systems) is more likely to lead to negative consequences of the technology within the organization (Symon & Clegg, 1991).

Organizational learning is likely to play a role in the acceptance of the technology (Attewell, 1992). Firms often delay the adoption of technologies until they obtain sufficient in-house expertise to implement and operate it effectively, especially organizations that previously experienced negative implementation episodes.

Technological change can sometimes polarize an organization's workforce. Skilled trade jobs may experience skill upgrading and increased responsibility, as happens with designers and CAD and CADCAM (Computer-Aided Design and Computer-Aided Manufacturing) systems, so that skilled trade workers are advanced to becoming office workers. Other production workers, however, may experience the negative aspects of deskilling and increasingly become subordinate to the technology. Managers can lead a successful transition to technologically modified jobs if they communicate to workers that technological systems are desirable and lead to job security (Davids & Martin, 1992), as opposed to job loss.

Jobs designed to include computer monitoring can have a potent effect on job satisfaction. Chalykoff and Kochan (1989) found that monitoring was *inherently* negative for some employees. For others, however, the negative impact was mitigated by management's paying increased attention to employees through feedback and the performance appraisal process. Further work needs to be done on how to minimize the negative impact of monitoring.

Training

Perhaps no human resource area is more important than training for understanding and managing the impact of technology on office workers. Recent reviews of the training area (Goldstein, 1991; Tannenbaum & Yukl, 1992) paid some attention to new training technologies. But what is critical is the rapid pace with which technologies can change or modify a job, particularly office jobs. Office workers routinely encounter new technologies—decision support systems; CAD and CADCAM systems; expert systems of various types; new versions of their word processors, spreadsheet programs, or desktop publishing systems; worker monitoring systems—which can change the way a job is performed.

There are two distinct issues under the training rubric. The first is how best to train people to use the new technologies. Are the traditional training issues—such as learning theory (for example, part versus whole), individual difference variables (for example, motivation, age; see Coovert, 1990), and outcome evaluation assessments—adequate when new technologies are being considered? The second issue is how to utilize new technologically advanced training devices, including multimedia and virtual reality systems. Put another way, the two primary issues are (1) training to use technologies, and (2) using technologies to train.

Training to Use Technologies: Animation

There has been considerable discussion regarding the best time to present a mental model to an individual learning a complex system or device. Consider a manager trying to learn a spreadsheet program for the first time. Should a trainer present a graphical model of the program and how it works followed by detailed instruction on its operation, or should the model be presented last, allowing the trainee to first develop a mental model? Augustine and Coovert (1991) examined this issue along with the effect of animating a graphical model. For example, when a print command was issued by individuals learning a computer environment, in the nonanimated condition the system instructed users that the file leaves the active work space and goes to the printer and pointed out those two components in a graphical depiction of the model. In the animated condition, the system showed the file leaving the active work space and traveling down a wire to the printer, where the printer printed it. Using a 2 x 2 design (mental model first/last by animation/no animation), the order of the presentation of the mental model had no effect on individuals' ability to learn during the training nor on their scores on a posttest. Animation, however, did have a significant effect on all measures of training and retention. It appears that making a mental model more vivid through the use of animation enriches it as a training strategy. Animation may make the process more concrete, or at least less abstract, and thus enhances retention and performance.

Training to Use Technologies: The Need for a Taxonomy

As emphasized previously, we need to develop and test rich models in order to understand the technology-job performance relationship. The same is true for training. Gattiker (1992) pointed out that most of what we know about training employees for computer-mediated work is the result of very narrow and fragmented studies. The author argued that this type of approach to building a body of knowledge could lead to our missing important intervening variables. Below is a brief review of studies focusing on age and training, presented to strengthen Gattiker's contention.

Even though many studies have looked at the issue of age and training to use a computer system, there is considerable inconsistency of findings. For example, Garfein, Schaie, and Willis (1988) obtained measures of fluid and crystallized intellectual ability on adults aged forty-nine to sixty-seven, and subsequently trained those individuals on using a microcomputer. Testing following the training revealed no significant age difference on the intellectual ability measures or in computer proficiency, leading the researchers to conclude that there is no reason to suspect age as a moderator when training individuals for computer-related jobs. Another study

(Czaja, Hammond, Blascovich, & Swede, 1989) reached quite the opposite conclusion. The researchers examined the ability of individuals aged twenty-five to seventy to learn a text editor. Younger individuals performed better on speed and accuracy measures than did older individuals. The authors concluded that older individuals may have difficulty in acquiring skills to use current computer technology and are therefore "at a disadvantage in work settings."

Although the differences in findings and conclusions on the part of these authors may be a function of different populations (Garfein et al. looked only at older workers, while Czaja et al. used a broad band of ages) or different training objectives (use of a microcomputer versus use of a text editor), there still might be another explanation. Staufer (1992) interviewed older office workers in a variety of occupations regarding their dominant view of computers and then classified these individuals by whether they viewed the computer as a challenge, a threat, or an irrelevant mechanism. This attitudinal difference toward computers turned out to be a useful moderator. Individuals who viewed the computer as a challenge favored information-seeking activities; those viewing it as a threat reacted passively and complained about health-related problems and increased time pressure; those who viewed the computer as irrelevant to their work had increased levels of job satisfaction. Of course, personality constructs may also be at work here, given the previously discussed linkage between locus of control and attitude toward computers.

Clearly, more extensive studies are called for, as well as studies that test models of exogenous and endogenous variables, including potential mediators. Only this way will we acquire the scientific base needed to make solid recommendations for training individuals to work in the technologically demanding office jobs of today and tomorrow.

Just-in-Time Training

Technologies increase demands on workers; they not only have to do their job, but they also have to learn new technologies associated with the job (for example, the secretary who learns the new release of a word processor). Many individuals report feeling increased pressure as a result of the new technology. One way to ease the time pressures associated with learning is to look at training from the same perspective as just-in-time manufacturing. That is, only train today what you need to know today (and perhaps tomorrow morning), forget training other information until it is needed, and never train something that will not be used.

Another technique, employing principles from cognitive science and adaptive testing, is to assess each individual immediately and identify the areas that need additional training. Brown and Campion (1986) trained in basic and job-related skills and then used a computerized dynamic assessment technique within the context of specific job demands to identify an individual's learning potential and the transferability of the learning to on-the-job requirements. The approach appears worthwhile, but the benefits must be balanced against the sometimes extreme development costs.

Training Technologies: Videodisc, Multimedia, and Virtual Reality

There are several new training technologies for the workplace. Pollard (1992), after examining a variety of studies in education, the military, and business, concluded that interactive videodisc instruction is an effective medium for training. Users have a positive attitude toward its use, and it tends to be more cost effective than traditional approaches.

Multimedia training systems are most commonly set up on personal computers with a sound card and speakers connected to a CD-ROM. These systems are receiving widespread attention as stand-alone training systems. Other multimedia technologies, similar to some CSCW systems, allow workers to meet and share data with colleagues from around the globe without having to leave their desks (see Cohen, 1993, for a description of cutting-edge multimedia systems).

Finally, there are virtual reality systems. This technology has received much attention recently, and anyone who ever donned a helmet and data glove to experience another reality will attest to how much fun such an experience can be. Virtual reality technologies in training systems are especially effective for situations where there is potential risk to humans (for example, an astronaut repairing a satellite) or worlds humans cannot physically enter (for example, Palfreman & Swade, 1991, described a world where a chemist can walk around a molecule to search for possible enzyme bonding sites).

To date, however, there have been few applications of virtual reality to office jobs. One notable exception is a system allowing architects to construct and walk through a virtual building to see what it will look like before actual construction begins (Palfreman & Swade, 1991). Once the costs of virtual reality technologies decrease and the resolution of the images increases, we are likely to see growing application of the technology for training purposes in office jobs.

Conclusion

The future promises exciting times for office workers as professional and clerical jobs continue to be modified by technologies. As long as workers retain control over aspects of the work, and the technologies are introduced in a positive manner by management, office work should be enhanced and worker skills augmented by the emerging technologies.

To the extent that any technological development furthers an office worker's ability to work naturally, either by relying on or augmenting existing knowledge, skills, and abilities, it will be embraced by office workers. That is the crux of the matter, and I draw a parallel from sports to clarify the point. Consider two football teams playing each other on a field of a certain width and length with the offense attempting to move a ball into a goal area defended by the opposing team. In the early days of football, players wore little, if any, equipment for protection and performance enhancement. Today's player, on the other hand, is literally covered with protective equipment—helmet; face mask; mouth guard; shoulder, hip, thigh, and knee pads—all designed to protect without inhibiting *natural* movement. Players' abilities are also augmented by their equipment, from different shoes for varying playing surfaces to "The Audiblizer," a microphone and transmitter built into a quarterback's shoulder pads that transmit what he says to an amplifier and speakers on either sideline. The speakers are loud enough to enable the offensive line to hear the quarterback change the play at the line of scrimmage, over the din of the crowd. These advances in equipment have not changed the game of football, but they have significantly enhanced an individual's capacity to use natural abilities and developed skills. The same is true for office jobs: technologies that allow individuals to work using existing knowledge, skills, and abilities, augmenting them if necessary, are the technologies emerging in the office of today and tomorrow.

The history of the development of user interfaces is a search for ways to allow individuals to work with a computer in a natural fashion. Major changes will continue to occur with interfaces and intelligent assistants, as will relatively minor adjustments, such as the new ergonomically designed mouse. Computer-supported cooperative work also developed out of concern for having workers work naturally. Little is done in isolation in today's organization; more often than not, people work together. Developments in computer-supported cooperative work focus on enabling individuals to work together naturally, while having their individual and group skills augmented and enhanced by powerful technologies.

We must begin, however, to move beyond the simple theoretical snapshots that have been taken to date of the relationship between workers, technology, and the organization. The development and testing of models expressing theoretically rich and meaningful relationships between our constructs is the only way we will ever be able to understand the complex set of variables and their relations to one another in this difficult arena. And only when we have developed models with rich explanatory power will we be in a position to effectively manage the changes that are being brought about by technology. It is also imperative that psychologists and management become involved early on with the systems being designed by engineers and computer scientists so that they can be proactive in design and implementation rather than reactive after the systems are introduced. By that time it is often too late to make meaningful changes in their design and/or functionality.

Will the promise of incredible and seemingly invisible computing power in the office come true, as proponents of ubiquitous computing claim? Absolutely, as long as we believe individuals are always looking for better tools with which to work, and that the best tool is one that does not take the focus from the problem at hand but allows people to work naturally.

Today's office workers have a lot to look forward to. Technology holds the promise of greatly enhancing the nature of work being performed in offices while at the same time increasing the quality of the office worker's life.

References

Alm, N., Elder, L., & Newell, A. F. (1993). Computer-aided conversation for severely physically impaired nonspeaking people. In S. Ashlund, K. Mullet, A. Henderson, E. Hollnagel, & T. White (Eds.), *Human factors in computing systems: INTERCHI '93 conference proceedings.* New York: Association for Computing Machinery.

Attewell, P. (1992). Technology diffusion and organizational learning: The case of business computing. *Organizational Science, 3,* 1–19.

Augustine, M. A., & Coovert, M. D. (1991). Simulation and information order as influences in the development of mental models. *Association for Computing Machinery SIGCHI Bulletin, 23,* 33–35.

Baecker, R. M. (Ed.). (1992). *Readings in groupware and computer-supported cooperative work.* San Mateo, CA: Morgan Kaufmann.

Baudel, T., & Beaudouin-Lafon, M. (1993). CHARADE: Remote control of objects using free-hand gestures. *Communications of the ACM, 36,* 28–35.

Brocklehurst, E. R. (1991). The NPL electronic paper project. *International Journal of Man-Machine Studies, 34,* 69–95.

Broome, B. J., & Chen, M. (1992). Guidelines for computer-assisted group problem solving: Meeting the challenges of complex issues. *Small Group Research, 23,* 216–236.

Brown, A., & Campion, J. C. (1986). Cognitive science principles and work force education. *Advances in Reading and Language Research, 4,* 217–229.

Chalykoff, J., & Kochan, T. A. (1989). Computer-aided monitoring: Its influence on employee job satisfaction and turnover. *Personnel Psychology, 42,* 807–834.

Cohen, J. (Ed.). (1993). Multimedia in the workplace. *Communications of the ACM, 36,* 28–77.

Collins, P. D., & King, D. C. (1988). Implications of computer-aided design for work and performance. *Journal of Applied Behavioral Science, 24,* 173–190.

Coovert, M. D. (1980). Locus of control as a predictor of users' attitudes toward computers. *Psychological Reports, 47,* 1167–1173.

Coovert, M. D. (1990). Development and evaluation of five user models of human-computer interaction. In U. Gattiker (Ed.), *End-user training.* Berlin: Walter de Gruyter.

Czaja, S. J., Hammond, K., Blascovich, J. J., & Swede, H. (1989). Age-related differences in learning to use a text-editing system. *Behaviour and Information Technology, 8,* 309–319.

Davids, K., & Martin, R. (1992). Shopfloor attitudes towards advanced manufacturing technology: The changing focus of industrial conflict? *Interacting with Computers, 4,* 200–208.

Edwards, A. D. (1989). Modeling blind users' interactions with an auditory computer interface. *International Journal of Man-Machine Studies, 30*, 575–589.

Feiner, S., MacIntyre, B., & Seligmann, D. (1993). Knowledge-based augmented reality. *Communications of the ACM, 36*, 52–62.

Fitzmaurice, G. W. (1993). Situated information spaces and spatially aware palmtop computers. *Communications of the ACM, 36*, 39–49.

Gallupe, R. B., Dennis, A. R., Cooper, W. H., Valacich, J. S., Bastianutti, L. M., & Nunamaker, J. F. (1992). Electronic brainstorming and group size. *Academy of Management Journal, 35*, 350–369.

Garfein, A. J., Schaie, K. W., & Willis, S. L. (1988). Microcomputer proficiency in later middle aged and older adults: Teaching old dogs new tricks. *Social Behavior, 3*, 131–148.

Gattiker, U. E. (1992). Computer skill acquisition: A review and future directions for research. *Journal of Management, 18*, 547–575.

Gattiker, U. E., & Howg, L. (1990). Information technology and quality of work life: Comparing users with non-users. *Journal of Business and Psychology, 5*, 237–260.

Gattiker, U. E., & Nelligan, T. W. (1988). Computerized offices in Canada and the United States: Investigating dispositional similarities and differences. *Journal of Organizational Behavior, 9*, 77–96.

Glinert, E. P., & York, B. W. (Eds.). (1992). Special section on computers and people with disabilities. *Communications of the ACM, 35*, 32–93.

Goldberg, D., & Richardson, C. (1993). Touch-typing with a stylus. In S. Ashlund, K. Mullet, A. Henderson, E. Hollnagel, & T. White (Eds.), *Human factors in computing systems: INTERCHI '93 conference proceedings*. New York: Association for Computing Machinery.

Goldstein, I. L. (1991). Training in work organizations. In M. D. Dunnette & L. M. Hough (Eds.), *Handbook of industrial and organizational psychology* (2nd ed., Vol. 2). Palo Alto, CA: Consulting Psychologists Press.

Grossman, L. M. (1993, August 3). Truck cabs turn into mobile offices as drivers take on white-collar tasks. *Wall Street Journal*, pp. B1, B5.

Hackett, E. J., Mirvis, P. H., & Sales, A. L. (1991). Women's and men's expectations about the effects of new technology at work. *Group and Organization Studies, 16*, 60–85.

Heath, C., & Luff, P. (1992). Media space and communicative asymmetries: Preliminary observations of video-mediated interaction. *Human-Computer Interaction, 7*, 315–346.

Hopper, A., Harter, A., & Blackie, T. (1993). The active badge system. In S. Ashlund, K. Mullet, A. Henderson, E. Hollnagel, & T. White (Eds.), *Human factors in computing systems: INTERCHI '93 conference proceedings*. New York: Association for Computing Machinery.

Idaszak, J. R., & Drasgow, F. (1987). A revision of the Job Diagnostic Survey: Elimination of a measurement artifact. *Journal of Applied Psychology, 72,* 69–74.

Kahn, H., & Cooper, C. L. (1991). The potential contribution of information technology to the mental health, job dissatisfaction, and alcohol intake of money market dealers: An exploratory study. *International Journal of Human-Computer Interaction, 3,* 321–338.

Kiesler, S., & Sproull, L. (1992). Group decision making and communication technology. *Organizational Behavior and Human Decision Processes, 52,* 96–123.

Kramer, T. J., Chibnall, J. T., & Pedersen, B. D. (1992). Managing computer integrated manufacturing (CIM): A review of themes, issues, and practices. *Journal of Business and Psychology, 6,* 415–442.

LaLomia, M. J., & Coovert, M. D. (1992). Problem solving performance as a function of display, number progression, and memory. *Behaviour and Information Technology, 11,* 268–280.

Linstrom, K. (1991). Well-being and computer-mediated work of various occupational groups in banking and insurance. *International Journal of Human-Computer Interaction, 3,* 339–361.

Mackay, W., Velay, G., Carter, K., Ma, C., & Pagani, D. (1993). Augmenting reality: Adding computational dimensions to paper. *Communications of the ACM, 36,* 96–97.

McInerney, W. D. (1989). Social and organizational effects of educational computing. *Journal of Educational Computing Research, 5,* 487–506.

Majchrzak, A., & Cotton, J. (1988). A longitudinal study of adjustment to technological change: From mass to computer-automated batch production. *Journal of Occupational Psychology, 61,* 43–66.

Martin, G. L. (1989). The utility of speech input in user-computer interfaces. *International Journal of Man-Machine Studies, 30,* 355–375.

Matias, E., MacKenzie, I. S., & Buxton, W. (1993). Half-QWERTY: A one handed keyboard facilitating skill transfer from QWERTY. In S. Ashlund, K. Mullet, A. Henderson, E. Hollnagel, & T. White (Eds.), *Human factors in computing systems: INTERCHI '93 conference proceedings.* New York: Association for Computing Machinery.

Milkman, R., & Pullman, C. (1991). Technological change in an auto assembly plant: The impact on workers' tasks and skills. *Work and Occupations, 18,* 123–147.

Nelson, D. L., & Kletke, M. G. (1990). Individual adjustment during technological innovation: A research framework. *Behaviour and Information Technology, 9,* 257–271.

Palfreman, J., & Swade, D. (1991). *The dream machine: Exploring the computer age.* London: BBC Books.

Pan, J. Y., & Tenenbaum, J. M. (1991). An intelligent agent framework for enterprise integration. *IEEE Transactions on Systems, Man, and Cybernetics, 21,* 1391–1408.

Perrolle, J. A. (1986). Intellectual assembly lines: The rationalization of managerial, professional, and technical work. *Computers and the Social Sciences, 2,* 111–121.

Pollard, C. (1992). Effects of interactive videodisc instruction on learner performance, learner attitude, and learning time. *Journal of Instructional Psychology, 19,* 189–196.

Raghavan, A. (1993, July 9). Amex specialists test hand-held computers. *Wall Street Journal,* p. B1.

Riecken, D. (Ed.). (1994). Intelligent agents [Special issue]. *Communications of the ACM, 37*(7).

Rivers, R. (1989). Embedded user models: Where next? *Interacting with Computers, 1,* 13–30.

Russo, P., & Boor, S. (1993). How fluent is your interface? Designing for international users. In S. Ashlund, K. Mullet, A. Henderson, E. Hollnagel, & T. White (Eds.), *Human factors in computing systems: INTER-CHI '93 conference proceedings.* New York: Association for Computing Machinery.

Saxton, M. J., Phillips, J. S., & Blakeney, R. N. (1991). Antecedents and consequences of emotional exhaustion in the airline reservations service sector. *Human Relations, 44,* 583–595.

Schneider, J. (1989). *Understanding the relationship between technological uncertainty and job satisfaction: Test of a model.* Unpublished master's thesis, University of South Florida, Tampa.

Schneiderman, B. B. (1980). *Software psychology: Human factors in computer and information systems.* Framingham, MA: Winthrop.

Schneiderman, B. B. (1987). *Designing the user interface: Strategies for effective human-computer interaction.* Reading, MA: Addison-Wesley.

Staufer, M. (1992). Technological change and the older employee: Implications for introduction and training. *Behaviour and Information Technology, 11,* 46–52.

Stefik, M., Foster, G., Bobrow, D. G., Kahn, K., Lanning, S., & Suchman, L. (1988). Beyond the chalkboard: Computer support for collaboration and problem solving in meeting. In I. Greif (Ed.), *Computer-supported cooperative work.* San Mateo, CA: Morgan Kaufmann.

Symon, G. J., & Clegg, C. W. (1991). Technology-led change: A study of the implementation of CADCAM. *Journal of Occupational Psychology, 64,* 273–290.

Tannenbaum, S. I., & Yukl, G. (1992). Training and development in work organizations. *Annual Review of Psychology, 43,* 399–441.

Taylor, J. C. (1986). Long-term sociotechnical systems change in a computer operations department. *Journal of Applied Behavioral Science, 22,* 303–313.

Valacich, J. S., Dennis, A. R., & Nunamaker, J. F. (1991). Electronic meeting support: The GroupSystems concept. *International Journal of Man-Machine Studies, 34,* 261–282.

Vallas, S. P., & Yarrow, M. (1987). Advanced technology and worker alienation: Comments on the Blauner/Marxism debate. *Work and Occupations, 14,* 126–142.

Weiser, M. (1991). The computer for the 21st century. *Scientific American, 265,* 94–104.

Weiser, M. (1993). Some computer science issues in ubiquitous computing. *Communications of the ACM, 36,* 74–84.

Wellner, P. (1993). Interacting with paper on the DigitalDesk. *Communications of the ACM, 36,* 86–96.

Welsh, J., & Toleman, M. (1992). Conceptual issues in language-based editor design. *International Journal of Man-Machine Studies, 37,* 419–430.

Yaverbaum, G. J., & Culpan, O. (1990). Exploring the dynamics of the end-user environment: The impact of education and task differences on change. *Human Relations, 43,* 439–454.

Part Three

Workers

Chapter Six

Human Resources and Their Skills

It does not take a scholar to recognize the potential mismatch between characteristics of the labor force in the United States (with some parallels in other industrialized countries, especially the Western democracies) and the work that post-industrial firms would like them to perform. These labor force characteristics include a shrinking proportion of young workers, a dearth of job candidates who are adequately prepared for knowledge work, a chronically unemployed or underemployed underclass, a rising number of educationally disadvantaged children, and an influx of legal and illegal immigrants unable to find work in rapidly growing third world countries who struggle with language, discrimination, and other adjustment problems. Demographic and educational factors are not just frustrating employers; they are to some extent determining the kind of work that is done in a given nation-state.

Demographic Changes

Using middle-range assumptions, the Bureau of Labor Statistics projects that the U.S. labor force will grow 19 percent between 1992 and 2005, slightly less than the 21 percent increase over the previous thirteen-year period, from 1979 to 1992 (Fullerton, 1993). In recent years, the recession overshadowed public concerns that slower population growth rates would produce a scarcity of workers to support the economy. Moreover, recurring rounds of organizational downsizing have inspired fears of too few jobs rather than too few workers to fill them. But even if there are enough people to fill upcoming jobs, they may not be the right people. Various demographic shifts suggest potential problems.

Aging

The working-age population in the United States accelerated in the 1960s and 1970s as the baby boom generation moved into their working years. But the boomers are now entering middle age, and the number of young people has declined. In 1965, the end of the baby boom, 29 percent of the population was forty-five and older; by 2005 this group will be nearly 40 percent of the population (Fullerton, 1993). The middle aging of the workforce in the 1990s could be a drag on productivity in a rapidly changing economy if the baby boomers become unwilling to move or take risks for work, as traditionally happened with older workers in the bureaucratic era (Howard & Bray, 1988; Johnston & Packer, 1987).

The aging of the population stems from causes beyond the baby boom. Life expectancy at birth increased from over forty-seven years to nearly seventy-five years between 1900 and 1986, and fertility declined from 3.9 births per woman to 1.8 (Fosler, Alonso, Meyer, & Kern, 1990). Although the number of elderly employed has increased, this is because of the size of the group, not their labor force participation rate, which has declined. In 1900, two of every three male and one of twelve female elderly worked; in 1985 the ratios were one in six for men and one in fourteen for women (Fosler et al., 1990).

Immigration

"Demographically, the United States is a small and shrinking national minority, within a shrinking Western minority, within a shrinking industrial (as traditionally defined) minority of the world's population" (Fosler et al., 1990, p. 11). The industrial countries together, capitalist and socialist, contain fewer than one-fourth of the world's population and will represent only one-fifth early in the next century. Contrarily, the workforces of Africa, Asia, and Latin America are projected to grow over the next twenty years by an amount (700 million) equal to the total workforce of the industrialized countries in 1985. Some 40 percent of the population of third world countries is under age fifteen compared to about 20 percent in the United States and Europe. If the developing countries are unable to generate jobs for their populations, a likely possibility, there will be increased pressure for migration, especially to the United States (Fosler et al., 1990).

During the peak years of immigration in the early twentieth century, annual counts of immigrants exceeded one million at six different times. These numbers were equaled in absolute terms in the last few years if illegal immigrants, newly arrived immigrants, and newly arrived refugees are included (Fosler et al., 1990; Mandel, 1994). The Census Bureau expects for its middle projections a net difference between immigration and emigration of 880,000 annually between 1992 and 2005 (Fullerton, 1993). About 70 percent will be Hispanics and Asians/Pacific Islanders, a decidedly different mix from the predominantly European immigrants early in the century.

The educational attainment of immigrants varies widely by country of origin. Consider, for example, the proportion of high school graduates among those who immigrated to the United States between 1980 and 1985: among those from India it was 89 percent; Africa, 82 percent; Asia, 73 percent; and Mexico, 21 percent. At the same time the U.S. graduation rate was 69 percent (Fosler et al., 1990). Obviously the United States has benefited from "brain gain" in a host of areas, such as the theoretical and applied sciences. But there is considerably more debate about whether unskilled and semiskilled workers take jobs away from indigenous workers or reduce wage rates. The 1990 Immigration Act boosted legal immigration 40 percent and doubled the slots for skilled workers, but the rules still favor family members of U. S. residents.

Economists generally agree that immigration has had a positive impact on the economy over the years, and other social scientists are generally favorable to its impact on the social fabric. Because immigrants typically come for economic reasons, their labor force participation rate is usually high. Other cited advantages are that they tend to save more, apply more effort during working hours, and are more inclined to start businesses and be self-employed. Fears that immigrants take away jobs from natives are seldom confirmed in studies and have small effects when they are found. Moreover, immigrants make jobs by starting businesses and injecting money into the economy. Nevertheless, the general public, especially in recent years, tends to believe immigration rates are too high (Simon, 1989).

There are, in effect, two immigrant economies (Mandel, 1994). The 800,000 or so who come in under the regular immigration system are generally well educated and depend little on welfare. But an additional 300,000 to 400,000 are illegal immigrants or refugees from ex-communist countries, such as Cambodia, Laos, Vietnam, and the former Soviet Union. This second group tends to have less education and earn lower wages. Moreover, the legal refugee group is more than twice as likely to be on welfare (16.1 percent in 1990) as the nonrefugee legal immigrants (7.8 percent) or natives (7.4 percent). According to immigration specialist George Borjas, the skill and wage deficits among the immigrants at the turn of the twentieth century persisted for several generations, which raises concerns about the prolonged economic effects of the illegal and refugee immigrants (Mandel, 1994).

Ethnic and Racial Groups

Demographers expect the proportion of non-Hispanic whites in the labor force to continue to decline, from 78 percent in 1992 to 73 percent in 2005 (Fullerton, 1993). This derives from both higher birth rates among other racial and ethnic groups and their greater immigration. The black labor force should grow more rapidly than average but less than Hispanics or Asian/other groups. In 2005, then, the labor force will be 11 percent black, 11 percent Hispanic, and 5 percent other minorities (Fullerton, 1993). This segment of the labor force has traditionally suffered most from discrimination and from educational underpreparation (except for Asians). Blacks and Hispanics tend to be concentrated in jobs that pay the least and offer the smallest number of opportunities for learning and development.

The increasing heterogeneity of the workforce and the protections of diverse groups by federal legislation (see Chapter Two) has led to a proliferation of diversity programs within organizations. A survey by *Training* magazine found that 56 percent of organizations offered such training, up from 40 percent in 1992.

Nevertheless these programs remain controversial (Filipczak, 1994). As organizations realize that their customers, too, are culturally diverse, they are more likely to view a heterogeneous workforce as a competitive advantage. Nevertheless, a Queens College study of over 300 corporations in the diverse New York area found that most companies were doing little more than necessary to comply with employment law. They discovered new needs to deal with the issue when they tried to incorporate diverse members into teams (Noble, 1994). Landy, Shankster-Cawley, and Moran shed some light on this issue in Chapter Seven.

Gender

The changing structure of jobs has been to women's advantage. With fewer jobs dependent on physical strength, women become viable candidates, and many of the service positions offer opportunities with which women are quite comfortable. They have continued to advance in education. Their numbers now exceed those of men receiving bachelor's and master's degrees, and they are expected to earn nearly as many doctorates as men by 2004 (NCES, 1993).

Women's increasing inclination to work outside the home contributed strongly to labor force growth from the 1960s on, but their entry rates are expected to slow in the future. Between 1979 and 1992, women's labor force participation rate increased from 51 percent to 58 percent; by 2005 it should be 63 percent participation compared to men's 75 percent (Fullerton, 1993). The leveling off of women's labor force participation could result in labor shortages if the economy continues to grow.

Although women have made tremendous gains in assuming jobs denied them in the past, they are still far from equal to men in the workplace. Many occupations are largely segmented by sex, and women are seldom seen in the top echelons of major corporations. During the first half of 1994, women's wages were 76 percent those of men's, up from 64 percent in 1980. The closing gap was, however, only partly due to women's gains: their earnings increased 12 percent but men's declined by 6 percent ("The Pay Gap Narrows," 1994).

Continuing sex segregation of the labor market lessens its flexibility. But so does the advent of dual-career families, who may be more reluctant to move (Johnston & Packer, 1987). Another wrinkle is the finding from several studies that men in dual-career families earn significantly less (approximately 20 percent) than men in traditional families. Traditional men may put in more time at work and push harder without the safety net of a working spouse. But some researchers, who have controlled for such variables, including relocation, conclude that corporate prejudice is at work (Lewin, 1994).

The Disabled

Proponents heralded the 1990 Americans with Disabilities Act as the great emancipator of the disabled that would smooth the entry of this marginalized group into the mainstream of American workers. Four years later, however, the number of disabled people entering the workforce has not significantly increased. A recent survey conducted for the National Organization on Disabilities found that among disabled people age sixteen to sixty-four, only 31 percent were working part time or full time compared to 33 percent in 1986. Although the recession was no doubt partly responsible for this lack of progress, knowledgeable professionals pointed to systemic causes. These included employer fears about driving up health insurance costs, fears among the disabled about losing their health benefits, and a culture of dependency not unlike that observed with welfare recipients. If disabled persons work, they pay a penalty in loss of benefits from complicated and poorly understood federal programs. This system, though well-meaning, has made taking a job work against the best interest of disabled people (Holmes, 1994). Unless the system is changed, employers may not reap the benefits of the disabled as a significant source of labor.

Labor Force Skills

High technology has stimulated more upskilling than downskilling of jobs, as discussed in Chapter Three. American employers decry the precipitous gap between the high demands of the new work and the shallow skills of workers. A survey by the National Association of Manufacturers disclosed that 30 percent of companies refrained from reorganizing work activities because their employees were unable to learn new jobs, and 25 percent could not upgrade their products because employees were unable to learn the necessary skills (Gerstner, 1994). A 1991 survey revealed that human resource professionals anticipated widespread problems in recruiting skilled talent. For example, 74 percent expected it would be at least somewhat difficult to recruit scientists and technologists, and more than half expected difficulty finding top managers or skilled blue-collar workers (Mirvis, 1993).

Education

At the March 1994 jobs conference of the Group of Seven leading industrial nations, government officials agreed that the only way to create good jobs in the face of technological change was to upgrade education, especially for those least skilled (Friedman, 1994). American youth spend more years in school than young people in other industrialized countries, but this does not necessarily translate into better education, for the quality of their schooling is typically inferior. Achievement tests consistently show that U.S. students do less well than their foreign counterparts. Moreover, the biennial National Assessment of Educational Progress has shown little improvement over time in student progress despite attentive hand-wringing, public debate, and improvement efforts over the last decade. The 1994 report, for example, found that fewer than 10 percent of seventeen-year-olds could do rigorous academic work in basic subjects and only 2 percent of eleventh graders could write well enough to meet national goals (Manegold, 1994). As a result of basic skills deficiencies, 22 percent of American organizations do remedial training in reading, writing, math, or English as a second language (Filipczak, 1994).

American youth vary more widely in achievement levels than those in other countries. Their college attendance rate is quite high, but so is their high school dropout rate (25 percent). Especially serious is the proportion of high school dropouts among blacks and Hispanics in poor inner-city neighborhoods, which ranges up to 45 percent. There is an educational underclass of not just minorities but white urban poor (Kochan & Osterman, 1991).

On the other hand, recent attempts to homogenize education—by eliminating tracking, promoting cooperative learning, and simplifying textbooks—have depressed the achievements of the most talented students. A study comparing students taking advanced courses in math and science in 13 countries (the top 1 percent of U.S. students compared to a larger proportion in other countries) ranked Americans eleventh to thirteenth in all subjects except physics, where they ranked ninth (Reis, 1994).

At the bottom of the educational ladder, some 13 percent of U.S. adults are functionally illiterate (Fosler et al., 1990); that is, their skills may be at fourth- to eighth-grade levels, but they are unable to perform fundamental tasks such as filling out a job application, using a train schedule, or understanding a newspaper. A national survey of adult literacy based on 26,000 interviews found that 21 percent to 23 percent demonstrated skills in the lowest of five levels of prose, document, and quantitative literacy. Only 18 percent to 21 percent were in the two highest levels (OERI, 1993). Clearly, a workforce that is functionally illiterate requires more expensive training than one with solid basic skills. And literacy demands keep increasing in the workplace. For example, an automobile mechanic had to be able to understand about 500 manual pages to perform the job in the 1950s, but 500,000 pages to do so in the 1990s (Filipczak, 1994).

Training

As Carnevale points out later in this chapter, education, even if good, is not enough. Research in cognitive and educational psychology emphasizes the importance of applying learning directly to the task at hand. In other words, people need organizational training connected to direct experience. An example illustrates why this is so important in the post-industrial firm (Kern & Schumann, 1992). As machines assume the "job" of making a product, the worker's job is to ensure that the system functions as efficiently as possible. This new breed of factory worker, called a systems controller, is in charge of complicated equipment. Whereas engineers acquire their competence primarily through theoretical knowledge, the systems controller relies on a synergy of theoretical and empirical knowledge derived from direct and sustained contact with the process. Moreover, the systems controller must exchange information with different categories of workers—an interaction that requires social competence, another skill that can be built by both practical training and on-the-job experience.

But Carnevale demonstrates further that organizations are not training enough. A *Training* magazine survey documented a five-year increase in training budgets of 11.2 percent (from $45.5 billion in 1990 to $50.6 billion in 1994), but the gain disappeared when adjusted for inflation (Filipczak, 1994). Constant change brought on by technological advances has accelerated the need for not just training but retraining. Certainly the predominance of the middle-aging baby boom in the workforce suggests that the need for retraining is likely to be considerable.

The Field of Dreams

Once again public policy comes to the fore. In his discussion of government regulation of human resources in Chapter Two, Ledvinka focused on the demand side of the labor market, where government tries to influence the hiring practices of firms. But employment policy can also emphasize the supply side. That is, governments can try to alter the distribution of outcomes by adding to the skills of workers (Osterman, 1988). This approach, steadily pushed by the Clinton administration and its Secretary of Labor Robert Reich, has been dubbed (after the fantasy baseball film) the Field of Dreams. That is, train the workers and the high-wage jobs will come. The notion that government can select the appropriate needed skills and support the training for workers to acquire them is parallel to the industrial policy idea of government's picking winning industries and subsidizing them.

In the next section of this chapter, Osterman and Carnevale discuss some of the ins and outs of this approach, which remains controversial. Critics note, for example, that there are already about 150 federal training programs, and only 7 percent to 12 percent of dislocated workers take advantage of retraining programs when they are offered. Workers may do just as well, detractors argue, with job-search assistance, which is considerably cheaper (Stamps, 1994).

Distribution of Work

How to reconcile workers with the new conditions of work is the subject of the next three chapters in Part Three. The purview of personnel selection methods, described by Landy, Shankster-Cawley, and Moran in Chapter Seven, is being expanded to encompass broader conceptions of cognitive ability and various noncognitive measures, particularly those that facilitate working in teams. The increasing sophistication of selection methodology could potentially differentiate workers to a higher degree, exacerbating what is considered a dangerous trend—the widening wage gap between skilled and unskilled workers.

Two Tiers

Policymakers from industrialized nations addressed the widening wage gap as a global problem for the first time at the Group of Seven jobs conference in March 1994. More educated workers are benefiting from the increasing pace of technological change, while lower-level workers are being displaced or poorly paid because of their low education levels (Friedman, 1994). The dollar payoff to high school and college graduates in the United States exemplifies the growing inequality that concerns policymakers. In 1979 a male college graduate earned 49 percent more than a man with only a high school diploma, but by 1992 the gap had widened to 83 percent. It is becoming difficult for both high school and college graduates to share the label "middle class" (Reich, 1994).

These trends raise concerns about society's becoming two-tiered: one tier highly successful and another group largely unable to compete. Reich (1991) identified three types of emerging workers: *routine production workers,* who are not just those in traditional blue-collar jobs but routine supervisory personnel; *in-person service workers,* who also do routine work but provide person-to-person services, such as retail sales workers, waiters and waitresses, hairdressers, flight attendants, and the like; and *symbolic analysts,* who solve, identify, and broker new problems, including research scientists, engineers, management consultants, and organization development specialists. These workers manipulate symbols, often work in teams, nearly always have at least a bachelor's degree, and are typically men. Those in the first category, routine production workers, are slipping badly in the emerging economy while those in the last category, symbolic analysts, are rising steadily, thus creating the two tiers. Reich holds the dramatic improvement in worldwide communications and transportation technologies largely responsible for the increasing demand for symbolic analysts. A two-tiered society unnerves policymakers because it threatens both general prosperity and social stability.

Organizational Segments

Organizational theorists also expect workers to be distributed differently across the organizational environment. Some conceptualize these segments as concentric circles, with core workers inside and contingent workers outside. Handy (1990) depicts core workers, contractors, and flexible part-time or temporary workers as three leaves of a shamrock.

Such segmentations have strong implications for the way workers will relate to organizations, a topic covered in depth by Rousseau and Wade-Benzoni in Chapter Eight. Add organizational segmentation to the growing needs for training and retraining emphasized by Carnevale, and radical new thinking about careers is needed. Hall and Mirvis engage us in this analysis in Chapter Nine.

References

Filipczak, B. (1994, October). Looking past the numbers. *Training,* pp. 67–74.

Fosler, R. S., Alonso, W., Meyer, J. A., & Kern, R. (1990). *Demographic change and the American future.* Pittsburgh: University of Pittsburgh Press.

Friedman, T. L. (1994, March 16). Accent is on education as global job talks end. *New York Times,* p. D2.

Fullerton, H. N., Jr. (1993, November). Another look at the labor force. *Monthly Labor Review,* pp. 31–40.

Gerstner, L. V., Jr. (1994, May 27). Our schools are failing. Do we care? *New York Times,* p. A27.

Handy, C. (1990). *The age of unreason.* Cambridge, MA: Harvard Business School Press.

Holmes, S. A. (1994, October 23). In 4 years, Disabilities Act hasn't improved jobs rate. *New York Times,* sec. 1, p. 22.

Howard, A., & Bray, D. W. (1988). *Managerial lives in transition: Advancing age and changing times.* New York: Guilford Press.

Johnston, W. B., & Packer, A. E. (1987). *Workforce 2000: Work and workers for the twenty-first century.* Indianapolis: Hudson Institute.

Kern, H., & Schumann, M. (1992). New concepts of production and the emergence of the systems controller. In P. S. Adler (Ed.), *Technology and the future of work.* New York: Oxford University Press.

Kochan, T. A., & Osterman, P. (1991). *Human resource development and utilization: Is there too little in the U.S.?* (Report prepared for the Council on Competitiveness) Sloan School of Management, Massachusetts Institute of Technology.

Lewin, T. (1994, October 12). Men whose wives work earn less, studies show. *New York Times,* pp. A1, A21.

Mandel, M. J. (1994, June 20). It's really two immigrant economies. *Business Week,* pp. 74–78.

Manegold, C. S. (1994, August 15). Students gain but fall short of goals. *New York Times,* p. B11.

Mirvis, P. H. (Ed.). (1993). *Building the competitive workforce: Investing in human capital for corporate success.* New York: Wiley.

NCES (National Center for Education Statistics). (1993). *Projection of education statistics to 2004.* Washington, DC: U.S. Superintendent of Documents.

Noble, B. P. (1994, November 6). Still in the dark on diversity. *New York Times,* sec. 3, p. 27.

OERI (Office of Educational Research and Improvement). (1993, Fall). How literate are American adults? *OERI Bulletin,* p. 1.

Osterman, P. (1988). *Employment futures: Reorganization, dislocation and public policy.* Cambridge, MA: MIT Press.

The pay gap narrows, but . . . (1994, September 19). *Fortune,* p. 32.

Reich, R. B. (1991). *The work of nations.* New York: Knopf.

Reich, R. B. (1994, August 31). The fracturing of the middle class. *New York Times,* p. A19.

Reis, S. M. (1994, April). How schools are shortchanging the gifted. *Technology Review,* pp. 38–45.

Simon, J. L. (1989). *The economic consequences of immigration.* Cambridge, MA: Blackwell.

Stamps, D. (1994, April). Reinventing training. *Training,* pp. 43–50.

The Youth Labor Market: Skill Deficiencies and Public Policy

Paul Osterman

The employment difficulties facing American youth have long been at the center of labor market policy, but in the past decade or so there has been a subtle shift in emphasis. Although no one would profess disinterest in the problems of inner-city youth—and a vigorous discussion of these difficulties has been incorporated in the debate around the underclass issue—more attention is being paid to the broader group of noncollege young people. This new emphasis is driven less by a concern with high unemployment or race/urban themes and more by the broader interest in competitiveness and skill. The consensus diagnosis of declining American competitiveness assigns important emphasis to inadequate American human resource practices within firms and the weak training of the labor force (see Kochan & Osterman, in press). The typical comparison is between the United States, Germany, and Japan with the United States coming off third best with respect to workforce preparation. This view has led to an explosion of national commissions and reform proposals centering on providing better vocational training to young people.

Note: An expanded version of this chapter, titled "Is There a Problem with the Youth Labor Market, and if So, What Should We Do About It?" will appear in *Poverty, Inequality, and the Crisis of Social Policy* (W. J. Wilson, R. Lawson, & K. McFate, Eds.). The version here is published with the permission of the Russell Sage Foundation.

An additional element in this new view is the argument that shifting product demand and technology have undercut opportunities for noncollege youth. This is seemingly reflected in wage data that show a decline in the relative wage of high school versus college young people (Blackburn, Bloom, & Freeman, 1990).

The foregoing represents what is perhaps the current mainstream view toward youth employment problems. There is, however, an alternative perspective. This holds that youth employment problems have always received much more attention than they deserve. The transition from school and living with parents to self-sufficiency and an adult job is bound to be full of stops and starts. This is particularly true in the United States, which has a much less structured entry process than do nations such as Germany and Japan. This lack of structure might seem to cause problems if viewed as a slice of time but, so the argument might go, over the longer term the vast majority of American youth successfully settle down with no discernible adverse effects. Although there may be particular groups, such as inner-city minorities, who have problems in general, for the majority there need be little concern.

The Transition from School to Work

How well does a given youth cohort manage the transition into adult status? The standard story for noncollege youth is that, regardless of the quality of general education, high school does not do much in the way of vocational training and preparation. Instead of learning job skills in school, youth go through an extended period of labor market adjustment when they leave the classroom environment. This transition includes casual work and nonwork associated with aging and maturation as well as serious search for an adult job (Osterman, 1980). Eventually youth settle down into an adult job, but the paths by which they get there are many and varied.

To assess these issues empirically, I tracked the progress of a cohort during the school-to-work transition (see Osterman, 1995) using data from the National Longitudinal Survey of Youth (NLSY), which followed 11,406 young people between the ages of fourteen and twenty-two in 1979 until 1988. The data showed steady progression with work commitment growing with age. For example, among the oldest group of the cohort, only 3.5 percent of the men and 4 percent of the women were unemployed at the time of the last interview. There is certainly little in these data to indicate a crisis in the school-to-work transition. However, we also want to know whether the jobs are steady and whether the young people enjoy long stretches without unemployment. The answer to this question is different.

A little over one-third of the men at the beginning of their thirties were in a job that had lasted for less than a year; another 16 percent had been in their job for only a year. Among high school graduates the picture is slightly better but still troubling: over 30 percent had not held a job for even a year and another 12 percent had only one year of tenure at their current job. The pattern for women is worse than it is for men for the total group but similar for women who had remained in the labor force for the four years prior to the survey.

The conclusion I would draw is that whether there is a school-to-work transition problem depends upon the standard. Most young people progress from school to work following the expected pattern. However, probing more deeply into the quality of the process raises difficult questions. Roughly a third of all high school graduates, and somewhat more high school dropouts, fail to find stable employment by the time they are thirty. Even if some of this group do better in the next few years, a substantial fraction of the cohort is still in trouble. For this group, the rather casual American system does not work well.

It is also true that we clearly face a crisis with respect to racial differences in employment outcomes for young people. Not only are the employment rates of minority youth well below those of whites (for example, in October 1990, among sixteen- to twenty-four-year-old high school graduates not enrolled in higher education, 79 percent of whites were employed compared to 56 percent of blacks), but the situation for some subgroups, particularly high school dropouts, worsened in the past decade.

The Skills of American Youth

The preceding section assessed the American system by looking at the experience of individuals. An alternative is to ask whether American youth as a group are receiving adequate skills to enable them, and the nation, to compete internationally.

There has been considerable discussion about whether new technologies and new production systems require greater skills and whether Americans receive these skills in equal measure to overseas youth (for a review, see Kochan & Osterman, in press). A fair summary would be that when new technologies are combined with new forms of work organization (emphasizing innovations such as team production, statistical process control, and total quality management), the skill demands on the labor force do indeed increase. This assessment is very much contrary to the spirit of the older, Braverman-inspired deskilling hypothesis. The conclusion is based partly on survey research of skill requirements, an exercise that provides mild support for the upskilling conclusion but which is likely to understate skill shifts. More striking evidence comes from case studies of firms that have undertaken these innovations. Contrasts with foreign firms also bring these points sharply home. In a number of industries researchers have created matched comparisons of American and foreign firms and have compared work organization and the skills of the labor force. American firms do not fare well in these comparisons.

Concerns about a skills gap are heightened by recent wage developments. The wage rates of both high school graduates and high school dropouts have fallen sharply relative to college graduates, with the fall being the sharpest for dropouts (Blackburn, Bloom, & Freeman, 1990).

The foregoing evidence suggests that there is a skills gap. However, several complications must be considered. The evidence on the link between the wage trends and skill deficits is indirect. It is hard to argue that the trends show a declining relative quality of schools or youth since older workers (who were in school many years earlier) show a comparable, though less dramatic, pattern. In addition, relative wages can decline for reasons unrelated to skill content (for example, shifts in product demand, decline in union power) and in fact recent research shows that in many occupations skills and wages moved in opposite directions (Howell & Wolff, 1991).

More fundamentally, fieldwork shows that higher levels of skill are associated with shifts in work organization aimed at utilizing those skills, and American firms are very uneven in their willingness to adopt these changes. The reasons for this reluctance are complicated and beyond the scope of this paper, but they include considerations such as managerial ideology, lack of strong employee voice, and the unwillingness of American firms to stabilize employment. Given this uneven adoption of new production systems, it is not clear how deep the skill deficit runs.

This point raises the most difficult issue in assessing any possible skills gap. Would an improvement in the skills of youth entering the labor force lead to a more widespread adoption of production systems that utilized those skills? Would supply create its own demand? I discuss this question at greater length in the following section, but it is important to understand that any strong belief in a skills gap rests on the implicit assumption that improved skills would be matched by an increase in the demand for them. If we can answer in the affirmative, then it is plausible to believe that we are in a low-level equilibrium trap which we can escape via training. If the answer is no, then the case for a skills gap is much weaker and we need to focus instead on policies that directly impact the creation of high-quality jobs.

Youth Labor Market Policy

There are two ways to think about youth labor market policy. The first is to believe that the overall structure is adequate, but there is a relatively small target group who are having troubles and that specific policies can be designed for them. The alternative view is to believe that something deep and fundamental is wrong with the entry process and that we need to consider more structural remedies. Which is the case in the United States?

To begin, it is obvious that there is an identifiable group, minority youth, whose problems run deeper than those of other segments. Whether there is a more general youth labor market problem rests more in the eye of the beholder. The fact that over 30 percent of thirty-year-old men, and a much larger fraction of thirty-year-old women, are in a job they have held for less than a year suggests that the settling-down process is not working well.

The evidence on skills and wages is equivocal although in another way. There is clearly a problem as the wages of young people with a high school degree or less are falling. However, it is not clear whether this is a problem of the youth labor market that can be addressed by attention to young workers' skills and the school-to-work transition, or whether it reflects broader shifts in the national economy that need to be tackled by other routes. Even if the problem is more general, as is suggested by the decline in the earnings of adult high school–educated workers, to the extent that we look to the supply side for a solution, it is to the youth labor market that we should turn because that is where it is most feasible to alter the characteristics of the labor force. However, to the extent that we want to find a response on the demand side—for example, by reinvigorating unions or industrial policy—a focus on the youth labor market is misleading.

These qualifications aside, I now discuss policy options. I begin with targeted programs aimed at disadvantaged youth and then turn to more general efforts to restructure the youth labor market.

Targeted Policies

One response is to emphasize programs aimed at identifiable target groups—clearly minority noncollege youth—and to leave alone other aspects of the youth labor market. Early youth programs, running to the beginning of the Youth Employment Demonstration Projects Act (YEDPA) in 1977, were characterized by substantial experimentation but relatively few evaluations that were adequate to produce conclusions about what works and what does not. The only youth employment program of the YEDPA era that had sustainable long-term gains was the Job Corps (Betsey et al., 1985). This expensive residential program appeared to pay off in employment and earnings as well as in decline of criminal activity and welfare receipt (although even here there is more uncertainty than the popular discussion suggests). Other programs either failed to achieve their objectives or had effects that decayed rapidly over time. An additional important (although negative) finding was that work experience—simply the experience of holding a job—had no long-term benefits. This is important because many youth programs are justified as providing such experience.

Although discouraging, the YEDPA experience left one major question unanswered: If a program like the Job Corps were run on a larger scale for out-of-school youth, would it work? To address this issue, the Manpower Demonstration Research Corporation launched the JobStart program, which provided intensive education and skills training to high school dropouts in thirteen sites. The results from this program, which was evaluated through random assignment, are also generally discouraging: the educational achievements did not translate into employment gains (Auspos, Cave, Doolittle, & Hoerz, 1989).

There are some more encouraging findings, notably the ability of some welfare-to-work programs to increase modestly the employability of young welfare mothers. Nonetheless, a review of American efforts to focus on disadvantaged youth leads to very unhappy conclusions. This does not imply, however, that we should just give up our efforts to help these groups; that would be morally unacceptable if nothing else. In small ways (and surely for some individuals in big ways) the programs help. But it does seem that in the end we are driven to consider more structural changes in the youth labor market. These structural changes, by their nature, will affect not only the disadvantaged but other youth more generally and thus will speak to the broader concern about the functioning of the youth labor market.

Two major strategies for structural change present themselves. These are (1) introducing new school-to-work transition systems, including an American adaptation of the German dual model; and (2) attempting to alter the broader allocation/stratification system that maps individuals into jobs of a given quality.

Linking School and Work

There has been an explosion of interest in altering the relationship between schools and the workplace, inspired in part by growing awareness of the German system. Today roughly 80 percent of all German youth go through this system. At about age fifteen youth choose one of approximately four hundred occupational tracks (which include training for everything from auto workers to bank tellers to accountants to electronics technicians). They then spend four days a week employed by a firm and receiving training, and one day a week in school. The training they receive is carefully structured and standardized nationally and is provided by specially trained and certified firm employees. At the end of this training period the young people take examinations, again nationally standardized and administered by a local business organization. This system is widely accepted by all segments of German society, and all actors in the labor market—firms, unions, and government—jointly participate in administering and supervising it. Occupational content and curriculum are continually reviewed through a series of joint consultative meetings.

A more complete discussion of this model would include greater balance in the treatment of its problems. Among the inadequacies in the German system that should be addressed are early tracking, substantial gender differences in occupational training, imbalances between occupations trained for and those demanded in the economy, the difficult situation of immigrants in Germany, and the sometimes slow response to technical change in updating the curriculum. However, the general picture conveyed here of deep training provided to a broad segment of entering workers is accurate. The key point is the high degree of seriousness accorded youth vocational training and the very considerable commitment given to quality, as reflected in the certification of trainers within firms, the careful attention given to curriculum, and the formal examination system. All of this stands in sharp contrast to the comparatively casual American system of vocational preparation.

The German dual model is attractive because it appears to represent a balance between firm- and school-based training. In addition, all observers agree that the quality of training is high. For these reasons, and because there appears to be a correlation between the dual system and German productivity, the recent American discussion has centered around efforts to transplant the German model here. Congress recently passed new school-to-work legislation along these lines.

What should we make of these efforts? At the broadest level these proposals are attractive because they speak directly to the inadequate skills that American youth bring to the workplace, and they do so in a way that promises a structural reform of the school-to-work transition process. It is for these compelling reasons—because the initiatives seem a way both to escape from the trap of remedial programs and to make a substantial shift in old patterns—that the ideas caught on so fast. Nonetheless, it does seem important to probe a little deeper at the level of both principles and practicality.

One of the strengths of the American entry system is the opportunities it gives young people to experiment and to change their minds. A second strength is its lack of tracking relative to European systems. Both of these advantages are at risk in a German model. It is very hard to imagine Americans willing to accept a system that required most youth to select occupations in the tenth or eleventh grade. To complicate matters further, even if American youth were to make such selections, the system would have to be designed to accommodate the enormous amount of mind-changing they would undoubtedly go through (such second thoughts are not a central part of the German system). This difference means that it would be impossible to specialize the occupational training or the classroom elements because everything would have to be transferable. Absent this specialization the program begins to look more like work experience and less like serious apprenticeships.

A related problem concerns portability. Americans are mobile, and any apprenticeship program must lead to credentials that are recognized throughout the country. This difficulty is exacerbated by the highly decentralized structure of American education, which means that the new apprenticeships have to be organized on a district-by-district basis. We are a long way from the German uniformity of four hundred recognized occupations and standard national examinations.

An additional concern is whether firms can be induced to cooperate and offer apprenticeship openings. After all, if firms do a poor job of providing quality training to their incumbent workforce—and most observers agree this is a problem—why should we expect them to do a good job for youth in apprenticeship programs?

This question in fact has two parts: whether the openings will be made available and whether quality training will be provided. In Germany, the national culture demands provision of training slots. Furthermore, firms have geared their production system around these slots, with large firms having training staffs and small firms counting on apprentices to help with production. The staff of employers have themselves gone through the program and hence are committed to the system and to quality training. Virtually none of the above applies in the United States. Employer motivations would have to be either public service or perceived labor shortages. Both are weak foundations upon which to build a fundamental transformation. In addition, even if the CEO committed the company to a given number of slots, the quality of that experience rests on the behavior of supervisors, and it is hard to see how mass production of quality training within firms can be assured.

A related concern is how firms would be compensated for the costs of training. In Germany, apprentices are paid but at rates very much below those of regular workers. Indeed, according to some estimates sixteen-year-old German apprentices are compensated at 20 percent of the adult rate and eighteen-year-olds at 33 percent (Casey, 1986). Because the youth are actually part of the production system, particularly in small firms, employers find the system worthwhile. American proposals tend to be silent on the issue of pay and the related issue of how to compensate firms for the costs of the training they provide. This issue is likely to exacerbate the concerns about quality.

Where is all of this likely to go? As a practical matter, it seems that even if successful in the end, these initiatives will devolve to a much more modest objective. Work experience in high school and the vocational skills content of the curriculum will be modestly enhanced. Programs will be offered that familiarize youth with alternative fields and try to interest them sufficiently to motivate them to continue after high school into community college programs in these areas.

Some advocates of American apprenticeship systems might argue their case from a different perspective. Returning to the themes raised earlier, they would describe apprenticeships as a way of constructing paths into the labor market for minorities who lack the informal contact networks enjoyed by whites. However, why should apprenticeships be able to meet this objective whereas vocational education programs failed in the past? The answer has to be that an apprenticeship system would be broad based, incorporating a large fraction of a youth cohort, and hence would avoid stigmatizing its clients. However, this immediately returns us to the earlier discussion and the doubts raised about whether it is possible to build such a system.

An additional qualification concerning the target group should be noted. The need to provide productive youth to employers as part of selling the program precludes targeting those most in trouble—people with very low academic skills who either have dropped out of the labor market or may be about to do so. Furthermore, despite much effort, no youth employment program has proved to have much effect on dropouts.

In short, I do not mean to imply that reforms of the school-work link are not desirable. The point is that they should be viewed in more modest terms than those now characterizing much of the current enthusiasm. Nonetheless, they hold the possibility of attracting a certain number of young people who might have graduated from high school and gone directly into the labor market with few skills, convincing them to continue instead in a serious vocational training program. This is all to the good, albeit far short of the implementation of German-style apprenticeship models.

The Broader Context

The second broad policy option is to try to alter the opportunity set into which youth move. To see the point, consider the following interpretation of the discussion thus far: there is a certain distribution of jobs in the economy and these jobs can be characterized by their wage/skill aspects. This distribution is fixed. A "good" youth labor system moves young people into this distribution without pain (for example, extended unemployment) and without discrimination (minority youth getting a larger share of the bad jobs than do white youth). In the end, however, the distribution is simply what it is and people are allocated into it. To alter this we would need to design policies that transform the underlying distribution of opportunities.

This topic touches on many deep issues, ranging from the sociological literature on whether social policy can influence social mobility to what determines the pattern of the firm's demand for labor. I obviously cannot do justice to these issues here. A more narrow formulation is whether any reforms of the youth labor market/school-to-work transition process are relevant. The question then becomes whether an increase in the skill of American youth will induce employers to alter the content of their jobs in a way that upgrades the quality of employment.

Advocates of increased training frequently argue that employers will respond to increased supply of skill by restructuring work, but the hard evidence on this is very scarce. It is obviously difficult using American evidence to prove the point because there are few, if any, identifiable local labor markets in which the experiment (to sharply improve training and then observe firm behavior) has been executed. Therefore advocates typically cite comparative research in which matched samples of firms in similar industries producing similar products are compared (for example, Maurice, Sorge, & Warner, 1980; Steedman & Wagner, 1987; Daly, Hitchens, & Wagner, 1985; MacDuffie & Krafcik, 1992). Most such studies find that firms with a more skilled labor force also have broader jobs, are more likely to devolve authority to employees and to use teams, and so forth. The problem, of course, is that it is very hard to know whether increased training induced firms to adopt these systems or whether firms for other reasons chose "transformed" production systems, then developed the skilled workforce that such systems require.

It seems to me that the best way to think about this issue is to conceptualize increases in the skill level of the workforce, or of potential new hires, as reductions in the costs firms face should they wish—for other reasons—to adopt new production systems. In this view improving skills increases the chances that such transformations will occur but in no way guarantees it.

There are several reasons for adopting this view. Any theory of why firms adopt production systems must identify a number of factors—such as worker voice, management values, and product market strategy—as important influences. And, indeed, those nations that have higher-skilled workforces and production systems with broadly skilled jobs also differ from the United States on these other dimensions. Hence, there is no reason to give skill any particular causal primacy. Indeed, there are reasons to think of it as secondary. Case studies of American firms that have chosen to move in new directions—firms such as Corning and Motorola—indicate that the decision to change came first and the firm then moved to train its workforce. Some international evidence also supports this view: Japanese youth do not leave school with high levels of vocational skills. Indeed, Japanese schools are known to be weak in vocational training. Rather, the graduates are strong academically and firms then provide the vocational training. Again, vocational training follows, not leads, production systems.

None of this is intended to imply that training does not help improve job quality. First, as already noted, it does reduce the cost of transformations and hence will improve the chances that change will occur. Second, training provides a useful platform from which public policy can work with firms on a variety of issues. It is an entree into the private sector and through this access other actions can be encouraged. Nonetheless, we should continue to hold modest expectations about the direct impact enhancing the skills of new entrants will have on the quality of jobs generated by the private economy.

Simply upskilling new entrants will not improve the distribution of job quality very much. There is, however, another European lesson with respect to the broader context. Until very recently, Europeans have used a combination of laws, union power, and custom to raise the bottom of the labor market. The consequence is that the earning distribution in Europe is narrower than in the United States, layoffs are typically more difficult, and temporary or short-contact work (and part-time work) is scarcer. It would seem reasonable to conclude that young people who do find work are better off relative to the average adult than is true in America. This suggests that a strategy of using political power to alter the distribution of labor market outcomes is feasible.

On the other hand, we have several reasons to be cautious of this conclusion. Until the mid-1970s, Europe also enjoyed full employment relative to the United States and therefore had it both ways: high-quality jobs and plenty of them. That condition changed and European unemployment has risen above American levels. While the quality of European jobs may still, on average, exceed that of jobs in the United States, young people have much more difficulty finding them. These difficulties have led Europeans to reconsider the optimum amount of labor market regulation that has been in effect, and in recent years they have loosened a number of restrictions. European labor markets remain more regulated than those in the United States and arguably still produce better jobs, but the case for emulating Europe is shakier than in the past.

Conclusion

Does America have a youth labor market problem, and if so, what do we know about how to deal with it? These are the central questions addressed in this chapter section and the answers are less clear than one might like.

In all countries, youth are marginalized in the labor market. France, for example, is very much like the United States in terms of youth entering isolated sectors and their high unemployment as they try to move into the adult economy. Even Germany marginalizes youth although in a more subtle way. Youth are also "confined" into a youth sector: they disproportionately undertake their apprenticeships in small firms, locations in which they will not remain as they age. In these small firms, youth are seen as low-wage labor as much as they are considered trainees enrolled in an educational process. Furthermore, while teen unemployment is low, the unemployment of young adults rises more sharply in Germany than it does in other nations because the effect of the dual system is to defer, not avoid, the entry process.

Youth are marginalized everywhere, partly because their skills (and maturity at work) are naturally lower than those of adults and partly because it is a reasonable distributional rule to parcel out a larger share of good jobs to adults rather than young people. Given these facts of life, it still remains the case that the process can be managed well or badly. To do it well means that the marginal phase is also a building one in which youth gain genuine skills appropriate to future economic demands. To do well also means that the process is fair and that no subgroup suffers disproportionately. By these standards, the United States still leaves much to be desired.

The real difficulties arise when it comes to considering solutions. The lessons of this review can best be summarized as follows: keep youth in school longer, connect them to the labor market earlier, and induce them at least to enroll in community colleges. These are the best lessons that can be drawn, but they are clearly not enough. It seems certain that substantial numbers of inner-city minority youth will not benefit. What we have learned, from here and abroad, suggests that interventions in the youth labor market are too narrow a way to approach this issue. A more expansive, macroeconomic policy and broader and deeper interventions in communities, families, and schools are required.

References

Auspos, P., Cave, G., Doolittle, F., & Hoerz, G. (1989). *Implementing Job-Start: A demonstration for school dropouts in the JTPA system.* New York: MDRC.

Betsey, C., et al. (1985). *Youth employment and training programs: The YEDPA years.* Washington, DC: National Research Council.

Blackburn, M., Bloom, D., & Freeman, R. (1990). The declining position of less-skilled American males. In G. Burtless (Ed.), *A future of lousy jobs.* Washington, DC: Brookings Institution.

Casey, B. (1986). The dual apprenticeship system and the recruitment and retention of young persons in West Germany. *British Journal of Industrial Relations, 24,* 63–81.

Daly, A., Hitchens, D. M., & Wagner, K. (1985, February). Productivity, machinery and skills in a sample of British and German manufacturing plants. *National Institute of Economic Review,* pp. 48–61.

Howell, D. & Wolff, E. (1991). Trends in the growth and distribution of skills in the U.S. workplace, 1960–85. *Industrial and Labor Relations Review, 44,* 486–502.

Kochan, T. A., & Osterman, P. (in press). *Human resource development and training: Is there too little in the U.S.?* Prepared for the American Council on Competitiveness. Cambridge, MA: Harvard Business School Press.

MacDuffie J. P., & Krafcik, J. (1992). Integrating technology and human resources for high performance manufacturing: Evidence from the international auto industry. In T. A. Kochan & M. Useem (Eds.), *Transforming organizations.* New York: Oxford University Press.

Maurice, M., Sorge, A., & Warner, M. (1980). Societal differences in organizing manufacturing units: A comparison of France, West Germany, and Great Britain. *Organization Studies, 1,* 59–86.

Osterman, P. (1980). *Getting started: The youth labor market.* Cambridge, MA: MIT Press.

Osterman, P. (1995). Is there a problem with the youth labor market, and if so, how should we fix it? In W. J. Wilson, R. Lawson, & K. McFate (Eds.), *Poverty, inequality, and the crisis of social policy.* New York: Russell Sage Foundation.

Steedman, H., & Wagner, K. (1987, November). A second look at productivity, machinery and skills in Britain and Germany. *National Institute Economic Review,* pp. 84–96.

Enhancing Skills in the New Economy

Anthony P. Carnevale

Something happened on the way to the second century of American economic dominance. The globalization of wealth and technology created a whole new economic ball game with new rules and an expanded set of competitive standards. In the old economy, America was preeminent because of our ability to consistently produce an increasing number of goods and services with the same or fewer resources. In the old mass production economy, higher volumes at lower costs per unit of output made products and services more affordable for an increasing share of the consuming public. In the new economy, both Americans and consumers in other nations have more money in their pockets and less time to spend it. As a result, they are demanding more than mass-produced goods and services.

Consumers will no longer accept products and services that are cheap and available but of low quality. Plain vanilla isn't good enough anymore. Consumers want variety and customization from companies that will tailor goods and services to their particular wants and needs. Consumers with more money but less time also want convenience built into the products and services they buy. They also want state-of-the-art products and services. They are loyal to the organizations they trust to get innovations off the drawing board and into their hands quickly. In the new competitive envi-

Note: Special thanks to Anita Cowley for her substantive contributions and editorial assistance.

ronment, consumers demand what new flexible technologies can deliver at mass production prices: quality, variety, customization, convenience, and speed. In addition, the globalization of competition assures that if Americans don't deliver on the new competitive standards, someone else will, and that someone else is likely to be a foreign worker in Europe or Asia. The new economy requires profound changes in American institutions. A substantial share of improvements in quality, variety, customization, convenience, and speed occur in the process of making the product, delivering the service, and interacting with the customer. As a result, top-down hierarchies that are the typical organizational format need to be replaced with high-performance work organizations that drive autonomy, skill, resources, and new, flexible technologies down the line toward the point of production, service delivery, and the interface with the customer.

The new economy will require a much more highly skilled workforce. First, we will need to provide effective education for the "other half" of our high school graduates who don't go on to postsecondary education. These are the students who ultimately make the products, deliver the services, and interact with customers. Skill requirements are going up fastest among this group, but they are afforded the least educational preparation. Our competitors are doing better. In Europe and Asia, noncollege youth get better schooling, and more than eight out of ten get formal training after high school (National Center for Education Statistics, 1994).

The Current Context of Education in America

The importance of integrating academic and applied learning has assumed a new urgency in the current environment for two reasons. First, the accumulation of research findings in the cognitive sciences asserts without qualification that a more experiential and applied pedagogy provides superior learning irrespective of the economic or social context in which skills will ultimately be used. Second, the organization and delivery of schooling have always been and need to be aligned with the organization of work in the interest of fulfilling both the educators' and the employers' mission in American society. Evidence of substantial change in the organization of work continues to accumulate, suggesting that schooling as presently structured may be out of sync with a new economic ethos, leaving employers and school graduates without the skills they need to succeed in the new economy.

Although there is a convergence between new research in the cognitive sciences and new functional requirements in cutting-edge, high-performance workplaces, the dominant pedagogy is still producing workers for traditional workplaces. Table 6.1 outlines how workers and their skills differ in typical production and service delivery systems.

In traditional workplaces, where jobs are designed narrowly and tasks are repetitive, there is little need to transfer general knowledge to a series of unique applications. In high-performance work systems, however, machines perform all the repetitive mental and physical tasks, and people spend their time deploying machine capabilities to produce variety and customize products and services. This requires workers who can transfer knowledge and prior experience to handle a continuous stream of exceptions. Every short production run or customized service is different and requires the transfer and tailoring of accumulated know-how to solve problems creatively. The hierarchical authority of the teacher instructing passive students is not unlike the world of bosses and workers in traditional workplaces. In both cases, passivity breeds boredom, poor performance, absenteeism, and sabotage. In high-performance work systems, employees are involved, not passive. Employees participate in setting outcome standards and take responsibility for quality of final products and services. Employees are also active participants in learning processes that drive continuous improvements, especially employees down the line at the point of production, at the point of service delivery, and at the interface with the customer where most incremental learning occurs.

Traditional pedagogy isolates students row on row, with each one looking at the back of the student's head in the row in front. Every student competes with all others in the war for grades and advancement. The classic image of the traditional assembly line is that of workers shoulder to shoulder facing the machinery they tend. Similarly, in traditional workplaces, individuals are assigned specific and separate responsibilities, and performance is judged one employee at a time in the competition for wages and promotion. In both cases, teamwork is discouraged, information is hoarded, and the high-performing "rate busters" are resented. In

Table 6.1. Characteristics of People at Work in Typical Production and Service Delivery Systems.

	Typical Production and Service Delivery Systems							
	Preindustrial Crafts	Mass Production			Service		Independent Sector	New Economy
Typical Worker	Artisans	White-collar workers, technical professionals	Skilled tradespeople	Blue-collar production employees	White-collar workers, service professionals	Nonsupervisory employees	Small business craft and professional workers	Teams of individuals alternating expert, brokering, and leadership roles
Skill Requirements	Deep occupational skills	Deep occupational skills, as well as broad group effectiveness, adaptability, and organizational skills	Deep technical skills, problem-solving skills	Narrow job-specific skills	Broad adaptability skills, interpersonal and organizational skills	Narrow job-specific skills, interpersonal skills	Deep occupational skills, personal management and adaptability skills	Deep technical skills, as well as learning, communication, adaptability, personal management, group effectiveness, and influencing skills
Use of Skills at Work	Hands on/concrete; specific and repetitive skill	Hands off/abstract; reserves of technical skills for handling exceptions	Hands on/concrete; reserves of technical skills for handling exceptions	Hands on/concrete; job-specific and repetitive skills	Hands off/abstract; broad and deep reserve skills	Hands on/concrete; job-specific and repetitive skills	Mix of hands-on and hands-off skills; reserve skills for handling exceptions	Hands off/abstract; general skills, reserves of technical and nontechnical skills for handling exceptions

Source: Adapted from Carnevale, 1991.

high-performance work systems employees work face-to-face, machines do the rote work, and people are left to deploy machine capabilities, spending most of their time interacting with co-workers or customers. Workers are more autonomous in order to exploit more flexible work structures and technologies. Because of the higher levels of human contact, work is more social, organized into teams and general community of practice. Performance and rewards are attached to groups and not individuals.

Traditional learning emphasizes correct responses to sets of particular questions. Similarly, traditional workplaces assign well-defined tasks and teach skills to match each task. More skilled workers are assigned more tasks and more skills, but roles are no less defined. Broader institutional goals and context are left to senior managers and technical personnel at the top of the organizational pyramid. In modern high-performance work systems, job assignments are overlapping, more open-ended and ambiguous. Everyone understands his or her role in the broader context of the entire work process from product design to customer, as well as the organization's strategy and vision. Everyone is responsible for the quality of the final product or service.

Traditional pedagogy emphasizes right answers with less attention to learning from mistakes and understanding processes for arriving at answers. Performance standards derive from tests that quantify and encourage right answers. The focus on right answers encourages superficial learning, and tests substitute for more applied diagnostic tools that can provide deeper assessments and prescribe further development. Similarly, traditional work structures emphasize performing assigned tasks without attention to alternative ways to get the job done that would improve work processes or product quality. Performance assessments are based on the ability of employees to finish tasks on time. Alternatively, in high-performance systems more attention is paid to understanding and improving work processes in the interest of embedding quality in the production process, rather than counting defects after work is done.

Taking all this into account, education will not be enough. Educational improvements have consistently accounted for about 20 percent of competitive improvements. This is impressive, but not enough to solve our competitive problem. Any education strategy all by itself would be too slow. School graduates replace existing workers at the rate of about 3 percent per year. At this rate, we will have to wait more than 33 years for a new workforce. In addition, more technology will be required (Denison, 1974; Baumol, Blackman, & Wolff, 1989). Currently Japanese workers have three times as much technology available to them on the job as American workers. Technology, like education, consistently accounts for about 20 percent of competitive improvements (Carnevale, 1991).

More education and technology will be nice but not enough. The lion's share of competitive advantage will come from the way we use our educated workers and technologies. Economists have known for a long time that about 40 percent of competitive improvements come from the resources we buy and about 60 percent come from the way we use those resources. In other words, about 40 percent of competitive improvements can be bought but 60 percent have to be learned in the real economy of workers, organizations, and machines (Denison, 1974).

Investment in education and technology are important in our competitive future, but innovation and know-how in the daily working environment are crucial. We can buy technologies and educate until we are blue in the face, but if employers don't build high-performance systems and design technologies that utilize skill, it's all for nothing. America's organizational adaptation to new competitive requirements has been minimal thus far. Currently only 1 percent of American employees work in a high-performance work setting that gives them the autonomy and skill necessary to meet new competitive standards and exploit the potential of new flexible technologies (Commission on the Skills, 1992).

Education, technology, and high-performance work organization will still not be enough. American employers will also need to train more. There are six main reasons why employees need training above and beyond schooling and what they learn informally from working together on the job in high-performance work systems.

1. *Employees need to be trained to handle organizational responsibilities* as they interact with subordinates, peers, and bosses. Four kinds of organizational training are required: executive development, management training, supervisory training, and in high-performance work systems, nonsupervisory worker training for employees who work in autonomous teams.
2. *Employees need training to optimize the use of technology.* Employees

must be able to design technologies successfully, install them effectively, make continuous improvements in their use, and develop new applications. This requires two kinds of training: technical training and skill training. More technical training will be required for those who need to understand the inner workings of technology: engineers, scientists, manufacturing technicians, and health technologists. For other workers, the inner workings of technology are as invisible as the carburetor is to the driver. These workers, most of us, will require skill training that teaches effective use of technologies.

3. *Employees need training to help them interact with customers.* Those who design and make or deliver goods and services need to empathize with customers if the wants, needs, and convenience of the customer are to be answered. Those with direct contact with customers need to develop both empathy and interpersonal skills that assure good customer service.

4. *Employees need training that allows them to meet specific strategic goals.* The current vogue for quality training is a case in point. The ability to provide variety or customize products and services requires training that enhances flexibility in skills such as problem solving and creativity. The organizational ability to provide customer service requires communication and interpersonal skills.

5. *Employees need basic skills training.* When new performance requirements, new technology, or new work processes outrun basic educational preparations, basic skills training is required.

6. *Employees need safety and other regulatory forms of training* in order to protect workers and communities.

Status of Training in America

There are eight categories of worker training and curricula that meet the aforementioned needs:

1. *Organizational training* for employees who have responsibilities for others or for work processes (for example, executive development, management and supervisory training, and team training)

2. *Technical training* to develop, install, and maintain new technology (for example, training for engineers, scientists, techni-

cians in manufacturing, technologists in health care, data processing workers, and skilled trades workers such as electricians and millwrights)
3. *Skill training* to teach employees to use new technology and software (for example, training for workers from machine operators to clerical workers)
4. *Customer interface training* for employees who work with customers (for example, salespeople, cashiers, and service workers)
5. *Strategic training* necessary to achieve specific goals (for example, quality training)
6. *Professional training* to help nontechnical professionals brush up and keep up (for example, retraining for accountants, architects, doctors, lawyers, and so forth)
7. *Basic skills training* for workers whose academic preparation in the three R's impedes performance and adaptation (notably this training accounts for only about $300 million of the $30 billion in employer training, Bureau of Labor Statistics, 1993)
8. *Regulated training* to comply with Occupational Safety and Health Administration (OSHA), environmental, or other governmental mandates.

A second set of curricula is organized by subject matter, but the content tends to be customized to the specific industry or occupational context:

- Academic basics: applied reading, writing, and computation
- Adaptability skills: learning, problem solving, creativity
- Listening and oral communication
- Interpersonal, negotiation, and teamwork skills
- Leadership and organizational effectiveness
- Career development, motivation, and goal setting
- Managing and valuing diversity

American employers spend about $30 billion a year on training—1.02 percent of payroll costs. By comparison, expenditures for new plants and equipment were projected at $552 billion for 1992. Training leaders like Motorola, IBM, Federal Express, and other high-training companies spend between 3 percent and 10 percent of payroll on training (Carnevale, 1992).

Large companies generally don't distribute training in an elitist fashion. As the previously listed categories show, much of the training goes to noncollege and nonsupervisory workers, especially if regulatory training is included. For instance, Bureau of Labor Statistics (BLS) data show that a higher proportion of technicians and technologists get formal retraining than executives. Employer-based training is elitist to the extent that technical and skill training is more job specific, and management and executive development is more general. But the real elitism in employer-based training rests in the reality that so few workers outside companies with over 10,000 employees get any. Only 16 percent of American employees have ever had any training from their employer.

Employer-based training is increasing, however. In 1983, BLS calculated that about 11 percent of workers had ever received formal training from their employer; this figure had grown to 16 percent by 1991—a 45 percent increase in training compared to a 17 percent increase in the size of the labor force. In addition, the training is longer. Between 1983 and 1991, the proportion of worker-trainees who received training of less than twelve weeks declined from 72 percent of trainees to 33 percent. At the same time, the proportion of worker-trainees who received twelve to twenty-five weeks of training increased from 8 percent of trainees to 32 percent (Bureau of Labor Statistics, 1993).

Although the increase in employer-based training is impressive, remember that it is limited to large organizations and skilled workers. As a result, natural increases in employer-based training fail to match resources to needs and do not align with specific components of our competitiveness and opportunity strategy.

While comparisons are difficult, it is clear that Americans don't train on the job nearly as much as their competitors do. European governments spend at least four times as much as American governments on workplace training. Comparisons are especially unfavorable for noncollege workers. For instance, 66 percent of German workers are involved in apprenticeship programs that include education and workplace training. Only two-tenths of one percent of Americans are involved in similar programs. The French employer-training mandate is currently set at 1.7 percent of payroll (Freeman, 1994). The Japanese embed training in work processes and equipment and still provide three to four times as much formal training as American employers.

Current and proposed policies to increase training require an employer-based involvement, including (1) the integration of schooling and work-based learning for noncollege youth as well as incumbent, disadvantaged, welfare-dependent, and dislocated workers; (2) developing curricula and education/training systems consistent with work-based skill standards; and (3) the inclusion of training elements in our high-performance work, small business development, and technology policy initiatives.

Conclusion

Current legislative proposals for training workers are proceeding along two tracks. One track proposes training for workers as well as the development of high-performance work systems as an integral part of legislative proposals for apprenticeship, job creation, trade, technology policy, and defense conversion. The inclusion of worker training and the installation of high-performance work systems as programmatic elements in legislative mandates emerging in a number of federal departments requires high levels of collaboration between the Department of Labor (DOL) and other federal departments as well as the development of new relationships with unions, trade associations, individual employers, and other public institutions in the field. The Department of Labor will need to collaborate with the Department of Education to provide the training complement to occupational education in developing apprenticeship and school-to-work programs. DOL will need to work with the Department of Commerce to assist in the high-performance work and training missions already included in legislation on technology policy. Similarly the Department of Defense conversion legislation includes substantial commitments to installation of training and high-performance systems in order to modernize the defense industrial base. Legislation contemplated for energy and transportation is likely to carry similar commitments. DOL will need strong technical assistance capabilities in Washington and in the field to collaborate successfully.

A second set of legislative proposals focuses on increasing the quantity and quality of training in general. Policies to leverage training in general are justified on the basis of the current underinvestment in worker training by employers. Proponents argue that increasing workers' skills through training can encourage employers to upgrade technology and work processes as well. Proposals to leverage training include employer mandates, tax incentives, and technical assistance.

Advocates of training mandates point to their proven effectiveness in France and Australia and claim that they would have the most dramatic impacts. The Clinton administration's mandate, for instance, would increase employer expenditures on training from $30 billion to $51 billion and would cover 75 percent of American workers. Training mandates are opposed by both business and organized labor, whose representatives argue that a training mandate overemphasizes training relative to job creation, trade, technology, and high-performance work policies that drive training. They contend further that incumbent worker training policies are most effective when integrated into these latter policy areas. In addition, opponents claim that a training mandate creates an antagonistic relationship with business in a new policy arena where collaborative relationships would be most effective, at least initially. They assert that mandates are premature and that policy for worker training should proceed apace with the introduction of new technology and high-performance work systems. Business interests, especially mid-sized and small businesses, also are opposed because they anticipate additional mandates for family leave and health care as well as OSHA and environmental restraints.

The most popular tax incentive for training is a tax credit to pay part of the cost for new training, modeled along the lines of the research and development (R&D) tax credit. Various commissions and a bipartisan series of federal legislators have consistently proposed tax credits for training since the 1970s. Recent discussions center on the inclusion of training as an eligible activity in a federal investment tax credit. Business tends to support tax credits, and indications from the AFL-CIO suggest that that organization might support a tax credit if suitable provisions for worker participation were included.

A general tax credit is likely to encourage most new training among large firms that already train. The challenge for framers of a training tax credit is to devise one that maximizes new spending for training, assures general training over job-specific training, and reaches more than large institutions that already train.

The consensus format for a training tax credit that would meet these requirements and would be both technically and politically feasible is this: it must be a proportional credit against tax liability for the direct costs of annual spending increases for frontline supervisory training as well as skill and team training for nonsupervisory workers. Eligible training would have to meet standards to assure quality and general (versus job-specific) applicability of training covered under the credit. Smaller organizations would be allowed to pool credits.

Other design features could be added to encourage more impact on overall training levels, more general versus job-specific training, and a greater complementarity with other policies that would benefit from a work-based training component. For example, the size of the tax credit could be varied or made exclusively available for employer training associated with school-to-work programs; work-based training to meet national skill standards; structured work experience and work-based training for upgrading the skills of Job Training Partnership Act or welfare clientele; part-time, temporary, or dislocated workers; structured on-the-job training or formal training necessary for workers to make the transition to high-performance work; and work-based training attached to a modernization effort in collaboration with federal small business development or industrial extension agencies. A system of grants and demonstrations could complement or provide a more incremental substitute on the way to a training mandate or a tax credit.

A leadership and technical assistance strategy would be a necessary complement to either a tax credit or grant-based approach to assure that new publicly subsidized training meets appropriate standards. A technical assistance agenda should be delivered through business and labor organizations and should focus on the following:

1. Inventory, benchmarking, analysis, standard setting, and the crafting of best-practice models and their dissemination in areas such as school-to-work, apprenticeships, skill standards, instructional systems design, informal high-performance learning systems, and curricula for supervisory, technical, and behavioral skills.
2. An examination of the above issues in the context of particular industries as well as product (for example, bio-technology) and production technologies with active industry and labor involvement.

3. A field strategy to integrate best practices through demonstrations and the facilitation of ongoing benchmarking among industry and labor institutions.

The notion of using loans to individuals and institutions for work-based training has received little attention, but deserves more. Loans are effective devices for funding long-term development for individuals and leveraging private organizational capital. There is evidence to suggest that loans have been effective in the retraining of dislocated workers, and recent proposals from lending authorities to expand their portfolios to corporate clients deserve further analysis.

Collaborative approaches to encourage worker training are cheapest and offer the path of least political resistance. These include the promotion of voluntary standards, research and development, technical assistance, dissemination of model practices, and demonstration projects. Collaborative approaches are inherently flexible because they can provide voluntary assistance on installing high-performance work designs as well as training; and with industry and labor participation, they can be customized to particular industry contexts. Moreover, they are voluntary and participatory, building public-private relationships in an incremental and nonintrusive fashion. Finally, they would build the institutional relationships and expertise that would allow DOL to be a strong partner working with other agencies, unions, trade associations, and delivery institutions in the field to leverage worker training and high-performance work systems in the full range of American workplaces.

References

Baumol, W. J., Blackman, S. A., & Wolff, E. N. (1989). *Productivity and American leadership: The long view.* Cambridge, MA: MIT Press.

Bureau of Labor Statistics (1993). *How workers get their training.* Washington, DC: U.S. Government Printing Office.

Carnevale, A. P. (1991). *America and the new economy: How new competitive standards are radically changing American workplaces.* San Francisco: Jossey-Bass.

Carnevale, A. P. (1992). What training means in an election year. *Training and Development Journal, 46*(10), 45–48.

Commission on the Skills of the American Workforce. (1992). *America's choice: High skill or low wages.* Rochester, NY: National Center on Education and the Economy.

Denison, E. (1974). *Accounting for United States economic growth, 1929–1969.* Washington, DC: Brookings Institution.

Freeman, R. B. (1994). *Working under different rules.* Cambridge, MA: National Bureau of Economic Research.

National Center for Education Statistics. (1994). *The condition of education.* Washington, DC: U.S. Government Printing Office.

Chapter Seven

Advancing Personnel Selection and Placement Methods

Frank J. Landy, Laura Shankster-Cawley, Stacey Kohler Moran

Trace personnel psychology from its earliest roots and you will notice major trends. The period from 1907 through 1920 was prescientific. Practitioners like Munsterberg, Thorndike, and Cattell simply transplanted findings from the laboratory to the workplace. There was no theory (beyond the inchoate recognition that individual differences might be useful as well as interesting) and even less empirical research. Burtt primed the inductive pump with disciplined correlational analyses of Munsterberg's casually collected test data (Landy, 1992). Viteles picked up and trumpeted this theme and launched the era of dustbowl empiricism. The period following World War II could be characterized as an epidemic of measurement that was not reined in until the early 1960s. During that period of empiricism, educational psychologists like Thorndike and Thurstone conducted the theoretical research. Guilford carried the banner through the 1960s with his nascent model of the intellect. It was not until the 1970s that theory-building in personnel

Note: We would like to acknowledge the contributions of David Day, Jim Farr, Rick Jacobs, and John Mathieu in reviewing early versions of this chapter as well as the substantial contributions of Ann Howard and Shelly Zedeck to later versions. In addition, the clerical and technical assistance of Joy Struble, Kirk Basehore, Michelle Albright, Adam Carroll, and Brian Cawley was invaluable.

psychology could function under its own power. The work of Schmidt and Hunter on differential validity, Fleishman on ability taxonomies, and Dunnette on the places of constructs in theories of work performance all represent this move toward a theoretical grounding for personnel practice.

In the past two decades, appreciation of the practical value of good theory has intensified. Analytic techniques like path analysis and meta-analysis have unlocked order and regularity that were previously obscured. These new "regularities" are forming the building blocks of new theories of industrial behavior. Similarly, the development of new techniques and measures has sharpened the definitions of antecedent and consequent variables of interest to personnel psychologists and practitioners. Meta-analyses have given new life to personality measurement. Innovative theories of cognitive functioning have led to new measurements and conceptualizations of mental ability. Elements of performance are better understood.

This is an exciting time for personnel practitioners and researchers alike. It is one of those periods when things are happening at such a rapid pace that the distinction between practice and theory is blurred. But with the excitement, there should also be apprehension. This point is where our predecessors were in 1945, but twenty years passed before real theoretical and practical progress began.

In this chapter, we identify the raw material that the current generation of personnel psychologists has to work with. We point out practical and theoretical advances as well as the challenges that we see to progress. In addition, we highlight the overarching theme of this book—change. As the heuristic model presented in Chapter One illustrates, two major forces will destabilize the environment for the personnel psychologist: technological advancement and demographic/social context transformation. The technological advancement (or demand) force will require new ways of thinking about predictors and criteria. The demographic/ social context force will require new ways of thinking about the interactions of workers and their environments.

Perhaps the best way of introducing our approach is to embrace the systems view of industrial and organizational psychology. Adopting a systems perspective requires that we discard the traditional view of selection and placement activities as neutral technologies to be inserted into a system in a rational manner. Personnel activities are part of a system, and as they change or are developed, they influence and are influenced by social, economic, and organizational contexts (Colarelli, 1994). We highlight the ways new research is beginning to adopt a more systems-oriented approach and the places still needing more work.

Job Analysis

As is so often the practice in personnel psychology, we begin with a consideration of the cornerstone of selection and placement: job analysis. Over the years, job analysis has changed its meaning. In the time of Viteles, it was primarily a consideration of attributes (that is, knowledge, skills, and abilities, or KSAs) and only peripherally a consideration of tasks. This began to change in the 1940s until it became primarily a consideration of tasks and only peripherally of attributes. McCormick and his colleagues (McCormick, Jeanneret, & Mecham, 1969, 1989) restored balance with the development of the Position Analysis Questionnaire (PAQ) system. Nevertheless, job analysts still tend to concentrate on tasks rather than attributes. This is a mistake. Psychologists are trained to make inferences based on knowledge of behavior, not job design. So, we begin our consideration of job analysis with an exhortation to use tasks as a way of getting to attributes. Tasks are a point of departure, not a point of arrival. Even though psychologists might develop content valid measures patterned after tasks, they should have a clear understanding of the attributes that underlie that task performance.

Despite its role as the cornerstone of personnel decision making, until recently job analysis was an intellectual wasteland. Fortunately, the systems view of personnel decision making has reinvigorated interest in job analysis. This new momentum can be seen in both tools and techniques.

Tools

For many years, the PAQ predominated as the standardized job analysis instrument of choice (McCormick et al., 1969). It was structured around a human factors model that included information input, information processing, and output or action. The actual elements of the system were generic task statements. These task statements were linked to KSA estimates, but the actual linkage was transparent to the user. So while there was some balance in terms of tasks and attributes, the attribute side remained somewhat mystical.

Fleishman and his colleagues have developed an alternative model that emphasizes attributes and anchors them in representative tasks (Fleishman, 1967; Fleishman & Quaintance, 1984). Fleishman and Mumford (1991) evaluated the construct validity of the abilities taxonomy, and Fleishman (1991) provided scales for use of the taxonomy in job analysis.

Because of its emphasis on attributes, Fleishman's model is more useful, from a psychological perspective, than the human factors model of the PAQ. Nevertheless, it is not a complete model because there is no place in that system for the "other" or "O" attributes that anchor the KSAO acronym. The O characteristics include such elements as values, personality characteristics, and motivational states. For many years, personnel psychologists gave the O components secondary status in job analyses, not so much because they considered these characteristics unimportant as because they had few measuring instruments for them that were normed or usable in the workplace. In addition, there had been little work on the conceptual and theoretical links between these characteristics and work performance. It was clear that these Os represented constructs, and employers feared using them in selection situations because the *Uniform Guidelines on Employee Selection Procedures* (1978) implied that construct validity was more difficult to demonstrate than either content or criterion-related validity. But times have changed. There are some good measures of O characteristics, these measures are linked to theory, and we should no longer be apprehensive about discussing constructs or construct validity.

Job analyses of the future will be well served by considering O attributes because of increasing needs for workers to take initiative and control their own work. The work of Inwald and Guion provides two examples of such efforts. Inwald (1992) developed the Hilson Job Analysis Questionnaire (HJAQ), which purports to identify the personality characteristics required for successful job performance in many occupations. As with any new instrument, more work on the underlying data base is needed before the merit of the instrument can be assessed. However, this initiative represents a broadening of the job analysis domain and should prove useful in an emerging environment that is placing more importance on personality variables. In a similar vein, Guion and his colleagues (personal communication, Guion to Landy, 1992) have been investigating the underlying personality characteristics of work behavior. The irony of this last effort is apparent to those who abandoned personality testing after Guion and Gottier's (1965) depressing review thirty years ago.

Questionnaires remain one of the most popular job analytic tools. They tend to use tasks as their raw material and measure parameters such as time spent on tasks, task difficulty, task importance, and the like. Although questionnaires have many positive characteristics, including apparent objectivity, facilitation of large-scale data collection, and associated time and cost efficiency, researchers have begun to examine the attributes of questionnaire data. In 1992, Sanchez and Fraser investigated the propriety of alternative parameters and found, surprisingly, a scale by job title interaction, which made it difficult to identify the superiority of any one scale. Even more interesting was their finding that each scale supplied useful and independent information about the job. These results suggest that questionnaires provide useful data, but that we still need to know more about the parameters of those questionnaires. This issue becomes even more salient in the context of the Americans with Disabilities Act of 1990 (ADA), which adds a new construct to the discussion, *essentiality*. There is little doubt that in the next several years there will be many heated courtroom discussions about how to calculate essentiality from job analysis data. Parameters will play a central role in that debate.

Little research has emerged that attempts to create new job analysis methodologies commensurate with ADA requirements. However, Robinson (1992) collaborated with PAQ Services in adapting the PAQ data base to address the problem of worker rehabilitation. The resulting Worker Rehabilitation Questionnaire is a counselor/therapist assessment of the current capacities of an individual used to identify jobs that a client might be able to perform. This technology should facilitate the placement of employees with disabilities and has promise for ADA compliance.

Sources of Data

An increasingly common source of information in job analysis is the subject matter expert (SME). Over the years there has been a consistent but generally fruitless search for a relationship between demographic characteristics of SMEs and job analysis results. But as has been the case with attempts to use demographic variables as predictors or covariates, there is no guiding theoretical framework. Demographic variables are simply boxcars that carry other important psychological characteristics, and we cannot seem to figure out what those psychological characteristics are. As a result, although we do not mean to close the door on such research, we see few implications for practitioners in this work.

Recently, some researchers have suggested that we need to move beyond examining simple demographic filters to other factors related to variability in SME ratings. Borman, Dorsey, and Ackerman (1992) investigated within-job interrater differences as a manifestation of time allocation strategies. They found associations between time-spent ratings and sales performance in the jobs they studied. This is an interesting avenue to pursue—SME task ratings as performance covariates.

The effect of SME attributes on job analysis ratings raises a larger issue. Industrial/organizational psychology is slowly moving toward development of a theory of human performance. But before we can hope to understand how people perform, we must apprehend how they perceive and interpret their jobs. And until we fully understand the psychometric and conceptual foundations for the ratings we choose to interpret, we will continue to be somewhat off target in our applications of job analysis data.

Team Analysis

There is a growing appreciation for the importance of team functioning in the workplace, regardless of whether these teams are formally constructed or are natural evolutions. Unfortunately, methods for analyzing teamwork are in short supply. Campion (1994) suggested that future job analysis studies should assess both the degree of team-oriented work required and the abilities required for teamwork. These abilities might include directing and controlling skills, such as planning/goal setting, task coordination, self-monitoring, and participation, as well as interpersonal skills, such as conflict resolution, collaborative problem solving, and communication (Stevens, 1992).

Job Analysis and Forecasting

In an age of rapid technological advancements and global competition, jobs are changing at an increasingly fast pace. One challenge job analysts will face with increasing frequency is the necessity to analyze jobs that do not yet exist. Two recent studies address this issue. Arvey, Salas, and Gialluca (1992) demonstrated how the task/ability intercorrelation matrix derived from current jobs can be used to forecast the ability demands of future jobs. They cautioned, however, that the utility of this approach is largely dependent on the comprehensiveness of the data base. This caveat suggests that organizations need to anticipate their needs and actively begin collecting large-scale task and ability data, a luxury available primarily to large organizations.

Taking a somewhat different approach, Manning and Broach (1992) illustrated the usefulness of expert teams in forecasting ability requirements. These researchers assembled a team of air traffic controllers and asked them to anticipate the changing ability demands of their jobs once an automated procedure is introduced into the control system. These studies represent a new era in job analysis research. With the creation of new jobs and introduction of new technology, job analysts will be forced to develop new methods of determining KSAOs.

Predictors

As we indicated earlier, the development of tests reached epidemic proportions during the 1940s and 1950s. This proliferation of newly developed tests led the American Psychological Association (APA) to consider providing consumers with information about how to evaluate their merits. The APA's effort produced two substantial products. The first was the now familiar conceptualization of validity models that were labeled criterion, content, and construct

(Cronbach & Meehl, 1955). These models set the intellectual foundation for evaluating the integrity of any particular test. The second product was the *Standards for Educational and Psychological Tests* (American Psychological Association, 1954), to be used as concrete guidelines for the evaluation of a test or form of measurement. The *Standards* are currently undergoing their third revision.

If the period of the 1950s was feast, the period from the 1960s on could be considered famine. Few tests entered the commercial market after the mid-1960s. This is unfortunate because our understanding of mental operations has increased considerably, yet we are still using devices patterned after a much more primitive model (and often, patterned after no model at all!). Fortunately, in the past few years, test development efforts have begun once again.

Cognitive Tests

An exciting development in the cognitive ability domain is a multi-ability paradigm, which is being investigated by several research teams. Ackerman, Kanfer, and their colleagues (see Ackerman, 1992; Ackerman & Humphreys, 1991; Kanfer & Ackerman, 1989) have been accumulating a solid body of field and experimental data demonstrating the relevance of a multi-ability framework for information processing tasks. In essence, they have constructed a modern version of a multiple factor theory of intelligence. Through their research they have demonstrated that different classes of abilities (general, broad content; psychomotor; perceptual speed) differentially predict task performance depending on the nature of the task and the stage of skill acquisition. Ackerman (1992) recommended studying the ability-predictor space and criterion space from this "componential" approach. In other words, we need to begin embracing both the complexity of cognitive abilities and the multifaceted nature of the criterion. This new paradigm is likely to lead to predictors specifically tailored to critical task components.

More recently, Ackerman and Kanfer (1993) again demonstrated the usefulness of this new paradigm, showing that general and broad content abilities are highly predictive of overall air traffic controller performance, especially when compared to the more traditional perceptual speed abilities. In addition, they demonstrated how laboratory and field studies can be combined to produce a validation strategy for use in the field. Given the difficulty in obtaining field samples of appreciable size, this combined approach holds promise for the future of cognitive ability test validation.

This new approach is compatible with Sternberg's more ambitious and engaging componential theory of intelligence. Sternberg and his colleagues (see Wagner & Sternberg, 1987; Sternberg, 1985; Sternberg, Wagner, & Okagaki, in press; Sternberg & Wagner, 1993) have given new life to the debate about general intelligence by broadening the scope. The roots of Sternberg's approach lie in his triarchic theory of intelligence (1985), which differentiates three types of abilities: academic, creative, and practical. Sternberg and his colleagues have shown that practical ability, or tacit knowledge, plays a role in job performance and must be distinguished from academic intelligence. They have identified three kinds of tacit knowledge, concerned with managing oneself, others, and tasks.

Sternberg and Wagner (1993) demonstrated that tacit knowledge predicts success in a variety of jobs, including academic psychology, management, and sales. It has particular relevance to ill-structured job domains such as management, which will play a greater role in most jobs in the future. "Right-sizing," reengineering, teamwork, and other initiatives make it clear that proficiency at one or more technical tasks will not be sufficient for the success of an individual worker. Each worker will need to be able to manage (that is, integrate and/or coordinate) individual efforts, the efforts of others, and/or multiple integrated and heterogeneous tasks. Sternberg has developed measures of practical intelligence and tacit knowledge (Wagner & Sternberg, 1987) that warrant inclusion in future studies of managerial performance. This work is novel and may prove quite useful in the emerging theories of work performance.

On the other side of the cognitive ability debate are those who adhere to the single factor view of intelligence and cognitive abilities (for example, Hunter, 1983; Gottfredson, 1986; Ree, Earles, & Teachout, 1992). Advocates of the univariate model argue that measures of general intelligence (g) remain the best way to predict training and job performance. They focus primarily on domains where large numbers of applicants/candidates must be processed and classified, which adds a utility rationale to enhance the attractiveness of a general intelligence approach. Schmidt and Hunter (in press) assert that tacit knowledge is not a new construct but what has been referred to for years as simply job knowledge. Regardless of the name of the construct, Schmidt, Hunter, and Sternberg all agree that job knowledge is predictive of performance variance otherwise unaccounted for with traditional measures of intellectual ability.

We feel the most useful and relevant question raised by these two lines of competing research is not whether the univariate, psychometric g approach is better at predicting job success than a multi-ability paradigm, but whether there are certain conditions under which one approach is better than the other. For example, Zeidner and Johnson (1991a, 1991b, 1994) have argued that the purpose of testing has an impact on the appropriateness of the competing models. They proposed that multi-ability cognitive tests or composites are most efficient if the purpose of the testing is differential placement rather than straightforward selection or screening. Alley and Teachout (1992) found with reanalyses of existing Armed Services Vocational Aptitude Battery (ASVAB) data sets that performance gains of one-third of a standard deviation above current assignment procedures were possible using a differential placement model. Scholarios (1992) also supported the composite approach using computer simulations.

This debate between the univariate and multi-ability camps has been a distraction from the more reasonable strategy of mapping cognitive activity in the work setting and developing measurement procedures and devices suitable for that newly mapped space. Because the psychological environment of the workplace is changing so rapidly, we cannot be sure what role g might play in the future relative to specific abilities. As an example, it may be that a certain amount of g is necessary to acquire specific knowledge in a continually changing technical environment, but that specific abilities will permit the application of that new knowledge. Thus the most effective position to take is that we will need to be able to measure g, specific cognitive abilities, and knowledge in future human resources applications. For that reason, the "debate" should be transformed into a collaborative effort of understanding and application.

Physical Abilities

Although physical ability testing has been credible for quite some time, it appeared in the employment arena relatively recently (Fleishman, 1988). Consequently, data on predictors of physically demanding tasks are sparse. This situation will change rapidly as a result of the passage of the Americans with Disabilities Act (1990), which permits employees and job applicants to claim accommodations in testing or job design for certain identified disabilities, after a demonstration that these covered disabilities are not essential to the performance of the job. Health care reform and changing insurance laws will also enhance organizational concerns with the relationship between physical performance and health.

Psychologists, exercise physiologists, ergonomists, biomechanists, and occupational medicine specialists increasingly collaborate in physical ability research. A recent contribution to the physical ability literature is Hogan's (1991) differentiation of the dimensions underlying performance in physically demanding tasks and jobs. Based on her analyses, she proposed a three-parameter model of strength, endurance, and movement quality (defined by flexibility, balance, and coordination requirements). Hogan's three-parameter model is congruent with the exercise physiology literature (McCardle, Katch, & Katch, 1991) and with Fleishman's taxonomy of physical abilities (Fleishman & Reilly, 1991), suggesting that physical abilities can be defined and measured using a finite set of theoretically meaningful dimensions.

Another group of researchers has provided construct validation evidence to the physical ability arena. Arvey and colleagues have published a series of articles illustrating physical ability test development and validation techniques (Arvey, 1992; Arvey, Landon, Nutting, & Maxwell, 1992; Arvey, Nutting, & Landon, 1992). Their target population has been public safety officers (for example, firefighters, police officers). As one would expect, they found that strength and endurance were implicated in successful public safety performance, and that women generally scored lower than men on both test and job performance relating to physical attributes. Using a combination of laboratory and field tests, Sothmann and colleagues (1990) were able to estimate the minimal oxygen consumption demands of firefighting tasks. Practitioners may be able to use this technology to decompose the demands of any physically taxing job. Landy and his co-workers (1992) conducted an extensive review of the physical demands of public safety positions as well as a consideration of the effect of aging on the decline of physical abilities. They concluded that chronological age per se (that is, devoid of effects of illness, injury, or lifestyle) has little impact on the decline of physical abilities. This finding contradicts the stereotype of physically demanding work as appropriate only for younger workers and is particularly salient considering that older workers will be more prevalent in the workforces of industrialized countries in the future.

Not all physical ability testing research deals with public safety. For example, Blakley, Quinones, and Jago (1992) confirmed the earlier findings of Arnold, Rauschenberger, Soubel, and Guion (1982) that isometric strength tests (grip, arm lift, shoulder lift, torso lift) are predictive of job performance. Blakley and colleagues demonstrated the value of isometric strength tests for predicting performance in a wide variety of physically demanding professions, including customer gas service employees, pipeline construction and maintenance workers, pipefitters, construction workers, and utility workers.

Biodata

As the workplace becomes increasingly diversified, we will need a more sophisticated understanding of values, attitudes, motivational forces, experiential bases, and so on. Biodata are clearly implicated in these investigations and practices. Fortunately, the volume of articles addressing the construct validity and theory underlying biodata predictors increased substantially in the past decade; a handbook of biodata was also produced (Stokes, Mumford, & Owens, 1994).

Today's biodata researchers raise questions that are considerably more insightful and theoretically grounded than those of the early investigators. For example, Mumford, Uhlman, and Kilcullen (1992) began with the most basic question: Why use biodata at all? Supported by a model that purports to explain the structure of life history, Mumford and colleagues argued that the application of construct validation principles yields useful and effective life history items. The ecology model presents people as organisms who actively seek opportunities and experiences to maximize long-term adaptation to their environment. The model further explains that given satisfactory outcomes, individuals will actively seek out similar situations in the future, producing coherent patterns of behavior (Mumford & Owens, 1987; Mumford, Stokes, & Owens, 1990; Mumford, Wesley, & Shaffer, 1987; Stokes, Mumford, & Owens, 1989). Researchers can use the ecology model to generate hypotheses for systematic construct-based item development. In other words, this approach uses theoretical rigor to develop useful biodata items.

Mael (1991) posed another basic question: What constitutes a biodata item? He suggested that historical content is the defining characteristic of biodata items. To support this contention, he identified ten specific parameters on which biodata items might be considered (for example, verifiable versus nonverifiable, job relevant versus not job relevant). We think this taxonomic aid will enlighten future research and discussion.

Recently, the Office of Personnel Management has embarked on an ambitious program of biodata development that incorporates theory-driven approaches we have been discussing. Dye (1991, 1992) provided strong evidence supporting the construct validity of the Individual Achievement Record (IAR), which measures four common factors: work competency, high school achievement, college achievement, and leadership skills. Research with 1,800 workers who took the IAR and a battery of marker variable tests showed that the two academic factors (high school and college achievement) tap reasoning abilities, and the other two components are associated with achievement and self-confidence. We feel that more research of this type should be conducted.

Personality

As Goldberg (1993) stated, "Once upon a time, we had no personalities. Fortunately, times change" (p. 26). New and more sophisticated meta-analytic techniques helped revive the use of personality variables in selection research. Schmitt, Gooding, Noe, and Kirsch (1984) began the resurrection of personality variables with their comprehensive review and meta-analysis that showed personality test scores were predictive of job performance. Articulation of the "Big Five" personality factors—neuroticism, extroversion, openness to experience, agreeableness, and conscientiousness—added structure to this reemerging domain (Digman, 1990).

Researchers have paid considerable attention to the Big Five model since its articulation and have confirmed its structure with several meta-analyses. Which dimension of the Big Five is most valuable for predicting job performance has been the subject of some debate. Barrick and Mount (1991) found that conscientiousness had the greatest predictive potential. Tett, Jackson, and Rothstein (1991) concluded that agreeableness was best, but Ones, Mount, Barrick, and Hunter (1994) criticized their methodology, analysis, and conceptual structure. Regardless of this dispute, examinations of the Big Five structure in predicting job performance should continue.

A challenge for the future is how to use personality test scores most effectively. Day and Bedeian (1993) argued that candidates' profiles should be compared with the profiles of others in the same organization rather than with some large normative population. The important issue, then, is whether a candidate is more or less agreeable, conscientious, and so forth than others in the organization or work group. In short, Day and Bedeian promoted the concept of "fit." (In earlier personality literature, this was known as the "nomothetic versus idiographic" debate.) The underlying proposition is that candidates are more likely to succeed in a given environment if their personalities fit with those of their co-workers and supervisors. Day and Bedeian suggested that this personality dissimilarity mechanism may account for the discrepancies between the Barrick and Mount (1991) and Tett and colleagues (1991) conclusions.

Two developments mentioned earlier suggest that good personality measures will be increasingly useful in the future. The first relates to the changing nature of work. It is clear that many, if not most, work environments are moving in the direction of team-based structures. This means that communication and interpersonal skills will need to be assessed as well as attributes like conflict resolution and empathy. In addition, as demographics change, the differences between races and age cohorts on traditional paper-and-pencil measures of cognitive abilities are likely to continue and to have more impact. That is not to say that these differences are indicators of discrimination. The point is that if we have only multiple-choice measures of cognitive ability available, adverse impact is likely to remain. But if we can measure job-related personal attributes like the Big Five, the proportional impact of traditional cognitive measures may very well be less substantial.

Integrity Tests

Just as personality tests have found new favor in the academic and applied communities, so have integrity tests, and for many of the same reasons. It seems clear that more trust will be invested in the employee of the future. Further, some usable operational definitions and measures of integrity have appeared. Goldberg, Grenier, Guion, Sechrest, and Wing (1991), working as an APA task force, wrote a favorable report on integrity testing. Ones, Viswesvaran, and Schmidt (1993) conducted a large-scale meta-analysis and concluded that integrity tests successfully predict a wide range of job behaviors. Their data covered more than 665 validity coefficients, over 180 studies, 25 different measures of integrity, and a wide range of criterion variables. The authors estimated the mean predictive validity coefficient to be .41 when integrity tests were used to predict supervisory ratings. This value compares favorably with more traditional test categories.

Integrity tests initially focused on predicting employee dishonesty (such as theft) but expansion of this narrow criterion domain proved favorable to test validity. Ones and colleagues (1993) demonstrated that integrity tests actually predict a vast array of organizationally disruptive behaviors (for example, absenteeism, tardiness, violence, substance abuse) better than they predict theft. Although moderators have some impact on estimated mean validities, the validity of both overt and personality-based integrity tests has been shown to generalize across situations.

Ones and colleagues (1993) also demonstrated substantial incremental validity when integrity tests are combined with cognitive ability tests. Because integrity tests have no adverse impact against minority job applicants, combining these scores with scores from cognitive ability tests both enhances utility and increases the number of minority applicants likely to be hired. Ones and colleagues concluded that most integrity tests measure the Big Five personality factor of conscientiousness. Thus the changing reputation of integrity tests can be seen as related to the changing reputation of personality tests at the construct level.

Safety Tests

With the criterion domain broadened to include counterproductive behaviors, researchers now face the challenge of developing selection tests to predict previously "unpredictable" behaviors, such as a tendency to be involved in accidents. Workplace safety has long been a concern of companies and employees alike. The economic and personal costs associated with annual workplace accidents are staggering: the National Safety Council (1991), for example, estimated that in 1990, a work-related injury occurred every eighteen seconds, at a cost to organizations of $63.8 billion. Recently, applied psychologists have begun a quest to approach safety from a personnel selection paradigm.

Jones and Wuebker (1988) and Jones (1991) related attitudes and personality traits to workplace safety. They found that candidates' scores on four related subscales correlated highly with accident history or lack thereof. Larson and Merritt (1991) demonstrated a positive relationship between the frequency of mental slips and driving safety. Mental slips were assessed using the Cognitive Failures Questionnaire, which assesses the frequency of everyday errors, such as bumping into people and forgetting names. More work on the construct of mental slips is needed before conclusive statements can be made, but this illustrates another method by which organizational safety can be investigated.

Arthur, Strong, and Williamson (1994) developed a computer-administered test of visual attention and found that test scores were significantly related to self-reported accident involvement. This research represents a move away from the attitudinal/personality-based measures and toward a more cognitive approach to accident prevention. Both approaches hold promise and should continue in the future.

Predictor Methodology

Ways to predict a number of different behaviors have been expanded by previously unavailable computer applications and new uses for old techniques such as the interview. These should enrich considerably the current predictive methods in use.

Computer Testing

Advances in computer technology have substantially enhanced testing methodologies. The most obvious enhancement is to the stimulus or test item. We can now create motion, depth, speed, and other characteristics that cannot be captured in paper-and-pencil tests. In addition, we can control the rate of information flow and observe changes in subject strategy as additional information is presented. On the response side, it is possible to measure response latencies, build examinations around response patterns (as with computerized adaptive testing), and avoid extra procedural steps, such as scoring of response sheets. We can only guess at what virtual reality technology will provide in the next decade, but we can be sure that it will be dramatic. The armed services use this technology for training, and it is not much of a stretch to adapt it for testing purposes.

Burke (1993) suggested that computer-based testing (CBT) and computer-adaptive testing (CAT) will affect the measurement of predictor variables and our inferences about future job performance based on selection test scores. For example, computers afford us the opportunity to present new forms of dynamic test stimuli (Hunter & Burke, 1987), computer simulations of reality (Wolfe, 1990), and video footage. This technology not only allows us to tap individual attributes and performance samples previously unmeasurable with paper-and-pencil tests, but also gives us a methodology that is completely transportable to even the most remote locations by means of computer notebook or desktop devices. The increased ability to measure more refined human attributes may lead to the development or expansion of categories of characteristics typically assessed during employment selection (Burke, 1993). Similarly, the ability of computers to accept multiple forms of responses (for example, mouse, keyboard, voice commands) may also enable easier testing of individuals with handicaps (Burke, 1993) as well as offer accommodation in job design.

Drasgow, Olson, Keenan, Moberg, and Mead (1993) envisioned personnel selection of the near future as multimedia assessment delivered by a personal computer (PC) equipped with a laser disc player, amplifier, and stereo speakers. Both Burke (1993) and Drasgow and colleagues (1993) pointed out that computers can present test material and assess candidates in an interactive medium. Companies currently evaluate communication skill and worker interaction from interviews or, if they have ample resources, from assessment center participation. The advantage of the computer is that it can present many dynamic variants of typical inter-actions based on the assessee's responses using either linear or nonlinear paths.

Examples of computerized testing have already begun to appear in the mainstream literature. Park and Lee (1992) described a computer-aided aptitude test for pilots that relies on a combina-tion of cognitive and perceptual motor tests. Arthur and colleagues (1994) predicted driving accidents using a PC-based test of visual attention. Bennett (in press) demonstrated the computer's ability to present a diverse array of stimulus material including computer programming problems, algebra problems, and ill-structured ver-bal problems.

Schmitt, Gilliland, Landis, and Devine (1993) used computer-based testing to select secretarial candidates. The selection pro-cedure required candidates to learn and use increasingly common electronic workplace devices, such as word processing pro-grams, electronic message software, and data bases. The authors contend that this testing format facilitates the rapid compilation of test score data, is fair to candidates who have used different types of computer systems in the past, and maximizes trans-portability of the tests.

Because the Americans with Disabilities Act (1990) is likely to increase pressure to administer tests in a nontraditional manner, testers must consider the comparability of computerized and paper-and-pencil cognitive ability tests. Mead and Drasgow (in press) discovered from a meta-analysis that results of power tests remain virtually identical across these testing modalities, but scores of those taking speed tests are affected by the mode of presenta-tion. Thus a speed test on a computer might not be a parallel form of the same test administered as a paper-and-pencil device.

It is disappointing that the applied psychology community has not embraced computer technology for personnel selection more extensively. Perhaps the new emphasis on the "information high-way" will accelerate the use of computer systems. Consider a mod-est initiative: there is no reason why a candidate could not apply for jobs across the country simply by accessing a selection system (appli-cation and tests) via Internet or some similar electronic mail system.

The Interview

Three recent meta-analyses combine to shed new light on the pre-dictive capability of the interview. McDaniel, Whetzel, Schmidt, and Maurer (in press), whose ambitious meta-analysis included over one hundred studies with a total N exceeding 17,000, found aver-age validities in the .40 to .50 range. Huffcutt and Arthur (1994) estimated from a meta-analysis of 112 validity coefficients that the structured interview has a mean validity of .57 (corrected for cri-terion unreliability, range restriction, and sampling error). This compares favorably with most other predictor categories and for-mats. Finally, Searcy, Woods, Gatewood, and Lance (1993), using highly restrictive inclusion rules, reviewed twenty-three studies and estimated the average validity to be in the high .40s.

In concert, the results of these meta-analyses suggest that the selection interview continues to be a useful predictor of job per-formance and will remain an important tool in the twenty-first cen-tury. The results support the increasing enthusiasm for the situational interview, which may be less vulnerable to bias from fac-tors such as race of applicant and/or interviewer (Lin, Dobbins, & Farh, 1992).

Assessment Centers

There has been a great deal of published research on assessment centers, including clear indications of predictive value. Neverthe-less, we still don't know why they work. Howard (1993) argued that assessment centers are well suited to face the challenges of the twenty-first century by refuting seven arguments against their continued use. She eloquently dismissed or provided convincing counterarguments for six of the seven concerns. But like other researchers, she had the most trouble dismissing the criticism that the construct validity of assessment centers has not been successfully demonstrated with any regularity. The overarching problem is that assessment center ratings reflect exercise factors that overwhelm common dimensions across exercises. In other words, assessor ratings of a dimension seem to be specific to each exercise and do not generalize across exercises as well as they should if they were tapping a single underlying construct representing a candidate attribute.

It is clear that assessment center technology is evolving in a way that will permit effective assessment in the work environments anticipated in the future. For example, assessment center practitioners have incorporated many new dimensions to reflect changing work responsibilities and have developed computerized exercises and scoring methods that enhance fidelity and efficiency (Howard, 1993). However, the nagging question of why assessment centers work plus an ancillary question of what independent contribution they make to the prediction of work performance will continue to challenge this approach. In the next section we consider further the issue of independent contribution.

Predictor Contributions: One Step Forward or Two Steps Back?

Although this may seem like a primitive issue, given the research base associated with various predictor types, it is not completely clear what is being measured by many of these devices or strategies. As examples, exactly what are we assessing in the interview or with an assessment center? Are we measuring general intelligence, motivation, personality, individual skills and abilities, knowledge, and/or experience? Does the interview tap process or substance? Given our increased sophistication in modeling, we should be able to answer with some confidence this question that was raised often in the 1950s and 1960s as speculation. If the validity of the interview generalizes across criteria and situations, and if the validity of measures of general intelligence generalize across criteria and situations, and if measures of Big Five personality constructs generalize across criteria and situations, it is reasonable to ask whether these predictors all make unique contributions or whether they share some core variance. Measures of knowledge and/or experience that seem to be undisputed contributors to performance likewise should be considered. How do all these components go together in predicting and understanding work behavior? It is tempting to create a large and diverse battery of predictors based on the results of the meta-analyses described here. But by doing so, we may be deluding ourselves as scientists and squandering valuable resources (money, administrative time and cost, applicant tolerance) as practitioners. We must learn more about the independent contributions of the various predictor groups.

Selection Processes

We are witnessing a paradigmatic revolution of sorts, which is more responsive to the needs of the better educated and more proactive workforce expected in the future. The classic approach to selection, with its emphasis on the methodological aspects of test development and validation, is being challenged or at least augmented by a new approach. Underlying this new approach is the recognition that not only do organizations use selection devices to gather information about applicants, but applicants also use them to gain information about the company (Thornton, 1994; Rynes & Miller, 1983).

Applicant Reactions

Most of the emerging research, focusing on how applicants use selection devices, is based on Schuler and Stehle's (1983) construct of *social validity*. A selection device is socially valid if the affected constituents (applicants, consultants, organizational decision makers) accept the selection process. Schuler and Stehle suggested that four components independently contribute to socially acceptable selection situations: (1) relevant information (for example, task requirements, organizational information), (2) participation in the development of the device (direct or representative), (3) transparency of the assessment tool, and (4) communication of results.

The new research paradigm is eclectic in nature. Contributing theories include attitude formation (see Ajzen & Fishbein, 1977), symbolic interactionism (Ashforth & Mael, 1989), justice theory (Folger, 1987), role-making (Katz & Kahn, 1978), psychological contracts (Argyris, 1960), and self-efficacy (Bandura, 1977). Unifying this research is the theme that selection exists within, and is influenced by, multiple contexts. As Herriot (1989) eloquently wrote, "Selection is not the gate through which applicants pass before they can relate to the organization; it is itself part of that relationship" (p. 171).

The point is that a selection strategy sends a message to the applicant; the issue for the practitioner is the nature of that message. As Rynes (1993) noted, "While experts debate the pros and cons of [selection] procedures in cool, scientific terminology (construct validity, empirical validity, item response theory, hit rates, validity scales, dollar-valued validity), applicant reactions to them are often vividly personal and highly emotional" (p. 241). Arvey and Sackett (1993) suggested that applicants' interpretation of what the selection strategy represents is influenced by the organizational context (for example, company hiring history), systemic context (such as types of tests), test specific context (such as specific test used), and the individual context (for example, the candidate's work history).

Arvey and Sackett (1993) and Rynes and Connerley (1992) discussed the form of applicant reactions to various selection procedures or strategies. In general, applicants react favorably to strategies that appear procedurally fair, face valid, and not unduly intrusive. Reactions of applicants toward the selection strategy do appear to influence reactions to the organization as a whole (Stoffey, Millsap, Smither, & Reilly, 1991).

It seems clear that (1) applicants gather information from selection procedures; (2) applicants form attitudes based on this information; (3) these attitudes differ depending on the type of test a person is exposed to and, in some instances, depending on characteristics of the individual; and (4) the reactions/attitudes have behavioral and/or intentional implications. By explicitly acknowledging the social process variables and contextual factors associated with selection testing, applied psychologists can begin to develop what Tissen (1994) referred to as a more "holistic approach to selection" (p. 189).

Cut Scores and Appointment Procedures

A relatively new addition to cut-score methodology is Cascio, Outtz, Zedeck, and Goldstein's (1991) notion of a sliding band. This method balances applicant appointments from eligible lists in a way that both recognizes social objectives like minority hiring and fulfills economic objectives associated with at least ordinal-level appointments. The procedure is based on the logic of standard errors and the procedures of a fixed-band appointment strategy. In the fixed-band approach, candidates are placed into score bands defined by the standard error statistic and selected from the highest band until that band is exhausted. In contrast, the sliding band allows decision makers to move the band down one point if all the applicants receiving the highest score in that band are appointed. This moving down of the band represents the "slide."

This approach has not been without criticism (see, for example, Schmidt, 1991; Sackett & Roth, 1991; Schmidt, 1992), and the debate is far from over. The argument against any band (fixed or sliding) is that the estimate of the true score of a candidate is still the observed score, regardless of its standard error. The rebuttal is that some (modest) precision can be traded off to realize the social goal of a diversified workforce.

The sliding band was supported in at least one recent federal discrimination lawsuit (*Officers for Justice and San Francisco Police Officers* v. *Civil Service Commission of San Francisco,* 1992). Because the Civil Rights Act of 1991 expressly forbids race norming (and possibly gender norming as well), employers may give the banding logic more careful consideration as they try to steer a course between profitability and a reduction in adverse impact.

Affirmative Action

On the surface, affirmative action applied to personnel selection and placement implies programs that will aggressively balance a workforce based on certain critical demographic characteristics (such as race and gender). But barely beneath the surface are concerns about preferential treatment and quotas. There are two separate issues to consider: the reactions and perceptions of the selected individual to the status of "affirmative action hire," and the reactions of co-workers and managers to that individual. Given the strength of the emotions generated by such concerns, this appears to be an area ripe for research.

Unfortunately, the little research that has been done often used student samples. Heilman and her colleagues (Heilman,

Rivero, & Brett, 1991; Heilman, Block, & Lucas, 1992) and Summers (1991) examined the issue of affirmative action "stigmatization" from a gender perspective, while Kravitz and Platania (1992) considered race-based affirmative action effects. Generally, the researchers concluded that the presence of affirmative action programs negatively influences perceptions of efficacy and competence. Nevertheless, the subject populations leave much to be desired, and the importance of the question requires more relevant experimental designs. To their credit, Heilman and colleagues (1992) conducted a follow-up field study of affirmative action status and perceived competence that confirmed the student result, but much more field study is warranted.

Selection and the Law

Adding to the constraints on selection are changes in law. Two of the most far-reaching ones affect the employment of people with disabilities and older workers.

Americans with Disabilities Act (ADA)

The ADA act has sent shock waves through the human resource community. There is a good deal of confusion about what disabilities are covered, how an essential task is defined, and what constitutes a medical test. As was the case with the Civil Rights Act of 1964, working definitions will emerge from a combination of administrative guidelines and clarification as well as relevant case law. Nevertheless, at a much deeper level, the law will likely stimulate research and theory.

As an example, Biersdorff and Radke (1991) addressed provisions of Canadian law similar to those of the ADA and questioned whether intelligence is essential for many jobs. If the answer is no, then various developmental disabilities might preclude the use of currently available screening devices. This, in turn, would substantially increase the demand for a comprehensive theory relating abilities to job performance. Similar questions are likely to arise with respect to perceptual-motor and motor abilities. It is also likely that ADA will require research and theory that integrate knowledge from diverse areas such as medicine, exercise physiology, education, and I/O psychology. Such integration and cross-disciplinary effort will be welcome and will likely lead to substantial progress in basic theory-building.

Age Discrimination in Employment Act (ADEA)

The ADEA, originally passed in 1967, was amended in 1986 to outlaw forced retirement based on age for all except tenured college faculty and public safety employees. Congress mandated that the Department of Labor and Equal Employment Opportunity Commision complete studies to determine the propriety of those exemptions. The National Research Council (Hammond & Morgan, 1991) and Landy and colleagues (1992) conducted studies that address these issues, the latter including a review of age relative to both cognitive and physical abilities. In both studies the researchers concluded that age was a poor predictor of performance and that the exemption should be eliminated. On December 31, 1993, Congress permitted the exemption to expire; new legislation to reinstate mandatory age-based retirement in public safety settings was subsequently defeated.

Nevertheless, age stereotypes continue to pervade business and industry. It is not clear what role these stereotypes will play as the workforce ages. Because age stereotypes are held just as firmly by older individuals as by younger ones, the simple aging of the workforce will not eliminate the problem. In fact, as older workers become more common, the problem may become more severe. In any event, researchers and practitioners should be aware that there is little credible evidence to suggest any substantial reduction in abilities (cognitive or physical) as a result of age per se.

Selection of Group Members

Perhaps one of the most dramatic changes in the nature of work has been the introduction of work teams, an idea that organizations are embracing enthusiastically. This way of work represents both a technological and sociological change. It is frustrating that psychologists have done little empirical study to evaluate the effectiveness of group work. Although more research is being done, there are few replicated findings with work groups. Researchers and practitioners need to negotiate an agenda for structuring research and application initiatives.

We see the beginnings of such an agenda in the work of Jackson and her colleagues (Bantel & Jackson, 1989; Jackson, 1991; Jackson et al., 1991; Jackson, Stone, & Alvarez, 1993). Taken as a whole, this body of literature presents a coherent framework, with supporting data, for the effect of group composition on task performance. This stream of research emphasizes heterogeneity among group members' abilities, skills, and personal attributes (Jackson, 1991). Two competing theories form the foundation of this research. On the one hand, the organizational demography model (Pfeffer, 1983) suggests that group member heterogeneity leads to lower cohesion, loyalty, performance, and satisfaction. On the other hand, the cognitive resources approach suggests that heterogeneity of group members leads to greater productivity through the increased exchange of ideas and knowledge bases (see Shaw, 1976).

Team member selection takes on even greater salience in light of the increasing diversification of the workforce (Jackson, 1991; Jackson et al., 1993). Heterogeneity is defined, in part, by personal attributes such as demographic characteristics; hence, organizational demography theory suggests that diversification has the potential to lower productivity, or at least keep it from maximization, while cognitive resources theory suggests that diversification will have a positive impact on productivity.

Jackson and her colleagues have shed new light on this apparent contradiction. For example, Bantel and Jackson (1989) found that group member heterogeneity in functional background (ability and knowledge) led to increased productivity. But Jackson (1991) found that group heterogeneity was also predictive of turnover within the group. In 1991, Jackson and colleagues integrated Schneider's (1983) Attraction-Selection-Attrition model with the organizational demography model to illustrate the complementary nature of these two research streams. The results of their study suggested once again that group heterogeneity (educational level, college curriculum, and industry experience) was predictive of turnover. Other personal attributes, with the exception of age, were not predictive of turnover.

Taken together, these results suggest that industrial psychologists are facing a new and perplexing challenge. On the one hand, workforce diversification has the potential to lead to greater productivity through the collaboration of many types of people and backgrounds. On the other hand, this same potential advantage may increase the likelihood that dissimilar people will leave the work group, ultimately resulting in greater homogeneity (and lower productivity).

Once again we see that demographic variables are simply boxcars carrying important differences in personality or values (Day & Bedeian, 1993), and it is on these latter differences that we should focus our attention. But contrary to traditional psychological conceptualization, Prieto (1994) argued that effective team performance is based not on a composite of effective individual performances but on five attributes of group members: (1) ability to gain group acceptance, (2) ability to increase group solidarity, (3) awareness of group consciousness, (4) willingness to share group identification, and (5) ability to manage the impressions of others. This new framework requires the creation of new assessment methodologies. Prieto recommended assessing these attributes using an assessment center format. This is a reasonable candidate methodology considering that the skills and abilities are most likely to manifest themselves in dynamic and ecologically valid situations.

This notion of team selection, of creating new assessment techniques to measure team ability, will seem unfamiliar to many I/O psychologists. Traditionally, we have pursued a science of individuals—individual differences and individual performance. It is this history that has made the marriage of the "I" and "O" sides of I/O psychology so difficult in the past several decades. Team selection is simply the latest manifestation of the different values and interests of I and O researchers and practitioners. And this may be the perfect stage on which to play out the final reconciliation of the two traditions, because there are interactive elements of both personnel and organizational research.

Morgan and Lassiter (1992) reviewed much of the social psychology literature in an attempt to suggest ways in which team selection and training might be done. They concluded that effective selection strategies cannot be developed solely on the basis of "difference variables" (such as ability, personality, and demographic characteristics) and that research is needed in the area of job analysis before substantial advances can be made.

While there is no strong empirical foundation for team selection and composition, there have been some successful initiatives. Shechtman (1992) selected teachers using a group assessment procedure based on assessment center methodology. The group assessment consisted of four activities: a nondirected group introduction, a directive group interview, a leaderless group discussion, and a provision of oral feedback to other members of the group. Assessors rated candidates on oral communication, human relationships, leadership, and overall fitness for the teaching profession.

In another recent initiative, Colarelli and Boos (1992) conducted a longitudinal field experiment to determine whether sociometric (self-formed work groups) and ability-based assignments differentially affect work group performance. Looking solely at the criterion of performance, they found no difference between those groups who selected their own members and those who were assembled based on their ability. However, when they broadened the criterion domain to include other outcomes, they found that the sociometric groups reported higher levels of communication, coordination, peer ratings, group cohesion, and job satisfaction. The results suggest that sociometric selection of work group members bears careful consideration.

If we were to identify one clear area of payoff for both researchers and practitioners contemplating the future, it would be that of team function—the selection, composition, training, performance measurement, and motivation of work teams.

Conclusion

Personnel selection and placement in the future will offer many challenges and opportunities. The first challenge is to understand the limits of meta-analytic approaches to theory-building and testing as well as the practical limits of its applied cousin, validity generalization. The meta-analytic approach is a powerful and illuminating procedure but will always be an aid to, and never a substitute for, logic.

Another challenge is to enhance applied research designs so that the movement from the research laboratory to the workplace is less strained. Paper people, video characters, student subjects, and strictly controlled stimulus elements are examples of the limiting characteristics of current research. A final challenge is to reinvigorate the search for novel predictors and selection procedures.

The opportunities are more exciting to consider. We desperately need a concentrated examination of group composition and group performance. For individual performance measurement, we need to reconsider the stability of performance over time and continue to examine different qualitative categories of performance (for example, task versus contextual).

On the predictor side of personnel selection, it is time to get down to the task of understanding cognitive activity in work settings. Fleishman's taxonomy is a good point of departure, but it should not be accepted as *the* structure of cognitive activity. Too little is known about this area to accept a convention at this time. Research on the Big Five personality factors will increase geometrically whether we endorse it or not, an action that is healthy and long overdue.

Applicant reactions to various personnel devices and procedures are worthy of additional study, and we encourage more attention to applicant behaviors rather than simply affective responses. We need to know a great deal more about how SMEs respond to job analysis questionnaires. It is not enough to know that experience makes a difference and race does not; we need to know more about the cognitive operations involved. There will be enormous payoffs from continued work on structural models representing the interaction of antecedent conditions (such as ability, experience, and personality) and consequent conditions (such as task performance, contextual performance, and individual development).

Perhaps the most obvious opportunity for learning more about the nature of work behavior comes from the impetus provided by the Americans with Disabilities Act (1990). Currently, personnel researchers have the attention of the business community, public policy advocates, regulatory agencies, and funding agencies by virtue of ADA. We should embrace the opportunity to do something good for society (integrate people with disabilities into the workplace on a rational basis), enhance both the science and practice of industrial and organizational psychology, and form alliances with other disciplines (such as occupational medicine, exercise physiology, biomechanics, and industrial engineering). The greatest advances in the science and practice of I/O psychology have occurred when we strove to meet a societal need. We should recognize this as one of those times.

References

Ackerman, P. L. (1992). Predicting individual differences in complex skill acquisition: Dynamics of ability determinants. *Journal of Applied Psychology, 77*(5), 598–614.

Ackerman, P. L., & Humphreys, L. G. (1991). Individual differences theory in industrial and organizational psychology. In M. D. Dunnette & L. M. Hough (Eds.), *Handbook of industrial and organizational psychology* (2nd ed., Vol. 1). Palo Alto, CA: Consulting Psychologists Press.

Ackerman, P. L., & Kanfer, R. (1993). Integrating laboratory and field study for improving selection: Development of a battery to predict air traffic controller success. *Journal of Applied Psychology, 78*(3), 413–432.

Ajzen, I., & Fishbein, M. (1977). Attitude-behavior relations: A theoretical analysis and review of empirical research. *Psychological Bulletin, 84,* 888–918.

Alley, W. E., & Teachout, M. S. (1992, August). *Differential assignment potential in the ASVAB.* Paper presented at the meeting of the American Psychological Association, Washington, DC.

American Psychological Association. (1954). *Standards for educational and psychological tests.* Washington, DC: Author.

Argyris, C. (1960). *Understanding organizational behavior.* Homewood, IL: Dorsey Press.

Arnold, J. D., Rauschenberger, J. M., Soubel, W. G. & Guion, R. M. (1982). Validation and utility of a strength test for selecting steelworkers. *Journal of Applied Psychology,* 1982, *67,* 588–604.

Arthur, W., Strong, M. H., & Williamson, J. (1994). Validation of a visual attention test as a predictor of driving accident involvement. *Journal of Occupational and Organizational Psychology, 67,* 173–182.

Arvey, R. D. (1992). Constructs and construct validation: Definitions and issues. *Human Performance, 5*(1–2), 59–69.

Arvey, R. D., Landon, T. E., Nutting, S. M., & Maxwell, S. E. (1992). Development of physical ability tests for police officers: A construct validation approach [Monograph]. *Journal of Applied Psychology, 77*(6), 996–1009.

Arvey, R. D., Nutting, S. M., & Landon, T. E. (1992). Validation strategies for physical ability testing in police and fire settings. *Public Personnel Management, 21*(3), 301–312.

Arvey, R. D., & Sackett, P. R. (1993). Fairness in selection: Current developments and perspectives. In N. Schmitt, W. C. Borman, & Associates, *Personnel selection in organizations*. San Francisco: Jossey-Bass.

Arvey, R. D., Salas, E., & Gialluca, K. A. (1992). Using task inventories to forecast skills and abilities. *Human Performance, 5*(3), 171–190.

Ashforth, B. E., & Mael, F. (1989). Social identity theory and the organization. *Academy of Management Review, 14,* 20–39.

Bandura, A. (1977). Self-efficacy: Toward a unifying theory of behavioral change. *Psychological Review, 84,* 191–215.

Bantel, K. & Jackson, S. (1989). Top management and innovations in banking: Does the composition of the top team make a difference? *Strategic Management Journal, 10,* 107–124.

Barrick, M. R., & Mount, M. K. (1991). The big five personality dimensions and job performance: A meta-analysis. *Personnel Psychology, 44*(1), 1–26.

Bennett, R. E. (in press). Environments for presenting and automatically scoring complex constructed-response items. In M. G. Rumsey & B. Walker (Eds.), *Directions for research in personnel measurement*. Hillsdale, NJ: Erlbaum.

Biersdorff, K. K., & Radke, S. A. (1991). Human rights legislation: Will intelligence become a bona fide occupational requirement? *Canadian Journal of Rehabilitation, 4*(4), 203–211.

Blakley, B. R., Quinones, M.A., & Jago, I. A. (1992, April). *The validity of isometric strength tests: Results of five studies*. Paper presented at the meeting of the Society for Industrial and Organizational Psychology, Montreal, Canada.

Borman, W. C., Dorsey, D., & Ackerman, L. (1992). Time spent responses as time allocation strategies: Relations with sales performance in a stockbroker sample. *Personnel Psychology, 45*(4), 763–778.

Burke, M. J. (1993). Computerized psychological testing: Impacts on measuring predictor constructs and future job behavior. In N. Schmitt, W. C. Borman, & Associates, *Personnel selection in organizations*. San Francisco: Jossey-Bass.

Campion, M. A. (1994). Job analysis for the future. In M. G. Rumsey, C. B. Walker, & J. H. Harris (Eds.), *Personnel selection and classification*. Hillsdale, NJ: Erlbaum.

Cascio, W. F., Outtz, J., Zedeck, S., & Goldstein, I. L. (1991). Statistical implications of six methods of test score use in personnel selection. *Human Performance, 4*(4), 233–264.

Colarelli, S. M. (1994). *The context of hiring practices*. Unpublished paper, Central Michigan University.

Colarelli, S. M., & Boos, A.L. (1992). Sociometric and ability-based assignment to work groups: Some implication for personnel selection. *Journal of Organizational Behavior, 13,* 187–196.

Cronbach, L. J., & Meehl, P. E. (1955). Construct validity in psychological tests. *Psychological Bulletin, 52,* 281–302.

Day, D. V., & Bedeian, A. G. (1993, April). *Effects of personality dissimilarity and psychological climate on role stress, job satisfaction, and job performance: An interactionist perspective.* Paper presented at the meeting of the Society for Industrial and Organizational Psychology, San Francisco.

Digman, J. M. (1990). Personality structure: Emergence of the five-factor model. In M. R. Rosenzweig & L. W. Porter (Eds.), *Annual review of psychology.* Palo Alto: Annual Reviews.

Drasgow, F., Olson, J. B., Keenan, P. A., Moberg, P., & Mead, A. D. (1993). Computerized assessment. In G. R. Ferris & K. M. Rowland (Eds.), *Research in personnel and human resource management.* Greenwich, CT: JAI Press.

Dye, D. A. (1991). Technical Report PRD-91–03. Washington, DC: U.S. Office of Personnel Management.

Dye, D. A. (1992). Technical Report PRD-92–14. Washington, DC: U.S. Office of Personnel Management.

Fleishman, E. A. (1967). Performance assessment based on an empirically-derived task taxonomy. *Human Factors, 9,* 349–366.

Fleishman, E. A. (1988). Some new frontiers in personnel selection research. *Personnel Psychology, 41,* 679–701.

Fleishman, E. A. (1991). *Manual for the ability requirement scales* (MARS, revised). Palo Alto, CA: Consulting Psychologists Press.

Fleishman, E. A., & Mumford, M. D. (1991). Evaluating classifications of job behavior: A construct validation of the ability requirement scales. *Personnel Psychology, 44*(3), 523–575.

Fleishman, E. A., & Quaintance, M. K. (1984). *Taxonomies of human performance: The description of human tasks.* Orlando, FL: Academic Press.

Fleishman, E. A., & Reilly, M. E. (1991). *Human abilities: Their definition, measurement, and job task requirements.* Palo Alto, CA: Consulting Psychologists Press.

Folger, R. (1987). Distributive and procedural justice in the workplace. *Social Justice Research, 1,* 143–159.

Goldberg, L. R. (1993). The structure of phenotypic personality traits. *American Psychologist, 48,* 26–34.

Goldberg, L. R., Grenier, J. R., Guion, R. M., Sechrest, L. B., & Wing, H. (1991). *Questionnaires used in the prediction of trustworthiness in preemployment selection decisions.* Washington, DC: American Psychological Association.

Gottfredson, L. S. (1986). Societal consequences of the *g* factor in employment. *Journal of Vocational Behavior, 29,* 379–410.

Guion, R. M., & Gottier, R. F. (1965). Validity and personality measures in personnel selection. *Personnel Psychology, 18,* 135–164.

Hammond, P., & Morgan, H. P. (Eds.). (1991). *Ending mandatory retirement for tenured faculty: The consequences for higher education.* Community Report from the National Research Council. Washington, DC: National Academy Press.

Heilman, M. E., Block, C. J., & Lucas, J. A. (1992). Presumed incompetent? Stigmatization and affirmative action efforts. *Journal of Applied Psychology, 77*(4), 536–544.

Heilman, M. E., Rivero, J. C., & Brett, J. F. (1991). Skirting the competence issue: Effects of sex-based preferential selection on task choices of women and men. *Journal of Applied Psychology, 76*(1), 99–105.

Herriot, P. (1989). Selection as a social process. In M. Smith & I. Robertson (Eds.), *Advances in selection and assessment.* New York: Wiley.

Hogan, J. (1991). Structure of physical performance in occupational tasks. *Journal of Applied Psychology, 76*(4), 495–507.

Howard, A. (1993). *Will assessment centers be obsolete in the 21st century? Replies to the critics.* Paper presented at the 21st International Congress on the Assessment Center Method, Atlanta.

Huffcutt, A. I., & Arthur, W., Jr. (1994). Hunter and Hunter (1984) revisited: Interview validity for entry-level jobs. *Journal of Applied Psychology, 79*(2), 184–190.

Hunter, D. R., & Burke, E. F. (1987). Computer-based selection testing in the Royal Air Force. *Behavior Research Methods, Instruments, and Computers, 19,* 243–245.

Hunter, J. (1983). A causal analysis of cognitive ability, job knowledge, job performance, and supervisor ratings. In F. Landy, S. Zedeck, & J. Cleveland (Eds.), *Performance measurement and theory.* Hillsdale, NJ: Erlbaum.

Inwald, R. E. (1992). *Hilson job analysis questionnaire.* Kew Gardens, NY: Hilson Research.

Jackson, S. (1991). Team composition in organizational settings: Issues in managing an increasingly diverse workforce. In S. Worchel, W. Woods, & J. Simpson (Eds.), *Group processes and productivity.* Newbury Park, CA: Sage.

Jackson, S. E., Brett, J. F., Sessa, V. I., Cooper, D. M., Julin, J. A., & Peyronnin, K. (1991). Some differences make a difference: Individual dissimilarity and group heterogeneity as correlates of recruitment, promotions, and turnover. *Journal of Applied Psychology, 76*(5), 675–689.

Jackson, S. E., Stone, V. K., & Alvarez, E. B. (1993). Socialization amidst diversity: The impact of demographics on work team oldtimers and newcomers. In L. L. Cummings & B. M. Staw (Eds.), *Research in organizational behavior* (Vol. 15). Greenwich, CT: JAI Press.

Jones, J. W. (1991). A personnel selection approach to industrial safety. In J. Jones (Ed.), *Preemployment honesty testing: Current research and future directions.* New York: Quorum Books.

Jones, J. W., & Wuebker, L. J. (1988). Accident prevention through personnel selection. *Journal of Business and Psychology, 3*(2), 187–198.

Kanfer, R., & Ackerman, P. L. (1989). Motivation and cognitive abilities: An integrative/aptitude-treatment interaction approach to skill acquisition [Monograph]. *Journal of Applied Psychology, 74*(4), 657–690.

Katz, D., & Kahn, R. (1978). *The social psychology of organizations* (2nd ed.). New York: Wiley.

Kravitz, D. A., & Platania, J. (1992, April). *Attitudes and beliefs about race-based affirmative action.* Paper presented at the meeting of the Society for Industrial and Organizational Psychology, Montreal, Canada.

Landy, F. J. (1992). Hugo Munsterberg: Victim or visionary? *Journal of Applied Psychology, 77*(6), 787–802.

Landy, F. J., et al. (1992). *Alternatives to chronological age in determining standards of suitability for public safety jobs.* University Park: Center for Applied Behavioral Sciences, Pennsylvania State University.

Larson, G. E., & Merritt, C. R. (1991). Can accidents be predicted? An empirical test of the cognitive failures questionnaire. *Applied Psychology, 40*(1), 37–45.

Lin, T. R., Dobbins, G. H., & Farh, J. L. (1992). A field study of race and age similarity effects on interview ratings in conventional and situational interviews. *Journal of Applied Psychology, 77*(3), 363–371.

McCardle, W. D., Katch, F. I., & Katch, V. L. (1991). *Exercise physiology: Energy, nutrition, and human performance.* Malvern, PA: Lea & Febiger.

McCormick, E. J., Jeanneret, P. R., & Mecham, R. C. (1969, 1989). *Position analysis questionnaire.* Palo Alto: Consulting Psychologists Press.

McDaniel, M., Whetzel, D., Schmidt, F., & Maurer, T. (in press). The validity of employment interviews: A comprehensive review and meta-analysis. *Journal of Applied Psychology.*

Mael, F. A. (1991). A conceptual rationale for the domain and attributes of biodata items. *Personnel Psychology, 44*(4), 763–792.

Manning, C. A., & Broach, D. (1992). *Identifying ability requirements for operators of future automated air traffic control systems.* (DOT/FAA/AM-92/26). Washington, DC: U. S. Government Printing Office.

Mead, A. D., & Drasgow, F. (in press). Equivalence of computerized and paper-and-pencil cognitive ability tests: A meta-analysis. *Psychological Bulletin.*

Morgan, B. & Lassiter, D. (1992). Team composition and staffing. In R. W. Swezey & E. Salas (Eds.), *Teams: Their training and performance.* Norwood, NJ: Ablex.

Mumford, M. D., & Owens, W. A. (1987). Methodology review: Principles, procedures, and findings in the application of background data measures. *Applied Psychological Measurement, 11,* 1–31.

Mumford, M. D., Stokes, G. S., & Owens, W. A. (1990). *Patterns of life adaptation: The ecology of human individuality.* Hillsdale, NJ: Erlbaum.

Mumford, M. D., Uhlman, C. E., & Kilcullen, R. N. (1992). The structure of life history: Implications for the construct validity of background data scales. *Human Performance, 5*(1–2), 109–137.

Mumford, M. D., Wesley, S. S., & Shaffer, G. S. (1987). Individuality in a developmental context II: The crystallization of developmental trajectories. *Human Development, 30,* 291–321.

National Safety Council. (1991). *Accident facts.* Chicago: Author.

Officers for Justice et al. and San Francisco Police Officers Association v. the Civil Service Commission of the City and County of San Francisco et al., City and County of San Francisco, 979 F.2d 721 (9th Cir. 1992).

Ones, D. S., Mount, M. K., Barrick, M. R., & Hunter, J. E. (1994). Personality and job performance: A critique of the Tett, Jackson, & Rothstein (1991) meta-analysis. *Personnel Psychology, 47*(1), 147–156.

Ones, D., Viswesvaran, C., & Schmidt, F. (1993). Meta-analysis of integrity test validities: Findings and implications for personnel selection and theories of job performance [Monograph]. *Journal of Applied Psychology, 78*(4), 679–703.

Park, K. S., & Lee, S. W. (1992). A computer-aided aptitude test for predicting flight performance of trainees. *Human Factors, 34*(2), 189–204.

Pfeffer, J. (1983). Organizational demography. In L. L. Cummings & B. M. Staw (Eds.), *Research in organizational behavior.* Greenwich, CT: JAI Press.

Prieto, J. (1994). The team perspective in selection and assessment. In H. Schuler, J. L. Farr, & M. Smith (Eds.), *Personnel selection and assessment: Industrial and organizational perspectives.* Hillsdale, NJ: Erlbaum.

Ree, M. J., Earles, J. A., & Teachout, M. S. (1992). *General cognitive ability predicts job performance* (interim technical report for November 1990–November 1991). Brooks Air Force Base, TX: Air Force Systems Command.

Robinson, D. D. (1992). *Worker Rehabilitation Questionnaire (WRQ) user's and technical manual.* Palo Alto: Consulting Psychologists Press.

Rynes, S. L. (1993). Who's selecting whom? Effects of selection practices in applicant attitudes and behavior. In N. Schmitt, W. Borman, & Associates, *Personnel selection in organizations.* San Francisco: Jossey-Bass.

Rynes, S. L., & Connerley, M. L. (1992). Applicant reactions to alternative selection procedures. *Journal of Business Psychology, 7*(3), 261–277.

Rynes, S., & Miller, H. (1983). Recruiter and job influences on candidates for employment. *Journal of Applied Psychology, 68,* 147–154.

Sackett, P. R., & Roth, L. (1991). A Monte Carlo examination of banding and rank order methods of test scores used in personnel selection. *Human Performance, 4*(4), 279–295.

Sanchez, J. I., & Fraser, S. L. (1992). On the choice of scales for task analysis. *Journal of Applied Psychology, 77*(4), 545–553.

Schmidt, F. L. (1991). Why all banding procedures in personnel selection are logically flawed. *Human Performance, 4*(4), 265–277.

Schmidt, F. L. (1992). What do data really mean? Research findings, meta-analysis, and cumulative knowledge in psychology. *American Psychologist, 47*(10), 1173–1181.

Schmidt, F. L., & Hunter, J. E. (in press). Tacit knowledge, practical intelligence, general mental ability, and job knowledge. *Current Directions in Psychological Science.*

Schmitt, N., Gilliland, S., Landis, R., & Devine, D. (1993). Computer-based testing applied to selection of secretarial applicants. *Personnel Psychology, 46*(1), 149–165.

Schmitt, N., Gooding, R. Z., Noe, R. A., & Kirsch, M. P. (1984). Meta-analyses of validity studies published between 1964 and 1982 and the investigation of study characteristics. *Personnel Psychology, 37,* 407–422.

Schneider, B. (1983). The people make the place. *Personnel Psychology, 40,* 437–453.

Scholarios, D. (1992, August). *A comparison of predictor selection methods for maximizing potential classification efficiency.* Paper presented at the meeting of American Psychological Association, Washington, DC.

Schuler, H., & Stehle, W. (1983). Recent developments in assessment centers: Evaluated under the aspect of social validity. *Zeitschrift für Arbeits- und Organisationpsychologie, 27,* 33–44.

Searcy, C., Woods, P. N., Gatewood, R., & Lance, C. (1993, April). *The validity of structured interviews: A meta-analytical search for moderators.* Paper presented at the meeting of the Society for Industrial and Organizational Psychology, San Francisco.

Shaw, M. E. (1976). *Group dynamics: The psychology of small group behavior* (2nd ed.). New York: McGraw-Hill.

Shechtman, Z. (1992). A group assessment procedure as a predictor of on-the-job performance of teachers. *Journal of Applied Psychology, 77*(3), 383–387.

Sothmann, M., et al. (1990). Advancing age and the cardiorespiratory stress of fire suppression: Determining a minimum standard for aerobic fitness. *Human Performance, 3,* 217–236.

Sternberg, R. J. (1985). *Beyond IQ: A triarchic theory of human intelligence.* New York: Cambridge University Press.

Sternberg, R. J., & Wagner, R. K. (1993). Practical intelligence and tacit knowledge. *Current Directions in Psychological Science, 2*(1), 1–4.

Sternberg, R. J., Wagner, R. K., & Okagaki, L. (in press). Practical intelligence: The nature and role of tacit knowledge in work and at school. In H. Reese & J. Puckett (Eds.), *Advances in lifespan development.* Hillsdale, NJ: Erlbaum.

Stevens, M. J. (1992). *Individual level knowledge, skill, and ability requirements for group-based work design systems.* Unpublished doctoral dissertation, Purdue University, West Lafayette, IN.

Stoffey, R., Millsap, R., Smither, J., & Reilly, R. (1991). *The influence of selection procedures on attitudes about the organizational and job pursuit intentions.* Paper presented at the meeting of the Society for Industrial and Organizational Psychology, St. Louis.

Stokes, G. S., Mumford, M. D., & Owens, W. A. (1989). Life history prototypes in the study of human individuality. *Journal of Personality, 57,* 509–545.

Stokes, G. S., Mumford, M. D., & Owens, W. A. (1994). *The biodata handbook: Theory, research, and application.* Palo Alto, CA: Consulting Psychologists Press.

Summers, R. J. (1991). The influence of affirmative action on perceptions of a beneficiary's qualifications. *Journal of Applied Social Psychology, 21*(15), 1265–1276.

Tett, R. P., Jackson, D. N., & Rothstein, M. (1991). Personality measures as predictors of job performance: A meta-analytic review. *Personnel Psychology, 44*(4), 703–742.

Thornton, G. (1994). The effect of selection practices on applicants' perceptions of organizational characteristics. In H. Schuler, J. L. Farr, & M. Smith (Eds.), *Personnel selection and assessment: Industrial and organizational perspectives.* Hillsdale, NJ: Erlbaum.

Tissen, R. (1994). Selection as a social process: From scapegoat to golden hen. In M. Smith & I. Robertson (Eds.), *Advances in selection and assessment.* New York: Wiley.

Uniform guidelines on employee selection procedures. (1978). *Federal Register, 43*(166), 38295–38309.

Wagner, R. K., & Sternberg, R. J. (1987). Tacit knowledge in managerial success. *Journal of Business Psychology, 1*(4), 301–312.

Wolfe, J. (1990). The evaluation of computer-based business games:

Methodology, findings, and future needs. In J. W. Gentry (Ed.), *ABSEL guide to experiential learning and simulation gaming.* New York: Nichols.

Zeidner, J., & Johnson, C. D. (1991a). *The economic benefits of predicting job performance, Vol. 1: Selection utility.* New York: Praeger.

Zeidner, J., & Johnson, C. D. (1991b). *The economic benefits of predicting job performance, Vol. 3: Estimating the gains of alternative policies.* New York: Praeger.

Zeidner, J., & Johnson, C. D. (1994). Is personnel classification a concept whose time has passed? In M. G. Rumsey, C. B. Walker, & J. H. Harris (Eds.), *Personnel selection and classification.* Hillsdale, NJ: Erlbaum.

Chapter Eight

Changing Individual-Organization Attachments

A Two-Way Street

Denise M. Rousseau, Kimberly A. Wade-Benzoni

Employment relations change whenever a fundamental change in work or the people doing work occurs. Today, breakthroughs in information technology and competitive forces are radically altering the nature of work (Davis, 1987). Lifestyle changes and demographic trends are modifying workforce values, skills, and expectations (Zuboff, 1988). The purpose of this chapter is to examine changing employee-organization attachments. It explores the meaning of and historical forces underlying individual-organization attachments, maps the forms these attachments take, and creates a lexicon for describing them. It also examines the relevance and limitations of current concepts in industrial/organizational (I/O) psychology for understanding emerging forms of attachment.

The Meaning of Attachment

Attachment is used here to refer to the link or bond between the individual and the organization (Mathieu & Zajac, 1990). Three basic features of this link are (1) parties to the attachment, (2)

Note: We thank Ann Howard, Brian Uzzi, and Shelly Zedeck for their very helpful comments. Katie Shonk did a marvelous job of editing and word processing.

strength or degree of involvement between the parties, and (3) duration or time frame. Attachment can occur in several domains, such as organization (Mathieu & Zajac, 1990) or union (Fukami & Larson, 1984), and involve a variety of parties (for example, organization, department, division, union, team) to which the person is attached.

With the advent of networked organizations (Snow, Miles, & Coleman, 1992), attachment can involve the individual's relations with multiple organizations, including customers and suppliers, as well as a primary employer. Strength or degree of involvement between the parties reflects the nature of their exchange, investments each makes in the other, and the amount of mutual impact (behavior change or influence) characterizing the relationship. Where organizations invest heavily in the training and development of members who in turn become socialized to the organization's culture, the degree of mutual involvement would be high. In contrast, employment relations where individuals provide limited services to the organization without training or development would be characterized by low involvement. Last, time frame reflects the duration of the individual-organization relationship. Duration involves both length of time (short-term versus long-term) as well as specificity (specific versus open-ended).

This chapter provides evidence of the considerable variation in these three dimensions of attachment throughout the history of modern organizations. We make a case for the consideration of all three elements of attachment in research on the employment relationship.

Attachment in Industrial/Organizational Psychology

Traditional I/O psychology research has tended to treat attachment as an individual-level phenomenon. Research on commitment and careers largely addresses *individual* perceptions, experiences, and values (Mathieu & Zajac, 1990). Increasingly, however, organizational researchers are recognizing that attachment is a two-way, not just an individual-level, phenomenon. For example, research on organizational citizenship recognizes the link between the "good soldier" (Organ, 1990) and the "good general" (Shore & Wayne, 1993). Organizational support in the form of training, ample rewards, and concern for individual welfare can create a sense of obligation on the part of employees, generating higher employee commitment and citizenship behaviors (Eisenberger, Huntington, Hutchison, & Sowa, 1986; Shore & Wayne, 1993). The meaning of attachment and its two-way character is particularly evident in recent findings from two arenas of organizational research: commitment and psychological contracts.

Commitment

Commitment has been widely studied in I/O psychology as an individual psychological state (for example, Mowday, Porter, & Steers, 1982). This research has been predicated on two assumptions: (1) there are only two parties to the attachment—the focal individual and the organization of which he or she is a member, and (2) high commitment is preferable to low commitment from the perspective of both the organization and the individual. Individual-level commitment has perhaps been most clearly defined and operationalized along two dimensions: continuance and affective commitment. *Continuance commitment* is the perceived need to remain in the organization because of costs incurred by leaving, such as loss of pay, pension, or promotion opportunities (Becker, 1960; Hrebiniak & Alutto, 1972). *Affective commitment* reflects the strength of an individual's identification and involvement with the organization and includes a strong belief in the organization's goals, a willingness to exert effort on the organization's behalf, and a desire to maintain membership (Meyer & Allen, 1984; Mowday et al., 1982; Barksdale & Shore, 1993).

From an attachment perspective, continuance commitment reflects the relationship's duration while affective commitment operationalizes its strength. Although continuance commitment has no systematic effect on behavior (Mathieu & Zajac, 1990), it does become increasingly correlated with affective commitment over time (as sunk costs increase and members become more emotionally involved with the organization). Affective commitment increases with age, job level, and job scope and is associated with more member contributions to the organization. Continuance commitment has more variable relations with other factors and appears to consist of two dimensions: low alternatives and high sacrifice. McGee and Ford (1987) reported a lower affective commitment for employees with fewer job alternatives but greater affective commitment for those making substantial sacrifices for the organization. This pattern implicates the nature of the exchange between employee and employer in shaping the form the employee's commitment takes.

Commitment research has frequently focused on the individual while ignoring the organization. However, affective commitment appears to increase with organizational supportiveness (for example, Shore & Wayne, 1993) and equitability in treatment (Organ, 1990). The role of the organization in shaping employee commitment is probably underestimated in commitment research: most studies have been done in single organizations offering little or no variance in factors such as human resource practices or organizational support (Mathieu & Zajac, 1990). Moreover, commitment researchers have assumed that both organizations and individuals value commitment. But some organizations and some individuals may not seek to foster high commitment (for example, among temporary employees whose termination dates are established the day they are hired). Thus we can conclude that current research neglects the situational and interactive underpinnings of commitment.

By highlighting the interactional nature of commitment and its link to organization-individual relations and exchanges, we can gain a deeper understanding of the experience of commitment. If we view commitment from the broader perspective of individual-organization attachments, it becomes apparent that operationalizations of the concept have underestimated the role played by the organization and the organization-individual exchange. Commitment is one manifestation of the attachment between individual and organization. As such, we need to focus on the features of that attachment. Recent research on the concept of the psychological contract addresses more specifically the nature of the individual-organization relationship and exchanges.

Psychological Contracts

Contracts are agreements to exchange services (for example, hard work, loyalty) for compensation (for example, pay, career opportunities, personal development). The rich array of possible exchanges (such as effort, learning, sacrificed opportunities elsewhere) and their duration (a day or indefinitely) create a variety of potential contracts between employee and employer. There are many levels of contract (Rousseau & Parks, 1993), among them the psychological contract reflecting the individual's (worker or employer) understanding of the employment relationship's terms, and the normative contract representing shared beliefs organization members may have about what they owe and are owed in turn. We focus here on the psychological contract.

Elsewhere, we have proposed that terms of psychological contracts typically take into account two key contract features very relevant to current organizational concerns: time frame and performance requirements (Rousseau, 1995; Rousseau & Wade-Benzoni, 1994). Time frame refers to one feature of the duration of the employment relationship—whether it is short-term or long-term. Another distinguishing feature in the individual-organization interaction is the extent to which particular performance requirements are specified as a condition of employment (well specified or weakly specified). Performance specifications are important contract features for two reasons: (1) they detail conditions under which the contract may be terminated (without specified performance terms the nature of the employee contribution is ambiguous and sanctions for substandard performance become difficult to enforce), and (2) they detail the employee's obligations in the exchange. When time frame and performance features are arranged in a 2 x 2 framework (see Table 8.1), four types of contracts can be identified: (1) *transactional contracts,* of limited duration with well-specified performance terms, (2) *relational contracts,* open-ended membership with incomplete or flexible performance requirements, (3) *balanced contracts,* open-ended, relationship-oriented employment with well-specified performance terms, and (4) *transitional contracts,* reflecting the absence of commitments and specific performance terms.

Transactional contracts focus on short-term and monetizable exchanges—"a fair day's work for a fair day's pay." Manpower, Kelly, Nursetemps, Accountemps, and other temporary employment services offer organizations the opportunity to create purely economic exchanges for a limited period of time. Transactional contracts are limited, arm's-length agreements, low on involvement and of short

Table 8.1. Types of Psychological Contracts.

		Performance Terms	
		Specified	*Not Specified*
Duration	*Short-term*	Transactional (for example, retail clerks hired during Christmas shopping season) • Low ambiguity • Easy exit • Low commitment • Freedom to enter new contracts • Little learning • Weak integration/ identification	Transitional (for example, employee experiences during organizational retrenchment or following merger or acquisition) • Ambiguity/uncertainty • Unstable • High turnover/ termination
	Long-term	Balanced (for example, high-involvement teams) • High affective commitment • High integration/ identification • High learning • Ongoing development • Mutual support	Relational (for example, family business members) • High continuous commitment • High affective commitment • Strong integration/ identification

duration. Relational contracts involve open-ended and often long-term relationships involving considerable investments (socioemotional as well as economic) by both employees (company-specific skills, long-term career development) and employers (extensive training and support). Such investments involve a high degree of mutual interdependence and barriers to exit. Balanced contracts reflect individual-organization attachments where extensive mutual exchanges (of time, effort, mutual contribution, and development) are conditioned on the capacity of the individual to provide requisite levels of performance and the organization's ability to develop and utilize the individual's capabilities. Transitional contracts reflect the inability of contract parties, especially the organization, to make commitments in the face of environmental uncertainty. The latter condition is apparent in industries eroded by competition and technological change.

These forms of contract yield distinct predictions about the behaviors of both individual and organization. Transactional contracts are expected to yield low commitment in all forms with the possible exception of continuance commitment when alternative jobs are few. When one party violates a transactional contract, the other typically terminates the interaction. Under transactional arrangements, incompetent employees are terminated, and employees quit untrustworthy organizations. In contrast, parties to a relational contract are more likely to react angrily to contract violation but remain in the relationship (Robinson & Rousseau, 1994; Brockner, Tyler, & Cooper-Schneider, 1992) due to high levels of affective commitment and the costliness of finding alternative relationships. Moreover, since relational contracts have fairly subjective terms (for example, "excellent training"), they offer more possibility for disagreement in interpretation. Balanced contracts assign responsibilities to both contract parties and as such are likely to create more mutuality because of the ongoing interactions, exchanges, and mutual support they require. Transitional contracts convey no guarantees. Thus they offer virtually no commitment and are a transition to another, more stable employment form. Which of these forms of contract emerges is linked to the organization's human resource practices and its broader business and strategic goals (Rousseau, 1995; Rousseau & Wade-Benzoni, 1994).

Commitment and the Nature of the Contract

Commitment has different meanings depending on the nature of the contract between individual and organization. In transactional situations, neither the individual nor the organization may seek continuance or affective commitment. However, in relational situations, high levels of both commitment forms are likely when the contract terms are met. The value of individual commitment to the organization depends on the type of attachment the organization and individuals seek.

Organization-employee attachment can take many forms depending on the goals of the organization and the needs of the individual. Attachment patterns also vary with changes in business strategy and broader societal changes. To understand changes in individual-organization attachment, we next consider the historical forces influencing organizational goals and individual needs.

Changing Forms of Attachment: A Brief Historical Overview

Employment relations in modern Western organizations have undergone transformation in the course of three major historical phases: Emergent, Bureaucratic, and Adhocratic. These phases have given rise to diverse forms of labor-organization attachments (see Table 8.2).

Emergent Phase

In the late eighteenth century, modern industrial production organizations began. Basic industries such as textiles and ceramics were each traditionally a cottage industry in which the farmer/craftsperson worked at home. Urban merchants traveled the countryside trying to purchase enough goods to satisfy the growing demand in town. Many goods were produced by people who farmed in good weather and produced handiwork in bad or when they felt inclined to do so. Although merchants often provided equipment and material to craftspeople (for example, looms and yarn), these middlemen had little control over such workers and, despite increases in demand, the merchants' means of increasing productivity were limited (Dickson, 1974). Factories were created to make supply more regular.

Table 8.2. Historical Phases and
Individual-Organization Attachment.

Phase	Commitment	Contract
Emergent	Continuance	Transactional
Bureaucratic	Affective and continuance	Relational
Adhocratic	Varies with type of relationship	

Historically, industrial organizations were a means of control, factories brought weavers under one roof and made it possible to monitor their work and ensure a steady supply of cloth. Predictability was a major driver. Factories concentrating labor and production in one spot *preceded* development of sophisticated technology such as power machinery (Dickson, 1974). Working in one place permitted production to be overseen by a foreman and provided consistency in output not available from individual craftspersons. Following the creation of factories it became possible to develop and use power machinery (for example, water-powered looms) and redesign work to improve the speed of production. Predictability was thus augmented by efficiency.

Factory efficiency made it difficult for craftspeople working at home to continue to compete, and within a few decades work in many industries changed from home-based crafts to centralized factories. Merchants had become factory owners and managerial work emerged in the form of foremen and overseers. Evolution in employment relationships had begun.

Several key features of employment relations were prominent in the emergent phase:

- A centralized workplace
- Worker/manager/owner distinction
- Managerial control over time and rate of production
- Organizational ownership over means of production
- Development of hierarchical controls enforcing regular hours and supervisor-subordinate relations
- Development of transactional contracts and employee commitment based on limited alternatives

Bureaucratic Phase

The next phase took predictability and efficiency to elaborate conclusions in the form of complex hierarchical organizations with internal labor markets (Hirsch, 1994). It is this bureaucratic phase from which modern organizational theory derives (for example, Barnard, 1938; Thompson, 1967). The traditional view of work in organizational theory is embedded in three fundamental notions:

administrative control over employees, development of long-term employment relationships, and physical proximity between organization and worker (Pfeffer & Baron, 1988).

This is the era portrayed by William Whyte's *Organization Man* (1956) and Rosabeth Moss Kanter's *Men and Women of the Corporation* (1977). Successful employees were those who developed organization-specific skills for working with both the technology and the social system that made up the organization. Successful managers at the most widely admired firms entered early, climbed the rungs of the company ladder, and fulfilled the role of "company men" (Hirsch, 1994). The organization's memory and distinctive competencies typically rested in the minds and skills of its employees and managers. Consistency, efficiency, and refinement of technology were facilitated by creation of internal labor markets (ILMs), where members who remained with the organization for indefinite periods of time developed norms for dealing with each other and for how they went about their work, and where managers oversaw the job they had once done. ILMs create not only predictable behaviors among workers but also a predictable supply of future talent, including the organization's managers. ILMs also create career paths that offer a promise of long-term employment as organization-specific skills are acquired. Workers became a core part of the organization, intrinsically a part of it because of the codes of behavior they had learned through socialization as well as the specific skills and technologies in which they had become proficient.

Key features of employment relations in the bureaucratic era included these:

- Internal labor markets involving early career entry into the organization, long-term retention, development of organization-specific skills, assimilation into an organization's culture to promote efficiency, and delayed rewards for contributions (seniority system)
- Organizational hierarchies facilitating control over behavior and career opportunities
- Slack resources as a source of competitive advantage: workers paid more than market wage and hierarchical levels expanded to reward retention of managers

- Development of relational contracts with employees (including managers) that expand employee commitment to be both affective and continuance (low opportunity and high sacrifice) and escalate organizational investment in individuals, creating organizational commitment to members (for example, desire to retain them)

Adhocratic Phase

Present and likely future employment relationships reflect a fundamental shift in the nature of work. Breakthroughs in information systems, global competition, and escalating interdependence between organizations and among people have created some new fundamentals: rapid change and tight time frames, along with multiple constituencies and decision makers. Speed of change makes predictability less valuable than adaptability. Diverse and segmented global markets make responsiveness critical. Flexibility is a major driver.

Established bureaucracies are slowly being replaced by adhocracies whose flexibility comes from looser structures and more individual autonomy. There are many labels for this "post-bureaucratic" phase—*adhocracies, high tech, post-industrial, networks* (Kanter, 1989; Venkatesh & Vitalari, 1992). Because these adaptations involve changes in the structure of occupations and the nature of work, organizational changes wrought by current technological, social, and economic forces are likely to be fundamental, not merely incremental (Venkatesh & Vitalari, 1992). By definition, fundamental changes conflict with structures created in an earlier time. This post-bureaucratic phase is not fully integrated in the organizational literature, where changes in administrative control/hierarchy, relationships, and location of work have not yet shaped fundamental constructs and models of organizational attachment. However, some key features of employment relations in post-bureaucratic adhocracies have been identified by Handy (1991) and Hall (1993):

- Development of differentiated employment relations within the same organization, including *core employees,* essential to organizational memory and continuity, with long-term relationships to the organization, and *peripheral employees,* providing flexibility as demand fluctuates or new opportunities emerge, who have limited relationships to the organization

- Altered forms of careers (less upward mobility but more alternative career paths including midcareer shifts, phased retirement, and the option of high- and low-involvement work roles)
- Emphasis on continuous skill development
- Boundaryless employment relations where work may be performed in the context of several organizations simultaneously (for example, customers serving on supplier design teams)
- Proliferation of contract forms and varying degrees of organizational commitment to labor and labor commitment to the organization

Lexicon

In the two hundred or so years since the beginning of the industrial revolution certain basic concepts and terms have characterized employment relations (Table 8.3). Charles Handy (1991) in *The Age of Unreason* has written: "One sign of the new type of organization is a perceptible shift in the language we use to talk about organizations. Organizations used to be perceived as gigantic pieces of engineering, with large interchangeable human parts. . . . Today the language is not of engineering but of politics, with talk of cultures and networks, of teams and coalitions" (p. 89). Despite the accuracy of Handy's observed shift in language, we are also struck by the continuity of employment terminology, even as its meaning and manifestations shift. Where once an employee was anyone within an organization who worked for a wage, trends give rise to partial and quasi employees (such as suppliers or customers and their individual representatives who work within an organization designing a product, as in the case of representatives from tire manufacturers serving on Mazda and Chrysler design teams; and military personnel working with defense contractors on product design and inspections). A diverse array of employment patterns necessitates attaching adjectives, descriptors, and modifiers to the term *employee* (core, peripheral, part time, temporary, and so forth). Organizations were once legal entities with employees inside and

Table 8.3. Organizational Constructs for Past and Future.

	Past	Future
Employee	One employed by another for wages; same meaning for all who worked for the organization.	Include customers as "partial employees" due to their participation in service production process (Bowen & Schneider, 1988). Organization will have many different kinds of employees (core, contractors, part-timers, temps, partial employees, and so forth).
Organization	Legal entity with employees inside and an external market outside its boundaries.	Many forms, legal as well as enacted, some with inclusion of customer/market inside boundaries, some with few employees within boundaries.
Management	Supervising and directing work of others.	Self-supervising employees; managers integrate work of others.
Career	Evolving sequence of work over time (Arthur, Hall, & Lawrence, 1989); can apply to all.	Different kinds of careers depending on employment status; part-timers and temps have jobs, not careers (Handy, 1990). Boundaryless careers—not contained within one organization or even one industry or occupation.
Status	Position or rank in relation to others, location in hierarchy.	Type of worker (core, contractor, and so forth).

Identification	Sense of self influenced by relationship with organization.	Sense of self varies with status: core employees are partners in organization; peripherals have stronger sense of relation to their work.
Networks	A system of interrelations.	Increasing interdependent relations, involving more people with different roles and different employment relations.
Office	A place where people work for their employers.	Access to common facilities for networked people, but fewer work centers and more decentralized work.

customers outside. Including customers within organizations for planning, design, and even production has created "boundaryless organizations" (see Davis, Chapter Three this volume), making the term *organization* more a metaphor than a concrete reality. Management once was the direction of the work of others, but now it can be performed by oneself (self-management, self-regulating teams, self-designing work systems; for example, Orsburn, Moran, Musselwhite, & Zenger, 1991). Careers were formerly an evolving sequence of phases and patterns (Crites, 1969); now they too have been described as boundaryless (Hirschhorn & Gilmer, 1992) or variously as multichannel, steady state, temporary (Hall, 1993), or protean (Hall & Mirvis, Chapter Nine this volume). Status is less a feature of position and more a description of the type of employment relationship (core or peripheral). Network once meant a system of interrelations—some social, some political. Increasingly, network refers to managed interdependence among persons in work roles whose employment status varies.

Finally, our notions of workplace, factory or office, home or workstation, have evolved, and with them have emerged not only new technologies and employment relations but also new forms of control (for example, computer-based monitoring; Venkatesh & Vitalari, 1992) and work motives (such as new definitions of psychological success; Hall, 1993). In the new combination of workplace elements, an office can be described as an "office factory" where standardized white-collar work is performed (for example, insurance claims processing). An office may be a "hollow," with people who work as free agents for various organizations sharing desks, computers, and a secretary, with no organizational relationship beyond time-shared space. Or an office may be one's home. The evident transformation of the workplace itself is somehow fitting. It was the movement of work from home to factory that initiated the industrial age. Changes in the workplace have been a signal throughout history of a change in the employment relationship.

We think it is appropriate that old terms continue to be applied in the evolving employment relationship, though connotations are changing quickly enough for organizational researchers to require a Rosetta stone to translate the meanings of employment concepts across eras. To understand the underpinnings of these changing employment dimensions we move next to emerging types of employment relationships.

Types of Employment Relations

Balancing control and flexibility are classic organizational challenges (Thompson, 1967). Bureaucratic organizations place a premium on behavioral control, valuing consistency and predictability more highly than adaptability, making them suitable to stable environments (for example, government agencies in first world nations). Adhocracies pursue adaptation through flexibility and frequent adjustments to products produced, results achieved, and the ways in which people are utilized, making them suitable for dynamic settings (for example, the early NASA space program, leading-edge software design firms). Many contemporary organizations seek some sort of balance between the two as they deal with changing environments while trying to meet demands of stockholders, governments, employees, and markets.

Two basic dimensions of employment relations that affect flexibility and control are (1) short- or long-term time frames and (2) embeddedness (internalization or externalization). So far, this chapter has used a variety of dimensions in characterizing attachment—long-term/short-term, specific/open-ended, weak/strong, internalized/externalized, and so on. The diversity of descriptors reflects the array of terms needed to express forms of the employment relationship. Certainly many of these terms overlap each other. Specific time frames are more likely to be short, and open-ended ones usually last longer. Internalized relations are likely to be stronger than externalized ones. To explore changing employment arrangements, we focus here on two dimensions (short-term/long-term and internalized/externalized) that link to organizational flexibility and control.

The time frame of employment relations will be longer when the organization's managers believe they can anticipate future market behavior and when development of organization-specific knowledge (technical and cultural) is seen as strategically desirable and possible. Rapidly fluctuating environments make predictability difficult and can lead to short-term employment arrangements to help firms adapt more quickly. Internalization/externalization is the degree to which the individual is embedded in the organization through membership (employment status, socialization, training and development). In common terms, internalization creates *insiders* and externalization makes for *outsiders*. Insiders, by their presence within the organization, are more subject to behavioral control, making them more predictable and better able to perform in ways interdependent with others. But control can be costly (for example, training, supervision) and long-term commitments can constrain flexibility. How organizations manage the competing demands of behavioral control and flexibility is evident in their human resource (HR) practices, and is particularly manifest in their employment relations. Based on the intersection of the time frame and embeddedness dimensions, a diverse array of employment relations can be mapped (Figure 8.1).

Traditional employees in internal labor markets were highly internalized and long-term: workers were embedded in the organization, working within its walls and its boundaries (legal and administrative), and with both a history and a future of employment with that firm. Outsourcing work has created short-term arrangements with high externalization: the organization's work is performed not by its members, but by those who work elsewhere often under someone else's guidance, with no history or future with that organization—a trend referred to as the "hollowing" of American industry (Bettis, Bradley, & Hamel, 1991).

Historically, control was built into the employment relationship. Bureaucratic organizations excelled at controlling technical processes and employee behavior, each of which requires employees to be insiders. Yet, despite our discussion of historic trends toward control through culture and long-term relationships, many short-duration, external relationships have existed and continue to exist. Perhaps the best exemplars are the entertainment industry (for example, music, television) and construction, where uncertainty in customer demands is dealt with by maintaining one's freedom to contract continually with others in a classic spot-market fashion. Construction organizations, too, are often truly hollow companies with virtually no employees.

Both long-term internalized (for example, civil servants) and short-term externalized relationships (for example, migrant farm workers) have existed for centuries. Innovations and expansions in

Figure 8.1. Attachment Map.

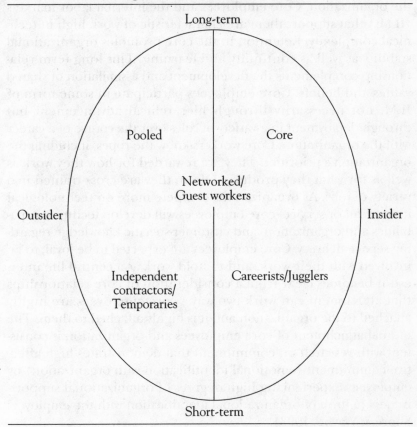

employment tend to occur in the off-quadrant domains (see Figure 8.1) of short-term internalized and long-term externalized relationships. Such patterns are becoming increasingly complex as organizations seek simultaneously to adapt and change while meeting demands for consistency and quality (as in "well-made," "supportively serviced," "reliable," and "environmentally sound"). Next we discuss the specific types of current and emerging employment relationships.

Long-Term Insiders: Core Employees

Core employees are those around whom the organization is built. They provide a focus for its activities based on their critical skills and expertise, and create a distinctive competitive advantage for the organization. Core employees and the internal labor markets (ILMs) that support them are characteristic of work high in technical complexity. Retention in the core promotes organizational stability as well as continuity and learning. This long-term relationship complements the development and assimilation of shared values and beliefs. Core employees participate in some form of ILM, not necessarily through hierarchical advancement but through deployment in a variety of roles over the course of a career with the organization. Core workers know the ropes, including the organization's priorities. They are rewarded for how they work as well as for what they produce. Often, they are cross-trained in a variety of jobs. As organizations compete more on technological innovation or service, core employees will develop technical capabilities and organization- and customer-specific knowledge regarding service delivery. Core employees are expected to be loyal, to be involved with their work, and to hold work as a central life interest. It becomes clear from a consideration of core relationships that attachment can work two ways: core employees are highly attached to the organization and it is highly attached to them. The mutual attachment of core employees and organization is consistent with research on commitment that demonstrates high affective commitment (emotional identification with organization) by employees experiencing high degrees of organizational supportiveness (a form of organizational identification with the employee; Shore & Wayne, 1993).

Organizations are currently reexamining their reliance on core employees in light of the overhead burden they bring and in the face of escalating demands for change and innovation. To cut costs and obtain flexibility, many firms have turned to outsourcing—that is, buying the competencies formerly provided by core workers. Outsourcing transfers the responsibilities for innovation and learning to another organization. Taken to the logical extreme, outsourcing as a general strategy to solve problems of cost and control can lead a firm to become a "hollow organization" with few distinctive competencies of its own (Bettis et al., 1992). Organizations that outsource as a matter of course fail to solve critical problems themselves and thus forgo opportunities down the road based on that learning. From a strategic human resources perspective, the issue seems to be whether the organization has sufficient core people proficient in areas representing its current and long-term strategic interests.

Short-Term Insiders: Careerists and Jugglers

Many short-term insiders are employees who expect to make their career in an industry, not necessarily with a specific firm (careerists). Others are people for whom employment is not a central life interest, such as students or parents with young children (jugglers). Changing performance demands and labor force demographics have created a need for flexibility evident in short-term insider roles. Short-term insiders are organization members but are not highly assimilated into an organizational culture. Both long-term and short-term insiders are required to demonstrate some degree of behavioral conformity, usually because they work interdependently with others. But behavioral demands on short-term employees are usually far less than on the long-term insider potentially in line to manage the organization in the future. Nonetheless, short-term insiders do usually need to manifest certain behaviors to maintain their employment—for example, regular work hours, adherence to organizational rules and procedures. This degree of behavioral consistency stops short of the socialization and in-depth organizational knowledge that characterize long-term insiders. The difference here is that whereas short-term members must exhibit behavioral consistency for effective performance, they do not reflect the organization's distinctive present and future competencies as core workers do. Short-term insiders offer organizations some flexibility in the face of unpredictable environmental changes by requiring fewer investments and commitments.

Hall (1993; Hall and Mirvis, Chapter Nine this volume) argues that short-term insider roles serve several purposes for individual job holders, too. Firms with careerist workers offer jobs that provide training as a stepping stone to jobs elsewhere, promoting individual career growth without creating internal labor markets (for example, consulting). They also offer employment opportunities to people seeking low involvement roles to help integrate work and family responsibilities. These and other short-term arrangements described in later sections offer a host of career options for people who seek psychological success through achieving personal goals other than promotion or advancement.

Long-Term Outsiders: Pooled Workers

Call-ins, substitutes, and other periodic employees can work irregularly for an organization, though in many cases they do so over some period of time. Pooled workers are often long-term employees whose time commitments have changed because of such factors as educational opportunities or family demands. Hospitals coping with nursing shortages create pools of nurses who want reduced hours and flexibility. Schools employ the same substitute teachers again and again to replace ill and absent ones. Many pooled workers actually are part-time employees with erratic schedules. Substitute teachers and other pooled workers have existed for many years. Use of such workers is expanding, but they have been the subject of little behavioral research.

Short-Term Outsiders: Temporaries and Independent Contractors

Externalization is a human resource strategy to promote flexibility and lower costs. Many varieties of temporary or "peripheral workers" have developed to promote flexibility for organizations as well as lifestyle options for individuals. Temporary work is used to meet various needs (for example, hires for seasonal work or special projects). Jobs where temporaries are employed typically are lower on technical and information complexity. There are two classes of temporary workers: those hired as individuals and those hired through agencies. Individual temporary workers tend to be younger or much older, low in experience, and women (Davis-Blake & Uzzi, 1993). Agency-based temporary workers are typically used when union-management relations are poor (Davis-Blake & Uzzi, 1993) or when there is no union (as in the case of nurses).

Extensive reliance on temporaries has been identified as a potential problem for both organizations and for employees. From the employee perspective, extensive use of temporaries creates two classes of employees: secure workers with high-paying employment and temporaries with sporadic and low-paying jobs. Bettis and others (1992) suggested that use of short-term outsiders presents a long-term threat to the well-being of the workforce economically as well as socially. Problems can emerge if temporaries are demographically different from core workers, especially regarding minority group and socioeconomic status. However, from the core employee perspective, hiring temporaries increases the core worker's mobility, with fewer people available to fill more responsible, managerial, and professional roles. (Note that most studies of mobility and employment status are between-firm studies; we do not have within-firm analyses to help explain why this effect occurs.) Prolonged reward inequality can potentially lower productivity and increase conflict within organizations (Cowherd & Levine, 1992).

An interesting challenge to the conventional wisdom on use of temporaries is found in research on employee benefits. Conventional wisdom argues that organizations use temporaries to avoid paying benefits (which can be 25 percent or more of total labor costs). Little evidence exists regarding the tangible benefits to firms from offering fringe benefits, and Davis-Blake and Uzzi (1993) reported little concern over benefits in firms using temporaries. However, use of temporaries is positively related to unionization. Temporaries may thus be a way of gaining flexibility in allocation of labor rather than a benefit cost-reduction strategy per se. Firms with formal mechanisms for joint union-management problem solving are less inclined to employ temporaries (Harrison & Kelley, 1991).

Independent contractors are another form of short-term outsider. People providing paid services to an organization without employment status are independent contractors. In effect, they work for themselves. Typically, they have a career within a profession such as accounting or consulting. Use of contractors permits firms to offer a range of products without risking large fixed investment in labor. Firms do not exercise day-to-day control over independent contractors and thus may not use them for tasks critical to their core business (Davis-Blake & Uzzi, 1993). Bureaucratic firms, larger organizations, and those with multiple sites tend to use independent contractors. However, use of contractors in core activities can occur when they have experience with the firm, as is often the case with consulting arrangements that develop into long-term relationships.

Some Floating Employment Arrangements

Some employee relationships cut across categories. Although core workers are by virtue of their key role long-term insiders, other types of relationships such as networked and long-distance employees or telecommuters can occur in virtually any quadrant. The term *networked employees* refers to individuals whose work is performed outside the boundaries of their home organization (Snow, Miles, & Coleman, 1992). Engineers who work on assignment as part of a client team, end users who serve on their supplier's design team, and others participating in interorganizational strategic alliances all can be classified as networked. Whether this network is short- or long-term affects the development of new memberships, skills, and work norms. Networked employees will in fact need to be able to discriminate among various role relationships in identifying what behaviors are appropriate in a specific assignment. Interestingly, commitment research may help explicate the experiences of networked employees. Studies of dual commitment, usually involving organization and union affiliation, indicate a positive relationship between affective commitments in these two domains (Angle & Perry, 1986). The highest levels of *joint* commitment were found in those members whose union and organization were most cooperative. Participation further moderates this relationship, as the most active participants have the highest levels of dual commitment.

Telecommuting has been described as a form of externalized employment (Pfeffer & Baron, 1988). Although it clearly is externalization of workplace, it is not necessarily a new or distinct employment relationship. Veteran employees may work at home not as part of a changed work relationship, but in order to do their work more effectively. A more general label for phenomena such as telecommuting is "distributed work arrangement." A distributed work arrangement is a decentralized organizational structure through which the core organization distributes a portion of its functions to a remote site (Venkatesh & Vitalari, 1992). This distributed work setting could be another organization or firm (via an interorganizational system), or a nontraditional work setting (for example, home, satellite office, or mobile-office vehicle).

Major reasons for working at home appear to be reduced work interruptions (Venkatesh & Vitalari, 1992), portability of work, and lessened commute time. Presence of children is negatively related to doing supplemental work at home, though the number of children present has no effect, leading Venkatesh and Vitalari to conclude that the objective is not to permit people to be with their families, but rather to achieve work-related objectives not fully attainable within the formal work environment. The authors noted that work externalization is more frequently reported by those in managerial and professional occupations due to their greater autonomy, control over schedules, and transportable work tasks along with incentive rewards such as bonuses and promotions. (Income is, in fact, positively related to performing supplemental work at home.) Telecommuting raises questions regarding how to balance work and nonwork life and how to manage their boundary.

Missing Workers Revisited: The Case of Part-Timers

Some have estimated that a quarter of the U.S. workforce is part time (Belous, 1989), making this one of the most common types of employment relationships. One of the few treatments of this group in the organizational literature (Rotchford & Roberts, 1982) referred to part-time employees as "missing workers." We have not mapped part-time workers in our relationship map, but we are not overlooking them here. Rather, we argue that part-time workers actually represent many distinct employment relationships. Some are veteran employees scaling back their work day as they begin their transition toward retirement. Some are parents of young children reducing their hours temporarily. Other part-timers are short-term employees (such as teenagers who work the lunch counters of fast food restaurants).

People with limited time commitments to the organization can vary in terms of their degree of both employment duration and internalization. Some part-timers evolved from full-time status to accommodate lifestyle factors such as children, health, or aging, whereas others begin and remain only marginally integrated into the organization. Part-time instructors in universities, scheduled to teach the same classes year after year, can come to have "moral tenure" by virtue of their long-standing relationship. Elsewhere, part-timers have temporary employment with limited involvement and virtually no training or orientation. Our analysis suggests that to understand the work experiences of part-time employees we must pay closer attention to the nature of their *particular* employment relationships.

The particular terms of the employment contract vary by time frame and degree of assimilation into and investment by the employing organization. Increasingly, organizations may have a mix of employment arrangements depending on the strategic concerns of the organization and its individual divisions and subunits, environmental stability, and emphasis placed on organizational learning and culture to obtain competitive advantage. The movement toward diversity in employment arrangements raises issues about the effects that the presence of both core and peripheral workers in the same organization have on each other. Do these arrangements provide desirable career options? Do they create relative deprivation for peripherals? Do they enhance the career mobility of the (fewer) core workers? Organizational issues arise regarding the impact of marginally connected employees on the firm's stability and its ability to create a nonreplicable competitive advantage. What is clear is that the development of particular employment relations reflects the organization's strategic choice. Moreover, as strategy changes, so too may change the relationships organizations have with their workers.

Transitions

The major dimensions of change in employment relationships are shifts in time frame and shifts in inclusion. Some shifts from core to peripheral status may signal a break with both key elements of the employment relationship. Although there are many issues relevant to such transitions (for example, *individual* job loss, stress, experienced psychological success or failure; *organizational* turbulence, loss of expertise), we focus here on two aspects of transition that affect both the individual and the organization: psychological contract violation and development of new schemata for employment, career, and job. Psychological contracts address changes *specific* to a particular individual and organization's employment relationship, and schemata address *broader* societal changes in attachments resulting from visible and widespread labor force experiences.

Individuals may experience a variety of changes in employment relationships. Employment security found in relational agreements may turn into "no guarantees." Jobs with limited performance requirements (fair day's work for a fair day's pay) may now require substantial personal development and learning with employees pressured to provide superior service and continuous improvement. Following massive layoffs, the workers who survive may have to work harder (more intensely and for more hours) for the same (or less) compensation. A major psychological feature of this transition for many individuals is its impact on the psychological contract.

Contract violation occurs in the context of the individual's experience with a specific organization. On being hired, people form understandings regarding the conditions of their employment, and despite some clarification and shift over time, these understandings remain relatively stable through the course of employment. Workers may view introduction of new performance requirements or threats to job security as contract violations if the initial contract did not specify the possibility of change or limits to job tenure. Unless individuals see changes in contract terms as legitimate and necessary (for example, the organization cannot survive unless it alters its relations with employees), they will likely view changes as contract violation (Rousseau & Aquino, 1993). How the organization manages the transition (for example, reasons it uses to justify changes) and its efforts to create alternative ways of honoring the spirit if not the letter of the contract (for example, generous severance packages and outplacement) influence the employee's response to the transition. Violated contracts are associated with erosion of trust, anger, and at times litigation (Rousseau, 1989; Kaufmann & Stern, 1988). Effectively managing the transition requires attention to issues of procedural (Tyler & Bies, 1990) and interpersonal justice (Bies & Moag, 1987).

Because contract violation engenders adverse reactions on the part of victims, establishment of new contract terms may be difficult. Contracts are created on the basis of trust, and new demands and commitments coming on the heels of layoffs or other adverse consequences ("take aways" in bonuses, career opportunities, and so forth) may not be credible. How the transition is managed may have a great impact on the viability of any new contracts. Features of effectively managed transitions between contracts include the following:

- *Conveying the necessity of change.* Are reasons understood and viewed as legitimate?
- *Choice.* Since contracts are voluntary, do affected individuals have any voice or influence over outcomes (for example, choice between alternatives such as retraining, new jobs, and so forth)?
- *Reestablishment of trust.* Has the employer made new commitments it has kept (often requiring some time to elapse before new employment arrangements are established and relied on)?

While contract violation affects the individual's relationship with a particular employer, changes in the schemata people use to understand and interpret employment relations influence broader cultural and societal patterns. *Schemata* represent ways in which people think about and interpret their experiences. There are schemata for family roles (spouse, parent), for friendships, and for a variety of other personal and social experiences. The lexicon presented earlier suggests that schemata regarding employment roles and relations are being transformed by people's own direct experiences as well as those they witness. Whereas a career once may have meant to work with one organization for life, it now has come to have different meanings. These new interpretations are rooted in both individual personal experiences and broader societal and cultural trends.

A common culture-based schema is the notion that employment is a relationship. Individuals across many cultures seek stable employment relationships (Herriot, 1992). Long-term employees at Motorola speak of being "Galvinized," after the founding Galvin family. Workers in the People's Republic of China speak of stable employment as "the iron rice bowl." Long-standing employment with one organization is a traditional value supported by many dominant cultural values. Loyalty, steadfastness, and good faith efforts all are value-full if not value-laden concepts, even in individualistic Western cultures. In a survey of recent business school graduates, a large proportion of alumni reported seeking a long-term stable relationship with a prospective employer, contrary to the job-hopping careerist motives popularly associated with young M.B.A. holders (Rousseau, 1990).

Yet many scholars note how difficult it is for people to sustain such relationship focus or loyalty in the face of environmental changes, fierce competition, deregulation, and restructurings (Hirsch, 1987; Reilly, Brett, & Stroh, 1993). The culture-based schema of relational employment is threatened both by individual experiences and well-publicized consequences of layoffs, downsizings, and restructurings. Turbulence in modern organizations has undermined this loyalist tendency, and often the most loyal are the most affected. Brockner, Tyler, and Cooper-Schneider (1992) identified a phenomenon they labeled "the bigger they are the harder they fall": individuals who have sought stable relations and been disappointed in the treatment they received are often less willing to commit to such relationships in the future. Robinson and Rousseau (1994) observed that employees who had wanted a committed relationship with their employer but had been poorly treated were much less trusting and considerably angrier at the employer than those employees who had been poorly treated but had valued the relationship less.

Loyalty to one's personal career may be the flip side of the high-commitment relationship with an organization (see Hall & Mirvis, Chapter Nine this volume). As an executive has said, "The old cradle-to-the-grave psychological contract—'if I work hard, the company will take care of me'—is absolutely gone" (Fisher, 1988, p. 42). This broken psychological contract can give rise to loyalty toward one's own career in place of the organization, a phenomenon Hirsch (1987, 1994) describes as "free agency." A free agent is an employee who takes personal responsibility for his or her future employment. Anticipating no security in the current (or in a future) job, free agents plan their own careers and look toward jobs as stepping stones to other positions with this (or another) organization.

Changing societal values regarding employment has long-term implications for human resource practices and future research. Handy (1991) foresees organizations built on loyal core employees who develop deep organization-specific knowledge and company loyalty. This core is supported by a host of peripherals with diverse temporary, networked relations—not insiders and yet not outsiders. How people will come to understand and interpret their employment relations compared with the relations of others who have very different contracts remains to be seen. The phenomenal growth of contingent workers (temporaries and contractors) can potentially fragment the employment system, widening the differences between the wages, training, and work experiences of cores and peripherals. The experiences of workers must be understood not only from the perspective of the individuals involved but through social comparison processes as well. How people perceive employment relations generally, how willing they are to trust and learn organization-specific skills, and how they understand their own roles compared with the different roles of co-workers will affect the ability of organizations to implement these multicontract employment arrangements. The challenges of multicontract organizations raise issues for twenty-first-century organization researchers.

Conclusion

Although employment research, particularly staffing and selection studies, often has an employer focus (Herriott, 1992), the employment relationship is a two-way street. Organizations choose employees and individuals elect to enter specific organizations. Organizations offer and individuals negotiate incentives and perform in ways largely consistent with the resultant reward system. Informed choice on the part of potential workers plays an increasingly important role in our thinking about recruitment and selection (Wanous, 1980) and in career development and performance management (Rousseau, 1995).

Organizational research must address attachment issues from the perspective of both the employer and employee. Specifically, research on commitment and contracts needs to raise questions such as the following about new employment forms and their link to individual experiences and organizational practices:

1. Can we expand the concept of commitment beyond its meaning in core employment relations? What forms will commitment take for peripheral arrangements? What impact do network relations have on the nature and meaning of commitment?

2. How do organizational factors such as supportiveness, strategic choice, and human resource practices affect individual commitment?
3. Can affective commitment be high even when continuance commitment is low, undesirable, or unrealistic?
4. In networked and other multi-organizational relations, what forms will attachment take? How do contracts function when workers network with more than one employing organization?
5. Bottom line: How will research on attachment have to change to understand new forms of work experience and relationships?

We also offer some questions for future research addressing how human resource (HR) practices affect organizational performance:

1. Does the presence of large proportions of peripherals undermine the stability of the organization and affect its ability to develop and retain expertise and manage its labor costs? Are there ratios of core to peripheral workers that optimally affect organizational performance?
2. What impact do distinct types of employment arrangements have on the organization's culture, shared values, ability to give consistent service or implement quality programs, and so forth?
3. How does the presence of distinct employment arrangements affect issues of organizational justice and legal claims?
4. How should those organizations with several distinct employment relationships manage their HR practices to send clear messages to workers?

One thing is highly likely: Future organizations and future workers will take less for granted in their relationship. From their first contact at recruitment, each will spend more time crafting and articulating the terms of their relationship.

References

Angle, H. L., & Perry, J. L. (1986). Dual commitment and labor-management relationship climates. *Academy of Management Journal, 29,* 31–50.

Barksdale, K., & Shore, L. M. (1993). *A comparison of the Meyer and Allen and O'Reilly and Chatman models of organizational commitment.* Unpublished manuscript, Georgia State University, Atlanta.

Barnard, C. (1938). *Functions of the executive.* Cambridge, MA: Harvard University Press.

Becker, H. S. (1960). Notes on the concept of commitment. *American Journal of Sociology, 66,* 32–42.

Belous, R. (1989, March). How human resource systems adjust to the shift toward contingent workers. *Monthly Labor Review,* pp. 7–12.

Bettis, R. A., Bradley, S. P., & Hamel, G. (1992). Outsourcing and industrial decline. *Academy of Management Executive, 6,* 7–21.

Bies, R. J., & Moag, J. S. (1987). Procedural justice: Communication criteria of fairness. In M. Bazerman, R. Lewicki, & B. Sheppard (Eds.), *Research on negotiations in organizations* (Vol. 1). Greenwich, CT: JAI Press.

Bowen, D. E., & Schneider, B. (1988). Services marketing and management: Implications for organizational behavior. In L. L. Cummings & B. M. Staw (Eds.), *Research in organizational behavior* (Vol. 10). Greenwich, CT: JAI Press.

Brockner, J., Tyler, T. R., & Cooper-Schneider, R. (1992). The influence of prior commitment to an institution on reactions to perceived unfairness: The higher they are, the harder they fall. *Administrative Science Quarterly, 37,* 241–261.

Cowherd, D. M., & Levine, D. I. (1992). Product quality and pay equity between lower-level employees and top management: An investigation of distributive justice theory. *Administrative Science Quarterly, 37,* 241–261.

Crites, J. O. (1969). *Vocational psychology.* New York: McGraw-Hill.

Davis, S. (1987). *Future perfect.* Reading, MA: Addison-Wesley.

Davis-Blake, A., & Uzzi, B. (1993). Employment externalization: The case of temporary workers and independent contractors. *Administrative Science Quarterly, 38,* 195–223.

Dickson, D. (1974). *The politics of alternative technology.* New York: Universe.

Eisenberger, R., Huntington, R., Hutchison, S., & Sowa, D. (1986). Perceived organizational support. *Journal of Applied Psychology, 71,* 500–507.

Fisher, A. B. (1988, May 23). The downside of downsizing. *Fortune,* pp. 42–45.

Fukami, C. V., & Larson, E. W. (1984). Commitment to company and union: Parallel models. *Journal of Applied Psychology, 69,* 367–371.

Hall, T. (1993, March). The *"new career contract:"* Alternative career paths. Paper presented at the Fourth German Business Congress, Cologne.

Handy, C. (1991). *The age of unreason.* London: Business Books.

Harrison, B., & Kelley, M. (1991). *Outsourcing and the search for flexibility.* Working paper, Carnegie-Mellon University, Pittsburgh.

Herriot, P. (1992). *The career management challenge.* London: Sage.

Hirsch, P. M. (1987). *Pack your own parachute.* Reading, MA: Addison-Wesley.

Hirsch, P. M. (1994). Undoing the managerial revolution? Needed research on the decline of middle management and internal labor markets. In R. Swedberg (Ed.), *Economic sociology.* New York: Russell Sage Foundation.

Hirschhorn, L., & Gilmer, T. (1992, March–April). The new boundaries of the "boundaryless" company. *Harvard Business Review,* pp. 104–115.

Hrebiniak, L. G., & Alutto, J. A. (1972). Personal and role-related factors in the development of organizational commitment. *Administrative Science Quarterly, 17,* 555–573.

Kanter, R. M. (1977). *Men and women of the corporation.* New York: Basic Books.

Kanter, R. M. (1989). *When giants learn to dance.* New York: Simon & Schuster.

Kaufmann, P. J., & Stern, L. W. (1988). Relational exchange norms, perceptions of unfairness, and retained hostility in commercial litigation. *Journal of Conflict Resolution, 32,* 534–552.

McGee, G. W., & Ford, R. C . (1987). Two (or more?) dimensions of organizational commitment: Reexamination of the affective and continuance commitment scales. *Journal of Applied Psychology, 72,* 638–642.

Mathieu, J. E., & Zajac, D. M. (1990). A review and meta-analysis of the antecedents, correlates and consequences of organizational commitment. *Psychological Bulletin, 108,* 171–194.

Meyer, J. P., & Allen, N. J. (1984). Testing the "side-bet theory" of organizational commitment: Some methodological considerations. *Journal of Applied Psychology, 69,* 372–378.

Mowday, R. T., Porter, L. W., & Steers, R. M. (1982). *Employee organization linkages: Psychology of commitment, absenteeism, and turnover.* Orlando, FL: Academic Press.

Organ, D. W. (1990). A motivational basis of organizational citizenship. In L. L. Cummings & B. M. Staw (Eds.), *Research in organizational behavior* (Vol. 12). Greenwich, CT: JAI Press.

Orsburn, J., Moran, L., Musselwhite, E., & Zenger, J. H. (1991). *Self-directed work teams.* Homewood, IL: Business One.

Pfeffer, J., & Baron, J. (1988). Taking the workers back out: Recent trends in the structure of employment. In L. L. Cummings & B. M. Staw (Eds.), *Research in organizational behavior* (Vol. 10). Greenwich, CT: JAI Press.

Reilly, A., Brett, J. M., & Stroh, L. (1993). The impact of corporate turbulence on managers' attitudes. *Strategic Management Journal, 14,* 167–179.

Robinson, S. L., & Rousseau, D. M. (1994). Violating the psychological contract: Not the exception but the norm. *Journal of Organizational Behavior, 15,* 245–259.

Rotchford, N. L., & Roberts, K. H. (1982). Part-time workers as missing persons in organizational research. *Academy of Management Review, 2,* 228–234.

Rousseau, D. M. (1989). Psychological and implied contracts in organizations. *The Employee Rights and Responsibilities Journal, 2,* 121–139.

Rousseau, D. M. (1990). New hire perceptions of their own and their employer's obligations: A study of psychological contracts. *Journal of Organizational Behavior, 11,* 389–400.

Rousseau, D. M. (1995). *Promises in action: Psychological contracts in organizations.* Newbury Park, CA: Sage.

Rousseau, D. M., & Aquino, K. (1993). Fairness and implied contract obligations in job termination: The role of remedies, social accounts, and procedural justice. *Human Performance, 6,* 135–149.

Rousseau, D. M., & Parks, J. M. (1993). The contracts of individuals and organizations. In L. L. Cummings & B. M. Staw (Eds.), *Research in organizational behavior* (Vol. 15). Greenwich, CT: JAI Press.

Rousseau, D. M., & Wade-Benzoni, K. (1994). Linking strategy and human resource practices: How employee and customer contracts are created. *Human Resource Management, 33,* 463–489.

Shore, L. M., & Wayne, S. J. (1993). Commitment and employee behavior: A comparison of affective commitment and continuance commitment with perceived organizational support. *Journal of Applied Psychology, 78,* 774–780.

Snow, C. C., Miles, R. E., & Coleman, H. J. (1992, Winter). Managing 21st century network organizations. *Organizational Dynamics,* pp. 5–20.

Thompson, J. D. (1967). *Organizations in action.* New York: McGraw-Hill.

Tyler, T. R., & Bies, R. J. (1990). Interpersonal aspects of procedural justice. In J. S. Carroll (Ed.), *Applied social psychology and organizational settings.* Hillsdale, NJ: Erlbaum.

Venkatesh, A., & Vitalari, N. P. (1992). An emerging distributed work arrangement: An investigation of computer-based supplemental work at home. *Management Science, 38,* 1687–1706.

Wanous, J. (1980). *Organizational entry: Recruitment, selection, and socialization of newcomers.* Reading, MA: Addison-Wesley.

Whyte, W. F. (1956). *Organization man.* New York: Simon & Schuster.

Zuboff, S. (1988). *In the age of the smart machine: The future of work and power.* New York: Basic Books.

Chapter Nine

Careers as Lifelong Learning

Douglas T. Hall, Philip H. Mirvis

The career is dead! Long live the career!

These statements represent the paradoxical state of careers in today's chaotic environment. With the decline and/or transformation of firms that have been the ultimate blue-chip providers of security to employees and pensioners—such as IBM, DEC, GM, even Lloyd's of London—the notion of a career as a series of upward moves based in a long-term employment relationship suddenly seems passé (Hall & Associates, in press).

However, if we think of a career more in terms of the development of a person's skills, capacities to learn, and self-identity—personal qualities that grow best under conditions of challenge—then today's turbulent environment provides far greater career development opportunities than one ever would have imagined in the heyday of the big blue-chip firms.

Following this line of reasoning, what we are witnessing is the shortening of the career cycle. As pointed out by Henry Morgan, Dean Emeritus of Boston University's School of Management, a career spanned several generations in the Middle Ages as crafts and occupations were passed down from father to son. With the rise of industrialization and creation of the modern corporation in the early to mid-twentieth century, a career spanned a lifetime as a person spent his or her (usually his) full career in one organization, doing one type of work. Now, with the rapid changes of the post-industrial information era, a person may have three or four careers in the span of his or her work life. This new scenario

raises a vital question: How can people learn to make the necessary and continual changes in their skills, self-picture, and employment to keep their careers alive?

In this chapter we explore the changing contours of contemporary careers. We begin by looking at the demise of the traditional career and psychological contract between people and their
organizations. Then we turn to how companies are adapting to
their turbulent environments and what this means for successful
career development. At the heart of this is a new strategy of career
development—continuous learning—embedded in a new way of
looking at and managing one's work over the life cycle, what Hall
calls the protean career (Hall & Associates, 1986). On the practical side, we examine career development priorities in this new
world of work and what organizations can do to help promote lifelong learning. This chapter closes with a look at emerging issues
in career development and the implications for how we conceptualize and study careers over the life course.

What Has Happened to Careers?

Constant corporate restructuring and downsizing, the outsourcing
of American jobs to foreign countries, heightened job demands,
and reductions in health and pension benefits have all taken their
toll on work careers in the past decade and a half. Start with job
loss: during the 1980s, 3.4 million jobs were eliminated from Fortune 500 companies, with many more positions erased in medium
and small farms. One recent study of over 400 employers found
that more than 80 percent downsized from 1986 to 1991, reducing
their workforce an average of 12.4 percent (Mirvis, 1993).

Economic recession, global competition, and U.S. deindustrial-
ization have had employers trimming staff, reducing hiring, shutting
down facilities, and making more use of consultants and the contingent workforce. The consequences ripple through the workforce:
U.S. workers are putting in more hours and earning less take-home
pay than a decade ago (Schor, 1991). To maintain their standard of
living, American families have had to borrow more and increasingly
depend, where feasible, on the earnings of two incomes.

The career horizons of those who continue to work in corporations have also deteriorated. Job insecurity is more pronounced

and notions of cradle-to-grave employment have been shattered (Mirvis, 1992). Pressures to perform have mounted as companies strive to be globally competitive and get more for less from their downsized workforce. Meanwhile, most American companies have cut back on their health benefits and many have reduced pensions and retirement health care coverage—all of which limits job mobility and makes retirement a less viable career option.

The rise of cynicism in the less stable and secure, and more fractious and competitive workplace has been amply documented in national surveys of the U.S. workforce (Kanter & Mirvis, 1989). Over half the American public believe that the leaders of big business are more interested in their own power and status than the needs of their company or their workforce. But nearly as many mistrust their own company executives and doubt the truth of what they are told by their own managers (Mirvis & Kanter, 1992). All of this has had a bearing on the loss of corporate loyalty among the workforce, the rise of "free agency" among job hoppers and career climbers, and pessimism about the future that permeates the nation's workforce ("Downward Mobility," 1992; Hirsch, 1987; Kanter & Mirvis, 1991).

What we today call the traditional employment arrangement, and its underlying psychological contract, were forged in the post–World War II era and maintained by people who grew up in or heard firsthand stories of the Great Depression and the Good War. Many entered the workforce in the 1950s, 1960s, and 1970s with the idea of a lifetime career with one employer. Experience mattered and maturity seemed to be valued in companies in the "good old days." Today, by comparison, these mature workers feel devalued at work and face an uncertain future on the job and in their lives.

In turn, new entrants to the workforce have, until recently, had expectations of onward and upward in their careers. While this reached its heights in the 1980s with young, upwardly mobile professionals (yuppies), expectations are falling fast in the 1990s for downwardly mobile professionals (dumpies). It seems doubtful that in the decade ahead corporations will offer as many employees as in the past the kinds of pay increases and long-term career opportunities they need to purchase homes, provide for their children's education, or satisfy their full range of consumer aspirations.

In sum, the traditional contract has been turned upside down in recent years. Consider this message (found posted on the bulletin board of a plant experiencing widespread layoffs) about what companies promise their workers today:

We can't promise you how long we'll be in business.

We can't promise you that we won't be bought by another company.

We can't promise that there'll be room for promotion.

We can't promise that your job will exist until you reach retirement age.

We can't promise that the money will be available for your pension.

We can't expect your undying loyalty and we aren't sure we want it.

Future Trends: Will Career Prospects Brighten?

The Bureau of Labor Statistics projects that the U.S. labor force will grow slowly in the 1990s. The big-growth decades of the 1970s (19 percent increase in the workforce) and 1980s (29 percent increase) saw baby boomers making their way into corporations. With the appearance of the "baby bust" generation, the workforce will grow only by 13 percent in the 1990s, even accounting for immigration. This has led to the prediction that industries will face labor shortages in entry-level workers in the 1990s and thereafter (Johnston & Packer, 1987).

Although labor shortages are evident in selected small businesses and services where "help wanted" notices abound, predictions of widespread shortages have proved inaccurate. On the contrary, the nation has experienced "job drought" (O'Reilly, 1992). A combination of extensive downsizing coupled with slowdowns in hiring has forestalled labor shortage problems for most companies. As a result, those counting on labor shortages to improve the near-term career prospects of today's workers and managers have been sadly disappointed. Furthermore, American workers' longer-term career prospects seem chancy. Nearly three-fourths of the firms in the study of 400 expect to downsize further in the 1990s and over half agree that periodic downsizing is essential to remaining competitive in the marketplace (Mirvis, 1993). In addition, many firms plan to open plants and offices overseas and expect an increasing share of their total workforce to be made up of non-U.S. employees.

There is, nonetheless, an emerging "skills gap" in the U.S. with many firms expecting trouble in finding enough high-skill professionals and blue-collar workers to meet projected demand (Mirvis, 1993). Already, new job designs and employee involvement efforts require an "upskilling" of the workforce that at least some firms have responded to with vigorous training and retraining programs. Looking ahead, as America continues its transformation from "brawn" to "brain" industries, studies project that the bulk of jobs created will require more education of jobholders than current ones and higher levels of language, math, and reasoning skills (see Johnston & Packer, 1987). Meanwhile, the educational preparation of high school and college graduates is declining and nearly half the population cannot read well enough or do the math necessary to meet these job demands.

Countless government commissions, industry councils, and research studies conclude that American workers urgently need to upgrade their knowledge and skills to be competitive with the global workforce. They call on corporations to become learning centers and to partner with school systems, universities, and nonprofit organizations to create an infrastructure wherein young, midcareer, and older workers can undergo lifelong learning. In this future scenario, to "earn a living" one must also "learn a living." Now, what does this mean for future careers? How will careers develop over the life course? No one knows for certain, but lines of theory and innovation are converging to the point that we can see some contours of careers unfolding in terms of lifelong learning.

New Environmental Conditions

Like the corporate giants in which they thrived, traditional career paths have become dinosaurs. Environmental changes are the cause of their demise. In the dinosaurs' case, a comet hit the earth and climatic upheaval proved deadly to a physiology that had adapted dinosaurs to one kind of earth but constrained their adaptability in another. In the case of traditional careers, the force of destruction comes from complex, rapid, and powerful global developments that have upset the prevailing industrial order and chilled employment relations. And, when it comes to physiology, we are discovering that the one-life, one-company career is too rigid and unwieldy to survive in today's world.

However, there is hope in the dinosaur metaphor. Scientists are learning, for instance, of extraordinary diversity that enhanced the adaptability of dinosaur species of ages ago and allowed for successive generations to reign as planetary conditions changed. It should not surprise us, then, that National Public Television serves up "Barney and friends" to provide lessons on getting along with others and coping with the complexities of life. Or that the popular book and movie *Jurassic Park* is a cautionary tale about resurrecting old life forms in a new environment. One message in this metaphor is that it is unlikely we can resurrect the traditional career; the other is that the career concept can possibly evolve and adapt to new environmental conditions. Indeed, there are likely as many dinosaurs on earth now as there were at the height of the creatures' prehistoric dominance: they are just smaller and fly through the air! Can careers go through such a dramatic metamorphosis?

Requirements for Adaptability

Some thirty years ago, specialists in organization theory found a mismatch between changes in the environment and the design of formal organizations (see Emery & Trist, 1965; Lawrence & Lorsch, 1967; Bennis & Slater, 1968). Their research confirmed that tightly structured, autocratic organizational forms were indeed effective in relatively simple, stable environments. However, when tasks become complex and the environment changes rapidly, a centralized structure cannot process enough information, close to the source, to figure out what is going on, and standard operating procedures limit the organization's capability to respond with innovation. In order to adapt quickly and effectively to turbulence, they reasoned, companies need more decentralized, flexible work arrangements where those closest to the action are more involved in intelligence gathering, analysis, and decision making. Their logic was purely Darwinian: the fittest are free, flexible, and fast.

Since that time, advances in systems theory and research have led to more sophisticated ideas about how organizations naturally adapt to turbulence in their environments (see Weick, 1977b; Cohen & March, 1986; Wheatley, 1993). First, there is the principle of requisite variety. As articulated originally by Ashby (1960), this means that a system must be as varied and complex as the environment it is trying to manage. One way that organizations accomplish this today is by differentiating their structure so that departments and business units can scan and respond to varied environmental conditions and, as the saying goes, be closer to their customers. Variety is further enhanced by employing people with different outlooks and expertise, giving an organization different pictures of its complex environment with different interpretations of how best to respond to changes. This is a prime argument in favor of increasing the diversity (by race, gender, nationality, and age) of a firm's workforce.

A second means of adapting to turbulence depends on enriching the response capability of organizations. This comes from what Emery (1969) called redundancy in function coupled with minimum critical specification of job duties and functional responsibilities. Here the organization bundles large sets of information processing and decision-making tasks into more or less self-contained work units where skilled operators have the capability and freedom to handle the demands of their task environment. In the old model of the hierarchical bureaucracy, workers worked, managers managed, and a cadre of top officials and staff specialists was assigned responsibility for scanning the environment and devising responses. However, the complexity of the environment today is so great that these multiple functions need to be brought into what some call a business-within-a-business. A common example is the semiautonomous work group that takes on a large range of planning and problem-solving duties typically assumed by management and corporate staff. Multidisciplinary project teams, joint ventures, and strategic alliances also exemplify enriched functions. The ultimate extension is in Davis and Davidson's (1991) formula where "every employee equals a business."

Building on these principles, design theorists (for example, Emery & Trist, 1973; Weick, 1977a) see a need for organizations to become self-designing systems that continuously invent responses to complexity and change. The keys to self-design are to (1) value impermanence, (2) remove information filters and promote new ways of seeing the environment, (3) encourage higher-order self-reflection and analysis, (4) facilitate member learning, and (5) focus commitment on the process of self-design. Expressed otherwise, these characteristics are embodied in models of organizational learning (Michael, 1973; Argyris & Schön, 1974; Senge, 1990).

Applying these requirements to careers, we contend that adaptability comes from adding variety and enrichment to career development, promoting career self-design, and enhancing the "learn-how" of working people. Variety and enrichment can be enhanced by diversifying the experiences of working people and emphasizing multiskilling (O'Toole, 1977). Capacities to self-design and develop career options, in turn, rest partly with the person and partly with an organization that also has responsibility for devising adaptive career development practices (Weick & Berlinger, 1989). And ongoing learning depends on the abilities of people and organizations to continuously reinvent career options in the face of environmental change and corporate upheavals (Hall, 1991). In short, the new career is about experience, skill, flexibility, and personal development. It does not involve predefined career paths, routine ticket punching, stability, or security.

The Adaptive Organization

Models of the free, flexible, and fast organization date from the 1960s when, for example, Bennis and Slater (1968) argued that "democracy is inevitable" and advised organizations to devise "temporary" structures to respond to rapid change in their environments. The 1970s witnessed "collateral" forms of organization where temporariness would be built into project groups; "parallel" structures where semipermanent committees of, say, workers and managers would oversee change efforts; and the "matrix" organization, which institutionalized cross-functional linkages to accomplish complex tasks (Zand, 1974; Galbraith, 1977; Davis & Lawrence, 1977). By the 1980s, change had sped up to the point that organizations began an era of continuous restructuring exemplified by new work designs, continuous improvement programs, and mergers, acquisitions, divestitures, and cross-company ventures in service of reinventing the corporation (see Lawler, Mohrman, & Ledford, 1992; Mirvis & Marks, 1992, for reviews).

In the 1990s, all of this is played out in the "boundaryless organization" (see Davis, Chapter Three this volume) that is continually self-designed around new markets, tasks, and situations. Handy (1992) has used the term "federal organization" to describe one such adaptive model emphasizing properties of decentralization, local empowerment, and self-reflection: "Federalism implies a variety of individual groups allied together under a common flag with some shared identity" (p. 117). The rationale here is that as organizations become more decentralized and functions gain local autonomy, their ultimate resource is people who have the skills, know-how, and discretion to manage the demands of novel work situations. Thus more and more, employees are coming to be viewed as semiautonomous, self-managing professionals whose security is not in corporate career paths but in their core competencies.

In his book, *The Age of Unreason*, Handy (1989) describes the configuration of human resources in the emerging organization as being like a shamrock, with three components. The first leaf of the shamrock, and the most important for continuity and organizational survival, is the core staff, a group increasingly made up of managers, technicians, and professionals. These are highly skilled individuals who have a major commitment to the organization and derive a lot of their sense of identity from it. The second leaf is contractors, specialized people and firms, often outside the organization, who serve a variety of needs, chiefly supply, distribution, and routine control functions. Their work is not part of the essential core technology and competence of the organization and can usually be done better by someone else in a smaller, more specialized, and autonomous position. The third leaf is the contingent labor force. These are part-timers and temporary workers who staff temporary structures and provide a "buffer" to the core workforce of a firm. This is the fastest growing component of the labor force and provides companies with a very efficient way to move quickly and flexibly to meet changing needs.

The federalist organization, with its three leaves of staff, provides a model of corporate adaptability. It aims to ensure that an organization is continually infused with a better picture of its environment and better able to respond to opportunities and threats—without a lot of overhead and bureaucracy. This means, of course, that restructuring will be an ongoing process in corporations in the future and that working people of all ages will face more job movement in, out, and around the boundaries of a corporation. One significant consequence is that people may in effect "age" over several employment cycles in their career and have to periodically acquire new skills and/or industry knowledge to renew their employability and value. This promises to change dramatically our definitions of upward mobility and will require new kinds of career management systems and strategies. Already, there are templates of this new organizational form. In turn, there are also new ideas on careers and career self-management to increase the adaptability of the workforce.

The Protean Career

What will constitute a career in this more flexible mode of organization? We would argue that the primary implication for employees is that careers have to become more protean (Hall, 1976; Hall & Associates, in press). The term *protean* is taken from the name of the Greek god Proteus, who could change shape at will—from fire to a wild boar to a tree, and so forth. This new form of career can be defined as follows: "The protean career is a process which the person, not the organization, is managing. It consists of all the person's varied experiences in education, training, work in several organizations, changes in occupational field, and so forth. The protean career is *not* what happens to the person in any one organization. . . . In short, the protean career is shaped more by the individual than by the organization and may be redirected from time to time to meet the needs of the person" (Hall, 1976, p. 201).

To be protean means to be proactive about career management. Consider some of the implications for working people in the future:

1.   *A new definition is needed for career progress and success.* Seymour Sarason (1977) makes the point that many people who came into the workforce in the 1950s had a "one-life, one-career" outlook. Those who have entered the workforce in the past thirty years have, to some extent, recognized the necessity of more frequent job changes. Most, however, are still imbued with the idea that a

career is marked by constant progress and that occupational success is defined by mastering a job and then savoring the recognition and perquisites that follow from seniority.

We contend that more and more careers in the future will be cyclical—involving periodic cycles of skill apprenticeship, mastery, and reskilling. In addition, we expect that lateral, rather than upward, movement will constitute career development and that late careers will increasingly be defined in terms of phased retirement. The problem is that this model of career progress is new and not yet accepted as the norm by many workers and managers. Indeed, it seems the antithesis of the onward-and-upward ideal that fires the American success ethic. What is more, it does not fit the more conservative but realistic notion that, through hard work and diligence, one can "make it" in a chosen field of endeavor.

Naturally, as the careers of more and more people unfold in peaks and valleys, and cross-functional moves gain currency as essential to multiskilling and continued employability, career progress of this sort will come to be acceptable and surely respectable to the American workforce. During this period of transition, however, working people must adjust their expectations about career progress and savor the intrinsic rewards and psychological success that come from challenging new assignments.

2.   *Development means "learning a living."* It seems inescapable that workers will have to change jobs, companies, and even careers over their life course in the decades ahead. With frequent job rotation, developmental assignments, lateral career moves, and the option of going from the first leaf of the adaptable company to the second and third leaves, the "new career" in corporations promises to tax even the most adaptable worker. Workers who cannot adapt to this kind of change will likely find themselves downwardly mobile at an earlier-than-expected age in their companies or simply ushered out.

This shift puts a premium on people's developing the "learn-how" to adapt to new situations. Tomorrow's versions of "color your own parachute" will emphasize the importance of varied experience on one's resume and advise jobholders to volunteer to serve on a committee or task force or project team. This self-responsibility also means continually networking across organizational boundaries and taking advantage of formal development and education programs that are offered.

It seems as though many older Americans are recognizing the importance of upgrading their skills. A recent survey found that 4.6 million workers age fifty-five to sixty-four would take classes to improve their employment opportunities and skills (Louis Harris & Associates, 1991). Continuous skill development is also essential to middle-age and younger people whom we have argued will age over several career cycles.

3. *Career development is personal development.* Most corporate development programs promote short-term task-related learning—the acquisition of performance skills—most commonly through classroom training. Such programs also usually have a socialization or attitude component, such as building corporate identification or a sense of teamwork. What is missing in these training programs, however, are long-term learning objectives: adaptability on the task side and a deeper sense of identity on the personal side.

Adaptability entails learning how to be open to change and how to cope with it by mastering new skills and managing new work relationships. Identity means gaining self-awareness and skills in self-management. The most familiar ways of promoting identity learning currently involve self-assessment and 360-degree feedback from, say, peers, subordinates, and superiors. Other, more esoteric methods, involving outward-bound-type training, journaling and creative writing, and personal growth workshops are also in vogue.

Hall refers to adaptability and identity as meta-skills because both equip the person to learn how to learn (Hall & Associates, 1986). These meta-skills are the essential career competencies of the future. Their recognition leads us to a nonobvious point: we would argue that it is fruitless to try to predict exactly which kinds of skills will be required in a given organization in the future. What is more practical is to help workers develop these two meta-skills so that they are equipped and empowered to learn job-specific skills for themselves as the need becomes apparent.

4. *The individual "owns" his or her career.* In the past, companies often paid lip service to the idea that the career was the employee's responsibility. Sometimes this was an excuse for the fact that the company was doing little or nothing to provide career assistance

for lower-level employees who were left to fend for themselves. Other times it was used as an escape clause in case managerial and professional employees were not promoted through the firm's succession planning process.

Career ownership takes on new meaning in the future, even for managers and professionals, because organizations will not be able to meaningfully plan a person's career. There is simply too much uncertainty about future organizational needs to chart out prospective career paths and steer people through precise developmental sequences. What is more, there is ample evidence that many working people today recognize that promises of future promotions are illusory. They would rather "pack their own parachute" than move through their corporation's definition of career development (Hirsch, 1987). All of this means that the individual is truly on his or her own in developing a career. What, therefore, can the organization do to promote adaptive career growth?

Flexible Career Development Practices

What exactly would it look like if a firm were more flexible in managing careers as it goes about continually restructuring itself? To begin, we have to consider seriously the idea that an organization should not be in the business of career planning—at least as this activity has been conventionally defined. Based on the adaptive requirements we have discussed, it is instead incumbent on firms to ensure that employees are exposed to a variety of challenging work assignments, develop both short-term performance-related skills and the meta-skills needed for long-term adaptability, and have the freedom and support to self-design their careers in line with the contours of a changing organization (Hall & Associates, in press).

In this light, it would be useful to think of a business as a portfolio of skills that can be applied to the demands of varied situations. This, of course, puts a premium on having adaptable and multiskilled people available to deploy on a moment's notice. Furthermore, it means developing relationships between units in an organization and with customers, suppliers, distributors, and so on, allowing human resources to move freely and fluidly across boundaries for the sake of immediate task accomplishment and the longer-term development of people. Finally, it means empowering employees with the responsibility to seek work opportunities and to acquire new skills as the occasion demands. Here are some of the other implications:

1. *Selection and placement are crucial to development.* The competencies required to manage and staff the adaptable company will differ from those needed in steady-as-she-goes companies. Many firms, for instance, hire people primarily for today's jobs and put a premium on their having today's skills. That approach can work in the case of contingent workers or where expertise is brought in from vendors on a temporary basis. To staff the core of the company, and to build a multiskilled workforce, however, requires that firms select and develop people who have an appetite for continuous learning and the capacity to cope with the ambiguity and challenge of shifting job assignments. To this point, companies usually hire a few designated "high potential" employees with this outlook and groom them through carefully selected job assignments. In adaptable corporations, many more workers of this type—at all levels—will be needed. And they will need the same sort of enriching on-the-job development.

Indeed, our feeling is that the best form of development is creative staffing, providing jobs that challenge and stretch workers over their life course. A large body of research has shown that the best source of development is the job itself (Hall & Associates, 1986). Rather than spend so much time worrying about what kinds of training and retraining programs are needed to keep people's skills current, we think it advisable to focus instead on providing information and support to help people get into jobs that will stretch them, and then those jobs will provide intrinsic opportunities for self-training and self-learning.

2. *Lifelong learning depends on mobility.* There are very few firms now that have pure promotion-from-within policies, but there are still many where the default option is to first look inside. This preference has been heightened in many firms that downsize through attrition and staff redeployment. And it is reinforced by corporate succession planning systems and electronic resume services. However, the adaptable corporation may have more options to con-

sider. For instance, its "internal" labor market would consist not only of core staff but also of persons on the second and third leaves who have knowledge of the corporation and close ties to existing units or projects.

The old model of career development was built on the expectation that employees would, at best, "plateau" in their contributions to an organization or else pass their peak and make lesser contributions through to their retirement. In the adaptable corporation, however, we expect workers to periodically plateau or pass their prime over their career age, rather than their chronological age. Research on plateauing indicates that a worker has become "mature" when she or he has become established in a line of work and chances of upward mobility slow or stop. Interestingly, in fields with drastically shorter product and technology cycle times, this process of becoming established happens when workers are in their twenties or thirties (Hall, 1985). Looking ahead, we project that just as the product life cycle is shortening in many industries, so too will the career cycle of many more employees. The implication is that we need to find new ways of maintaining career adaptability not only for chronologically older workers but also for the much larger group of employees at an advanced "career age."

One way to promote lifelong learning is to keep people moving through a number of career cycles of exploration-establishment-maintenance-disengagement, rather than trying to prolong the maintenance stage of their career. Companies can do this by encouraging exploration of new areas of work, even while a person is thriving in the present one; and they can legitimize the process of planning for disengaging and moving on, even while one is still performing well in one's current work. Indeed, we can foresee a time when employees might move in and out of their organizations by perhaps working in core areas for a time, taking a job in a supplier company or consulting firm, working as an individual contractor on selected projects, and then returning to the fold as a senior core contributor.

3. *Job assignments provide "real-time" learning.* The "silver lining" in the difficulties of promoting lifelong learning for workers is the critical finding emerging from years of research on career learning:

the best development occurs on the job (Hall & Associates, 1986; McCall, Lombardo, & Morrison, 1988). Therefore, a critical task is to promote "real-time" learning through participation in projects emphasizing adaptive skills. For example, action-learning programs at 3M, Motorola, and General Electric have utilized a variety of formats to incorporate personal development into work projects. Eli Lilly has for years utilized real work projects, often related to a total quality or continuous improvement process; these are chosen by the individual for the purpose of learning new skills. However, they are done in addition to the person's regular work assignments, and the person enlists the aid of other people (coaches) whom she or he can ask for help as needed.

In most of these applications, workers-cum-trainees operate in project teams, which builds their skills in managing complex relationships. So-called 360-degree feedback (because it comes from multiple sources and directions), teamwork and leadership skill training, and change management concepts are usually included as part of the learning program. In addition to such specialized assignments, real-time learning is also enhanced in companies that feature team-based work and encourage employees to help each other learn the new skills. While some of this learning has to come from formal training (delivered "just in time"), much of it depends on peer-assisted self-directed learning.

4. *Mentoring, coaching, and relationships are integral to learning.* Mentoring and other relationship-based forms of learning play a critical role in career development and are becoming more widely used in a variety of real-time learning situations. At ARCO, for example, personal consultants provide very focused skill-building coaching to older managers in very short (two-hour) sessions. In addition, mentoring is especially useful as a form of development under conditions of organizational stress—the environments of most firms today (Kram & Hall, 1991).

The problem with mentoring is that it cannot be forced: you can't assign someone to be someone else's mentor. The trick is to create conditions that encourage and reward the natural development of mentoring relationships. And, to be most effective, the mentoring relationship should be tied to specific job-learning needs and to the strategic direction of the firm (Kram, 1988). But, if managed well, mentoring is an ideal learning form in today's under-resourced organization: it promotes learning for both parties, it develops support and community through good relationships, and—best of all—it's free!

5. *People need information and support to self-manage their careers.* Although an organization cannot do much directly to develop a person's career, it can do a great deal to provide empowering resources for career development. The two most important resources are information about opportunities throughout the organization and support in taking developmental action. With advanced information technology, it is possible for employees to learn about the strategic direction of the business, work opportunities in different areas, specific position openings, and upcoming training and development programs. Electronic resume systems make it possible for a person to be considered for a position even without the person's knowing about it. There is also a vast array of career software (CareerSearch, SIGI, Discover, and so forth) that can help individuals to engage in self-assessment and to obtain information about career opportunities outside their own organizations.

Add to this a network of educational institutions, professional associations, community organizations, and the like and a firm can promote career development simply by encouraging employees to take advantage of the full range of career-enhancing resources available inside and outside the organization. In this way, companies shift from being a direct provider of career services to being a career resource and referral agent.

6. *Career moves should be valued.* Furthermore, we would argue that turnover needs to be viewed as a positive, not a negative, in the adaptive corporation. Of course, there is always a risk that companies, having continuously enriched the skills and experiences of their employees, will lose them before these investments have been recouped. In this sense, firms that do not invest in their people, but perhaps pay top dollar for talent, would seem to be "free riders." Our feeling is that, on the contrary, firms with developmental cultures are more apt to retain talented people and certainly be attractive to eager-to-learn people of all ages who have reached a plateau in firms that do not emphasize development.

Another consideration concerns the appropriate skill mix within work units in a company. To this point, many firms strive to have peak performers in place in all their work units. We contend that the adaptable corporation will have to have a culture that values being a learner as much as being a peak performer. Indeed, key criteria in selection decisions should be a person's ability to learn and move rapidly and easily from job to job.

These changes raise a complication in organizations that offer skill-based pay and performance-based compensation. If, for example, too much stress is given to skill mastery within a specific job, this could create a disincentive for moving to a new job where the person would be starting over as a learner. This problem might be addressed through the payment of a "learning bonus" and a premium for the new skills that are mastered. In addition, companies that primarily compensate current performance will have to find ways to reward developmental work. The point is to put less stress on skill mastery and current performance (as ends in themselves) and more emphasis on learning and developing in new areas.

7. *Older workers need not be "deadwood."* Certainly periodic downsizing will mark the adaptable corporation. Rather than just emphasizing cost-cutting in these efforts, adaptive companies will also put considerable time and money into retraining and redeploying their workers over their working life course. At present, companies faced with the choice between retiring older workers early or retraining and redeploying them generally favor the seemingly more cost-effective option of getting rid of them. The rationalization is that because older workers have fewer remaining years of employment, the benefits of further investment may not be recouped before they retire (Barth, McNaught, & Rizzi, 1993).

This economic logic is turned on its head in the adaptable company. For instance, what we call retraining and redeployment today would be a more or less continuous process in companies, proactively planned for and thoughtfully designed, rather than a reactive, one-shot undertaking. Indeed, we expect that as employees age through several career cycles, companies will apply cost-benefit criteria to their continued employment and development. Ironically, older workers, having benefited from continuous development, may prove to be more expensive to replace than early career employees.

In addition, adaptable companies may have more options about where to redeploy aging workers. Given that corporations will have closer relationships with supplier plants, distributors, and other firms on their second leaf, it is possible that movement of older workers to these organizations could become part of a phased retirement career plan. Indeed, it is not hard to imagine companies using these firms much like the "farm system" in professional baseball: drawing in young people after they have gained some seasoning and sending back older workers who might well serve as mentors and coaches in addition to performing day-to-day chores.

Challenges for Adaptive Career Development

There are bound to be difficulties in transforming the concepts and practices of career development to match new environmental conditions. For example, with corporate staffs becoming smaller and business decisions and power being delegated to fairly autonomous business units, it is becoming more difficult to make staffing decisions for key jobs based on corporatewide development needs. We are seeing more tugs and pulls between the requirements for immediate staffing of the business units and the necessity for the corporation as a whole to plan for its future human resource needs.

Our prediction, however, is that this will not be as serious a problem as it now appears. We expect that corporate human resource development planners will focus their attention on a small group of core contributors and, at the same time, provide resources and broker opportunities for large pools of employees of all ages in the business units to upgrade their skills. There will also be more human resource development planning at the business unit level, as staff resources gravitate to where key business decisions are made. The function of the corporate planners, accordingly, will be to interconnect business unit and corporate staff development plans.

There are, nonetheless, some corporatewide issues that will need careful consideration:

1. *Can companies provide careers in the face of continuing cutbacks?* Plainly there is a need for a new kind of compact between employers and employees in this downsizing era. There are leading companies, of course, that have avoided layoffs by investing in productivity, curbing new hires, reducing pay rates or increases, and instituting job

sharing. And some who have gone through major downsizing now strive to run lean and have created a multiskilled workforce so that more people can be redeployed rather than outplaced. Yet it seems that large-scale dislocation is inevitable through the 1990s and maybe thereafter. Accordingly, some firms are revising their corporate philosophies to take account of "new realities." Digital Equipment and Hewlett-Packard—once committed to full employment—now emphasize that they offer top-notch training and a good work environment and promise only that they will be honest with people about business conditions and assist them with outplacement in the event of layoffs or early retirement. This, at least, clearly redefines the corporate culture and gives employees a realistic picture of what they can expect from their employers. Good intentions aside, these firms cannot expect, nor do we think they will get, the kind of loyalty that they once had from employees.

Absent guarantees of lifetime job security, there are nevertheless other measures companies can take to create a corporate culture that is attractive to lifelong learners. In the past, for instance, "regular" employees have been defined as organization members, bound by job descriptions and rules, and obliged to render specific services in return for payment. Distinctions have usually been made between, say, managers and nonmanagers, exempt and nonexempt workers, and part- and full-time staff.

The adaptive organization may abandon some of these traditional distinctions. For instance, some employees might be treated like "partners," with a share in ownership, participation in profit sharing, and even emeritus status on eventual retirement. Now these terms generally apply to top-level managers and high-level individual contributors. In the future they may also extend to customer service representatives, lathe operators, or computer programmers who are on a career learning path and acquiring varied skills and experience needed for flexible assignment throughout an organization. By contrast, otherwise highly paid professionals and managers, deemed specialists, might work on a fee-for-service basis and be treated as more or less casual labor. Designation of status would hinge on the long-term value of employees' skills and what kind of relationship best serves their interests and those of the organization.

Moreover, some companies that strive for an egalitarian culture may choose to classify all their employees as salaried, whereas others, under the principle of equity, could provide managers and exempt employees an equivalent to overtime pay. Looking ahead, it is possible that firms will have long-term contracts with perhaps a consultant or key service provider and just offer short-term employment to an executive or professional. In turn, employees in a valued supplier plant or consulting firm, or even seasonal workers, might be accorded a kind of "dual-citizenship"—eligible for enhanced training and benefits from a corporation though otherwise employed by a vendor or self-employed. Again, people's status would hinge on their value to a corporation and what might be "self-designed" through negotiation.

It is plain enough that most employers in the future will not be able to guarantee lifetime job security for even their core employees, let alone ensure continued business for contractors or opportunities for temporary and part-time workers. Nevertheless, they can manage valued employees as if they were lifelong contributors and invest in their continued employability. This means investing in their core skills and development and, when necessary, assisting them in moving in and out of the organization. Indeed, we can imagine a day when employers will offer to "trade" employees, or even whole groups, on a temporary or permanent basis as job opportunities ebb and flow between companies.

2. *Can corporations accommodate the diverse career needs of employees?* A recent survey finds that three in five American workers rate the effect of a job on their personal and family life as "very important" in making employment decisions—far more so than wages, benefits, and even job security (Galinsky & Friedman, 1993). With 87 percent of the American workforce living with at least one family member, finding time for spouses, children, parents, or partners is a major priority for more and more people. The survey reports that nearly half the workforce rate the family-supportive policies of employers as a key consideration in their job choice.

Demographic shifts in the workforce, coupled with the increased priority many people place on maintaining a semblance of family and personal life, make it imperative that adaptable companies respond to work/family issues. Hall and Parker (1993) make the case that just as companies are becoming more flexible in their structure, staffing, and work systems, so also they need to be more flexible in matters of time and space. Indications are that more and more firms are offering flextime, work-at-home options, part-time employment, and even job sharing and career breaks under the rubric of work/family programming (Parker & Hall, 1993). In the past, work/family and dual-career-couple issues were seen as an employee's problem; now that they are viewed as affecting company competitiveness, they are also a company problem.

What are the implications for career development? The option of entering a "mommy track" or "daddy track" has of course been advanced as one means of accommodating the career preferences of working parents (see Schwartz, 1989). We also estimate that the very "temporariness" of work assignments in adaptable companies, coupled with advances in telecommunication technology, will afford many more people the opportunity to work part time, or from their homes, or on a seasonal basis. This kind of flexibility will help people to control their work time and location. It will also help them manage their commitment and psychic energy. Research on social identity (Lobel, 1991) suggests that work/family conflicts can be minimized to the extent that people achieve some congruence with their work and nonwork roles. Workplace flexibility makes this easier.

As we use jobs to promote development for workers over their careers, however, we need also to recognize that there are great individual differences in what employees look for from a job in general and at particular points in their career (Hall & Rabinowitz, 1988). For some, the goal might be a continuously high level of challenge, growth, and development—the so-called intrinsic rewards of work. Accordingly, they would be oriented to what is called a high-involvement career path. However, another segment of workers is keyed to extrinsic rewards: steady pay, good benefits, congenial working conditions, and the like. The solution, where feasible, is to find ways to match these people to jobs suited to their talents and needs. Certainly companies will continue to have jobs in the future that are less demanding psychologically. These might offer flexible work schedules, job rotation for variety, the option of work at home and, in later career stages, the opportunity for job-holders to move downward, to lower-level, less demanding positions. Thus a low-involvement career path, while likely not as remunerative as in the past, could nonetheless provide a feasible, low-stress alternative to staying on the fast track.

It is important, however, to recognize that an exclusively high- or low-involvement career is not the answer. Already, companies are making informal accommodations for parents of young children that enable them to take on less demanding assignments for a period of years (in lower-involvement jobs) and then resume more intensive work (in high-involvement jobs). In addition, more companies are expected to offer sabbaticals to workers in the years ahead, more chances to work part time, if desired, and alternative career paths that enable them to take on less demanding responsibilities for a commensurate decrease in pay (see Parker & Hall, 1993). These kinds of options will certainly aid mature employees who want to combine work and schooling, and they could extend the careers of older workers.

3. *What is the future of "socially useful" careers?* Back in the mid-1960s, the great majority of college students had hopes of finding work that was "socially useful" and afforded them the opportunity to cultivate a "meaningful philosophy of life." In the mid-1980s, by comparison, students' chief aims were money and status—period (Higher Education Research Institute, 1967–1987). Today, however, it appears that values are shifting once again: many more students are taking an interest in the environment and social causes, and aspire to work in more socially responsible businesses.

In turn, there are some signs that business is assuming important social responsibilities. More and more companies, for example, are going "green" and making environmental protection an integral part of their sourcing, packaging, and manufacturing strategies. "Cause-related" marketing is also catching on as Reebok's human rights efforts and Coors's literacy campaigns have caught the attention of both the market and marketeers. Indeed, surveys find that consumers are willing to pay 5 percent to 10 percent more for products produced by environmentally oriented and socially responsible companies (Gary, 1990; Clancy, 1991).

Socially responsible human resource management is also on the rise. At present this includes "family friendly" practices, programs to hire and train disabled and disadvantaged employees, and employee involvement in public schools. In Los Angeles, as an example, 125 Arco Oil & Gas Company employees volunteer time at the Tenth Street Elementary School. Honeywell sponsors a summer Teacher's Academy where high school math and science teachers team up with industry people to develop work-relevant projects for students ("Needed: Human Capital," 1988).

A few smaller companies, like The Body Shop, pay employees for up to ten hours a week to work on human needs in their communities, and some bigger firms, like Polaroid, have employees "adopt" community groups and manage them as part of their job. Carrying this a step further, Vermont ice cream maker Ben & Jerry's regularly educates its employees on social issues and has made contributions to the firm's social mission a part of everyone's job and performance appraisal. The company also has a seven-to-one salary ratio whereby top executives can earn only seven times more than entry hourly employees. This is part of their belief in "caring capitalism." This policy has had a profound effect on employees at Ben & Jerry's, where it has kindled a spirit of generosity and become a prime contributor to satisfaction and commitment (Mirvis, Sales, & Ross, 1991). There is also some evidence that companies with a smaller gap between the pay of top executives and mainline workers achieve better results in product quality (Cowherd & Levine, 1992). Businesses for Social Responsibility, a new kind of chamber of commerce for socially responsible firms, predicts that the opportunity to do "socially significant" work could become a prime means of recruiting and motivating at least a segment of the workforce in the future.

In our view, this movement also has ramifications for career development. For instance, as firms develop partnerships with local school systems, for example, or band together with other businesses and nonprofits to tackle social problems, they provide people with the opportunity to take on new and challenging assignments that promise to expand their horizons and give fuller expression to their personal interests and values. In Rochester, New York, as an example, Kodak and the school board launched a wholesale restructuring of the local school system (Marshall & Tucker, 1992). Hundreds of Kodak people worked on task forces and volunteered time in schools to improve school performance and create apprenticeship-type programs for students in local industries. This may not seem to be the core work of Kodak but it is essential to upgrading its future workforce, enhances the attractiveness of the local community to Kodak employees, and, we believe, enhances the personal development of Kodak contributors.

In Corning, New York, as another illustration, members of a quality team at Corning Glass worked with nonprofit organizations in housing, education, and social service to enhance the attractiveness of the area for African Americans—a growing segment of their workforce (Hall & Parker, 1993). This was part of a larger effort in Corning to "value diversity." A recent survey finds that one-fifth of the minority workers in the United States believe that they have been discriminated against by their employers. Moreover, over half the workforce prefer working with people of the same race, gender, age, and education as their own (Galinksy & Friedman, 1993). At the same time, employers who understand the demographic trends see programs aimed at managing diversity as competitive necessities. As a result, mentoring programs aimed at minority workers and training for all employers on the management of diversity are becoming commonplace in these companies. Such efforts, exemplified by the outreach undertaken by Corning, help to promote social integration within companies, have a competitive payoff for the organization, and provide employees with new and rich experiences integral to success in the multicultural workplace of the future (see Cox, 1993).

It would be ennobling to see social responsibility spread from a thin segment of companies to the mainstream of American industry in this decade and thereafter. Certainly leading theorists are exploring new models of economic behavior—reaching beyond the conventional image of people as self-interested "utility maximizers" to recognize their altruistic and moral dimensions (Kohn, 1990). In the same way, a "communitarian" model of social organization is being advanced as an alternative to the highly individualistic "contractual" model favored by neoclassical management theories (Etzioni, 1988). Still, the ideas behind this movement are controversial, evidence of the impact of new practices is sparse, and what it might mean for vocational choice and career development is speculative at best. On this last point, however, one thing is clear: we need new ideas on how to conceptualize and study careers and career development in the future.

A New Stage in Career Research?

The earliest research on work careers concerned the relationship of people's knowledge and aptitudes to their choice of occupations and success therein. Studies by psychologists such as Super, Holland, Tiedeman, and Crites, and by sociologists such as Oswald Hall, Merton, and Becker, focused largely on the match between the person and the occupation (Hall, 1976). The aim of psychologists was to predict people's career choices and success. Sociologists wanted to understand the flow of people into and through occupations and how economic, educational, and supply-demand factors affected these flows.

The next stage of research concerned the match between the person and the job (Bray, Campbell, & Grant, 1974; Hall, 1976; Schein, 1978). Such studies introduced the concept of job choice into the mix and delineated the many factors bearing on people's self-selection into jobs. In turn, job analyses detailed the skill and performance requirements of jobs and were used to develop selection and placement instruments and to counsel new entrants and ongoing employees about the fit of their job choices to their capabilities.

Then came studies of career stages, life cycles, and ladders (see Hall & Associates, 1986). The intent here was to find a better match of person and organization over the course of a long-term career. In addition to considering skills, aptitudes, and interests, researchers considered how a person's age, experiences, and temperament might fit with career development trajectories in organizations. Chartrand and Camp (1991) report that researchers also became more interested in organizational processes bearing on career development. They found that the most frequently studied construct in career research reported in the *Journal of Vocational Behavior* from 1986 to 1990 was organizational commitment. Thus the psychological contract was being defined in terms of single employer-employee relations and commitment was still seen as central to "doing a career."

We wonder whether this interest in commitment has researchers locked into "organizational era" research whose time has come and gone. Already there are new inquiries into how people view commitment among their work, co-workers, and companies and into their different levels of attachment to their profession versus employing organization (see Rousseau and Wade-Benzoni, Chapter Eight this volume). We would propose a new stage in career research concerned with the match between the person and his or her life's work. Here the emphasis shifts from people's specific jobs and organizations to their "fitness" in handling the full range of their life interests and situations, including "work" as spouses, parents, and members of various communities.

In this frame, a person's work career consists of a whole set of activities (part-time jobs, self-employed undertakings, temporary assignments, three-year team projects, work-at-home periods, sabbaticals, and so forth), which may not and probably will not come neatly packaged and defined as a "job" in one "organization" but which can constitute full employment, provide adequate compensation, and afford deep satisfaction to the individual. Furthermore, a focus on life's work also takes account of how people's activities as spouses, parents, neighbors, and volunteers shape work choices, add to skills, promote or tax adaptability, and otherwise influence their self-pictures. This expanded frame invites new lines of thinking and research about tomorrow's careers.

Implications for Future Career Research

A major implication of these ideas for future research is that the study of careers has to get better connected to the career environment—and become more varied, multidisciplinary, and self-designed. Like the old careers they studied, the neat, orderly research designs predicting career choice, progress, and outcomes do not fit the turbulence of today's organizations. Hence, the nature of the research will have to match the nature of its subject: rapidly changing, fast learning, and complex.

One implication is that we will need more short-term longitudinal studies that capture the complex processes of lifelong learning. By short-term, we mean intensive studies of career learning occasioned by such events as lateral job movement, a major corporate restructuring, a personal crisis, or other circumstances where the research homes in on the microlearning and adaptive processes of a wide range of people. Longitudinal studies would enable us to see these processes at work over time as people age, chronologically and over career stages, encounter new situations that call on past learning, and make decisions about how much commitment and psychic energy to invest in their work and their current organization.

Consider some issues we might usefully investigate further:

1.   *How and what do people learn from "real-time" experience?* Recognizing that work challenges and relationships are keys to continuous learning, we need to study exactly how people learn from such experiences—and what they actually learn. Differences in the ways people perceive information, sort, assemble, and compare it against past experience, and draw generalizations about it are a function of their cognitive styles and the environment in which they operate. We know a lot about these matters in general but less about how workers translate their real-time experiences into career learning.

When, for example, are the skills developed on a challenging assignment incorporated fully into a person's behavioral repertoire, partially or totally forgotten, or compartmentalized as relevant to a discrete set of future situations? When is difficulty handling relationships treated as a sign that one should try out new interpersonal strategies, persevere in anticipation of working things out, or give up notions of becoming a manager? These elemental learning processes, and the cues that stimulate and inform them, need closer study in real time as people consider and prepare for new work regimens, take stock of their careers and contemplate changing them, deal with new superiors, subordinates, and themselves in highly charged situations, and in other respects learn about their weaknesses and strengths.

Such research has practical implications for organizations aiming to enhance the career learning of their members. One problem with using job assignments and relationships for learning, for instance, is that they are hard to document and frame as learning (in contrast to formal education and training, which at least can be incorporated into the resume). The result: real-time learning does not always "take" or generalize to new experiences. More research on such elements as critical incident learning could help workers at every career stage learn how to distill valuable lessons and assess their applicability to new situations. Advanced skill certification exercises might also be developed that capture learnings about interpersonal relations or about crisis management—learnings that are more subtle than those usually measured in skill certification programs. On this point, Robinson and Wick (1992) offer many other valuable ideas, ranging from personal journaling to buddying up with a co-learner, on how to help people learn how they learn from experience.

Another area for application concerns placement. We have argued that it is important for organizations to vary the work experiences of employees to deepen their perspectives and enrich their skill-sets—the aim being to match people and work in service of long-term development. At this point, however, we do not know very much about the intrinsic learning potential of complex work assignments. Competency models provide a roster of the skills and attitudes needed in certain kinds of complex work. But they do not, of themselves, detail what kind of work stimulates the development of these skills and attitudes. Can we develop a new generation of job analyses that delineate the learning potential embedded in different tasks and situations? Such research would not only help in matching people to work but also to learning experiences of utmost relevance.

2.   *Can people learn to be adaptable?* We contend that career development is anchored in personal development and have urged jobholders to acquire the meta-skills needed to adapt to new situations and to learn how to learn. This, however, raises a question: Is adaptability a characteristic of the individual that is relatively fixed or can it be developed? There are plenty of instruments that purport to measure the flexibility and adaptability of jobholders and thus their suitability for particular positions, situations, and organizations. Do these measures indeed predict how people cope with corporate restructuring, rapid job movement, career path ambiguity, and the like? There are also plenty of "natural experiments" under way that would put such predictions to a test—and help refine the concept of career adaptability.

Researchers are identifying what prevents people from learning how to learn. Argyris's in-depth studies (1982, 1985) of single-loop learning, defensive reasoning, and skilled incompetence, for instance, suggest that many so-called learning deficiencies are learned from experience. His interventions aimed at bringing assumptions to the surface and promoting double-loop learning hold out the potential for systematic "unlearning" of these deficiencies and for increasing people's adaptability (Argyris, 1991). Donald Bohm's "dialogue" group discussion methodology is another promising way to enhance people's capacities to learn how to learn (cited in Senge, 1990). Do these studies mean that people can be taught to be adaptable?

One survey of U.S. firms with one hundred or more employees found that 56 percent offered personal growth training to their employees (Gordon, 1988). More in-depth studies of these kinds of programs would help to determine whether rafting through white water, an exercise on stereotyping, an evocative film, thoughtful meditation, or a communal encounter with the spirit—just a sample of the fare in personal growth training—enhances people's adaptability. Back in the work environment, research shows that some people, some of the time, go through periods of self-examination, seek feedback from others, and consciously plan personal change (McCall et al., 1988). Self-reflection or examining one's assumptions, testing out definitions of a situation, and being open to feedback seem to be crucial elements in learning how to learn. We need to better understand what triggers serious self-reflection, how it is best conducted, and how it might be encouraged in the context of career learning.

The corporate world provides plenty of opportunities to study self-reflection in the context of rapid change. One problem, however, is that too much change generates ambiguity and threat that can inhibit self-reflection, constrain higher-order thinking, and undermine people's capacities to cope. Many ideas have been advanced on how to counteract the threat associated with change, ranging from giving people emotional inoculations and realistic previews to helping them systematically consider worst- versus best-case scenarios. Future research needs to amplify the ways people learn from trauma and crises and what this means for their future job, career, and work/life decisions. The findings may also guide refinement of interventions aimed at promoting personal growth in situations that would otherwise lead people to crawl into a shell.

3.   *What company practices really help people adapt and learn to learn?* We have argued that companies can help their employees gain varied and multiple skills by matching them to appropriate learning experiences and empowering them to self-design their careers. More research is needed to identify what kinds of policies and practices serve this purpose, and to determine their respective costs and benefits. Should companies, for example, insist that all employees be continuous learners and treat them as they have "high-potential" employees in the past? Or is it better to have high- and low-involvement career options available so that people can self-select into different tracks depending on their needs, capabilities, and interests at different points in time?

The latter would, of course, seem most respectful of individual differences and give people needed flexibility to attend to family and personal concerns. But can companies keep people securely employed on low-involvement career tracks, given the benefits of farming this work out or moving offshore? Is it likely that many who are on the high-involvement track would risk, say, taking an extended family leave or a sabbatical to smell the roses when peers are building a reputation as estimable workaholics who thrive under pressure? Comparative studies would help to identify the kinds of firms and industries in which it makes strategic sense to create high- and low-involvement career options and even where steady-but-reliable performance, as opposed to continuous learning, is the better course. Studies might also reveal what it takes for executives in a "family friendly" company to spend more time with their children: Maybe a role model or two? A critical mass of child-minded executives? A tragedy? Or simply quiet, collective complicity?

In order to become learning centers, companies would seemingly have to tailor training and work assignments to people's learning styles, taking account of age, gender, race, and all the other factors that impinge on individual and group learning, and set up systems of advanced skill certification, mentoring, and so on. We know that schools and universities do a lousy job in these regards. Is there reason to believe that corporations can do this any better?

Probably not by expanding the corporate training and development function. But much has been made about the "learning organization" and how it will cultivate and capitalize on learning to gain a sustained competitive advantage. Certainly the norms and practices of organizational learning (Michael, 1973; Senge, 1990) would seem to support the more or less organic development of innovations in career learning. Longitudinal studies are thus needed to show the many and different ways that companies develop lifelong learning norms, and whether this is typically an incremental versus transformational process. It would also be interesting to see whether current career development systems can be adapted to the contours of the new career or if they have to be scrapped. Or to learn the pluses and minuses when companies build up their in-house career development capability, put the responsibility fully in the hands of managers and employers, or hire expert assistance.

Large-scale longitudinal research is also needed to assess the learning system that will surround corporations in the future. Obviously schools and community colleges will be called on to do much more to meet the needs of workers for continuing education. Business-public school partnerships, now geared primarily to young people, will likely expand to focus on the needs of mid-career and aging workers. It is foreseeable that a consortia of businesses in a local community, in partnership with high schools, trade schools, and community colleges, will establish programs whereby workers, at several career stages, will move seamlessly in, out, and among businesses and educational institutions. Already several national and many local nonprofits help to place executives and professionals in part- or full-time positions following their retirement, early or otherwise, and selected ones serve the needs of the neediest youth. Many unions assist displaced members and offer them training and social support to aid in their reemployment. We expect that these institutions will be more tightly connected in the future and serve as a broad resource network for people and corporations. More studies are needed about how these learning systems develop and function (see Marshall & Tucker, 1992) and how much they contribute to career learning and adaptability.

4.   *Will the concept of career have any meaning in the future?* To begin this chapter, we hailed the birth of the "new" career. It is also important to look at its downsides. By now, the young, "new-breed" workforce of the late 1960s and 1970s are well along in their careers. Surveys in those times found many of them infused with the belief that interesting and challenging work was central to their identity (Yankelovich, 1981). This trend seemed to hold through the 1980s as the "new achievers" (Pascarella, 1984) moved up in organizations or else moved out to entrepreneurial ventures. Today, the "new generation" makes up the lion's share of the workforce and Maccoby (1988) finds a new character type, the self-developer, emerging among them. Self-developers, he reports, balance mastery and play, strive for knowledge, but also seek balance in their lives. They are also the problem solvers in organizations, the most customer centered, and those most suited to the techno-service work that will increasingly be the work of the future.

As such, they have taken hold of what we have termed the *new* career. The question that we must confront, then, is why self-developers are often unhappy with their circumstances and find themselves making repeated and unsatisfying compromises (see Sarason, 1977). It may be, of course, that work is not of itself that much fun and that self-developers simply have not "grown up" and accepted this unpleasant reality. Alternatively, it could be that not enough organizations have yet accepted the notion, advanced by Harman and Hormann (1990), that in a technologically advanced society "employment exists primarily for self-development" (p. 26). Certainly many executives, pressed to compete globally, would quarrel with that notion.

A third hypothesis, and one that needs imaginative study, is that interesting and challenging work is simply not the end-all and be-all of self-development. Current aspirations with getting more time with family and pursuing personal goals hint at other dimensions to self-development. Moreover, if we can set aside the idea that "self-actualization" is the pinnacle of human motivation, we make room to consider whether community, transpersonal connectedness, and even spirituality are the transcendent aims of human development.

The new stage of career research we are pointing to concerns not only the development of one's work work but also one's life work. The two, in our view, connect deeply in the work/life intersection—a subject given only the barest scrutiny by career researchers. In this light, of course, distinctions between career and life stages, for example, and indeed between career and self-development, may prove arbitrary and ultimately meaningless.

And what of those for whom a career of lifelong learning in several adaptive organizations is unimaginable? Labor Secretary Robert Reich (1991) suggests that enhanced opportunities may be limited to a "fortunate fifth" of the U.S. population unless the nation makes a deep commitment to create high-skill/high-wage jobs, enhance the academic preparation of entry-level workers, and retrain vast numbers of current employees. Meanwhile, the continuing loss of jobs in heavy industry, the ongoing reduction in corporate staff and management, coupled with increases in minimum wage, part-time, and temporary employment, threaten to consign the less fortunate four-fifths of the U.S. workforce to limited opportunity or dead-end jobs.

There are plenty of studies of the trauma of job loss, the anomie of bumping along from job to job, and the problems people have finding and keeping work in today's society. Studies of programs designed to train welfare mothers for jobs, improve the work ethic and skills of disadvantaged youth, retrain displaced employees, or enhance the employability of older, prematurely retired workers all fit into the category of research on careers. Will research on the "new" career address these issues? It's one more element to think about when planning the next generation of career research.

Conclusion

Some of the ideas advanced here about continuous corporate restructuring, the lifelong development and multiskilling of workers, career paths between the three leaves of the adaptable company, and the notion that people will move from job to job and even employer to employer may seem far off into the future and even farfetched. On this point, however, it is worth noting that ideas about participative management, semiautonomous work groups, skill certification, flexible hours, and retraining and redeployment seemed just as far out and farfetched twenty years ago.

Still, the adaptable corporation we have been describing may seem excessively cold and calculating in its human resource outlook—welcoming, perhaps, of its "fittest" workers but rather instrumental in its handling of the seemingly less adaptable and able. Two factors will likely work against corporations' treating older workers in a purely instrumental way. First, firms are constantly being judged not just on how they manage their stars but also their everyday earthlings. On this count, it is worth noting that companies that downsized in the late 1980s but did not retrain and redeploy their people are having a hard time recruiting new employees; they have acquired a bad reputation (Marks, 1993).

Second, companies who have taken a lead in responding to new environmental conditions facing their business also tend to be human resource leaders in all respects (Mirvis, 1993; Denison, 1990). Most seem to foster human development in their corporate culture. Still, it will be incumbent on adaptive corporations to reaffirm the value of people in an age of instability. With the traditional psychological contract in tatters (see De Meuse & Tornow, 1990; Rousseau & Wade-Benzoni, Chapter Eight this volume), a clearly articulated set of values around career development for employees is an important first step in redefining the employment relationship.

We expect there will be many and varied opportunities to study the new career in organizations in the future. However, one of the difficulties of doing research on this subject is that when individuals and organizations are undergoing such fundamental change, participating in a research study is not generally a high-priority activity. As a result, it has to be clear to the organizations and individuals involved that the research will be of value for them. In the more stable past, people often participated in research to contribute to knowledge or for the intrinsic interest of being part of a study. By now, many people have been "surveyed to death" (as we have often heard), and contributing to knowledge is seen as far less important than contributing to one's own survival. Thus the burden is on us as researchers to be more customer-minded in our research. This means collaborative planning with participants, using data-collection methods that will provide useful data to all concerned, and providing useful "products" of the research to participants as well as to the academic community. Such an approach should be especially attractive in the study of careers, because the issues are so important to so many people and organizations.

References

Argyris, C. (1982). *Reasoning, learning, and action: Individual and organizational.* San Francisco: Jossey-Bass.

Argyris, C. (1985). *Strategy, change, and defensive routines.* Cambridge, MA: Ballinger.

Argyris, C. (1991, May–June). Teaching smart people how to learn. *Harvard Business Review,* pp. 99–109.

Argyris, C., & Schön, D. A. (1974). *Theory in practice: Increasing professional effectiveness.* San Francisco: Jossey-Bass.

Ashby, W. R. (1960). *An introduction to cybernetics.* London: Chapman & Hall.

Barth, M. C., McNaught, W., & Rizzi, P. (1993). Corporations and the aging workforce. In P. Mirvis (Ed.), *Building the competitive work force.* New York: Wiley.

Bennis, W. G., & Slater, P. (1968). *The temporary society.* New York: Harper.

Bray, D. W., Campbell, R. J., & Grant, D. L. (1974). *Formative years in business: A long-term AT&T study of managerial lives.* New York: Wiley.

Chartrand, J. M., & Camp, C. C. (1991). Advances in the measurement of career development constructs: A 20-year review. *Journal of Vocational Behavior, 39,* 1–39.

Clancy, K. J. (1991). *The green revolution: Its impact on your pricing decisions.* New York: Yankelovich, Skelly & White/Clancy.

Cohen, M. D., & March, J. G. (1986). *Leadership and ambiguity* (2nd ed.). Cambridge, MA: Harvard Business School Press.

Cowherd, D. M., & Levine, D. I. (1992). Product quality and pay equity between lower level employees and top management: An investigation of distributive justice theory. *Administrative Science Quarterly, 37,* 302–320.

Cox, T. (1993). *The multicultural organization.* San Francisco: Berrett-Koehler.

Davis, S. M., & Davidson, B. (1991). *2020 vision.* New York: Simon & Schuster.

Davis, S. M., & Lawrence, P. R. (1977). *Matrix.* Reading, MA: Addison-Wesley.

De Meuse, K. P., & Tornow, W. W. (1990). The tie that binds—has become very, very frayed! *Human Resource Planning, 13,* 203–213.

Denison, D. (1990). *Corporate culture and organizational effectiveness.* New York: Wiley.

Downward mobility. (1992, March 23). *Business Week,* pp. 56–63.

Emery, F. E. (Ed.). (1969). *Systems thinking.* Harmondsworth, England: Penguin.

Emery, F. E., & Trist, E. L. (1965). The causal texture of organizational environments. *Human Relations, 18,* 21–32.

Emery, F. E., & Trist, E. L. (1973). *Toward a social ecology.* London: Tavistock.

Etzioni, A. (1988). *The moral dimension.* New York: Free Press.

Galbraith, J. R. (1977). *Organizational design.* Reading, MA: Addison-Wesley.

Galinsky, E., & Friedman, D. (1993). *National study of the changing workforce.* New York: Families & Work Institute.

Gary, L. (1990). Consumers turning green: J. Walter Thompson's Greenwatch survey. *Advertising Age, 61*(41), 74.

Gordon, J. (1988, October). Who's being trained to do what? *Training,* pp. 51–60.

Hall, D. T. (1976). *Careers in organizations.* Glenview, IL: Scott, Foresman.

Hall, D. T. (1985). Project work as an antidote to career plateauing in a declining engineering organization. *Human Resource Management, 24,* 271–292.

Hall, D. T. (1991). Business restructuring and strategic human resource development. In P. B. Doeringer (Ed.), *Turbulence in the American workplace.* New York: Oxford University Press.

Hall, D. T., & Associates. (1986). *Career development in organizations.* San Francisco: Jossey-Bass.

Hall, D. T., & Associates. (in press). *The career is dead! Long live the career! A relational approach to careers.* San Francisco: Jossey-Bass.

Hall, D. T., & Parker, V. A. (1993, Summer). The role of workplace flexibility in managing diversity. *Organizational Dynamics,* pp. 4–18.

Hall, D. T., & Rabinowitz, S. (1988). Maintaining employee involvement in a plateaued career. In M. London & E. Mone (Eds.), *Career growth and human resource strategies: The role of the human resource professional in employee development.* New York: Quorum.

Handy, C. (1989). *The age of unreason.* Cambridge, MA: Harvard Business School Press.

Handy, C. (1992, November–December). Balancing corporate power: A new Federalist Paper. *Harvard Business Review, 70,* 59–72.

Harmon, W., & Hormann, J. (1990). *Creative work.* Indianapolis: Knowledge Systems.

Higher Education Research Institute. (1967–1987). *Annual survey of college freshmen.* Los Angeles: University of California.

Hirsch, P. (1987). *Pack your own parachute.* Reading, MA: Addison-Wesley.

Johnston, W. B., & Packer, A. E. (1987). *Workforce 2000.* Indianapolis: Hudson Institute.

Kanter, D. L., & Mirvis, P. H. (1989). *The cynical Americans: Living and working in an age of discontent and disillusion.* San Francisco: Jossey-Bass.

Kanter, D. L., & Mirvis, P. H. (1991, Spring). Cynicism: The new American malaise. *Business and Society Review,* pp. 57–61.

Kohn, A. (1990). *The brighter side of human nature.* New York: Basic Books.

Kram, K. E. (1988). *Mentoring at work: Developmental relationships in organizational life.* Lanham, MD: University Press of America.

Kram, K. E., & Hall, D. T. (1991). Mentoring as an antidote to stress during corporate trauma. *Human Resource Management, 28,* 493–510.

Lawler, E. E., III, Mohrman, S. A., & Ledford, G. E. (1992). *Employee involvement and total quality management: Practices and results in Fortune 1000 companies.* San Francisco: Jossey-Bass.

Lawrence, P. R., & Lorsch, J. W. (1967). *Organization and environment.* Cambridge, MA: Harvard Graduate School of Business Administration.

Lobel, S. A. (1991). Allocation of investment in work and family roles: Alternative theories and implications for research. *Academy of Management Review, 16*(3), 507–521.

Louis Harris & Associates. (1991). *Productive aging: A survey of Americans age 55 and over* (Study no. 902061). New York: Author.

McCall, M. W., Jr., Lombardo, M. M., & Morrison, A. M. (1988). *The lessons of experience: How successful executives develop on the job.* Lexington, MA: Lexington Books.

Maccoby, M. (1988). *Why work.* New York: Simon & Schuster.

Marks, M. L. (1993). Restructuring and downsizing. In P. Mirvis (Ed.), *Building the competitive work force.* New York: Wiley.

Marshall, R., & Tucker, M. (1992). *Thinking for a living.* New York: Basic Books.

Michael, D. N. (1973). *Learning to plan and planning to learn.* San Francisco: Jossey-Bass.

Mirvis, P. H. (1992). Job security: Current trends. In L. K. Jones (Ed.), *The encyclopedia of career change and work issues.* Phoenix: Oryx Press.

Mirvis, P. H. (Ed.). (1993). *Building a competitive workforce: Investing in human capital for corporate success.* New York: Wiley.

Mirvis, P. H., & Kanter, D. L. (1992). Beyond demographics: A psychographic profile of the workforce. *Human Resource Management, 30*(1), 45–68.

Mirvis, P. H., & Marks, M. L. (1992). *Managing the merger.* Englewood Cliffs, NJ: Prentice Hall.

Mirvis, P. H., Sales, A. S., & Ross, D. (1991). Work life at Ben & Jerry's. In R. Marx, T. Jick, & P. Frost (Eds.), *Management live!* Englewood Cliffs, NJ: Prentice Hall.

Needed: Human capital. (1988, September 19). *Business Week,* pp. 100–141.

O'Reilly, B. (1992, August 24). The job drought. *Fortune,* pp. 62–74.

O'Toole, J. (1977). *Work, learning, and the American future.* San Francisco: Jossey-Bass.

Parker, V., & Hall, D. T. (1993). Workplace flexibility: Faddish or fundamental? In P. Mirvis (Ed.), *Building the competitive work force.* New York: Wiley.

Pascarella, P. (1984). *The new achievers.* New York: Free Press.

Reich, R. (1991). *The work of nations: Preparing ourselves for 21st century capitalism.* New York: Knopf.

Robinson, G. S., & Wick, C. W. (1992). Executive development that makes a business difference. *Human Resource Planning, 15,* 63–76.

Sarason, S. (1977). *Work, aging, and social change.* New York: Free Press.

Schein, E. H. (1978). *Career dynamics.* Reading, MA: Addison-Wesley.

Schor, J. B. (1991). *The overworked American.* New York: Basic Books.

Schwartz, F. (1989). Management women and the new facts of life. *Harvard Business Review, 67*(1), 65–76.

Senge, P. (1990). *The fifth discipline.* New York: Doubleday.

Weick, K. E. (1977a, Autumn). Organization design: Organizations as self-designing systems. *Organizational Dynamics,* pp. 38–49.

Weick, K. E. (1977b). *Social psychology of organizing.* Reading, MA: Addison-Wesley.

Weick, K. E., & Berlinger, L. R. (1989). Career improvisation in self-designing organizations. In M. B. Arthur, D. T. Hall, & B. S. Lawrence (Eds.), *Handbook of career theory.* New York: Cambridge University Press.

Wheatley, M. J. (1993). *Leadership and the new science: Learning about organization from an orderly universe.* San Francisco: Berrett-Koehler.

Yankelovich, D. (1981). *The new rules.* New York: Random House.

Zand, D. (1974). Collateral organization: A new change strategy. *Journal of Applied Behavioral Science, 10,* 63–89.

Part Four

Working

Chapter Ten

When People Get Out of the Box

New Relationships, New Systems

Susan Albers Mohrman, Susan G. Cohen

Environmental and technological changes are leading to fundamental upheaval in organizations. New approaches to designing and managing organizations are changing the assumptions that have been built into traditional hierarchical organizations and the performance required from organizational participants. Organizational change is leading to new patterns of interaction and new integrating mechanisms that are fundamentally changing the relationships among the individuals in an organization and the relationship of the individual to the organization. The broad parameters of the emerging organizational architecture have been articulated (for example, Nadler, Gerstein, & Shaw, 1992; Galbraith, Lawler, & Associates, 1993). Organizations will assume a variety of forms that are determined by dynamic competitive requirements and strategy. People will, in effect, work in organizations that are continually transforming themselves. Organizations will be flatter, giving rise to increasing use of teams and other lateral organizing mechanisms. These changes will require the creation of high-involvement organizations in which people are empowered to influence performance (Lawler, 1992; Galbraith, 1994).

This new organizational architecture (Nadler et al., 1992) will require substantial change in the human resource practices that shape and manage the employment relationship and in the work that is performed by the individuals in the firm. The relationships among organizational members are also in flux because of the change in the organizational context in which individuals perform their work. This chapter examines the nature of these changes in the way people relate to each other in the organization.

The essence of the change is depicted as "people emerging from the box," to reflect a shift away from portraying an organization as a set of boxes and lines, with jobs, job descriptions, boss-subordinate relations, and departmental allegiances determining how work is done. The chapter explores what happens to people and their relationships with one another when the boxes no longer determine how work is done or managed. Ultimately, the boxes may not even exist.

Out of the Box: The Contours of the Change

Organizational identity that derives from the box occupied on the organizational chart has become part of the psyche of employees in most large organizations. Figure 10.1 illustrates this depiction of the organization. It is a standard organization chart that conveys meaning and shapes relationships in a very powerful way. It has led to practices consistent with this meaning, including the following:

1. *People occupy boxes.* Job descriptions identify people's role in the organization and attempt to capture the contribution that is expected from a box. The entire set of tasks of the organization is, in a sense, broken down into boxes. Job evaluation systems evaluate the market value of particular job skills and grade jobs to establish internal equity.

2. *The individual's relationship to the organization is mediated by the boss (as the line connects their boxes).* The boss represents the organization in managing subordinates' performance, including assigning and directing work, formulating work goals, providing feedback and direction, attending to developmental needs, evaluating the work and assessing the performer, and determining rewards. The boss is the employee's most direct link to organizational information needed to perform the job and provides the opportunities for visibility and development that can help the employee advance through the organization.

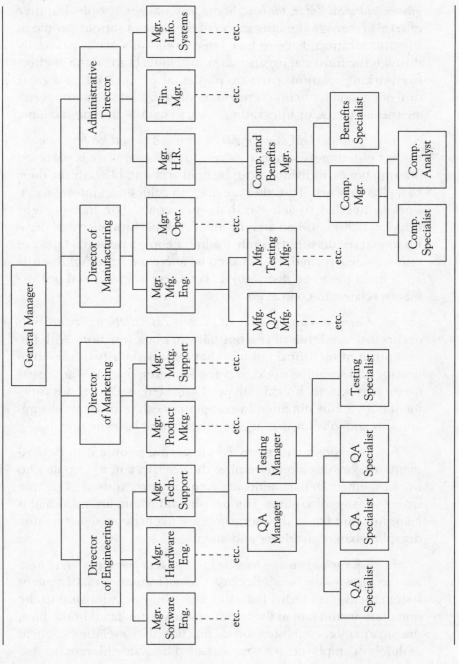

Figure 10.1. (Partial) Box and Line Organization.

3.   *The individual's relationship to others in the organization is to a great extent mediated by the boss.* Managers manage people, but they often also manage the integration of the work of various people in the organization. Face-to-face lateral relations occur primarily through the informal organization, and failures to establish effective working relations carry no particular penalty. When a great deal of lateral interaction is required, organizations sometimes create special boxes, or integrating roles, to handle the transactions.

4.   *People are held accountable for their individual job performance,* not for system performance or results. Because work is parceled out into boxes, individuals can be held accountable only for their own piece of work. Thus they are likely to cultivate an informal network as needed to achieve their own goals. The line of sight (Lawler, 1990) between an individual's job performance and organizational results often is quite distant. People's personal fates are only remotely related, or may even be at cross-purposes if rewards are a fixed pie to be distributed according to individual performance relative to co-workers.

5.   *Career advancement is in the vertical direction.* Promotion occurs through levels of responsibility in one's function. With the exception of technical ladders that exist primarily in the engineering and scientific world, very few advancement paths are based on increases in technical skills and knowledge. Career advancement is generally obtained by competing with individuals of similar skills and jobs for management boxes that become open.

6.   *Diversity is minimized.* By clustering people into departments, the organization minimizes the diversity among people who work together. Departments are frequently composed of people from the same discipline. The people with whom an individual is colocated and has daily interaction are likely to possess the same discipline-based worldview and language.

7.   *A key role of human resource practices is to promote equity of treatment and equal opportunity.* Because the performance management system focuses on individuals in a box whose relationship to the organization and fate in the organization are mediated by the boss, the organization establishes formal practices that level the treatment of different employees who are managed by quite different bosses.

These elements of the traditional "box and line" organization give an overall impression of segmentation: between individuals, levels, functions, disciplines, and units. The notion is to self-contain and predescribe an individual's task as much as possible in order to reduce the time spent interacting and increase the time spent doing "productive work." A sense of rigidity also is present. Such an organization depends on stability so that its boxes and their job descriptions and evaluations continue to fit the tasks. Environmental changes that lead to reorganization can set off thousands of hours of reworking job descriptions and job evaluations in a large, complex organization. On the other hand, employees know what is expected of them, and the organization knows what it holds people accountable for and on what it can base personnel action.

This box and line organization is very hierarchical in orientation. It fits Lawler's depiction of the "low-involvement" or traditional organization, in which the line worker performs the organization's work, middle managers control that work, and top management plans, designs, and leads the organization (Lawler, 1986). In this kind of organization, little employee involvement in the success of the organization can be expected. Employees at best are involved in the effectiveness of their own job performance. Organizations train them to do their own job, provide information necessary to do that job, and reward them for individual performance. Employees have little power to influence work processes or their context because their work is, often artificially, segmented from the entire process and the set of co-workers whom their work affects. Employees may not even understand how their work fits with the work of others in the organization.

Organizations have existed with this form of enterprise even as they have experimented with ways to compensate for its inherent weaknesses. Job enrichment programs have been employed to offset the negative motivational impact of tightly constrained jobs. Survey feedback and participation groups have been established to provide opportunity for employees to influence the organization and for managers to become aware of the reality their employees experience. Managers have been trained to administer human resource systems and manage performance in an equitable and motivating way. Human resource systems have been designed and redesigned, as if some magical format will lead to equity and motivation in the organization (Mohrman, Resnick-West, & Lawler, 1989; Teel, 1980). The "flavor of the month" has been an endless stream of programs designed to compensate for the pitfalls of this way of organizing.

This line and box organization has some advantages. When executed well, it is a landscape where the rules of the game are clear, and people are able to calculate their own self-interest and to "know where they stand." It has a predictability and stability that allows people to plan their lives, and a clear psychological contract that enables people to gauge the amount of effort they must exert to be perceived as doing a good job. It simplifies the organization for the individual, who knows that the boss has to be kept happy and who can deal with a predictable network of others.

Nevertheless, the pitfalls of the line and box organization—rigidity, segmentation, and failure to get people involved in the success of the enterprise—have been its Achilles' heel as today's markets demand ever-higher levels of performance and great flexibility from organizations. While it would be wrong to say that the day of boxes and lines is gone, a different conceptualization of organization is slowly emerging, one that stresses the interconnections within the organization rather than its segments (for example, Rummler & Brache, 1990).

In today's rapidly changing environment with a market requirement for quick response and rapid cycle time, the hierarchy is simply too slow. In response, organizations have introduced a complex assortment of teams: cross-functional teams, work teams, quality improvement teams, task teams, and so forth. They have also introduced other mechanisms that link various parts of the organization laterally in order to achieve focus on organizational issues such as products, customers, and geographies and to make trade-offs between them. The dynamic global organizations of today are too complex to rely on hierarchical resolution of multidimensional issues (Galbraith, 1994).

The application of teams to deal with the shortcomings of the line and box model has a developmental history that is continuing to unfold. During the 1970s and early 1980s, most American organizations set up "quality circles" and other kinds of parallel structures in huge numbers (Ledford, Lawler, & Mohrman, 1988).

There was great disappointment with their results, largely because these efforts were swimming upstream against a hierarchical logic that made it difficult for them to have meaningful impact in organizations (Lawler & Mohrman, 1985; 1987). Nevertheless, parallel structures did not go away. Organizations have adopted a more sophisticated approach to self-improvement, Total Quality Management (Deming, 1986; Juran, 1989), that relies on teams and cross-functional integration but attempts to create a context in which these teams can be effective. It tries to refocus attention on the work processes rather than the performance of individuals.

In the 1960s and 1970s a small number of manufacturing companies experimented with self-managing work teams (Lawler, 1987). By the late 1980s and early 1990s, this small number had grown extensively, and organizations in all sectors of the economy were adopting similar approaches (Cohen, 1994). Project teams have long been used in the aerospace and defense industries; they are now being used extensively in many industries, including almost all companies that have a new product development process. The latest iteration of this evolution is the emergence of cross-functional teams to manage organizational processes (Hammer & Champy, 1993).

As these approaches proliferate, organizations are taking on a different shape. Figure 10.2 is a depiction of a "team organization" (Mohrman, Cohen, & Mohrman, 1995). Instead of focusing on boxes and lines and who reports to whom (the segments), it stresses the connectedness of the organization. Increasingly, the performing units of the organization are becoming collectives of people rather than individuals (Mohrman, Mohrman, & Cohen, 1992), and the organization is parceling work to teams rather than to the individuals who compose the teams. Boxes and lines may still exist in this organization, but depicting them does not give much information about how the work is actually done. Operational direction increasingly occurs through the team structure, even if reporting relationships do not change.

In organizations whose operating design is composed of teams and teaming arrangements nested in bigger business units, as illustrated in Figure 10.2, employees begin to think of their organizational identity as being determined at least in part by the teams of which they are members. Following are some of the emerging elements of this kind of organization.

Figure 10.2. Team-Based Organization.

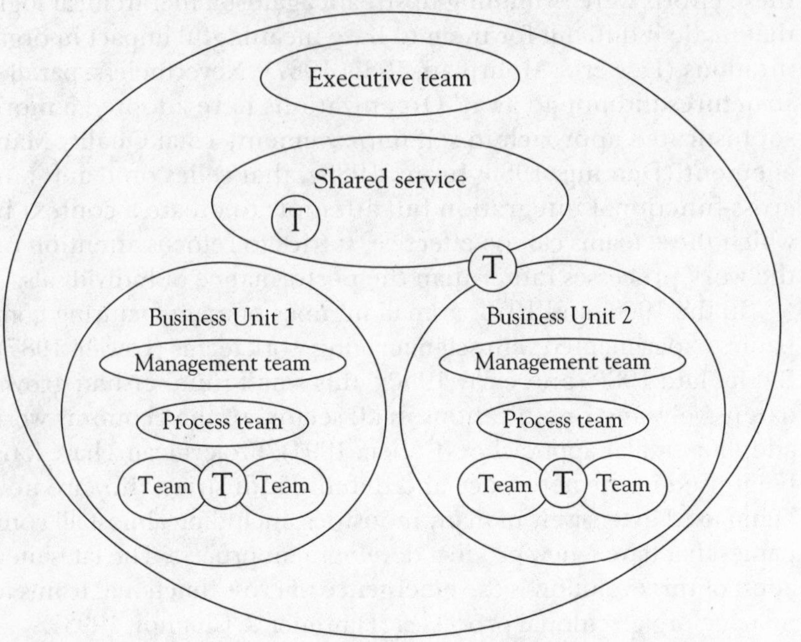

Source: Adapted from Mohrman, Cohen, and Mohrman, 1995.

1.   *People belong to a team or teams as part or all of their organizational role.* People's role in the team may be described by the competencies they bring to the team and the manner in which the team chooses to apply its members to the set of required tasks. Individuals can play different roles in different teams.

2.   *Compensation is determined by competencies employees have developed,* which are valued relative to the labor market but also in relation to their criticality to the company and its logic of operation. For example, cross-functional knowledge is more critical and provides more leverage in a team organization than in a box and line organization; consequently, it is valued higher.

3.   *The individual's relationship to the organization is to a great extent mediated by the team.* Team performance is managed: the team has goals, gets feedback, gets appraised, and gets rewarded. Team

members play an active role in managing each other's performance. The team depends on higher-level teams or managers to keep it informed. Employees may continue to rely on a functional manager for functional information, for help making trade-offs between priorities, and for technical feedback and development, but not for operational direction.

4.   *Individuals relate directly to others in the organization with whom they are interdependent.* This interaction includes other team members but extends beyond the team to others in the organization whose work must fit with the work of the team. The team members do not rely on managers to mediate interactions. Failure to establish good working relations carries a big penalty, because the collective product is evaluated, not the piece parts that can be controlled by a single individual.

5.   *People are held accountable for collective results.* These results may be at the team or business unit level. It is assumed that results accrue from a complex set of transactions between people and teams as they integrate their work to produce a whole product or service or manage a whole process. Individuals also may be held accountable, but in the context of the units of which they are a part.

6.   *Career growth and advancement occurs through the development of increased competency to contribute.* People who develop more competencies can play more roles in teams and can participate in teams with a larger scope, such as business unit or cross-team teams. Cross-functional competencies play a vital role as teams now become the locus of resolution of cross-functional issues. Skill-based pay systems (Jenkins, Ledford, Gupta, & Doty, 1992) formalize the increased value attached to competency development and provide a basis for advancement through competency levels and increasing scope of responsibility.

7.   *People have to deal with a more diverse set of co-workers in getting the task done.* Teams bring together the contributors required to produce the whole product or service. That often includes multiple functions and disciplines as well as ethnic and cultural diversity. It leads to greater intensity of interaction with people who have different worldviews, algorithms, and languages.

8.   *A key role of human resource practices is the development and placement into teams of people with needed skill-sets.* Equitable treatment and equal opportunity take on a new meaning that is defined by accurate assessment of competencies that enable people to play particular roles in a dynamic configuration of teams. The relevant equal opportunity is access to the development and application of new competencies rather than simply access to promotions.

9.   *Contributors who must integrate their work with a broad network of co-workers often rely on electronic methods.* People often cannot be colocated with all their co-performers. Work is integrated through shared systems and data bases and by electronic communication rather than face-to-face interaction.

This kind of organization is emerging to promote the flexibility and integration that were so difficult to achieve in the box and line organization. The transition is not easy. Clearly, moving to a team organization requires more than identifying teams and determining their missions. The next section gives a brief overview of the elements of effectiveness of a team organization.

Out of the Box: Factors Contributing to Effectiveness in the Team-Based Organization

Years of research have confirmed the importance of the internal dynamics of teams. The team-building literature has stressed clarity regarding the mission and goals of the team, the roles of the individuals who compose the team, the manner in which decisions are made, and the norms that are established (Dyer, 1987). The team effectiveness literature stresses the factors contributing to three aspects of team functioning: the effort of team members, the knowledge and skills possessed by team members, and the appropriateness of their performance strategies (Hackman, 1987; Hackman & Associates, 1990). This framework takes us beyond the internal processes of the team in understanding team effectiveness, and points out the need to have well-designed teams and adequate contextual support provided through the reward, educational, and information systems.

In our research on team-based organizations (Mohrman et al., 1995), we observed that some teams that appear to have textbook processes, leadership, and effective internal dynamics can fail to achieve their mission because of the organizational context in which they exist. For example, some new product development teams were well designed for concurrent engineering, but the functional managers in the division could not agree to support design directions that came out of the team. Inconsistent direction from different managers was a frequent factor contributing to the derailment of teams.

The importance of the context results in part from the high levels of interdependence in some knowledge work settings, which make it impossible to create teams that can achieve their mission independently (Mohrman, 1995). A product distribution team that we studied was poised to release and distribute a new product, but it treaded water (and the company lost potential market share) while an understaffed marketing support team awaited direction from a process improvement team regarding aspects of the uniform product documentation procedures for families of products. Figure 10.2 depicts some of the complexity of these settings by illustrating the requirement for teams that link teams, teams that link central services with the business units that are their clients, and teams that integrate processes that cut across multiple teams. Thus employees in team-based organizations exist in a constellation of teams, and the work of teams and their individual members is influenced by the work of other teams.

The important design features in a team organization are those that "point people in the same direction" (Mohrman et al., 1995). They make it more likely that people in teams and across teams will integrate and coordinate with one another. They create a shared understanding of what the organization or business unit is trying to accomplish and how it is going about it—both the ends and the means of the organization. These design features include the following:

1. Knowledge throughout the organization of the *strategy and goals* of the organization
2. *Aligned and measurable goals* for the various performing units in the organization
3. *Systematic decision processes* based on data from multiple stakeholders, reflecting multiple perspectives, and yielding decisions that various parties have agreed to accept

4. *Clarity of decision processes,* including where authority lies for which decisions and what escalation paths exist if a team is unable to reach a decision
5. *Computer connectedness among interdependent parts of the organization,* including shared data bases and common languages
6. *Performance management practices that operate at the collective level,* by creating shared goals, providing teams and business units with performance information and feedback, and by evaluating and rewarding performing units

The second set of features that promote effectiveness in a team-based organization are those that "empower" the performing units by providing clear direction and building the capability of the unit to act. Our research upheld the pieces of the high-involvement model of Lawler (1986, 1992). Teams need to have the appropriate skills and knowledge, acquired in part through the staffing of the team and in part through development. They need to be well informed, particularly about goals and performance. They need to have power to make decisions about how they go about their work and to influence other decisions that impact them but are made beyond the team. Finally, they must be rewarded for performance.

In summary, one strength of a laterally oriented organization is that it can integrate across multiple functions and perspectives. Another strength is that decisions can be made closer to where the work is done.

This view of the organization has profound implications for its people, who may have been quite comfortable living in their boxes. First, hierarchy does not go away, but its role shifts to clarifying ends and involving people in determining common means. Thus people are much more responsible for contributing to the "how" of the organization, and they are held accountable for results. Second, people now have to learn to operate as part of a complex collective web. They can no longer rely on the organization to manage the relations between the pieces of that web; rather, they are required to help resolve the lateral issues of the organization. Finally, individuals are expected to contribute to the organization in many more ways, in interactions that require a continual orientation to learning and expanding competencies. Advancement will depend on the willingness of people to expend energy learning.

The remainder of this chapter examines more closely what these changes mean for the relations between people in the organization.

People Who Have Been Let Out of the Box

People who have been "let out of the box" find themselves in the dynamic lattice of relationships that is the lateral organization. These relationships cut across departments, functions, disciplines, and personal backgrounds. The ability to work laterally is the key to personal success. Developing this capacity requires a new mindset about who individuals are and what they do at work. People have the opportunity for personal growth, skill development, and connectedness to others, but they also confront a lack of security, ambiguity, competing demands, and unrelenting work pressures.

In the old line and box organization, people could truly be individual contributors. The lateral organization is a collective organization. Individuals' fates are based on their competencies and their ability to execute these in a collective setting. Whether an individual is a member of a permanent work team, belongs to multiple work teams, is a member of several temporary task forces, or just networks with others to get work done, results are achieved collectively. A person's success or failure depends on collective success or failure. An individual's fate is inextricably (and very proximately) linked to that of his or her co-workers.

This dependency on co-workers is uncomfortable for most of us. We have been socialized to value individual responsibility and individual achievement, and feel discomfort with the thought of relying on others (Katzenbach & Smith, 1993). The rugged individualist is an American symbol, one that is still held in high regard in many U.S. corporations. The fear of dependency has deeper roots. Psychoanalytical theorists (Freud, 1922; Bion, 1961) and group theorists (Gibbard, 1974; Slater, 1966; Smith & Berg, 1987) have clinically documented that people are intrinsically ambivalent about their membership in groups. Groups bring to the surface early feelings of engulfment and abandonment, which people defend against by alternately moving away from and moving toward their group memberships. Although this perspective has not been empirically tested, these dynamics have been described by clinical researchers observing therapy groups and training laboratory groups (Benne, 1964; Bennis & Shepard, 1956; Gibbard, 1974; Schermer, 1985; Smith & Berg, 1987). Katzenbach and Smith (1993) found that many team members reported anxiety when joining and working in a team.

Understanding the human dynamics of work teams and developing supporting human resource systems is of paramount importance, given that working in teams may not come naturally, comfortably, or easily to people. This section begins a discussion of some of the key factors that underpin people's ability to work collaboratively in the lateral organizations, and the skills development issues that are implied. It is not meant to be exhaustive. In fact, there are many unanswered questions about interpersonal dynamics when people are no longer in boxes.

The psychological contract has changed in today's organizations. Decreasing loyalty between organization and employee is one factor in this redefinition; greater emphasis on the lateral organization is another. Loyalty to employer required a willingness to put in long hours filling your box, to move between boxes at the will of the employer, and to accept hierarchical decisions without question. In return, employees anticipated a career with the company. As the conditions that fostered this two-way loyalty have changed, the requirements for successful performance in an organization have escalated. Strong commitments to one's work and to co-workers are requisite for successful performance in the lateral organization. Organizational members can no longer rely on the hierarchy to mediate their work in the organization; teams and team members must rely on each other's initiative and responsibility to coordinate and integrate their work. Establishing the needed levels of interpersonal and task commitment is a challenge of the lateral organization.

Three clusters of factors underpin the ability of people to work collaboratively and laterally: competence (the task capabilities that people bring to the work); cognition (conceptual and learning dynamics); and caring and commitment (the affective relationship to task and people). In the following sections we briefly describe the import of these issues in a lateral organization, mention some of the streams of organizational psychology work that relate to these issues, and raise some of the questions that need to be examined.

Competence

Competence is continual development of underlying skills and abilities. Clearly, in all organizational designs people need to have technical competence. In the lateral organization they need to have a body of knowledge that can be applied to a variety of projects, problems, and opportunities encountered in various teams and roles. Breaking down the barriers between the segments of the organization does not reduce the need for state-of-the-art specialty knowledge. Organizations hire laser physicists, computer specialists, marketers, software engineers, and so on, and expect them to apply these skills to a variety of projects. Especially in its knowledge work components, the lateral organization continues to rely on workers with advanced knowledge, expecting them to be able to apply their expertise to the task at hand and take responsibility for continually updating their learning.

Although technical competence is also critical for task effectiveness in the line and box organization, it takes on additional importance in the lateral organization, where co-workers are dependent on the skills and abilities of one another to perform the collective task. In the hierarchical organization, lack of competence is an issue to be dealt with between the manager and the performer. In the lateral organization, the fates of team members depend on collective results, so failures of competence have direct relevance to co-workers.

In some settings that use self-managing teams, co-workers become integrally involved in developing and certifying each other's skills through cross-training schemes. Here, it is also the responsibility of the team to plan work in a manner that utilizes and keeps current members' skills. So far, however, there is little empirical work about how co-workers go about influencing each others' competence. But it is clear that in the lateral organization a whole host of interpersonal issues will be introduced because employees are dealing directly with these issues.

In some settings, teams have the opportunity to select their members. The mix of skills on a team will likely affect team performance as well as co-worker relations. Should teams be composed of members who are all highly technically competent, or is a mix of skills superior? Not surprisingly, some research evidence suggests that technical competence of group members is positively related to group performance (Hill, 1982; Laughlin, 1980), particularly if members can be assigned to tasks that best utilize their technical skills (Voiers, 1956). The evidence is mixed, however, as to whether groups composed of members similarly high in technical competence perform better than groups that are heterogeneous in ability levels (Jackson, 1992). For example, Tziner and Eden (1985) found that a highly skilled military crew member contributed to performance more when the other members were similarly of high ability. In contrast, in laboratory studies of intellectual tasks, teams composed of members with mixed levels of ability performed better than groups made up of individuals with similarly high levels of ability (Laughlin, Branch, & Johnson, 1969). The impact of skill mixture on relations among co-workers in actual work settings warrants further research.

Lateral organizations expand the notion of job competency. Other skills related to the collective task are important, many for responsibilities that have traditionally been the province of managers. A key skill for co-workers is to plan and set goals together, a process that is ultimately related to team effectiveness (Mohrman et al., 1995). Because part of the planning process is to determine the individual assignments and goals within the team, people find themselves negotiating their tasks and goals with co-workers rather than managers. Most studies of goal setting and planning have been conducted in a hierarchical setting; even studies of participative management have looked at how managers can enact these roles more participatively, not at how they can be conducted laterally. There is almost no information about how these activities occur when they are not hierarchically mediated.

Another key skill contributing to team and business unit effectiveness is knowing and using systematic decision-making processes, in which decisions are data based, costs and benefits are considered, and trade-offs are rigorously made (Mohrman et al., 1995). These processes provide a shared understanding of how decisions are made and a structured approach to collecting and processing input from all relevant contributors. Individuals will have to be willing to approach tasks using strategies and decision processes that enable the work of all contributors to be interpreted and used. At times this requires giving up favorite approaches or a preference just to complete a task alone. Research is needed on how people make the transition from viewing themselves as individual contributors to seeing themselves as part of a collective, and on the relationship issues that emerge when work is so closely intertwined.

Cognition

Cognition is the process of knowing in the broadest sense (Neufeldt & Guralnick, 1988). It includes observation, perception, memory, judgment, and learning. The lateral organization demands intelligence that goes beyond knowledge of a specialty. In order to work with people across organizational interfaces and disciplines, individuals have to develop an understanding of ideas and frameworks different from their own. In a qualitative study of new product development efforts in five firms, Dougherty (1992) identified how organizational innovators were able to transcend their separate disciplinary "thought-worlds" by interacting extensively, learning about each other's perspectives, adopting a customer orientation, and developing a new shared understanding of the product design. Specialty engineers who visit customers, for example, are better prepared to engage in problem solving regarding design trade-offs because they bring a broader perspective to the decisions.

To create value from the synthesis of disparate ideas, cognitive leaps are needed. Perhaps most critical is the ability to learn. Charles Handy (1989) argued that discontinuous change calls for discontinuous thinking, which necessitates learning. Learning involves grappling with questions and problems to be solved. New ideas, theories, and frameworks are generated and tested, reflected on, evaluated, and improved. Ethnographic studies of service technicians (Orr, 1990) and insurance claims processors (Wenger, 1991) found that learning and innovation occurred from interacting with others in a "community of practice." These ethnographic studies are intriguing in their assertion that learning and innovation occur in the process of doing one's work and talking about it with co-workers. Learning may result more from collective informal processes among co-workers than from training classes or review of company manuals (Brown & Duguid, 1991). Research is needed concerning how people working laterally can communicate across their perspectives and worldviews and learn from one another.

Caring and Commitment to Work and Co-Workers

The lateral organization presents a more ambiguous and complex environment where people conduct many transactions and establish direct relationships laterally that were once mediated by management. People are collectively responsible for doing what's necessary for successful task performance. People rely on their co-workers to care about and be committed to each other and to their work.

People who are highly committed to work are personally identified with and engaged in what they do. Who they are as individuals is consistent with what they do in a work setting. Work must have personal meaning in order for commitment to be high. At the highest levels of commitment, people view what they are doing as moral and can express themselves in their work (Etzioni, 1961; Walton, 1980). Little distance exists between a personal sense of self and a work role (Kahn, 1990).

Psychological meaningfulness and a sense of responsibility for the outcomes of one's work have been found to predict internal work motivation (Fried & Ferris, 1986; Wall, Clegg, & Jackson, 1978; Williams & Bunker, 1993). The concept of internal motivation comes from the job characteristics theory of Hackman and Oldham (1976). People with high internal work motivation feel good when they perform well and care about the quality of the product or service they and their team provide. Some data suggest that people with internal work motivation perform better, are more willing to perform "extra-role" tasks (Williams & Bunker, 1993), and are more likely to innovate and solve problems (Amabile, 1988; Quinn, 1985). Being internally motivated may fuel a willingness to work through difficult lateral transactions in order to determine the best course of action.

In ethnographic studies of counselors at a summer camp and members of an architectural firm, Kahn (1990) found that personal engagement was related to deriving a sense of meaning from work. Both characteristics depended on interpersonal relationships with co-workers. Meaningful co-worker interactions involved both personal and professional elements and a connection to people's emotional lives. These interactions fostered a sense of worth, self-appreciation, personal dignity, and mutuality. Commitment to work went hand in hand with commitment to co-workers.

Katzenbach and Smith (1993) found that members of high-performing teams develop a commitment and dedication to each other as well as to the purpose of the team. Members of several teams stated in interviews that they genuinely enjoyed each other's company, had fun together, and supported and relied on one another. In our qualitative study of new product development at a high-technology firm (Cohen, Mohrman, Mohrman, & Feyerherm, 1992), many team members from the more successful teams reported that they had worked together on previous projects and knew each other well. They claimed that their familiarity with one another helped them to work together more effectively.

There has been a long history of research regarding group cohesiveness—that is, the degree to which members of a group are attracted to other members and are motivated to stay in the group (Organ & Hammer, 1950). Many (but not all) studies have found group cohesiveness to be positively related to performance outcomes (Evans & Dion, 1991), including job satisfaction and organizational productivity (Summers, Coffelt, & Horton, 1988). Some of the earliest studies found cohesiveness and performance to be related, but the direction of the relationship depended on whether group norms supported high or low productivity (Seashore, 1954; Schachter, Ellerston, McBride, & Gregory, 1951). The relationship between cohesiveness and performance may be mediated by several contingencies (Guzzo & Shea, 1992).

Although there have been few empirical studies, some psychologists have argued that cohesive groups are more likely to be innovative because they provide psychological safety for their members, which enables them to deal with uncertainty in a more creative way (Dailey, 1979; Nystrom, 1979; West & Farr, 1989). On the other hand, one factor that leads to group cohesiveness, homogeneity of membership, has been found to restrict creativity and innovation (Jackson, 1992). In a study of innovation in primary health care teams, West and Wallace (1991) found that team innovation was predicted by tolerance of diversity, team cohesiveness, and team commitment.

Caring about co-workers may require a willingness to deal with difficult, emotional issues. Personal and professional differences will at times lead to disagreements that need to be openly discussed and resolved. Strong feelings may be expressed, including anger. If an emotional bond exists among co-workers, anger may be viewed as providing the emotional energy to confront differences. Dealing with the emotions that may arise in the process of doing collaborative work can strengthen co-worker relationships (Tsovold, 1991). Research is needed that explores the "emotional work" that takes place in teams and its impact on relationships and performance.

Caring and commitment of co-workers implies mutual respect and trust. When the chips are down, can an individual rely on co-workers? Will people do what they say? Will co-workers put the collective interest ahead of separate interests? Mutual respect is built from believing in one another's competence and sharing values. Mishra (1993) conceptualized mutual trust as consisting of competence, openness, caring, and reliability; he found that mutual trust within a top management team and between customers and suppliers was positively related to collaboration during a crisis situation. Trust develops through working together for mutual benefit (Tsovold, 1992).

The depth of relationship being described goes beyond people's typically superficial involvements at work. It is not effective for managers to exhort employees to care for and be committed to their peers. It cannot be a direct result of team-building or training. Although team-building can help co-workers to have an initial appreciation of each other or a better understanding of personal differences, team-building does not create this type of deep bond. Although training events can foster interpersonal sharing, they alone cannot create relatedness. This depth of relationship among co-workers emerges at least in part through a history of shared experiences in the pursuit of common goals. It takes time to develop. Working effectively with co-workers requires moving beyond individualism and anxiety to partnership and mutual trust. Certain skills make it more likely that an individual can make this journey.

Interpersonal Skills

Interpersonal skills are a necessity. An individual needs to be able to communicate with others, listen to others, influence others, and so forth. Collaboration requires effective communication.

Negotiation and conflict-resolution skills are at the heart of what is required to work collaboratively. People may conflict about

goals, methods, task assignments, evaluations, workloads, responsibilities, feedback, and rewards. People with conflict-resolution
skills know how to deal openly with their frustrations and grievances, listen and understand others' feelings and complaints, work
for solutions that are mutually advantageous, and reach agreements (Van Berklom & Tsovold, 1981). Conflict resolution among
co-workers was related to a team's ability to make improvements
(Mohrman et al., 1995).

Conflicts among co-workers are more likely to occur in the lateral organization, because people from different functions, disciplines, departments, and personal backgrounds view their worlds
in dissimilar ways. Dougherty (1992) documented the different
thought-worlds of research and development, sales, manufacturing, and marketing participants in new product development
projects. They viewed uncertainty, critical issues, and the development process itself in qualitatively different ways. These differences
may lead to conflict, but dealing with and resolving these conflicts
can lead to innovation.

Innovation theorists (Kanter, 1985; Pinchot, 1985) have argued
that resolving conflicts across functional and disciplinary boundaries
enables innovation by permitting different perspectives to be combined in novel ways and allowing multiple aspects of complex problems to be addressed simultaneously. In our qualitative study of new
product development we found cyclical processes of divergence and
convergence to be critical to perceived project effectiveness. Early
in a project phase, it was critical that divergent information from all
relevant functions or disciplines be brought up and evaluated. Then
it was important that participants converge on or reach a shared
agreement as to the output and method for that phase (Cohen et
al., 1992). Achieving convergence required a mechanism to resolve
the conflicts that emerged when differences surfaced.

In addition, changing demographic patterns mean that people
collaborate with those of different age, race, ethnicity, nationality,
and gender. People from different demographic groups are socialized to exhibit behaviors "appropriate" to their group identities,
and to respond differentially to members of varying demographic
groups (Maccoby & Jacklin, 1974; Jacklin, 1989). These differences
in behaviors and responses to others may create conflict or simply
interpersonal distance that prevents people from collaboration.

Being able to discuss constructively and resolve these issues may lead to improved effectiveness. Resolving the conflicts associated with differences in backgrounds becomes a strategic business imperative (Copeland, 1988; DeLuca & McDowell, 1992; Jackson, May, & Whitney, 1995).

The Challenge

Effective collaboration requires more than interpersonal and task-related skills. It implies a commitment to work and to co-workers— a willingness to exert effort to accomplish what the people in your work network need from you in order for the collective work to go forward. It is a process that typically takes time to develop. However, a scarce resource in the lateral organization is time. Many linkages among co-workers are temporary. Many teams are in existence for short periods of time. Many projects have life cycles of weeks. Co-workers in these efforts will not have the opportunity to develop this deeper understanding and commitment to one another unless they have a previous experience of working together What, if anything, can be done to substitute for depth of relationship with co-workers?

There may not be any substitute. However, people who have sufficient interpersonal skills, conflict-resolution skills, and task-related skills have an advantage for working effectively with co-workers. In addition, the use of agreed-on shared systematic decision-making processes can expedite task-focused interactions. These skills can help co-workers to focus on their task and begin a process of learning to relate to one another. Much more applied work needs to be done to develop and validate approaches to inter-personal skills attainment and to develop systematic processes and tools for conducting collaborative work.

What is being described involves responding to increased relationship and task demands. Success in the lateral organization depends on deeper relationships with co-workers and a deeper relationship to work. In order to coordinate and integrate effectively with others, people must rely on each other's task competence, cognitive abilities, caring, and commitment about their work and each other. This is a tall order.

The attachment to work and to co-workers needs to occur without expectations of organizational loyalty and career security. In the downsized and flattened organizational environment, traditional career advancement and security cannot be promised. Although individuals may have the opportunity to learn new skills and to work in new areas, vertical movement is limited. Whether competition among peers will diminish or increase is unknown. Fewer vertical opportunities may create more competition. On the other hand, greater lateral opportunities combined with mutual reliance and closeness among co-workers may reduce peer competition. The impact of the changing shape of the organization on collaborative behavior warrants research.

Out of the Box: The Special Case of Managers

Relationships between employees and managers dramatically change in the lateral organization. In the old box and line organization, both managers and employees were in their "boxes" and there was a simple one-to-one relationship between them. In the lateral organization, people relate to a complex array of "bosses," including those to whom they report and those in quasi-managerial roles without hierarchical authority, such as team leaders and facilitators. The distinction between individual contributors and managers is no longer clear, and roles shift depending on organizational needs. The managerial function is performed both by individuals and by management teams, and employees rely on the direction provided by teams. Managers work closely with other managers from different functions and disciplines. These changes are profound and dramatically affect the relationships between managers and employees and among managers.

Although there have been thousands of studies pertaining to management and leadership and possibly hundreds of theories, few pertain to the dynamics found in the new organization. Most leadership research is concerned with leadership effectiveness and not with the impact of leadership on the relationships and dynamics among people. For example, recent work has emphasized that leaders and managers need to do more to build employee commitment and to rely less on compliance and control (Bennis & Nanus, 1985; Kotter, 1982; Lawler, 1992; Walton, 1985). As an example of this stream of work, Bennis and Nanus (1985) described how effective leaders manage people's attention through establishing a vision, creating meaning through communication, and developing trust. This work describes what leaders do, but it does not deal with the impact of the change in leadership behaviors on the relationships between managers and employees.

In this section, we describe the changing roles and relationships for managers in the lateral, team-based organization. First we focus on the vertical dimension, the relationships between managers and employees. Then we examine the horizontal dimension, the lateral roles and relations among managers. We describe key aspects of changing managerial roles, identify major issues, and briefly summarize some streams of leadership research that relate to these issues.

Relations Between Managers and Employees

Everyone in a lateral organization will undergo a learning process as the roles of managers and employees shift. For employees accustomed to one vertical reporting relationship, this shift can be traumatic initially. Many people will at times assume managerial roles, and reporting to more than one managerial actor will not be uncommon.

Multiple Reporting Relationships

In the team-based organization, people may report to more than one manager. An individual on a project team may report to a project manager but get technical supervision from a functional manager, or report to a functional manager, but get day-to-day direction from a project manager. An individual may report to both a functional and project manager as in a matrix organization. The dual reporting relationship found in the matrix organization is relatively simple, however, when compared to the potential complexities of reporting in the lateral organization. A person may report to a management team in addition to or instead of reporting to an individual manager. Individuals may not be physically colocated with their managers. For example, a marketer on a cross-functional project team may report to a marketing functional manager about marketing concerns and report to a cross-functional business strategy team about a project whose members are in several locations. Teams may report to other teams without individual reporting relationships being defined.

Multiple reporting relationships and team-based hierarchies change the relationship between individuals and the organization's authority structure. Employees, as individuals and in teams, need to be more self-managing, making decisions about how to do things as they go about their work. Reporting relationships are likely to be conflictual, with individuals needing to negotiate expectations and priorities with multiple managers and with management teams. Managers have subordinates who take direction from multiple sources and need to work laterally to negotiate priorities with their peers. The key question raised is this: What impact do multiple reporting relationships have on the dynamics between managers and employees?

Quasi-Managerial Roles

Quasi-managerial roles are those in which individuals perform managerial functions but do not have hierarchical authority. These roles are typically established in organizations that have removed a level of management and formed self-managing teams, but still require individuals to perform team leadership and integrating functions. These roles are called by different names in different organizations—for example, team facilitators or team leaders. These labels may be used interchangeably or may reflect a different constellation of duties. Team facilitators may be responsible for leading meetings, making sure the discussions stay on track, and that task assignments are clearly made. They might not even be members of the team. Team leaders may be responsible for internal coordination of work, linkages to key stakeholders, and coaching and developing team members. In addition to their leadership functions, team leaders or facilitators who are team members typically have responsibilities to make technical contributions and do their part of the collective task. Teams may have one designated leadership role or multiple leadership roles shared among members of the team. Sometimes internal team leader roles are established to supplement external team leadership roles. Organizations frequently place former first-level supervisors in team leader roles and expect them to manage in new "empowering" ways. Individuals in these quasi-managerial roles need to influence team members to get things done without being able to rely on hierarchical authority. In some cases, team leaders may head groups with some members who have higher rank in the organization than that of the team leader. Team members need to relate and accept direction from peers who lack the legitimacy that derives from organizational rank.

Other quasi-managerial roles involve integrating across teams and components of a business unit. These integrating roles may be performed by individuals or teams. Integrators make decisions that establish the direction, context, and constraints for work teams. People who perform these integrating roles may not have hierarchical authority. They may be from the same level in the organizational hierarchy as the teams and people whose work they are charged with integrating.

Quasi-managerial roles raise the issue of the legitimacy of authority that is not based on a line and box position. In research relevant to this issue, Manz and Sims (1987) conducted a study of leadership of self-managing teams in which there were dual leadership roles. In the manufacturing plant they studied, the external coordinator had reporting authority, but was expected to lead in an empowering way. The internal team leader was in a quasi-managerial role, and worked alongside other team members. From Manz and Sims's perspective, a leader's role is to facilitate the development of employee self-controls so that employees can lead themselves. Interestingly, employees perceived the coordinators as encouraging more self-management than they perceived from team leaders.

Self-managing leadership behaviors were positively correlated with leadership effectiveness of the external leaders in a manufacturing plant (Manz & Sims, 1987), and with team effectiveness and quality of work life in a telephone company (Chang, Cohen, & Ledford, 1994). This perspective is useful for identifying the behavioral repertoire involved in encouraging self-management and specifying what individuals in quasi-managerial roles need to do to influence performance when they cannot rely on hierarchical authority. It also suggests, however, that people who have the legitimacy that comes from hierarchical position will be more likely to provide coaching that encourages self-management, possibly an indication of the difficulty of enacting a quasi-managerial role. This perspective does not address the relationship between team leaders and employees nor deal with the issues involved when former supervisors are asked to be team leaders without hierarchical authority. These issues warrant future research.

Multiple and Dynamic Roles

Traditionally, when people were promoted to management, they no longer were responsible for making direct technical contributions to the business. They may have contributed ideas in the process of supervising technical or professional employees, but they were not given technical or professional assignments. In the flattened, lateral organization, the distinction between the managerial role and professional role has begun to blur. Roles are fluid. A manager may be responsible for managing one project and be a team member for another. Increasingly, managers will be expected to have and apply technical or professional expertise, and technical and professional contributors will be given responsibility for budgets, people, or projects. As Handy (1989) stated, in the organization of the future everyone will have to be a manager, and no one will be able to afford being only a manager. Although this overstates the present reality, many managers have assignments on teams as direct contributors. Subordinates may need to relate to their manager as a peer on one project and as their boss on another. In some situations subordinates may lead teams where their boss is a member. This means that individuals and managers need to negotiate multiple and changing role relationships with one another. These circumstances raise the following question: What is the impact of changing and multiple roles on the relationship between managers and employees?

Research has shed some light on this question by delineating sources of power and relating them to influence attempts. Bass (1960) differentiated between personal power stemming from the attributes of the person and position power stemming from the attributes of the position. Supporting this distinction, Yukl and Falbe (1991) found that personal power was more important than position power as a determinant of task commitment and ratings of managerial effectiveness. French and Raven's (1959) original taxonomy differentiated five sources of power: legitimate, reward, coercive, expert, and referent. Researchers have found support for two additional power sources: agent persuasiveness and control over information. People reported that they were more likely to do things requested by a manager who had legitimate power, expert power, and was persuasive (Yukl & Falbe, 1991).

The implications of this stream of research are intriguing. The new organization, characterized by multiple reporting relationships, changing roles, and quasi-managers, depends more on personal power than position power to get things done. Position is an unstable source of power in today's organizations. Managers who demonstrate the characteristics that we have argued are needed by all employees—competence, cognition, and caring and commitment—are more likely to be able to exert personal influence to get things done. In addition, interpersonal, communication, and conflict-resolution skills are important for persuasiveness. Yet, the picture is mixed. Subordinates still evaluated legitimate power, the power that comes from position and job responsibilities, as critical for influencing them. This suggests that people in quasi-managerial roles and in shifting relationships have an extra burden to carry. Unless the organization defines quasi-managerial roles as legitimate positions, the people in these roles will lack a vital source of power.

Relations Among Managers: Management Teams and Lateral Relationships

Increasingly, teams report to and/or receive direction from management teams in the lateral organization. Management teams are responsible for the coordinated management of teams or other subunits that are interdependent in the accomplishment of a collective output. The team's members are managers with hierarchical authority who typically come from the different functions that need to cooperate to produce a product or service. Managers work laterally with other managers from different functions or disciplines on these teams. They need to build effective working relationships with people whose experiences, values, and viewpoints differ from their own. Individual managers, who may be used to managing their piece of the organization independently, are now dependent on one another for team success. This mutual dependency coexists with diversity. What enables management teams to be effective? What impact does the coexistence of dependency and diversity have on the relationships and dynamics among managers?

Even when formal management teams have not been established, managers still need to work directly with other managers with whom they are interdependent. Effective lateral relationships among managers are critical for success in the new organization.

The research on the nature of managerial work has noted the importance and frequency of lateral interactions (Kanter, 1989; Kotter, 1982; Mintzberg, 1973). The ability of managers to get things done depends on their involvement in informal networks that cut across organizational boundaries (Kanter, 1989). Researchers have identified communication, negotiation, and conflict-resolution skills as critical for lateral integration (Courtright, Fairhurst, & Rogers, 1989; Lax & Sibenius, 1986; Walton, 1987). For example, communication researchers have found that managers who develop effective lateral relations communicate in a way to minimize social distance and status differentials (Fairhurst & Chandler, 1989). Recent work identified five interrelated sets of managerial behavior as contributing to effective lateral integration: relationship-building, proactive agenda development, active listening and sharing of information, "win-win" negotiation strategies, and directly addressing conflict (Steckler & Preston, 1993). The Yukl and Falbe (1991) study found, not surprisingly, that managers had less legitimate and coercive power over peers than over subordinates. Building effective lateral relations depends more on the personal skills and strategies that managers use than the positions they happen to occupy.

Some research has focused on management teams. Working laterally with other managers from different functions or disciplines requires a decision-making process that considers divergent functional perspectives and interests, but forges a consensus based on the needs of the broader business unit. Managers in effective management teams are open to learning, have good problem-solving and conflict-resolution skills, and are willing to use a disciplined approach to decision making (Mohrman et al., 1995). Ancona and Nadler (1989) described management team effectiveness as depending on three key processes: work management, relationship management, and boundary management. They argued that the criticality of each process depends on environmental and structural contingencies. For example, if an organization has high internal coordination requirements and high environmental demands, all three processes are critical.

Members of these teams meet more frequently with one another and with outsiders than do members of management teams confronting less complex environments. Thus they need sophisticated interpersonal, negotiation, and conflict-resolution skills and the capacity to blend action and analysis (Bourgeois & Eisenhardt, 1988). One study found that management team performance varied over time as a function of members' openness to learning, and that capacity depended on the amount of trust among members and with the top executive (Eisenstat & Cohen, 1990). Certainly, the skills and relationships demanded of managers in management teams go beyond what was required in the old line and box organization. In general, research on management teams is in its infancy. More work is needed to understand the internal dynamics of management teams and external relations with key stakeholders.

Out of the Box: New Systems, New Relationships

In the team-based organization, new systems are required to support the new way of doing business. These systems help organizational members enact their new roles, but they also shape relationships between people. In this section we deal very briefly with the impacts of two major systems, performance management and information systems.

Performance Management

Organizations are beginning to implement performance management systems that reflect the new shape of the organization and its emphasis on integration of work, multidirectional influence, and flexible jobs that reflect competencies (Mohrman, Mohrman, & Cohen, 1992; Mohrman, Mohrman, & Lawler, 1992). These include new appraisal systems (peer appraisal; 360-degree systems that collect input from peers, managers, subordinates, and customers; and team appraisals) and new reward systems (skill-based pay; team bonuses; gainsharing; and multilevel rewards based on individual, team, and organization performance). Pay is based on collective performance and/or on appraisals of individual performance that are based in part on peer input. Appraisals and rewards are related to business results to a greater extent than in traditional systems. New relationships between co-workers result from putting them in a common fate pool and making them legitimate stakeholders in the determination of the requirements for each other's work and the judgment of that work. Close bonds and formal relationships result.

A question that arises in organizations undergoing a transition to lateral functioning concerns accountability. When people are let out of their boxes, managers wonder how blame or credit can be attributed, and what it means to hold collectives of people accountable. In the lateral organization, the accountability system is the multiple-level performance management system. This includes the manner in which goals are established and aligned, progress is tracked and fed back, results are measured and performance is assessed, and rewards for performance are given at the individual, group, and/or organizational levels.

When the team performs well, positive outcomes accrue to the members. When it fails to achieve results, the team members are not rewarded, but the consequences may be more serious. If a team is unsuccessful, organizational results are not being achieved. That may have a ripple effect through the organization. The analog of replacing the person in the box is reconstituting the collectives of people who are working together to produce a product or service. This can be initiated by the team itself or externally by managers, whose responsibilities include ensuring that the performing units of the organization are designed for effective performance. Thus individuals will have a compelling reason to learn to work with one another effectively, since their ongoing role in the team depends on the ability of the team collectively to develop its capabilities and accomplish its goals. Managers and team members alike will have to learn to deal with team performance problems.

To become comfortable with the new ways of managing, people will have to develop a different way of thinking about equity in the organization. For this to happen, the organization will have to put systems in place to shape and support this new social definition. Attributions of equity are essentially subjective feelings that have been shaped by experience, primarily in an environment that stresses individual performance and reward. In that context, equity has meant treatment considered commensurate with one's individual talents and performance, both in an absolute sense (personal equity) and in relation to the others in the organization (internal equity) and in other organizations (external equity) (Lawler, 1981). This attribution of equity is a socially constructed meaning.

The new definition of equity that may evolve in a laterally oriented organization will be based on an understanding that the success of the organization depends on the performance of teams and networks of contributors who are collectively responsible for doing what is necessary to achieve results, and a view that equitable assessment of performance and determination of rewards occur at least in part at the collective level, with a focus on results. In studies of organizations implementing team-based structures, high performance was associated with lateral co-worker processes and not with manager processes, but satisfaction was more strongly linked to managers' processes (Mohrman et al., 1995). Feelings of equitable treatment were related to both team-oriented and individual-oriented performance management practices.

Given the gap between the traditional and emerging definitions of equity, it is not surprising early in the transition to team organizations to hear managers express fear of losing excellence if individuals are not rewarded based on their individual performance, and to hear employees express concern about being "dragged down by poor performers." The organizational members have not yet internalized new assumptions: that excellent individual performance helps the organization only if it is integrated into the overall collective performance of the organization in such a way that it impacts results; and that it is the responsibility of the collective of individuals, including the excellent performers, to ensure that the work of all contributors is integrated and that poor performance is addressed. Although there is some research evidence that these new organizational understandings do begin to develop in team organizations, work in this area is rudimentary.

Information and Communication Systems

The lateral organization depends on new information systems to connect people and to analyze and distribute information. Achieving high performance requires increased and more effective use of teams and information systems, and each is necessary to harness the potential of the other (Mankin, Cohen, & Bikson, in press). New computer technology provides the infrastructure for collaboration and changes how co-workers work and relate to one another.

In the new organization, people are generally networked together electronically. They can have access to shared data bases, applications, and each other (Sproull & Kiesler, 1991). People can communicate with one another and work together without having to be physically colocated. Team members in different locations, on different schedules, and working in different organizations may rarely meet, but can still access the same customer data sets, use network software to do financial analyses, and share results on their electronic mail network.

One impact of new information systems on people is a broadening of perspective. When data bases are shared and systems are networked together, people can obtain information from different departments and different levels. People can participate in electronic networks of those with similar interests but often very different backgrounds. Relationships may develop that can be harnessed for goal-directed activities. People can use this medium to send the same message to hundreds of people as simply as sending it to one person. The information people receive is no longer limited to where their box falls on the organizational chart. People may develop an increased understanding of the "big picture" and how their activities relate to it.

Increasingly, software is being developed to expedite and facilitate collaborative work. Analysts describe these groupware products in terms of the environments for group activity (Johansen, 1988), ranging from products designed to augment face-to-face meetings to technology intended to support dispersed people doing collaborative work (different places, different times). Various electronic data bases, writing and editing programs, and group calendars are examples of the latter. The use of groupware programs changes interactions among co-workers. Because groupware is relatively new and continuing to develop, little systematic research has been done on its impact on co-worker relations.

Some research has suggested that computer-mediated communication reduces status differences (Sproull & Kiesler, 1991). People pay less attention to organizational rank, demographic features, and appearance when they receive electronic mail or share information using groupware programs (McGuire, Kiesler, & Siegel, 1987; Zuboff, 1988). People pay more attention to the substantive value of a contribution when they are not distracted by status or appearance. Computer-mediated communication helps keep decision making based on task expertise (Bikson & Eveland, 1990) and calls for high levels of competence. People may build reputations on the quality of their contributions and their helpfulness to others.

Thus network technology expedites connectedness and commitment among co-workers. It also can facilitate empowerment. Information that was available only to executives in the old organization may be distributed broadly. People may access data sets about customers, markets, financial projections, and so on, that enable decision making to be distributed throughout the network. Information technology helps individuals and teams make decisions at the point of action.

Of course, there are downsides. Just about anyone who is connected to others through electronic mail, voice mail, and fax machines complains about the number of messages to read, hear, and respond to. If information is disseminated widely with little thought to its utility, receivers' time will be wasted in reading and responding to it. Five minutes of time spent by each of three hundred individuals can be quite costly to an organization. Information overload can strain the capacity of employees to get work done. People also tend to be less polite when they communicate with others electronically. Messages can be blunt and aggressive and undermine collaboration (Sproull & Kiesler, 1991). New barriers can develop between "information haves" and "information have-nots," and these can severely curtail cooperativeness among people who need to work together. Finally, computer technology can be used to disempower and deskill. Computers can extend the capability of managers to monitor individual activities and can reduce individual or workgroup discretion (Zuboff, 1988).

Despite these potential downsides, the major impact of computer technology has been to enhance connectedness, collaboration, empowerment, and integration in the lateral organization. Adequacy of computer systems and their ability to connect people influence team effectiveness (Mohrman et al., 1995). They help people to coordinate effectively across functional, hierarchical and discipline-based organizational boundaries. Information technology can be a powerful tool for collaboration. Much more research is required, however, to fully understand its influence on relations between people in the organization.

New Frontiers for Organizational Research

Organizations are moving toward this new reality in fits and starts to be sure, but they are beginning to let people out of the box. Practice is far outstripping the capacity of theory and research to provide it with solid underpinnings. Organizations are providing potentially rich laboratories in which to develop and test badly needed theories and applications. The central concern is to learn what happens to people when the focus in the organization moves away from lines and boxes to connections.

Until recently, most research about the effectiveness of human resource systems has been conducted in and/or to support the line and box organization. Predominant topics have included job design, dyadic boss-subordinate relationships, the impact of various pay schemes on individual performance, validation of selection and placement techniques for jobs (boxes), and individual appraisal systems. Furthermore, exploration of theoretical issues such as motivation has been predominantly in settings where individual performance is the focus and hierarchy the context. Even team research, though clearly in the arena of the lateral organization, has often examined the effectiveness and building of teams within line and box organizations.

There are some pockets of research that have focused explicitly on theory and practice to support the lateral organization. For example, research on the effectiveness of skill-based pay (Gupta, Ledford, Jenkins, & Doty, 1992) and gainsharing (Graham-Moore & Ross, 1990) has produced knowledge about the effectiveness of these approaches and the conditions that impact their success. Leading effective teams has lately received much attention. Research on teams, including self-managing, cross-functional project, and process management teams, has increased and is occurring more frequently in organizations that are purposefully moving toward a more lateral logic. Furthermore, organizational research is beginning to come to grips with the levels-of-analysis issue, providing a methodological base for examining individual, group, and organization-level phenomena and their relationships (Rousseau, 1985).

Much remains to be learned if organizational psychology and personnel research are to provide solid knowledge for understanding and guiding the connected organization. In the following sections we briefly describe a few of the theoretical and human resource systems issues that need to be explored.

Theoretical Issues

A number of theoretical issues arise in the lateral organization. These include peer and managerial relationships and roles, the development of new kinds of cognitive learning to support collaborative work, and the effective application of information technology to facilitate and mediate collaborative work.

Team-based organizations place far greater demands on relationships at work than does the line and box organization. With co-worker interactions no longer mediated by management and demands for collective accountability high, attachment to co-workers and the exchange of emotion intensify. Will co-workers be able and willing to do the affective work necessary to collaborate effectively with their peers, or with their managers? Will closer attachments to co-workers help or get in the way of achieving performance results? The lateral organization requires people to manage multiple relationships and serve on multiple teams. Can workers effectively deal with multiple affective relationships at work? What about burnout? Can organizations help employees deal with the affective dimensions of work? Should they? We are at the very beginning of understanding how relationships are changing and what their impact will be on people and work.

Leadership and management issues pose particularly large challenges in the lateral organization. A promising stream of research is work on power and influence. Subordinates and peers are more influenced by a manager's personal power than his or her position power. This work should be extended to look at the impact of changing and multiple roles. For example, do sources of power shift when managers take on professional roles and vice versa? When first-level supervisors are placed in team leader roles, has their source of power changed? What replaces position in an organizational hierarchy as a source of legitimacy? What behaviors will enable managers and subordinates to develop effective collaborative relations when they are working together as peers on projects? What is the impact of functional diversity on the dynamics in management teams? This list of questions could be much longer because much remains to be learned.

Information technology has dramatically changed the way people communicate and connect with one another, eliminating barriers to information exchange based on geography, structure, hierarchy, and organization. Social relations change, power becomes more diffuse, and status differences diminish on the electronic network. We do not yet know how to set up the working arrangements that fully take advantage of the capabilities offered by groupware and electronic networking. We also are just beginning to understand how relationships change when they are mediated electronically, and what can be done to build effective communities along the information highway.

The lateral organization poses learning and development challenges unparalleled in the line and box organization. As collectives of individuals are increasingly expected to process complex, multidimensional information and make complicated trade-offs, a premium will be placed on ability to handle ambiguity and complexity. Can these cognitive capabilities be developed? In individuals? In teams? Teams may need instrumented approaches like those provided by simulations and other forms of artificial intelligence to assist in collective, cross-discipline decision making (for example, Boland & Tenkasi, 1993). Organizations may require career paths that systematically expand cognition. How do these approaches affect the ability of team members to collaborate?

Team-based organizations require the development of team skills but also of teams. The challenge is to develop team capabilities that transcend particular teams, such as by training people in shared, systematic team processes that enable them to be "anchored" as they go between teams. An issue to be examined is whether team commitment and trust is team specific or whether it can be developed as an organizational characteristic that transcends teams.

Human Resource Systems

There are several areas where human resource practices need to be informed by more robust theory and supporting research. A few are highlighted here. The first concerns motivation and compensation theory. One key issue concerns levels of analysis: we need to know more about what motivates *collective* performance. The more people's fates are linked together, the more important this question becomes. If rewards are applied at multiple levels of analysis, are they complementary, or do they work at cross-purposes? When business performance is the result of collective performance, what role do individual rewards play in promoting collective performance? Do team rewards stifle individual excellence? Do individual rewards undermine the trust and collaboration required for lateral interaction?

Peer and multiple-stakeholder review processes are another fruitful area for investigation. How do individuals and teams process conflicting feedback and make sense of conflicting expectations from different stakeholders? What is the impact of peer review on team performance and on the trust and commitment between team members? What dynamic is established when team members negotiate their goals with members rather than managers? Under what conditions are these goals viewed as legitimate?

A number of human resource systems need to be developed to support lateral functioning. For example, organizations must find a classification system to replace job grading systems that conformed to the hierarchy. Skill-based pay systems offer a glimpse into the principles of such a system, but the application of these principles organizationwide remains a challenge. Systems to forecast skill needs and inventory current skills and development needs for a laterally oriented organization remain rudimentary. This system will determine opportunity and whether people feel that they are in competition with each other for scarce developmental/advancement opportunities. Ultimately, these issues will in part define the sense of equity and opportunity in the organization.

Perhaps the biggest challenge is to develop a selection system for composing teams rather than filling jobs. What issues of team composition affect the ability of the team to collaborate? What kind of job experiences build the capability of people to collaborate cross-functionally, and how extensive should the development of cross-functional backgrounds be? What issues of selection and evaluation validity exist in the new organization, and what safeguards for equality of opportunity are required? What difference does it make if team members select team members? Many of these issues have not yet been conceptualized in a systematic fashion.

Conclusion

Organizations that are built to emphasize connections between people rather than divisions between them yield new ways of operating and new relations among their members. Employees come out of the boxes and are much less influenced by the lines that have been the core structural concepts of traditional hierarchical organizations.

Connections between co-workers increase radically through the use of teams, collective accountability mechanisms, and information systems that tie people of all levels and locations together. In the new organization, people are forced to count on each other, highlighting the importance of competence, cognition, caring, and commitment for effective performance. Managers become co-workers, and co-workers become managers. Management as well as the core transformation processes of the organization become collective processes.

The new organization is one where people sink or swim together. It is a frontier, but not one of rugged individualism. Rather, it requires community and collective risk taking. Organizational members constitute a learning community, puzzling through their new landscape, designing it as they go, and collaborating in dealing with the task and social aspects of the changes they are experiencing. Co-workers with a direct line of sight to organizational performance and possibly to its survival relate differently, using different skills and tools, to one another.

There are many areas in which theory and research lag behind practice, and where theoretical development is required to underpin new organizational systems. The challenges facing organizational psychology are daunting and exhilarating. Methodological advances and an understanding of the new organizational landscape will help in the investigation of what happens when people get out of their boxes.

References

Amabile, T. M. (1988). A model of creativity and innovation in organizations. In B. M. Staw & L. L. Cummings (Eds.), *Research in organizational behavior* (Vol. 10). Greenwich, CT: JAI Press.

Ancona, D. G., & Nadler, D. A. (1989). Top hats and executive tales: Designing the senior team. *Sloan Management Review, 31*(1), 19–28.

Bass, B. M. (1960). *Leadership, psychology, and organizational behavior.* New York: Harper.

Benne, K. D. (1964). From polarization to paradox. In L. P. Bradford, J. R. Gibb, & K. D. Benne (Eds.), *T-group theory and laboratory method.* New York: Wiley.

Bennis, W., & Nanus, B. (1985). *Leaders: The strategies for taking charge.* New York: Harper.

Bennis, W. G., & Shepard, H. A. (1956). A theory of group development. *Human Relations, 9,* 415–437.

Bikson, T., & Eveland, J. D. (1990). The interplay of work group structures and computer support. In J. Galegher, R. E. Kraut, & C. Egido (Eds.), *Intellectual teamwork: Social and technological foundations of cooperative work.* Hillsdale, NJ: Erlbaum.

Bion, W. R. (1961). *Experiences in groups.* New York: Basic Books.

Boland, R., & Tenkasi, R. (1993). *Perspective making and perspective taking in communities of knowing.* Unpublished manuscript, Center for Effective Organizations, University of Southern California, Los Angeles.

Bourgeois, L. J., & Eisenhardt, K. M. (1988). Strategic decision processes in high velocity environments: Four cases in the microcomputer industry. *Management Science, 34,* 816–835.

Brown, J. S., & Duguid, P. (1991). Organizational learning and communities-of-practice: Toward a unified view of working, learning, and innovation. *Organizational Science, 2*(1), 40–57.

Chang, L., Cohen, S. G., & Ledford, G. E., Jr. (1994). *A hierarchical construct of self-management leadership and its relationship to quality of work life and perceived work group effectiveness* (Tech. Rep. No. 94–6 [249]). Los Angeles: Center for Effective Organizations, University of Southern California.

Cohen, S. G. (1994). Designing effective self-managing work teams. In *Advances in interdisciplinary studies of work teams: Vol. 1. Series on self-managed work teams.* Greenwich, CT: JAI Press.

Cohen, S. G., Mohrman, S. A., Mohrman, A. M., & Feyerherm, A. (1992, June). *Integration in new product development: Managing the convergence/divergence cycle.* Paper presented at the meeting of the Western Academy of Management, Leuven, Belgium.

Copeland, L. (1988). Valuing diversity, Part 1: Making the most of cultural differences in the workplace. *Personnel, 65,* 52–60.

Courtright, J. A., Fairhurst, G. T., & Rogers, L. E. (1989). Interaction patterns in organic and mechanistic systems. *Academy of Management Journal, 32,* 773–802.

Dailey, R. C. (1979). Group, task and personality correlates of boundary-spanning activities. *Human Relations, 32,* 273–285.

DeLuca, J. M., & McDowell, R. N. (1992). Managing diversity: A strategic "grass-roots" approach. In S. E. Jackson & Associates, *Diversity in the workplace: Human resources initiatives.* New York: Guilford Press.

Deming, W. E. (1986). *Out of crisis.* Cambridge, MA: MIT Press.

Dougherty, D. (1992). Interpretive barriers to successful product innovation in large firms. *Organization Science, 3*(2), 179–202.

Dyer, W. G. (1987). *Team building: Issues and alternatives* (2nd ed.). Reading, MA: Addison-Wesley.

Eisenstat, R. A., & Cohen, S. G. (1990). Summary: Top management groups. In J. R. Hackman (Ed.), *Groups that work (and those that don't): Creating conditions for effective teamwork.* San Francisco: Jossey-Bass.

Etzioni, A. A. (1961). *A comparative analysis of complex organizations.* New York: Free Press.

Evans, C. R., & Dion, K. L. (1991). Group cohesion and performance: A meta-analysis. *Small Group Research, 22,* 175–186.

Fairhurst, G. T., & Chandler, T. A. (1989). Social structure in leader-member interaction. *Communication Monographs, 56*(3), 215–239.

French, J. R., & Raven, B. (1959). The bases of social power. In D. Cartwright & A. Zander (Eds.), *Group dynamics.* New York: Harper.

Freud, S. (1922). *Group psychology and the analysis of the ego.* London: International Psychoanalytical Press.

Fried, Y., & Ferris, G. R. (1986). The dimensionality of job characteristics: Some neglected issues. *Journal of Applied Psychology, 71,* 419–426.

Galbraith, J. R. (1994). *Competing with flexible lateral organizations* (2nd ed.). Reading, MA: Addison-Wesley.

Galbraith, J. R., Lawler, E. E., III, & Associates. (1993). *Organizing for the future: The new logic for managing complex organizations.* San Francisco: Jossey-Bass.

Gibbard, G. S. (1974). Individuation, fusion and role specialization. In G. S. Gibbard, J. J. Hartman, & R. D. Mann (Eds.), *Analysis of groups: Contributions to theory, research, and practice.* San Francisco: Jossey-Bass.

Graham-Moore, B., & Ross, T. L. (1990). *Gainsharing: Plans for improving performance.* Washington, DC: BNA.

Gupta, N., Ledford, G. E., Jenkins, G. D., Jr., & Doty, D. H. (1992). Survey-based prescriptions for skill-based pay. *ACA Journal, 1*(1), 50–61.

Guzzo, R. A., & Shea, G. P. (1992). Group performance and intergroup relations in organizations. In M. D. Dunnette & L. M. Hough (Eds.),

Handbook of industrial and organizational psychology (2nd ed., Vol. 3). Palo Alto, CA: Consulting Psychologists Press.

Hackman, J. R. (1987). The design of work teams. In J. W. Lorsh (Ed.), *Handbook of organizational behavior.* Englewood Cliffs, NJ: Prentice Hall.

Hackman, J. R., & Associates. (1990). *Groups that work (and those that don't): Creating conditions for effective teamwork.* San Francisco: Jossey-Bass.

Hackman, J. R., & Oldham, G. R. (1976). Motivation through the design of work: Test of a theory. *Organizational behavior and human performance, 16,* 250–279.

Hammer, M., & Champy, J. (1993). *Reengineering the corporation.* New York: Harper.

Handy, C. (1989). *The age of unreason.* Cambridge, MA: Harvard Business School Press.

Hill, M. (1982). Groups versus individual performance. Are $N + 1$ heads better than one? *Psychological Bulletin, 91,* 517–539.

Jacklin, C. N. (1989). Female and male: Issues of gender. *American Psychologist, 44,* 127–133.

Jackson, S. E. (1992). Team composition in organizational settings: Issues in managing an increasingly diverse work force. In S. Worchel, W. Wood, & J. A. Simpson (Eds.), *Group process and productivity.* Newbury Park, CA: Sage.

Jackson, S. E., May, K. E., & Whitney, K. (1995). Understanding the dynamics of diversity in decision-making teams. In R. A. Guzzo & E. Salas (Eds.), *Team decision-making effectiveness in organizations.* San Francisco: Jossey-Bass.

Jenkins, G. D., Jr., Ledford, G. E., Jr., Gupta, N., & Doty, D. H. (1992). *Skill-based pay practices, payoffs, pitfalls, and prospects.* Scottsdale, AZ: American Compensation Association.

Johansen, R. (1988). *Groupware: Computer support for business teams.* New York: Free Press.

Juran, J. M. (1989). *Juran on leadership for quality.* New York: Free Press.

Kahn, W. A. (1990). Psychological conditions of personal engagement and disengagement at work. *Academy of Management Journal, 33*(4), 692–724.

Kanter, R. M. (1985). *Change masters: Innovation for productivity in the American workplace.* New York: Simon & Schuster.

Kanter, R. M. (1989). The new managerial work. *Harvard Business Review, 67*(6), 85–92.

Katzenbach, J. R., & Smith, D. K. (1993). *The wisdom of teams: Creating the high-performance organization.* Cambridge, MA: Harvard Business School Press.

Kotter, J. P. (1982). *The general managers.* New York: Free Press.

Laughlin, P. R. (1980). Social combination processes of cooperative problem-solving groups on verbal intellective tasks. In M. Fishbein (Ed.), *Progress in social psychology* (Vol. 1). Hillsdale, NJ: Erlbaum.

Laughlin, P. R., Branch, L. G., & Johnson, H. H. (1969). Individual versus triadic performance on a unidimensional complementary task as a function of initial ability level. *Journal of Personality and Social Psychology, 12,* 144–150.

Lawler, E. E., III. (1981). *Pay and organization development.* Reading, MA: Addison-Wesley.

Lawler, E. E., III. (1986). *High-involvement management: Participative strategies for improving organizational performance.* San Francisco: Jossey-Bass.

Lawler, E. E., III. (1987). The new plant revolution. *Organizational Dynamics, 6*(3), 2–12.

Lawler, E. E., III. (1990). *Strategic pay: Aligning organizational strategies and pay systems.* San Francisco: Jossey-Bass.

Lawler, E. E., III. (1992). *The ultimate advantage: Creating the high-involvement organization.* San Francisco: Jossey-Bass.

Lawler, E. E., III, & Mohrman, S. A. (1985). Quality circles after the fad. *Harvard Business Review, 63*(1), 64–76.

Lawler, E. E., III, & Mohrman, S. A. (1987). Quality circles: After the honeymoon. *Organizational Dynamics, 15*(4), 42–55.

Lax, D. A., & Sibenius, J. K. (1986). *The manager as negotiator: Bargaining for cooperation and competitive gain.* New York: Free Press.

Ledford, G. E., Lawler, E. E., III, & Mohrman, S. A. (1988). The quality circle and its variations. In J. P. Campbell, R. J. Campbell, & Associates, *Productivity in organizations: New perspectives from industrial and organizational psychology.* San Francisco: Jossey-Bass.

Maccoby, E. E., & Jacklin, C. N. (1974). *The psychology of sex differences.* Stanford, CA: Stanford University Press.

McGuire, T., Kiesler, S., & Siegel, J. (1987). Group and computer-mediated discussion effects in risk decision making. *Journal of Personality and Social Psychology, 52*(5), 917–930.

Mankin, D., Cohen, S. G., & Bikson, T. K. (in press). *Teams and new technology: Developing information systems for collaborative work.* Cambridge, MA: Harvard Business School Press.

Manz, C. C., & Sims, H. P. (1987). Leading workers to lead themselves: The external leadership of self-managing work teams. *Administrative Science Quarterly, 32,* 106–128.

Mintzberg, H. (1973). *The nature of managerial work.* New York: Harper.

Mishra, A. K. (1993, August). *Breaking down organizational boundaries during crisis: The role of mutual trust.* Paper presented at the meeting of the Academy of Management, Atlanta.

Mohrman, A. M., Mohrman, S. A., & Lawler, E. E., III. (1992). The performance management of teams. In W. Bruns (Ed.), *Performance measurement, evaluation, and incentives.* Cambridge, MA: Harvard Business School Press.

Mohrman, A. M., Resnick-West, S. M., & Lawler, E. E., III. (1989). *Designing performance appraisal systems: Aligning appraisals and organizational realities.* San Francisco: Jossey-Bass.

Mohrman, S. A. (1995). Designing work teams. In H. Risher & C. Fay (Eds.), *Enhancing workplace effectiveness.* San Francisco: Jossey-Bass.

Mohrman, S. A., Cohen, S. G., & Mohrman, A. M. (1995). *Designing team-based organizations: New forms for knowledge work.* San Francisco: Jossey-Bass.

Mohrman, S. A., Mohrman, A. M., & Cohen, S. G. (1992). Human resources strategies for lateral integration in high technology settings. In L. R. Gomez & M. W. Lawless (Eds.), *Advances in global high-technology management: Human resource strategy in high technology* (Vol. 1). Greenwich, CT: JAI Press.

Nadler, D., Gerstein, M. S., & Shaw, R. B. (1992). *Organizational architecture: Designs for changing organizations.* San Francisco: Jossey-Bass.

Neufeldt, V., & Guralnick, D. B. (Eds.). (1988). *Webster's New World dictionary of American English* (3rd coll. ed.). New York: Simon & Schuster.

Nystrom, H. (1979). *Creativity and innovation.* London: Wiley.

Organ, D., & Hammer, W. C. (1950). *Organizational behavior.* Plano, TX: Business Publications.

Orr, J. (1990). Sharing knowledge, celebrating identity: War stories and community memory in a service culture. In D. S. Middleton & D. Edwards (Eds.), *Collective remembering: Memory in society.* Newbury Park, CA: Sage.

Pinchot, G., III. (1985). *Intrapreneuring.* New York: Harper.

Quinn, J. B. (1985, May–June). Managing innovation: Controlled chaos. *Harvard Business Review,* pp. 73–84.

Rousseau, D. M. (1985). Issues of level in organizational research: Multi-level and cross-level perspectives. In L. L. Cummings & B. M. Staw (Eds.), *Research in organizational behavior* (Vol. 7). Greenwich, CT: JAI Press.

Rummler, G. A., & Brache, A. P. (1990). *Improving performance: How to manage the white space on the organization chart.* San Francisco: Jossey-Bass.

Schachter, S., Ellerston, N., McBride, D., & Gregory, D. (1951). An experimental study of cohesiveness and productivity. *Human Relations, 4,* 229–238.

Schermer, V. L. (1985). Beyond Bion: The basic assumption states revisited. In M. Pines (Ed.), *Bion and group psychotherapy.* New York: Routledge.

Seashore, S. E. (1954). *Group cohesiveness in the industrial work group.* Ann Arbor: University of Michigan Press.

Slater, P. E. (1966). *Microcosms.* New York: Wiley.

Smith, K. E., & Berg, D. N. (1987). *Paradoxes of group life: Understanding conflict, paralysis, and movement in group dynamics.* San Francisco: Jossey-Bass.

Sproull, L., & Kiesler, S. (1991). *Connections: New ways of working in the networked organization.* Cambridge, MA: MIT Press.

Steckler, N., & Preston, D. (1993, August). *Middle managers and lateral integration in the boundaryless organization.* Paper presented at the meeting of the Academy of Management, Atlanta.

Summers, I., Coffelt, T., & Horton, R. E. (1988). Work-group cohesion. *Psychological Reports, 63,* 627–636.

Teel, K. S. (1980). Performance appraisal: Current trends, persistent progress. *Personnel Journal, 59*(4), 296–316.

Tsovold, D. (1991). *The conflict-positive organization: Stimulate diversity and create unity.* Reading, MA: Addison-Wesley.

Tsovold, D. (1992). *Team organization: An enduring competitive advantage.* Chichester, England: Wiley.

Tziner, A., & Eden, D. (1985). Effects of crew composition on crew performance: Does the whole equal the sum of its parts? *Journal of Applied Psychology, 70,* 85–93.

Van Berklom, M., & Tsovold, D. (1981). The effects of social context on engaging in controversy. *Journal of Psychology, 107,* 141–145.

Voiers, W. D. (1956). *Bombing accuracy as a function of the ground-school proficiency structure of the B-29 bomb team* (Research report AFDTRC-TN-56–4). Lackland Air Force Base, TX: Air Force Personnel and Training Research Center.

Wall, T. D., Clegg, C. W., & Jackson, P. R. (1978). An evaluation of the job characteristics model. *Journal of Occupational Psychology, 51,* 183–196.

Walton, R. E. (1980). Establishing and maintaining high commitment work systems. In J. R. Kimberly, R. H. Miles, & Associates, *The organizational life cycle: Issues in the creation, transformation, and decline of organizations.* San Francisco: Jossey-Bass.

Walton, R. E. (1985). From control to commitment in the workplace. *Harvard Business Review, 63*(2), 77–84.

Walton, R. E. (1987). *Managing conflict: Interpersonal dialogue and third-party roles.* Reading, MA: Addison-Wesley.

Wenger, E. (1991, Fall). Communities of practice: Where learning happens. *Benchmark,* pp. 82–84.

West, M. A., & Farr, J. L. (1989). Innovation at work: Psychological perspectives. *Social Behavior, 4,* 15–30.

West, M. A., & Wallace, M. (1991). Innovation in health care teams. *European Journal of Social Psychology, 21,* 303–315.

Williams, E. S., & Bunker, D. R. (1993, August). Sorting outcomes: A revision of the JCM. In D. R. Bunker & E. D. Williams (Co-Chairs), *The Job Characteristics Model: Recent work and new directions.* Symposium conducted at the meeting of the Academy of Management, Atlanta.

Yukl, G., & Falbe, C. M. (1991). Importance of different power sources in downward and lateral relations. *Journal of Applied Psychology, 76*(3), 416–423.

Zuboff, S. (1988). *In the age of the smart machine.* New York: Basic Books.

Chapter Eleven

Leadership in the Twenty-First Century

A Speculative Inquiry

Robert J. House

Scholars and practitioners of management generally concur that organizational leaders in the twenty-first century will face a number of important changes that will impose substantial new role demands. These changes include greater demographic diversity of workforces, a faster pace of environmental and technological change, more frequent geopolitical shifts affecting borders and distribution of power among nation states, and increased international competition.

The popular and business press expect these changes to result in new and different relationships between employers and employees, organizations and resource suppliers, government and business, and buyers and sellers. If this is the case, business, government, and military organizations will need to adopt new strategic approaches and organizational forms. These changes will place new demands on the leaders of tomorrow.

A significant consequence of impending technological change is that most routine work will be done by automated processes, leaving nonroutine work to humans. Moreover, work largely will not be subject to process control. Because much twenty-first century work will be intellectual rather than physical, to observe, monitor, and control the processes and behavior by which organizational members accomplish their tasks will be difficult if not impossible. As a result, a substantial proportion of organizational members will work without direct supervision. These individuals will be key to organizational success—they will perform the organization's most important work, be in greatest demand, and not be easily replaceable.

Because work will be predominantly nonroutine and intellectual, effective performers must adjust to variable role demands and engage in frequent problem solving. Consequently, individual initiative, motivation, and willingness to take personal responsibility for task accomplishment will primarily determine both the quality and quantity of nonroutine work. The end result of this scenario is that organizations that are able to instill in their members internalized commitment to their work and to the organization will have a significant competitive advantage.

Elsewhere, Boas Shamir, Michael Arthur, and I have argued that strong internalized commitment is a function of the extent to which individuals (1) identify with the values for which their organizations or leaders stand, (2) possess intrinsic nonconscious motivation, and (3) experience self-worth contingent on their contributions to their organization (Shamir, House, & Arthur, 1993). We further contended that these motivational components, and consequently internalized commitment, are determined in significant part by the leadership of organizations and work units (House & Shamir, 1993; Shamir et al., 1993).

Plan of This Chapter

This chapter presents a review of theoretical and empirical literature that describes leader behaviors I believe will be called for in the twenty-first century. I first distinguish among general leadership, work unit or supervisory leadership, and management, then speculate on leader behaviors that will differentiate unusually effective leaders from others in the post-industrial world. These speculations derive from two theories that have been advanced elsewhere: a theory of the nature of outstanding leadership, commonly referred to as charismatic, visionary, transformational, or inspirational leadership (House & Shamir, 1994); and a theory that concerns day-to-day supervision of work units, which originated as path-goal theory (House, in press).

Following these speculations, I identify previously unstudied topics that warrant serious theoretical and empirical inquiry. Major conclusions are italicized throughout this chapter.

Leadership, Management, and Supervision

Despite some three thousand empirical studies of leadership conducted by academic researchers, this literature has gone largely unnoticed or ignored by policymakers, the press, and practicing managers. In 1988 and again in 1993 *Time* magazine published cover articles addressing the need for leadership in the U.S. political system. Not a single reference was made to any academic studies conducted by leadership scholars.

Failure to distinguish between management, supervisory leadership, and general leadership largely accounts for this neglect of the academic literature. What lay persons view as leadership (Lord & Maher, 1991) is a far cry from the traditional trait descriptions and task-person orientation of supervisors that dominated the leadership literature until about the mid-1970s.

In this chapter *management* is defined as behavior of a person in a position of formal authority that results in compliance of organizational members with their normal role or position requirements. *Supervisory leadership* is behavior intended to provide guidance, support, and corrective feedback for the day-to-day activities of work unit members. *General leadership* is behavior of individuals that gives purpose, meaning, and guidance to collectivities by articulating a collective vision that appeals to ideological values, motives, and self-perceptions of followers resulting in (1) the infusion of values into organizations and work, (2) unusual levels of effort on the part of followers above and beyond their normal role or position requirements, and (3) follower willingness to forgo self-interest and make significant personal sacrifices in the interest of a collective vision. Throughout this chapter, the term *leadership* refers to general leadership as defined here.

Managers and supervisors have positions of formal authority and subordinates who are obliged to comply with a set of role or position requirements. In contrast, leaders may or may not hold positions of formal authority. Leaders assert influence by virtue of unique personal attributes, values, and behaviors rather than, or in addition to, positional authority. Leaders are followed willingly;

therefore, those whom they motivate to action are referred to as followers rather than subordinates. Of course, some individuals in positions of authority need to function as managers, supervisors, and leaders. Such individuals will likely have some subordinates who minimally comply with normal levels of position requirements as well as some followers who voluntarily go above and beyond the call of duty in the interest of a collective vision.

In the following section, leader behaviors that I believe will be especially relevant to general leadership in the twenty-first century are described. Also indicated are the conditions under which they are likely to be accepted by followers and lead to effective organizational performance.

The Neocharismatic Leadership Paradigm

Since the mid-1970s, a substantial body of theoretical and empirical literature concerning the behavior that distinguishes outstanding leadership has emerged. Several leadership scholars have advanced theories to explain how leaders attain extraordinary accomplishments, such as turning losing industrial firms into profit makers, winning military battles against larger and stronger armies, leading organizations successfully through times of crisis, gaining large market shares in the face of severe competition, or revitalizing stagnant and foundering organizations. With surprising consistency these theories have been supported by empirical investigation (for reviews, see Bass & Avolio, 1993; House & Shamir, 1993). The theories referenced are the 1976 theory of charismatic leadership (House, 1977), the attributional theory of charisma (Conger & Kanungo, 1987), and the transformational (Bass, 1985; Burns, 1978) and visionary theories of leadership (Bennis & Nanus, 1985; Sashkin, 1988).

This general class of theory, although rooted in the past (Selznick, 1957; Weber, 1947), constitutes a new paradigm for the study of leadership, one that emphasizes leader appeal to follower values, motives, and dearly held self-concepts. Leaders articulate an ideological vision and stress the values inherent in the vision and identification with the collective.

This new genre of theory is referred to here as the *neocharismatic paradigm* because Weber's (1947) conceptualization of charisma is either implicitly or explicitly a central concept. The theories of the neocharismatic paradigm assert that exceptionally effective leaders are visionary, offer innovative solutions to major social problems, stand for nonconservative if not radical change, generally emerge as more effective under conditions of social stress and crisis, and induce significant social and organizational changes.

Assumptions

The following assumptions concerning the nature of human motivation (Shamir, House, & Arthur, 1993) provide the foundation for the selection of leader behaviors described in this chapter.

1.   Humans are not only pragmatic and goal-oriented but self-expressive. Behavior is not just instrumental-calculative but expressive of feelings, aesthetic values, and self-concepts. We do things because of what we are—because by doing them we establish and affirm an identity for ourselves, even when our behavior doesn't serve materialistic or pragmatic self-interests.

2.   People are motivated to maintain and enhance their self-esteem and self-worth. Self-esteem is based on a sense of competence, power, achievement, or ability to cope with and control one's environment. Self-worth is based on a sense of virtue and moral worth and is grounded in norms and values concerning conduct.

3.   People are motivated to retain and increase their sense of self-consistency. Self-consistency refers to correspondence among components of the self-concept at a given time, continuity of the self-concept over time, and correspondence between the self-concept and behavior. People derive a sense of meaning from continuity between the past, the present, and the projected future, and from the correspondence between their behavior and self-concept.

4.   Self-concepts are composed, in part, of identities. Along with values, identities (or role-identities) link the self-concept to society. Social identities locate the self in socially recognizable categories such as nations, organizations, and occupations, thus enabling people to derive meaning from being linked to social collectives.

5.   Humans may be motivated by faith. When goals cannot be clearly specified or the subjective probabilities of accomplishment and rewards are not high, people may be motivated by faith because being hopeful—having faith in a better future—is an intrinsically satisfying condition.

Generic Behaviors That Characterize Outstanding Leadership

The behaviors described by the neocharismatic leadership paradigm are expected to differentiate outstanding leaders from others in terms of their effects on followers and social systems. The following leadership behaviors were selected for this chapter because they are expected to have strong effects on follower values, motives, and dearly held self-concepts such as self-worth and self-efficacy, and because there is substantial evidence of their effectiveness from empirical research or historical sources.

Two of the behaviors of this paradigm—the formulation and articulation of a vision and extraordinary risk taking—are likely limited to the leadership of entire organizations or autonomous subunits of organizations. The remaining behaviors are generic to outstanding leadership for all kinds of collectivities, including dyads; small informal groups or formal work units; autonomous divisions of large organizations; social movements; business, political, religious, and military organizations; and nation states.

Vision

Outstanding leaders articulate a vision or serve as a catalyst to facilitate the development of a vision that expresses cherished end values shared by leaders and followers. It is a vision of a better future to which followers have a *moral right*; thus, it embraces a set of ideological values that resonate with the values and emotions of followers. Such visions need not be grandiose. Outstanding leaders in the normal work world have visions that embrace such ideological values as honesty, fairness, craftsmanship, high-quality services or products, a challenging and rewarding work environment, professional development for organizational members, freedom from highly controlling rules and supervision, a fair return to major constituencies, respect for organizational members and customers, and regard for the environment in which the organization functions (Berlew, 1974). Several studies have shown that articulation of an ideological vision differentiates outstanding leaders from others (Curphy, 1990; House, Spangler, & Woycke, 1991; Howell & Avolio, 1993; Howell & Frost, 1989).

Visions need not be formulated exclusively by the leader. The leader may instead be a catalyst and facilitator of follower contributions to the formulation of the vision. The leader may also inherit the vision developed by prior members of the collective and perpetuate it by institutional means, such as strategies, policies, norms, ceremonies, and symbols.

Leaders' articulation of a collective vision, regardless of its source, results in synergy among members of the collective and contributions to the collective greater than the sum of individual contributions. Managers or leaders at any organizational level can formulate an ideological vision, although leaders of entire organizations or autonomous subunits of organizations are better positioned to do so.

Passion and Self-Sacrifice

Outstanding leaders make extraordinary self-sacrifices in the interest of their vision, the mission they lead, and the collective. By making such sacrifices leaders demonstrate their passion for, and commitment to, the collective vision and earn credibility and respect of followers.

Confidence, Determination, and Persistence

Outstanding leaders display a high degree of confidence in themselves and in the attainment of the collective vision. Such leaders need strong self-confidence and moral conviction because their mission is usually unconventional and likely to encounter powerful opposition from those who have a stake in preserving the status quo. By displaying determination and persistence, change-oriented leaders demonstrate courage and conviction in the vision and mission, which inspires, empowers, and motivates followers.

Selective Motive Arousal

Outstanding leaders selectively arouse followers' motives that are of special relevance to successful accomplishment of the vision and mission. McClelland (1985) and his associates have demonstrated that three nonconscious motives—affiliation, power, and achievement—have substantial effects on individual short- and long-term behavior (McClelland & Boyatzis, 1982; McClelland, Koestner, & Weinberger, 1989). The affiliative motive is relevant to group cohesiveness, collaborative behavior, and interpersonal attraction and support among group members; the power motive is relevant to persuasive and competitive interpersonal behavior and to combat; and the achievement motive is relevant to behavior that is innovative and directed toward continuous improvement of performance. Motive arousal by leaders facilitates, energizes, and directs behavior of followers.

Such motive arousal is achieved differentially for each of the three motives. The achievement motive has been aroused by suggesting to subjects that an experimental task is a measure of personal competence, or that the task is a standard against which one can measure one's general level of ability (McClelland, 1985). The affiliative motive is aroused by making salient the importance of mutual acceptance and identification with the vision and the collective. The power motive has been aroused experimentally by (1) evoking the image of an enemy, (2) having subjects observe the exercise of power by one person over another, (3) allowing subjects to exercise power over another (Winter, 1973), or (4) having subjects witness inspirational speeches (Steele, 1973).

When leaders are viewed as credible, trusted, admired, and respected, they can have profound motive arousal effects on followers. For example, Gandhi's exhortations and role modeling of love and acceptance of others likely aroused the need for affiliation, a need especially relevant to the goal of uniting Hindus, Moslems, and Christians. Military leaders often employ symbols of authoritarianism and evoke the image of the enemy, which arouses the power motive, one especially relevant to effective combat performance. General George Patton, when addressing infantry recruits, would dramatically point out the threat of the enemy. He told his biographer, "As in all my talks, I stressed fighting and killing" (Blumenson, 1985, p. 222). Industrial leaders and leaders of scientists frequently stress challenge and excellence of performance as a measure of one's self-worth. Such leader behavior arouses the achievement motive, a motive especially relevant to the assumption of personal responsibility, persistence, and pride in high-quality work performance.

Risk Taking
Both attributional charismatic theory (Conger & Kanungo, 1987) and visionary theory (Sashkin, 1988) assert that outstanding lead-

ers are more prone to take risks than others. They often take significant career risks by introducing change, challenging the status quo, and serving as champions of innovative projects. Howell and Higgins (1990) found that informal project champions were more risk oriented than other members of their project teams, and House, Spangler, and Woycke (1991) found that charismatic U.S. presidents were more risk oriented than noncharismatic presidents.

Expectations of and Confidence in Followers

Outstanding leaders expect a great deal from their followers: commitment, determination, persistence, self-sacrifice, and performance above and beyond the call of duty. At the same time they communicate these high expectations, they also express strong confidence in their followers' ability to meet them. Leaders empower followers through this combination of high performance expectations and high confidence. Individuals are clearly more motivated when they have confidence in their ability to contribute to or accomplish important goals (Bandura, 1986). There is substantial, even dramatic, evidence that followers rise to the challenge of high performance expectations of their leaders and, as a consequence, accomplish goals they never dreamed they could attain (Eden, 1990; Korman, 1971; Rosenthal & Jacobson, 1968).

Developmental Orientation

As the rate of technological change quickens in the twenty-first century, there will be increased demands on organizational members to develop and maintain occupational skills and abilities. Leaders express developmental orientation by analyzing follower skill and ability levels and providing coaching, training, and developmental experiences. Because developmental efforts stress the importance of follower competence, such leader efforts are likely to arouse follower achievement motivation as well as increase follower competence and self-efficacy.

Bass and Avolio (1993) reviewed a number of studies demonstrating that highly effective leaders devote substantial effort toward the development of follower competence. Such developmentally oriented leaders generally have high-performing work units and satisfied and committed followers.

Role Modeling

Outstanding leaders set a personal example of the beliefs and values inherent in the organization's vision. According to Shamir and associates (1993, pp. 585–586), "The leader becomes a 'representative character' . . . a symbol . . . that helps define for the followers just what kinds of traits, values, beliefs and behaviors it is good and legitimate to develop." There is substantial evidence that individuals fashion their behavior after people they perceive positively (Bandura, 1986).

Demonstration of Integrity

Outstanding leaders demonstrate integrity toward their followers both individually and collectively. Integrity is manifested in many ways: absence of greed and exploitation of others; fairness; honesty; consistency in word and action; courage in the face of adversity; and meeting obligations and carrying out responsibilities. Followers won't trust leaders they perceive as not having integrity. Without trust, followers won't accept the vision and values of their leaders or put forth extra effort in the interest of the leader's vision (Harris & Hogan, 1992; Kouzes & Posner, 1987; Podsakoff, MacKenzie, Moorman, & Fetter, 1990).

Frame Alignment

Frames, or schemata of interpretation, enable individuals to interpret and understand events as part of a coherent perspective on life (Goffman, 1974). Outstanding leaders engage in persuasive communications to align follower attitudes, values, and perspectives to their own. They do this by articulating an ideology clearly, using labels and slogans, providing a vivid image of a better future (Willner, 1984), and invoking end values and moral justifications (Burns, 1978; Klemp & McClelland, 1986).

Symbolic Behavior

Outstanding leaders serve as symbolic figureheads and spokespersons for the collective. Their positive self-presentation helps develop follower identification with the collective and with the values inherent in the collective vision.

The preceding leader behaviors have differentiated outstanding leaders of leader-follower dyads (Howell & Frost, 1989), small informal groups (Howell & Higgins, 1990; Pillai & Meindl, 1991), formal work units (Curphy, 1990), complex organizations (Bass & Avolio, 1993; Bennis & Nanus, 1985; Sashkin & Fulmer, 1988), social movements (Smelser, 1963), voluntary organizations (Trice & Beyer, 1986), educational organizations (Koh, Terborg, & Steers, 1991; Roberts, 1985), political organizations (Willner, 1984), and nation states (House et al., 1991; Siminton, 1988). The leader behaviors predicted significant follower self-sacrifice and effort above and beyond the call of duty, thus meeting the theoretical definition of leadership advanced previously.

These behaviors have also differentiated outstanding leaders from others in the Netherlands (Koene, Pennings, & Schreuder, 1991), India (Pereira, 1987), and Singapore (Koh et al., 1991), but variables in other cultures possibly could negate or mute their motivational effects on followers. Whether these behaviors are universal to general leadership remains to be established empirically. Based on the logic and evidence presented thus far, *the aforementioned leader behaviors will differentiate outstanding leaders from others in the twenty-first century.*

Outstanding leaders do not necessarily use an assertive, flamboyant style. Some outstanding leaders, such as Jesse Jackson, John F. Kennedy, and Martin Luther King, Jr., communicate their messages in an inspirational manner with a high degree of emotion and nonverbal expressiveness. However, Kirkpatrick (1992) demonstrated in a laboratory experiment that leaders induced motivation on the part of followers not by their nonverbal behavioral style but by the content of their message. George Washington, Abraham Lincoln, Albert Schweitzer, Indira Gandhi, Mahatma Gandhi, Nelson Mandela, and Mother Teresa are examples of soft-spoken yet undisputed, outstanding leaders who appeal to followers on the basis of their vision and its values.

Social Conditions That Favor Outstanding Leadership

Weber (1947), House (1977), and Burns (1978) argued that charismatic or transformational leadership is born out of crises and stressful situations facing followers. Theoretically, when people experience stressful crises, oppression, discrimination, extremely poor working conditions, or unfair and harsh treatment by management, they feel a need for a courageous leader who will challenge the established order and offer a radical, or at least innovative, solution to alleviate their plight. Weber and Burns argued that if a leader emerges who expresses sentiments deeply held by followers and offers a solution that followers believe will solve the crisis or eliminate the stressful conditions, such a leader is likely to be viewed as an outstanding, even charismatic, leader. Two empirical studies demonstrated that crisis indeed facilitated the emergence of charismatic leadership (House et al., 1991; Pillai & Meindl, 1991).

The argument can also be made that leaders are more likely to emerge and be effective under ambiguous conditions, when followers theoretically have a need to reduce stressful uncertainty. Waldman and Ramirez (1992) found that chief executives' charismatic leadership predicted the economic performance of organizations facing high uncertainty but not those in relatively certain environments. Therefore, *when followers experience a high degree of stress or stressful uncertainty, the emergence and perceived effectiveness of leaders who engage in the aforementioned leadership behaviors will be enhanced.*

Roles requiring highly routine, nonthinking effort in exclusively economic-oriented organizations do not usually evoke an ideological orientation from their occupants. For example, clerks or assembly line workers in profit-making firms do not usually perceive their roles as ideologically oriented. But the same work, if directed toward an ideological goal, can lend itself to outstanding leadership. For example, in World War II "Rosie the Riveter" expressed the ideological contribution of an assembly line worker to the war effort. Similarly, such menial efforts as stuffing envelopes frequently are directed toward ideological goals in political and religious organizations. Awareness of the need for ideological value orientation to elicit strong motivation is, perhaps, one of the major reasons the popular management literature stresses the importance of an organization's culture to its effectiveness. Therefore, *whenever the roles of followers can be authentically described or defined as providing an opportunity for moral involvement, the potential leader can articulate ideological goals and values and have a strong influence on the motivational states of followers.*

Shamir and colleagues (1993) argued that charismatic leadership is more likely to be relevant under conditions that do not favor the use of extrinsic rewards by leaders—conditions that Mischel

(1973) called weak psychological situations. Leadership that relies primarily on extrinsic motivation can be exercised only when leaders (1) are able to specify clear goals, (2) understand the means by which goals are achieved, (3) have objective or highly consensual ways of measuring performance, (4) have discretion over the allocation of rewards, and (5) are able to link extrinsic rewards to individual performance. Shamir and others (1993) argued that when the above conditions do not exist, "followers' self-concepts, values and identities can be more readily appealed to, engaged, and expressed behaviorally. Furthermore, in the absence of extrinsic incentives followers are more likely to look for self-related justifications for their efforts (Bem, 1982) and thus become more prone to the influence of charismatic leadership" (p. 589).

These conditions present an apparent dilemma for the management of compensation in organizations led by leaders who appeal to ideological values for motivational purposes. Current literature stresses the need for consistent alignment between organizational values inherent in corporate strategies and extrinsic rewards. Further, total quality management programs include specific goals and measurement of goal attainment. Yet both dissonance theory (Aronson, 1980) and self-perception theory (Bem, 1982) suggest that the addition of transactional compensation practices to transformational or charismatic behaviors would constitute overjustification and induce dissonance. Accordingly, contingent extrinsic compensation conflicts with and undermines value-oriented leadership, decreases intrinsic follower motivation, and results in reduced extra effort. Perhaps the solution to this dilemma is to stress the attainment of specific organizational goals when that is under the control of organizational members, but also to reward more general contributions to the organization, including organizational citizenship, contributions to teams, and efforts over and above the attainment of specific operational goals.

Leadership directed toward attainment of internalized follower commitment is more effective in situations that require a combination of highly involved and active leadership and extraordinary effort by both leaders and followers. Under conditions requiring routine but reliable performance in the pursuit of pragmatic goals, commitment-oriented leadership is less likely to be required and may even be dysfunctional.

Therefore, *the emergence and effectiveness of outstanding leadership will be enhanced to the extent that (1) performance goals cannot be easily specified and measured, (2) extrinsic rewards cannot be made clearly contingent on individual performance, (3) few situational cues, constraints, and reinforcers exist to guide behavior and provide incentives for specific performance, (4) exceptional effort, behavior, and sacrifices are required of both leaders and followers, and (5) potential followers experience feelings of unfair treatment, persecution, and oppression from sources other than the leader.*

One additional condition under which leaders are likely to emerge and be effective applies specifically to formal complex organizations. Recall that leadership gives meaning to efforts and goals by connecting them to followers' values. The values of leaders in complex organizations must be congruent with dominant societal values when these are reflected in the values of organizational members.

The following example illustrates this assertion. Given the Dutch passion for flowers and pride in their canals, we would expect most Dutch citizens to oppose organizations that produce wastes and smoke emissions that threaten the natural environment in flower-producing regions or pollute the canals and waterlands of the Netherlands. Further, we would expect ideologically oriented leaders to emerge in flower-producing organizations and in social movements that oppose environmental pollution. Therefore, *a necessary condition for leaders to introduce changes in organizational structures, strategies, practices, and cultures is that the values inherent in such changes are compatible with the dominant values of the society.*

Managerial Behaviors in Formal Organizations: A Special Case

In addition to the above *leader* behaviors that theoretically influence the values, motives, and self-concepts of followers, individuals in positions of authority in nonvoluntary organizations must engage in a number of *managerial* behaviors. In contrast to leader behaviors, managerial behaviors are not interpersonal in nature. They are rational-analytic behaviors concerned with the development and implementation of organizational strategies, tactics, and policies. Examples include planning, organizing, and establishing administrative systems. Managerial behaviors provide the intellectual content necessary for organizations to perform effectively. In empirical studies the following managerial behaviors have distinguished outstanding leaders from others, even though the behaviors are not interpersonal in nature.

Intellectual Stimulation

Formal organizations of the twenty-first century will need members who exercise independent initiative, autonomous judgment and decision making, analytical thinking, and innovative approaches to tasks and problems. Consequently, leaders will need to stimulate followers intellectually and develop their competence and independence (Bass, 1985). Intellectual stimulation involves challenging followers' assumptions, asking them to see the world from a different perspective, encouraging them to challenge stereotypes and previously accepted generalizations, and even inviting people to think independently of and question their leaders.

A number of studies have shown leader intellectual stimulation to be positively related to leader and follower performance, but other studies found it either unrelated (Avolio, Waldman, & Einstein, 1988; Hater & Bass, 1988) or negatively related (Seltzer & Bass, 1990) to follower satisfaction. Unless they trust their leaders, followers are likely to experience intimidation, stress, and dissatisfaction and to reject leaders' attempts to stimulate and develop them intellectually (Podsakoff et al., 1990).

It follows, then, that leaders in formal organizations need to provide intellectual stimulation when followers are required to be innovative or to act independent of supervision. Followers will accept such attempts, however, only when they have a high degree of trust in their leaders.

Environmental Monitoring

Conger and Kanungo (1987, 1988) assert that charismatic leaders are more sensitive to and more likely to monitor the environment than are noncharismatic leaders. I maintain that environmental sensitivity and monitoring are *managerial* attributes required in open systems in uncertain and changing environments. Because such conditions are expected to typify organizations in the future, environmental monitoring behavior will be an important managerial behavior necessary for effective leadership in the twenty-first century. Environmental monitoring helps leaders formulate effective strategies, build credibility with followers, take risks intelligently, and perform the role of spokespersons for the collective.

Shared Strategy Formulation

Effective strategy formulation is based on an implicit or explicit vision of the organization of the future. The formulation of visions is a managerial behavior while the communication and implementation of visions are leader behaviors. This distinction is consistent with the argument that managerial behaviors are rational-analytic and leader behaviors are interpersonal in nature, although these behaviors generally occur together and are enacted by the same individual. An individual could, however, articulate and lead the implementation of a vision conceived by a predecessor or some other individual or group, such as a strategy task force or a board of directors.

Flawed strategy often leads to the downfall of charismatic leaders. Napoleon Bonaparte failed to consider the severity of the winters when he invaded Russia. Henry Ford's strategy of a single mass-produced automobile model (any color as long as it is black) and highly centralized organization led to the near downfall of his empire.

Klemp and McClelland (1986) found that outstanding chief executives of large organizations involved their followers in the development of the organizational strategy and jointly shared problem solving and decision making with followers more often than did other chief executives. Sharing strategy formulation with the top management team most probably stimulates negative feedback and serves as a check on the implementation of flawed strategies. Therefore, *leaders in the twenty-first century will be required to stimulate followers intellectually, monitor the environments of their organizations, and formulate strategies jointly with their top management teams.*

Management of Infrastructure

Nadler and Tushman (1990) argued persuasively that in complex formal organizations leader appeal to follower values, motives, and self-concepts is insufficient unless the leader is also able to conceive of and manage a complex infrastructure to support the vision and encourage change in managerial behavior. They recommended that leaders must be able to take the following measures:

- Select appropriate individuals to staff a supporting top management team
- Structure information and control systems and processes to be consistent with the collective vision
- Involve others in leadership roles
- Develop skills for effective team member performance and group problem solving
- Build competent teams throughout the organization
- Clarify required behaviors
- Provide incentives
- Establish measurements
- Administer rewards and punishments

While these managerial behaviors are largely rational-analytic in nature, they clearly complement the leadership behaviors described previously and are most likely necessary for leaders to be effective and sustained in complex formal organizations. Therefore, *leaders of formal organizations in the twenty-first century will need the knowledge and skills to design, implement, and manage complex infrastructures.*

Work Unit Supervision

Leaders usually perform supervisory as well as general leadership and managerial roles. *Supervisory* leader behaviors are concerned with monitoring, guiding, and providing corrective feedback for work unit members in their day-to-day activities.

Work unit leaders will be effective to the extent that they complement their subordinates' environment to ensure that they are able and motivated to attain work goals, experience intrinsic satisfaction, and receive valued rewards as a result of work goal attainment. If the environment does not provide clear causal linkages between effort and goal attainment and between goal attainment and extrinsic rewards, it is the leader's function to arrange such linkages. If work unit members don't perceive such linkages when they do indeed exist, it is the leader's function to clarify such perceptions. Finally, if work unit members lack abilities, cooperation from others, support, or needed resources, it is the leader's function to provide such support and resources. Thus, consistent with Katz and Kahn's (1978) definition of leadership, the role of the supervisory leader is to provide the necessary incremental information, support, and resources over and above those provided by the formal organization or the work unit members' environment to ensure both work unit member satisfaction and effective performance.

Assumptions

The following assumptions about individual and work unit effectiveness are taken as axiomatic and provide the foundation for subsequent propositions.

1.   Leader behavior is acceptable and satisfying to subordinates to the extent that the work unit members see such behavior as either an immediate source of satisfaction or as instrumental to future satisfaction.

2.   Leader behavior will enhance work unit member goal-oriented performance to the extent that such behavior (a) enhances the motivation of work unit members, (b) enhances task-relevant abilities of work unit members, (c) provides guidance, (d) reduces obstacles, and (e) provides resources required for effective performance.

3.   Leader behavior will enhance work unit member motivation to the extent that such behavior (a) makes satisfaction of work unit members' needs and preferences contingent on effective performance, (b) makes work unit members' tasks intrinsically satisfying, (c) makes goal attainment intrinsically satisfying, (d) makes rewards contingent on goal accomplishment, and (e) complements the environment of work unit members by providing psychological structure, support, and rewards necessary for effective performance.

4.   Leader behavior will enhance task-relevant abilities of work unit members to the extent that the leader engages in development of work unit members or serves as a role model from whom work unit members can learn appropriate task-relevant behavior.

5.   Leader behavior will enhance work unit performance to the extent that such behavior (a) facilitates collaborative relationships among unit members, (b) maintains positive relationships

between the unit and the larger organizations in which it is embedded, (c) ensures that adequate resources are available to the work unit, and (d) enhances the legitimacy of the work unit in the eyes of other members of the organization.

Supervisory Work Unit Leader Behaviors

The following supervisory leader behaviors (specified in more detail in House, in press) were selected because of their relevance to leadership of organizations in the twenty-first century. Specified here are several organizational conditions that make these behaviors necessary and effective, and some conditions that render them unnecessary or dysfunctional.

Path-Goal Clarifying Behaviors

Leaders will increasingly need to clarify paths and goals of work unit members in the twenty-first century as task demands become more ambiguous, unpredictable, complex, and interdependent, and as work becomes more knowledge based. Many leader behaviors are intended to clarify work unit members' role demands and make the satisfaction of their needs and preferences contingent on effective performance. These include (1) clarifying performance goals, (2) clarifying means by which work unit members can effectively carry out tasks, (3) clarifying standards by which subordinates' performance will be judged, (4) clarifying expectancies that others have for work unit members to which the members should and should not respond, and (5) judicious use of rewards and punishment, contingent on performance.

Path-goal clarifying behaviors will have a positive effect on work unit members when work role and task demands are ambiguous and intrinsically satisfying and when work unit members feel unable to clarify such ambiguity. Under such conditions subordinates are likely to see path-goal clarifying behavior as helpful and instrumental to task performance.

In contrast, when subordinates' task and role demands are unambiguous and not intrinsically satisfying, subordinates will see path-goal clarifying behavior as redundant and overcontrolling. Further, when subordinates' tasks are dissatisfying, they will see path-goal clarifying behavior as an attempt to induce them to work harder at distasteful tasks and then resent, resist, and be demotivated by such leader behaviors. Subordinates who consider that they have high task-relevant ability will perceive path-goal clarifying behavior as excessively controlling.

Leaders can enact path-goal clarifying behaviors in a nonauthoritarian directive manner or in a participative manner. Directive behavior provides psychological structure for work unit members by (1) letting subordinates know what they are expected to do, (2) scheduling and coordinating work, (3) giving specific guidance, (4) clarifying policies, rules, and procedures, (5) clarifying the degree to which effort will result in successful performance (goal attainment), and (6) clarifying the degree to which performance will be extrinsically rewarded with recognition by the leader through pay, advancement, job security, and the like.

Participative path-goal clarifying behavior encourages work unit members to influence decision making and work unit operations. Participative leaders consult with work unit members and take their opinions and suggestions into account when making decisions. House and Mitchell (1974) asserted that participative leader behavior has the following effects:

- Clarifies path-goal relationships between effort and goal attainment and between goal attainment and extrinsic rewards (topics ordinarily discussed as part of the participative leadership process)
- Increases congruence between individual and organizational goals (work unit members will select goals they value highly)
- Increases individual autonomy and ability to carry out their intentions (leading to greater effort and performance)
- Increases motivation for organizational performance (by increasing involvement, commitment, and the social pressure of peers involved in the participative process)

Whether nonauthoritarian directive leadership or participative leadership will be motivational to work unit members will depend on their level of personal involvement in their work. When individuals are highly involved in their work, they take personal responsibility for work quality, take pride in their work, and exercise initiative and creativity to ensure that work is accomplished. They want to influence decisions that affect their tasks or themselves at work, so they prefer to clarify paths and goals through participation with their supervisors. Therefore, *participative leadership will have a positive effect on the satisfaction and motivation of subordinates who are highly personally involved in a decision or task that is ambiguous and satisfying.*

When work unit members with ambiguous and satisfying tasks are *not* highly involved in their work, the appropriate level of directive versus participative leadership will depend on their level of preference for independence and self-directed behavior. Many personality traits are associated with such preferences: need for independence, (Abdel-Halim, 1981; Vroom, 1959), authoritarianism (Vroom, 1959), achievement motivation (McClelland, 1985), and internal locus of control (Runyon, 1973). Individuals with strong preferences for independence and self-direction find participative leadership to be satisfying, whereas individuals with strong preferences for dependence and direction from others find directive leadership to be persuasive (Abdel-Halim, 1981; Runyon, 1973; Tannenbaum & Allport, 1956; Vroom, 1959). Therefore, *when task demands are ambiguous and satisfying, and individuals are not involved in their work, directive leadership will motivate individuals with a low preference for independence and self-direction, and participative leadership will motivate individuals with a high preference for independence and self-direction.* These speculations assume that individuals choose the level of effort they will expend depending on the satisfaction or rewards they expect as a result of their efforts. However, under conditions of stress or uncertainty, individuals are unable to assess accurately the probability that their effort will lead to valued rewards. Therefore, the preceding speculation holds only under conditions of certainty or low stress, when probabilities can be assessed rationally.

Supportive Leader Behavior

Supportive leader behavior is directed toward satisfying the needs and preferences of work unit members, creating a friendly and psychologically supportive work environment, and developing good relationships with work unit members. Supportive leader behavior is theoretically a source of self-confidence and social satisfaction and a means for stress reduction and alleviation of frustration. It is especially needed when tasks or relationships are psychologically or physically distressing. Under such conditions individuals are less able to use their intelligence and rely primarily on experience, so that intelligence becomes negatively related to performance (Fiedler & Garcia, 1987). Supportive leader behavior theoretically offsets the negative effects of stressful situations and permits individuals to maximize the application of their intelligence.

Therefore, *when work unit members' tasks or work environments are dangerous, monotonous, stressful, or frustrating, supportive leader behavior will lead to increased effort and satisfaction by (1) increasing work unit member self-confidence, (2) enhancing the quality of relationships between leaders and work unit members, (3) lowering stress and anxiety, and (4) compensating for unpleasant aspects of the work. When tasks are intrinsically satisfying or environmental conditions are not stressful, supportive leader behavior will have less effect on follower satisfaction, motivation, or performance.* The assertions concerning the effects of path-goal clarification and supportive leader behavior have been supported in a number of studies (House, in press).

Work Facilitation

Leader behaviors that facilitate work consist of providing mentoring, developmental experiences, guidance, coaching, counseling, and feedback to assist work unit members; eliminating roadblocks and bottlenecks; providing resources; and authorizing work unit members to take actions and make decisions necessary to perform effectively. As interdependencies between work units and among work unit members increase in the twenty-first century, many of these facilitating leader behaviors will take on increased importance. In current practice, managers and supervisors are often referred to as facilitators rather than superiors.

When the work of the unit is free of technological uncertainty and external demands are predictable, leader planning, scheduling, organizing, and establishment of formal coordination mechanisms will facilitate the work of the unit members. In contrast, when the work of the unit is characterized by technological uncertainty or external demands are unpredictable, personal coordination of the work by the leader or reciprocal coordination by members of the work unit will facilitate work unit goal accomplishment. Which of these two modes of coordination will be most effective will depend on the ability level of the work unit members. Therefore, *when work unit members do not have task-relevant knowledge and experience, personal coordination of uncertain work by the leader will facilitate work unit goal accomplishment; when work unit members have substantial task-relevant knowledge and experience, coordination of uncertain work by work unit members will facilitate work unit goal accomplishment. Under conditions of uncertainty and change, leaders will enhance work unit effectiveness by delegating responsibility for reciprocal coordination to work unit members.*

Similarly, the degree to which leaders need to facilitate the development of subordinates or remove obstacles to their effective performance depends on the work unit members' task-relevant knowledge and experience. *When work unit members do not have task-relevant knowledge and experience, supervisors' efforts to develop subordinates or remove obstacles to their effective functioning will enhance work unit effectiveness. When work unit members have task-relevant knowledge and experience, supervisory delegation of authority to reduce work-related obstacles will facilitate work unit accomplishment.*

Achievement-Oriented Leader Behavior

In the twenty-first century individuals increasingly will need to take initiative, complete tasks independently, and assume personal responsibility for goal accomplishment. Leaders can motivate such achievement-oriented behavior by setting challenging goals, seeking improvement, emphasizing excellence in performance, and showing confidence that work unit members will attain high standards of performance. Achievement-oriented leader behavior motivates work unit members to strive for higher standards of performance and to have more confidence in their ability to meet challenging goals, but its effect depends on the achievement motivation of work unit members. Specifically, achievement arousal stimuli enhance the valence of efforts and goals for individuals who have moderate to high levels of achievement motivation (McClelland, 1985).

Individuals with high achievement motivation respond to tasks that allow them to assume personal responsibility, reflect positively on their competence (if they perform well), require moderate levels of risk (are challenging), and provide opportunities for performance feedback. They do not obtain satisfaction from, and usually become frustrated by, tasks that rely on others for effective performance and by political and social influence activities. Consequently, a high level of achievement motivation is dysfunctional for higher-level managers whose effectiveness depends primarily on delegation and social influence (House et al., 1991; Spangler & House, 1991). The achievement motive is most predictive of performance for technical personnel, salespersons, scientists and engineers, and owners of entrepreneurial firms.

Therefore, *achievement-oriented leader behavior will motivate work unit members who have individual responsibility and control over their work. It will be most motivational for individuals who are moderately or highly achievement motivated. Achievement-oriented leader behavior will enhance the valence of performance and increase the intrinsic satisfaction of those individuals with moderate to high achievement motivation.*

Interaction Facilitation

Leader behavior that facilitates collaborative and positive interaction consists of resolving disputes; facilitating communication; giving minority groups or individuals a chance to be heard; emphasizing the importance of collaboration and teamwork; and encouraging close, satisfying relationships among work unit members. These behaviors are especially relevant when the group members' work is interdependent.

Interaction facilitation by supervisors will become increasingly important in the twenty-first century because of the enhanced complexity of work and proliferation of autonomous team-oriented work groups. Therefore, *leader interaction facilitation will increase work unit cohesiveness and reduce voluntary absenteeism and attrition. Such behavior will increase work unit effectiveness when unit members' work is interdependent and the norms of the work group encourage unit members' performance; when the work of the unit members is not interdependent, leader interaction facilitation will increase social non-task-related communication but will not increase work unit effectiveness.*

Group-Oriented Decision Process

Group-oriented decision making substantially increases acceptance of decisions as well as technical and economic decision quality

(Maier, 1967). Group decision making is a special case of participative leadership requiring leader skills beyond those exercised between superiors and work unit members as dyads. As organizations seek to empower their members and rely on autonomous work group designs, the group-oriented decision process will increase in importance.

The group-oriented decision process consists of a number of specific behaviors by group or work unit leaders: posing problems, not solutions, to the group; searching for and identifying mutual interests of group members with respect to solving problems; encouraging all members of the group to participate in the discussion; ensuring that participation is balanced; searching for alternatives; delaying evaluation of alternatives until group members have exhausted their ability to generate alternatives; and encouraging the group to evaluate the advantages and disadvantages of each alternative and combine the advantages into a creative solution. When problems can be segmented into parts for analysis, effective group leaders also allocate parts of the problems to individuals or subgroups with special expertise.

Research suggests that *the group decision process will increase both decision quality and decision acceptance when work unit members have mutual interests in the problems or decisions. Decision acceptance will be increased by including in the group decision process those who will implement the decision. Decision quality will be increased by including in the group decision process those with relevant technical or economic expertise.*

Representation and Networking

Work units require resources to perform their tasks. Their ability to acquire necessary resources depends on their relative power within the organization and perceived legitimacy by their suppliers. Work units on whom others depend for resources, performance, or information enjoy a relatively high degree of power and, therefore, are able to obtain resources needed to perform their functions and reward work unit members for effective performance (Mintzberg, 1983; Pfeffer, 1981). Work units that do not control resources, information, or performance of other units must rely on their perceived legitimacy in order to acquire such resources. Effective representation of work units contributes to their perceived legitimacy. Consequently, a critical function of work unit leaders is representation of their work units.

Group representation includes presenting the group in a favorable manner and communicating the importance of its work to other organizational members. According to Yukl (1994a), work unit leaders can enhance such representation by effective networking, which involves maintaining positive relationships with influential others. Leaders develop positive relationships by entering into exchanges with others and being effective trading partners, keeping in touch with network members, joining groups that offer opportunities to make contacts, participating in organizationwide social functions and ceremonies, giving others unconditional favors, showing appreciation for favors and the work of others, and showing positive regard for others (Yukl, 1994b). Therefore, *active representation and networking by work unit leaders will enhance work unit legitimacy and ability to obtain resources. It will have a more positive effect for work units with lower interorganizational power.*

Shared Leadership

Leadership behaviors need not be performed only by formally appointed work unit leaders. The increased complexity and interdependence of work in the twenty-first century is likely to require that work unit members informally assume leadership roles. Bowers and Seashore (1967) found strong correlations between the extent to which insurance agency managers and peers enacted supportive leadership, goal emphasis, work facilitation, and interaction facilitation. Peer leadership often correlated more highly with agency performance than leadership exercised by the formal manager. Therefore, *when work unit members have interdependent work, leader encouragement of collaborative shared responsibility for the exercise of leader behaviors will enhance work unit cohesiveness and performance.*

Some Relevant Considerations

Several considerations should be mentioned with respect to the discussion thus far. No claim is made that this chapter includes an exhaustive set of leader behaviors or contingency moderators. Nevertheless, it is improbable that any one leader will have the ability to engage in all the described leadership behaviors all or even most of the time. Effective leaders likely share leadership with work unit members and enact those behaviors with which they are most comfortable, based on their personalities and repertoire of abilities.

It is also likely that some of the behaviors can substitute for each other. For example, leaders may substitute articulation of a vision coupled with role modeling for path-goal clarifying behaviors. Or, leader interaction facilitation or peer supportiveness may substitute for, or make unnecessary, supportive leadership. Some of the moderating variables specified by the theory may also replace each other. For example, individual self-perceived abilities and task-relevant knowledge may substitute for task structure.

In the absence of additional empirical evidence, speculations concerning the interaction among leader behaviors or among the moderating variables of the theory would be overly complex. It is hoped that future empirical research will clarify how such interactions occur.

Empowerment

The assertions advanced here specify several ways that empowerment, emphasized in current managerial literature, can be accomplished.

- Neocharismatic leadership behavior strengthens subordinates' self-efficacy and conviction in the appropriateness of their actions.
- Neocharismatic leader behavior strengthens collective identification and the motivation for work unit members to contribute to collective goals.
- Path-goal clarification establishes comprehensibility necessary for delegation of authority and responsibility.
- Work facilitation enhances individual development and ability to work autonomously.
- Supportive leadership enhances psychological security.
- Achievement-oriented leader behavior arouses achievement-oriented behavior among subordinates and encourages them to take moderate calculated risks.
- Interaction facilitation empowers followers to engage in reciprocal coordination and interdependent action.
- Work unit representation enhances the legitimacy of work units and the resources available to work unit members.
- The group decision process allows work unit members to influence decision making.

Clearly, there are numerous ways of empowering individuals at work.

Two Parsimonious Integrative Propositions

The essential underlying rationale from which the above assertions are derived is strikingly parsimonious. The essence of the theoretical argument with respect to supervisory leadership is the following meta-proposition: *Leaders, to be effective, engage in behaviors that complement work unit members' environments and abilities in a manner that compensates for deficiencies and is instrumental to individual satisfaction and work unit performance.* In other words, effective work unit leaders focus on what is lacking in the environment of work unit members. This meta-proposition, and the specific assertions relating leader behavior to responses of work unit members, decision effectiveness, superior-subordinate relationships, and work unit behavior, are consistent with and integrate the predictions of current task- and person-oriented theories of leadership (Fiedler & Garcia, 1987; Graen & Scandura, 1987; House, 1977; Kerr & Jermier, 1978; Vroom & Jago, 1988). Further, the above assertions are consistent with empirical generalizations resulting from earlier task- and person-oriented research (Bass, 1990; Bowers & Seashore, 1967; Fleishman, 1973; Likert, 1977, Yukl, 1994a).

The essence of the theoretical argument with respect to general (or neocharismatic) leadership is this: *such leadership causes followers to recognize values that are shared with the leader and among the members of the collective, arouses in followers powerful nonconscious motives, engages followers' strongly held self-concepts such as self-efficacy and self-worth, and brings about strong follower identification with the vision and the collective.*

The assertions advanced with respect to general leadership are consistent with the predictions of charismatic, visionary, transformational, and inspirational theories (Bass, 1985; Bennis & Nanus, 1985; Burns, 1978; Conger & Kanungo, 1987; House, 1977; House & Shamir, 1993; Kouzes & Posner, 1987; Sashkin, 1988; Yukl, 1994b). Further, the above assertions are consistent with empirical findings resulting from a substantial number of studies (see Bass & Avolio, 1993, and House & Shamir, 1993, for overviews of the empirical literature).

Directions for Future Research

This section presents some of the deficiencies in our current knowledge about leadership that I believe warrant continued theoretical and empirical inquiry.

Rationality Assumptions

With the exception of cognitive resource utilization theory (Fiedler & Garcia, 1987) and the decision selection theory (Vroom & Jago, 1988), all extant theories of supervision, management, and leadership ignore the effect of contextual variables on follower cognitive processing as well as individual tendencies to respond emotionally rather than rationally to contextual variables and to the behavior of others. Extant theories assume that supervisors, managers, and leaders are able to calculate correctly or learn expected outcomes associated with the exercise of theoretically specified behaviors. They also assume that supervisors, managers, and leaders are able to enact task-oriented and supportive leader behaviors at their discretion. These theories, then, make strong implicit rationality assumptions despite substantial empirical evidence that humans are subject to a myriad of cognitive biases and limitations (Nisbett & Ross, 1980; Simon, 1987; Tversky & Kannaman, 1974) and that emotions and affect can be strong determinants of behavior. *An important question concerning extant theories is the validity of their underlying assumptions about rationality on the part of both leaders and followers.*

Context

The preceding discussion suggests that the validity of supervisory management and leadership theories may be limited to a narrow set of conditions. Contingency theory (Fiedler, 1967), path-goal theory (House, 1971; House & Mitchell, 1974), and substitutes theory (Kerr & Jermier, 1978) assert that contextual variables either limit or moderate the influence of leaders on followers. Supervisors, managers, and leaders need not just leadership behaviors in their repertoires but also a sufficiently unrestrictive context in which they can enact such behaviors. *An important topic for future research concerns the degree to which contextual conditions impede or facilitate the enactment of leader behaviors.*

Lack of Attention to Process

In contrast to earlier theories, the neocharismatic paradigm asserts that leaders have profound effects on both cognitive and affective motivational states of followers, which are taken as intervening variables. These theories assert that leaders appeal to values that are of major importance to followers, cause followers to change their values and preferences, arouse follower motives and emotions, and enhance follower self-esteem. They also claim that leaders increase followers' commitment to their organizations, their attraction to the mission articulated by the leader, and their trust and confidence in the leader. The effect of leaders on these intervening variables is asserted to account for outcome variables such as leader and work unit performance and follower satisfaction. *While neocharismatic theories enjoy a substantial amount of support with respect to outcome variables such as follower satisfaction or measures of work unit and leader effectiveness, the effect of leaders on the theoretical intervening variables remains to be tested.*

Exclusive Focus on Dyads

With the exception of contingency theory (Fiedler, 1967) and charismatic theory (House, 1977), prevailing theories of leadership focus almost exclusively on dyadic relationships between leaders and followers rather than relationships between leaders and groups of followers or leader effects on organizational performance. Prevailing theories are generally silent with respect to the processes or theoretical mechanisms by which leaders affect small groups, work units, total organizations, or the environments in which organizations exist. *Research on how leaders affect the various kinds of collectivities remains to be conducted and is clearly warranted.*

Psychological Bias

Earlier theories as well as those of the neocharismatic paradigm reflect a psychological bias: they focus on leaders' effect on immediate followers to the exclusion of contextual environmental variables and macro-organizational variables. Little attention has been paid to the processes by which leaders affect organizational variables. *Additional research is required to determine the effects of leaders on the macro attributes of organizations such as structures, strategies, policies, culture, and incentive and control systems.*

Conflict in Organizations

Both earlier theories and those of the neocharismatic paradigm ignore the possibility of conflict in organizations. Little scholarly attention has been devoted to how leaders induce conflict to their advantage or how they resolve conflict. While there is a rich literature on conflict and conflict resolution in complex organizations, this literature has not been integrated into the currently available theories of leadership. *Additional theoretical and empirical attention needs to be directed toward the effect of conflict on the exercise of leadership and the role of the leader in inducing and resolving conflict.*

Change

Earlier theories of leadership are silent with respect to the processes by which leaders bring about large-scale change in organizations. While theories of the neocharismatic paradigm assert that outstanding leaders inspire followers to implement such change, these theories are vague with respect to the processes by which such change occurs. *The role of leaders in introducing and implementing change remains an important topic for future research.*

Diplomatic Social-Political Leadership

Although leaders employ a variety of power tactics (Kipnis, Schmidt, & Wilkinson, 1980; Yukl, 1994a) and higher-level management involves substantial negotiation, coalition formation, and consensus building, the leadership literature has paid little attention to the style of leadership that relies on consensus development among constituencies, including followers. This deficiency in current theory stems from both implicit assumptions of rationality in many of the current theories and from the almost exclusive focus on leader-follower relationships rather than the context within which leaders function, including their peers and other constituencies. *Research is needed concerning how the political context influences leader behavior and how leaders enact diplomatic and political processes in organizations.*

Strategic Leadership

There is a dearth of theory and empirical evidence relevant to the strategic functioning and behavior of top-level leaders, despite widespread recognition of the importance of such leadership. While there is substantial theory on managerial decision making (March, 1988) and some theory on how managers formulate strategies and policies (Hofer & Schendel, 1978; Narayan & Fahey, 1982), this literature is largely ignored by current leadership theory. *Research needs to be directed toward the role of leaders in the strategy formulation process and how leaders effectively formulate and implement strategy.*

Effects of Culture on the Exercise of Leadership

There is strong reason to believe that cultural values, beliefs, and norms limit the kind of behavior that supervisors, managers, and leaders can enact. Leadership is defined in such varied ways within the U.S. culture that it surely is expressed in different ways across cultures. The following are paraphrased statements drawn from interviews I have conducted with members of other cultures:

- The Dutch culture is highly egalitarian, and people are skeptical about the value of leadership. Terms like *leader* and *manager* carry a stigma. If a Dutch father is employed as a manager, his children will not admit it to their schoolmates.
- When the Canadian and Swedish hockey teams had to break their tie with a "shootout," the Canadian coach selected his players, whereas the Swedish coach consulted with all members of the team and selected players on the basis of consensual decision making among equals. This clearly reflects basic differences in the two cultures. (Incidentally, the Swedish team won.)
- The Arabs worship their leaders—*as long as they are in power.* For a leader to show kindness or be generous without being asked to do so is a sign of weakness. Generosity should be bestowed as a sign of strength in response to expressions of dependence by followers.
- The Iranians seek power and strength in their leaders. Delegating authority, consulting with followers, inviting followers to participate in decision making, or empowering followers are signs of weakness.
- The Japanese leader is expected to behave in a manner that is humble, modest, and dignified and to speak infrequently and only on critical occasions. When things go seriously wrong, the Japanese leader is expected to accept responsibility and possibly even resign, even if he or she is not the cause.

- The French appreciate two kinds of leaders, of which de Gaulle and Mitterrand are examples. De Gaulle represents a strong charismatic leader; Mitterrand is an example of a consensus builder, coalition former, and effective negotiator. In either case, the French expect their leaders to be cultured and well educated.
- Citizens of many Latin American nations expect leaders to be paternalistic—to be concerned with and look after the needs of followers, including providing protection, assistance when in trouble with the law, and intervention when followers have family and personal problems. In addition, leaders are expected to look good—to have bearing and be well dressed and well groomed.
- The Portuguese are suspicious of leaders; they see them as potentially despotic and dangerous. They prefer to have mundane managers rather than visionary, creative, and risk-taking leaders.
- The Americans appreciate two kinds of leaders. They seek empowerment from a leader who grants autonomy and delegates with confidence. They also respect the bold, forceful, confident, and risk-taking leader as personified by John Wayne and the robber barons.

To date, little is known about leadership in countries and cultures other than those of North America and Europe. Further, all extant theories of leadership have originated in the United States and have embedded within them dominant American cultural assumptions and values: stressing individualism rather than collectivism; emphasizing rationality rather than asceticism, spirituality, religion, or superstition; stated in terms of individual rather than group incentives; stressing follower responsibilities rather than rights; assuming hedonistic rather than altruistic motivation; and assuming centrality of work and democratic value orientation.

A substantial body of cross-cultural, social-psychological, sociological, and anthropological research informs us that many cultures do not share these assumptions. As a result, there is a growing awareness of the need for a better understanding of the way in which leadership is enacted in various cultures and for an empirically grounded theory to explain differential leader behavior and effectiveness across cultures (Bass, 1990; Boyacigillar & Adler, 1991; Dorfman & Ronen, 1991). *Thus there is a need for theoretical and empirical inquiry with respect to cultural influences on what leader behaviors can be enacted and what leader behaviors will be accepted and effective.*

Management of Diversity

Finally, attention needs to be devoted to the unique problems and processes associated with the management of diversity. The U.S. workforce will be much more diverse in the twenty-first century with a substantially higher proportion of minorities and women. Partly as a result of affirmative action, the proportion of minorities and women represented in professional and management positions will also be higher. Increased globalization of business will require managers to do business across cultures and manage individuals from diverse cultures. *Scholars need to generate understanding of such issues as (1) how individuals view managers of the opposite gender, (2) how cultural expectations affect the acceptance of leaders by individuals, (3) how leaders can negotiate and resolve differences in cultural expectations, and (4) how leaders can meet the challenge of managing multiple subordinates or groups from different cultures. Changes in the demography of the U.S. workforce and the globalization of management calls for research concerning issues of diversity.*

Conclusion

In this chapter, I advanced a set of theoretical speculations relevant to the leadership of organizations beyond the year 2000. These assertions are informed in part by theoretical and empirical knowledge regarding the practice of unusually effective or outstanding leadership, and in part by a speculative inquiry into the various ways that leadership might be behaviorally enacted in the next century.

I hope that some will find this speculative inquiry interesting and challenging, and that controversial issues will be resolved by empirical inquiry and new theoretical developments. If the chapter stimulates such scholarly inquiry, it will have accomplished its objective.

References

Abdel-Halim, A. A. (1981). Personality and task moderators of subordinate responses to perceived leader behavior. *Human Relations, 34,* 73–88.

Aronson, E. (1980). Persuasion by self-justification: Large commitments for small rewards. In L. Festinger (Ed.), *Retrospections on social psychology*. New York: Oxford University Press.

Avolio, B. J., Waldman, D. A., & Einstein, W. O. (1988). Transformational leadership in a management game simulation. *Group and Organization Studies, 13,* 59–80.

Bandura, A. (1986). *Social foundations of thought and action: A social cognitive theory*. Englewood Cliffs, NJ: Prentice Hall.

Bass, B. M. (1985). *Leadership and performance beyond expectations*. New York: Free Press.

Bass, B. M. (1990). *Bass and Stogdill's handbook of leadership: Theory, research, and managerial applications* (3rd ed.). New York: Free Press.

Bass, B. M., & Avolio, B. J. (1993). Transformational leadership: A response to critiques. In M. Chemmers & R. Ayman (Eds.), *Leadership theory and research perspectives and directions*. Orlando, FL: Academic Press.

Bem, D. J. (1982). Self-perception theory. In L. Berkowitz (Ed.), *Advances in experimental social psychology* (Vol. 6). Orlando, FL: Academic Press.

Bennis, W., & Nanus, B. (1985). *Leaders: The strategies for taking charge*. New York: Harper.

Berlew, D. E. (1974). Leadership and organizational excitement. *California Management Review, 17*(2), 21–30.

Blumenson, M. (1985). *Patton: The man behind the legend*. New York: Morrow.

Bowers, D. G., & Seashore, S. E. (1967). Predicting organizational effectiveness with a four-factor theory of leadership. *Administrative Science Quarterly, 11,* 238–263.

Boyacigillar, N., & Adler, N. (1991). The parochial dinosaur: Organizational science in a global context. *Academy of Management Review, 16,* 262–290.

Burns, J. M. (1978). *Leadership*. New York: Harper.

Conger, J. A., & Kanungo, R. A. (1987). Toward a behavioral theory of charismatic leadership in organizational settings. *Academy of Management Review, 12,* 637–647.

Conger, J. A., & Kanungo, R. A. (1988). Behavioral dimensions of charismatic leadership. In J. A. Conger & R. A. Kanungo (Eds.), *Charismatic leadership: The elusive factor in organizational effectiveness*. San Francisco: Jossey-Bass.

Curphy, G. J. (1990). *An empirical evaluation of Bass's (1985) theory of transformational and transactional leadership*. Unpublished doctoral dissertation, University of Minnesota, Minneapolis.

Dorfman, P. W., & Ronen, S. (1991, August). *The universality of leadership theories: Challenges and paradoxes*. Paper presented at the meeting of the Academy of Management, Miami, FL.

Eden, D. (1990). *Pygmalion in management.* Lexington, MA: Heath.

Fiedler, F. E. (1967). *A theory of leadership effectiveness.* New York: McGraw-Hill.

Fiedler, F. E., & Garcia, J. E. (1987). *New approaches to effective leadership: Cognitive resources and organizational performance.* New York: Wiley.

Fleishman, E. A. (1973). Twenty years of consideration and structure. In E. A. Fleishman & J. G. Hunt (Eds.), *Current developments in the study of leadership.* Carbondale: Southern Illinois University Press.

Goffman, E. (1974). *Frame analysis.* Cambridge, MA: Harvard University Press.

Graen, G. B., & Scandura, T. (1987). Toward a psychology of dyadic organizing. In B. M. Staw & L. L. Cummings (Eds.), *Research in organizational behavior* (Vol. 9). Greenwich, CT: JAI Press.

Harris, G., & Hogan, J. (1992). *Perceptions and personality correlates of managerial effectiveness.* Paper presented at the 13th Annual Department of Defense Psychological Symposium, Colorado Springs, CO.

Hater, J. J., & Bass, B. M. (1988). Supervisors' evaluations and subordinates' perceptions of transformational leadership. *Journal of Applied Psychology, 73,* 695–702.

Hofer, C. H., & Schendel, D. (1978). *Strategy formulation: Analytical concepts.* St. Paul, MN: West.

House, R. J. (1971). A path-goal theory of leader effectiveness. *Administrative Science Quarterly, 16*(3), 321–338.

House, R. J. (1977). A 1976 theory of charismatic leadership. In J. G. Hunt & L. L. Larson (Eds.), *Leadership: The cutting edge.* Carbondale: Southern Illinois University Press.

House, R. J. (in press). Path-goal theory of leadership: Lessons learned, legacies, and a reformulated theory. *Leadership Quarterly*

House, R. J., & Mitchell, J. R. (1974). Path-goal theory of leadership. *Journal of Contemporary Business, 5,* 81–92.

House, R. J., & Shamir, B. (1993). Toward the integration of transformational, charismatic, and visionary theories. In M. Chemmers & R. Ayman (Eds.), *Leadership theory and research: Perspectives and directions.* Orlando, FL: Academic Press.

House, R. J., & Shamir, B. (1994). A value, motives, and self-concept theory of leadership. In A. Kieser, G. Raber, R. Wunderer, & U. Mitarbeit (Eds.), *Handwörterbuch der führung (Encyclopedia of leadership).* Stuttgart: Poeschel.

House, R. J., Spangler, W. D., & Woycke, J. (1991). Personality and charisma in the U.S. presidency: A psychological theory of leadership effectiveness. *Administrative Science Quarterly, 36*(3), 364–396.

Howell, J. M., & Avolio, B. J. (1993). Transformational leadership, transactional leadership, locus of control, and support for innovation:

Key predictors of consolidated-business-unit performance. *Journal of Applied Psychology, 78,* 891–902.

Howell, J. M., & Frost, P. J. (1989). A laboratory study of charismatic leadership. *Organizational Behavior and Human Decision Processes, 43*(2), 243–269.

Howell, J. M., & Higgins, C. A. (1990). Champions of technological innovation. *Administrative Science Quarterly, 35,* 317–341.

Katz, D., & Kahn, R. L. (1978). *The social psychology of organizations.* New York: Wiley.

Kerr, S., & Jermier, J. M. (1978). Substitutes for leadership: Their meaning and measurement. *Organizational Behavior and Human Performance, 22,* 375–403.

Kipnis, D., Schmidt, S. M., & Wilkinson, I. (1980). Intraorganizational influence tactics: Explorations in getting one's way. *Journal of Applied Psychology, 6,* 440–451.

Kirkpatrick, S. A. (1992). *Decomposing charismatic leadership: The effects of leader content and process on follower performance, attitudes, and perceptions.* Unpublished doctoral dissertation, University of Maryland, College Park.

Klemp, G. O., & McClelland, D. C. (1986). What characterizes intelligent functioning among senior managers? In R. J. Sternberg & R. K. Wagner (Eds.), *Practical intelligence: Nature and origins of competence in the everyday world.* Cambridge: Cambridge University Press.

Koene, H., Pennings, H., & Schreuder, M. (1991). *Leadership, culture, and organizational effectiveness.* Paper presented at the Center for Creative Leadership Conference, Boulder, CO.

Koh, W. L., Terborg, J. R., & Steers, R. M. (1991). *The impact of transformational leaders on organizational commitment, organizational citizenship behavior, teacher satisfaction, and student performance in Singapore.* Paper presented at the meeting of the Academy of Management, Miami, FL.

Korman, A. K. (1971). Expectancies as determinants of performance. *Journal of Applied Psychology, 55,* 218–222.

Kouzes, J. M., & Posner, B. Z. (1987). *The leadership challenge: How to get extraordinary things done in organizations.* San Francisco: Jossey-Bass.

Likert, R. (1977). Management styles and the human component. *Management Review, 66,* 23–28.

Lord, R. G., & Maher, K. J. (1991). *Leadership and information processing: Linking perceptions and performance.* New York: Unwin Hyman.

McClelland, D. C. (1985). *Human motivation.* Glenview, IL: Scott, Foresman.

McClelland, D. C., & Boyatzis, R. (1982). The leadership pattern and long-term success in management. *Journal of Applied Psychology, 67,* 737–743.

McClelland, D. C., Koestner, R., & Weinberger, J. (1989). How do self-attributed and implicit motives differ? *Psychological Review, 96*(4), 690–702.

Maier, N.R.F. (1967). Assets and liabilities in group problem solving: The need for an integrative function. *Psychological Review, 74*, 239–249.

March, J. G. (1988). *Decisions and organizations.* Cambridge, MA: Blackwell.

Mintzberg, H. (1983). *Power in and around organizations.* Englewood Cliffs, NJ: Prentice Hall.

Mischel, W. (1973). Toward a cognitive social learning reconceptualization of personality. *Psychological Review, 80*, 252–283.

Nadler, D. A., & Tushman, M. L. (1990). Beyond the charismatic leader. *California Management Review, 32*(2), 77–97.

Narayan, V. K., & Fahey, L. (1982). The micro politics of strategy formation. *Academy of Management Review, 7*, 25–34.

Nisbett, R., & Ross, L. (1980). *Human inferences: Strategies and shortcomings of social judgment.* Englewood Cliffs, NJ: Prentice Hall.

Pereira, D. (1987). *Factors associated with transformational leadership in an Indian engineering firm.* Paper presented at the meeting of the Administrative Science Association of Canada, Vancouver.

Pfeffer, J. (1981). *Power in organizations.* Boston: Pitman.

Pillai, R., & Meindl, J. R. (1991). The effects of a crisis on the emergence of charismatic leadership: A laboratory study. *Best Paper Proceedings of the Academy of Management,* pp. 420–425.

Podsakoff, P. M., MacKenzie, S. B., Moorman, R. H., & Fetter, R. (1990). Transformational leader behaviors and their effects on followers' trust in leader, satisfaction, and organizational citizenship behaviors. *Leadership Quarterly, 1*(2), 107–142.

Roberts, N. C. (1985). Transforming leadership: A process of collective action. *Human Relations, 38*, 1023–1046.

Rosenthal, R., & Jacobson, L. (1968). *Pygmalion in the classroom: Teacher expectation and pupils' intellectual development.* Fort Worth, TX: Holt, Rinehart and Winston.

Runyon, K. E. (1973). Some interactions between personality variables and management styles. *Journal of Applied Psychology, 57*(3), 288–294.

Sashkin, M. (1988). The visionary leader. In J. A. Conger & R. A. Kanungo (Eds.), *Charismatic leadership: The elusive factor in organizational effectiveness.* San Francisco: Jossey-Bass.

Sashkin, M., & Fulmer, R. M. (1988). Toward an organizational leadership theory. In J. A. Conger & R. A. Kanungo (Eds.), *Charismatic leadership: The elusive factor in organizational effectiveness.* San Francisco: Jossey-Bass.

Seltzer, J., & Bass, B. M. (1990). Transformational leadership: Beyond initiation and consideration. *Journal of Management, 16,* 693–703.

Selznick, P. (1957). *Leadership in administration: A sociological interpretation.* New York: Harper.

Shamir, B., House, R. J., & Arthur, M. (1993). The motivational effects of charismatic leadership: A self-concept based theory. *Organizational Science, 4,* 577–594.

Siminton, D. K. (1988). Presidential style: Personality, biography, and performance. *Journal of Personality and Social Psychology, 55*(6), 928–936.

Simon, H. A. (1987). Making management decisions: The role of intuition and emotion. *Academy of Management Executive, 1,* 57–64.

Smelser, N. (1963). *A theory of collective behavior.* New York: Free Press.

Spangler, W. D., & House, R. J. (1991). Presidential effectiveness and the leadership motive profile. *Journal of Personality and Social Psychology, 60*(30), 439–455.

Steele, R. S. (1973). *The physiological concomitants of psychogenic motive arousal in college males.* Unpublished doctoral dissertation, Harvard University, Cambridge, MA.

Tannenbaum, A. S., & Allport, F. H. (1956). Personality structure and group structure: An interpretive study of their relationship through an event-structure hypothesis. *Journal of Abnormal and Social Psychology, 53,* 272–280.

Trice, H. M., & Beyer, J. M. (1986). Charisma and its routinization in two social movement organizations. In B. M. Staw & L. L. Cummings (Eds.), *Research in organizational behavior* (Vol. 8). Greenwich, CT: JAI Press.

Tversky, A., & Kannaman, D. (1974). Judgement under uncertainty: Heuristics and biases. *Science, 185,* 1124–1131.

Vroom, V. H. (1959). Some personality determinants of the effects of participation. *Journal of Abnormal and Social Psychology, 59,* 322–327.

Vroom, V. H., & Jago, A. G. (1988). *The new leadership: Management practices in organizations.* Englewood Cliffs, NJ: Prentice Hall.

Waldman, D. A., & Ramirez, G. (1992). *CEO leadership and organizational performance: The moderating effect of environmental uncertainty.* Working paper #92–10, Concordia University, Montreal, Canada.

Weber, M. (1947). *The theory of social and economic organization* (A. M. Henderson & T. Parsons, Trans.). New York: Free Press. (Original work published 1924.)

Willner, A. R. (1984). *The spellbinders: Charismatic political leadership.* New Haven, CT: Yale University Press.

Winter, D. G. (1973). *The power motive.* New York: Free Press.

Yukl, G. (1994a). *Leadership in organizations* (3rd ed.). Englewood Cliffs, NJ: Prentice Hall.

Yukl, G. (1994b). A retrospective on Robert House's 1976 theory of charismatic leadership and recent revisions. *Leadership Quarterly, 4*(3–4), 367–373.

Chapter Twelve

Changing Conceptions and Practices in Performance Appraisal

Jerry W. Hedge, Walter C. Borman

As the world of work is transformed to reflect changes in technologies, in the society, and in the demographics of the workforce, our opinion is that *the need* for evaluating job performance will remain constant. However, the way we go about the process of gathering accurate performance data will require new thinking about old approaches and innovative ideas about new approaches. Based on some current and projected trends in the nature of work, we speculate in this chapter on some of the issues and answers for performance evaluation in the future. First we present a brief overview of these trends.

Everywhere we turn we hear that corporate America is in the process of reinventing itself for the twenty-first century. A fundamental economic change is afoot: the replacement of industry's century-old electromechanical base by the computer-based service infrastructure, the replacement of the tradesman by the technician. Constant technological advances are changing work patterns, making flexible hours and working from home more commonplace. Workers will be expected to have a variety of skills, be subjected to frequent retraining, and be more self-directed. Management will change, with new priorities of product quality and customer satisfaction reflecting a shift from manufacturing to service (Goldstein & Gilliam, 1990). In the future, flexibility, in addition to the traditional skills and abilities, will be a hallmark of employment (Lewthwaite, 1993).

We believe that several present and likely future trends in organizations and in the U.S. economy, many of them described in other chapters of this book, will lead to significant changes in the way performance appraisal is accomplished. The following trends seem especially important for influencing future performance appraisal research and practice: (1) the increasing pace of technological change in many jobs and organizations in the United States and elsewhere (Gattiker, 1990); (2) as a consequence of technological change, the accelerating need for worker training and retraining, with the accompanying need to evaluate success in training (London & Bassman, 1989); (3) the movement revolving around worker empowerment, partnerships between management and employees, the encouragement of self-management, and stewardship (Block, 1993; "Empowering Workers," 1991); (4) alternative formats to the traditional office, including working at home (Calem, 1993), telecommuting (Leyden, 1993), "virtual organizations" (Offermann & Gowing, 1990), and other variants; (5) the rapidly increasing use of temporary workers (Diesenhouse, 1993), even at highly skilled and professional levels (for example, "elite temps"); and (6) the burgeoning amount of attention paid to customer satisfaction, with the continuing shift from a manufacturing to a service economy (Peters & Waterman, 1982; Peters & Austin, 1985).

We turn now to a more specific look at performance appraisal, recognizing that how we work and where we work are becoming more diversified than ever before. Within this context, we examine the usefulness of different performance rating sources, including supervisor, peer, self, subordinate, and customer. We also discuss the potential use of other methods of evaluation, such as electronic performance monitoring and work sample testing. Because of the increased reliance on work teams, we examine the concept of team performance and productivity as well. We also discuss the need for a more thorough coverage of the criterion space (for example, prosocial and contextual performance), and how these continued and rapid changes in the workplace are affecting workers' attitudes about, and reactions to, performance appraisal.

Performance Ratings

Ideally, ratings can provide performance scores that are free from contamination *and* deficiency—that is, perfectly relevant. This is because, first, as long as performance requirements for a job can be articulated and defined, rating scales can be developed to reflect those performance requirements. Second, the rater or raters using these dimensions to make evaluations can, again ideally, average performance levels observed over time and in different job situations to arrive at a rating on each dimension.

This assessment of ratings reflects the potential the method has for yielding accurate performance scores. Unfortunately, rater errors, biases, and other inaccuracies detract from the scores' validity. Still, it is safe to assume that performance ratings will continue to retain their predominance, if for no other reasons than ease of acquisition and cost, as has always been the case. However, the usefulness or accuracy of a particular rating source may vary considerably according to the structure of the work environment. For example, it may be perfectly appropriate to ask customers to rate the performance of a retail sales clerk, but inappropriate to rely on peer ratings for a telecommuter who spends 75 percent of the work week at home.

In addition, the purpose for which performance ratings are intended appears to play a role in their usefulness. Management uses evaluations for general personnel decisions, such as promotions and terminations. Evaluations also identify training and development needs, pinpointing employee skills and competencies that are currently inadequate but for which programs can be developed. Finally, performance evaluations can be used as a criterion against which selection and development programs are validated. As we discuss the usefulness of different appraisal methods, we do so with an eye to purpose.

The usual practice in most organizations is for an employee to be evaluated by an immediate supervisor. In recent years some organizations have come to realize that other sources besides an employee's boss can provide appraisals. Because of the dramatic changes affecting the workplace, problems of relying on any one source of appraisal alone may become amplified. The use of multiple sources for performance ratings has continued to gain acceptance over the last decade and numerous advantages have been cited. It is even becoming fashionable to talk about 360-degree feedback, where evaluations are sought from supervisors, peers, and even subordinates and customers in the belief that feedback from these individuals is enriched by including multiple sources of input. In organizations where 360-degree feedback has been adopted, its primary focus has been developmental, although it has been used for administrative and validation purposes as well (Tornow, 1993a).

While the notion of ratings from multiple sources is not new, the initiative for a formalized program of feedback to managers from their constituents is in its infancy. Much still needs to be done to make such programs viable (see London & Beatty, 1993; Moses, Hollenbeck, & Sorcher, 1993; Tornow, 1993a).

We recommend reliance on more than one source of ratings whenever possible. As the workplace continues to change, we need to be flexible and innovative by using different sources, alone or in combination, as the work environment and purpose of appraisal dictate. We turn now to a closer look at each rating source in terms of its usefulness in the future world of work.

Supervisory Ratings

Changes in the technology of work are likely to have a significant impact on supervisory performance appraisal. In particular, computer-based technologies often allow employees to work with minimal supervision, sometimes at home. In situations such as telecommuting, or even where semiautonomous work groups are in place, the supervisor will not be in a good position to observe the worker's performance on a regular basis, and other methods of evaluation may be needed.

In other cases the structure of the organization may facilitate close supervision, but because of rapidly changing technologies, supervisors may be less familiar with the technology than are their subordinates. Consequently, technology may undermine the role of the supervisor in performance appraisal (Murphy & Cleveland, 1991). As a result, the supervisor may not be perceived as a competent judge of the technical aspects of subordinates' performance. In such situations, other sources (such as peers) or methods of appraisal (for example, work sample tests using expert evaluators) must be relied on to provide information about technical performance to supplement the supervisory evaluation.

Still, it seems likely to us that the supervisor will remain the primary source of performance appraisal in the workplace of the future. Companies will not abandon supervisor appraisals merely because appraisal accuracy may be affected. Regardless of whether the purpose of appraisal is validation, administrative decision making, or employee development, supervisors will likely retain the responsibility of maintaining close enough contact with subordinates that sufficient information about some technical, motivational, and interpersonal aspects of performance can be gathered as a basis for evaluation. Consequently, research must continue to explore ways to enhance supervisory appraisal accuracy.

Peer Ratings

Peer appraisals have consistently been shown to be reliable. Because multiple peer ratings tend to be collected for each person evaluated, such assessments frequently provide a stable measure relatively free of the bias and idiosyncrasies of a single rater. Also, Latham (1986) has argued that reliability is affected positively by the daily interactions among peers. Not only do peers see how the employee interacts with them, but they also observe how that employee interacts with subordinates and supervisors. Thus peers often have access to more job-relevant information on which to base an evaluation than do other sources.

In terms of the future, peer ratings may be out of the question for employees who work at home, especially those who work in isolation. However, it is conceivable that telecommuters may be linked together and communicate by telephones or computers. In such cases, peers could have access to some aspects of their co-workers' behavior, or the products of that behavior, and thereby provide a relevant evaluation of performance.

The usefulness of peer evaluations may be greater in a team-oriented workplace. Because work groups, to varying degrees, tend to monitor and manage their own performance processes, peer evaluations would seem to be especially relevant with them. Group members work in close proximity, are able to observe each other's technical and interpersonal job behaviors, and should therefore be in an excellent position to rate their co-workers. Unfortunately, McEvoy and Buller (1987) noted that peer ratings are not well accepted by raters or those rated except when they are used for developmental purposes. The problem here focuses on asking group members to play a major role in the administrative decision process. Appraising and rewarding individual performance using a peer-rating system may hinder coordination and increase intragroup conflict.

Thus in spite of certain attractive features of peer ratings in a team environment, caution may be advised in the *administrative* use of performance ratings from peers. The problem associated with acceptance of peer ratings by the peers themselves should be less onerous when the focus is either developmental or for validation/research purposes, or in situations where the team concept is not an integral part of the organizational structure.

Self-Ratings

Much has been written about self-appraisals. Researchers have suggested that self-ratings are unreliable, biased, and inaccurate compared to other ratings sources or more "objective" criteria (for example, De Nisi & Shaw, 1977; Levine, Flory, & Ash, 1977; Nilsen & Campbell, 1993). Other researchers paint a more favorable picture of self-ratings (for example, Carroll & Schneier, 1982; Latham & Wexley, 1981; Shrauger & Osberg, 1981).

Much of the empirical research cited suggests that self-ratings differ from other types of ratings; a major question is whether *different* means *less accurate*. Dunnette (1993) concluded that self-descriptions do, indeed, possess accurate components, and suggested that it is premature to presume that others' ratings should always be used to assess the validity of self-ratings.

Self-ratings have certain advantages. Latham and Wexley (1981) have noted that, from a developmental perspective, self-ratings force the employee to focus on what's expected in the job. Also, they allow the supervisor to see how subordinates perceive their level of effectiveness. Thus self-appraisals may help clarify and even resolve differences of opinion between the subordinate and boss concerning performance requirements. In addition, self-appraisal helps employees to think about strengths and weaknesses in their performance and, ideally, stimulates activity toward self-improvement. In fact, the recent research on procedural justice suggests that giving the employee an opportunity to provide performance information to the supervisor should also increase the employee's perceptions of evaluation fairness (Greenberg, 1986).

Self-appraisals may be especially appropriate for employees working in isolation, a scenario that will occur more often as we look toward a future of increased telecommunication. In such work environments, what are the options for assessing performance? Employees working in isolation may know more about their own performance than anyone else and should at least be capable of providing information about their own strengths and weaknesses (Campbell & Lee, 1988).

When performance appraisal is being done for administrative purposes and work is relatively independent, self-ratings may be a necessary component of the appraisal, along with other sources of information. For example, later in the chapter we discuss the use of electronic performance monitoring, a method that can capture product or process aspects of employee performance. An employee working at home could be monitored by computer, and that information along with a self-appraisal could be used to evaluate the individual's performance. In such instances, if the employees know that self-ratings make up only part of the evaluation, the presence of other performance data may increase the chances that the self-ratings will be accurate.

Subordinate Ratings

Despite evidence that use of subordinate appraisal is on the increase, there is almost no empirical research to support upward appraisal for any purpose. A recent study by Bernardin, Dahmus, and Redmon (1993) does provide reaction data showing that supervisors were supportive of subordinate appraisal as a useful source of data, except when used as a basis for determining pay.

A number of years ago, Latham and Wexley (1981) suggested that subordinate ratings can aid management in identifying supervisors who are promotable because of their skill in managing people. More recently, Tornow (1993b) suggested that subordinates can be seen as providing the most direct source of feedback regarding the target manager's leadership behavior.

Despite the lack of supportive research on subordinate appraisal, a growing number of companies now use this source for appraising supervisors and managers; these include Amoco, Bank of America, Du Pont, Wells Fargo, Exxon, Tenneco, the World Bank, Johnson & Johnson, and GTE (Bernardin, Dahmus, & Redmon, 1993; Michels, 1991). Such appraisals are seen as valuable because they can foster team-building, force supervisors and subordinates to gain a better understanding of each other's jobs, and supply information about a manager's "people" skills from the subordinate's point of view.

If organizations of the future increasingly encourage team-based environments, as recent trends suggest (for example, Tannenbaum, Beard, & Salas, 1992), subordinates can contribute useful performance data to the appraisal process. Subordinate appraisals can support team-building by challenging workers and their bosses to discuss and resolve problems of mutual concern. Also, when subordinates must evaluate their bosses on a variety of work performance dimensions, it encourages them to view problems through the eyes of their supervisor, thus allowing them to gain a fuller appreciation of the supervisor's job. Equally important, once the feedback is received, the supervisor can begin to see concerns from the perspective of subordinates.

Probably the biggest potential problem with subordinate appraisals is the fear that supervisors will exact retribution if an honest but unfavorable appraisal is received. Thus it is critical that organizations maintain anonymity when using such ratings. Unfortunately, ensuring anonymity can become problematic if the work group is small.

At the very least, all should recognize that subordinates may provide valuable information about some aspects of the supervisor's performance but probably not all dimensions because of their somewhat limited perspective. Obviously, much additional research is needed in this area.

Customer Appraisals

Some organizations elicit performance appraisals from persons outside the immediate work environment. Customers are in a unique position to judge what the performance expectations are and how well they have been met, as this reflects customer satisfaction (Tornow, 1993a). Unfortunately, very little research is available to support or refute the use of these types of ratings. A study by Bernardin (1992) provided some support for customer-based appraisals as a source of added and unique information beyond that provided by top-down appraisal.

Ratings by customers or clients are probably the least used or studied source, but with the continued move toward a service economy, such evaluations make good sense. Customers provide another valuable perspective to be used in conjunction with other means of evaluating performance. Most service organizations acknowledge that customer satisfaction is critical for the survival of their business, yet few of them take formal steps to gather information about it. In some ways customer ratings may not face many of the problems associated with accuracy of other rating sources. If any source of appraisal would be brutally honest in its ratings, it is probably customers! Such ratings should be limited to customer service dimensions, however, as customers do not see all aspects of an employee's job performance. Customer ratings can be used for developmental, administrative, or validation purposes. Again, much additional research is needed in this area.

Electronic Performance Monitoring

A relatively new method of gathering performance data about individuals in the workplace is known as electronic performance monitoring. It is already gaining in popularity; according to a 1988 report to the U.S. Congress by the Office of Technology Assessment, approximately 10 million U.S. workers were subjected to secret electronic monitoring that year. Rather than being observed directly by supervisors, employees can be monitored electronically in a variety of ways. Probably the first kind used in industry was telephone monitoring, whereby supervisors (sitting next to the employee, or in their own office) listened in on employee telephone calls. Alternatively, rather than listening to the conversation at the time it occurs, an audiotape of a worker's telephone call can be made for later analysis. Video cameras can also be used to capture employee activities on tape. Computer monitoring has evolved to the point that some computer systems are designed to record and evaluate information as detailed as the number of keystrokes made per minute and the number of breaks a computer user takes; other systems allow managers to access an employee's computer screen and watch work from a distance (Laabs, 1992).

Electronic performance monitoring has become one of the more controversial areas involved with new technology in the workplace. Critics charge that computerized employee monitoring is an invasion of privacy and disregards human rights, undermines trust, reduces autonomy, and emphasizes quantity to the exclusion of quality. Other critics suggest that electronic performance monitoring causes stress and is counterproductive because its use leads to declines in employee morale and productivity. Forester and Morrison (1990) described an organization in which the main computer records how long each clerk spends on each call and how much time separates one call from the next. Workers earn negative points for spending more than a predetermined target time handling a call, or taking more time than allowed for breaks.

Supporters of computer monitoring argue that it provides concrete, accurate performance measurement and a mechanism around which managers can motivate employees by providing incentives and effective rewards based on merit and effort. They also point out that what is being measured is factual, and that many workers favor such systems because they allow diligent workers to legitimately argue a case for better pay and benefits, with the case not relying on personal opinions or personalities (Forester & Morrison, 1990).

Data to support or refute the usefulness of the method are scarce. Laabs's (1992) interviews with management and employees subject to performance monitoring in a number of organizations (including Duke Power Company, AT&T, Toyota, Avis, and Charles Schwab) suggest that electronic monitoring is especially useful if its primary purpose is employee development. Managers in these organizations argued, for example, that a useful way to improve individuals' selling skills is to listen and critique their performance on sales calls. Some organizations listen in and provide immediate feedback in the form of noting strengths and weaknesses. Others (such as Duke Power Company), according to Laabs, rate performance on a nine-point scale across a number of dimensions such as courtesy, listening ability, empathy, job knowledge, professional and positive attitude, communication skills, documentation and follow-up, marketing, and closing statement.

Murphy and Cleveland (1991) suggested that automatic monitoring may be regarded negatively by employees, but little is known about the conditions under which it will cause major problems (for example, employee stress or lowered morale). Turnage (1990) proposed that if it is used for evaluation, monitoring may cause distress and affect individual motives, goals, and performance; if it is used to give workers accurate, meaningful, nonevaluative feedback, however, it could serve to increase goal setting, allow greater control over individual performance, and thus increase motivation.

What additional influences could automatic monitoring of employees' behavior have on that behavior and performance appraisal? Grant, Higgins, and Irving (1988) examined the behavior and attitudes of monitored and unmonitored claims processors in a large insurance company. They found that monitored employees rated production quantity as the most important factor in their jobs, while unmonitored employees identified customer service and teamwork as their most important job factors. The authors suggested that monitored workers reasoned that unmonitored job factors did not count. A similarly negative outcome could be that supervisors will feel compelled to bring their evaluations in line with the objective data, even if they know that this depiction tells only part of the story regarding performance.

Grant and colleagues (1988) suggested that systems not monitoring all aspects of a job should be supplemented by other means of appraisal. They also noted that failure to provide frequent feedback on unmonitored performance dimensions will convince the employee that those dimensions are not important. These researchers also found that monitored employees were often aware that the performance data being collected through monitoring did not measure all parts of their job and perceived this as unfair.

As mentioned earlier, one of the consequences of new office communications technology is the ability to work at locations away from the traditional office. Computer monitoring may be especially appropriate as a means for gathering performance information about individuals who work in relative isolation or who spend much of their work week away from the traditional office. In addition, it may help to keep individuals "honest" if they are asked to complete self-ratings. Clearly, much additional research is needed on this method before we can reach any definitive conclusions about its usefulness.

Work Samples

Historically, work samples or performance tests have been used more commonly as predictors than as criterion measures (for example, Asher & Sciarrino, 1974). However, in one sense they represent a compelling criterion measurement method. What could be a fairer measure of job performance than to ask incumbents to complete several of the most important job tasks and then evaluate their performance on them? Performance tests appear to address directly the incumbent's ability to do the job. Performance or work sample testing has been referred to as a "high-fidelity" criterion measurement method, and other methods, such as job knowledge tests and performance ratings, as "surrogates" to performance tests (Wigdor & Green, 1991). In fact, researchers (for example, Ghiselli & Brown, 1948; Guion, 1979; Robertson & Kandola, 1982; Siegel, 1986) have advocated work sample tests because they are direct, relevant measures of job proficiency that extract samples of behavior under realistic job conditions.

The most frequently used work sample methodology is hands-on testing. Individuals are asked to demonstrate proficiency on a set of tasks by performing the steps required for successful completion. Hands-on tests have been used as criteria for evaluating training programs (for example, Goldstein, 1974), validating selection devices (for example, Siegel & Jensen, 1955), identifying individual skill deficiencies (for example, Goldstein, 1980), and establishing worker job/task certification (for example, Guion, 1979).

The major advantage of using work sample methods is that they permit the employee's skills and knowledge to be compared to known standards under controlled and uniform conditions. Their main drawback is that the employee's performance during testing may not accurately reflect that person's daily performance on the job. In addition, work sample measures rarely cover all aspects of the criterion space.

Recent work by Hedge and Teachout (1992) on a measure of individual technical job competence may provide further support for the use of work sample methodology. Their approach, known as Walk-Through Performance Testing, is a task-level job performance measurement system that combines hands-on task performance and interview procedures. The hands-on component resembles a traditional hands-on work sample test designed to measure proficiency on a set of critical tasks. The interview component of the test requires incumbents to *describe* in detail how they would perform a job-related task. The administrator evaluates their *show and tell* descriptions for proficiency-based strengths and weaknesses related to the performance of that task. Just as with the hands-on component, the test administrator records correct or incorrect completion of each step of the task. One potential benefit of this interview testing methodology is that it combines the rigors of work sample testing with measurement efficiency (that is, time/cost savings). In addition, it affords the opportunity to assess proficiencies on tasks that cannot be measured feasibly in a hands-on mode.

In the future, as technologies continue to evolve rapidly, technical skills may become obsolete more quickly, and the need will increase for frequent evaluation of the employee's performance. However, because of their own skill obsolescence, supervisors may find it difficult to evaluate their subordinates' technical proficiency accurately. In such situations, a work sample criterion measure and "certified evaluators" may be an especially useful supplement to supervisory ratings for administrative or developmental purposes.

Productive Capacity

In 1989 the Air Force began to examine time-based measures of job performance (Carpenter, Monaco, O'Mara, & Teachout, 1989). The notion here was that a quality-based metric (that is, the usual 1–5, 1–7, 1–9 rating scale) was not as suited to addressing certain manpower issues as was a quantity-based metric. Consider, for example, the problem of estimating repair time for four F-111s with certain specified problems. How long will it take five average airman mechanics to do the work? Or conversely, given that we must get the four F-111s in the air in sixteen hours to meet mission requirements, how many average-performance-level airman mechanics will be required, how many high-performance-level mechanics, and so on?

Carpenter and various colleagues (Carpenter et al., 1989; Skinner, Faneuff, & Demetriades, 1991; Harville & Skinner, 1993) reasoned that individuals could be evaluated on each of a number of tasks according to how quickly they could complete the task (above a certain minimum level of quality). A person's productive capacity could then be determined for a task or series of tasks. A rating scale developed by Skinner and co-workers (1991) gave raters an absolute standard against which to compare the time required by each person evaluated to complete each task. The benchmarks were time estimates to complete a task successfully at three different competency levels: fastest possible, average or normal, and slowest possible. Skinner and her associates demonstrated that these benchmarks could be reliably estimated for several tasks associated with four Air Force jobs and thus could serve as useful reference points for raters judging the amount of time required for *their* airman being evaluated to complete a task successfully. Harville and Skinner (1993) subsequently demonstrated that time-to-complete estimates, made using benchmarked scales, correlated moderately with the actual times taken to complete work samples of the corresponding tasks for three of the four jobs studied.

These productive capacity ratings have the potential to address directly the manpower questions presented earlier and therefore may be quite useful for some organizational applications in the future (Borman & Hedge, 1993). Certainly in the U.S. military, more and more attention is being paid to manpower planning issues. The productive capacity, quantity-based measurement system is much more relevant for addressing these issues than are our usual quality-based rating methods. One could generate a productive capacity index for the individual, the work unit, or even the entire organization.

Team Appraisal

Interest in organizing work around teams has increased in the last few years. Generally, a team is defined as an interdependent collection of individuals, assigned specific roles and functions, who work toward a common goal or objective (see Salas, Dickinson, Converse, & Tannenbaum, 1992; Sundstrom, De Meuse, & Futrell, 1990). Various researchers have postulated models that describe the variables necessary for effective team performance (for example, Hackman, 1983, as described in Salas et al., 1992; Morgan, Glickman, Woodard, Blaiwes, & Salas, 1986; Tannenbaum et al., 1992). For instance, the integrative model of Tannenbaum and others (1992) views team effectiveness as a product of multiple factors (examples are in parentheses): the organizational and situational context (organizational climate; reward systems), task characteristics (task complexity), work structure (team norms), individual characteristics (ability; motivation), team characteristics (team cohesiveness; member homogeneity), and team processes (coordination; communication). Outputs (and examples) are team performance (quantity; quality; errors), team changes (new norms; new communication patterns), and individual changes (attitudes; motivation). These models have much in common, and for our purposes serve to demonstrate the additional levels of complexity associated with team performance appraisal.

In some situations, team performance can be measured as an average of individual outputs, but in other situations such a strategy can be misleading. For example, Salas and others (1992) noted that individual skills are necessary for team success but are not sufficient for good team performance. In fact, Steiner (1972) defined "process loss" as occurring whenever team member efforts are wasted or duplicated in the course of meeting team coordination and communication requirements. Thus Steiner described team performance as a function of the ability of team members to perform their individual tasks, coordinate their work flow, and communicate effectively with one another.

The team evolution and maturation model developed by Morgan and others (1986) aptly describes this process as consisting of two basic tracks that must be successfully integrated for satisfactory team performance to be reached. One track deals with task-oriented skills that members must understand and acquire for task performance; the other track reflects the behaviors and attitudes that team members must develop before they can function effectively as a team. Specific teamwork behaviors include coordination, adaptation to varying situational demands, effective communication, compensatory behaviors, mutual performance monitoring, and giving/receiving feedback.

Individual performance within the team obviously can be appraised by any of the methods previously described. For example, supervisors could evaluate each of the team members under them. What is more interesting, and what may become more common in the future, is to evaluate *the team's* performance. With the emergence of work teams, managers' objectives increasingly may be tied to team goals. Consequently, it may be important to assess work group performance as well as individual performance. Overall team performance might be assessed, or multiple dimensions could be rated (for example, Morgan's task-oriented and teamwork dimensions).

An innovative method developed by Pritchard, Jones, Roth, Stuebing, and Ekeberg (1988) provides a measure of team or unit overall performance by merging specific indicators into an index of percentage. Briefly, they had organization members identify multiple outcomes or products from the organization. Then, in an especially appealing feature of the method, they scaled different levels of the outcomes according to the degree of effectiveness represented. Consider, for example, a repair facility unit, one of the organizations for which Pritchard and colleagues developed a productivity measurement system. Organization members, with the help of a consultant, first identified seven indicators that they believed reflected reasonable indexes of the unit's productivity. For example, one of the indicators was the number of units per week returned for re-repair. The unit members then constructed for each indicator what the researchers called a *contingency*, as illustrated in Figure 12.1.

In the example in Figure 12.1, unit members believed that five returns per week are expected, essentially an average outcome, and this was assigned an effectiveness score of 0. They thought the best possible return rate was two per week, and assigned a +80 score to that outcome; they judged the worst realistically possible to be ten per week and assigned that a -70 effectiveness score. The group then scored the remaining outcomes, resulting in the contingency appearing in Figure 12.1. As is evident from the example, contingencies may be nonlinear. Here two returns per week is not much more effective than three per week. The importance of the outcome to organizational effectiveness is represented by the slope of the curve, with a steep slope indicating a relatively important outcome. Using the contingencies, organizations can score individual

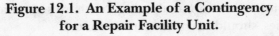

**Figure 12.1. An Example of a Contingency
for a Repair Facility Unit.**

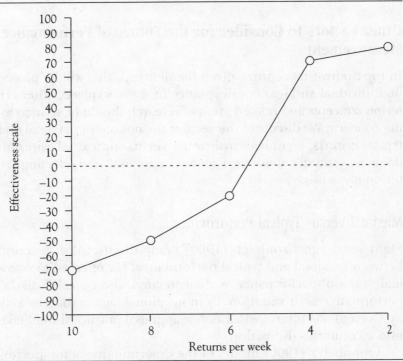

units on their outcomes and pool these scores to provide a single effectiveness value. The main advantage of this method is that multiple indicators of productivity can be pooled in a meaningful and psychometrically sound way.

Pritchard and colleagues (1988) have used the method primarily in productivity improvement programs, but it may also be employed in group performance appraisal. Different contingencies can be generated for different performance dimensions, and overall effectiveness scores computed for individual units. This method ties in nicely with the notion of rewarding performance at the team rather than the individual level. For example, assigning pay or bonuses based on appraised group performance should foster teamwork and encourage cooperation and support among team members. With increasing emphasis on teams in organizations, group performance appraisal, using Pritchard's approach or similar strategies, should become more common.

Other Factors to Consider for the Future of Performance Measurement

In the twenty-first century, given the demands that will be placed on individual and team performance in the workplace, other criterion concepts and related areas of research should be of increasing concern. We discuss in this section the notions of maximal and typical criteria, technical proficiency versus contextual criterion domains, attitudes about performance appraisal, and selecting criterion measures.

Maximal Versus Typical Performance

Many years ago Cronbach (1960) made the useful distinction between maximal and typical performance. He referred to maximal, "can-do" performance as ability-related, and typical, "will-do" performance as driven more by motivational factors than by ability. Current *and* future performance appraisal practice should take into account this distinction.

Campbell's (1990) model of the determinants of job performance clarifies the distinction. The model implies that performance is a function of declarative or factual knowledge, procedural knowledge (that is, knowing how to do a task), and motivation. Maximal performance is involved in the first two components, and the motivation component is important for typical performance. Maximal performance measures, such as work samples and hands-on performance tests, usually constrain those tested to try hard for the short duration of the test, and thus motivation is essentially held constant. Typical performance, on the other hand, depends substantially on motivation. Will-do performance-over-time requires job knowledge certainly, but also requires sustained, motivated effort in a setting where motivation is *not* constrained and can clearly vary across job incumbents.

How does ability fit in here? Performance models offered and confirmed by Hunter (1983), Schmidt, Hunter, and Outerbridge

(1986), and Borman, White, Pulakos, and Oppler (1991) demonstrate a clear path from ability (that is, general cognitive ability) to job knowledge to technical proficiency, where the proficiency variable is a maximum performance measure. Interestingly, when Borman and associates included supervisory performance ratings with selected personality measures and behavioral variables reflecting mostly typical performance, a model emerged with achievement orientation, dependability, and technical proficiency all influencing the ratings (see Figure 12.2).

One way to interpret these results, within the framework of maximal/typical performance and their antecedents, is as follows. The ratings are likely measures of both maximal and typical performance. They are meant to tap typical performance, but raters may consider can-do performance when rating such dimensions as Technical Knowledge and Technical Skill. Accordingly, maximal performance (technical proficiency) appears to be a function of ability and job knowledge, but not so much a function of personality. Typical

Figure 12.2. Antecedents of Maximal and Typical Performance.

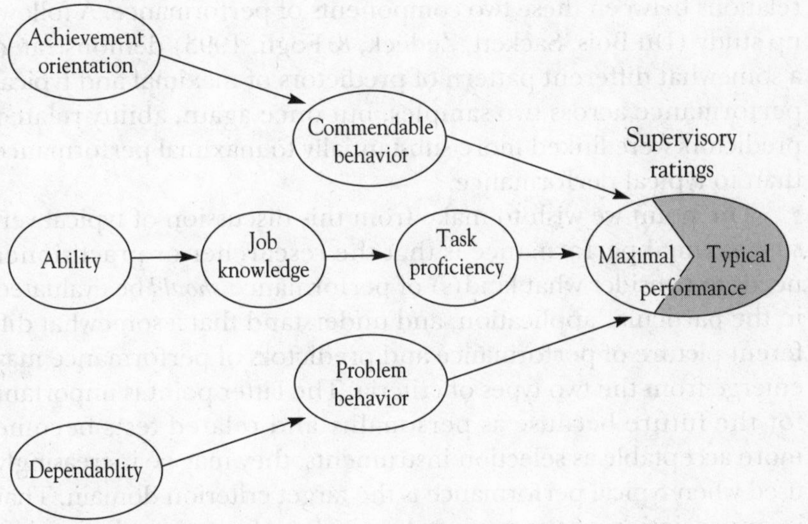

Source: Adapted from Borman, White, Pulakos, & Oppler, 1991.

performance, as captured in the ratings, has as antecedents both the ability/job knowledge/technical proficiency sequence of variables *and* personality through the typical performance behavioral variables. It may be that the technical proficiency-ratings path would not be as large if the ratings reflected only typical performance, although this is clearly speculation. Nonetheless, what this performance model suggests is that maximal and typical performance can be distinguished because they have somewhat different antecedents. They are both very important for organizational functioning and may not be highly correlated.

A study by Sackett, Zedeck, and Fogli (1988) provides a more direct picture of the maximal-typical performance linkage. Working with grocery clerks, these researchers designed a maximal performance work sample test that consisted of ringing up items in a standardized shopping cart. Measures of speed (total time to complete the cart) and accuracy (number of voids and incorrect entries) were derived from this test. For the typical performance measure, a computer-monitored system kept track of each grocery clerk's performance over a thirty-day period. Speed (number of items rung up per minute) and accuracy (number of voids per day) were measured. The most striking finding here is the generally low correlations between these two components of performance. A follow-up study (Du Bois, Sackett, Zedeck, & Fogli, 1993) demonstrated a somewhat different pattern of predictors of maximal and typical performance across two samples, but once again, ability-related predictors were linked more substantially to maximal performance than to typical performance.

The point we wish to make from this discussion of typical versus maximal performance is that the researcher or practitioner needs to consider what kind(s) of performance *should* be evaluated in the particular application, and understand that a somewhat different picture of performance and predictors of performance may emerge from the two types of criteria. The latter point is important for the future because as personality and related tests become more acceptable as selection instruments, they may be increasingly used when typical performance is the target criterion domain. That is, appreciation of the maximal-typical performance distinction should make it even more likely that personality predictors are seen as appropriate for personnel selection because of their link with typical, will-do performance.

Technical Proficiency Versus Contextual Criterion Domains

Another construct distinction is between task performance and contextual performance. Borman and Motowidlo (1993a) discussed this distinction and its implications for personnel selection. Task performance relates to the proficiency with which job incumbents perform the core technical activities that are important for their jobs. The authors defined contextual performance as extra-task proficiency that contributes more to the organizational, social, and psychological environment to help accomplish organizational goals. Integrating elements of organizational citizenship (for example, Organ, 1988), prosocial organizational behavior (for example, Brief & Motowidlo, 1986), and a model of soldier effectiveness (Borman, Motowidlo, & Hanser, 1983), Borman and Motowidlo (1992) identified the following contextual dimensions:

- Persisting with enthusiasm and extra effort as necessary to complete one's own task activities successfully
- Volunteering to carry out task activities that are not formally part of one's own job
- Helping and cooperating with others
- Following organizational rules and procedures
- Endorsing, supporting, and defending organizational objectives

There are conceptual and some limited empirical arguments to suggest that contextual performance is related to organizational effectiveness. That is, organizations with members effective in the contextual performance domain will tend to be more successful than organizations whose incumbents are ineffective in this domain (Borman & Motowidlo, 1993a). A recent study of U.S. Air Force enlisted personnel by Motowidlo and Van Scotter (described in Borman & Motowidlo, 1993b) found that the correlation for task and contextual performance was only .17, indicating that contextual performance cannot be "covered" by measuring technical proficiency alone.

Our view is that contextual performance will be seen as more important in the future. As the global economy demands that organizations become even more competitive, more will be expected of employees. As work teams become more prevalent, cooperation and working smoothly with others will be increasingly important.

Finally, as customer service continues to be a major emphasis in organizations, going "above and beyond the call" for customers will be increasingly expected of organization members.

Attitudes About Performance Appraisal

Workers' desires for autonomy and self-development are increasing, and today's workers have a growing sense of entitlement to be involved in the decisions pertaining to their work (Offermann & Gowing, 1990). Consequently, worker attitudes toward performance appraisal may play an increasingly important role in performance appraisal in the future. Murphy and Cleveland (1991) noted that the dominance of psychometric and accuracy criteria have diverted researchers' attention away from three classes of criteria that might be critical in determining the success of an appraisal system: reactions, practicality, and decision processes. They argued that reaction criteria (such as perceptions of fairness and accuracy of appraisal systems) probably place a ceiling on the effectiveness of the system; that is, acceptance of the system by raters and those rated may be necessary but not sufficient for the system to be effective. Dickinson (1993) suggested that if negative attitudes about performance appraisal prevail among organizational members, its use may hinder rather than help achieve outcomes.

In spite of the commonsense logic that acceptance of a personnel procedure is crucial to its effective use, the notion that attitudes toward performance ratings could affect their validity was not noted until 1967, when Lawler proposed a model of the factors that affect the construct validity of ratings. Central to the model was the belief that attitudes toward the equity and acceptability of a rating system are a function of organizational and individual characteristics as well as the rating format.

Landy, Barnes, and Murphy (1978) were among the first researchers to relate attitudinal factors empirically to job performance measurement. They identified four significant predictors of perceived fairness and accuracy of performance appraisals: (1) frequency of appraisal, (2) plans developed with the supervisor for eliminating weaknesses, (3) supervisor's knowledge of the job duties of the person rated, and (4) supervisor's knowledge of the level of performance of the person rated. In a follow-up study with the same population, researchers found that the level of the performance rating did not affect these relationships (Landy, Barnes-Farrell, & Cleveland, 1980). Dipboye and de Pontbriand (1981) further distinguished employees' opinions as to whether they related to the performance appraisal system or to the appraisal itself. They found that four factors related to the two dependent variables: (1) favorability of the appraisal, (2) opportunity for employees to state their own perspective in the appraisal interview, (3) job relevance of appraisal factors, and (4) discussion of plans and objectives with the supervisor.

A series of studies by Kavanagh and colleagues (Kavanagh & Hedge, 1983; Kavanagh, Hedge, Ree, Earles, & De Biasi, 1985) found that several attitudes toward the appraisal system were significant predictors of appraisal acceptability across studies. These included attitudes about whether (1) the appraisal system facilitates fair and accurate appraisals, (2) the appraisal system allows raters to distinguish between workers' proficiencies, (3) the appraisal system provides clear performance standards, (4) the individuals rated receive satisfactory feedback, and (5) they receive a satisfactory performance evaluation.

A related body of literature, which has received renewed attention of late with its translation into performance appraisal terms, concerns organizational justice (Thibaut & Walker, 1975). This research is directed at identifying the features of organizational procedures that affect perceptions of fairness, work attitudes, and behavior. The literature suggests that there are two dimensions of perceived justice to any policy: distributive justice and procedural justice. Interpreted in performance appraisal terms, *distributive justice* focuses on the fairness of the evaluations received relative to the work performed. *Procedural justice* focuses on the fairness of the evaluation procedures used to determine the ratings (Greenberg, 1986).

Giles and Mossholder (1990) identified four important organizational actions related to satisfaction with appraisals: removing excessive complexity from appraisal systems, properly introducing them into organizations, ensuring that supervisors conduct appraisal sessions, and linking salary adjustments with appraisal results. They suggested that if such actions are neglected, it is likely that the impact of the appraisal system will be substantially reduced.

A number of years ago Jacobs, Kafry, and Zedeck (1980) noted their own disappointing experiences with organizations that abandoned recently developed appraisal systems. They suggested that many organizations revert to evaluation systems in use prior to intervention because of organization policy and the excessive personnel time and energy requirements associated with, for example, behaviorally anchored rating scales. These frustrations, in a very applied way, speak to the issue of acceptability, and suggest its importance as a criterion when evaluating the effectiveness of an appraisal system. After all, if a psychometrically sound system is unacceptable to its users, it might never be used, or it might be used improperly. As Banks and Murphy (1985), and Longenecker, Sims, and Gioia (1987) have noted, raters must not only be capable, but they must also be *willing* to provide accurate ratings.

As the future work environment pushes us toward use of new and different appraisal techniques, it would be wise not to lose sight of how these approaches may be perceived by all parties involved in the appraisal process. Acceptance of a particular method or methods may be critical for successful implementation and use.

Identifying Additional Criteria for Criterion Measures

Over the years, researchers have identified and/or developed many examples of "criteria for criteria," or standards on which to assess the quality of criterion measures (Weitz, 1961). Bellows (1954) suggested that criterion measures be reliable, realistic, representative, related to other criteria, acceptable to the job analyst, acceptable to management, consistent from one situation to another, and predictable. Blum and Naylor (1968) proposed that criterion measures should also be inexpensive, understandable, measurable, relevant, uncontaminated and bias-free, and discriminating. Bernardin and Beatty (1984) compiled a large list of variables and clustered them into three primary categories of criteria: quantitative (for example, reliability, validity, discriminability); utilization (for example, feedback, merit pay, adverse impact); and qualitative (for example, amount of documentation, user acceptability, maintenance costs).

Although researchers have periodically called attention to the importance of using multiple criteria to judge criterion measures, they have seldom provided operational definitions of these variables. If some form of empirical evaluation is included, it is typically dominated by considerations of reliability and validity. Several researchers have attempted to apply a more systematic process to the use of multiple criteria to judge performance measures.

McAfee and Green (1977) applied sixteen criteria to aid the selection of a performance appraisal method for use in a large midwestern hospital. They rated ten different appraisal methods on criteria such as usefulness for counseling and employee development, expense to develop, reliability, and freedom from psychometric errors. They used a weighted sum to identify the best method for the job and organization under consideration. Drawing on this work, Kavanagh (1982) proposed nineteen criteria, each operationally defined, against which to judge the value of performance appraisal systems. Included were such things as psychometric quality, developmental costs, user acceptance, periodic review/feedback, meeting guidelines of the Equal Employment Opportunity Commission (EEOC), and susceptibility to inflation of ratings.

As dramatic changes continue to occur in the structure and function of the workplace, changes may also be required in how we approach the measurement of job performance. In this chapter we have suggested that performance appraisal in the workplace of the future may, by necessity, become much more varied and multifaceted. As such, reliance on a more formalized process of applying the type of criteria described by McAfee and Green (1977) and Kavanagh (1982) for selecting performance measures should improve the chances that adequate measures are chosen and that accurate, useful performance information is obtained.

Conclusion

Our focus in this chapter has been on the need for, and use of, performance appraisal strategies for enhancing the effectiveness of organizations. We believe that efforts devoted to evaluating performance are critical for workforce productivity. The measurement of employees has played and is likely to continue to play a major role in organizations, unless future jobs get structured to (1) eliminate performance variability or (2) severely reduce the control over performance by the worker.

Consequently, as we move toward the twenty-first century, rapidly changing job requirements and job environments demand that our performance appraisal systems reflect these changes. The performance appraisal system can help connect employees to the organization during these changing times; it can help them to identify how changes will affect their jobs, how performance expectations/goals will change, and how they will need to adapt to changing job requirements.

Regarding research, we must be open to investigating different measurement methods such as electronic performance monitoring, team effectiveness indexes, and subordinate and customer ratings. Research on objective performance measures and supervisor and peer ratings will remain important, but some of our attention should be focused on emerging methods as well.

Many organizations wisely employ a variety of strategies to increase individuals' productivity and organizational effectiveness. From the perspective of this chapter, we conclude by noting that only through carefully developed and implemented performance appraisal programs can we hope to utilize human resources efficiently in changing organizations.

References

Asher, J. J., & Sciarrino, J. A. (1974). Realistic work sample tests: A review. *Personnel Psychology, 27,* 519–533.

Banks, C. G., & Murphy, K. R. (1985). Toward narrowing the research-practice gap in performance appraisal. *Personnel Psychology, 38,* 335–345.

Bellows, R. M. (1954). *Psychology of personnel in business and industry* (2nd ed.). Englewood Cliffs, NJ: Prentice Hall.

Bernardin, H. J. (1992). An "analytic" framework for customer-based performance content development and appraisal. *Human Resource Management Review, 2,* 81–102.

Bernardin, H. J., & Beatty, R. W. (1984). *Performance appraisal: Assessing human behavior at work.* Boston: Kent.

Bernardin, H. J., Dahmus, S. A., & Redmon, G. (1993). Attitudes of first-line supervisors toward subordinate appraisals. *Human Resource Management, 32,* 315–324.

Block, P. (1993). *Stewardship: Choosing service over self-interest.* San Francisco: Berrett-Koehler.

Blum, M. L., & Naylor, J. C. (1968). *Industrial psychology.* New York: Harper.

Borman, W. C., & Hedge, J. W. (1993). *Exploring the concept of productive capacity measurement* (Institute Report no. 239). Minneapolis: Personnel Decisions Research Institute.

Borman, W. C., & Motowidlo, S. J. (1993a). Expanding the criterion domain to include elements of contextual performance. In N. Schmitt, W.

C. Borman, & Associates (Eds.), *Personnel selection in organizations*. San Francisco: Jossey-Bass.

Borman, W. C., & Motowidlo, S. J. (1993b, April). *Does personality predict job performance? It depends on the criterion.* Paper presented at the meeting of the Society for Industrial and Organizational Psychology, San Francisco.

Borman, W. C., Motowidlo, S. J., & Hanser, L. M. (1983, August). A model of individual performance effectiveness: Thoughts about expanding the criterion space. In N. K. Eaton & J. P. Campbell (Chairs), *Integrated criterion measurement for large scale computerized selection and classification.* Symposium conducted at the meeting of the American Psychological Association, Anaheim, CA.

Borman, W. C., White, L. A., Pulakos, E. D., & Oppler, S. H. (1991). Models of supervisory job performance ratings. *Journal of Applied Psychology, 76,* 863–872.

Brief, A. P., & Motowidlo, S. J. (1986). Prosocial organizational behaviors. *Academy of Management Review, 11,* 710–725.

Calem, R. E. (1993, April 25). Technology allows more to bring jobs home. *Star Tribune,* p. 1J.

Campbell, D. J., & Lee, C. (1988). Self-appraisal in performance evaluation: Development versus evaluation. *Academy of Management Review, 13,* 302–314.

Campbell, J. P. (1990). Modeling the performance prediction problem in industrial and organizational psychology. In M. D. Dunnette & L. M. Hough (Eds.), *Handbook of industrial and organizational psychology* (Vol. 1). Palo Alto, CA: Consulting Psychologists Press.

Carpenter, M. A., Monaco, S. J., O'Mara, F. E., & Teachout, M. S. (1989). *Time to job proficiency: A preliminary investigation of the effects of aptitude and experience on productive capacity* (AFHRL-TP-88–17). Brooks Air Force Base, TX: Training Systems Division, Air Force Human Resources Laboratory.

Carroll, S. J., & Schneier, C. E. (1982). *Performance appraisal and review systems: The identification, measurement, and development of performance in organizations.* Glenview, IL: Scott, Foresman.

Cronbach, L. J. (1960). *Essentials of psychological testing* (2nd ed.). New York: Harper.

De Nisi, A., & Shaw, J. B. (1977). Investigation of the uses of self-reports of abilities. *Journal of Applied Psychology, 62,* 641–644.

Dickinson, T. L. (1993). Attitudes about performance appraisal. In H. Schuler, J. L. Farr, & M. Smith (Eds.), *Personnel selection and assessment: Individual and organizational perspectives.* Hillsdale, NJ: Erlbaum.

Diesenhouse, S. (1993, May 31). More Americans leave mainstream for "elite" temporary corps. *Saint Paul Pioneer Press,* p. 6.

Dipboye, R., & de Pontbriand, R. (1981). Correlates of employee reactions to performance appraisals and appraisal systems. *Journal of Applied Psychology, 66,* 248–251.

Du Bois, D., Sackett, P. R., Zedeck, S., & Fogli, L. (1993). Further exploration of typical and maximum performance criteria: Definitional issues, prediction, and white-black differences. *Journal of Applied Psychology, 78,* 205–211.

Dunnette, M. D. (1993). My hammer or your hammer? *Human Resource Management, 32,* 373–384.

Empowering workers: Is it real or overplayed? (1991, June 18). *Wall Street Journal,* p. A1.

Forester, T., & Morrison, P. (1990). *Computer ethics: Cautionary tales and ethical dilemmas in computing.* Cambridge, MA: MIT Press.

Gattiker, U. E. (1990). *Technology management in organizations.* London: Sage.

Ghiselli, E. E., & Brown, C. W. (1948). *Personnel and industrial psychology.* New York: McGraw-Hill.

Giles, W. F., & Mossholder, K. W. (1990). Employee reactions to contextual and session components of performance appraisal. *Journal of Applied Psychology, 75,* 371–377.

Goldstein, I. L. (1974). *Training: Program development and evaluation.* Pacific Grove, CA: Brooks/Cole.

Goldstein, I. L. (1980). Training in work organizations. *Annual Review of Psychology, 31,* 229–272.

Goldstein, I. L., & Gilliam, P. (1990). Training system issues in the year 2000. *American Psychologist, 45,* 134–143.

Grant, R. A., Higgins, C. A., & Irving, R. H. (1988). Computerized performance monitors: Are they costing you customers? *Sloan Management Review, 29,* 39–45.

Greenberg, J. (1986). Determinants of perceived fairness of performance evaluations. *Journal of Applied Psychology, 71,* 340–342.

Guion, R. M. (1979, April). *Principles of work sample testing: I. A non-empirical taxonomy of test uses* (ARI-TR-79-A8). Alexandria, VA: Army Research Institute for the Behavioral and Social Sciences.

Hackman, J. R. (1983). *A normative model of work team effectiveness* (Technical Report no. 2). New Haven, CT: Yale University.

Harville, D. L., & Skinner, J. (1993, August). *Using supervisor estimates of time to job proficiency to set entry standards.* Paper presented at the annual meeting of the Academy of Management.

Hedge, J. W., & Teachout, M. S. (1992). An interview approach to work sample criterion measurement. *Journal of Applied Psychology, 77,* 453–461.

Hunter, J. E. (1983). A causal analysis of cognitive ability, job knowledge, job performance, and supervisory ratings. In F. Landy, S. Zedeck, & J. Cleveland (Eds.), *Performance measurement and theory*. Hillsdale, NJ: Erlbaum.

Jacobs, R., Kafry, D., & Zedeck, S. (1980). Expectations of behaviorally anchored rating scales. *Personnel Psychology, 33,* 595–640.

Kavanagh, M. J. (1982). Evaluating performance. In K. M. Rowland & G. R. Ferris (Eds.), *Personnel management*. Boston: Allyn & Bacon.

Kavanagh, M. J., & Hedge, J. W. (1983, May). *A closer look at correlates of performance appraisal system acceptability*. Paper presented at the meeting of the Eastern Academy of Management, Pittsburgh.

Kavanagh, M. J., Hedge, J. W., Ree, M., Earles, J., & De Biasi, G. L. (1985, May). *Clarification of some issues in regard to employee acceptability of performance appraisal: Results from five samples*. Paper presented at the meeting of the Eastern Academy of Management, Albany, NY.

Laabs, J. J. (1992). Surveillance: Tool or trap? *Personnel Journal, 71,* 96–104.

Landy, F. J., Barnes, J. R., & Murphy, K. R. (1978). Correlates of perceived fairness and accuracy of performance evaluation. *Journal of Applied Psychology, 63,* 751–754.

Landy, F. J., Barnes-Farrell, J. R., & Cleveland, J. N. (1980). Perceived fairness and accuracy of performance evaluation: A follow-up. *Journal of Applied Psychology, 65,* 355–356.

Latham, G. L. (1986). Job performance and appraisal. In C. L. Cooper & I. Robertson (Eds.), *International review of industrial and organizational psychology* (Vol. 1). Chichester, England: Wiley.

Latham, G. L., & Wexley, K. N. (1981). *Increasing productivity through performance appraisal*. Reading, MA: Addison-Wesley.

Lawler, E. E., III. (1967). The multitrait-multirater approach to measuring managerial job performance. *Journal of Applied Psychology, 51,* 369–381.

Levine, E. L., Flory, A., & Ash, R. A. (1977). Self-assessment in personnel selection. *Journal of Applied Psychology, 62,* 428–435.

Lewthwaite, G.A. (1993, September 5). Workers of the future will be multifunctional. *Star Tribune,* p. 1J.

Leyden, P. (1993, September 5). Teleworking could turn our cities inside out. *Star Tribune,* pp. 1A, 16A.

London, M., & Bassman, E. (1989). Retraining midcareer workers for the future workplace. In I. L. Goldstein & Associates, *Training and development in organizations*. San Francisco: Jossey-Bass.

London, M., & Beatty, R. (1993). 360-degree feedback as a competitive advantage. *Human Resource Management, 32,* 353–372.

Longenecker, C. O., Sims, H. P., & Gioia, D. A. (1987). Behind the mask: The politics of employee appraisal. *Academy of Management Executive, 1,* 183–193.

McAfee, B., & Green, B. (1977). Selecting a performance appraisal method. *Personnel Administrator, 22,* 61–64.

McEvoy, G. M., & Buller, P. F. (1987). User acceptance of peer appraisals in an industrial setting. *Personnel Psychology, 40,* 785–797.

Michels, A. J. (1991, July 29). More employees evaluate the boss. *Fortune,* p. 13.

Morgan, B. B., Jr., Glickman, A. S., Woodard, E. A., Blaiwes, A. S., & Salas, E. (1986). *Measurement of team behaviors in a Navy environment* (Technical Report NTSC TR-86–014). Orlando, FL: Naval Training Systems Center.

Moses, J., Hollenbeck, G., & Sorcher, M. (1993). Other people's expectations. *Human Resource Management, 32,* 283–297.

Murphy, K. R., & Cleveland, J. (1991). *Performance appraisal: An organizational perspective.* Boston: Allyn & Bacon.

Nilsen, D., & Campbell, D. (1993). Self-observer rating discrepancies: Once an overrater, always an overrater? *Human Resource Management, 32,* 265–281.

Offermann, L. R., & Gowing, M. K. (1990). Organizations of the future. In L. Offermann & M. Gowing (Eds.), *American Psychologist* [special issue], *45,* 95–108.

Office of Technology Assessment. (1988). *Computerized manufacturing automation.* Washington, DC: U.S. Government Printing Office.

Organ, D. W. (1988). *Organizational citizenship behavior: The good soldier syndrome.* Lexington, MA: Lexington Books.

Peters, T. J., & Austin, N. (1985). *A passion for excellence: The leadership difference.* New York: Random House.

Peters, T. J., & Waterman, R. H. (1982). *In search of excellence: Lessons from America's best-run companies.* New York: Harper.

Pritchard, R. D., Jones, S. D., Roth, P. L., Stuebing, K. K., & Ekeberg, S. E. (1988). Effect of group feedback, goal setting, and incentives on organizational productivity [Monograph]. *Journal of Applied Psychology, 73,* 337–358.

Robertson, I. T., & Kandola, R. S. (1982). Work sample tests: Validity, adverse impact and applicant reaction. *Journal of Occupational Psychology, 55,* 171–183.

Sackett, P. R., Zedeck, S., & Fogli, L. (1988). Relations between measures of typical and maximum job performance. *Journal of Applied Psychology, 73*(3), 482–486.

Salas, E., Dickinson, T. L., Converse, S. A., & Tannenbaum, S. I. (1992).

Toward an understanding of team performance and training. In R. W. Swezey & E. Salas (Eds.), *Teams: Their training and performance.* Norwood, NJ: Ablex.

Schmidt, F. L., Hunter, J. E., & Outerbridge, A. N. (1986). Impact of job experience and ability on job knowledge work sample performance, and supervisory ratings of job performance. *Journal of Applied Psychology, 71,* 432–439.

Shrauger, J., & Osberg, T. (1981). The relative accuracy of self-predictions and judgments by others in psychological assessment. *Psychological Bulletin, 90,* 322–351.

Siegel, A. I. (1986). Performance tests. In R. A. Berk (Ed.), *Performance assessment: Methods and applications.* Baltimore: Johns Hopkins University Press.

Siegel, A. I., & Jensen, J. (1955). The development of a job sample trouble-shooting performance examination. *Journal of Applied Psychology, 39,* 343–347.

Skinner, J., Faneuff, R. S., & Demetriades, E. T. (1991). Developing benchmarks to scale task performance times. *Proceedings of the 33rd annual conference of the Military Testing Association, 33,* 399–404.

Steiner, I. D. (1972). *Group processes and productivity.* Orlando, FL: Academic Press.

Sundstrom, E., De Meuse, K. P., & Futrell, D. (1990). Work teams: Applications and effectiveness. *American Psychologist, 45,* 120–133.

Tannenbaum, S. I., Beard, R. L., & Salas, E. (1992). Team building and its influence on team effectiveness: An examination of conceptual and empirical developments. In K. Kelley (Ed.), *Issues, theory, and research in industrial/organizational psychology.* Amsterdam: Elsevier North-Holland.

Thibaut, J., & Walker, L. (1975). *Procedural justice: A psychological analysis.* Hillsdale, NJ: Erlbaum.

Tornow, W. W. (1993a). Editor's note: Introduction to special issue on 360-degree feedback. *Human Resource Management, 32,* 211–219.

Tornow, W. W. (1993b). Perceptions or reality: Is multi-perspective measurement a means or an end? *Human Resource Management, 32,* 221–229.

Turnage, J. J. (1990). The challenge of new workplace technology for psychology. In L. Offermann & M. Gowing (Eds.), *American Psychologist* [special issue], *45,* 171–178.

Weitz, J. (1961). Criteria for criteria. *American Psychologist, 16,* 228–231.

Wigdor, A. K., & Green, B. F. (Eds.). (1991). *Performance assessment for the workplace: Report of the committee on the performance of military personnel* (Vol. I). Washington, DC: National Academy Press.

Part Five

Reflections

Chapter Thirteen

Post-Industrial Lives

New Demands, New Prescriptions

Jerald Hage

The workplace is not the only context in which the large sea changes that have been variously labeled post-industrial (Bell, 1973; Piore & Sabel, 1984; Naisbitt, 1982), post-modern (Feather-stone, 1988a, 1988b; Feher, 1987; Kellner, 1990; Lyotard, 1984), or the third wave (Toffler, 1981) have been felt. In this book, much of the emphasis has been placed on post-industrial changes in technology, changes in work, and how individuals and groups of workers relate to these changes. Post-modernism as distinct from post-industrialism refers more to changes in the character of the mind and the way in which it perceives reality. One of the objectives of this chapter is to relate these two perspectives by suggesting that the effects of post-industrialization are altering the character of our minds, including its cognitive structure, our sense of selves, and particularly our awareness of the diversity that defines our social identity, resulting in our capacity to perceive reality in more complex ways that can be defined as post-modern. The two most common attributes of a post-modern perspective are that it involves the combination of multiple styles and that there is a

Note: This chapter is an original abstraction from the book *Post-Industrial Lives* by Jerald Hage and Charles Powers (1992). A large debt is owed to Madeleine Hage, who made the prose so much more intelligible; for that I am extremely grateful. I also want to thank Ann Howard and Sheldon Zedeck for their very helpful comments, which forced me to think more deeply about some of our causal arguments.

capacity to appreciate both the beautiful and the ugly—the good and the bad. This is exactly what is required in any perception of reality, especially of others, if we are to interpret symbolic communication correctly.

Not everyone agrees that we are living in a new epoch, regardless of how it is labeled. The evidence usually offered for the existence of post-industrial society refers to the presence of new technologies and new kinds of work (see many examples in this book) or a vision of a bright and somewhat painless future (see Naisbitt, 1982; Toffler, 1981). But a more striking set of evidence for a new world order is the *role failures* observable in the family and in the community. Signs of these include the rise in violent crimes (car thefts, drive-by shootings, drug slayings, and so forth); the number of all children, a staggering one-fourth, now being born out of wedlock; the steady divorce rate, which is approaching nearly 50 percent in California, considered the bellwether of the United States; and perhaps most important, the large number of children being raised in single-parent situations, many of them in poverty. The thesis of this chapter is that these role failures reflect the inability of individuals to adjust to the new societal contradictions associated with post-industrialization or are the consequence of role failures in other sectors of society, most critically the rising levels of chronic unemployment produced by the new technologies and the substitution of low-paying service jobs for high-paying manufacturing work. Chronic unemployment is higher in Europe than the United States, but the low pay and frequent periods of layoffs in the United States are the functional equivalents. What has convinced a large number of Americans of the rising uncertainty of stable employment is the dismissal of many middle managers. Middle-class families now feel threatened.

The long-term implications of these adjustment failures in the United States and other advanced industrialized societies—where the same processes are occurring but at a slower rate because of their larger and more generous welfare programs—are even grimmer. Children raised in single-parent families will live in poverty for at least part of their childhood, leave school earlier than their parents, be more likely to engage in some form of criminal behavior, experience longer periods of unemployment, and have teenage pregnancies, thus starting another generation in the cycle

(Furstenberg, 1990). Because, in the United States, people of the same social class tend to congregate in the same local areas, and many educational and social services are based on local taxes, these problems are concentrating in areas that do not have the resources to deal with them effectively (Kozol, 1991). In *The Truly Disadvantaged,* Wilson (1987) chronicles the consequences of these conditions for black children and can provide a perspective on the future for white children as well.

The signs of family breakup and community breakdown, and their implications for the future of society, have begun to trouble large numbers of people—evidenced by the emphasis placed on family values in the 1992 presidential campaign and the large amount of media attention paid to them since then—and for good reason. These are omens of the eventual collapse of society. Although everyone may be quite troubled, the solution of family values ignores the new realities of post-industrial families. Essentially, the advocates of family values deny that there are large structural changes in society that make it difficult for people to live by the old rules and family scripts.

This chapter takes the opposite tack and suggests that we must understand the new demands of post-industrial society before we can provide new prescriptions for the family. Divorce, plant closings, poor quality schools, and the like represent failures to adjust to new societal conditions in either the family or various kinds of private and public organizations (Hage & Powers, 1992). The central argument is that in shifting from industrial to post-industrial society, people must learn to live in complex role-sets, each with a large number of role-relationships in which negotiations about role expectations or behavior become one of the major capacities for successful role behavior. Furthermore, to adjust to the constant changes in a society that provides the context for both the family and the workplace, people in post-industrial society need to have complex and creative minds, be adaptive and flexible, and know how to understand symbolic communications.

By contrast, in industrial societies individuals could rely more easily on well-prescribed scripts for the roles of father, mother, worker, neighbor, and the like, for there were relatively few roles that had to be enacted, making negotiations about expectations largely unnecessary. Role scripts might be defined as social schemata, allowing people to learn quickly what is expected of them in much the same way that schemata allow people to read. In this instance, the "reading" consists of understanding social behavior appropriate for each role and how to respond to various social cues. The role scripts in industrial society did not allow for much individual variation; to a large extent, there was one script for a male and another for a female, for example. As much as the advocates of family values want to return to the simpler world of role scripts, this solution will not work in a world of constant and rapid change.

The inability of many to shift from relatively simple role scripts to complex negotiations about expectations in a variety of role-relationships or role-sets has led to the role failures (such as divorce) that are at the root of many of the problems that have been outlined. In the family, many men—despite their verbal statements—find it difficult to meet their wives' demands for equal participation in the onerous chores of housekeeping and child rearing. Conversely, many women—and again despite their verbal statements—find it equally unacceptable to support unemployed husbands. In both instances, the stereotypical role scripts for husband/provider and wife/homemaker are being challenged by much more complex views of alternation and of equality. In the business world, Argyris and Schön (1974) have demonstrated that many managers cannot shift from single-loop to double-loop thinking, another sign of the inability to perceive a more complex reality. Further evidence of this inflexibility or nonadaptiveness can be observed in the relatively small numbers of unemployed men and women who enroll in high-technology training programs, which are available in many community colleges. But also, in many states, the community colleges have been slow to create new training programs for the high-tech jobs that exist.

The objective of this chapter is to suggest a normative solution and indicate how one can adjust to the "new world order." Some major assumptions underlie this normative solution. First, as more complex institutions are constructed, there is a need for more complex minds and selves. Second, as these institutions themselves change rapidly, there is a need for more creative minds and more flexible selves.

The nature and character of post-industrial society (PIS) are described in the first section, where the basic theme is the rapid expansion in knowledge, the growth in the intractableness of the societal problems, and the complexity of the social institutions and organizations required both to utilize this new knowledge and to solve these intricate problems. The second section describes the many parallel changes occurring on what might be called the micro-sociological level—that is, in the interactions, roles, networks, role-sets, and social groups, whether work teams, associations, families, or others. Finally, the chapter concludes with a discussion of what is required at the individual or what might be labeled the psychological level—creative and complex minds, complex and adaptive selves, and the capacity to understand symbolic communications—for survival and the avoidance of role failure in PIS.

The Macro Context: Knowledge, Diversity, and Complexity

The thesis of post-industrial society has now been debated for some twenty years, ever since the publication of Daniel Bell's (1973) *The Coming of Post-Industrial Society*. Although Bell did emphasize research and development as an important defining characteristic of post-industrial society, his argument concentrated on the continuation of trends that have been present for some time, especially the growth of the service sector. Hage and Powers (1992) argue that, rather than the continuity of various trends, it is the *discontinuities* that are more striking. Specifically, they suggest that the large number of institutional failures—political gridlock, budget deficits, trade deficits, high levels of business failure, large unemployment levels, plus the many signs of family breakup and community breakdown previously discussed—is more convincing evidence of the emergence of a new society with new "rules of the game" because these failures are proof that the industrial institutions no longer suffice.

The cause of these institutional failures is, again, another discontinuity—namely, a rapid increase in the level of knowledge in society, which is manifested in three areas: (1) the level of college-educated people, which rose very rapidly during the 1960s and

1970s; (2) a number of sophisticated technologies such as flexible manufacturing (Piore & Sabel, 1984), robots, telecommunications, and bio-technologies (bio-tech) and the like; and (3) a surge in the amount of money invested in research and development, especially overseas (National Science Foundation, 1989).

Most discussions of PIS imply that it is occurring everywhere. This is not true. For better or worse, the major societal changes are felt more keenly in some institutional sectors of society than in others, in different regions, with disparate impacts among the social classes, and of course at the individual level as well. Indeed, it is the *unevenness* of the advance of PIS that has made many miss the connection between the numerous signs of role failure and institutional breakdown and the more positive features that have tended to dominate discussions of PIS, as in the work of Toffler (1981), Bell (1973), Naisbitt (1982), and others. The failure to adapt has been concentrated more in the working class than in the middle class, more among general managers than professionals, more among blacks than whites, and so forth. Evidence for this is the higher divorce rate among the working class—even higher among blacks—and the higher layoff rate for general managers in large corporations than for professionals.

There are several reasons for this. The new technologies had differential adverse effects—first on blacks, second on members of the working class, and third on general managers. Flexible manufacturing and computers have eliminated the need for large numbers of people, as demonstrated by studies of the employment rates (both blue collar and white collar) in the automobile, rubber tire, cement, and other old assembly line industries. Beyond this, these groups have lacked specialized skills and experience that would protect them from being dismissed. But more fundamentally, without a college education, people have fewer opportunities and diminished adaptive skills.

One way of measuring the differential advance of the post-industrial society is to examine the growth in knowledge along the three distinct dimensions listed earlier, specifically education, technology, and research and development. Each of these three dimensions has affected the societal context in diverse ways, only some of which can be described in this brief essay. Rising levels of education have encouraged both women and blacks to make new demands for social equality. The same social force of college-educated people has generated various political demands for a cleaner environment, safer products, and conservation of scarce global resources, prompting a wide variety of social movements as well as new kinds of demands for the business world. Educated consumers now want highly specialized products, customized service, and the latest technological advance. These same consumers are making similar demands in the public sector, wanting high-quality education, customized health care, effective police and prisons, and so forth.

Most discussions of PIS have emphasized the many new sophisticated technologies—in particular computers, robots, specialized and flexible manufacturing, and bio-tech—as almost the definition of what is meant by post-industrial. But what they generally have not stressed is that sophisticated technologies are designed to provide constant change in production systems and highly flexible responses to shifting consumer demands. Most of the examples that come to mind as high-tech products—bio-tech, sports technologies, computers, drugs, and so forth—have short product lives and highly specialized markets, which means that the companies that make them must worry about constant product innovation.

The meaning of technology and of rapid technological change for the family has not received as much discussion in the literature on PIS, except perhaps for the role of technology in allowing people to work at home. But there are many more impacts than this, especially on the roles within the family. New products—frozen foods, microwaves, videocasssette recorders (VCRs), washing machines—have made it possible for women to leave the role of housewife as a full-time occupation and enter the labor force just as rising levels of education have encouraged them to look for careers rather than just part-time jobs for the sake of earning money. College education in both men and women exposes them to various aspects of themselves, awakening needs that earlier had been perceived only dimly. Again, the stress is on the multiplicity of selves that are discovered. Both television and VCRs have become "adjuncts" to baby-sitting. Unfortunately, they have probably been misused in this capacity by the first generation of post-industrial families, with quite negative consequences for the children and their capacity to read and write. The presence of a new technology does not always mean that it is immediately employed in correct ways—again the theme of role failure.

In contrast, the constant technological change in computers has made the personal computer (PC) a consumer product; the rapid technological spin-offs—CD-ROMS, modems, faxes, various kinds of graphic software, games—are entering the home and providing new ways of learning. One of the more interesting developments is the role of computer games in developing children's capacity to handle situations that are quite complex and dynamic, making computer games probably one of the more subtle and profound mechanisms for preparing children for a world of constant change. Similarly, the development of new products such as mobile telephones, large-screen televisions, fax machines, and so forth are altering the way in which people interact and experience their family life. They do allow people to "reach out and touch someone," as the phone now does.

It is not just the *quantity* of college-educated people, money spent on research and development, or automated production systems that affects the nature of society, but it is also the *qualitative* differentiation that is occurring. With growth have also emerged diverse new disciplines and occupational specialties with their associated technologies, as well as quite distinct and varied research and development projects. This sheer diversity means that we have moved away from the mass society of the industrial age to a highly differentiated society where individuals demand and live a customized lifestyle, perhaps best represented by their leisure time activities.

Skiing, scuba diving, secondary residences, and sailboats represent huge investments of money, for in most of these new leisure time activities, one finds highly sophisticated technologies. Attached to each leisure time lifestyle are costly and specialized clothes—one is tempted to say post-industrial uniforms—magazines, clubs, travel to particular geographical locations, and the like. Given the amount of money invested, the effort needed to select the correct equipment and clothing, and the time in the role, these leisure time pursuits become critical dimensions in the definition of the self.

But the development of new occupations has also meant a number of specialties that have implications for the family as well. In health care, gerontology is now a major specialty. Hospice services and nursing homes have also developed. In the raising of children, the increase in the number of family therapists is perhaps one of the most interesting developments, as is the general expansion of community mental health programs. Within the schools, a variety of special education specialists now exist to help children learn. This wide array of experts has implications for the nature of the family role-sets, making them larger and more complex, and facilitates the ability to adjust to the demands of PIS—for part of the task of these many new specialties is to reduce the scope of role failure or to deal with its consequences.

Finally, still another repercussion of the growth in knowledge, whether in the form of higher education, new technologies, or research, is the enormous complexity of the world in which we now live. Many of the problems associated with industrial society—childhood illnesses, illiteracy, high death rates, lack of electricity and indoor plumbing, little political freedom—have been solved for many if not most members of society. But for each problem of industrial society that has been solved, two or more new ones have emerged. A number of examples will make this point clear. A standardized primary school curriculum allowed industrialized societies to provide mass literacy to the population. But how does one give each college student individualized, diverse, and flexible instruction that will help him or her meet the requirements of the workforce, to say nothing about the specialized needs of the learning disabled? Again, mass vaccinations in the schools and water purification plants and sewage systems in the cities allowed for rapid rises in longevity, but now we must solve the problem of what to do with an aging population. Not only does their presence create enormous burdens on the health care system, but it has implications for the very foundations of the welfare state, most notably its pension system. Mentally ill persons were simply thrown into large hospitals and kept under guard in the industrial society: now the post-industrial society attempts to provide community mental health care systems that are quite complex (Morrissey, Tausig, & Lindsey, 1984; Alter & Hage, 1993) and diversified.

While two or three political parties used to suffice for most countries, there is now a wide variety of social movements supporting an amazing array of causes ranging from the homeless to animal protection, from anti-nuclear to pro-choice, from the National Rifle Association to the Greens, and so forth. Etzioni (1968) argued some twenty-five years ago that we were moving into an age of the "active society," that is, one in which many people are mobilized into various social causes that put pressure on the political system or parts of society to change in various ways. The current struggle between pro-choice and anti-abortion proponents is, perhaps, only the most dramatic illustration in the United States, and the ethnic and religious conflicts the most frightening ones in Europe.

The complexity of these problems is compounded by the increasing interdependence of the world. Solutions for each country cannot be adopted without considering their implications for others. Thus acid rain, terrorism, ethnic conflicts, interest rates, unification, unemployment, and a host of other issues have become internationalized because their causes or solutions have repercussions for many other countries. So far, this interrelatedness appears to have produced mostly stalemates in crises such as the defense of the European Monetary Union, the solution of the Bosnia conflict, the elimination of whale killing, and so forth as opposed to the arguably singular success of the Gulf War.

The complexity of the problems, the need to engage in constant research and development, and the input of highly specialized occupations have altered the shape and form of business organizations, again a topic that is discussed throughout this book (also see Hage, 1988; Hage & Powers, 1992; Hollingsworth, 1991; Powell, 1990). Here I can note only four fundamental and, I believe, enduring changes: the reduction in size of the effective business unit, usually a profit center; the movement toward an organic structure as typified in small high-tech businesses; the creation of joint ventures, usually between small and large businesses and between large businesses across international boundaries; and the emergence of networks of organizations (see Alter & Hage, 1993). These shifts can be characterized as movements toward much more complex structures and institutional arrangements.

Less discussed is a parallel movement in the family structure along basically the same dimensions: the decreased size of the family, as with single parents; the increased complexity of most kinds of families; the development of joint ventures among some divorced parents; and the emergence of networks of support groups and even multiple family structures. Nor are these mutually exclusive; the single-parent or the dual-career family may be involved in a number of support and/or self-help groups as well as receive services from service delivery networks (Alter & Hage, 1993). Increasingly, raising children is a group effort involving not only one or more parents or stepparents, but day care personnel, teachers, psychologists, social workers, and other professionals.

And just as the business world is characterized by the diversity of product markets, the family can also be described by its diversity of kinds; this includes the increasing provision for the third generation—the elderly surviving parent or conversely the younger generation living with their parents after a divorce or because they are not able to support themselves financially; cohabiting couples; the homosexual couple and family; the never-married single parent raising adopted children as well as couples who adopt; and so forth. All of these variations are far removed from the social reality of the American family in the 1950s as portrayed in television series (remember the Cleavers or the Nelsons?).

At the macro level of society, the growth in knowledge in its three distinctive dimensions has led to the solution of many of the old problems associated with the industrialization of society but has in turn generated a variety of new problems requiring complex solutions. It has also generated a diversity of products, markets, organizations, and family structures. But what implications does this have for the micro level, the level of roles and relationships, networks and groups?

The Micro Level: Role-Relationships, Role-Sets, Networks, and Teams

Throughout this book, a great deal has been written about the nature of work roles. Here I highlight only a few of the basic changes, dimensions that have parallels within families and leisure time roles, our two main concerns. Most of the post-industrial work roles now emphasize mental rather than physical activity, involve a great deal of time in information gathering and processing, and entail very large amounts of interaction either with clients or in work teams—interactions not programmed or defined by rules manuals, job descriptions, or other kinds of role scripts.

Work roles have neither physical nor temporal boundaries, resulting in the interpenetration of work, family, leisure, and other kinds of roles that in the industrial age were effectively segregated.

The use of the computer at home, flexible hours, and the nature of professional and managerial work that never seems to end have moved the workplace into the home. Meanwhile, the problems of day care for parents and the need to juggle complicated schedules attached to careers have moved the home into the workplace. In the dual-career family, the complexity of handling two careers has brought work into the decision-making process for the family. In the single-parent family, the absence of someone to help with the work of the family has had the same effect.

Furthermore, technology in the workplace, one of the themes of this book, impacts the family in two specific ways. In those industries that have not adopted new technologies, plants are closing and both men and women, often unskilled, are losing their jobs; the aftermath is often divorce, the uprooting of the family, and a number of other consequences previously described. In contrast, in those sectors of society that have adapted, the pace of technological change is accelerating continually, altering the nature of the workplace in the process, which in turn again impacts the careers of the individuals involved and thus their families. Short product lives mean constant changes in work schedules. The sudden growth and decline of many small high-tech companies frequently require shifting places of work, with all the adjustments that this implies.

In a variety of sectors, existing role scripts have had to give way because the social situations have become too complex and diverse to handle with a clear set of rules appropriate for everyone. The constant technological change in those industrial sectors that have adapted and the interpenetration of work and the family (as well as leisure and cultural roles, as suggested in the next section) have added a complexity that makes role scripts inappropriate. Beyond this and for a variety of reasons, society has allowed most social roles to become detached from social sanctions, letting instead a "thousand flowers bloom." Perhaps the most spectacular example of this are the current debates over the legality of gay marriages and families. In general, the wide variety of role behaviors associated with now-acceptable gender roles is a fundamental sign of shifts in societal attitudes.

The growth in education among women has often led to their unwillingness to accept the housewife role; in many cases, they want careers of their own. More critically, women have rejected the role of superwoman, insisting instead that the men in their lives share in the work associated with the house and the raising of children. Finally, the ability to pursue a career has made the woman much less dependent on the man; she is capable of providing support for both herself and her children, thus again changing the gender role. Not all men have been able to adjust to these new role expectations, which has led to increasing divorce rates and new and different kinds of family arrangements.

But those men and women who have continued to be married or have remarried have discovered that role redefinition is a continual process; to resolve role conflicts, they must engage in constant negotiations about who will do what, when, and how. These conflicts are most intense in dual-career families because both father and mother have to juggle work and household maintenance (and as yet men have not in general absorbed their share of the burden, placing the women under considerable strain). These negotiations cannot be concluded once and for all at the beginning of the marriage because new work situations and career opportunities are always presenting themselves and new problems emerge relative to the children as they advance through the stages of life, all of which necessitate a careful rethinking of individual responsibilities. For example, it is not at all uncommon for men, even divorced men, to become important figures in raising children during adolescence, a fact that even estranged wives come to recognize. At this moment there may have to be a renegotiation of visiting rights in the best interests of the child. Unfortunately, many of these negotiations are handled in the courts—another sign of role failure—because the participants have not learned how to negotiate role expectations in the family.

Most of the new family arrangements make family roles much more complex than the traditional gender-based arrangements. A single parent may have to play several parental roles as well as worry about a career. Rather than role conflict between two individuals, single parents may then experience this conflict intrapsychically. In both the single-parent family and the dual-career family, the role strains created by lack of time are another common feature of post-industrial families. Such strain may lead parents to choose unfortunate solutions, such as allowing children unrestricted use of television, VCRs, and video games, supplemented by parental substitutes such as day care, baby-sitters, and au pair girls. Often a sense of parental guilt ensues, which in turn can lead to acquiescing to many of the child's demands.

Nor are these the only sources of role complexity, conflict, and strain in PIS families. Interracial and international marriages are now more and more common. They pose unusual problems as people attempt to deal with the difficulties associated with integrating two or more cultures. Furthermore, interracial marriages have to confront the problems of racism, while international marriages may have to resolve the issue of linguistic choice. Nor are these simply decisions made once and for all. As the children grow up, new sides of their own identities emerge and they may want to establish contact with a part of their heritage that has been denied them. In the process, both international and interracial marriages force family members to confront the problem of multiple identities. Though they do so to a greater degree than other kinds of families, all types of families in PIS are increasingly faced with this very issue of "who am I?"

Another source of complexity for family roles is the existence of numerous specialists now available, whether in the school, the day care center, mental health centers, or other places. This has made the task of family living much more complicated than previously because these experts frequently suggest new behaviors and adjustments for parents. Certainly, these should be viewed as opportunities rather than just additional pressures. But for their recommendations to be effectively utilized, these experts must be brought into the decision-making processes about child rearing; when they are, temporary "work" teams may be created relative to the problem of how to raise children. These family teams will have to be constituted at disparate stages, depending on the nature of the crisis. Unfortunately, we tend not to think of the parents or kin, associated experts, friends, and others who are consulted in the process as a problem-solving team, yet they are.

If we were to code the parental discussions (or the amount of time spent thinking in the single-parent situation) while their children are growing up, we would probably find most of the discussions revolve around either education or finances. Certainly, discussions on education are not just limited to the issues of whether Johnny is learning to read but include the broader problems of the development of children's personalities, overcoming their learning disabilities (which increasingly involve a larger and larger proportion of children), and enhancing their special qualities. As the routine of housework has been diminished by various technologies, a new and very complex goal has been added: raising children as distinct and unique human beings who will choose among a variety of occupations, gender roles, and lifestyles, and are encouraged to express their abilities and talents, avoiding the use of preprogrammed role scripts. Admittedly, this is most often a characteristic of upper-middle-class families, where the growth in education has changed perceptions about how to raise children. The children nurtured with the ideas of Dr. Benjamin Spock are now beginning to have their own children, and they know that individualized socialization is a much more complex task than teaching children to be well-mannered and polite "little adults," the goal of many families during the 1940s and 1950s. In particular, raising individualized human beings requires much higher rates of family interaction, especially with the children, than used to be the case.

One of the more striking examples of how parents are altering their views on education (and a sign of role failure in the public schools) is the increase in private school enrollments. For the middle class, some advantages of private schools are the small classes, personal attention to individual abilities and talents, and the much higher levels of communication about the progress of the children than one finds in the public schools.

So far we have stressed the diversity of the post-industrial society. Yet, across the many kinds of families, some common themes emerge. One is the increased amount of interaction among the members of the family, however constituted. With more leisure time now available both during the summer and at other times of the year (with the many long weekends), the frequency of interaction is greater and, more important, the interactions last longer. The evidence for this increased leisure time is the average length of the work week, the large growth in part-time work (not always by choice), and the number of holidays and vacation days. Yet, it is equally true that many professionals and top managers work very long days and on weekends (see Schor, 1991). However, these overworked professionals tend to invest large amounts of money in their leisure time activities and to take many small but expensive vacations.

As interactions increase in length, the nature of communications changes as well. Having lived both here and abroad, I have often been struck by how conversations shift in tone and in the nature of topics during the long meals in France every Sunday and in the United States on holidays. Psychiatrists report that patients always reveal more in the last few minutes of the fifty-minute session, one reason why some therapists have experimented with marathon therapy. Swimming pools, boats, vacation homes, camping trips, attendance at major sports events, and fishing—places and events where longer interactions are more likely—are examples of how leisure time can shape and form children. A particularly critical activity is games (and while these games may vary by social class and type of family, their effects are the same), especially if all family members can participate. Families that "play together" have lower divorce rates and the children have fewer problems. One has to admit that perhaps the causal order is the reverse: families without problems can more easily participate in leisure time activities together whereas those with deep-seated conflicts cannot. But I would still argue that games are mechanisms for handling these conflicts and bringing them out into the open.

A further qualitative shift in the nature of parent-child social relationships has been occurring, at least among those middle-class families that have entered the post-industrial society. Not only is more time spent in this relationship, but it has broadened considerably in the diversity of activities that parents and children perform together. As variety expands, the scope of the relationship alters, and so does the involvement of the individuals. In many instances family rituals have developed at the same time that role scripts have disappeared, but these rituals are now individually designed rather than imposed by society on everyone. Divorced parents, when they do visit their children, are likely to spend much more time with them—in part because of guilt and in part because they are limited to specific visits—and likely to engage in a greater range of activities than they would have had they remained married to the child's other parent. Again, this behavior changes the whole nature of the relationship.

Another very common pattern in PIS families is group problem solving among the parents (stepparents) and various others (teachers, social workers, therapists) relative to difficulties that children may encounter as they mature, whether these be reading problems in school, fights, drugs, or sex. (Industrial society was in general a less dangerous world for children.) For divorced parents, when visitation rights exist, there are considerable opportunities for communications relative to sharing the children's supervision (on what days and under what conditions). In dual-career families, parents may be involved in group problem solving particularly at times when career choices may impact the needs of each family member. Other indicators, such as the growth of family therapists—the fastest growing segment of the mental health network—as well as other forms of team or group efforts, including the various self-help groups for single parents and for children themselves who are victims of drug addiction, alcoholism, or family violence, all point to the existence of intricate networks involving families and others external to the family in problem-solving situations.

With these developments has come change in the role-sets— all the relationships associated with a particular role, such as those of either father or mother—which have grown larger in size. There may be one or more stepparents or live-in companions in the home. Furthermore, given the greater integration of work and family, the children may become acquainted with various members of either the father's or mother's work role-set—that is, the various individuals with whom they interact, especially if day care exists at the workplace. Cooperative baby-sitting arrangements are common among parents with young children, which in turn extends the variety of adults involved in the life of the children; this presents considerable contrast to the industrial age, when the mother was the sole responsible baby-sitter. Beyond this, vacations, especially if they involve relatively large investments such as vacation homes, boats, skiing, camping trips, and the like, are likely to include friends, many of whom may also belong to the work role-set.

Not only is the role-set larger but so is the social network—the string of individuals connected to various family friendships. These networks become particularly important during times of crisis when the family is confronted with a new problem to solve. At these times, network members can be vital sources of information on how to resolve the crisis. So far, the best-known article discussing this process is by Granovetter (1973), who suggested that these weak ties—that is, friends of friends—are precisely those that become important when people search for jobs. But his idea can be extended to other areas in which families seek information.

Each time a family crisis emerges or a new stage of development occurs, search behavior becomes critical. Families with extensive interpersonal social networks have what is now called social capital (Coleman, 1990) and for this reason they are more likely to adapt successfully.

However, increases in the size of the social network and of the role-set for children can result in a number of advantages, provided there is not too much fluidity in the number of role partners. When the single parent has a succession of partners, there is correspondingly little stability in the nature of the social network and the child can become afraid of investing any emotional energy in any relationship. On the other hand, a few long-term relationships provide the child with alternative parental models. One final note on this point: social networks established around day care, school, or extracurricular activities offer the same opportunities for alternative role models.

We find that in the family, as in the workplace, successful adaptation to the many changes occurring requires the development of teams to help make decisions jointly about the raising of children to become individuals. Social networks and large role-sets fulfill a useful service in providing information about options, especially during the inevitable crises that occur as children mature in a world that has become more dangerous, whether the reason be police brutality, AIDS, drugs on the playground, or guns in the school.

Also analogous to changes occurring in the workplace, where the impact of the post-industrial society is being felt most acutely, is the emergence in the family of much more complex roles, of relationships with greater scope, of extended networks, and of joint decision making in those families that are more successful in adapting to the requirements of their present environment.

The Normative Model: Creative Minds, Complex Selves, and Symbolic Interaction

Given complex and large role-sets in a variety of family settings and constant role redefinition through negotiation, what kinds of individuals will survive in the post-industrial society, in the sense of reducing or avoiding role failure? My answer, which builds on the work of George Hubert Mead (1934/1964), is that only creative minds, complex selves, and individuals who have the ability to "read" symbolic communication are likely to be able to negotiate expectations and thus reduce the stresses and strains of the continual change associated with post-industrial society. Each of these ideas needs to be expanded.

Creative Minds and Flexible Selves

In the industrial society, much emphasis was (and still is) placed on intelligence as measured by the standard tests. But to solve problems successfully, creativity becomes a much more critical life skill, necessary not only in the family but also in the work teams that have been discussed throughout this book. Creativity is difficult to define (see Hage & Powers, 1992), but its major characteristic seems to be the ability to devise new symbols or perceive new relationships or develop new techniques. Admittedly, there are gradations of creativity from the simple to the quite complex, but the ability to develop a new and unique solution for a problem that one's child faces is an extremely important kind of creativity for the post-industrial family and one that does not receive the credit it deserves.

The number of problems faced by the post-modern family is endless, each requiring a new solution appropriate for the individual child in his or her particular situation. Insofar as each child is raised to be an individual rather than fitted into some social role, general solutions are not possible, just as they are not in high-tech companies that are on the cutting edge of the post-industrial society. Generalizing the concept of learning strategies to cover the idea of maturation strategies or stages of development, we can understand that some children may not become adults until they are thirty whereas others are mature when they are thirteen. Furthermore, given the amount of interpenetration of work and family, the choice of solutions frequently must be made with a considerable number of constraints that vary from one family to the next. Again, making appropriate decisions necessitates creativity.

Creativity is also required for the continual family role redefinitions associated with altering circumstances of work, careers, and various opportunities in the community that arise. The decision on how best to allocate work among the various family members depending upon the situation, the choice of a day care center or school, the handling of family crises, and so forth all require a considerable amount of problem solving in which creativity is the key. Perhaps the greatest demands for creativity are being placed on the single-parent families, who suffer from the lack of both time and money and who do not have role scripts or societal experience available to them, in part because these are new kinds of families. Furthermore, the social roles must be constructed to fit the specific circumstances, tailor-made to the individualized lifestyles of the family and successfully integrated with work and leisure roles. Again, creative solutions are required. How does one become both a father and a mother, for example?

In finding creative definitions for these social roles in new families, social networks or funds become critical. Single parents not only lack time, which produces role strain, and money, which generates family conflict, but social capital, which reduces their opportunities to find solutions. Unquestionably, other people cope with similar kinds of problems, but without access to a network, an individual has no way to profit from their experience. Self-help groups are therefore a critical institutional innovation because they compensate for this lack of social capital.

Finally, creativity lies at the heart of developing flexible selves. It is easy enough to develop a solution for various problems that the family faces as the children advance through the stages of life and the wage earner(s) move through the stages of their career(s). But it is much more difficult to find the right solution for the particular individuals involved that takes into account what they can and cannot do. For example, some women are better mechanics than their husbands and some men are better cooks than their wives. The essence of flexibility is knowing how to proceed within the limits of our capabilities and prior histories. In the division of work within the family, rigid gender definitions have to be broken down. To demand from individuals what they cannot do guarantees rigidity and thus role failure. Creativity consists of finding the solution that is flexible enough to allow for individual variations.

Complex Selves and Minds

Rather than stress the idea of the situational self, in which individuals think of only one social role at a time, complex selves are aware of their multiple social roles. A complex self has affective roles (gender, age, family, religion, friendship), work roles, leisure roles, and cultural roles (ethnic, racial, nation-state). Given the interpenetration of work and the family, the only way these spheres can be integrated successfully is for individuals to maintain simultaneously their awareness of their different role-sets associated with these social roles. The same is true for leisure and cultural roles. Interracial or international marriages cannot survive without an increase in the number of social roles that define each of the individuals involved, for defining oneself in terms of one role only—religion, ethnicity, nationality, race—leaves no room for accommodation, which at a larger level is precisely the cause of ethnic conflicts in eastern Europe.

Although interracial and international marriages may create special forms of role conflict and role strain, they have special advantages as well. If problems are successfully resolved, the children in such marriages may develop more complex minds and selves and become true post-modern men and women: they can more easily read symbolic communication, take the role of the other, and successfully negotiate social conflicts.

Particularly important for the definition of the self are the various leisure roles. In PIS, it is not just work but play also that provides meaning to life, explaining why more and more of the family budget is allocated to leisure time activities. The evidence for this is in the explosion during the past decade of money spent on trips, skiing, scuba diving, and camping equipment, swimming pools and second homes, recreational vehicles, and so forth. Play, of course, was extremely important in traditional and even the industrial society. But in these contexts, the distinctive characteristic is that everyone had to play the same game and be interested in the same sport. Now choice is provided and the range of alternatives is quite large, varying from rugby to bicycle racing to canoeing. In other words, the traditional games from many societies are now available to post-industrial men and women. A prominent indicator of this is the large number of sports opportunities now being presented to women.

One of the reasons that leisure roles provide more meaning now than previously is a consequence of the increased choices available to us, both because of higher living standards for those who have stable employment and because of the new low transportation costs. Another reason is that leisure time allows us to express sides of our personalities that are not represented in either the family or work roles, providing an enrichment of both mind and self. Consider the man who plays revolutionary soldier or the woman who rides a Harley-Davidson or the girl who plays basketball or the boy who dances. One could multiply the examples endlessly. Also, leisure time, regardless of the activity involved, replenishes the emotional energy that has been depleted by the stress of role conflict, role strain, and the negotiations about role redefinitions in the family or at work.

There is a mistaken notion that the family is where individuals draw their emotional sustenance, but this is an often untrue and idealized image of family life. Instead, mother and father (whether divorced or not) are constantly discussing, negotiating, and coping with the problems presented by their children. Think of the dangers that modern-day children face—crack, learning disabilities, AIDS, rape, violence on the streets—and one appreciates how stressful it is to raise children in a post-industrial world where childhood has lost its innocence. And this stress is one reason that family interactions can drain the emotions of family members.

Another reason that the emotional stock must be replenished is the loss of emotional energy associated with defining new roles and role prescriptions in both family and work roles. In an industrial society, enacting rigidly prescribed role scripts that were stable across time demanded little energy. Social control of deviant acts in either the family (punish the child) or in business (fire the employee) demanded little thought or energy because they were all programmed. But when one attempts to provide high-quality customer service, each customer has to be treated as a special case. In the family, attempting to raise each child as an individual has the same consequences; each child necessitates special handling, adapted to his or her personality and particular strengths and weaknesses. Anyone who teaches and has individual conferences with each student about term papers in which, together, they search for unique solutions is aware of how much energy is consumed in the process. The drain of continual interaction is the cause of burnout, very much an ailment of the post-industrial society.

The literature on burnout has placed emphasis on service roles. But what has been missed is that increasingly all work roles involve customer service, at least in the more successful PIS firms. Furthermore, teamwork and the other group situations, including committee meetings, joint decision making, and the rest, drain emotional energy. They do so precisely as they become real attempts to negotiate between conflicting demands and constraints in a complex world. This is not a new argument; Simmel (1955) made it long ago. But what is new is the *increasing* amount of time spent in problem solving and therefore difficult interactions in the family and in work. Therefore, the more we interact in problem solving, the more we need leisure time.

Another source of lost emotional energy is creative problem solving. One cannot be creative all day. In the industrial society, many family and work problems were handled in routine ways; routine or habitual responses to events do not require much energy, emotional or otherwise. But creative problem solving does because we must weigh the various alternatives and their consequences. It is this cathectic quality—to use Parsons's (1951) term—that makes problem solving not just a mental effort but an emotional one.

As yet there is little research to support this line of reasoning, but it would appear that creative thought is dependent on intuition, which has its basis in emotions or feelings. Furthermore, in post-industrial society, creative problem solving is done in teams. To make these teams work effectively requires that each member be "tuned into" the ideas and feelings of the other members. When groups work well, the experience can be exhilarating, and so generate emotion that replenishes. Much teamwork, however, is exhausting, requiring renewal time for the affected employees if they are to avoid burnout. Thus leisure time becomes one of the major equilibrating forces in the social life of post-modern people, explaining why leisure roles have become so important.

But just as work and the family must be integrated, so do play and work, and play and the family inasmuch as the various demands of work and family tend to crowd out leisure for dual-career and single-parent families (see Schor, 1991). Beyond this, the periodicities of these various spheres of our life are quite disparate. Fortunately, as flextime becomes more common and with the spread of computers at home, it is becoming easier to handle the problems of integration. Integration also becomes more feasible precisely because society has largely eliminated its control over the definition of family roles, leisure roles, and affective roles. Even in work roles, much more self-control is now available to individual members; the professions, one of the fastest growing segments of the labor force, are an example. This greater independence of definition, of course, creates problems—how will these roles be defined and redefined—but the lack of societal control facilitates the process of integration. Furthermore, the lack of societal control allows for the fluidity in role partners, activities, and the like that are characteristic of post-modern families.

Complex selves imply that there are also complex minds and thus multiple perspectives on social reality. It is not by accident that the thesis of post-modernism has emerged at the same time as that of post-industrialism but their causes are different. A post-modernist's view of reality reflects a more complex mind and one that can assume a more critical distance. This same mental complexity facilitates the processes of social negotiations between multiple role-sets in different spheres of one's social life, thus aiding the processes of social and psychological integration. Finally, complex minds are also more creative ones, precisely because of the dialectic between alternative perspectives. One of the important themes of Mead (1934/1964) was the capacity to take the role of the other. Individuals with complex selves are more likely to be able to perceive the world from multiple vantage points, empathizing with the position of the other. Clearly, this capacity facilitates negotiating role expectations and encourages creativity.

Indeed, it is exactly this growth in the complexity of the mind and of the self that has made the striking increase in biracial and international marriages possible. Furthermore, this same characteristic underlines the radical shift in the kinds of product demands that have in turn affected organizations' competitive strategies. More complex minds are more interested in the quality of the product, perceive that the product has multiple consequences for the environment as well as for one's health and safety, and desire customized service. Finally, more complex minds have quite disparate views on a variety of subjects, breaking down the simplistic political labels of left and right.

Understanding Symbolic Communication

Understanding symbolic communication means being able not only to hear the verbal content but to "read" the nonverbal messages, the emotional messages. These messages explain how important the conversation is to the individual who is speaking, regardless of whether he or she believes what is being said, the particular kinds of emotions, and finally the relative importance of the listener to the speaker. Complex minds can more easily perceive both the verbal and nonverbal messages, especially the emotional content of what is being said, because they can more easily "take the role of the other." The more ways in which we view the other person—that is, as occupying multiple roles, itself a consequence of the number of ways in which we ourselves are relating—the more likely we are to be able to interpret what is being said, especially at the nonverbal level. Furthermore, to understand emotional messages, we must be in contact with our own feelings and send symbolic messages, which in turn encourages the other person to do likewise. When we are open, then our respondents are open as well. Awareness of symbolic communication is thus the essence of post-modern communication because it allows us to perceive multiple layers, such as levels of irony and both the positive side and the dark side (that is, dishonesty or negative feelings) of what is being communicated.

Why is the nonverbal or emotional aspect of symbolic communication so critical for successful negotiation? It allows us to understand what is negotiable and what is not, even if the individuals involved only dimly perceive this. In other words, these emotional messages allow us to appreciate the constraints that are inherent in each situation. Furthermore, the emotional messages are critical for effective, creative problem solving because when individuals propose solutions, they cannot always argue effectively. The nonverbal side will allow us to perceive more deeply the relative importance of each proposal to each participant. Nonverbal communications are more likely to make us aware of role conflicts, role strains, and burnout before it is necessary to have verbal communications about them and thus before they become too large to handle effectively.

Conclusion

One of the major themes of this chapter is that the arrival of the post-industrial society is observable in the large number of failures, in particular in the breakup of families and the breakdown of communities, and discontinuities between industrial and post-industrial societies. But these role failures are understandable given the new societal conditions that the new kinds of families confront: role conflict over expectations, role strain because of the absence of time, and burnout because of the high social interaction rates in the teams and networks attached to work. The shift from an industrial to a post-industrial society has been too quick to allow many people to adjust to the new demands for rapid flexibility and continuous negotiation about role expectations. Furthermore, given the large emotional drain of these new work and family conditions, those that do not have enough leisure are likely to suffer even more.

The normative model proposed here is a relatively simple one. Given the complexity of role-sets, people need to have complex minds and selves. Given the rapidity of role redefinition, people need to have creative minds for problem solving and adaptive selves. Finally, to be successful in adapting, solving problems, and handling the negotiations involved in role redefinitions so as to reduce role conflict, role strain, and burnout, people must be able to perceive symbolic communications, that is, the two-dimensional reality of social interaction. Again, developing leisure activities has been suggested as a way to increase the capacity to withstand the stresses of post-industrial life.

Although role failures, burnout, and role strain are visible signs of the post-industrial society, it is also true that in many ways the children of post-modern families are being prepared much more adequately for the future than their parents were for the present. A number of specialized occupations have developed to facilitate the process of socialization and the problem solving associated with various crises. Video games are teaching children fast reactions. Complex family situations—multiple families, dual-career families—are exposing children to much more variety in social roles and at least the need to learn how to negotiate expectations. Thus there are signs of hope as well. Regardless, this normative model provides a number of insights on how to help people avoid role failure and what they can do to improve their adjustments to a rapidly changing society.

References

Alter, C., & Hage, J. (1993). *Organizations working together.* Newbury Park, CA: Sage.

Argyris, C., & Schön, D. (1974). *Theory in practice.* San Francisco: Jossey-Bass.

Bell, D. (1973). *The coming of post-industrial society.* New York: Basic Books.

Coleman, J. S. (1990). *Foundations of social theory.* Cambridge, MA: Belknap Press.

Etzioni, A. (1968). *The active society.* New York: Free Press.

Featherstone, M. (Ed.). (1988a). In pursuit of the post-modern. *Theory, Culture, and Society, 5,* 195–216.

Featherstone, M. (Ed.). (1988b). *Postmodernism.* Newbury Park, CA: Sage.

Feher, F. (1987). The status of post modernity. *Philosophy and Social Criticism, 13*(2), 195–206.

Furstenberg, F., Jr. (1990). Divorce and the American family. In W. R. Scott & J. Blake (Eds.), *Annual review of sociology, 16.*

Granovetter, M. S. (1973). The strength of weak ties. *American Journal of Sociology, 78*(6), 1360–1380.

Hage, J. (1988). *The futures of organizations.* Lexington, MA: Heath.

Hage, J., & Powers, C. (1992). *Post-industrial lives.* Newbury Park, CA: Sage.

Hollingsworth, J. R. (1991). The logic of coordinating American manufacturing sectors. In J. L. Campbell, J. R. Hollingsworth, & L. N. Lindberg (Eds.), *The governance of the American economy.* New York: Cambridge University Press.

Kellner, D. (1990). The postmodern turn: Positions, problems, and prospects. In G. Ritzer (Ed.), *Frontiers of social theory.* New York: Columbia University Press.

Kozol, J. (1991). *Savage inequalities: Children in America's schools.* New York: Crown.

Lyotard, J. (1984). *The postmodern condition.* Minneapolis: University of Minnesota Press.

Mead, G. H. (1964). *Mind, self, and society.* (C. Morris, Ed.). Chicago: University of Chicago Press. (Original work published 1934.)

Morrissey, J. P., Tausig, M., & Lindsey, M. L. (1984). *Interorganizational networks in mental health systems: Assessing community support programs for the chronically mentally ill.* Washington, DC: Community Support Rehabilitation Branch, Division of Mental Health Service Programs.

Naisbitt, J. (1982). *Megatrends: Ten new directions transforming our lives.* New York: Warner Books.

National Science Foundation, National Science Board. (1989). *Science indicators.* Washington, DC: U.S. Government Printing Office.

Parsons, T. (1951). *The social system.* New York: Free Press.

Piore, M. J., & Sabel, C. F. (1984). *The second industrial divide: Possibilities for prosperity.* New York: Basic Books.

Powell, W. W. (1990). Neither market nor hierarchy: Network forms of organization. In L. L. Cummings & B. Staw (Eds.), *Research in organizational behavior.* Greenwich, CT: JAI Press.

Schor, J. B. (1991). *The overworked American.* New York: Basic Books.

Simmel, G. (1955). *Conflict and the web of group affiliations.* (K. Wolff, Trans.). New York: Free Press.

Toffler, A. (1981). *The third wave.* New York: Bantam Books.

Wilson, W. J. (1987). *The truly disadvantaged: The inner city, the underclass, and public policy.* Chicago: University of Chicago Press.

Chapter Fourteen

Rethinking the Psychology of Work

Ann Howard

Workers should delight in the way work is changing. After all, their traditional enemies, machines and managers, are now their servants and friends. At the turn of the last century, humans had to adjust to crude and uncompromising machines; Frederick Taylor regulated the muscles and motions, and welfare workers attuned the spirits. In the next century, machines will adjust to humans. Adaptable computer technology will further people's ability to work naturally (Coovert, Chapter Five; Van der Spiegel, Chapter Three). During the industrial and bureaucratic eras, managers gave orders and workers complied; in the new high-involvement workplaces, workers are empowered and managers offer inspiration and support (Mohrman & Cohen, Chapter Ten; House, Chapter Eleven). Social and economic goals have converged, declared Wall and Jackson (Chapter Four).

Then why are people so anxious? Opinion polls in the United States continually document people's cynicism and mistrust (Hall & Mirvis, Chapter Nine), pessimism about the future, and search for scapegoats. Voters in 1994 switched the reins of congressional power from Democrats to Republicans, and Californians voted to deny schooling and health care to the children of illegal immigrants. People sense that the world is destabilized. Hage (Chapter Thirteen) identified widespread signs of role failure in the family and other social institutions—an upsurge in children born out of wedlock, divorce, violent crime, political gridlock. Family breakup and community breakdown are omens of the collapse of society, he warns.

Jobs are a major source of anxiety in the volatile political-economic-societal environment. Will there be enough jobs? Will they be well-paying and rewarding? Workers fear that their jobs will be taken away by immigrants or by trade agreements that let firms more easily outsource low-skilled work to less-developed countries with cheaper labor. But high-skilled jobs are also threatened—by electronic immigrants in developing countries who handle accounting, legal research, and the like by telecommuting; by robots that can negotiate production schedules with other computers and manage business transactions without human intervention; by eager technicians and engineers in low-wage, high-skill countries like China and India (*Business Week,* 1994). Neither flexible machines nor friendly managers offer workers security.

The Edge of Chaos

The winds of change are buffeting the terms and conditions of work, its content, and its context. This chapter portrays the human side of the changing nature of work, weaving together common threads from this volume. This section draws on complexity theory to expose order underlying what now appears as chaos in the workplace and broader society. The next three sections highlight themes within the book's central parts—work, workers, and working—followed by a discussion of their political, economic, and societal implications. The chapter concludes with recommendations for generating psychological knowledge and rethinking the psychology of work.

Discontinuity

The changes under way in the political-economic-societal context are not only more frequent but different in kind from what we have known in the past. It is the discontinuity of change that provokes institutional and role failure (Hage, Chapter Thirteen). As Havel (1994, p. A27) expressed it, "Many things indicate that we are going through a transitional period, when it seems that something is on the way out and something else is painfully being born. It is as if something were crumbling, decaying and exhausting itself, while something else, still indistinct, were arising from the rubble." Discontinuous change is uncomfortable change because the past is no longer a guide to the future (Handy, 1989).

Discontinuity is not foreign to human history but new to its current players. According to Drucker (1993), every few hundred years in Western civilization a sharp transformation or divide, lasting about fifty years, creates a very different world. We are in the middle of a transformation now that won't be complete, if history repeats itself, until 2010 or 2020—not yet a new world order, just a new world disorder. Globalism is commingling cultures and values, currently adding more perplexity than definition to social structure.

What are the roots of this discontinuity? A primary culprit is the mysterious new economic resource called knowledge (useful information). Hage (Chapter Thirteen) traces the growth in knowledge to higher levels of education, new technologies, and increased research and development; Davis (Chapter Three) views the growth of knowledge, information technology, and global competition as contributing to change both directly and interactively. They agree that information technology has been a catalyst to the explosion of knowledge; not only does it allow rapid processing and widespread communication of information, but it also lets scientists model phenomena and manipulate vast quantities of data.

Compared to previous economic resources—land and capital—knowledge has peculiar qualities, still incompletely understood. Knowledge creates knowledge. In the language of economist Brian Arthur, it follows the principle of increasing returns, where initial gains lead to even more gains (Waldrop, 1992). It grows when shared because recipients feed back questions, amplifications, and modifications (Quinn, 1992). You can give knowledge away and still have it. Moreover, you can't will knowledge to your children, and the government can't redistribute it (Handy, 1994).

The collapse of communism and the turn of many countries toward a freer market have also provoked discontinuous change. Here, too, information technology has been an underlying force because it links nations and peoples and creates openness, which is anathema to totalitarianism. Developing countries are now reducing tariffs, taxes, and other barriers to foreign investment and trade (*Business Week,* 1994), revving up the motor of global competition.

Complexity Theory

Some of the confusing signals of the current political-economic-societal context can be made comprehensible if interpreted within the developing theory of complexity (Lewin, 1992; Waldrop, 1992). Scientists of various mathematically based disciplines, drawn together by the Santa Fe Institute, are pursuing general laws that underlie the emergence of complex systems. Complexity theory maintains that individual components or agents (for example, physical particles or firms in a global economy) interact according to a few simple rules. The system operates from the bottom up without a central controller, but a global property emerges and feeds back to influence the behavior of the individual components. In Adam Smith's economic theory, for example, individual buyers and sellers operate by simple principles of self-interest, and an invisible hand, the global emergent property, guides the market toward a balance of supply and demand.

Complex systems advance not gradually but through what paleontologists call punctuated equilibrium. That is, a period of stability is interrupted by an environmental jolt that pushes the system into chaos. During a chaotic period there is an avalanche of change and burst of differentiation, like the Cambrian explosion of complex creatures that resulted from the onset of multicellularity 570 million years ago, or the currently experienced rush of discontinuity described by Havel (1994), Drucker (1993), and Hage (Chapter Thirteen). Punctuated equilibrium is also the pattern of innovation, which progresses in fits and starts rather than a steady stream. Phase transitions are like a period of trial and error, where some differentiating components survive and others become extinct.

Complex systems evolve through self-organization and selection to what is called the edge of chaos. This is a balance point between stagnation and anarchy where the system can be spontaneous and adaptive; it is neither locked into place nor dissolved in turbulence (Waldrop, 1992). It is a point of maximal differentiation and integration, where the parts differ significantly in structure and function but can still communicate and enhance each other's goals (Csikszentmihalyi, 1993).

Work organizations should likewise seek their way to the edge of chaos. The deeply ordered line and box organizations described by Mohrman and Cohen (Chapter Ten) grant employees little latitude and incline toward stagnation. At the opposite extreme lie organizations wide open to change but poorly integrated, in which people are unsure of what to do and work at cross-purposes. How to achieve the optimal balance of differentiation and integration at the edge of chaos is an organization's primary challenge. Davis (Chapter Three) speculates that emerging organizational forms, such as virtual organizations composed of temporary partnerships, may demonstrate evolutionary superiority in the long run.

What, then, would work be like at the edge of chaos? Figure 14.1 provides an overview of themes elaborated in the next three sections. Recapitulating the model of Figure 1.1 in the opening chapter, Figure 14.1 shows light beams that reflect demand and supply joining in the spotlight of work, workers, and working. Not every organization will fit this model; it represents those in turbulent environments who must constantly adapt to survive.

Figure 14.1. Model of Adaptive Work.

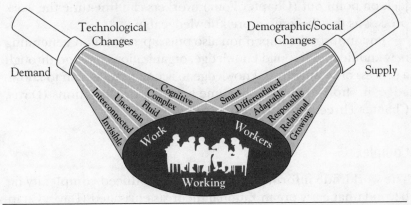

Work

The left side of Figure 14.1 summarizes work demands in an adaptive organization in the post-industrial economy. These demands derive from technological and other changes discussed in Chapters Three through Five.

Cognitive

McKinsey and company have estimated that by the year 2000, 70 percent of jobs in Europe and 80 percent of those in the United States will require primarily cerebral skills rather than manual skills (Handy, 1989), estimates that Quinn (1992) finds low. Although organizations can implement technology in ways that either deskill or upskill work, the overall trend is toward upskilling (see Chapter Three). Work based on knowledge will require reasoning and judgment; it will be cognitive.

Information technology is changing the nature of both the tools that workers use and the problems they must solve (Hirschhorn & Mokray, 1992). Factory tools are evolving from single mechanisms that provide sensory feedback to systems of tools that present cognitive feedback. Similarly, problems involve more parameters across several, not solitary, operations. The worker is responsible for preventing variances, not just correcting them, and for detecting patterns in the process flow rather than solving single puzzles. In order to plan ahead, monitor, and inspect, the worker must consciously picture in the abstract the whole nature of the run. As Wall and Jackson point out (Chapter Four), workers can fine-tune the work process as they become more knowledgeable.

Post-industrial competition also puts a premium on generating new knowledge. To build knowledge, organizations must go through a process of moving from knowledge to action to reflection to knowledge; in short, they must become learning organizations (Davis, Chapter Three; Hall & Mirvis, Chapter Nine).

Complex

The worldwide information system has produced complexity far beyond what early organizational theorists envisaged (Davis, Chapter Three). According to the principle of requisite variety, a system must be as varied and complex as the environment it is trying to manage (Hall & Mirvis, Chapter Nine). Simple role scripts dictated by social norms or line and box organizational charts are no longer sufficient. Scripts have to give way to new role negotiations when the environment becomes too complex and diverse to handle with a clear set of rules appropriate for everyone. In the social sphere, Hage (Chapter Thirteen) notes that managing change by a return to "family values," with one fixed script for men and one for women, is doomed to failure. Workers and managers likewise must negotiate new role expectations about issues such as psychological contracts (Rousseau & Wade-Benzoni, Chapter Eight), teamwork (Mohrman & Cohen, Chapter Ten), leadership (House, Chapter Eleven), and careers (Hall & Mirvis, Chapter Nine).

The increasing differentiation of knowledge and reduction of organizations to their core competencies suggest that specialization of work will increase. The most effective knowledge workers are specialists (Drucker, 1993), and occupations are increasingly specialized (Hage, Chapter Thirteen). On the other hand, teams often work best with multiskilling, so that team members can handle shifting requirements and cover for each other (Wellins, Byham, & Wilson, 1991). These two seemingly contradictory forces raise questions about how best to deal with complexity: Should there be more generalists or more specialists?

The answer is both: adaptive organizations need specialists with additional competencies. Specialization provides depth of expertise, but organizational flexibility requires each worker to expand in outlook, assume additional roles, and exercise a broader array of skills. For example, team members take on roles that require interpersonal skills like conflict resolution or leadership. Teams should not spread tasks too widely lest members become masters of none. But the complexity of tasks and functions and requirements for special skills should pose natural limits on multiskilling (Wellins et al., 1991).

Fluid

An accelerating spiral of knowledge, propelled by global competition, will keep work fluid and create difficulty in tying down a "job." Various other forces are contributing to the job's demise (Ilgen, 1992; Bridges, 1994). Mergers and acquisitions, downsizing, and outsourcing of corporate activities to niche firms keep jobs churning.

Customization requires that companies regularly recast tasks. Teams rather than individuals are assuming work responsibilities, especially where cross-functional problem solving and collaboration are critical. Social institutions are also playing a role: the decline in unions has shrunk reliance on jobs as entities for bargaining and grievances, and the Americans with Disabilities Act of 1990 compels employers to individualize jobs.

Boundaries around a job induce rigidities into the system; environmental changes can lead to thousands of hours of reworking job descriptions (Mohrman & Cohen, Chapter Ten). By contrast, a field of organizational work that needs to be done takes its cues from the changing demands of the project, not from a job description or the boss's orders, just as farm families during the agricultural era took care of shifting clusters of tasks according to the weather and the needs of the day (see Chapter One). The job is, after all, an artifact of the industrial age, created to package work in factories and bureaucratic organizations (Bridges, 1994).

In contrast to the rigid, crystalline structures of American firms, Nissan's CEO likens fluid Japanese organizations to mud, always in flux, with ill-defined separations between functions (Handy, 1994). Like mud, work responsibilities are seeping out of their traditional containers. Rather than repeating well-structured routines, workers in lateral organizations float from team to team while managers may manage one project and be a team member for another (Mohrman & Cohen, Chapter Ten). Jobs represent one more boundary to be eliminated (Davis, Chapter Three), one more box to get out of (Mohrman & Cohen, Chapter Ten).

As bounded jobs disappear, people are likely to overextend themselves. Dejobbed work lacks edges that signal when a worker has done enough (Bridges, 1994). In Handy's (1994) terminology, work is like an inside-out doughnut, with an essential core of formal duties and an outer area of discretionary space. Jobs in bureaucratic organizations are mostly core with meager space. But if work has little core and unlimited space, then workers can never do enough.

The absence of a well-defined job has serious implications for the practice of industrial/organizational (I/O) psychology, which relies on job analyses to set the criteria for many other human resource systems, including recruiting, selection and placement, training and development, performance appraisal, compensation, and human resource planning. The Civil Rights Act of 1964, as interpreted in EEOC guidelines and case law, requires establishment of job relatedness for employment practices, and the 1978 Uniform Guidelines on Employee Selection Procedures require objective job analyses to justify selection testing and performance appraisal. Fluid jobs undermine compliance with these standards. One electronics company, for example, uses job descriptions for hiring and setting initial salaries but then ignores them for guiding work activities, all the while nervous about being sued for misrepresentation (Bridges, 1994).

Dejobbing suggests that job analyses based on specific tasks must yield to those targeted at more general functions. Without bounded jobs there can be no stable, well-defined tasks. How to define broader functions is likely to stimulate debate, some of which has already appeared in discussions of validity generalization. Schmidt, Hunter, and Pearlman (1981) have argued that only superficial, holistic job analyses are required to support use of general ability tests, but this approach clearly will not pass muster with current law.

Job analyses have importance beyond justifying validity generalization, and more detail is useful for such purposes as training and performance appraisal. As Landy, Shankster-Cawley, and Moran point out in Chapter Seven, psychological attributes are the focus of interest, and tasks should be seen only as means to get to attributes. This raises the question of whether attributes can be identified directly without jumping through the hoops of defining tasks or more general task-related functions. Again, case law clearly says "no" to such a practice, but this has not kept psychologists from developing methods to do so. Harvey (1991) has argued against leaping to attributes, reasoning that job analysis should describe work behavior independent of personal characteristics to provide an objective grounding for personnel practices and to assure that there is no criterion contamination or deficiency.

Uncertain

Environmental uncertainty requires organizations to be more ad hoc in formulating strategies and structuring work. Complex adaptive systems evolve according to what complexity theorists call the Darwinian principle of relativity; that is, each agent is constantly adapting to other agents (Waldrop, 1992). As evolutionary biologists put it, organisms don't evolve; they co-evolve. An organism's survival doesn't depend on overall "fitness," which is impossible to define, but on the niche it is filling, what other organisms are around, what resources it can gather, and to some extent its past history. Organizations likewise must engage in this dance of co-evolution with their wafting webs of economic and political dependencies. They must keep open as many options as possible and strive for what is not necessarily optimal, but advantageous and workable.

The road to organizational flexibility is strewn with jettisoned external and internal boundaries. Companies have reduced external barriers between competitors and collaborators, around their suppliers and customers, even between work and home; they have dismantled internal boundaries between groups and departments, levels of authority, cultures, permanent and temporary employees, and time periods (Davis, Chapter Three). Mohrman and Cohen (Chapter Ten) express boundary reduction in terms of getting out of the boxes on the organizational chart and into the fluid arrangements of the lateral organization.

Boundary reduction provides flexibility to respond more quickly to customer and competitive demands. At the same time, it introduces uncertainty into work roles. It is often unclear, for example, who has the legitimacy to require performance of employees or where to get information about individual performance (Mohrman & Cohen, Chapter Ten). Tasks also contain more uncertainty. One reason that the cognitive demands of work are rising is because problems are less routine and their resolution less automatic (Hirschhorn & Mokray, 1992).

Workers confront additional uncertainty from the dismantling of the internal labor market, which offered them long-term relationships with organizations and rewards based on seniority (Rousseau & Wade-Benzoni, Chapter Eight). As organizations turn to external vendors to replace support services and even more essential functions, they invite in external market forces in which employees become competitors (Bridges, 1994). Careerists become short-term rather than long-term insiders (Rousseau & Wade-Benzoni, Chapter Eight). In fact, organizations facing uncertainty become unable to plan an individual's career (Hall & Mirvis, Chapter Nine).

Interconnected

Information technology has enabled instantaneous, far-reaching communications and the collaboration of organizations in a world-wide web (Davis, Chapter Three). Internally, organizations are adopting teams and operating laterally (Mohrman & Cohen, Chapter Ten). Work is thus interconnected with people and entities both outside and inside the organization.

Interconnected work requires integrative mechanisms. Groupware technologies facilitate relational work, and communication and information systems should unite people into a collective (Coovert, Chapter Five; Mohrman & Cohen, Chapter Ten). Falling boundaries enhance the diversity of interconnected people and entities, adding another layer of complexity to communication and collaboration.

The upsurge in interconnections as well as the demise of the bounded job suggest that analyses of work should differentiate tasks from roles. Hirschhorn and Mokray (1992), for example, view skills (knowledge, know-how, and abilities) as shaped by an organization's technical infrastructure and roles as shaped by the social system. Similarly, Ilgen and Hollenbeck (1991) treat jobs as sets of task elements and roles as expected behaviors that exist in people's minds. Hedge and Borman (Chapter Twelve) imply this separation when they distinguish functional from contextual performance.

Interconnected work shifts emphasis away from doing a job and toward taking roles (Hirschhorn & Mokray, 1992). "Jobs" or work clusters would maintain a core of essential tasks but have an expanding outer circle of roles that evolve out of the interaction of the job incumbent with others in the work setting (Ilgen, 1992).

Invisible

Knowledge and service work are by nature intangible. The abstraction of work from hands-on, manual labor to manipulation of electronic images on a computer screen is making work invisible. Moreover, the context in which work is performed is increasingly obscure. As previously discussed, the job is disappearing in favor of an amorphous collection of work. The central office is shrinking as more work is conducted in mobile offices and by telecommuting.

Ubiquitous computers in the workplace will be invisibly nestled within ceilings, walls, book spines, and other locations (Coovert, Chapter Five). Virtual and boundaryless organizations are more a metaphor than a concrete reality (Rousseau & Wade-Benzoni, Chapter Eight); they may disaggregate to the point of almost ceasing to exist (Quinn, 1992). Organizations are populated by internal and external virtual staff.

Invisible work creates visible problems for managers and psychologists. Some argue that psychology has always dealt with unobservables (Landy, 1986; Schmidt et al., 1981), but emerging work conditions add new dimensions to old problems. How can you perform a job analysis if there is no job? How can you select or train people for invisible work? How can you coordinate or appraise the performance of workers you can't observe? How can you validate selection or training systems if you can't measure performance?

In some cases, work can be made more visible. Assessment centers have traditionally done this for unobservable processes such as decision making; after assessees complete an in-basket exercise, assessors interview them to learn how they arrived at their decisions in the exercise. Computer-generated augmented reality and animation can dramatize processes for training purposes (Coovert, Chapter Five), and multimedia can add realism to various human resource systems. Sources other than a remote boss can be used for performance appraisal (Hedge & Borman, Chapter Twelve).

Invisible work nevertheless provides opportunities for mischief. Nord and Brief (1990) have suggested, for example, that where individual skills and outputs are less clearly measured and interdependency assumes greater importance, social construction can play a larger role in judging contributions. But invisibility can also have benefits. Telecommuters report lower stress, better ability to focus on the task, greater efficiency, and increased flexibility in balancing personal and work demands (Davis, Chapter Three).

Summary

Post-industrial work in adaptive organizations will be cognitively demanding and complex. It will be fluid and constantly changing; in this environment, tying down stable jobs will be difficult.

Uncertainty and invisibility will enhance the abstract nature of work, but interconnections to others will engender new roles and relationships.

Workers

The right side of Figure 14.1 illustrates the nature of workers suited to adaptive organizations in the post-industrial economy, as discussed in Chapters Six through Nine.

Smart

Cognitive, complex work requires smart people. Workers must be intelligent enough to capitalize on powerful new tools and technologies and to solve multidimensional problems. They must be able to acquire and apply knowledge and do so continuously, because technology and work are constantly changing. More and more, workers must be capable of reasoning and learning.

An unavoidable conclusion is that most work in adaptive organizations will require higher levels of general mental ability (g) than in the past. Other classes of abilities, including psychomotor skill and perceptual speed, may also be important for certain tasks and levels of skill acquisition (Ackerman, 1992; Ackerman & Humphreys, 1990). Landy, Shankster-Cawley, and Moran (Chapter Seven) hypothesize that in a constantly changing technical environment g may be necessary to acquire specific knowledge, but that special abilities will permit application of that knowledge. This will depend, however, on the extent of uncertainty and novelty involved. Lower-level abilities are important in the performance of practiced tasks subject to automatic processing. When tasks are too complex or uncertain to be automatized and require attention or cognitive effort (controlled processing), g best predicts performance over time (Ackerman & Humphreys, 1990).

The discontinuity of change makes it difficult to forecast the specific skills needed for post-industrial work. Moreover, Osterman (Chapter Six) points out that providing unemployed youth with specific skills is no guarantee that jobs will be created to use them; this "field of dreams" approach, popularized by Labor Secretary Reich, appears made of quicksand. A consensus seems to be forming that basic skills and education are prerequisite to preparing workers to learn on the job the specific skills that they will need (Carnevale, Chapter Six; Hammer & Champy, 1993; Quinn, 1992). But those basic skills are essential. A novice typist, for example, will never acquire a high level of speed and accuracy if that person's knowledge of the language is at the sixth-grade level or below (Ackerman & Humphreys, 1990). "Train and the jobs will come" may be fantasy, but a case can be made for "Fail to educate and the jobs will go."

This conclusion cannot help generating despair among Americans pummeled with the unrelenting documentation of mediocre outcomes of public primary and secondary education. In addition to basic literacy and numeracy, young people should be learning how to reason (Glaser, 1989). Carnevale (Chapter Six) faults traditional pedagogy's similarity to the old assembly line economy: it poses authoritative teachers in front of passive students, focuses on getting the right answers rather than understanding processes, and encourages superficial learning. Also contributing to educational mediocrity has been a deemphasis of standards in favor of social amelioration despite evidence that many disadvantaged children can learn considerably more if it is expected and demanded of them (Drucker, 1993; Sharf, in press). Sharf argues further that employers cannot signal the value of education and grades in their selection criteria because such standards are treated like tests and subject to civil rights enforcement.

Although employer-based training increased over the last decade, it was mostly confined to large organizations and skilled employees. Its limited application has prompted the government to seek ways to force widespread employer training, including training mandates (which are strongly opposed by business and labor), tax credits, or grants (Carnevale, Chapter Six). Hall and Mirvis (Chapter Nine) propose instead creative staffing; that is, organizations should help people get into jobs that will stretch them and let the jobs provide self-training and self-learning.

Coovert (Chapter Five) recommends just-in-time training. This option becomes feasible with technologically based instruction, available in packaged products or through twenty-four-hour access to the Infobahn (high-speed information highway). A worldwide workforce could even engage in distant learning with remote instructors (Van der Spiegel, Chapter Three).

Differentiated

Massive differentiation, characteristic of today's products, markets, organizations, families, leisure lifestyles, and other aspects of society (Hage, Chapter Thirteen), extends across workers as well. (Differentiation within individuals is discussed in the later section of this chapter entitled Growing.) A knowledge-based global economy will accentuate inequalities in ability.

Workforce differentiation is already evident in the increasing inequality in wages in mature economies, most pronounced in the United States and Britain, where the social safety net is thinner (Handy, 1994). The decline in wages of high school graduates relative to college graduates has been well documented (Chapter Six). Even within various professions, the gap between the top achievers and others has been widening as globalization enhances competition and its rewards (Mandel, 1992). That the rich get richer and the poor get poorer (relatively or absolutely) was also characteristic of bureaucratic careers (Howard & Bray, 1988), but the principle of increasing returns is operating more aggressively in the post-industrial era.

Several writers have predicted a two-tiered workforce. Reich (1991), for example, contrasts the competitive symbolic analysts to those in personal service or routine production jobs, and Drucker (1993) contrasts knowledge and service workers. Handy (1989) foresees a privileged world of core employees juxtaposed against the more perilous existence of workers peripheral to the organization, a theme emphasized by Rousseau and Wade-Benzoni in their discussion of organization attachments (Chapter Eight) as well as by Hall and Mirvis relative to careers (Chapter Nine).

A repeated refrain in global business circles is that half the people will be permanently overworked, the other half permanently unemployed (Sasseen, 1994). Handy (1989) proposed that the core workforce will consist of half the people, paid twice as much, working three times as effectively. Peripheral workers, by contrast, may have great difficulty finding enough employment. There could be mutual envy, he notes: the poor but leisured may be envious of the rich and busy, while the rich and busy may resent having to support the poor and envy their leisure time. Hage's prescription for the burnout and energy drain of post-industrial life is more leisure (Chapter Thirteen), but core workers may have no time for it. Peripheral workers will have pressing concerns about not only earning a living but replacing the sense of identity, purpose, and self-esteem that work has traditionally provided (Bridges, 1994; Dumaine, 1994). There is already evidence that despite overall current unemployment of less than 6 percent in the United States, rising proportions of prime working-age men, particularly less-educated minorities, are working sporadically or not at all (Nasar, 1994).

Work demands for adaptability and speed could also stratify the workforce by age, even though physical and cognitive abilities are unrelated to age per se (Landy, Shankster-Cawley, & Moran, Chapter Seven). Handy (1989) predicts that core workers will be considered too old for their high-paced jobs by age fifty. They will have short but hard careers and then move on to seek relief from the pressure as well as to make room for younger, more energetic, and more up-to-date people. Many professionals attain peak performance in their twenties through forties (Ericsson & Charness, 1994); great software developers are said to do their best work before age thirty (Deutschman & Tetzeli, 1994). In heated global competition, these differences may matter. This does not necessarily imply that workers will retire by their fiftieth birthday; their wisdom should be valuable (Sterns & Sterns, in press), and they could be deployed as coaches and mentors (Hall & Mirvis, Chapter Nine). But age discrimination may increasingly trigger lawsuits.

Given a strong economy, young, well-educated workers could be in short supply, according to demographic trends. Moreover, the peak years of working will overlap with the prime years of child rearing, a juxtaposition that may further restrict the supply of workers, especially women, willing to subject themselves to excessive workloads. Competition for the top tier of workers will be high, and accurate selection methods much in demand.

Adaptable

If work is constantly changing, then workers will have to be adaptable. Because organizations won't be able to specify what kinds of skills they will need for future work, Hall and Mirvis (Chapter Nine) suggest teaching adaptability as a meta-skill to enable workers to cope with change. At the same time, they question whether people can learn to be adaptable. A clue to possibly teachable behaviors may come from research on learning how to learn.

Organizations may be able to use personality tests, behavioral interviews, simulations, or other measures to select more adaptable people. For example, openness to experience, one of the Big Five personality factors, was found to correlate with a training criterion, but its simultaneous correlation with cognitive ability clouded whether the factor reflects being willing or able to engage in learning experiences (Barrick & Mount, 1991).

Adaptability may have an upper limit. Lifton (1993) warns that believing a person can do anything or be anybody could render the self incoherent and immobile in the face of an overwhelming and chaotic field of possibilities. He propounds integrative proteanism to hold together disparate elements of the self. In the parlance of complexity theory, proteanism should be taken just to the edge of chaos, where there is order that doesn't block the flow of change.

Responsible

For organizations to be flexible enough to respond to an uncertain environment, employees must be motivated to take the initiative and be responsible for their own work. Shopfloor workers must be responsible for production, given the high cost of errors with expensive machinery and the dire consequences of poor quality or timing (Wall & Jackson, Chapter Four). Self-directed teams must assume responsibility for the company's success (Mohrman & Cohen, Chapter Ten). Self-discipline must replace social cues when workers telecommute (Davis, Chapter Three). And individuals must take responsibility for redefining their social roles in an era of breakdown of traditional norms and institutions (Hage, Chapter Thirteen). In short, the post-industrial society can offer space and freedom, but with freedom goes responsibility.

Hall and Mirvis (Chapter Nine) emphasize in their definition of the protean career that people must take responsibility for their own self-development and career plans because the organization will no longer assume that role. This is not to deny the importance of leaders, who should analyze the skill levels of their followers and help them toward appropriate developmental experiences (House, Chapter Eleven). But post-industrial leaders must also encourage followers to be self-managing (Mohrman & Cohen, Chapter Ten). Actually, people learn most rapidly when they are responsible for their actions; helplessness undermines the incentive to learn (Senge, 1990).

There will undoubtedly be considerable social debate about the extent to which workers should assume individual responsibility for the fringe benefits that organizations have traditionally provided. Bridges (1994) and Roberts (1994) call for people to take responsibility for their own health insurance and pensions (replacing Social Security) as if they were self-employed. Organizations are already cutting back health benefits, pensions, and retirees' health care coverage (Hall & Mirvis, Chapter Nine).

Taking on individual responsibility will undoubtedly suit some people better than others, and organizations would do well to assess applicants' inclinations to do so. A measure of responsibility might, in fact, generalize across post-industrial work. Meta-analyses have been somewhat inconsistent, however, in demonstrating this for the Big Five's conscientiousness factor (Landy, Shankster-Cawley, & Moran, Chapter Seven).

If workers assume more responsibility, they will want and deserve respect for their newly independent status. Recognition of the duality of the person-organization relationship should encourage studies of applicant reactions (Landy, Shankster-Cawley, & Moran, Chapter Seven) and psychological contracts (Rousseau & Wade-Benzoni, Chapter Eight). Hall and Mirvis (Chapter Nine) suggest several ways in which organizations can help employees self-manage their careers, such as assigning projects that promote real-time learning, providing career information, and investing in workers' core skills and development to make them more employable.

Relational

Employee commitment, according to Mohrman and Cohen (Chapter Ten), must shift from the organization to the work and co-workers. This latter commitment is made necessary as work becomes more interconnected and organizations emphasize teams.

Where relationships to others are mediated not by the boss but by the team, people who fail to establish good working relations will suffer big penalties.

Carnevale (Chapter Six) cites a number of required relational skills, including communication, group effectiveness (interpersonal skills, negotiation, teamwork), and influencing skills. Mohrman and Cohen (Chapter Ten) add conflict resolution skills, anticipating that diversity will increase conflict. Many workers will have to relate to others who may be quite different from themselves. Beyond ethnic and cultural diversity, co-workers on cross-functional teams will represent multiple disciplines and have different worldviews. In work, as in other aspects of life, people must learn to live in complex role-sets, each with role-relationships requiring negotiations about expectations and behavior (Hage, Chapter Thirteen). Moreover, people must be sensitive to the emotional, noncognitive messages of symbolic communication to understand what is negotiable.

The composition of a team can affect its ability to collaborate (Landy, Shankster-Cawley, & Moran, Chapter Seven; Mohrman & Cohen, Chapter Ten). Psychologists have only begun to explore issues related to team selection. Assessment centers should provide a useful technology for this purpose, but the dimensions and criteria for selecting members are not yet well defined. This is a complex issue given the research findings that group heterogeneity aids productivity but hurts turnover; apparently, being with different kinds of people can stimulate creativity but may not be as enjoyable (see Landy, Shankster-Cawley, & Moran, Chapter Seven). In a similar dynamic, selection of members by teams can facilitate collaboration but may not assure heterogeneity.

Growing

Complex post-industrial life requires complex selves, states Hage (Chapter Thirteen). To develop complexity, workers must grow through dialectical motion between their own differentiation and integration (Csikszentmihalyi, 1993). Differentiation for an individual involves recognizing an opportunity for action or challenge; being open to, even seeking, possibilities; and being willing to experiment and take risks. To master a challenge, individuals must acquire skills and meld them into their repertoire of abilities, which is the process of integration. But complex skills can be built up only by complex activities; boring jobs or oppressive work environments would prohibit this process from taking place. Much post-industrial work, then, should facilitate growing.

Davis (Chapter Three) refers to this growth process as personal mastery, which he likens to constant refinement with self-reflection as practiced in the Asian martial arts. Personality may play a role in this process. Davis suggests that conscientiousness is related to personal mastery, and Hedge and Borman (Chapter Twelve) report that dependability is modestly related to acquiring job knowledge. Here are more grounds, then, for a generalized personality factor important to future work.

It may be an overgeneralization to assume that all people are motivated to grow and self-develop and that challenging work fulfills this need. Nord, Brief, Atieh, and Doherty (1990) argued that this neoconventional view is a social construction of middle-class writers that blinds adherents to conflicts surrounding experiences of work. Gordon (1993) complained that there is a tendency in the training business to equate personal growth with more investment in any job, no matter how trivial. "Would a self-actualized individual really be more likely than a spiritually stunted one to seek bliss and fulfillment in the act of answering a phone by the third ring?" (p. 8). Self-developers are often unhappy with their circumstances and make repeated and unsatisfying compromises, according to Hall and Mirvis (Chapter Nine). These authors suggest that community, transpersonal connectedness, and spirituality may provide additional sources of meaning. Thus for core employees, work may not be enough; for those on the periphery, there may not be enough work.

Summary

The ability to reason and learn will be essential for the future workplace. But greater task complexity, novelty, and inconsistency increase the influence on performance of not just ability but motivational variables (Ackerman & Humphreys, 1990). Workers must take the initiative and assume additional responsibilities. Moreover, they must relate to others effectively and adapt readily to changing circumstances. Besides cognitive variables, both conative (motivational) and affective (personality) factors will be important. Put another way, *g will be more necessary but less sufficient.*

Working

The spotlight in Figure 14.1 brings work and workers together in the act of working, as discussed in Chapters Ten through Twelve. In adaptive organizations, workers are empowered but interdependent. The challenge for managers and leaders is to coordinate and integrate the organization without toppling these precarious roles and relationships.

Empowerment

The word *empowerment* has not been entirely satisfactory because it implies that someone on high gives away power that he or she could later take away. Alternative terms, such as *high involvement* (Lawler, 1992) or *subsidiarity* (Handy, 1994) dodge this connotation but unfortunately lack cachet. What should be communicated is that power properly belongs further out from the central coordination of the organization and should be taken back only as a last resort (Handy, 1994). Mary Parker Follett (1949) conceptualized this principle in the 1920s; she believed that authority derives from the function or task and argued for "power with" rather than "power over" others. Today's movement of responsibility and authority to those lower down in the organization is not simply part of a general empowerment of the disenfranchised (Vaill, 1989), because the latter implies "power over" through political means. Rather, empowerment is a different way of conceptualizing control over work that offers organizational and psychological benefits not yet fully explored.

Work must be controlled from somewhere, and if workers are expected to perform with higher responsibility and skill, they must be able to control the process (Chapter Three). Various technological and organizational factors have either mandated or enabled local control. Reengineering, for example, inevitably leads to empowerment of individuals and self-directing teams because performance of whole processes requires people to think, interact, use their judgment, and make decisions (Hammer & Champy, 1993). Quality improvement efforts use employee involvement as a way of taking advantage of knowledge within an organization (Davis, Chapter Three). Information technology brings instantaneous data to frontline workers, enabling them to make informed, timely decisions. Moreover, software can conduct quality checks, allowing less-trained employees to perform to higher standards without supervision (Quinn, 1992).

I/O psychologists have rallied behind empowerment for some time as a way to enhance employee motivation (for example, Byham, 1988; Lawler, 1992). Research psychologists from various other traditions have converged on related concepts. Internal locus of control, competence, self-efficacy, and learned helplessness and hopelessness represent a line of thought that explores more fully how people can become agents rather than patients (Smith, 1991). Wall and Jackson (Chapter Four) suggest building further bridges to the psychology of learning and research on stress. Thanks largely to their cogent analyses, we can now identify a number of ways, summarized in the following sections, in which empowerment can be anchored in organizational, psychological, and other theory.

Flexibility

The flexibility needed to confront production uncertainty is achieved by devolved decision making and higher employee discretion (Wall & Jackson, Chapter Four). Moreover, as competition puts a premium on speed, organizations benefit directly if employees at the point of customer contact can make needed decisions and take appropriate actions. Organizations are constrained if individual workers lack the power to act. Alternatively, organizations enrich their response capability by bundling multiple functions and placing them in the hands of skilled operators (Hall & Mirvis, Chapter Nine).

Natural Process

Natural complex systems, which operate without a central controller, provide metaphors for human efforts. Van der Spiegel (Chapter Three), for example, described how engineers are escaping the limits of the centrally controlled classic computer architecture by using biological systems as models for intelligent machines. Neural network systems can handle noisy, incomplete, and ill-defined problems, much like those in adaptive organizations, by relying on dispersed information processing. Similarly, managers need to understand that local control is a natural process, despite their predilections to keep a tight grip on the organizational reins.

Wheatley (1992) draws another metaphor from quantum theory, where reality emerges from the process of observation. Workers, too, become aware of the reality of a plan or strategy only by interacting with it and creating different possibilities from their personal observations.

Motivation

As Wall and Jackson (Chapter Four) make clear, psychological theories of job design have focused exclusively on enhancing motivation. Both the job characteristics model, which focuses on individuals, and sociotechnical systems theory, which emphasizes group and organizational factors, have inspired empirical investigations that justify this emphasis, and it remains the classic psychological rationale for current treatises on empowerment (for example, Byham, 1988; Lawler, 1992). Other theorists have tied empowerment to constructs from expectancy theories of motivation (Conger & Kanungo, 1988; Thomas & Velthouse, 1990).

Although job design is a key source of empowerment, leadership can also motivate and support employees' empowering behavior. As Mohrman and Cohen (Chapter Ten) point out, managers have significantly different roles in a lateral organization compared to a line and box organization, and they need to strike an appropriate balance between exerting too much and too little authority. As Handy (1994) puts it, the power belongs to the people; it is the manager's challenge to help them exercise it responsibly.

House (Chapter Eleven) provides various theoretical mechanisms through which leaders support empowerment. These are either directly motivational and tied to neocharismatic theory (for example, strengthening self-efficacy and collective identification; arousing achievement-oriented behavior) or facilitative and tied to path-goal theory (for example, establishing comprehensibility through path-goal clarification; empowering interdependent action through interaction facilitation). Similarly,

Howard and Wellins (1994) identify eleven roles for empowering leaders that range from inspirer (directly motivational) to team-builder (enabling). Mohrman and Cohen (Chapter Ten) also emphasize the need for leaders to perform enabling roles such as coach or facilitator.

Regardless of the approaches leaders take, the underlying psychological impact on the empowered is presumed to be motivational. The enabling role of leaders helps employees to feel that they can perform their work competently, and the inspirational role helps employees to believe that the work is worth doing well.

Learning

Both the job characteristics model and sociotechnical systems theory arose in an era of concern that job simplification was destructive to employee attitudes and behavior. Wall and Jackson (Chapter Four) make the compelling case that psychologists need to supplement their emphasis on motivation in job design theory with a cognitive perspective, including knowledge-based and learning processes. They suggest that job design can affect not just willingness to work but ability to work. In other words, job control enables employees to work smarter, not harder.

In support of a knowledge-based mechanism, Wall and Jackson note that integrated manufacturing initiatives work best when they capitalize on workers' experience and tacit knowledge. Workers with control can see the relationship between their actions and consequences, develop an understanding of the dynamic properties of systems, and thus anticipate, avoid, and prevent production difficulties. The authors' field experiments have demonstrated that empowered workers apply existing knowledge more quickly as well as engage in more fault prevention over time.

Expanding the psychological underpinnings of empowerment from motivation to learning has particular appeal for post-industrial work. First of all, if knowledge is the new resource for the emerging economy, then an objective of working should be to increase knowledge. Second, emerging work conditions suggest that in many situations motivation to work harder may not require the same level of concern that it evoked in the 1970s. For example, Howard and Wellins (1994) found in a twenty-five-organization study that high-involvement leadership enhanced employees' satisfaction and job involvement, but it had no relationship to employees' level of effort. Most respondents thought they exerted considerable effort, and the similarity of their responses created little variance to correlate with leader behaviors. A national study of nearly 3,400 workers found that 80 percent agreed or strongly agreed that their jobs require them to work very hard, and 42 percent indicated that they often or very often felt used up at the end of the workday (Galinsky, Bond, & Friedman, 1993). Schor (1991) found that today compared to twenty years ago, the average American works about one month more per year. In short, the economy's frantic pace, work demands, and anxiety about organizational failure and job security may have lit motivational fires under many employees that require little additional fuel.

The existence of these changes in the environment does not negate the importance of empowerment to other aspects of motivation or to job satisfaction. But it may help to explain why satisfaction and performance have been only weakly correlated despite the presumption of classic job design theory that they have common determinants. An alternative theoretical model might specify (1) the conditions under which *perceived empowerment* enhances motivation and satisfaction, and (2) the conditions under which *objective empowerment* leads to learning and thence enhances performance. Individual differences moderating each process should differ. Growth need strength is a proposed moderator in the motivation model; Coovert (Chapter Five) identifies locus of control, gender, and culture as other possibilities. Ability to learn might moderate a learning model. An important linking mechanism across the motivation and learning branches is knowledge of results, or feedback. As Wall and Jackson (Chapter Four) state, feedback in the job characteristics model is interpreted in motivational terms, yet another important purpose of feedback is to provide direction for learning. Hedge and Borman (Chapter Twelve) called attention to different antecedents of typical and maximal performance (personality and ability, respectively); there may similarly be different causal paths to satisfaction and performance from the motivational and learning processes stimulated by empowerment and individual control.

Stress Tolerance

Drawing on the demand-control model from the job stress literature, Wall and Jackson (Chapter Four) note that in highly demanding situations, low worker control produces strain and symptoms whereas high control helps people avert or become more resistant to stress. Coovert (Chapter Five) also cited research that related tight managerial control to exhaustion. Once again a key mechanism is learning: workers with control can learn to predict and avoid stressful situations, and their greater competence and feelings of mastery make them more resistant to the aversive demands that remain. Here, then, is another branch for the theoretical tree proposed in the previous section—a mental health consequence of empowerment under conditions of uncertainty.

Several chapter authors recommended that workers develop personal mastery and competence to deal with the stress and demands of post-industrial life. This approach was emphasized by Davis (Chapter Three) as a response to complexity and uncertainty, by Mohrman and Cohen (Chapter Ten) for handling the demands of the lateral organization, and by Hall and Mirvis (Chapter Nine) for managing careers in fluid organizations. The connection between empowerment, personal mastery, and stress tolerance needs to be made more explicit.

Summary

For organizations striving to be optimally adaptive, empowerment will be an important strategy for working. Not only will it help workers tolerate the inevitable stress that they will face, but it will also help to motivate them, channel their learning, develop important competencies, and provide the organization with the flexibility it needs to survive. Empowerment can function without organizational contortions because it is a natural process.

Interdependence

New manufacturing practices lead to much greater work interdependence (Wall & Jackson, Chapter Four). Just-in-time deliveries reduce the buffers of work-in-progress and make workers more dependent on each other to complete the task; total quality management magnifies the importance of pleasing internal and external customers; total quality initiatives and advanced manufacturing technology require close links between shopfloor and support staff. In the office, computer-supported cooperative work facilitates interdependence and allows larger groups to work together (Coovert, Chapter Five).

Mohrman and Cohen (Chapter Ten) vividly portray the requirements for working interdependently in team-based firms. The collective, not the individual, becomes the performing unit. People are held accountable for collective results, and team members manage each other's performance.

Interdependence can be highly rewarding to those who relish the opportunity to connect with others. But Mohrman and Cohen (Chapter Ten) warn that those who have been socialized to value individual responsibility may find dependency on co-workers uncomfortable. There is something of a paradox here in that many previously discussed circumstances require workers to take individual responsibility—for expensive machinery, the company's success, their own psychological contracts, their career development—at the same time that interconnected work demands shared accountability and accommodation. When individuals' fates are linked to those of co-workers, they must move beyond individualism to partnership and mutual trust, advise Mohrman and Cohen (Chapter Ten), but this process will not necessarily be welcomed nor easily undertaken. House (Chapter Eleven) suggests that neocharismatic leadership can help arouse affiliation motives, strengthen collective identification, and stimulate contributions to collective goals.

There is some risk that organizational teams could substitute a new tyranny for the old. Team or peer performance appraisals, for example, can provide useful feedback for learning and development, but they can quickly degenerate into destructive political tools if tied directly to strong outcomes such as pay and promotion (Hedge & Borman, Chapter Twelve; Howard, Byham, & Hauenstein, 1994). There are other pitfalls to using teams, including unclear accountability, overemphasis on multiskilling that overloads workers and ignores their preferences, groupthink, the tendency for teamwork to become an end in itself, and a stifling team atmosphere that drives out creative and independent individuals (Gordon, 1994).

When interdependence works well, it can promote learning. People learn by interacting, and relationships are important sources of new knowledge (Mohrman & Cohen, Chapter Ten). Networks seem to be particularly effective for knowledge growth; they are, after all, how knowledge-dependent professions organize themselves (Lifson, 1992). But team learning is poorly understood. Psychologists need to explore how people communicate across diverse perspectives and learn from each other (Mohrman & Cohen, Chapter Ten), and how to tap the potential for many minds to become more intelligent than one (Senge, 1990).

Interdependence poses many other challenges for psychological research and practice. Mohrman and Cohen (Chapter Ten) cite the need for research and theory around such issues as the motivation of collective performance, the role of individual and team rewards, attributions of equity, and the sort of job experiences that build people's capability to collaborate cross-functionally. Measurement of team performance is another challenge; it can be misleading to simply average individual outputs because team members have responsibilities beyond undertaking individual tasks (Hedge & Borman, Chapter Twelve). Team members must, for example, coordinate work flow, communicate effectively with one another, engage in compensatory behaviors, give and receive feedback, and participate in mutual performance monitoring. Clearly the individual-based tenets of I/O psychology will need to be reexamined if the group becomes the primary unit of analysis. Even leadership theory has focused mainly on dyads, and there is a need to understand the mechanisms and processes by which leaders affect groups and work units (House, Chapter Eleven).

Holism

The biggest design challenge in the lateral organization is to keep multiple functions moving in the same direction (Mohrman & Cohen, Chapter Ten). With individuals and groups empowered, how does management accomplish its coordination function? How can an organization achieve what Mary Parker Follett (1949) called integrative unity, where each of the interrelated parts is engaged in efficiently pursuing the common goals?

New approaches to science, expressed in theories of complexity and chaos, embrace holism—examinations of whole systems and the relationships among their parts. Complex systems create holistic order not by elaborate controls but by a few guiding principles. Wheatley (1992) claims that organizations have confused control with order, drawing on a mechanistic and boundary-filled machine model when they should have been emulating an organic model of fluid and boundaryless living systems with self-renewing capabilities. Moreover, the notion of controlling an organization from the top is an illusion; no one could master its dynamic and detailed complexity (Senge, 1990). As organizations flatten, a manager's span of control often ranges over twenty to twenty-five employees, even one hundred in service organizations. Quinn (1992) argues that "span of control" in such situations is an anachronism; at best it is a "span of coordination" (p. 113).

Following an organic model, coordination of a post-industrial organization relies on self-organization or self-reference. That is, each part of a system should remain consistent with itself and with all other parts of the system as it changes (Wheatley, 1992). In the absence of specific rules, people need mental models that will help them handle the situations they face; thus, an organization must communicate a framework for its members that represents guiding principles for their behavior. Current prescriptions for creating mental models and a common identity for employees typically revolve around the articulation and communication of the organization's vision and values.

Wheatley (1992) conceptualizes a properly disseminated vision as an invisible force field that permeates through the entire organization, influencing every employee who bumps up against it. But an organizational vision is also highly vulnerable to being nothing more than a cliche. Senge (1990) warns that a vision without systems thinking can paint lovely pictures of the future with no deep understanding of the forces that must be mastered to move the organization there.

Holistic organizations can be likened to fractals—geometrical forms generated by computers from just a few equations that feed back on themselves. The iterative process of evolving feedback reveals complexity underneath, as when organizational survey data are fed back and amplified by different interpretations. Fractal organizations trust in the power of guiding principles or values and expect to see similar behaviors show up among their members (Wheatley, 1992). Bray (1994) was relying on fractal qualities when he recommended diagnosing organizations by observing a subset of members in a special assessment center.

Creating the fractal organization requires paying special attention to values and attitude management. This begins with recruitment and selection and extends through indoctrination, training and retraining, and alignment of systems, such as compensation and rewards, information, and communications (Mohrman & Cohen, Chapter Ten).

Responsibility for disseminating a coherent framework rests with management. Neocharismatic leaders, described by House (Chapter Eleven), are particularly well suited to this role. Such leaders communicate a powerful vision, cause followers to recognize values shared among the collective, and bring about strong follower identification with the vision. They align frames (mental models) among followers by using labels and slogans, providing vivid images of a better future, and invoking moral justifications and end values.

Post-industrial leaders thus shape their organizations through concepts and feelings rather than through rules or structures. They depend more on personal power than on position power (Mohrman & Cohen, Chapter Ten). In a world of invisible work and empowered workers, the organization must use invisible force fields to create holistic coherence and coordination.

Political, Economic, and Societal Implications

If the speculations in this volume are realized, what will be the overall impact of the changing nature of work on workers and society? The following potential problems could surface:

- *Insecurity:* downsizing, psychological contract violation, cutbacks of pensions and health benefits, part-time and temporary work for many, few long-term employment relationships
- *Uncertainty:* constant change, multiple reporting relationships, inability to forecast the future
- *Stress:* competing demands, long work hours, exhaustion, global competition
- *Social friction:* two-tiered society, sharp differentiation on ability, insufficient work for the low-skilled, family breakups and

community breakdowns unless new roles and contracts are negotiated

But work could provide the following compensations:

- *Challenge:* endless opportunities for stretching, growing, developing skills, keeping interested
- *Creativity:* opportunity to generate novel solutions to new problems, self-expression
- *Flexibility:* individualization of careers and person-organization contracts, personal time and space arrangements, multiple careers
- *Control:* empowerment, decision-making responsibility, directing one's life
- *Interrelatedness:* global communication, group and team collaboration, end of isolation

The future world of work offers exciting opportunities to meet needs at the higher levels of Maslow's hierarchy—social, esteem, self-actualization—at the expense of meeting needs at the lower levels—security and safety. It will not be a world for the timid, insecure, or low-skilled but for capable risk takers who thrive on challenge and responsibility. Security will come not in preplanned career paths but in developing competencies (Hall & Mirvis, Chapter Nine). Such conditions cannot help engendering serious social consequences.

Impact of Psychological Interventions

Psychological interventions will not play a neutral role in the scenario just described. Personnel selection, of course, exacerbates worker differences, which is the reason the government tries to regulate it (Ledvinka, Chapter Two). Increasing needs for workers who can reason and learn could enhance the demand for overt or covert measures of g. As the average level of complexity rises at work, g will become more predictive of job performance, and adverse impact will increase. With promotional opportunities sparse in lateral organizations, equal treatment issues, including litigation, are likely to be focused on opportunities to develop competencies for more complex work (Mohrman & Cohen, Chapter Ten; Sharf, in press).

Less obviously related to differentiation is the impact of empowerment. This intervention in the environment is more palatable to the government than interventions that rely on individual differences, according to Ledvinka's analysis (Chapter Two). Moreover, it is a democratizing force; it levels the status differences between workers and management. One impediment to empowerment is the Wagner Act, which forbids company unions; whether an agreement can be reached to modify the act in a way that will satisfy both unions and management remains to be seen (see Chapter Two).

Assuming that any legal hurdles can be overcome, empowerment may have the unintended consequences of accentuating the importance of cognitive ability and further differentiating workers. Two considerations suggest this hypothesis. First, organizations often empower workers so that they can take advantage of the information available in new technology. The jobs of these empowered workers then become more complex, and stronger cognitive ability is needed to handle them. A second effect comes about as different workers perform in these upskilled jobs. With more opportunity to use their abilities, those with the best reasoning and learning skills will outshine others. There will be a higher payoff from hiring smart workers for jobs that challenge their intellect than for jobs that are more routine.

This is an example of how forces of democracy inevitably lead to meritocracy (Herrnstein & Murray, 1994), a fact not well understood by government regulators. There is other evidence of this phenomenon in the changing nature of work. Electronic communications deemphasize status, as do cross-functional teams. Both end up putting considerably more emphasis on individual competence (Mohrman & Cohen, Chapter Ten).

Buffers and Brakes

As Ledvinka documented in Chapter Two, U.S. law seeks to avoid conflict and ensure equality. With competitive forces pushing inexorably toward inequality, the instinctual direction of public policy may be, as Ledvinka predicts (Chapter Two), to establish ever more impediments to selection in the workplace. On the other hand, the availability of alternatives such as electronic immigrants, automation, and outsourcing to foreign lands suggests that too much regulation may drive away employment opportunities that the government wants to ensure.

As both Wever and Ledvinka pointed out (Chapter Two), institutions of public policy and labor relations do not change readily. Yet current institutions are less effective than in the past as buffers for workers against exploitation by the private sector. The horrendous working conditions that inspired government intervention and union organizing at the turn of the last century are increasingly rare as technology improves and employers become more enlightened about people and work conditions. Union membership has declined markedly in the private sector (see Chapter Two). Although unions are now trying to center themselves in the middle of the empowerment movement, their role is unclear. Wever (Chapter Two) suggests that organized labor needs to expand its concerns beyond job control unionism. Bridges (1994) proposes that unions abandon collective bargaining and become public advocacy and educational institutions, much like professional organizations.

Private firms increasingly see both unions and U.S. government workplace regulations as brakes on the flexibility that they need to compete in the post-industrial global market. This problem stems partly from the presumptive adversarial relationship between employees and employers, noted by both Ledvinka and Wever (Chapter Two). The detailed nature of U.S. regulation also promotes inflexibility (Wever, Chapter Two). Compounding the problem for personnel selection are the false assumptions and outdated scientific understandings that underlie regulation. Affirmative action policies assume that it is possible to compensate for cognitive deficits, but there is no research evidence that supports this assumption (Ackerman & Humphreys, 1990; Herrnstein & Murray, 1994). They also incorrectly assume that standard tests are highly likely to be biased against minorities.

Some government regulations have become nonsensical and mutually contradictory. Valid, unbiased ability tests inevitably lead to disparate impact; this is prima facie evidence of discrimination as the Civil Rights Act of 1964 has been interpreted by the Equal Employment Opportunity Commission (EEOC) guidelines and the courts. At the same time disparate treatment (race norming) to remedy the situation is forbidden by the Civil Rights Act of 1991, even though favoring minorities to remedy previous imbalances is acceptable (Sackett & Wilk, 1994). Similarly, Landy (1986), commenting on the "trinitarian" view of content, criterion-related, and construct validity in the Uniform Guidelines, concluded that the regulations cause psychologists to "accept a set of rules, premises, and assumptions that often make no sense" (p. 1190).

Affirmative action achieved laudable goals in the early years of its implementation. There is evidence that women and minorities advanced into jobs for which they were qualified but denied previously by discriminatory practices (Herrnstein & Murray, 1994). It also inspired psychologists to undertake a great deal of valuable research into possible test bias, adverse impact, validity generalization, and related issues. Now, however, there is reason to suggest not just diminishing returns but negative returns of government regulation as companies are forced to play hide-and-seek with de facto quotas, psychologists are constrained in applying their tools wisely, the EEOC is hopelessly backlogged with complaints (Kilborn, 1994), and minorities suffer bruised self-esteem from being placed in situations where they risk failure or the condescension of co-workers who assume they are less capable than they truly are. It is difficult to find winners in the current situation. Following Hage's prescriptions (Chapter Thirteen), post-modern men and women from the public and private sectors need to apply their creative minds to renegotiating outdated, adversarial role scripts.

Expanding Psychological Knowledge

I/O psychologists alone lack the political clout to forge solutions to government regulation of human resource practices (Ledvinka, Chapter Two), but they can add value in the post-industrial economy by continuing to do what they do best—conduct objective, scientific research that sheds light on psychological issues related to work. This last section explores ideas for rethinking and redoing psychology for a changing world of work.

Societal and Scientific Responsibilities

An important way to lessen the adverse impact of g-loaded selection methods is to add other predictors that can account for additional variance in performance. Lower-level abilities that help sustain automatic processing are one promising avenue, and identifying the kinds of work where such abilities play a significant role will be important.

As concluded earlier, g will be more necessary but less sufficient for post-industrial work; this reality opens the door to adding noncognitive measures to personnel selection that can reduce overall adverse impact. Assessment centers have made clear the importance of administrative and interpersonal skills for managers; these competencies will be needed by a wide variety of interdependent workers in lateral organizations where leadership is shared or rotated. Howard and Bray (1988) found, for example, that race and ethnic group differences among young telephone company managers were negligible for interpersonal skills. Various measures of motivation, personality, values, and other noncognitive measures may also help reduce the adverse impact of cognitive tests for minorities. Considerably more evidence needs to be gathered about the predictive bias or adverse impact of such measures (Sackett & Wilk, 1994).

In training, an important avenue to pursue is aptitude-treatment-interaction research, which computer technology will facilitate (Coovert, Chapter Five). It may be possible to individualize training in ways that could benefit those who have difficulty learning from standard instruction.

Practice

Over the last few years, practicing I/O psychologists have been gradually leaving the employ of business organizations and increasing their affiliations with consulting firms (Balzer & Howard, 1994). This trend is consistent with the move by organizations to strip themselves down to core competencies and outsource other work to contractors or temporary personnel. It is not necessarily a bad turn of events for the profession, for it allows more specialization, encourages cross-organizational comparisons, and facilitates frame-bending and creative thinking that might be discouraged in the trenches of one organization's culture. What might be lost is the understanding of an organization in depth, especially that gained from experiential learning that informs the cognitive unconscious (Epstein, 1994).

Some organizations are beginning to embed training within operating departments, bypassing centralized professional staffs. This trend signals not just downsizing of internal staff but increased interest in just-in-time solutions for performance problems rather than generalized skill development (Galagan, 1994). Just-in-time training should be particularly important as jobs dissolve into fluid work clusters.

For virtual staff assembled quickly for specific projects or assignments, selection will become more important than training (Davis, Chapter Three). Thus selection methods must not only be accurate; they must also be fast and just in time. Besides being readily available, human resource programs will need to be amenable to mass customization—that is, be readily tailored to work unit or individual needs. In short, the practice of I/O psychology in the twenty-first century will need to be more like the work environment (as Hall & Mirvis, Chapter Nine, advised for career research)—fluid, varied, and complex, but customer oriented and just in time.

Technology

Computer technology is a boon to mass-customized and just-in-time solutions. There are already job ads on the Internet, and provisions could be made for candidates to complete applications or take tests by computer network also (Landy, Shankster-Cawley, & Moran, Chapter Seven). Selection and assessment systems are beginning to take advantage of computerization and could embellish their face validity and user-friendliness with comfortable interfaces (see Coovert, Chapter Five) and multimedia enhancements. Work sample tests and situational exercises could emerge naturally from operation technologies (Coovert, Chapter Five). Virtual reality exercises in future assessment centers could efficiently allow assessees to respond behaviorally to realistic workplace simulations (Howard, 1993).

Many expert systems can bring human resource applications to large or small organizations. Software systems now deliver tailorable instruments for purposes such as job analyses, multirater assessments, performance management, interview guide generation, and attitude surveys. Career software helps self-assessment, provides guides to getting career information, and supports electronic resumes (Hall & Mirvis, Chapter Nine). For training, Coovert (Chapter Five) demonstrated that animation can enrich learning and retention by making mental models more vivid.

Using sophisticated computer systems, psychologists could also create microworlds that model the complexity of organizations as adaptive systems (Senge, 1990). Telephone company managers, for example, use a computer simulation (Telesim) based on artificial life technology, incorporating principles of adaptive agents and increasing returns, to think through looming issues like mergers between telecommunications and cable (Ditlea, 1994).

Variables and Models

Variables used for personnel selection are to an unknown degree overlapping because they come from different methodological traditions, such as biodata, assessment centers, or personality tests (Landy, Shankster-Cawley, & Moran, Chapter Seven). A parsimonious reduction of constructs would be beneficial, as would identification of major domains of human performance and their primary predictors. The controversy over assessment center construct validity is readily resolved, for example, if one concedes that dimensions cluster within different performance domains (as factor analyses demonstrate), each exercise usually focuses on only one domain, and the strong intercorrelations of dimensions within an exercise are simply a reflection of that one performance domain (Howard, 1993).

Various authors in this volume indicated that psychologists' variables have been too narrow and their models too limited. Coovert (Chapter Five) suggests models with more moderators and mediators. Wall and Jackson (Chapter Four) point to new contingencies and constructs from a broader range of theoretical inquiry. Other authors point to entire arenas that are relatively unexplored; for example, teams as units of performance

(Mohrman & Cohen, Chapter Ten) and cross-cultural differences in leadership (House, Chapter Eleven).

Both the industrial and organizational sides of I/O psychology could benefit from a more holistic frame of reference—the whole person and the whole organization, interacting with each other and with the broader environment. Indeed, a goal of this volume has been to take a more comprehensive view of the political-economic-societal context in which work takes place. It is time to leave the age of Frederick Taylor, to stop perfecting minute pieces of the human resource apparatus when the entire organizational system is reinventing itself to grow and adapt in a new world order. Like biologists, we needed to understand the parts of the system before we could look at the whole, but it is time to look at the whole again (Lewin, 1992).

Distilling the various lessons in this volume, we should be wary of constructing models that put too much reliance on the following aspects:

- Mechanical forces toward equilibrium
- "One best way" solutions
- Exclusive emphasis on one psychological mechanism (for example, motivation)
- Optimal computation (requiring consideration of all possible alternatives)
- All people the same
- Individuals isolated from systems
- The "job" or local influences as accounting for all variance
- Exclusively linear effects

Instead we should consider models that take these things into account:

- Learning
- Dynamic growth
- Ad hoc approaches to problem solving
- Differentiation and individual differences
- Aptitude-treatment interactions
- Cognitive, conative, and affective determinants of behavior
- Groups and teams

- Organizational and extra-organizational systems
- Nonlinear and reciprocal effects

Research about learning at work seems especially critical, whether to explicate job control, personnel selection and skill acquisition, lifelong self-development, reward systems, working laterally, organizational adaptation, or other factors. For the first time in history, the fundamental economic resource, knowledge, is directly acquired through psychological processes. Psychologists need to enhance knowledge about acquiring and using knowledge at work.

Conclusion

Despite our admonitions that the future is not predictable, in this volume we have forecast the future world of work. We could, of course, be quite erroneous in our assumptions and conclusions. After all, one hundred years ago a prominent U.S. journalist predicted that by now the law would be simplified, the number of lawyers diminished, and their fees vastly curtailed (Walter, 1992). We accept the risks of poor prediction with equanimity.

If our projections are even moderately on target, psychologists should find unlimited challenges in the changing nature of work. Education and technology alone cannot make organizations competitive; the most important factor will be the way organizations use their educated workers and technologies (Carnevale, Chapter Six). Many of the skills workers will need are in nontechnical areas in which psychologists can add significant value: learning, communications, responsibility, adaptability, personal mastery, group effectiveness, influencing, negotiating, and so forth. The larger social consequences of the changing nature of work should be neither underestimated nor ignored. But most psychologists will embrace the prospect of realizing individual and organizational potentials in a newly liberated workplace. With creativity and courage, we can help make that prospect a reality. We have much work to do.

References

Ackerman, P. L. (1992). Predicting individual differences in complex skill acquisition: Dynamics of ability determinants. *Journal of Applied Psychology, 77*(5), 598–614.

Ackerman, P. L., & Humphreys, L. G. (1990). Individual differences theory in industrial and organizational psychology. In M. D. Dunnette & L. M. Hough (Eds.), *Handbook of industrial and organizational psychology.* Palo Alto, CA: Consulting Psychologists Press.

Balzer, W. K., & Howard, A. (1994). 1993 profile of Division 14 members: Noteworthy trends. *The Industrial-Organizational Psychologist, 31*(3), 95–97.

Barrick, M. R., & Mount, M. K. (1991). The big five personality dimensions and job performance. *Personnel Psychology, 44*(1), 1–26.

Bray, D. W. (1994). Personnel-centered organizational diagnosis. In A. Howard & Associates, *Diagnosis for organizational change: Methods and models.* New York: Guilford Press.

Bridges, W. (1994). *JobShift: How to prosper in a workplace without jobs.* Reading, MA: Addison-Wesley.

Business Week. (1994). 21st century capitalism (Special issue).

Byham, W. C. (1988). *Zapp! The human lightning of empowerment (and how to make it work for you).* Pittsburgh: Development Dimensions International.

Conger, J. A., & Kanungo, R. A. (1988). The empowerment process: Integrating theory and practice. *Academy of Management Review, 13*, 471–482.

Csikszentmihalyi, M. (1993). *The evolving self: A psychology for the third millennium.* New York: Harper.

Deutschman, A., & Tetzeli, R. (1994, July 11). Your desktop in the year 1996. *Fortune,* pp. 86–98.

Ditlea, S. (1994, November). Imitation of life. *Upside,* pp. 48–60.

Drucker, P. F. (1993). *Post-capitalist society.* New York: Harper.

Dumaine, B. (1994, December 26). Why do we work? *Fortune,* pp. 196–204.

Epstein, S. (1994). Integration of the cognitive and the psychodynamic unconscious. *American Psychologist, 49*(8), 709–724.

Ericsson, K. A., & Charness, N. (1994). Expert performance. *American Psychologist, 49*(8), 725–747.

Follett, M. P. (1949). *Freedom and co-ordination: Lectures in business organisation.* London: Management Publications.

Galagan, P. A. (1994). Reinventing the profession. *Training and Development, 48*(12), 20–27.

Galinsky, E., Bond, J. T., & Friedman, D. E. (1993). *The changing workforce.* New York: Families and Work Institute.

Glaser, R. (1989). *The fourth R, the ability to reason.* Washington, DC: Federation of Behavioral, Psychological and Cognitive Sciences.

Gordon, J. (1993, September). The organization man: A sequel. *Training,* p. 8.

Gordon, J. (1994, August). The team troubles that won't go away. *Training*, pp. 25–34.

Hammer, M., & Champy, J. (1993). *Reengineering the corporation: A manifesto for business revolution.* New York: Harper.

Handy, C. (1989). *The age of unreason.* Cambridge, MA: Harvard Business School Press.

Handy, C. (1994). *The age of paradox.* Cambridge, MA: Harvard Business School Press.

Harvey, R. J. (1991). Job analysis. In M. D. Dunnette & L. M. Hough (Eds.), *Handbook of industrial and organizational psychology.* Palo Alto, CA: Consulting Psychologists Press.

Havel, V. (1994, July 8). The new measure of man. *The New York Times*, p. A27.

Herrnstein, R. J., & Murray, C. (1994). *The bell curve: Intelligence and class structure in American life.* New York: Free Press.

Hirschhorn, L., & Mokray, J. (1992). Automation and competency requirements in manufacturing: A case study. In P. S. Adler (Ed.), *Technology and the future of work.* New York: Oxford University Press.

Howard, A. (1993). *Will assessment centers be obsolete in the twenty-first century?* Paper presented at the International Congress on the Assessment Center Method, Atlanta.

Howard, A., & Bray, D. W. (1988). *Managerial lives in transition: Advancing age and changing times.* New York: Guilford Press.

Howard, A., Byham, W. C., & Hauenstein, P. (1994). *Multirater assessment and feedback: Applications, implementation, and implications* [Monograph]. Pittsburgh: Development Dimensions International.

Howard, A., & Wellins, R. S. (1994). *High-involvement leadership: Changing roles for changing times.* Pittsburgh: Development Dimensions International.

Ilgen, D. R. (1992). *Jobs and roles: Accepting and coping with the changing structure of organizations.* Paper presented at the Army Research Institute Selection and Placement Conference, Alexandria, VA.

Ilgen, D. R., & Hollenbeck, J. R. (1991). The structure of work: Design and roles. In M. D. Dunnette & L. M. Hough (Eds.), *Handbook of industrial and organizational psychology.* Palo Alto, CA: Consulting Psychologists Press.

Kilborn, P. T. (1994, November 26). Backlog of cases is overwhelming jobs-bias agency. *New York Times*, pp. 1, 10.

Landy, F. J. (1986). Stamp collecting versus science: Validation as hypothesis testing. *American Psychologist, 41*(11), 1183–1192.

Lawler, E. E., III. (1992). *The ultimate advantage: Creating the high-involvement organization.* San Francisco: Jossey-Bass.

Lewin, R. (1992). *Complexity: Life at the edge of chaos.* New York: Collier/Macmillan.

Lifson, T. B. (1992). Innovation and institutions: Notes on the Japanese paradigm. In P. S. Adler (Ed.), *Technology and the future of work*. New York: Oxford University Press.

Lifton, R. J. (1993). *The protean self: Human resilience in an age of fragmentation*. New York: Basic Books.

Mandel, M. J. (1992, June 8). Who'll get the lion's share of wealth in the '90s? The lions. *Business Week*, pp. 86–88.

Nasar, S. (1994, December 1). More men in prime of life spend less time working. *New York Times*, pp. A1, D15.

Nord, W. R., & Brief, A. P. (1990). On the reciprocal relationship between the meaning of work and political economy. In A. P. Brief & W. R. Nord (Eds.), *Meanings of occupational work: A collection of essays*. Lexington, MA: Lexington Books.

Nord, W. R., Brief, A. P., Atieh, J. M., & Doherty, E. M. (1990). Studying meanings of work: The case of work values. In A. P. Brief & W. R. Nord (Eds.), *Meanings of occupational work: A collection of essays*. Lexington, MA: Lexington Books.

Quinn, J. B. (1992). *Intelligent enterprise*. New York: Free Press.

Reich, R. B. (1991). *The work of nations*. New York: Knopf.

Roberts, P. C. (1994, December 3). The G.O.P. contract is too timid. *New York Times*, p. 23.

Sackett, P. R., & Wilk, S. L. (1994). Within-group norming and other forms of score adjustment in preemployment testing. *American Psychologist, 49*(11), 929–954.

Sasseen, J. A. (1994, October 17). The winds of change blow everywhere. *Business Week*, pp. 92–93.

Schmidt, F. L., Hunter, J. E., & Pearlman, K. (1981). Task differences as moderators of aptitude test validity in selection: A red herring. *Journal of Applied Psychology, 66*, 166–185.

Schor, J. B. (1991). *The overworked American*. New York: Basic Books.

Senge, P. M. (1990). *The fifth discipline: The art and practice of the learning organization*. New York: Doubleday/Currency.

Sharf, J. C. (in press). Training and the law (beancounting disincentives to human capital investment). In R. Craig (Ed.), *Training and development handbook*. New York: McGraw-Hill.

Smith, M. B. (1991). *"Human science"—really!* Paper presented at the meeting of the American Psychological Association, San Francisco.

Sterns, H. L., & Sterns, A. A. (in press). Age, health, and employment capability of older Americans. In S. Bass, M. Barth, P. Rizzi, & B. McNaught (Eds.), *Aging and active*. New Haven, CT: Yale University Press.

Thomas, K. W., & Velthouse, B. A. (1990). Cognitive elements of empowerment: An "interpretive" model of intrinsic task motivation. *Academy of Management Review, 15*(4), 666–681.

Vaill, P. B. (1989). *Managing as a performing art: New ideas for a world of chaotic change.* San Francisco: Jossey-Bass.

Waldrop, M. M. (1992). *Complexity: The emerging science at the edge of order and chaos.* New York: Simon & Schuster.

Walter, D. (Ed.). (1992). *Today then: America's best minds look 100 years into the future on the occasion of the 1893 World's Columbian Exposition.* Helena, MT: American & World Geographic.

Wellins, R. S., Byham, W. C., & Wilson, J. M. (1991). *Empowered teams: Creating self-directed work groups that improve quality, productivity, and participation.* San Francisco: Jossey-Bass.

Wheatley, M. J. (1992). *Leadership and the new science: Learning about organization from an orderly universe.* San Francisco: Berrett-Koehler.

Name Index

Subject Index

in, 377–387; factors in effective, 374–377; information technology for, 396–399, 401; and management teams, 392–394; managers for, 387–394; performance management for, 394–396; research needed on, 399–403; systems for, 394–399; theoretical issues for, 400–401

Latin America: and globalization, 118; leadership in, 443; workforces of, 212–213

Law of Scattering, 116

Leadership: aspects of, 411–450; and attention to process, 440; background on, 411–412; behaviors for, 416–421; conclusion on, 444; considerations in, 436–438; in dyads, 440; and empowerment, 437–438; integrative views of, 438; management and supervision related to, 413–414; neocharismatic, 414–427; participative, 430–431, 435; research needed on, 439–444; self-managing, 390–391; shared, 436; and social conditions, 421–424, 441; strategic, 441–442

Learning: bonus for, 340; and empowerment, 536–537; how to learn, 116, 352, 353–354; lifelong, in careers, 323–361; a living, 333–334; organizational practices for, 353–354; real-time, 337–338, 350–351, 381. See also Cognition; Education; Knowledge

Legislation: bureaucracy context for, 16–17; and employment relations, 70–86; impact of, 47, 67–86; in industrial age, 7; in post-industrial age, 30–31, 36; on school-work transition, 230; and selection processes, 275–276; and workforce skills, 213, 214, 216, 247–248

Leisure, in post-industrial lives, 499–500, 505–506

Level of analysis: in employment mod-

els, 70, 72, 74, 85–86; job design as, 156

Lexis, 119

Literacy, survey of, 218

Liveboards, for ubiquitous computing, 193–194

Lloyd's of London, and careers, 323

Locus of control, and attitudes toward computers, 179

Lordstown, Ohio, strike in, 21

Los Angeles, social responsibility in, 346

Louis Harris & Associates, 334, 360

M

McKinsey survey, 46–47, 518

Maine, working in, 15

Managers: behaviors of, 424–427; employment relations of, 388–392; issues for, 400–401; for lateral organizations, 387–394; leaders and supervisors related to, 413–414; participation by, 22; reporting relationships of, 388–389; roles of, 391–392; scientific, 13–15

Manpower, and transactional contracts, 294

Manpower Demonstration Research Corporation, JobStart program of, 228–229

Manufacturing. See Factories

Maryland, workers' compensation law in, 7

Mastery, personal, 131–132, 532

Mazda, and employment relations, 301

Mentoring, in career development, 338–339, 341, 347

Mergers and acquisitions, and external boundaries, 126

Mexico: and educational attainment, 213; and globalization, 118

Microchip development, 98–100

Microsoft: beta-testing by, 128; and workplace technologies, 107

Minnesota Multiphasic Personality Inventory, 80